THE POLITICAL ECONOMY OF ANTITRUST

CONTRIBUTIONS TO ECONOMIC ANALYSIS

282

THE POLITICAL ECONOMY OF ANITITRUST

Edited by

Vivek Ghosal
Georgia Institute of Technology, Atlanta, USA & CESifo, Munich, Germany

John Stennek
Research Institute for Industrial Economics, Stockholm, Sweden & CEPR, London, UK

Emerald

United Kingdom – North America – Japan
India – Malaysia – China

Emerald Group Publishing Limited
Howard House, Wagon Lane, Bingley BD16 1WA, UK

Reprints and permission service
Contact: booksandseries@emeraldinsight.com

Printed and bound by CPI Group (UK) Ltd, Croydon, CR0 4YY

British Library Cataloguing in Publication Data
A catalogue record for this book is available from the British Library

ISBN: 978-0-444-53093-6

Introduction to the Series

This series consists of a number of hitherto unpublished studies, which are introduced by the editors in the belief that they represent fresh contributions to economic science.

The term 'economic analysis' as used in the title of the series has been adopted because it covers both the activities of the theoretical economist and the research worker.

Although the analytical method used by the various contributors are not the same, they are nevertheless conditioned by the common origin of their studies, namely theoretical problems encountered in practical research. Since for this reason, business cycle research and national accounting, research work on behalf of economic policy, and problems of planning are the main sources of the subjects dealt with, they necessarily determine the manner of approach adopted by the authors. Their methods tend to be 'practical' in the sense of not being too far remote from application to actual economic conditions. In addition, they are quantitative.

It is the hope of the editors that the publication of these studies will help to stimulate the exchange of scientific information and to reinforce international cooperation in the field of economics.

The Editors

Acknowledgements

A book of this scope and magnitude can only be made possible by the generous contributions of time and effort by many. The editors, Vivek Ghosal and Johan Stennek, express their deep gratitude to Joe Harrington for providing invaluable help and guidance during many stages of the development of this volume as well as very generously agreeing to contribute to the first chapter. Apart from Chapter 1, all the papers in this volume were subject to a single-blind refereeing process meeting international standards. We thank each of the authors in this volume for their contributions and for showing patience and understanding as the chapters went through the extensive refereeing and editorial process. We express our gratitude to Russell Pittman (Antitrust Division, U.S. Department of Justice), Michele Polo (University of Bocconi) and Lucía Quesada (University of Wisconsin, Madison) for providing us with valuable comments on some of the specific contributions included in this volume. Finally, we thank Joy Ideler, Jeroen Loos, Tomas Martišius, Lisa Muscolino, Mark Newson and Valerie Teng at North-Holland for providing expert help and guidance through the different stages of the development of this volume.

Contents

List of Contributors

Numbers in parenthesis indicate the pages where the authors' contributions can be found.

Cécile Aubert (123) Université Paris Dauphine (EURIsCO), Dpt. Economie Appliquée, 75 016 Paris, France. E-mail: Cecile.Aubert@dauphine.fr

Timothy J. Brennan (417) Professor of Public Policy and Economics, University of Maryland Baltimore County; Senior Fellow, Resources for the Future. E-mail: brennan@umbc.edu

Paolo Buccirossi (81) Lear—Laboratorio di economia, antitrust, regolamentazione. E-mail: paolo.buccirossi@learlab.it

Joe Chen (59) Faculty of Economics, University of Tokyo, Tokyo, 113-0033 Japan. E-mail: joechen@e.u-tokyo.ac.jp

Jay Pil Choi (241) Department of Economics, Michigan State University, East Lansing, MI 48824. E-mail: choijay@msu.edu

John M. Connor (177) Purdue University, West Lafayette, IN. E-mail: jconnor@purdue.edu

Tomaso Duso (303) Humboldt University, Berlin, and WZB, Germany. E-mail: duso@wz-berlin.de

Antoine Faure-Grimaud (383) London School of Economics, FMG and CEPR, UK.

Jérôme Foncel (349) GREMARS, University of Lille 3, France.

Joseph Francois (463) Tinbergen Institute, Rotterdam, and CEPR.

Sven-Olof Fridolfsson (287) Research Institute of Industrial Economics, Stockholm, Sweden. E-mail: sof@industrialeconomics.se

Luke Froeb (369) Owen Graduate School of Management, Vanderbilt University, Nashville, TN 37203. E-mail: luke.froeb@vanderbilt.edu

Vivek Ghosal (1) Georgia Institute of Technology, Atlanta, GA, USA.

Klaus Gugler (303) University of Vienna, Austria. E-mail: klaus.gugler@univie.ac.at

Joseph E. Harrington Jr. (1, 59) Johns Hopkins University, Baltimore, MD, USA. E-mail: joe.harrington@jhu.edu

Henrik Horn (259) Research Institute of Industrial Economics, Stockholm, and CEPR, London.

Henrik Horn (463) IIES Stockholm University, The Research Institute of Industrial Economics (IUI), and CEPR, Sweden.

Marc Ivaldi (217, 349) University of Toulouse, EHESS and IDEI, Toulouse, France.

Bruno Jullien (217) IDEI, Toulouse, France.

William E. Kovacic (149) U.S. Federal Trade Commission.

Robert C. Marshall (149) Pennsylvania State University, USA.

David Martimort (383) Université de Toulouse, and IUF, France.

Stephen Martin (25) Department of Economics, Purdue University, West Lafayette, IN 47907-2056, USA. E-mail: smartin@purdue.edu

Leslie M. Marx (149) Duke University, USA.

R. Preston McAfee (453) Humanities and Social Sciences, California Institute of Technology, Pasadena, CA 91125. E-mail: preston@mcafee.cc

Hugo M. Mialon (453) Department of Economics, Emory University, Atlanta, GA 30322-2240. E-mail: hmialon@emory.edu

Sue H. Mialon (453) Department of Economics, University of North Dakota, Grand Forks, ND 58202. E-mail: sue.mialon@und.edn

Valérie Rabassa (349) European Commission, Chief Economist Office, Directorate General for Competition, Belgium.

Matthew E. Raiff (149) Bates White, LLC.

Patrick Rey (217) IDEI, Toulouse, France.

Paul Seabright (217) IDEI, Toulouse, France.

Giancarlo Spagnolo (81) Stockholm School of Economics, Consip Research Unit, and CEPR. E-mail: giancarlo.spagnolo@yahoo.it

Johan Stennek (1, 259) Research Institute of Industrial Economics, Stockholm, and CEPR, London.

Jean Tirole (217) IDEI, Toulouse, France.

Steven Tschantz (369) Department of Mathematics, Vanderbilt University, Nashville, TN 37203. E-mail: tschantz@math.vanderbilt.edu

Gregory J. Werden (369) U.S. Department of Justice, Washington, DC 20530. E-mail: gregory.werden@usdoj.gov

Burcin Yurtoglu (303) University of Vienna, Austria. E-mail: burcin.yurtoglu@univie.ac.at

CHAPTER 1

Issues in Antitrust Enforcement

Vivek Ghosal[a], Joseph E. Harrington Jr.[b] and Johan Stennek[c]

[a]*Georgia Institute of Technology, Atlanta, GA, USA*
[b]*Johns Hopkins University, Baltimore, MD, USA*
[c]*Research Institute of Industrial Economics, Stockholm, Sweden*

Motivated by recent events and experiences in antitrust enforcement and policy in the United States and the European Union, and new insights and findings from academic research, this book presents a collection of theoretical, empirical and public policy-oriented articles representing recent research on the political-economy of antitrust. Political-economy is defined broadly to include the demand-side drivers of antitrust activity such as market failures and interest-groups, along with supply-side drivers including ideology and partisan politics as well as the importance of informational limitations in antitrust enforcement and the institutional structure of the antitrust agencies. Examining issues related to the political-economy of antitrust is important as antitrust policy and enforcement provide a key mechanism for preserving the competitiveness of markets, with implications for innovation, efficiency, growth and welfare. This book brings together contributions by leading academic researchers in the areas of political-economy, cartels, merger and non-merger enforcement, as well as economists working with antitrust authorities in the U.S. and E.U., to make a timely contribution for researchers and practitioners.

The chapters in this volume cover the full range of topics: enforcement of cartels; merger control; monopolization and abuse of dominance; and systemic issues in antitrust enforcement and policy. Since the last few years have seen significant changes in both the U.S. and E.U. in the attitudes towards cartels, the book places emphasis on antitrust enforcement of cartels, including topics such as the corporate leniency programs that have recently been introduced in the U.S. and E.U., optimal deterrence mechanisms against cartels and detection of cartels. While the individual chapters of the book make independent contributions and may be read separately, the book brings together articles from various sub-areas to present a more encompassing picture. This chapter provides an overview of some the trends and recent research in antitrust enforcement and policy and highlights the contributions made by the chapters in this volume.

CONTRIBUTIONS TO ECONOMIC ANALYSIS
VOLUME 282 ISSN: 0573-8555
DOI: 10.1016/S0573-8555(06)82001-8

1.1. Shifting winds in antitrust

Changes in intellectual thinking in economics, law and politics have produced significant shifts in antitrust enforcement and policy in the U.S. over the last several decades. The intellectual underpinnings of some of the key changes can be traced back to the rising tide of criticisms of the U.S. antitrust enforcement in the 1950s and 1960s by the Chicago-School scholars, and the genesis of their law and economics movement is often recognized to be Aaron Director and Edward Levi.[1] Director and Levi (1956) criticized the state of antitrust, disagreed with a variety of business practices like tying and vertical restrictions being anti-competitive and abuse of monopoly power, downplayed the likelihood of predatory pricing, emphasized efficiencies and noted flaws in key antitrust decisions like Standard Oil (1911) and Alcoa (1947).[2] In similar tone, Director (1957) criticized the United Shoe Machinery (1918) decision. Many of these arguments went on to become guideposts for the Chicago-School's law and economics thrust. The influential contributions by Stigler (1964) and Williamson (1969), along with Demsetz (1973, 1974), Bork (1966, 1978)[3] and Posner (1969, 1974, 1976) among others, solidified the modern law and economics framework in the U.S. Overall, the thinking shifted in two important ways. First, vertical and conglomerate mergers, resale price maintenance, vertical restrictions and other conduct that were often viewed as anti-competitive under the older antitrust regime were given pro-competitive and efficiency interpretations. Second, the focus shifted to areas of clearer harm to welfare such as horizontal mergers in concentrated markets and price-fixing.[4] Ghosal (2006a) presents an empirical analysis of the long-term patterns of enforcement and finds noticeable structural-breaks in the U.S. enforcement data in the mid-to-late-1970s, symptomatic of a regime-shift in enforcement towards greater emphasis on prosecuting cartels and lesser emphasis on merger and non-merger (civil) enforcement. While there are competing explanations of this shift, the Chicago-School engineered rethinking

---

[1] Director joined the Chicago Law faculty in 1946, founded the *Journal of Law and Economics* in 1958, and his students included Robert Bork, Frank Easterbrook and Richard Posner—legal scholars and judges who greatly influenced antitrust. Bork notes: "*[Director's] teachings ... made him the seminal figure in launching the law and economics movement, which transformed wide areas of legal scholarship.*" (From: Aaron Director, Founder of the Field of Law and Economics, University of Chicago Press, 2004.)

[2] Influenced by Director's hypothesis that firms would prefer mergers and other practices to attain monopoly status as opposed to predatory pricing, McGee (1958) tested whether Standard Oil engaged in predatory pricing, a key issue in the 1911 antitrust decision. His results suggested this was not the case.

[3] It is noteworthy that while Bork's book was published in 1978, it was completed much earlier in 1968–69.

[4] As Baker (1997) notes: "*Our own discipline, antitrust, underwent its Copernican revolution within the professional experience of all but the most recent antitrust practitioners. I am speaking, of course, of the rise of the Chicago school approach.*" Baker (2002, 2003), Crandall and Winston (2003), Kovacic and Shapiro (2000) and Motta (2004, pp. 2–9) provide discussion of these shifts.

about the role of antitrust and emphasis on the efficiency aspects of business conduct is an important explanation. While the changes in the U.S. intellectual and enforcement mindset pre-dates changes in any other country, recent years have seen broadly comparable changes in enforcement patterns in several other countries and the E.U. Symptomatically, criminal enforcement and merger control are also the main focus of this volume.

The second chapter by Stephen Martin provides an overview of the development of antitrust and industrial economics, the interdependencies between the two and some of the political-economy aspects. In particular, Martin addresses the question of what antitrust has contributed to the study of industrial economics. He notes that industry deconcentration proposals were widely supported by mainstream economists in the 1950s and 1960s and that opposition to such proposals was critical to the evolution of the First Chicago School approach from the "Positive Program for Laissez Faire" of Henry Simons (which, equally suspicious of public and private power, regarded antitrust as an essential element of public policy) to that of the Second Chicago School (which emphasized distrust of public power at the expense of distrust of private power). Reaction to the Second Chicago School emphasis on the neoclassical models of perfect competition and monopoly was one motivating factor in the displacement of the structure–conduct–performance framework by game-theoretic models in the late 1970s and 1980s.

1.2. Enforcement of cartels

The last 15 years has witnessed a new era in fighting cartels. In the case of the United States, two complementary events were responsible for this sea change. The first event was the 1991 revision of the Federal Sentencing Guidelines which allowed for a ratcheting up of penalties to be levied. Government fines, which were historically paltry, have risen to as high as $500 million for a single firm and fines in the tens of millions of dollars are now commonplace. At the same time, the incarceration of price-fixers has become routine, even of foreign citizens, and the average length of a sentence has noticeably increased to about 18 months.

The second event was the 1992 revision of the U.S. Department of Justice's Corporate Leniency Program. This program waives all government penalties to the first cartel member to come forward and cooperate fully. As noted by then Deputy Assistant Attorney General James Griffin (Griffin, 2003), the revision encompassed three significant changes: (1) amnesty is automatic if there is no pre-existing investigation; (2) amnesty may still be available even if cooperation begins after the investigation is underway; and (3) all officers, directors, and employees who cooperate are protected from criminal prosecution. In response to this revision, the application rate went from about one per year to about two per month. As a leniency program is more effective when it permits the avoidance of more severe penalties, the increase in penalties and the revision of the leniency program reinforced each other in creating a more effective anti-cartel policy.

To take a big picture look at some of the changes in the U.S. enforcement of cartels, we present Figures 1.1–1.3 (from Ghosal, 2006b). Figure 1.1 displays the data on the total number of price-fixing cases prosecuted in the post-war era, 1948–2003. These data reveal a sharp increase in the number of criminal antitrust cases prosecuted starting in the late-1970s and the early-1980s. Figures 1.2 and 1.3 present data on the average fine per corporation and per individual convicted over the 1968–2003 period. While the fines were typically very low for most of the sample period, there were dramatic increases starting around mid-1990s.

Though the key policy and enforcement initiatives may have originated in the U.S., the movement to a tougher policy against cartels has occurred in many industrialized countries. The E.U. initiated a leniency program in 1996 and experienced a near-doubling of the annual rate of convictions between 1990–95

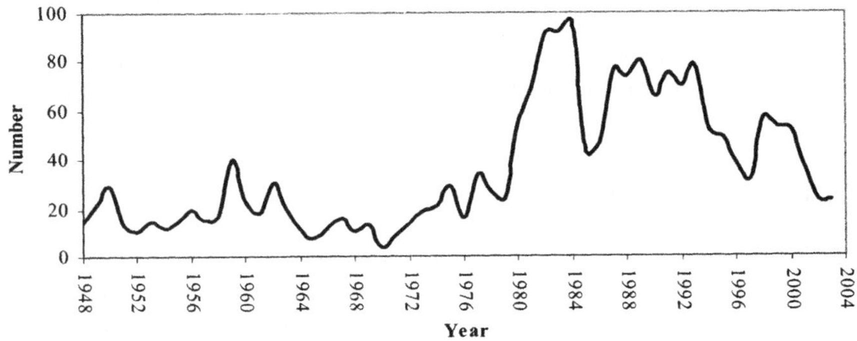

Fig. 1.1: U.S.: Total criminal antitrust cases filed.

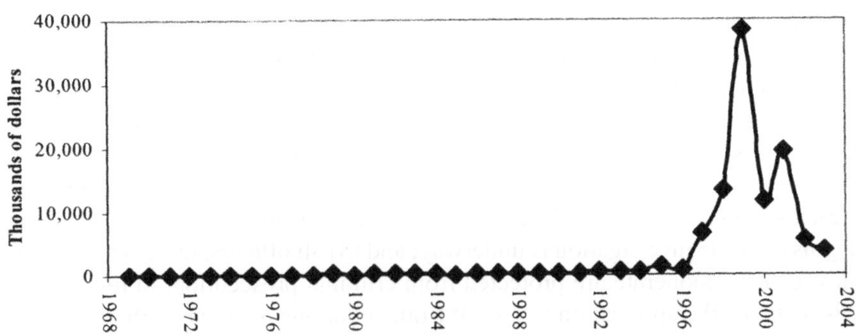

Fig. 1.2: U.S.: Fine per corporation.

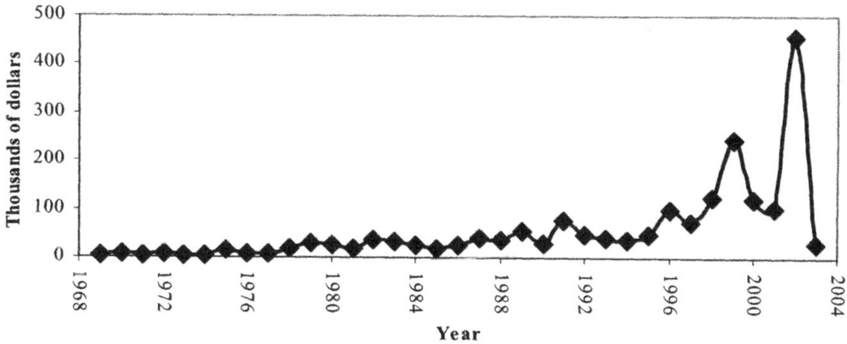

Fig. 1.3: U.S.: Fine per individual.

and 1996–2003 (Brenner, 2005).[5] Leniency programs have been implemented in Australia, Brazil, Canada, France, and Korea as well as many other countries. Even countries like the Netherlands and Japan, long known as cozy environments for cartels, have become quite inhospitable. As of January 2006, the Fair Trade Commission of Japan is empowered with a leniency program and the capacity to levy a penalty equal to 10% of (total) firm revenue, up from the previous mark of 6%.

In evaluating these developments, one must recognize that there are three essential stages in battling hard-core cartels. Cartels must be discovered, discovered cartels must be successfully prosecuted, and successfully prosecuted cartels must be penalized. Operating effectively at all three stages is crucial to disrupting existing cartels and deterring new cartels from forming. The primary impact of the recent changes mentioned above has been in prosecution and penalization. It is perhaps important to note that while there have been cases in which a leniency program was responsible for the actual discovery of the cartel—such as the spontaneous reporting with the monochloroacetic acid cartel—well-documented cases are rare. The power of a leniency program lies more in aiding investigation and prosecution when there is already some knowledge or suspicion about collusion. The leniency program can also help ferret out confessions by firms in instances where there is some evidence/information that the government is investigating a cartel—potentially triggering a race to the competition authority or courthouse to avail of leniency.

A next natural policy step is then to improve methods of detection. One approach is screening industries, which refers to the analysis of market data—such as prices and market shares—to find evidence suggestive of collusion. A flagged industry would be one that warrants further investigation. Though antitrust authorities have not generally engaged in screening, there have been some recent attempts. At the Bureau of Economics of the U.S. Federal Trade Commission,

---

[5] Also see Harding and Joshua (2004) for discussion of changes in the enforcement of cartels in Europe.

former Director Jonathan Baker used price increases after an industry-specific trough in demand to identify the exercise of market power (FTC History, 2003, pp. 108–110), while former Director Luke Froeb made progress in developing a screen in terms of the price variance (Abrantes-Metz et al., 2005). In the Netherlands, the competition authority recently uncovered collusion in the shrimp industry using screening. The time is right to invest in developing screening methods as leniency programs and screening are complements. If an antitrust authority identifies an industry for further scrutiny through some form of screening and conveys these suspicions to the suspected firms, it could well induce some cartel members to come forward and apply for leniency. Harrington (2006) presents analysis and discussion of various facets of detection.

In the broad area of discovery of cartels, Ghosal (2006b) focuses on the genesis and taxonomy of criminal investigations and discusses the various avenues via which information may flow to the Antitrust Division about possible cartel activities leading to investigations and prosecutions. Using time-series data, he examines the interrelationships between the criminal enforcement variables as well as the potential linkages between civil and criminal enforcement. The findings include: (1) current period increases in grand jury investigations or criminal cases initiated or the number of individuals or firms convicted generates increases in most of these variables in future periods. This suggests that information unearthed during a given criminal investigation often reveals information about other conspiracies leading to future investigations; and (2) an increase in civil enforcement leads to future increases in the criminal prosecutions and firms and individuals convicted, suggesting that information gleaned during civil (e.g., mergers or monopolization) investigations may sometimes reveal information about collusive behavior in markets leading to criminal investigations. The results point to potentially important complementarities in the antitrust investigative processes. The findings appear to offer some practical advice for firms: (1) if you are neck-deep in a price-fixing agreement, be very careful about submitting a merger application to the DOJ or FTC; and (2) if you are caught price-fixing in one market and you are engaged in similar activities in other markets, you may want to quickly head for the corporate leniency door![6]

---

[6] See Ghosal (2006b) for some examples from actual cases. For example, the Antitrust Division's investigation of the lysine cartel involving Archer-Daniels Midlands and several Asian firms uncovered evidence on the vitamins and related cartels leading to their prosecution including large multinationals like Hoffman-La Roche and Rhone-Poulenc. Block and Feinstein (1986), for example, present evidence on spillover investigations in the highway construction industry where the Antitrust Division prosecuted about 200 contractors on charges of bid-rigging. Regarding the interface between civil and criminal investigations, some examples include the Division's successful challenge of the UPM Kymmene-Bemis MACtac merger a few years back due to price-fixing allegations. Further, it spawned a grand jury investigation into the alleged price fixing. Another was the FTC's "3 Tenors" case which came out of an HSR investigation of a proposed merger between Time Warner & EMI. The contracts that were ultimately challenged were discovered during the HSR investigation.

The recent progress in fighting cartels has led not to complacency but rather an ambition in policy circles and academia to make further improvements. The E.C. revised its leniency program in 2002 and currently there are discussions about adopting the U.S. model of private customer damages. Criminalization of price-fixing is on the rise; as of 2002, Ireland and the U.K. joined Canada, Israel, and the U.S. in having prison sentences as an instrument to punish managers for colluding. With the Antitrust Criminal Penalty Enforcement and Reform Act of 2004, the U.S. increased the maximum prison sentence from three to ten years and expanded leniency by reducing liability from treble customer damages to single damages.

That the development of stronger anti-cartel policies is high on the policy agenda makes the papers in this volume all the more timely and valuable. By generating a better understanding about collusion and how antitrust policy influences firm behavior, they provide the foundation for making further innovations in the battle against cartels.

The chapter by John Connor takes stock as to the magnitude of penalties levied since 1990 along with other dimensions to enforcement. He finds vast differences between the E.U. and the U.S. The time between "first notice" and the first cartel member being sanctioned is around two years in the E.U. which is noticeably longer than in the U.S. In addition, government fines and private damage recovery in the U.S. are more than four times as large as in the E.U. Connor estimates for the U.S. that total penalties are about 150% of damages which is insufficient to make collusion unprofitable. Though progress has been made, we are still far short of penalties being big enough and detection being likely enough to make collusion exclusively a topic for economic historians.

In asking how severe the penalty must be to deter cartel formation, the usual approach is to find that value whereby the cartel participation constraint (CPC) is violated; that is, the minimum expected penalty that exceeds the incremental expected gain in profit from colluding. The chapter by Paolo Buccirossi and Giancarlo Spagnolo questions the validity of this approach. With most cartels, the biggest challenge is maintaining internal stability, which is modeled using the incentive compatibility constraint (ICC); the satisfaction of which ensures that a firm prefers to collude than to cheat. A leniency program can significantly affect the ICC because a firm that cheats can, at the same time, apply for leniency. In this way, a leniency program can disrupt cartel stability and deter cartels from forming. What Buccirossi and Spagnolo show is that it is generally the ICC that is binding and not the CPC. Thus, expected penalties can be such that collusion is profitable but a cartel still may not form because the ICC is violated; the cartel would be unstable. By calibrating a simple model, they are able to show that, with a leniency program, the necessary penalty to violate the ICC is a mere fraction of that required to violate the CPC. In spite of the ability of a leniency program to amplify the impact of penalties, the authors conclude that E.U. fines are still too low to deter cartel formation, which reinforces the conclusion of Connor.

An exploration into the effect of leniency programs is also conducted in the chapters by Cécile Aubert and Joe Chen and Joseph Harrington. While they both find a leniency program can enhance welfare, they also find some perverse effects that may generate inefficiencies. Previous theoretical research examining leniency programs has, for reasons of tractability, restricted the model so that there is only one collusive price (thus, firms cannot control the degree of collusion) and both the penalty and the probability of detection and conviction are fixed and independent of firm behavior. The general conclusion of that work is the optimality of maximal leniency—waiving all fines to the first firm to apply. Using numerical analysis, the chapter by Chen and Harrington explores a richer model that allows for a range of collusive prices and for the penalty and the probability of detection and conviction to be sensitive to the collusive price path; higher prices result in a larger penalty and larger price changes imply a higher probability of detection. With this model they not only consider the effect of a leniency program on cartel formation but also its effect on the price path when a cartel does form. Supportive of previous work, maximal leniency is shown to be optimal. However, they also find that partial leniency can, relative to a policy of no leniency, actually make collusion easier which is reflected in a higher cartel price path. It is important to note that the U.S. does not provide full leniency since a firm is still liable for single customer damages which are often substantial.

A very different approach to modeling firm behavior is taken in the chapter by Aubert. Building on the earlier work of Aubert et al. (2006), she takes account of the important fact that those agents who are colluding are almost never significant shareholders. Rather, they are managers whose interest is dictated by their compensation scheme and this inevitably means they care about more than just expected profit. This approach permits one to explore how antitrust policy influences compensation schemes and thereby the incentives of managers to collude. The agency problem lies in that a manager can deliver reasonably high profit by either colluding with low effort or competing with high effort. Society prefers the latter though the manager prefers the former since effort is costly. Without antitrust penalties, there is no way to induce competition and high effort. Introduction of penalties allows the manager's payoff to differ between collusion/low effort and competition/high effort which then makes it possible to induce the socially preferred outcome. The introduction of a leniency program can deter collusion when it would have occurred otherwise but it can also result in inefficiencies that would not have occurred if there were penalties but no leniency. Taking account of the fact that managers, not shareholders, are the ones colluding—as done in this chapter—is an important direction for future research.

Though our attention thus far has focused on explicit collusion, tacit collusion can be just as welfare-reducing in spite of being legal. Tacit collusion is of particular relevance to merger analysis since a primary consideration is whether a proposed merger would have coordinated effects by making tacit collusion more likely. This issue is addressed in the chapters by William Kovacic, Robert Marshall, Leslie Marx, and Matthew Raiff and Marc Ivaldi, Bruno Jullien, Patrick Rey, Paul Seabright, and Jean Tirole.

As the distinction between tacit and explicit collusion is not one that the existing theoretical framework can easily accommodate, empirical work pertaining to tacit collusion is especially valuable and the chapter by Kovacic et al. offers a novel analysis. They build on the idea that firms, upon discovery that they had been operating a cartel, might substitute tacit collusion for explicit collusion. Identifying the circumstances under which they are able to make that transition could be informative towards identifying the circumstances under which tacit collusion is sustainable. They focus on 30 vitamins markets that were involved in the vitamins cartel of the 1990s. Vitamins markets with only two firms are found to maintain prices after the plea period, which is consistent with having replaced explicit with tacit collusion; while markets with three or more firms experience a large drop in price. This suggests that concerns about coordinated effects from a proposed merger are particularly relevant when it means reducing the number of firms to two.

Finally, the chapter by Marc Ivaldi et al. is an excellent primer on the theory of collusion; it is comprehensive yet concise, rigorous yet readable. For the reader who is not knowledgeable about how industrial organization economists think about collusion, this chapter will let you in on our little secrets. The chapter is of particular value in identifying the structural variables relevant to evaluating the possible coordinated effects of a merger.

1.3. Merger control

Merger control in the U.S. has seen significant milestones. The first Merger Guidelines were introduced in 1968. Among the important objectives were to inform the markets and the public of the use of the federal antitrust laws to the evaluation of mergers and to streamline the procedures to provide more transparency about the process. Implementation under the 1968 guidelines largely reflected the structure–conduct–performance paradigm with heavy emphasis on market shares and concentration and a near-paranoia on entry barriers (Williamson, 2002). Shifts in economic and legal thinking—for example, away from narrow-minded market concentration based evaluations to a broader understanding of business practices—eventually led to changes in the guidelines.

The 1982 Merger Guidelines introduced several innovations. An important one was the hypothetical monopolist test. As noted by Werden (2002):

> The hypothetical monopolist paradigm became a major organizing principle of the 1982 Merger Guidelines, and the hypothetical monopolist paradigm came to provide the sole test for market delineation ... The hypothetical monopolist paradigm was the lens through which all evidence was to be viewed ... the contribution of the 1982 Merger Guidelines was not the hypothetical monopolist paradigm itself, but rather a carefully constructed algorithm for merger analysis built around that paradigm.

Werden goes on to note that, due to the 1982 Merger Guidelines, the hypothetical monopolist paradigm was embraced, in varying degrees, by competition authorities in many countries. The innovation in the 1984 revision of the Merger Guidelines was to place significant focus on efficiencies and made it an integral part of the competitive effects analysis. As noted by Kolasky and Dick (2002), this focus remained intact until 1997 when the DOJ and FTC revised the Merger Guidelines to elaborate on the tools they had developed to evaluate efficiency claims.

The 1992 incarnation of the Merger Guidelines produced enhanced emphasis on qualitative competitive effects analysis and an even greater openness to considering efficiency arguments (Kolasky and Dick, 2002). The 1992 Horizontal Merger Guidelines also distinguished between anti-competitive mergers that may make it more likely for firms to coordinate their actions versus mergers that make it profitable for the merging firms to reduce output and raise price *unilaterally*. The unilateral effects theories and the methods for their evaluation gained currency starting the 1992 guidelines. Baker (1997) provides an insightful discussion of unilateral effects and notes two key factors that made this development possible: (1) the theoretical literature started by Salant et al. (1983); and (2) the econometric methodology and point-of-sale scanner data that made it possible to identify the extent to which consumers consider individual products close substitutes. Baker goes on to note:

> The 1992 Horizontal Merger Guidelines recognize these economic developments by setting forth several ways in which mergers may "less[en] competition through unilateral effects." The settings in which this may occur include two in which competition is localized—a spatial location model of competition among sellers of differentiated products, and an auction model variant—and a third in which firms sell homogeneous products and are distinguished primarily by their capacities.

Finally, an important refinement in the 1997 revision of the Merger Guidelines (1997) related to whether the efficiencies had to be passed on to consumers in order for it to matter. Some interpreted the 1997 revisions as adopting a "consumer welfare" approach to efficiencies in which efficiencies would count only to the extent they are likely to be passed on to consumers in the form of lower prices and expanded output. However, Kolasky and Dick (2002) note that "a close reading of the 1997 revisions shows that the agencies preserved the possibility of weighing positively efficiencies that would not immediately be passed on to consumers. Significantly, the revisions did not include a pass-on requirement in defining cognizable efficiencies." They label the 1997 revisions "a hybrid consumer welfare/total welfare model."

To look at the big picture of merger enforcement, we present Figures 1.4–1.6 (from Ghosal, 2006c). Figure 1.4 presents data on the total number of mergers challenged in court by the U.S. Department of Justice over the period 1958–2003.[7] The data show a significant cooling-off of merger challenges from about

---

[7] U.S. merger enforcement is jointly carried out by the U.S. Department of Justice and the Federal Trade Commission. On average the task is probably split evenly. Here, to take a quick look, we only present the DOJ data.

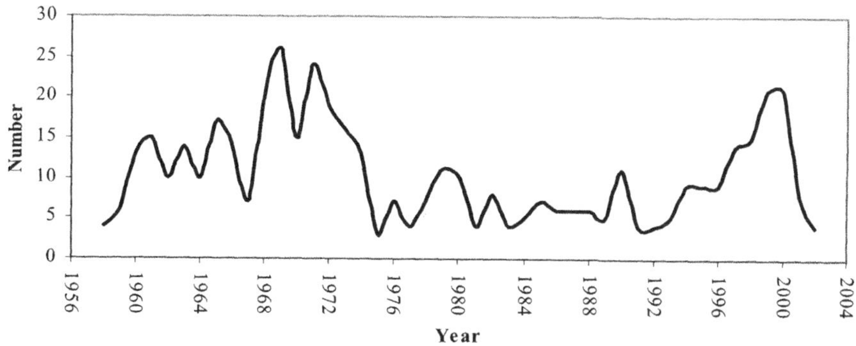

Fig. 1.4: U.S.: Total number of mergers challenged.

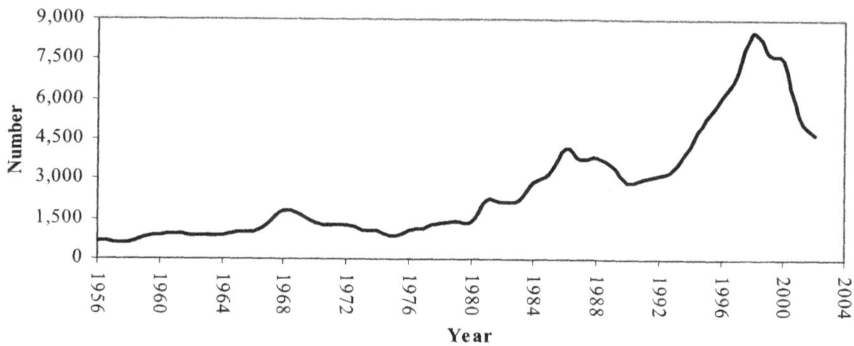

Fig. 1.5: U.S.: Total number of mergers.

the mid-1970s to the mid-1990s, after which the data show a small increase before falling off again.[8] The absolute number of mergers challenged of course is not the best indicator of the intensity of merger enforcement because the total number of mergers in the U.S. varies a lot over time. To take a look at this, Figure 1.5 presents the total number of mergers in the U.S. over the same time

[8] In an early case—*U.S. v. General Dynamics Co. (1974)*—the Supreme Court went against the antitrust mindset of the 1950s and 1960s and did not find a violation even thought the existing market shares were high. The Antitrust Division had defined the product market as "coal." The Court disagreed with this definition and considered the market to be the more overarching "energy" which included oil, gas, nuclear and geothermal power. The Antitrust Division had defined the geographic market narrowly. The Court disagreed with the geographic market definition and broadened it considerably arguing that the market area should be defined in terms of the transportation networks and freight charges that determine the cost of delivering coal and other energy. In addition, the Court examined in detail the actual and potential competition and entry conditions in the markets under consideration. This wide ranging evaluation of market conditions, and considering significantly wider product and geographic markets, was a radical departure from the narrow concentration based mindset of the earlier decades and set the stage for significant changes in future merger evaluations.

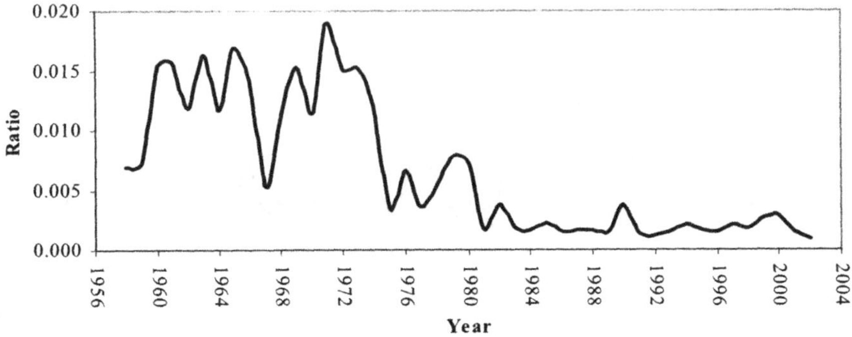

Fig. 1.6: U.S.: Ratio of merger challenges to merger wave.

period. These data show a merger wave in the 1980s and another in the late-1990s. To take a more accurate look at the intensity of merger enforcement, Figure 1.6 presents the ratio of mergers challenged by the DOJ to the total number of mergers in the U.S. The data in Figure 1.6 show a dramatic drop in the intensity of merger challenges in the mid-1970s and remain low thereafter. Ghosal (2006c) discusses the evolution of merger control and conducts an econometric analysis to shed light on the political-economy of merger enforcement. Kovacic (2003) presents a lucid discussion about the underlying forces that affected the path of the U.S. merger enforcement as well as myriad enforcement issues that are not easily captured in a simple count of mergers challenged by the government.

Traversing the Atlantic, the European Union's merger policy is enshrined in the so-called Merger Regulation.[9] As merger control is not specifically provided for in the Treaty, the Commission attempted to fill this lacuna by developing the law under Articles 81 (anticompetitive agreements) and 82 (abuse of dominance) to scrutinize mergers. However, these tools were deemed inadequate and the first Merger Regulation was adopted in 1989. The E.U. has seen significant changes in the intensity of screening of mergers as well as numerous administrative changes. Motta (2004, Ch. 1) and Wish (2001) present some of the details. To provide a quick look at recent patterns in E.U. merger enforcement, Figures 1.7 and 1.8 present the total number of merger investigations that reached the Phase I and the more critical Phase II stage of evaluation.[10] These data point to a steady rise in scrutiny from 1990 to 2001 before tapering off in recent years.

In recent years, merger policy in Europe has taken on a somewhat controversial turn. The year 2002 was exceptional as The Court of First Instance annulled

---

[9] Council Regulation No 139/2004 of 20 January 2004 on the control of concentrations between undertakings, which entered into force on May 1, 2004.

[10] These data are from Duso et al. (this volume). Phase I refers to the initial (roughly one month) investigation and Phase II refers to the more substantive (roughly four month) investigation.

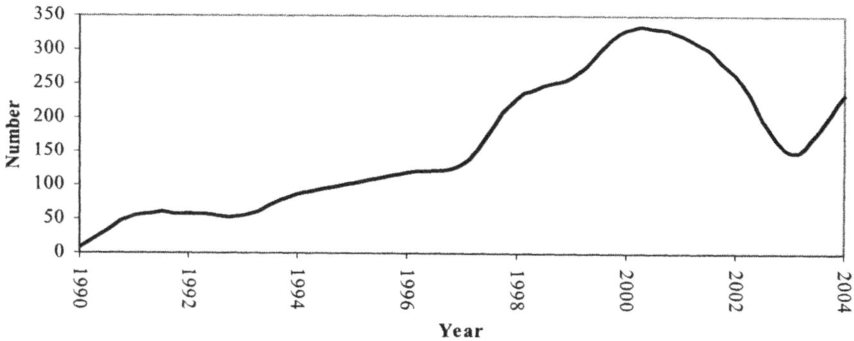

Fig. 1.7: E.U.: Total number of Phase I merger investigations.

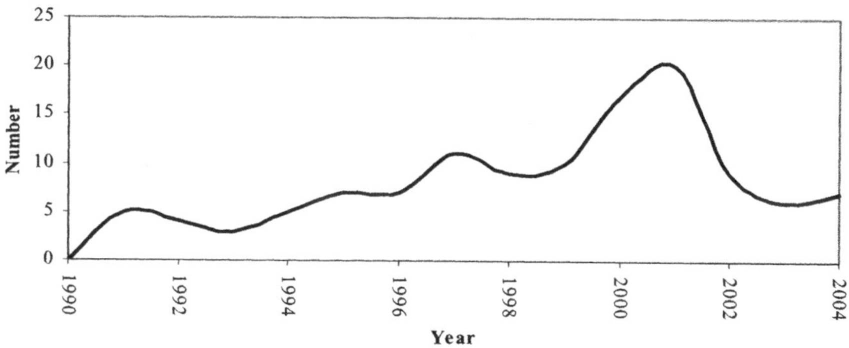

Fig. 1.8: E.U.: Total number of Phase II merger investigations.

three of the Commission's merger decisions: Airtours and First Choice; Schneider and Legrand; and Tetra Laval and Sidel. In 2004, the Court annulled the prohibition of the WorldCom (now MCI) and Sprint merger. Even the Commission's decision to block the merger between Volvo and Scania was criticized by some due to the Commission's narrow focus on market shares in specific countries and ignoring broader issues related to demand and supply substitution. Finally, the E.C. blocked the merger between two U.S.-based companies, General Electric and Honeywell. While the Court of First Instance upheld the Commission's decision, they noted that the Commission had committed manifest errors of assessing the conglomerate effects of the GE/Honeywell merger.

The cumulative impact of these events called for a reform of the European merger control system and the E.U. decided on a major reform package which entered into force in 2004. Several elements of this package also appear to reduce the differences between the U.S. and the E.U. The new merger regulation now includes a new substantive test including unilateral effects. The Commission also issued horizontal merger guidelines which elaborate on the analysis of unilateral effects and efficiency gains as part of the competition test, and make clear that it will use a consumer welfare standard. And, for the first time, a Chief Competition Economist was appointed. It is, however, somewhat unclear whether the new regulation signifies a shift in policy. The new Significantly Impeding Effective Competition test (the SIEC test) appears to superficially rearrange the terms of the old dominance test. An innovation, however, is to increase legal certainty. The new regulation clarifies that mergers in oligopolistic markets may harm competition, even in the absence of collusion. The courts had not expressly interpreted the old regulation to include such unilateral effects. Therefore, the new regulation explicitly states that the substantive test extends beyond dominance (recital 25). It is also declared that the guidance that may be drawn from past judgments of the courts and Commission decisions pursuant to the old regulation should be preserved, and therefore the substantial test still refers to dominance (recital 26). Thus, although it might be unclear whether the old regulation included unilateral effect, it should be clear the new one does.[11]

Several of the chapters in this volume contribute to the analysis of some of the important issues in the development of merger control.

The blocking of the proposed merger between General Electric and Honeywell —two U.S. based companies—by the E.U. generated a transatlantic war of words with some accusing the E.U. of placing greater weight on protecting European competitors. The chapter by Jay Pil Choi analyzes the political economy aspect of international antitrust in light of the GE/Honeywell decision. Choi argues that this case demonstrates the need for consistent simple rules and better coordination by harmonizing antitrust controls across antitrust enforcement agencies in different jurisdictions, especially between Europe and the United States. One reason is that with the current system, the enforcement decision on a merger does not reflect the majority view and any international merger will be essentially determined by the least permissive agency. Another reason is that efficient mergers can be blocked since each agency ignores the external effects of the merger in other jurisdictions.

The European Commission has intervened against a number of domestic mergers in small Member States. Against this backdrop, Henrik Horn and Johan Stennek discuss regional aspects of merger control. For instance, the Commission prohibited Volvo's acquisition of Scania, arguing that competition would be reduced in nationally defined markets. These interventions triggered a political debate about merger control and market definitions. Smaller countries accused

---

[11] Since the 1992 Merger Guidelines, the U.S. "significant lessening of competition test" (SLC) has been interpreted to include unilateral effects. But the recent Oracle decision has caused some controversy. According to this decision a plaintiff must demonstrate that the merging parties would enjoy a post-merger monopoly or dominant position at least in a "localized competition space" in order to prove unilateral effects. Still, the decision does acknowledge that economic analyses such as merger simulations or econometric estimates of diversion ratios (that do not rely on the identification of a market or submarket) may be useful to address unilateral effects. (Useful discussions of this can be found in the issue of Antitrust (Spring 2005; Vol. 19, No. 2) published by the American Bar Association.)

the Commission of making it impossible for their companies to merge and obtain leading global positions. The E.U. officials responded that companies in smaller countries can obtain leading positions, by merging with companies from other countries. The Volvo/Renault and Scania/Volkswagen partnerships that followed the prohibition of the Volvo/Scania merger, clearly showed that there were alternative ways for these companies to grow. The critics acknowledge that international mergers may indeed constitute an alternative. But international mergers may be less advantageous for smaller countries. They may have adverse effects on employment and the location of both head quarters and production. E.U. officials concede that E.U. merger control does not take into account a possible move of firms abroad and that mergers are controlled for the interest of consumers. Horn and Stennek note that international firms have an incentive to locate their production to the larger countries with the larger markets. They may serve also the smaller markets from the same production facilities to avoid duplication of plant-specific fixed costs. The consumers in smaller markets will then have to pay higher prices, to cover the trade costs incurred when exporting goods from the larger to the smaller countries.

Since the beginning of antitrust enforcement starting with the U.S. Sherman Act of 1890, there has been a debate about the objectives of antitrust in general and merger control in particular. The debates have centered around issues related to consumer welfare, total welfare, redistribution of wealth, protection of small businesses, among other considerations. The chapter by Sven-Olof Fridolfsson discusses the goal of merger control. The goal in the U.S. is typically perceived to be to protect the consumers. Also the new horizontal merger guidelines clearly indicate that the E.C. will use a consumer welfare standard. The question is why firms' profits are not considered? The answer perhaps lies in the concern for the distribution of wealth in society, combined with the belief that firm owners typically are wealthier than consumers. It is far from clear, however, that merger control can influence distribution much. And, in any case, taxes and transfers are probably more effective. Many economists have advocated a shift of focus to economic efficiency—that is, merger control should attempt to maximize the sum of the firms' profits and the consumers' surplus. But maybe the authorities are right after all and there should be a consumer bias even though the ultimate goal may be overall efficiency. Fridolfsson notes that firms can be expected to propose the most profitable mergers, among those that would be accepted by the authorities. By demanding mergers to also benefit consumers the firms are forced to propose mergers that are profitable because of important synergetic gains, as opposed to being profitable due to lessening of competition. This is efficiency enhancing.

Some mergers that should have been blocked may have been cleared by the authorities. Other mergers that were cleared probably should have been challenged. Finally, if mergers were cleared subject to remedies, were they the right one's? How do we know that the competition authority made the right decision? Tomaso Duso, Klaus Gugler and Burcin Yurtoglu notice that problematic mergers today are often cleared, but subject to conditions that remove competitive concerns such as the divestiture of some assets or other behavioral obligations like licensing agreement or access to essential facilities. For instance, during its fiscal years 1998 and 1999, the Federal Trade Commission challenged 63 mergers. Of these 41 (65%) involved negotiated restructuring, 18 (29%) were abandoned, and only four (6%) were litigated. In Europe, only 19 mergers have been blocked since 1990. During the same time more than half of Phase II decisions (72 out of 121, or 59%) are cleared subject to commitments. Duso et al. provide an international comparison of institutional arrangements and regulatory approaches to deal with remedies in merger control. They conclude that there is a clear convergence on some shared principles that guide competition authorities in the application of remedies. They also provide a first empirical assessment of the use of remedies in European merger control, using an event study methodology to identify the competitive effects of mergers and remedies. They suggest that the Commission's views on competitive effects quite often appear to differ from the view of the market, as it is expressed by the movements in stock-prices. Moreover, stock markets seem to evaluate remedies to be on average effective only when applied in the first investigation phase and not so when adopted after an in depth inquiry.[12]

Evaluating the unilateral effects of mergers became important in the U.S. starting with the 1992 Merger Guidelines and the E.U., in recent years, has taken similar steps in this direction. The chapter by Jérôme Foncel, Marc Ivaldi and Valérie Rabassa provides an extensive discussion of the new substantive test of the new European Merger Regulation, with an empirical illustration from the Lagardère/Editis case. They argue that this case demonstrates an enhanced interest of the European Commission for the measurement of unilateral effects. They also argue that the use of an econometric model based on unilateral effects clarifies and complements the traditional dominance approach, by providing explicit measures of the predicted price increases.

Finally, the chapter by Luke Froeb, Steven Tschantz, and Gregory Werden discusses the effects of mergers between competing manufacturers of differentiated consumer products that are sold through retailers. They demonstrate that the effects of the mergers on consumers are determined to a large extent by the manufacturers' relationships with their retailers. The paper illustrates how the sort of formal modeling that has become common with differentiated products mergers must account for vertical issues relating to horizontal mergers.

1.4. Non-merger enforcement

Non-merger enforcement in the U.S.—under the Sherman Act Section 1 and Section 2—has seen some landmark antitrust cases such as Standard Oil (1911), Aluminum Corp. of America (1947), AT&T (1980), Microsoft (1999), to name a few. In the more recent era, however, non-merger enforcement in the U.S. has

[12] Also see Duso et al. (2006) on using stock price data to evaluate merger control decisions.

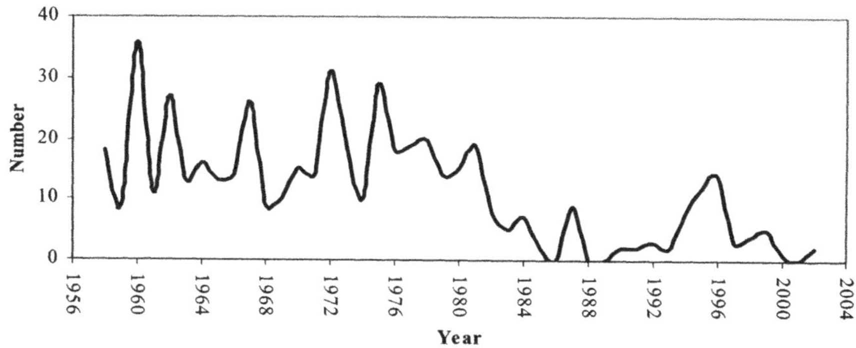

Fig. 1.9: U.S.: Sherman Act Section 1 cases.

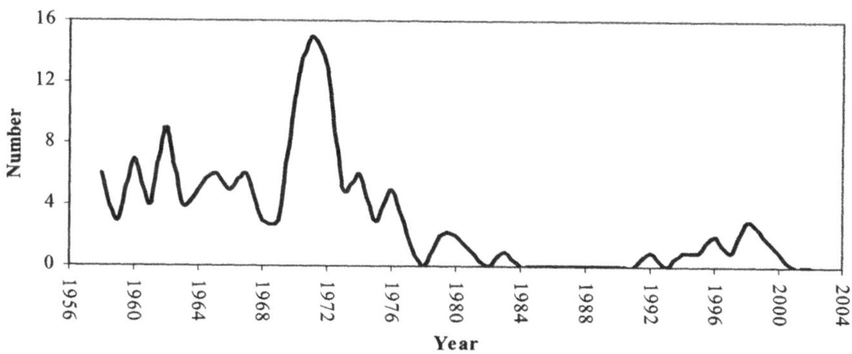

Fig. 1.10: U.S.: Sherman Act Section 2 cases.

experienced a marked decline. In significant part, the Chicago-school's focus on examining the efficiency aspects of business practices provided the initial impetus that de-emphasized non-merger civil antitrust enforcement. Probably the most significant early case that dwelled on efficiency issues is Continental TV v. GTE Sylvania (1977). In this case the Supreme Court emphasized concepts related to competition in the market and argued that vertical restrictions are likely to promote interbrand competition by allowing producers to achieve efficiencies in distribution. This is the first time that the Court explicitly noted efficiencies to argue in favor of the pro-competitive effects. Figures 1.9 and 1.10 (from Ghosal, 2006a) provide a bird's-eye view which reveal clear declines in non-merger enforcement. Ghosal (2006a) conducts an econometric analysis of these patterns and finds that both political and economic factors appear to play an important role in the shifts in enforcement.

Turning to non-merger enforcement in the E.U., we begin by taking a quick look at the E.C. antitrust decisions by the type of alleged infringement. These data are presented in Table 1.1 and Figure 1.11, both of which are from Schinkel et al. (2006). Schinkel et al. present one of the most comprehensive analyses of

Table 1.1: E.C. antitrust decisions specified by the type of alleged infringement (adapted from Schinkel et al., 2006).

	Negative clearance	Exemption	Infringement	Interim measure
Horizontal constraints	31	58	136	0
Abuse of dominance	0	0	44	3
Vertical restraints	29	31	61	1
Licensing	6	12	11	0
Joint ventures	12	46	3	0
Procedural issue	0	0	30	0

European enforcement to date and survey the development of European competition law enforcement of Articles 81, 82 and 86—excluding merger control and state aid—since its foundation in the Treaty of Rome of 1957. Their time-series data reveal a stepped up enforcement by the E.U. in recent decades, a shift from notifications and third party complaints to decisions in investigations started at the Commission's own initiative, and an exponential increase in fines. Unlike some of the findings for the U.S., they do not find evidence of political cycles in the E.U. enforcement. They also relate the types of infringements to the OECD sector classification and the probability of an appeal being lodged with the European Court of Justice and the Court of First Instance.

The E.C. is currently reviewing its policies against dominant companies' exclusionary conduct, such as predatory pricing, rebates, tying and bundling, and refusal to supply (part of Article 82). A recent discussion paper (E.C., 2005) outlines a more effects-based (or economic) approach and clarifies that the objective of the rules against abuses of dominant positions is to protect the consumers, and not the competitors of the dominant companies. The suggested framework for analysis is quite detailed, with three tests. The first step is to test if the conduct has the capability to foreclose competitors from the market. The second step is to establish actual or likely foreclosure effects. At this point the market coverage (incidence) of the conduct, network effects and other circumstances are investigated. In the third step, the dominant companies will have the opportunity to rebut a presumption of abuse, for example, by demonstrating efficiencies.

During the consultation following the publication of the discussion paper and the public hearing, several issues were discussed.[13] For instance, consistency with economic principles may come at the cost of legal uncertainty. A too complicated system may also mean that enforcement decisions may come too late to protect the rivals of much stronger dominant firms. Some new entrants are afraid that not using per-se rules and presumptions will make it more difficult for them. But many commentators also call for safe harbors (e.g., in terms of market

---

[13] The comments are published at: http://ec.europa.eu/comm/competition/antitrust/others/article_82_review.html.

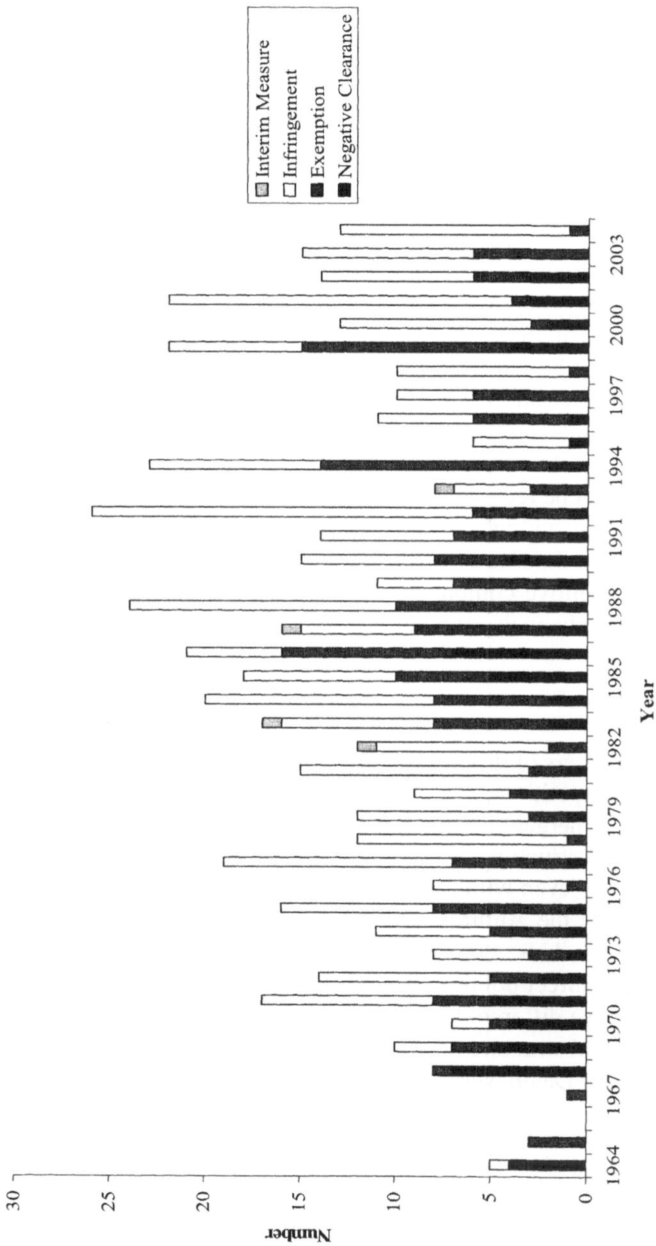

Fig. 1.11: E.C. antitrust decisions by type (from Schinkel et al., 2006).

shares) for potentially dominant firms. One of the more specific issues with the economic approach is whether and how efficiencies should be included in the analysis of abuse of dominance. Unlike the rules on anticompetitive agreements (Article 81) and on mergers, Article 82 does not explicitly refer to efficiencies. Still, the discussion paper does outline an efficiency defense, similar to that of the other competition policy areas. A difficulty in designing an efficiency defense is that, on the one hand, efficiencies should be an integral part of the Commission's investigation of anticompetitive effects. On the other hand the dominant companies have an informational advantage and should bear the burden of proof.

In the arena of non-merger enforcement, the chapter by Timothy Brennan dwells on the important issue of monopolization law. Brennan notes that U.S. monopolization law is controversial as evidenced by the AT&T and Microsoft cases. He argues that monopolization is typically portrayed as a dominant firm protecting itself by harming nascent rivals. Since the competitive process itself—offering more and better products at lower prices—also harms rivals, antitrust observers fall into two warring camps. Brennan argues that we could potentially limit the controversy and avoid these spurious requirements if monopolization law can be recast to make it akin to the relatively less controversial branches of collusion and merger law. Brennan argues that this entails rejecting the focus on rivals and instead treating Section 1 cases as about monopolization of otherwise competitive complementary markets, for example, in production inputs, distribution channels, or retail outlets.

1.5. Systemic issues

The final three chapters of this volume cover general topics that are of relevance for all areas of competition policy—which include non-merger enforcement as well as cartels and merger control.

The institutional structure of competition and regulatory agencies can vary across countries and even within countries. For example, the Assistant Attorney General who heads the Antitrust Division of the U.S. Department of Justice is appointed by the U.S. President, whereas the E.U. competition commissioner has no such direct political affiliation. In the event that different political principal's may have different views about intervention in markets, such differences in institutional structure may affect enforcement. The chapter by Antoine Faure-Grimaud and David Martimort discusses the pros and cons of politically independent competition agencies. Independence may for example mean the right to open and close a merger review on clear and pre-specified criteria. Issues of political influence often surface in connection to international mergers. In the United States concerns about foreign ownership of ports and oil facilities blocked two foreign acquisitions. In Germany the Ministry of Economics overruled the antitrust authority's recommendation to prohibit Eon's takeover of Ruhrgas on the ground that the merger would create a substantial export powerhouse. Faure-Grimaud and Martimort argue that independence of the regulator stabilizes regulatory policies and avoids much of the fluctuations induced by an exogenous political uncertainty on the electoral outcomes. However, independence also increases the cost of preventing regulatory capture. Adding up both effects, independence nevertheless increases ex ante social welfare.

The U.S. has seen a dramatic increase in private antitrust litigation over the last few decades. One view of this trend is that these lawsuits purportedly are for gaining respite from anti-competitive activities by market participants. A competing view is that many of these lawsuits are for strategic reasons. Preston McAfee, Hugo Mialon and Sue Mialon discuss firms' incentives to use antitrust lawsuits for strategic purposes—to prevent procompetitive efficiency improvements by rival firms. They argue that smaller firms in more fragmented industries are more likely to use the antitrust laws strategically than larger firms in concentrated industries.

Finally, the chapter by Joseph Francois and Henrik Horn explores important linkages between competition policy and international trade and discusses the scope for an international agreement to curb the beggar-thy-neighbor competition policies. They argue that countries that are net exporters in the sectors that are more easily cartelized do have incentives to pursue such policies. In addition, there is a certain political logic to the fact that there are attempts to bring such an agreement into a structure like the WTO. This is, in part, because such an agreement would enhance trade. This is also because a competition policy agreement may require side payments, and a trade agreement, like the WTO or regional schemes, offers plenty of scope for members to trade off gains under one agreement with losses under another agreement. There is reason to believe that support for such an agreement could come from a wide spectrum of factor owners in both exporting and importing countries.

Acknowledgements

We are grateful to Hugo Mialon and Maarten Pieter Schinkel for helpful comments.

References

Abrantes-Metz, R.M., Froeb, L., Geweke, J., Taylor, C. (2005), A variance screen for collusion. U.S. Federal Trade Commission, Bureau of Economics Working Paper No. 275, March.

Aubert, C., Rey, P., Kovacic, W. (2006), The impact of leniency and whistle-blowing programs on cartels, *International Journal of Industrial Organization*, in press.

Baker, J. (1997), Unilateral competitive effects theories in merger analysis. *Antitrust* 11, 21–26.

Baker, J. (2002), A preface to post-Chicago antitrust. In: van den Bergh, R., Pardolesi, R., Cucinotta, A. (Eds.), *Post-Chicago Developments in Antitrust Analysis*. Edward Elgar.

Baker, J. (2003), The case for antitrust enforcement. *Journal of Economic Perspectives* 17, 27–50.

Block, M., Feinstein, J. (1986), The spillover effect of antitrust enforcement. *The Review of Economics and Statistics* 68, 122–131.

Bork, R. (1966), Legislative intent and the policy of the Sherman Act. *Journal of Law and Economics* 9, 7–48.

Bork, R. (1978), *The Antitrust Paradox*. Basic Books, New York.

Brenner, S. (2005), An empirical study of the European corporate leniency program. Humboldt-University Working Paper, March.

Crandall, W., Winston, C. (2003), Does antitrust policy improve consumer welfare? Assessing the evidence. *Journal of Economic Perspectives* 17, 3–26.

Demsetz, H. (1973), Industry structure, market rivalry and public policy. *Journal of Law and Economics* 16, 1–9.

Demsetz, H. (1974), Two systems of belief about monopoly. In: Goldschmidt, H., Mann, H.M., Weston, J.F. (Eds.), *Industrial Concentration: New Learning*.

Director, A. (1957), United States v. United Show Machinery Corporation: An economic analysis of an antitrust case. *The University of Chicago Law Review* 24, 606–611.

Director, A., Levi, E. (1956), Law and the future: Trade regulation. *Northwestern University Law Review*, 281–256.

Duso, T., Neven, D., Röller, L.-H. (2006), The political economy of European merger control: Evidence using stock market data. *Journal of Law and Economics*, in press.

European Commission (2005), DG Competition discussion paper on the application of Article 82 of the treaty to exclusionary abuses. http://ec.europa.eu/comm/competition/antitrust/others/discpaper2005.pdf.

FTC History (2003), Bureau of Economics Contributions to Law Enforcement, Research, and Economic Knowledge and Policy, Transcript of Roundtable with Former Directors of the Bureau of Economics, September 4. http://www.ftc.gov/be/workshops/directorsconference/index.htm.

Ghosal, V. (2006a), Regime shift in antitrust. Georgia Institute of Technology, Working Paper.

Ghosal, V. (2006b), Uncovering dynamic interrelationships in the process of criminal antitrust investigations. Georgia Institute of Technology, Working Paper.

Ghosal, V. (2006c), Economics, politics and merger control. In: Jay, Pil, Choi (Eds.), *Recent Developments in Antitrust*. MIT Press, Cambridge.

Griffin, J. (2003), The modern leniency program after ten years: A summary overview of the antitrust divisions criminal enforcement program. U.S. Department of Justice.

Harding, C., Joshua, J. (2004), *Regulating Cartels in Europe: A Study of Legal Control of Corporate Delinquency*. Oxford University Press, Cambridge.

Harrington, J.E. Jr. (2006), Detecting cartels. In: Buccirossi, P. (Ed.), *Handbook of Antitrust Economics*, The MIT Press, in press.

Kolasky, W., Dick, A. (2002), The Merger Guidelines and the integration of efficiencies into antitrust review of horizontal mergers. Paper presented at the 20th Anniversary of the 1982 Merger Guidelines, The Contribution of the Merger Guidelines to the Evolution of Antitrust Doctrine.

Kovacic, W. (2003), The modern evolution of U.S. competition policy evolution norms. *Antitrust Law Journal* 71, 377–478.

Kovacic, W., Shapiro, C. (2000), A century of antitrust and legal thinking. *Journal of Economic Perspectives* 14, 43–60.

McGee, J.S. (1958), Predatory price cutting: The standard oil case. *Journal of Law and Economics* 1, 137–168.

Merger Guidelines (1997), Federal Trade Commission and U.S. Department of Justice. http://www.ftc.gov/bc/docs/horizmer.htm.

Motta, M. (2004), *Competition Policy*. Cambridge University Press.

Posner, R.A. (1969), Oligopoly and the antitrust laws: A suggested approach. *Stanford Law Review* 21, 1562–1606.

Posner, R.A. (1974), Exclusionary practices and the antitrust laws. *University of Chicago Law Review* 41, 506–535.

Posner, R.A. (1976), *Antitrust Law: An Economic Perspective*. University of Chicago Press, Chicago.

Salant, S., Switzer, S., Reynolds, R. (1983), Losses from horizontal merger: The effects of an exogenous change in industry structure on Cournot–Nash equilibrium. *Quarterly Journal of Economics* 98, 185–199.

Schinkel, M.P., Carree, M., Günster, A.M. (2006), European antitrust policy: An analysis of commission decisions, 1962–2004. Amsterdam Center for Law and Economics Working Paper Series.

Stigler, G. (1964), A theory of oligopoly. *Journal of Political Economy* 72, 44–61.

Werden, G. (2002), The 1982 Merger Guidelines and the ascent of the hypothetical monopolist paradigm. Paper presented at the 20th Anniversary of the 1982 Merger Guidelines, The Contribution of the Merger Guidelines to the Evolution of Antitrust Doctrine.

Williamson, O. (1969), Economies as an antitrust defense: The welfare tradeoffs. *American Economic Review* 58, 18–36.

Williamson, O. (2002), The Merger Guidelines of the U.S. Department of Justice: In perspective. Paper presented at the 20th Anniversary of the 1982 Merger Guidelines, The Contribution of the Merger Guidelines to the Evolution of Antitrust Doctrine.

Wish, R. (2001), *Competition Law*, 4th ed. Butterworths.

CHAPTER 2

Remembrance of Things Past: Antitrust, Ideology, and the Development of Industrial Economics

Stephen Martin

Department of Economics, Purdue University, 403 West State Street, West Lafayette, IN 47907-2056, USA
E-mail address: smartin@purdue.edu

Keywords: antitrust, industrial economics, ideology

JEL classifications: B2, L0, L4

> Why study the mistakes of the past?
> Reaction in a faculty meeting to the suggestion that the Ph.D. program include a required course on the history of economic thought.[1]

2.1. Introduction

What it is that economics can, does, or should bring to antitrust is a topic that turns up fairly often in the literature.[2] The question of what antitrust has brought to industrial economics has received less attention, and it is that question to which I devote myself in this essay.

Stigler (1982, p. 6) has noted the income redistribution consequences of antitrust for the economics profession. Such transfers accrue to individual members of the profession, and are not my topic. Closer to what I have in mind is the invaluable role of antitrust as a rich source of raw material for industrial economists (Coase, quoted in Kitch, 1983, p. 193):

> I think you can often learn more about how the economic system works by reading law books and cases in law books than you can be reading economics books because you do get descriptions of actual business practices which are difficult to explain.

---

[1] I owe this heading to an anecdote of my late teacher and onetime colleague Walter Adams.

[2] See among others Bok (1960), Sullivan (1977), Baxter (1983), Turner et al. (1983) and Rowe et al. (1984). Let me note here that anonymous referees have suggested that I include in this chapter a discussion of the impacts of contrasting schools of thought in industrial economics on antitrust. That is an interesting topic, and one I take up in Martin (2007).

CONTRIBUTIONS TO ECONOMIC ANALYSIS
VOLUME 282 ISSN: 0573-8555
DOI: 10.1016/S0573-8555(06)82002-X

But this raw material is not without its price. I will argue that the antitrust policy implications that can be drawn from scientific research by industrial economists have drawn ideological currents into academic debate as moths are drawn to a flame, and that this phenomenon contributes to explaining a puzzle that has continued for a period now going on thirty years. This puzzle is the ability of advocates who favor a minimal role of antitrust enforcement in the economy to portray their views, to the legal community, as generally accepted by economists, when this claim is now and has always been manifestly incorrect.

Concerning the current views of the profession, Bolton et al. (2000, p. 2242) write

> A powerful tension has arisen between the foundations of current legal policy and modern economic theory. The courts adhere to a static, non-strategic view of predatory pricing, believing this view to be an economic consensus. This consensus, however, is one most economists no longer accept.

U.S. courts continue to be heavily influenced by what Posner (2001, p. 194, fn. 2) terms "orthodox 'Chicago School'" views toward most strategic behavior, not merely predatory pricing. Bolton et al. are correct that most economists do not now accept the orthodox Chicago School analysis. Consideration of the literature suggests that orthodox Chicago School views were *never* accepted by mainstream economists.

Of course, scientific validity is not a matter of majority vote, and as John Bates Clark wrote long ago (1887, p. 45) "Conclusions reached by valid reasoning are always as true as the hypotheses from which they are deduced. If we admit the fact of unlimited competition, we concede in advance many doctrines which current opinion is now disposed to reject." Mainstream economists have never disputed that the policy recommendations of the orthodox Chicago School follow as a matter of logic from the assumption that observed prices and quantities can be treated as good approximations to long-run competitive equilibrium values (see the discussion, below, of Reder, 1982). What has never been accepted by most industrial economists is that it is appropriate to make this "good approximation" assumption.

In Section 2.2, I discuss the rise of industrial economics as a branch of microeconomics. In Section 2.3, I review the rise of the first Chicago School of industrial economics, which advocated affirmative government action to obtain and maintain good market performance. In Section 2.4, I turn to the rise of the Second Chicago School, which argued that no such government action was needed, and that markets could, with few exceptions, be treated as if they were in long-run perfectly competitive equilibrium (the "good approximation" assumption). Section 2.5 discusses the oligopoly problem, its role in dislodging the structure–conduct–performance paradigm by the Second Chicago School as a source of antitrust advice and in the rise of game theoretic approaches to the analysis of imperfectly competitive markets by economists. Section 2.6 discusses the evolution of the Second Chicago School in the face of the evident failure of mainstream economists to accept the good approximation assumption.

Section 2.7 concludes with a few remarks on ideology and its impact on industrial economics.

2.2. Early development of industrial economics [3]

2.2.1. Origins

Industrial economics is generally said to have emerged as a distinct branch of microeconomics with Edward S. Mason's Harvard seminar of the 1930s (Markham and Papanek, 1970, pp. vii–viii), but the topics that occupy industrial economists have concerned economists since before the emergence of political economy as a distinct branch of the social sciences in 1776.

Policy questions that remain at the heart of industrial organization were the subject of widespread academic and popular debate in the United States between 1880 and 1900, a debate that continued at only a slightly less intense level between 1900 and 1920. Seven of the first 10 presidents of the American Economic Association played active roles in this debate.[4] Marshall's 1919 *Industry and Trade* made international comparisons in industrial organization and drew conclusions for economic development. Like the bourgeois gentleman who spoke prose without realizing it, economists who studied "railway problems" (Ripley, 1907) or "trust and corporation problems" (Burns, 1937, p. 663) studied industrial economics in everything but name.

But they did so using analytical tools that seemed to them to be ill-suited to the task. The mainstream price theory of the early twentieth century consisted of a theory of competitive markets and a theory of monopoly, with a vast wasteland in between.[5] This theory of competitive markets was not the modern model of perfect competition, but its Marshallian predecessor. To classify a market as competitive in this sense required only that it (Andrews, 1951 , p. 141) "would be possible for other businesses to produce a commodity with the same technical specifications as the product of any particular firm, and to offer it for sale to that firm's customers." If this condition were met (Andrews, 1951, pp. 141–142), "the possibility of entry of other producers would ensure that long-run price would be equal to the normal average cost of production."

Economists of the period were aware of the disconnect between the implications of this theory of competitive markets and the industrial world around them (Marshall, 1925 [written in 1890], p. 268):

---

[3] For discussions of the development of the field of industrial economics, see Bain (1949a, pp. 129–133), E.T. Grether (1970), Phillips and Stevenson (1974), David Dale Martin (1976), Hay and Morris (1979), Schmalensee (1982a, 1982b, 1987, 1988), Davies and Lyons (1989), Bonanno and Brandolini (1990), and, from a perspective of legal scholarship, Hovenkamp (1991, Chapter 22).

[4] These are Francis A. Walker, John Bates Clark, Henry C. Adams, Arthur T. Hadley, Richard T. Ely, Edwin R.A. Seligman, and Jeremiah W. Jenks. The works of two others (Tassig and Patten) on tariff policy touched upon topics that would now be classified in industrial economics.

[5] Schumpeter (1934, p. 249); Bain (1944, p. 4); Stigler (1949, p. 12); Andrews (1951, p. 141; 1952, p. 72); Schneider (1967, p. 139).

> it is chiefly from America that a cry has been coming with constantly increasing force for the last fifteen years or more, that in manufactures free competition favours the growth of large firms ... ; that such firms, if driven into a corner, will bid for custom at any sacrifice; that, rather than not sell their goods at all, they will sell them at [marginal cost]..., which is sometimes very little; that, when there is not enough work for all, these manufacturers will turn their bidding recklessly against one another, and will lower prices so far that the weaker of them will be killed out, and all of them injured; so that when trade revives they will be able, even without any combination amongst themselves, to put up prices to a high level; that these intense fluctuations injure both the public and the producers; and the producers, being themselves comparatively few in number, are irresistibly drawn to some of those many kinds of combinations to which, nowadays, the name Trust is commonly ... applied.

Spurred by this perceived disconnect, some economists developed new theoretical tools, while others turned to empirical approaches.

2.2.2. Monopolistic competition

An initial theoretical response was the attempt to refine the cost curve apparatus of Marshall's theories of the firm and of industry supply. Sraffa, commenting on these efforts, drew attention to the importance of the demand side of the market for market performance (1926, p. 543):

> The chief obstacle against which [businessmen] have to contend when they want gradually to increase their production does not lie in the cost of production—which, indeed, generally favours them in that direction—but in the difficulty of selling the larger quantity of goods without reducing the price, or without having to face increased marketing expenses. This necessity of reducing prices in order to sell a larger quantity of one's own product is only an aspect of the usual descending demand curve, with the difference that instead of concerning the whole of a commodity, whatever its origin, it relates only to the goods produced by a particular firm; and the marketing expenses necessary for the extension of its market are merely costly efforts ... to increase the willingness of the market to buy from it—that is, to raise that demand curve artificially.

Two books published in 1933, Edward Chamberlin's *The Theory of Monopolistic Competition* and Joan Robinson's *The Economics of Imperfect Competition*, followed up on Sraffa's theme.[6] Both put forward analytical frameworks

---

[6] On the relation between the two works, see White (1936) and Fisher (1989, p. 114, fn. 2, emphasis in original):

> It is interesting to note that Joan Robinson, in her *The Economics of Imperfect Competition* (1933) which is often paired with Chamberlin's book, simply failed to understand the oligopoly problem altogether. She assumed (p. 21) that the behavior of each oligopolist can be modelled by creating a demand curve taking the optimal reactions of rivals into account and then having the oligopolist set marginal revenue equal to marginal cost. This totally begs the question of what those optimal reactions are—and the fact that one cannot know the answer to that before creating the theory is the central core of the oligopoly problem. Chamberlin made considerable efforts to differentiate his product from that of Joan Robinson. In the oligopoly dimension, at least, he was right.

that incorporated firm-specific downward sloping demand curves and costly sales efforts as essential aspects of the firm's environment.

Robinson (1969, p. xiii) acknowledges her debt to Sraffa (1926) and the literature of which it was a part. Chamberlin (1961, pp. 517–518) denies any connection between his work and the cost curve controversy. He traces it instead to a much earlier debate on railroad rates, a debate that drew his attention to both oligopoly and product differentiation as features of industrial markets.[7] Railroads were the first wave in the rise of large-scale industry in the United States, and to this extent Chamberlin's work may be more directly connected than that of Robinson with the underlying industrial developments that prompted economists to explore new analytical frameworks.

Samuelson (1967, p. 138) writes of the theory of monopolistic competition as a revolution, leading "economists into a new land," the land of imperfect competition (Samuelson, 1967, p. 108, fn. 5):

> If the real world displays the variety of behavior that the Chamberlin–Robinson models permit ... then reality will falsify many of the important qualitative and quantitative predictions of the competitive model. Hence, by the pragmatic test of prediction adequacy, the perfect-competition model fails to be an adequate approximation.

Stigler offers a more measured assessment (1949, p. 24):

> The general contribution of the theory of monopolistic competition ... seems to me indisputable: it has led to reorientation and refinement of our thinking on monopoly. We are now more careful to pay attention to the logical niceties of definitions of industries and commodities. We are now more careful to apply monopoly theory where it is appropriate. The importance of the trade mark and of advertising, and the need for the study of product structure and evolution, have become more generally recognized.

Most economists would probably credit the theory of monopolistic competition with a greater impact than Stigler is willing to concede. If it appears less than revolutionary to contemporary economists, that may well be because they have grown up accustomed to having monopolistic competition as part of their intellectual landscape.[8]

2.2.3. Structure–conduct–performance

The analytical framework that came out of the 1930s was the *structure–conduct–performance* (S–C–P) paradigm. It was formulated in literary rather than mathematical form, and it held center stage in industrial economics for some 40 years.

---

[7] The relation between the railroad rate controversy and Chamberlin's work is discussed by Ekelund and Hébert (1990).

[8] For elements of one debate on monopolistic competition, see Archibald (1961, 1963), Stigler (1963), Friedman (1963), and also Chamberlin (1957, Chapter 15). I do not pursue this and other such skirmishes, as they proved to be false starts in the debate between Chicago and the rest of the profession. The seed planted by Chamberlin did not fully flower until much later (Dixit and Stiglitz, 1977; Salop, 1979; Wolinsky, 1986).

The economists who erected the S–C–P framework were interested in explaining the way prices were determined in imperfectly competitive markets. This interest was explicitly motivated by contemporary industrial developments (Mason, 1939, p. 63):

> The growth of corporate bureaucracies (with the consequent institutionalization of management decisions), the separation of ownership from control, and the growing influence of labor organization on policy making are all factors "internal to the firm" which may and do affect its reaction to market situations.

Their view was that the models of competitive markets and of monopoly that economists had to work with were not suited for this purpose (Mason, 1939, p. 61):

> In perfect markets, whether monopolistic or competitive, price is hardly a matter of judgment and where there is no judgment there is no policy. The area of price policy, then, embraces the deliberative action of buyers and sellers able to influence price; that is to say, it covers practically the whole field of industrial prices.

They rejected early formal theoretical models of imperfectly competitive markets as inapplicable in practice (Mason, 1939, p. 62):[9]

> It would no doubt be extremely convenient if economists knew the shape of individual demand and cost curves and could proceed forthwith, by comparisons of price and marginal cost, to conclusions regarding the existing degree of monopoly power. The extent to which the monopoly theorists, however, refrain from an empirical application of their formulae is rather striking. The alternative, if more pedestrian, route follows the direction of ascertainable facts and makes use only of empirically applicable concepts.

They also rejected the then-common institutional approach to industry studies, which they felt was primarily descriptive (Burns, 1937, p. 664, emphasis added):

> studies of particular industries assumed a conventional pattern. ... The technical processes of production were described. The organization of the industry was discussed in terms of the size and location of plants, the scope of ownership control (the size and extent of integration of firms), the organization of marketing, labor conditions, and the history of mergers in the industry.... The discussion of wages and possibly profits implied an interest in the functioning of the industry, *but the aspect of its functioning most vital to theorists and purchasers, namely its price policy, received scant attention.*

Mason (1939, p. 61) specifically rejects the institutionalist approach.

Economists of the time called for a general analytical framework (Burns, 1937, p. 665):[10]

> The primary necessity ... is some broad framework within which price behavior can be analyzed in various industries. It must explain the relationship between the organization of production and distribution and the behavior of buyers and of prices.

---

[9] See similarly Bain (1944, p. 5). For later calls for "a return to the data," see Andrews (1951, p. 172; 1952, p. 75) and Coase (1972).

[10] See similarly Mason (1939, p. 61) and Andrews (1952, p. 75).

The structure–conduct–performance paradigm developed out of Mason's seminar. It was the organizing framework of research in industrial organization from the 1930s to the 1970s, and was the basis of the two successive leading textbooks in the field.[11]

The earliest research in what became the S–C–P tradition were book-length studies of single industries. Subsequently, Bain (1956) published a comparative study of a small number of industries. He did not employ regression analysis. Other industrial economists soon turned to the econometric analysis of cross-section samples of industry data, first of small numbers of industries, and later of large samples covering essentially all manufacturing.

2.2.4. Did the S–C–P paradigm treat market structure as endogenous or exogenous?

Because of the role the issue played in the dislodging of the S–C–P approach by what I will call the Second Chicago School and the subsequent dislodging of the Second Chicago School by game-theoretic analysis, I wish to deal explicitly with the question whether the S–C–P paradigm treated market structure as being determined by economic forces, or as exogenous, determined outside the marketplace?

Some economists have taken the view that the S–C–P approach paid scant attention to the determinants of market structure. McGee (1988, p. 2, emphasis in original) takes the view that causation in the S–C–P paradigm was mostly in one direction: "In the beginning, most economists seem to have believed that the structure–conduct–performance relationship was largely or altogether one way: to a significant degree the *structure* of an industry determines the *conduct* of firms in it; and how firms behave to a significant degree determines how well the industry *performs*." Davies and Lyons (1996, p. 89) write that economists who worked in the S–C–P tradition "gave relatively little thought to the fundamental determinants of concentration itself."

This is a difficult position to defend. Heflebower's (1954) "Theory of industrial markets and prices" was as much about factors determining market structure as about factors determining market performance. A widely-known and generally-accepted schematic representation of the S–C–P framework shows clear feedback links from firm conduct to market structure (Scherer, 1970, p. 5). A key theoretical element of the S–C–P analytical framework was the limit price model, associated with Bain (1949b).[12] In its simplest version (Modigliani,

---

[11] Bain (1959); Scherer (1970, 1980), and Scherer and Ross (1990).

[12] There are many anticipations of the limit price model, including Marshall (1925/1890, p. 270):

> The leaders in the movement towards forming Trusts seem to be resolved to aim in the future at prices which will be not very tempting to any one who has not the economies which a large combination claims to derive . . . from its vast scale of business and its careful organization. . . .

1958; Sylos-Labini, 1957, 1962) the limit price model supposes that an incumbent firm or several incumbent firms can discourage future entry by setting a low current price. While this formulation has been subject to criticism from the game-theoretic perspective (Friedman, 1979; see also Bain, 1949b, pp. 452–453), it may be mentioned here simply to note that it explicitly makes the number of firms on the supply side of the market depend on business conduct, so that supply-side market structure is endogenous.

Passing from the theoretical to the empirical, there is a large literature in the structure–conduct–performance tradition that seeks to explain cross-industry differences in market structure in terms of technological and conduct variables. What may be the earliest of these, Fuchs (1961), studies the impact of multiplant operation on market structure. A prominent paper, Comanor and Wilson (1967), in research that Ekelund and Hébert (1990, p. 28, footnote 3) describe as "continuing the Harvard tradition," argued that advertising was a factor causing seller concentration. Research seeking to explain the causes of market structure is difficult to reconcile with the claim that the S–C–P approach took market structure to be exogenous.

S–C–P economists thought market structure changed slowly (Bain, 1970).[13] But they generally recognized that the nature and rate of change of market structure was affected by economic forces, including underlying demand- and supply-side conditions and the conduct of firms in the market.

2.3. The First Chicago School

While it is customary to write of "the Chicago School," at least two can be distinguished (Bronfenbrenner, 1962, pp. 72–73).[14] The First Chicago School may be dated roughly to the 1930s and 1940s, the Second, insofar as industrial economics is concerned, from immediate post-World War II period.[15]

The First and Second Chicago Schools had in common beliefs in the efficacy of the market system of organizing economic activity and that the role of government should be as limited as possible, consistent with making the market

---

[13] Later empirical evidence suggests they were correct about this.

[14] Reder (1982, p. 1) writes that

> The influence of specialty upon one's perspective of Chicago economics is not trivial. . . . [the] Chicago corner of the economics profession can look quite different to someone in Monetary Theory or International Trade than to a specialist in Labor, Industrial Organization or Law and Economics.

When I discuss the Chicago School or Schools, I refer to what Posner (1979) terms "the Chicago School of antitrust analysis."

[15] The 1946 appointment of Aaron Director to the University of Chicago Law School was critical to the transition from the First to the Second Chicago Schools; see Coase (1998), Peltzman (2005). See also Stigler (2005).

system work.[16] Where they differed was in their views on what is the minimum necessary role of the government. Economists associated with the First Chicago School were advocates of a *laissez faire* government policy, which (Lange, 1945–1946, pp. 31–32):[17]

> maintains that the capitalist economy, provided it is not hampered by government planning, spontaneously operates in such a way that it secures the maximum of public welfare.

They were also convinced that government should set the ground rules for private competition by means of a strong antitrust policy.

The essential views of the First Chicago School on this matter are laid out in Henry C. Simons' 1934 essay *A Positive Program for Laissez Faire*. Simons defended the market mechanism of resource allocation on the grounds that it was more effective than other systems and that it was essential for the preservation of a free society. *A Positive Program* took the view that government had to play an affirmative (positive) role to maintain the functioning of a market economy. This view was a child of its time (Director, 1948, p. 6):

> There may once have been substantial merit in the notion that the free-market system would steadily gain in strength if only it were freed of widespread state interference. By 1934 it became evident that a combination of [this] negative attitude, which permitted the proliferation of monopoly power, and promiscuous political interference, which strengthened such power, threatened "disintegration and collapse" of the economic organization. And only the "wisest measures by the state" could restore and maintain a free-market system.

Simons' positive program envisaged government making a clear distinction between parts of the economy where competition could be an effective resource allocation mechanism and parts of the economy where it could not. Where competition *could* be effective, Simons would have had the government pursue an activist antitrust policy, to ensure that competition *would* be effective. Not only should the government prohibit collusion, and punish it if detected, it should proactively control the size of firms to maintain a market structure consistent with competitive outcomes (1936, pp. 70–71):

> There must be vigorous and vigilant prosecution of conspiracy in restraint of trade...
> Sharp separation must be made between operating companies and investment trusts ... Operating companies should be denied the right to own securities of other such companies... Operating companies must be limited in size, under special limitations prescribed for particular industries by the Federal Trade Commission, in accordance with the policy of preserving real competition.

---

[16] Compare Friedman (1974, p. 11):

> In discussions of economic policy, "Chicago" stands for belief in the efficiency of the free market as a means for organizing resources, for scepticism about government intervention into economic affairs, and for emphasis on the quantity of money as a key factor in producing inflation.

[17] Director (1964, p. 2) writes that "Laissez faire has never been more than a slogan in defense of the proposition that every extension of state activity should be examined under a presumption of error."

Where the underlying technology dictated that competition could not be an effective resource allocation mechanism,[18] Simons saw the policy choice as being between regulation and public ownership. His view of regulation, based on observation of the way regulation worked in practice, was largely negative (Simons, 1948, pp. 50–51):

> With the railroads, the abuse of private monopoly power led finally to real control over the prices of services. We have developed in the Interstate Commerce Commission an unusually competent and scrupulous public body. Even here, however, the preposterous system of relative charges (freight classification), and the disastrous rigidity of freight rates during the depression, testify eloquently to the shortcomings of the regulation expedient; the intrenched position of the railway brotherhoods indicates clearly how governments reconcile the interests of small, organized groups and those of the community at large. In the field of local utilities a half-century of effort at regulation yields up a heritage of results, a cursory inspection of which should suffice to dampen anyone's enthusiasm for a system of private monopoly with superimposed government regulation.

Simons therefore reluctantly came down on the side of public ownership of natural monopoly industries (1936, p. 74):

> In my pamphlet, I suggested early transition to government ownership for the railroads, and gradual movement in that direction with the other utilities. Candidly, I feel that our situation with respect to these industries will always be unhappy, at best; and I have no genuine enthusiasm for public ownership. My advocacy of the change is motivated primarily as an attack upon the notion, now common in high places, that our arrangements with respect to the railroads provide a simple and admirable model for the control of other industries generally.

For Simons, the political and economic justifications for his positive program were inextricably intertwined (1936, p. 75):

> This is the compelling reason for stamping out private monopoly. For every suppression of competition gives rise to an apparent need for regulation; and every venture in regulation creates the necessity of more regulation; and every interference by government on behalf of one group necessitates, in the orderly routine of democratic corruption, additional interference on behalf of others. The outcome ... is: an accumulation of governmental regulation which yields, in many industries, all the afflictions of socialization and none of its possible benefits; an enterprise economy paralyzed by political control; the moral disintegration of representative government in the endless contest of innumerable pressure groups for special political favors; and dictatorship.

2.4. The Second Chicago School

The Second Chicago School carried further the antipathy of the First toward government involvement in the marketplace, rejecting any antitrust policy beyond a prohibition of collusion and mergers to monopoly or near-monopoly,[19] rejecting government regulation of natural monopoly, and certainly rejecting public enterprise.

---

[18] Here, notice, we come up against the endogeneity of market structure.

[19] Posner (1979, p. 928). Posner also writes that opposition to cartels was (p. 932) "[p]artly, perhaps, for tactical reasons (not to seem to reject antitrust policy in its entirety)... ".

Reder writes that a distinguishing characteristic of the Second Chicago School was what he calls the "Tight Prior equilibrium" assumption, the view that the economy could be treated as if it were essentially *Pareto optimal*, that (1982, p. 11): "decision makers so allocate the resources under their control that there is no alternative allocation such that any one decision maker could have his expected utility increased without a reduction occurring in the expected utility of at least one other decision maker."

The view that the economy can be treated as if it is Pareto optimal follows from four assumptions that Reder ascribes to Chicago economists (1982, p. 11, emphasis in original, footnotes omitted):

> (1) *most* individual transactors treat the prices of all goods and services that they buy or sell, as independent of the quantities that they transact;
> (2) the prices at which individuals *currently agree* to transact are market clearing prices that are consistent with optimization by all decision makers;
> (3) information bearing on prices and qualities of all things bought and sold, present and future, is acquired in the quantity that markets its marginal cost equal to its price; i.e., information is treated like any other commodity;
> (4) neither monopoly nor governmental action (through taxation or otherwise) affects relative prices or quantities sufficiently to prevent either marginal products or compensation of identical resources from being approximately equal in all uses.

As Reder sees it, students of the Chicago School of antitrust policy took the view that (1982, p. 12):

> in applied work, . . . in the absence of sufficient evidence to the contrary, one may treat observed prices and quantities as good approximations to their long-run competitive equilibrium values. Call this the "good approximation assumption."

2.4.1. Chicago I and Chicago II

The Second Chicago School repudiated Simons' *Positive Program for Laissez Faire*, on the ground that it advocated an interventionist role for government. This shift may reflect a change in the political atmosphere (Friedman, in Kitch, 1983, p. 178):

> You have to recognize what the environment was at the time. By comparison with almost everybody else [Simons] was very free market oriented. I've gone back and reread the *Positive Program* and been astounded at what I read. To think that I thought at the time that it was strongly free market in its orientation!

It may also reflect evidence about the importance of economies of large scale production, or experience with the ability (or inability) of government to intervene effectively in the economy, that accumulated after the appearance of *A Positive Program* (Friedman, 1982, p. 32). In any case, the claim that later advocates of a government role essentially the same as that put forward by Simons were making recommendations inconsistent with economic theory would seem to be a delicate one for the Second Chicago School to make.[20]

2.4.2. Methodology

A methodological debate associated with Friedman (1953) surfaces in connection with the later rise of game theory: is a theory to be judged by the realism of its assumptions, or by the adequacy of its predictions?[21]

Blaug (1986, p. 265) has written that "Methodology is like medicine. We tolerate it because it is supposed to be good for us, but we secretly despise it." Like many medicines, methodology is probably also best if taken in small doses, and that is what will be offered here.

Stigler states the Chicago position (1949, p. 23):

> The purpose of the study of economics is to permit us to make predictions about the behaviour of economic phenomena under specified conditions. The sole test of the usefulness of an economic theory is the concordance between its predictions and the observable course of events. Often a theory is criticized or rejected because its assumptions are "unrealistic." Granting for a moment that this charge has meaning, it burdens theory with an additional function, that of description. This is a most unreasonable burden to place upon a theory: the rôle of description is to particularize, while the rôle of theory is to generalize—to disregard an infinite number of differences and capture the important common element in different phenomena.

As suggested by the qualification "granting that the charge of unrealism has meaning," it may first be noted that all theory is unrealistic. It is the essence of theory that it abstracts from reality. While it may be possible to say that the assumptions underlying one theory are more or less realistic than those underlying another theory, all theory is based upon assumptions that are, to some extent, unrealistic. Otherwise, it would not be theory, it would be a list.

At the same time, it is difficult to see how one could evaluate the validity of theoretical predictions except within the framework of a model that permits examination of what are thought to be the interesting alternative hypotheses (Friedman, 1953, p. 38, emphasis added):[22]

---

[20] The assertion that Simons should be thought of as an interventionist rather than an advocate of *laissez faire* has not gone unchallenged. de Long (1990) argues that Simons has a legitimate claim to the label "classical liberal." de Long's view is that what separates the First and the Second Chicago schools is not their positions about where to go, but rather their positions on how to get there (1990, p. 618): "The conflict between Chicago then and Chicago today is about what the necessary foundations for a competitive free market economy are, and not about the desirability of such an economic order."

[21] On Friedman's methodology, see Samuelson (1963), Machlup (1964), Wong (1973), Boland (1979), Frazer and Boland (1983), as well as comments and replies on the latter in the September 1984 issue of the *American Economic Review*.

[22] This passage is quoted by Chamberlin (1957, p. 16). Friedman continues (1953, p. 38) "To perform this function, the more general theory must have content and substance; it must have implications susceptible to empirical contradiction and of substantive interest and importance." As an example of substantive implications that are subject to empirical contradiction and could not be

> It would be highly desirable to have a more general theory than Marshall's, one that would cover at the same time both those cases in which differentiation of product of fewness of numbers makes an essential difference and those in which it does not. *Such a theory would enable us to handle problems we now cannot and, in addition, facilitate determination of the range of circumstances under which the simply theory can be regarded as a good enough approximation.*

Koopmans (1957, p. 142) writes of economic theory "as a sequence of conceptual *models* that seek to express in simplified form different aspects of an always more complicated reality." Industrial economists generally work with models that are less simplified than the neoclassical model of perfectly competitive markets.[23]

2.5. Confronting the oligopoly problem

2.5.1. S–C–P to Chicago

Since the industrial revolution, a central problem for public policy toward business has been that (Second Chicago School assumptions to the contrary notwithstanding), performance in markets supplied by a few large firms seems often to resemble that which results from collusion, without collusion taking place (Mason, 1949, p. 1277):

> high overhead costs, large cyclical variations in the volume of sales, and immobility of resources are combined in a substantial number of industrial markets. Given these conditions, together with a small number of firms, some economists have contended that such phenomena as price uniformity, price leadership and the relative inflexibility of prices ... are frequently compatible with the independent action of firms all recognizing their interdependence.

The problem is, given such an industry, what to do about it (Mason, 1949, p. 1277):[24]

> If the behavior is really the result of agreement, enjoining the agreement may, by securing independence of action, change the market behavior. But if the action of firms is already independent, this remedy is useless.

One answer, of course, may be to do nothing. Simons argued that regulation often begins with the goal of protecting the consumer from the regulated industry and ends up protecting the regulated industry from competition. Government planning may crash on the shoals of information problems and bureaucracy.

---

obtained in analysis that begins from the premise that prices and quantities in the U.S. automobile industry can be treated as if they are long-run competitive equilibrium values, one might cite Bresnahan's (1981) estimate of consumer welfare losses due to quality downshifting.

[23] It is mainly in the analysis of dynamic models of entry that the literature works with an explicit "as if competitive" assumption, and even in that literature the assumption is far from universal.

[24] Posner (1976, 2001), and *In re High Fructose Corn Syrup* 295 F.3d 651 (2001), is willing to infer collusion from evidence of market performance that would result from explicit collusion. This position may reflect the view that collusion can never be entirely tacit. It is a policy view that seems to confront *Theatre Enterprises* (346 U.S. 537 1954).

Breaking up large, efficient firms for the sake of artificially maintaining a larger number of smaller and less-efficient firms imposes unnecessarily high production costs on society. If regulation, government ownership, and imposed limits on firm size are the only policy options, then perhaps to do nothing is best.

But from the 1950s through the 1970s, mainstream economists championed the kind of deconcentration plan that had been put forward by Henry Simons. Stigler (1952, pp. 162, 164) wrote that few disinterested people would deny the facts that

1. Big businesses often possess and use monopoly power.
2. Big businesses weaken the political support for a private-enterprise system.
3. Big businesses are not appreciably more efficient or enterprising than medium-size businesses.

He continued that (1952, p. 164) "to deal with the problems raised by big business" "The obvious and economical solution ... is to break up the giant companies."[25]

Stigler came to feel that these views were mistaken (1988, pp. 97–108). But the fact that he held them in the early 1950s suggests that they were not the hallmark of atheoretical pseudo-economists who did not understand neoclassical economic theory. It *is* probably fair to say that economists who advanced deconcentration proposals did not accept the position that prices and quantities in most industries, most of the time, could be treated as if they were at their competitive equilibrium values. But that assumption is not part of neoclassical economic theory.

Kaysen and Turner put forward a detailed deconcentration proposal (1959, pp. 113–114):

> The logic of our policy goal ... calls for a widespread application of dissolution remedies, on the ground that an increase in numbers and reduction of concentration is the surest and most durable way of reducing market power.

They would not, however, have broken up existing firms if that had meant the loss of economies of large scale production (1959, p. 114).

A government advisory panel (White House Task Force on Antitrust Policy, 1968–69) subsequently recommended adoption of a law very much like the one suggested by Kaysen and Turner.[26] A bill proposing such a law, Senate Bill 1167 ("The Hart Bill") was introduced in the United States Senate in 1967.[27]

---

[25] Stigler apparently held these views at least through December 1955, when he concluded his contribution to an American Economic Association panel discussion with the statement (Stocking et al., 1956, p. 507) "Those of us who wish to see greater use made of what is often the only real remedy are not reckless innovators; we are simply traditionalists who wish to regain the 1911 level of use of the remedy of dissolution."

[26] The task force recommendation is commonly known as the Neal Report, after its chairman, Phil C. Neal, then Dean of the University of Chicago Law School.

[27] For the text of the Hart bill, see Goldschmid et al. (1974, pp. 444–448). Perusal of this volume brings to mind Viner's description of an earlier conference (this is quoted by Reder, 1982, footnote 19, from Patinkin, 1981, p. 266; emphasis in original):

The reaction of the Second Chicago School was to attack the S–C–P paradigm, and the case for the deconcentration bill, on two fronts.

The first was to argue on several grounds that the results of empirical research in the S–C–P tradition were invalid. Some of these grounds were technical in nature, and need not detain us here.[28] The part of this critique that has made the most lasting impression was that S–C–P researchers had misinterpreted the consistent finding that profit rates tended to be higher where markets were supplied by a small number of firms. In the Second Chicago School view, far from demonstrating the greater ease of tacit or overt collusion in more concentrated markets, this result reflected a causal link going in the other direction, from firm performance to market structure. This causal link instead demonstrated the endogeneity of market structure, an endogeneity which, according to the Second Chicago School caricaturization, the S–C–P paradigm had ignored. The alternative causal mechanism put forward is that more efficient firms, which are more profitable because they are more efficient, also tend to grow large. Comparing different industries, industries supplied by a few large firms will have higher profit rates, on average, than industries supplied by many small firms, but this is a sign of differential efficiency, not market power.[29]

The idea of a deconcentration policy is not now on anybody's radar screen. But many of the same issues arise if an antitrust authority is faced with a decision whether or not to permit a merger, or if dissolution is proposed as a remedy when a firm has been found guilty of monopolization or abuse of a dominant position.

Since there is a good case to be made that the S–C–P school did in fact regard market structure as endogenous, there are really two pertinent questions to ask. The first is, taking it as given that market structure in any industry tends to converge to an equilibrium configuration, must that configuration necessarily be efficient? Since the Second Chicago School rejected the possibility of

---

> It was not until after I left Chicago in 1946 that I began to hear rumors about a 'Chicago School' which was engaged in *organized* battle for laissez faire and the 'quantity theory of money' and against 'imperfect competition' theorizing and 'Keynesianism.' I remained sceptical about this until I attended a conference sponsored by University of Chicago professors in 1951. The invited participants were a varied lot of academics, bureaucrats, businessmen, etc., but the program for discussion, the selection of chairmen, and everything about the conference except the unscheduled statements and protests from individual participants were so patently rigidly structured, so loaded, that I got more amusement from the conference than from any other I ever attended. Even the source of the financing of the Conference, as I found out later, was ideologically loaded. There is a published account of the proceedings of the Conference, but it does not include the program, etc., as presented to the participants to direct their discussion. From then on, I was willing to consider the existence of a 'Chicago School'...

[28] See Martin (2002, Chapter 6) for discussion.

[29] This argument is particularly associated with Demsetz (1973, 1974), whose work was primitive by the standards of its time (Rosenbluth, 1976). Subsequent research that controls for efficiency differences finds evidence of market power and efficiency effects on profitability.

single-firm action to obtain or enhance market power (Posner, 1979, p. 928), their answer to this question was yes.[30]

The second question is how quickly market structure approaches its equilibrium configuration. If market structure is endogenous and market structure adjusts very quickly to the most efficient arrangement, a deconcentration bill or a vigilant merger policy is unnecessary. The market will get to the efficient configuration on its own, before government can nudge it along.

On the other hand, if market structure is endogenous but market structure adjusts slowly to the most efficient arrangement, one might make a case for a deconcentration bill or a rigorous merger policy, provided policymakers can identify cases in which firms are larger than required for efficient operation. The Second Chicago School rejected this possibility (McGee, 1974, p. 104):[31]

> I see little reason to spend much more time estimating optimum plant or firm sizes except perhaps, in a completely centralized and governmentally controlled economy in which the State tries hard to keep markets from working and consumers from expressing preferences. When property and markets are at work, and consumers are permitted to choose what and from whom to buy, it is, as far as I am concerned, a trivial matter what the facts of technical economies are, or what economists have to say about them.

This view reflects the Second Chicago School assumption that real world data can be treated as if the real world is Pareto optimal. Thus the Second Chicago School criticized the empirical research that had been used to argue in favor of a deconcentration bill.[32]

It also criticized the deconcentration bill on the ground that its theoretical underpinning, the S–C–P approach, was inconsistent with the tight prior equilibrium assumption (Posner, 1979, p. 929):[33]

> Casual observation of business behavior, colorful characterizations (such as the term "barrier to entry"), eclectic forays into sociology and psychology, descriptive statistics, and verification by plausibility took the place of the careful definitions and parsimonious logical structure of

---

[30] Posner (2001, p. 251) writes that the accusation that the "Chicago School" denies the possibility of single-firm exclusion of efficient competitors reflects a misunderstanding that has endured for at least a quarter-century. If the indicated view of the orthodox Chicago School position is a misunderstanding, it is at least one of respectable vintage.

[31] See also Friedman (1955, p. 237):

> If we ask what size firm has minimum costs, and define "minimum costs" in a sense in which it is in a firm's own interest to achieve it, surely the obvious answer is: firms of existing size.

[32] This criticism should perhaps be viewed in light of Reder's (1982, pp. 12–13, footnote 28) comments on the likely reaction of students of the Chicago approach if Harberger's (1954) estimates of welfare losses in the U.S. economy had suggested significant losses:

> But suppose the losses had been "large" (say, 25 per [cent] of potential GNP), would this have lead to an abandonment of [the Tight Prior Equilibrium]? My conjecture is negative; the measurement would have been attacked, both substantively and methodologically, and research would have proceeded on the assumption that the measurements were incorrect.

[33] See also the remarks of Becker quoted at page 173 in Kitch (1983).

economic theory. The result was that industrial organization regularly advanced propositions that contradicted economic theory.

What is meant here by "economic theory" is the neoclassical theory of perfectly competitive markets.

The Hart deconcentration bill never saw the light of day, and for a period of perhaps 10–12 years from the mid-1970s, the Second Chicago School monopolized the giving of antitrust advice to U.S. courts and policymakers.

One can find statements from this period that the Chicago approach had become the mainstream approach among professional economists (Posner, 1979, p. 925):

> I shall argue in this paper that although there was a time when the "Chicago" school stood for a distinctive approach to antitrust policy, especially in regard to economic questions, and when other schools, particularly a "Harvard" school, could be discerned and contrasted with it, the distinctions between these schools have greatly diminished. This has occurred largely as a result of the maturing of economics as a social science, and, as a corollary thereto, the waning of the sort of industrial organization that provided the intellectual foundations of the Harvard School.

The reference to "the Harvard School" is disingenuous, since the S–C–P approach was subscribed to by the bulk of the profession.

Nelson's reaction to Posner's assertion included (1979, p. 949):

> Posner contrasts the "old" school of industrial organization (Harvard) which he proposes was atheoretic with the "new" school (Chicago) which based itself rigorously on price theory. But the price theory to which Posner refers is the old fashioned price theory of the textbooks of twenty years ago. What Posner does not see is that over the last decade or so a newer price theory is replacing the old. I suggest that the new price theory probably provides better support for the old industrial organization than it does for what Posner calls the new. Indeed, the journals are full of a "new new" industrial organization literature based on the newer price theory, viewing the problem in a way that is more consistent with old Harvard than with new Chicago.

Table 2.1 reports the results of an examination of 117 articles on industrial economics, price theory, and antitrust published in the Papers and Proceedings issue of the *American Economic Review* between 1951 and 1982.[34] I classified these papers in three groups: those consistent with the good approximation assumption, those inconsistent with the good approximation assumption and

---

[34] Details of the classification are given in the Appendix. I began the survey with 1951 as the first year of the first postwar decade. I ended the survey in 1982 on the ground that Schmalensee's statement suggests that if ever Chicago had commanded the mainstream of industrial economics, that moment had by then passed (1982b, p. 24):

> Recent work follows Harvard in acknowledging the possibility of markets not well described by either perfect competition or pure monopoly, and it follows Chicago in stressing the value of deductive analysis of explicit economic models.

I did not include papers on regulation in the survey, and I did not include discussions.

Table 2.1: Classification of 117 articles from the papers and proceedings issues of the *American Economic Review*, 1951–1982.

	1950s	1960s	1970–1982	Total
Chicago	7	9	6	22
Mainstream	24	17	20	61
"Think outside the box"	11	9	14	34

consistent with the structure–conduct–performance approach, and those inconsistent with the good approximation assumption and also urging the advantages of heterodox alternative approaches.

There is of course an element of judgment in this classification. Few positions are so straightforward as Nutter's (1954, p. 70):

> We must certainly be struck by the fact that, when we are faced with concrete problems, we place our trust overwhelmingly in the simple and familiar tools of supply and demand, with results that are generally quite satisfactory for most purposes,

as Miller's (1954, p. 15):

> It has become clear that the competitive process is no simple thing and that market structures and behavior defy reduction in either law or economics to a simple dichotomy of monopoly and competition,

or as Simon's (1962, pp. 14–15):

> ... conclusions about welfare in such areas as tax and antitrust policy depend in an important way upon the underlying postulates about the behavior of the individual firm. The picture of the firm that is emerging from the new research is that of a searching, information processing, allocating mechanism. It is doubtful that the propositions that hold under the assumption of static, profit-maximizing firms under conditions of certainty hold for such firms.

Where classification is ambiguous, my intention has been to give the benefit of the doubt to either the first or the third category, as appropriate. The message of Table 2.1, however, seems clear: it has never been the case that the tenets of the Chicago School were the mainstream view of industrial economics.[35]

In retrospect, it seems entirely possible that the views of industrial economists about the Chicago School of antitrust policy were something to which Chicago scholars were in some measure indifferent. In its manifestation that is discussed here,[36] the Chicago School was primarily a school of *antitrust analysis*, and

[35] I have not included Kearl et al. (1979) in the sample classified in Table 2.1. They report the results of a survey of a stratified random sample of 600 1974 members of the American Economic Association. Statement 12 in their survey is "Antitrust laws should be used vigorously to reduce monopoly power from its current level." They report that 49 per cent of respondents generally agreed with the statement, 36 per cent agreed with provisions, and 15 per cent generally disagreed. For comparison purposes, the 22 papers I have classified as consistent with the good approximation assumption are 19 per cent of the 117 papers examined.

[36] See footnote 14.

only secondarily a school of thought in industrial economics. Chicago advocates found that (Bork, at p. 8 in Shapiro et al., 1984) "... basic price theory ... is really a quite simple and logical system that can be applied by judges" and that is what appears to have interested them.

2.5.2. Chicago to game theory

While the Second Chicago School was disputing policy primacy with the S–C–P paradigm, there were developments in another part of the forest (Shubik, 1980, p. 21):

> There is a history of mathematical models of oligopolistic competition dating from Cournot (1838) to the theory of games. There is also a literature generated by institutional economists, lawyers, and administrators interested in formulating and implementing public policy. It has been the tendency of these groups to work almost as though the other did not exist.

The founders of the S–C–P approach had rejected contemporary economic theory as inadequate for the analysis of imperfectly competitive markets. So, perhaps, it was.[37] But game theory, which extends neoclassical price theory to environments of incomplete and imperfect information, provides a natural framework for the analysis of strategic behavior. Mainstream industrial economists, having faced criticism for the failure to use formal models, were not slow to turn to game theory as an alternative approach. Game theory directs attention toward the realism of a model's assumptions (Fudenberg and Tirole, 1987, p. 176, emphasis added):

> Game theory has had a deep impact on the theory of industrial organization ... The reason it has been embraced by a majority of researchers in the field is that it imposes some discipline on theoretical thinking. It forces economists to specify the strategic variables, their timing, and the information structure faced by firms. As is often the case in economics, the researcher learns as much from constructing the model ... as from solving it because *in constructing the model one is led to examine its realism.* (Is the timing of entry plausible? Which variables are costly to change in the short run? Can firms observe their rivals' prices, capacities, or technologies in the industry under consideration? Etc.)

This may be contrasted with the Friedman (1953) view that the realism of a model's assumptions is immaterial, what matters is the accuracy of its predictions.

Like Pandora, who loosed the ills of the world and found they could not be closed up again, the Second Chicago School invoked formal theory in its contest with the S–C–P approach, and found it could not close it up again. Faced with the fact that game theoretic models reproduce, as often as not, the conclusions of the S–C–P paradigm, the reaction of the Second Chicago School was to reject the use of game-theoretic models (Baxter, 1983, p. 320):

---

[37] See Nelson (1979, p. 952) for a similar view.

> What concerns me is that the economists have rather lapped the bar and the courts. Quite frankly, I do not want them back in the courts talking about new and not well-understood justifications for intervention, some of which sounds [sic] like the half-baked oligopoly theories of twenty years ago (although they are not).

2.6. Chicago transformed

Having lost the high ground of theoretical rigor, Chicago turned to empirical research. Coase (1972, p. 62) criticized mainstream industrial organization for its focus on price, an element of market performance: "Industrial organization has become the study of the pricing and output policies of firms, especially in oligopolistic situations. . . ." As we have seen, this focus was intentional on the part of those who developed the S–C–P paradigm.

Coase buttressed his critique of mainstream industrial economics with the plea that attention to market performance was misplaced (1972, p. 60):[38]

> We all know what is meant by industrial organization. It describes the way in which activities undertaken within the economy are divided between firms. As we know, some firms embrace many different activities; while for others, the field is narrowly circumscribed. Some firms are vertically integrated; others are not. This is the organization of industry or—as it used to be called—the structure of industry. What one would expect to learn from a study of industrial organization would be how industry is organized now, and how this differs from what it used to be in earlier periods; what forces were operative in bringing about this organization, and how these forces have been changing over time; what the effects would be of proposals to change, through legal action of various kinds, the forms of industrial organization.

He argued that it was empirical rather than theoretical research that was most likely to generate progress (1972, pp. 70–71):

> it is unlikely that we shall see significant advances in our theory of the organization of industry until we know more about what it is that we must explain. An inspired theoretician might do as well without empirical work, but my own feeling is that the inspiration is most likely to come through the stimulus provided by the patterns, puzzles, and anomalies revealed by systematic data-gathering.

Further, he argued for a specific rather than a general approach (1972, p. 73):

> In my view, what is wanted in industrial organization is a direct approach to the problem. This would concentrate on what activities firms undertake, and would endeavor to discover the characteristics of the groupings of activities within firms. Which activities tend to be associated, and which do not? The answer may well differ for different kinds of firm; for example, for firms of different size, or for those with a different corporate structure, or for firms in different industries.

The position taken by Coase in 1972 has much in common with the position taken by Mason and his students in the 1930s: the theory we have is not satisfactory, let us turn to empirical analysis as a way of laying the foundation for an adequate theory. But the kind of industry study Coase calls for sounds very

---

[38] In the same place, Coase calls for the study of the division of activity between profit and nonprofit firms and between the private sector and government.

much like the primarily descriptive industry studies rejected by the developers of the S–C–P approach.[39]

2.7. Final thoughts

Industrial economics is a contentious field, as are many other branches of economics. Lange (1945–1946, pp. 22–23), discusses four reasons economists may differ in the policy recommendations they draw from economic analysis.

First, Lange writes, economists may differ about social objectives. Two economists who agree about the impact of a tariff on the domestic market will differ in their recommendations for the appropriate tariff level if one economist recommends a policy to maximize consumer welfare and another recommends a policy to protect domestic firms from foreign competition.

Second, economists may disagree about facts. One economist may think that it is possible for economists to evaluate the minimum size firm needed in (say) electric power generation to obtain the lowest possible average cost, and that this size is small relative to the size of the market. Another economist may think that it is not possible for economists to measure the minimum lowest-average cost firm size, or that if such measurement is possible, that the indicated size is large relative to the size of the market. Economists with such alternative views would make different recommendations about merger policy in the electric power industry.

Third, some economists may fail to apply scientific procedures correctly. The remedy for this is straightforward, and will manifest itself if the usual process of give-and-take in academic journals runs its course.

Finally, economists' policy recommendations may differ for reasons of ideology.[40] Wiles (1983, pp. 61–62) defines an ideology as

> a general and coherent *Weltanschauung*, felt passionately and defended unscrupulously. It contains *sacred propositions* of a factual sort. In the face of contrary evidence, the words in these propositions will be redefined, or the philosophical status of the propositions will even be changed, in order not to abandon the original concatenation of words. A special methodology and vocabulary will also grow up, the use of which confines the devotees to problems and approaches that cannot threaten the sacred propositions.

Discussing the impact of ideology on economics, Lange (1945–1946, p. 23) writes:

> The really important influences, however, are those which are subconscious. The economist subject to them is unaware of their existence; the influences operate through processes of rationalisation of subconscious motivations. The result is the production of *ideologies*, i.e. systems

---

[39] Posner (1979, p. 931), is quite critical of S–C–P industry studies, which in his view had the characteristic that "The powerful simplifications of economic theory—rationality, profit maximization, the downward-sloping demand curve—were discarded, or at least downplayed, in favor of microscopic examination of the idiosyncrasies of particular markets."

[40] For a call for greater attention to the impact of ideology on policy, see North (1983).

> of beliefs which are held not on grounds of their conformity to scientific procedure but as rationalisations of subconscious, non-logical motives. ... [Ideologies] convince only those who share the same subconscious motivations and undergo the same processes of rationalisation.

Ideology permeates economics. It influences the research topics individual economists find interesting. It influences the reactions of journal editors and referees to research results that are subject to the winnowing process of scientific screening (Schumpeter, 1949, p. 349):

> The majority of economists ... are ready enough to admit [ideology's] presence though, like Marx, they find it only in others and never in themselves; but they do not admit that it is an inescapable curse and vitiates economics to its core.

Arguments that are made for ideological reasons may nonetheless be correct. The conclusions reached on the basis of those arguments may be correct, in a scientific sense. As Schumpeter also wrote, with the bluntness that a great mind can permit itself (1949, p. 349):

> *...ideologies are not simply lies*; they are truthful statements about what a man thinks he sees.

Such arguments should not, therefore, be dismissed simply on the ground that they are ideological. They should be considered on the merits.

I began this essay by asking "What has antitrust brought to industrial economics?" "Ideology" is a central part of any answer to that question.

It is interesting to speculate how the field of industrial economics might have developed if deconcentration proposals of the kind put forward by Simons, Stigler, Kaysen and Turner, and others had never seemed to approach a tangible possibility of adoption. I have suggested above (Section 2.5.1) that "the Chicago School was primarily a school of *antitrust analysis*, and only secondarily a school of thought in industrial economics." One alternative reality is that without the target provided by deconcentration proposals, no full-blown attack (footnote 32) on the structure–conduct–performance approach would have taken place. Initiatives like Phillips (1960, 1961), Williamson (1965), and Richardson (1972), which in varying ways pointed out that firms operate not only in product markets but also within a dense network of interfirm contracts, and that this network has efficiency as well as market power implications, might very well have had a greater direct following than has been the case.[41] The theoretical tools to formally model imperfectly competitive markets that did not exist in the 1930s had been developed by the early 1970s, and game theory would in any case have supplanted the structure–conduct–performance paradigm.[42] The antitrust policy positions supported by mainstream industrial economics would be very much

[41] In this alternative state of the world, transaction cost economics would certainly have emphasized the efficiency aspects of interfirm relations. It may well be that the transaction cost economics message that enduring institutional arrangements may have efficiency implications has been garbled by the hard-core Chicago message that enduring institutional arrangements can have *only* efficiency implications.

[42] This is at least suggested by the size of the "think outside the box" category in Table 2.1.

what they are today. What would be absent would be the misinterpretation of mainstream economic views embodied in some U.S. antitrust precedents.

The Second Chicago School did change the landscape of professional industrial economics. Mainstream industrial economists now look for efficiency as well as market power explanations of real-world observations. Mainstream industrial economists now expect theoretical research to be carried out using formal models that are consistent with mainstream microeconomic theory, and are likely to look askance at theory formulated in the discursive style that characterized the S–C–P paradigm.[43] But mainstream industrial economic theory is not neoclassical price theory, nor is it the theory of perfectly competitive markets. Mainstream industrial economists today reject the Second Chicago School "good approximation" assumption that prices and quantities in real-world markets can, most of the time, be treated as if they are competitive equilibrium values.

Acknowledgements

I am grateful for comments received from William S. Comanor, John Connor, F.M. Scherer, John T. Scott, at the Università degli Studi di Lecce, and from two anonymous referees. Responsibility for errors is my own.

Appendix

This appendix lists by group the classification of papers reported in Table 2.1. All papers are from the *American Economic Review*.

(1) Implicitly or explicitly consistent with the view that the good approximation assumption is appropriate for industry analysis, or with policy positions implied by the good approximation assumption.

Ratchford, B.U. "An economist's view," 41(2), May 1951, pp. 299–306.
Taylor, O.H. "The future of economic liberalism," 42(2), May 1952, pp. 1–15.
Knight, F.H. "Institutionalism and empiricism in economics," 42(2), May 1952, pp. 45–55.
Reder, M.W. "Rehabilitation of partial equilibrium theory," 42(2), May 1952, pp. 182–197.
Brozen, Y. "Determinants of the direction of technological change," 43(2), May 1953, pp. 288–302.
Nutter, G.W. "Competition: Direct and devious," 44(2), May 1954, pp. 69–76.
Levi, E.H. "The monopoly problem as viewed by a lawyer," 47(2), May 1957, pp. 293–302.

[43] If usage of discursive theory now appears in the literature, it is likely to be employed in an institutionalist/transaction cost analysis that is in many ways the successor of the Second Chicago School.

Telser, L.G. "How much does it pay whom to advertise?" 51(2), May 1961, pp. 194–205.

Holton, R.H. "Scale, specialization, and costs in Retailing," 51(2), May 1961, pp. 206–212.

Adelman, M.A. "The antimerger act, 1950-60," 51(2), May 1961, pp. 236–244.

Dewey, D. "Mergers and cartels: Some reservations about policy," 51(2), May 1961, pp. 255–262.

Heady, E.O. "Efficiency of the farm firm," 54(3), May 1964, pp. 97–106.

Massel, M.S. "Anniversaries of the Patent and Sherman Acts: Competitive policies and limited monopolies," 56(1/2), March 1966, pp. 284–290.

Blank, D.M. "The quest for quantity and diversity in television programming," 56(1/2), March 1966, pp. 448–456.

Telser, L.G. "Supply and demand for advertising messages," 56(1/2), March 1966, pp. 457–466.

Bork, R.H. "The goals of antitrust policy," 57(2), May 1967, pp. 242–253.

Telser, L.G. "Searching for the lowest price," 63(2), May 1973, pp. 40–49.

Williamson, O.E. "Markets and hierarchies: Some elementary considerations," 63(2), May 1973, pp. 316–325.

Carlton, D.W. "Uncertainty, production lags, and pricing," 67(1), February 1977, pp. 244–249.

Klein, B. "Transaction cost determinants of 'unfair' contractual arrangements," 70(2), May 1980, pp. 356–362.

Bailey, E.E. "Contestability and the design of regulatory and antitrust policy," 71(2), May 1981, pp. 178–183.

Stigler, G.J. "The economists and the problem of monopoly," 72(2), May 1982, pp. 1–11.

(2) Inconsistent with Chicago School positions.

Rostow, W.W. "A historian's perspective on modern economic theory," 42(2), May 1952, pp. 16–29.

Kaysen, C. "Dynamic aspects of oligopoly price theory," 42(2), May 1952, pp. 198–210.

Galbraith, J.K. "Countervailing power," 44(2), May 1954, pp. 1–6.

Stigler, G.J. "The economist plays with blocs," 44(2), May 1954, pp. 7–14.

Miller, J.P. "Competition and countervailing power: Their roles in the American economy," 44(2), May 1954, pp. 15–25.

Harberger, A.C. "Monopoly and resource allocation," 44(2), May 1954, pp. 77–87.

Heflebower, R.B. "Toward a theory of industrial markets and prices," 44(2), May 1954, pp. 121–139.

Clark, J.M. "Competition: Static models and dynamic aspects," 45(2), May 1955, pp. 450–462.

Weintraub, S. "Revised doctrines of competition," 45(2), May 1955, pp. 463–479.

Whitney, S.N. "Vertical disintegration in the motion picture industry," 45(2), May 1955, pp. 491–498.

McKie, J.W. "The decline of monopoly in the metal container industry," 45(2), May 1955, pp. 499–508.
Marengo, L. "The basing point decisions and the steel industry," 45(2), May 1955, pp. 509–522.
Penrose, E. "Limits to the growth and size of firms," 45(2), May 1955, pp. 531–543.
Blair, J. "Economic concentration and depression price rigidity," 45(2), May 1955, pp. 566–582.
Mason, E.S. "Market power and business conduct: Some comments," 46(2), May 1956, pp. 471–481.
Brewster, K. Jr. "Enforceable competition: Unruly reason or reasonable rules?" 46(2), May 1956, pp. 482–489.
Adelman, M.A. "The 'product' and 'price' in distribution," 47(2), May 1957, pp. 266–273.
Heflebower, R.B. "Mass distribution: A phase of bilateral oligopoly or of competition?" 47(2), May 1957, pp. 274–285.
Kaysen, C. "The social significance of the modern corporation," 47(2), May 1957, pp. 311–319.
Clark, J.M. "The uses of diversity: Competitive bearings of diversities in cost and demand functions," 48(2), May 1958, pp. 474–482.
Fusfeld, D.R. "Joint subsidiaries in the iron and steel industry," 48(2), May 1958, pp. 578–587.
Worcester, D.A. Jr. "A partial theory of collusion," 48(2), May 1958, pp. 588–597.
Ackley, G. "Administered prices and the inflationary process," 49(2), May 1959, pp. 419–430.
Blair, J.M. "Administered prices: A phenomenon in search of a theory," 49(2), May 1959, pp. 431–450.
Gustafson, W.E. "Research and development, new products, and productivity change," 52(2), May 1962, pp. 177–185.
Scitovsky, T. "On the principle of consumers' sovereignty," 52(2), May 1962, pp. 262–268.
Healy, K.T. "The merger movement in transportation," 52(2), May 1962, pp. 436–444.
Grether, E.T. "Consistency in public economic policy with respect to private unregulated industries," 53(2), May 1963, pp. 26–37.
Bain, J.S. "The impact on industrial organization," 54(3), May 1964, pp. 28–32.
Bishop, R.L. "The impact on general theory," 54(3), May 1964, pp. 33–43.
Baumol, W.J. "Monopolistic competition and welfare economics," 54(3), May 1964, pp. 44–52.
Markham, J.W. "Market structure, business conduct, and innovation," 55(1/2), March 1965, pp. 323–332.
Markham, J.W. "The joint effect of antitrust and patent laws upon innovation," 56(1/2), March 1966, pp. 291–300.

Phillips, A. "Patents, potential competition, and technical progress," 56(1/2), March 1966, pp. 301–310.
Horvitz, P.M. "The pricing of textbooks and the remuneration of authors," 56(1/2), March 1966, pp. 412–420.
Hurt, R.M., Schuchman, R.M. "The economic rationale of copyright," 56(1/2), March 1966, pp. 421–432.
Comanor, W.S. "Vertical mergers, market powers, and the antitrust laws," 57(2), May 1967, pp. 254–265.
Hamburger, W. "Conscious parallelism and the kinked oligopoly demand curve," 57(2), May 1967, pp. 266–268.
Leibenstein, H. "Entrepreneurship and development," 58(2), May 1968, pp. 72–83.
Comanor, W.S., Wilson, T.A. "Advertising and the advantages of size," 59(2), May 1969, pp. 87–98.
Bain, J.S. "Survival-ability as a test of efficiency," 59(2), May 1969, pp. 99–104.
Grether, E.T. "Industrial organization: Past history and future problems," 60(2), May 1970, pp. 83–89.
Hirshleifer, J. "Where are we in the theory of information?" 63(2), May 1973, pp. 31–39.
Vernon, R. "Competition policy toward multinational corporations," 64(2), May 1974, pp. 276–282.
Shubik, M. "Oligopoly theory, communication, and information," 65(2), May 1975, pp. 280–283.
Salop, S. "Information and monopolistic competition," 66(2), May 1976, pp. 240–245.
Grossman, S.J., Stiglitz, J.E. "Information and competitive price systems," 66(2), May 1976, pp. 246–253.
Porter, M.E. "Interbrand choice, media mix and market performance," 66(2), May 1976, pp. 398–406.
Spence, M. "Product differentiation and welfare," 66(2), May 1976, pp. 407–414.
Spence, M. "Nonprice competition," 67(1), February 1977, pp. 255–259.
Leibenstein, H. "On the basic proposition of X-efficiency theory," 68(2), May 1978, pp. 328–332.
Pollak, R.A. "Endogenous tastes in demand and welfare analysis," 68(2), May 1978 pp. 374–379.
Panzar, J.C. "Equilibrium and welfare in unregulated airline markets," 69(2), May 1979, pp. 92–95.
Pindyck, R.S. "The cartelization of world commodity markets," 69(2), May 1979, pp. 154–158.
Salop, S.C. "Strategic entry deterrence," 69(2), May 1979, pp. 335–338.
Stiglitz, J.E. "Equilibrium in product markets with imperfect information," 6(2), May 1979, pp. 339–345.
Fraumeni, B., Fraumeni, M., Jorgenson, D.W. "Rates of return by industrial sector in the United States, 1948–76," 70(2), May 1980, pp. 326–330.

Grether, D.M., Isaac, R.M., Plott, C.R. "The allocation of landing rights by unanimity among competitors," 71(2), May 1981, pp. 166–171.
Gilbert, R.J., Harris, R.G. "Investment decisions with economies of scale and learning," 71(2), May 1981, pp. 172–177.
Dixit, A. "Recent developments in oligopoly theory," 72(2), May 1982, pp. 12–17.
Schwartz, A., Wilde, L.L. "Imperfect information, monopolistic competition, and public policy," 72(2), May 1982, pp. 18–23.

(3) Inconsistent with Chicago School positions, also suggesting need to expand received analytical approaches.

Bowman, M.J. "The consumer in the history of economic doctrine," 41(2), May 1951, pp. 1–18.
Hildebrand, G.H. "Consumer sovereignty in modern times," 41(2), May 1951, pp. 19–33.
Boulding, K.E. "Implications for general economics of more realistic theories of the firm," 42(2), May 1952, pp. 35–44.
Ayres, C.E. "The role of technology in economic theory," 43(2), May 1953, pp. 279–287.
Spengler, J.J. "Sociological value theory, economic analyses, and economic policy," 43(2), May 1953, pp. 340–349.
Cole, A.H. "Twentieth-century entrepreneurship in the United States and economic growth," 44(2), May 1954, pp. 35–50.
Robertson, R.M. "On the changing apparatus of competition," 44(2), May 1954, pp. 51–62.
Hoover, E.M. "Some institutional factors in business investment decisions," 44(2), May 1954, pp. 201–213.
Hickman, C.A. "Managerial motivation and the theory of the firm," 45(2), May 1955, pp. 544–554.
Hollander, S.C. "Theoretical implications of empirical research on retail pricing," 47(2), May 1957, pp. 252–265.
Lewis, B.W. "Economics by admonition," 49(2), May 1959, pp. 384–398.
Margolis, J. "Sequential decision making in the firm," 50(2), May 1960, pp. 526–533.
Cohen, K.J. "Simulation of the firm," 50(2), May 1960, pp. 534–540.
Marschak, J. "Theory of an efficient several-person firm," 50(2), May 1960, pp. 541–548.
Whitin, T.M. "Managerial economics and the firm," 50(2), May 1960, pp. 549–555.
Shubik, M. "Game theory as an approach to the firm," 50(2), May 1960, pp. 556–559.
Phillips, A. "Policy implications of the theory of interfirm organization," 51(2), May 1961, pp. 245–254.
Simon, H.A. "New developments in the theory of the firm," 52(2), May 1962, pp. 1–15.

Baumol, W.J. "Entrepreneurship in economic theory," 58(2), May 1968, pp. 64–71.

Williamson O.E. "Allocative efficiency and the limits of antitrust," 59(2), May 1969, pp. 105–118.

Singer, E.M. "Industrial organization: Price models and public policy," 60(2), May 1970, pp. 90–99.

Grabowski, H., Mueller, D. "Industrial organization: The role and contribution of econometrics," 60(2), May 1970, pp. 100–104.

Lintner, J. "Expectations, mergers and equilibrium in purely competitive securities markets," 61(2), May 1971, pp. 101–111.

Williamson, O.E. "Vertical integration of production: Market failure considerations," 61(2), May 1971, pp. 112–123.

Marris, R. "Is the corporate economy a Corporate State?" 62(1/2), 1972, pp. 103–115.

Smith, V.L. "Economic theory and its discontents," 64(2), May 1974, pp. 320–322.

Buchanan, J.M. "A contractarian paradigm for applying economic theory," 65(2), May 1975, pp. 225–230.

Foley, D.K. "Problems vs. conflicts: Economic theory and ideology," 65(2), May 1975, pp. 231–236.

Joskow, P.L. "Firm decision-making processes and oligopoly theory," 65(2), May 1975, pp. 270–279.

Williamson, O.E. "The economics of internal organization: Exit and voice in relation to markets and hierarchies," 66(2), May 1976, pp. 369–377.

Butters, G.R. "A survey of advertising and market structure," 66(2), May 1976, pp. 392–397.

Bower, J.L. "The business of business is serving markets," 68(2), May 1978, pp. 322–327.

Stiglitz, J.E. "Potential competition may reduce welfare," 71(2), May 1981, pp. 184–189.

Schmalensee, R. "Antitrust and the new industrial economics," 72(2), May 1982, pp. 24–28.

References

Andrews, P.W.S. (1951), Industrial analysis in economics. In: Wilson, T., Andrews, P.W.S. (Eds.), *Oxford Studies in the Price Mechanism*. Clarendon Press, Oxford, pp. 139–172.

Andrews, P.W.S. (1952), Industrial economics as a specialist subject. *Journal of Industrial Economics* 1 (1), 72–79. November.

Archibald, G.C. (1961), Chamberlin versus Chicago. *Review of Economic Studies* 29 (1), 2–28. October.

Archibald, G.C. (1963), Reply to Chicago. *Review of Economic Studies* 30 (1), 68–71. February.

Bain, J.S. (1944), *The Economics of the Pacific Coast Petroleum Industry. Part I: Market Structure*. University of California Press, Berkeley and Los Angeles.

Bain, J.S. (1949a), Price and production policies. In: Ellis, H.S. (Ed.), *A Survey of Contemporary Economics*. The Blakiston Company, Philadelphia, pp. 129–173.

Bain, J.S. (1949b), A note on pricing in monopoly and oligopoly. *American Economic Review* 39 (1), 448–469. March.

Bain, J.S. (1956), *Barriers to New Competition*. Harvard University Press, Cambridge, MA.

Bain, J.S. (1959), *Industrial Organization*. John Wiley & Sons, Inc., New York and London.

Bain, J.S. (1970), The comparative stability of market structures. In: Markham, J.W., Papanek, G.F. (Eds.), *Industrial Organization and Economic Development, in honor of E.S. Mason*. Houghton Mifflin Company, Boston, pp. 38–46.

Baxter, W.F. (1983), Reflection's upon Professor Williamson's comments. *St. Louis University Law Journal* 27 (2), 315–320. April.

Blaug, M. (1986), Economic methodology in one easy lesson. In: Blaug, M. (Ed.), *Economic History and the History of Economics*. New York University Press, Washington Square, New York, pp. 265–279.

Bok, D.C. (1960), Section 7 of the Clayton Act and the merging of law and economics. *Harvard Law Review* 74 (2), 226–355. December.

Boland, L.A. (1979), A critique of Friedman's critics. *Journal of Economic Literature* 17 (2), 503–522. June.

Bolton, P., Brodley, J.F., Riordan, M.H. (2000), Predatory pricing: Strategic theory and legal policy. *Georgetown Law Journal* 88, 2239–2330. August.

Bonanno, G., Brandolini, D. (1990), Introduction. In: Bonanno, G., Brandolini, D. (Eds.), *Industrial Structure in the New Industrial Economics*. Clarendon Press, Oxford, pp. 1–21.

Bresnahan, T.F. (1981), Departures from marginal-cost pricing in the American automobile industry. *Journal of Econometrics* 17, 201–227.

Bronfenbrenner, M. (1962), Observations on the 'Chicago School(s)'. *Journal of Political Economy* 70 (1), 72–75. February.

Burns, A.R. (1937), The organization of industry and the theory of prices. *Journal of Political Economy* 45 (5), 662–680. October.

Chamberlin, E.H. (1933), *The Theory of Monopolistic Competition*. Harvard University Press, Cambridge, MA.

Chamberlin, E.H. (1957), *Towards a More General Theory of Value*. Oxford University Press, New York.

Chamberlin, E.H. (1961), The origin and early development of monopolistic competition theory. *Quarterly Journal of Economics* 75 (4), 515–543.

Clark, J.B. (1887), The limits of competition. *Political Science Quarterly* 2 (1), 45–61. March.

Coase, R.H. (1972), Industrial organization: A proposal for research. In: Fuchs, V.R. (Ed.), *Policy Issues and Research Opportunities in Industrial Organization*. NBER, New York.

Coase, R.H. (1998), Aaron Director. In: Newman, P. (Ed.), *The New Palgrave Dictionary of Economics and the Law. Vol. 1*. Macmillan Reference Limited, London, pp. 601–605.

Comanor, W.S., Wilson, T.A. (1967), Advertising market structure and performance. *Review of Economics and Statistics* 49 (4), 423–440. November.

Cournot, A. (1838), *Researches into the Mathematical Principles of the Theory of Wealth*. L. Hachette, Original Paris. English translation by Nathaniel T. Bacon, The Macmillan Company, New York, 1897; reprinted 1927 by The Macmillan Company, New York with notes by Irving Fisher; reprinted 1960, 1964, 1971 by Augustus M. Kelley, New York.

Davies, S., Lyons, B. (1989), Introduction. In: Davies, S., Lyons, B., Dixon, H., Geroski, P. (Eds.), *Economics of Industrial Organization*. Longman, London and New York, pp. 1–25.

Davies, S., Lyons, B. (1996), *Industrial Organization in the European Union*. Clarendon Press, Oxford.

de Long, J.B. (1990), In defense of Henry Simons' standing as a classical liberal. *Cato Journal*, 601–618. Winter.

Demsetz, H. (1973), Industry structure, market rivalry, and public policy. *Journal of Law and Economics* 16 (1), 1–9. April.

Demsetz, H. (1974), Two systems of belief about monopoly. In: Goldschmid, H.J., Mann, H.M., Weston, J.F. (Eds.), *Industrial Concentration: The New Learning*. Little, Brown & Company, Boston.

Director, A. (1948), Prefatory note. In: Simons, H.C. (Ed.), *Economic Policy for a Free Society*. University of Chicago Press, Chicago & London, pp. 5–7.
Director, A. (1964), The parity of the economic market place. *Journal of Law and Economics* 7, 1–10. October.
Dixit, A., Stiglitz, J.E. (1977), Monopolistic competition and optimum product diversity. *American Economic Review* 67, 297–308.
Ekelund, R.B. Jr., Hébert, R.F. (1990), E.H. Chamberlin and contemporary industrial organisation theory. *Journal of Economic Studies* 17 (2), 20–31.
Fisher, F.M. (1989), Games economists play. *RAND Journal of Economics* 20 (1), 113–124. Spring.
Frazer, W.J., Boland, L.A. (1983), An essay on the foundations of Friedman's methodology. *American Economic Review* 73 (1), 129–144. March.
Friedman, J.W. (1979), On entry preventing behavior and limit price models of entry. In: Brams, S.J., Schwodiauer, G. (Eds.), *Applied Game Theory*. Physica-Verlag, Wurzburg-Wien, pp. 236–253.
Friedman, M. (1953), The methodology of positive economics. In: Friedman, M. (Ed.), *Essays in Positive Economics*. University of Chicago Press, Chicago and London, pp. 3–43.
Friedman, M. (1955), Comment on economies of scale. In: *Business Concentration and Price Policy*. Princeton University Press, Princeton, pp. 230–238.
Friedman, M. (1963), More on Archibald versus Chicago. *Review of Economic Studies* 30 (1), 65–67. February.
Friedman, M. (1974), Schools at Chicago. *University of Chicago Alumni Magazine*, 11–16. Autumn.
Friedman, M. (1982), *Capitalism and Freedom*. University of Chicago Press, Chicago and London. First published 1962.
Fuchs, V.R. (1961), Integration, concentration, and profits in manufacturing industries. *Quarterly Journal of Economics* 75 (2), 278–291. May.
Fudenberg, D., Tirole, J. (1987), Understanding rent dissipation: On the use of game theory in industrial organization. *American Economic Review* 77 (2), 176–183. May.
Goldschmid, H.J., Mann, H.M., Weston, J.F. (Eds.) (1974), *Industrial Concentration: The New Learning*. Little, Brown & Company, Boston.
Grether, E.T. (1970), Industrial organization: Past history and future problems. *American Economic Review* 60 (2), 83–89. May.
Harberger, A.C. (1954), Monopoly and resource allocation. *American Economic Review* 44 (2), 75–87. May.
Hay, D.A., Morris, D.J. (1979), *Industrial Economics*. Oxford University Press, Oxford.
Heflebower, R.B. (1954), Toward a theory of industrial markets and prices. *American Economic Review* 44 (2), 121–139. May.
Hovenkamp, H. (1991), *Enterprise and American Law 1836–1937*. Harvard University Press, Cambridge, MA and London, England.
Kaysen, C., Turner, D.F. (1959), *Antitrust Policy: An Economic and Legal Analysis*. Harvard University Press, Cambridge, MA.
Kearl, J.R., Pope, C.L., Whiting, G.C., Wimmer, L.T. (1979), A confusion of economists? *American Economic Review* 69 (2), 28–37. May.
Kitch, E.W. (1983), The fire of truth: A remembrance of law and economics at Chicago, 1932–1970. *Journal of Law and Economics* 26 (1), 163–234. April.
Koopmans, T.C. (1957), *Three Essays on the State of Economic Science*. McGraw-Hill Book Company, Inc., New York.
Lange, O. (1945–1946), The scope and method of economics. *Review of Economic Studies* 13 (1), 19–32.
Machlup, F. (1964), Professor Samuelson on theory and realism. *American Economic Review* 54 (5), 733–735. September.
Markham, J.W., Papanek, G.F. (1970), *Industrial Organization and Economic Development, in honor of E.S. Mason*. Houghton Mifflin Company, Boston.
Marshall, A. (1919), *Industry and Trade*. Macmillan and Co. Limited, London.
Marshall, A. (1925), Some aspects of competition. (Presidential Address to the Economic Science and Statistics Section of the British Association, at Leeds, 1890) In: Pigou, A.C. (Ed.), *Memorials of Alfred Marshall*. Macmillan, London, pp. 256–291.

Martin, D.D. (1976), Industrial organization and reorganization. In: Samuels, W.J. (Ed.), *The Chicago School of Political Economy*. Association for Evolutionary Economics and Division of Research, Graduate School of Business Administration, Michigan State University. Chapter 13.

Martin, S. (2002), *Advanced Industrial Economics*, 2nd ed. Basil Blackwell.

Martin, S. (2007), The goals of antitrust policy. In: Collins, W.D. (Ed.), *Issues in Competition Law and Policy*. American Bar Association.

Mason, E.S. (1939), Price and production policies of large-scale enterprise. *American Economic Review* 29 (1), 61–74. March.

Mason, E.S. (1949), The current status of the monopoly problem in the United States. *Harvard Law Review* 62 (8), 1265–1285. June.

McGee, J.S. (1974), Commentary. In: Goldschmid, H.J., Mann, H.M., Weston, J.F. (Eds.), *Industrial Concentration: The New Learning*. Little, Brown & Company, Boston, pp. 101–104.

McGee, J.S. (1988), *Industrial Organization*. Prentice-Hall, Englewood Cliffs, NJ.

Miller, J.P. (1954), Competition and countervailing power: Their roles in the American economy. *American Economic Review* 44 (2), 15–25. May.

Modigliani, F. (1958), New developments on the oligopoly front. *Journal of Political Economy* 66 (3), 215–232. June.

Nelson, R.R. (1979), Comments on a paper by Posner. *University of Pennsylvania Law Review* 127, 949–952.

North, D.C. (1983), Comment on Stigler and Friedland, 'The literature of economics: The case of Berle and Means'. *Journal of Law and Economics* 26 (2), 269–271. June.

Nutter, G.W. (1954), Competition: Direct and devious. *American Economic Review* 44 (2), 69–76. May.

Patinkin D. (1981), *Essays On and In the Chicago Tradition*. Durham, North Carolina.

Peltzman, S. (2005), Aaron Director's influence on antitrust policy. *Journal of Law and Economics* 48, 313–330. October.

Phillips, A. (1960), A theory of interfirm organization. *Quarterly Journal of Economics* 74 (4), 602–613. November.

Phillips, A. (1961), Policy implications of the theory of interfirm organization. *American Economic Review* 51 (2), 245–254. May.

Phillips, A., Stevenson, R.E. (1974), The historical development of industrial organization. *History of Political Economy* 6 (3), 324–342. Fall.

Posner, R.A. (1976), *Antitrust Law*, first edition. University of Chicago Press.

Posner, R.A. (1979), The Chicago School of antitrust analysis. *University of Pennsylvania Law Review* 127, 925–948.

Posner, R.A. (2001), *Antitrust Law*, second edition. University of Chicago Press.

Reder, M.W. (1982), Chicago economics: Permanence and change. *Journal of Economic Literature* 20 (1), 1–38. March.

Richardson, G.B. (1972), The organisation of industry. *Economic Journal* 82 (327), 883–896. September.

Ripley, W.Z. (1907), Introduction. In: *Railway Problems*. Ginn and Company, Boston.

Robinson, J. (1969), *The Economics of Imperfect Competition*, 2nd ed. Macmillan, St. Martin's Press, London. First edition 1933.

Rosenbluth, G. (1976), Comment. *Journal of Law and Economics* 19 (2), 389–392. August.

Rowe, F.M., Brozen, Y., Areeda, P.E., Millstein, I.M. (1984), Are economists taking over? In: Fox, E.M., Halverson, J.T. (Eds.), *Antitrust Policy in Transition: The Convergence of Law and Economics*. ABA Press, pp. 23–41.

Salop, S.C. (1979), Monopolistic competition with outside goods. *Bell Journal of Economics* 10 (1), 141–156. Spring.

Samuelson, P.A. (1963), Problems of methodology—discussion. *American Economic Review* 53, 231–236.

Samuelson, P.A. (1967), The monopolistic competition revolution. In: Kuenne, R.E. (Ed.), *Monopolistic Competition Theory: Studies in Impact*. John Wiley & Sons, New York, pp. 105–138.

Scherer, F.M. (1970), *Industrial Market Structure and Economic Performance*, 1st ed. Rand McNally, Chicago.
Scherer, F.M. (1980), *Industrial Market Structure and Economic Performance*, 2nd ed. Rand McNally, Chicago.
Scherer, F.M., Ross, D. (1990), *Industrial Market Structure and Economic Performance*, 3rd ed. Houghton Mifflin Company, Boston.
Schmalensee, R.C. (1982a), The new industrial organization and the economic analysis of modern markets. In: Hildebrand, W. (Ed.), *Advances in Economic Theory*. Cambridge University Press, Cambridge, pp. 253–284.
Schmalensee, R.C. (1982b), Antitrust and the new industrial economics. *American Economic Review* 72 (2), 24–28. May.
Schmalensee, R.C. (1987), Industrial organization. In: Eatwell, J., Milgate, M., Newman, P. (Eds.), *The New Palgrave*. Macmillan Press Limited, London, pp. 803–808.
Schmalensee, R.C. (1988), Industrial economics: An overview. *Economic Journal* 98 (392), 643–681. September.
Schneider, E. (1967), Milestones on the way to the theory of monopolistic competition. In: Kuenne, R.E. (Ed.), *Monopolistic Competition Theory: Studies in Impact*. John Wiley & Sons, New York, pp. 139–144.
Schumpeter, J.A. (1934), Review of Robinson's "Economics of Imperfect Competition". *Journal of Political Economy*, 249–257. Reprinted in Clemence, R.V. (Ed.), *Essays of J.A. Schumpeter*. Cambridge, MA, 1951, pp. 125–133.
Schumpeter, J.A. (1949), Science and ideology. *American Economic Review* 39 (2), 345–359. March.
Shapiro, R.B., Bork, R.H., Breyer, S.G. (1984), Judicial precedent and the new economics. In: Fox, E.M., Halverson, J.T. (Eds.), *Antitrust Policy in Transition: The Convergence of Law and Economics*. ABA Press, pp. 5–21.
Shubik, M. (1980), *Structure and Behavior*. Harvard University Press, Cambridge, MA.
Simon, H.A. (1962), New developments in the theory of the firm. *American Economic Review* 52 (2), 1–15. May.
Simons H.C. (1934), *A Positive Program for Laissez Faire*, Public Policy Pamphlet No. 15. Gideonse, H.D. (Ed.). University of Chicago Press, Chicago. Reprinted in Simons, H.C., *Economic Policy for a Free Society*. University of Chicago Press, Chicago & London, 1948.
Simons, H.C. (1936), The requisites of free competition. *American Economic Review* 26 (1), 68–76. March.
Simons, H.C. (1948), *Economic Policy for a Free Society*. University of Chicago Press, Chicago & London. Reprinted from *A Positive Program for Laissez Faire*, Public Policy Pamphlet No. 15, Gideonse, H.D. (Ed.), University of Chicago Press, Chicago, 1934.
Sraffa, P. (1926), The laws of returns under competitive conditions. *Economic Journal* 36 (144), 535–550. December.
Stigler, G.J. (1949), Monopolistic competition in retrospect. In: *Five Lectures on Economic Problems*. Longmans, Green and Co., London, pp. 12–24;
Reprinted in Stigler, G.J., *The Organization of Industry*. Richard D. Irwin, Inc., Homewood, IL, 1968.
Stigler G.J. (1952), The case against big business. *Fortune* pp. 123, 158, 162, 164, 167. May.
Stigler, G.J. (1963), Archibald versus Chicago. *Review of Economic Studies* 30 (1), 63–64. February.
Stigler, G.J. (1982), The economists and the problem of monopoly. *American Economic Review* 72 (2), 1–11. May.
Stigler, G.J. (1988), *Memoirs of an Unregulated Economist*. Basic Books, New York.
Stigler, S.M. (2005), Aaron Director remembered. *Journal of Law and Economics* 48, 307–311. October.
Stocking, G.W., Kahn, A.E., Griffin, C.E., Stigler, G.W. (1956), Report of the Attorney General's Committee on Antitrust Policy: Discussion. *American Economic Review* 46 (2), 496–507. May.
Sullivan, L.A. (1977), Economics and more humanistic disciplines: What are the sources of wisdom for antitrust. *University of Pennsylvania Law Review* 125 (6), 1214–1243. June.

Sylos-Labini, P. (1957), *Oligopolio e progresso tecnico*. Giuffrè, Milan.

Sylos-Labini, P. (1962), *Oligopoly and Technical Progress*. Harvard University Press, Cambridge.

Turner, D.F., Pitofsky, R., Campbell, T.J. (1983), Has economics rationalized antitrust? *Antitrust Law Journal* 52 (3), 607–622. September 29–30.

White, H.G. Jr. (1936), A review of monopolistic and imperfect competition theories. *American Economic Review* 26 (4), 637–649. December.

White House Task Force on Antitrust Policy (1968–69), "Report", ("Neal Report"). *Antitrust Law & Economics Review* 2, 11–76. Winter.

Wiles, P. (1983), Ideology, methodology, and neoclassical economics. In: Eichner, A.S. (Ed.), *Why Economics Is Not Yet a Science*. M.E. Sharpe, Inc., Armonk, NY, pp. 61–89.

Williamson, O.E. (1965), A dynamic theory of interfirm behavior. *Quarterly Journal of Economics* 79 (4), 579–607. November.

Wolinsky, A. (1986), True monopolistic competition as a result of imperfect information. *Quarterly Journal of Economics* 101 (3), 493–512. August.

Wong, S. (1973), The 'F-twist' and the methodology of Paul Samuelson. *American Economic Review* 63 (3), 312–325. June.

CHAPTER 3

The Impact of the Corporate Leniency Program on Cartel Formation and the Cartel Price Path

Joe Chen[a] and Joseph E. Harrington Jr.[b]

[a]*Faculty of Economics, University of Tokyo, 7-3-1 Hongo, Bunkyo-ku, Tokyo, 113-0033 Japan*
E-mail address: joechen@e.u-tokyo.ac.jp
[b]*Johns Hopkins University, Baltimore, MD 21218, USA*
E-mail address: joe.harrington@jhu.edu

Abstract

Previous research exploring the effect of corporate leniency programs has modeled the oligopoly stage game as a Prisoners' Dilemma. Using numerical analysis, we consider the Bertrand price game and allow the probability of detection and penalties to be sensitive to firms' prices. Consistent with earlier results, a maximal leniency program necessarily makes collusion more difficult. However, we also find that partial leniency programs—such as in the U.S.—can make collusion easier compared to offering no leniency. We also show that even if cartel formation is not deterred, a leniency program can reduce the prices charged by firms.

3.1. Introduction

One of the most important policy developments in antitrust policy in recent decades is the revision of the Corporate Leniency Program by the U.S. Department of Justice (DOJ) in 1993. Originally instituted in 1978, this program allows corporations and individuals, who were engaging in illegal antitrust activity (such as price-fixing), to receive amnesty from government penalties. This means that a corporation can avoid government fines, while individuals escape fines and prison sentences. The 1993 revision made it possible for amnesty to be awarded even when an investigation had been started and made it a condition that the DOJ "has not received information about the illegal activity being reported from any other source." This means that amnesty is limited to one firm per cartel. Leniency programs have proliferated as the European Commission instituted one in 1996 and an increasing number of industrialized countries have some form of leniency program. While it is difficult to assess the role of these programs on cartel formation and collapse, we do know that it has been widely

CONTRIBUTIONS TO ECONOMIC ANALYSIS
VOLUME 282 ISSN: 0573-8555
DOI: 10.1016/S0573-8555(06)82003-1

used. Notable examples include Rhône-Poulenc in the vitamins case, Christie's in the fine arts auctions case, and Carbide/Graphite in the graphite electrodes case.[1]

In light of the influence of leniency programs, it is not surprising that there has been a growing amount of research exploring how such programs destabilize collusion. Recent work includes Aubert et al. (2003), Motta and Polo (2003), Spagnolo (2003), Feess and Walzl (2004), Motchenkova (2004), and Harrington (2005a). This research has generally shown that leniency does reduce cartel stability. In the context of a stationary environment (that is, the probability of conviction without use of the leniency program is fixed over time), Spagnolo (2003) shows that, if there is a budget-balancing constraint, a first-best solution can be achieved by giving the first firm to come forward a reward equal to the fines levied on the remaining firms. Motta and Polo (2003) allow the probability of conviction to stochastically change over time though it is restricted to take only two values, one of which is zero (which corresponds to the event that there is no investigation). Their analysis provides qualified support for leniency. In some cases, waiving a sufficiently high fraction of penalties can prevent cartel formation, in which case such a policy is optimal. However, if it cannot prevent cartel formation then no leniency should be provided. Harrington (2005a) also allows the probability of detection and conviction to vary over time but it can take any value from [0, 1]. This introduces a new effect absent from Motta and Polo (2003) which has the implication that, under certain conditions, more leniency can enhance cartel stability. It is then possible for partial leniency to be optimal though plausible sufficient conditions are provided for it to be optimal to waive all penalties for the first firm to come forward. It is also shown that restrictions should be placed on when amnesty is awarded, though it can be optimal to award amnesty even when the antitrust authority is very likely to win the case without insider testimony.

A common limitation to all of this research is that the impact of leniency programs is explored in a restrictive setting: The stage game modeling oligopolistic interaction is the Prisoners' Dilemma. This means that the collusive price and profit are fixed, as are the price and profit associated with a firm cheating on the cartel. It has the implication that the probability of the cartel being discovered is exogenous to how the cartel behaves as is the penalty in the event of discovery and successful prosecution. All of these restrictions affect the influence of a leniency program. While a leniency program may be able to prevent cartel formation, by fiat it cannot impact the cartel price in the event a cartel forms. Furthermore, while a leniency program may prevent cartel formation when the collusive price path is fixed (as it is with the Prisoners' Dilemma), it may not be able to do so if firms can strategically adjust the cartel price path so as to counteract the destabilizing effect of a leniency program. Previous work has shown

---

[1] A good review of the status of leniency programs is provided in Hard Core Cartels (2003). A critical description of the U.S. program can be found in Kobayashi (2001).

that leniency programs destabilize cartels by tightening the incentive compatibility constraint and the issue is to what extent can a strategically-minded cartel counteract it by appropriately lowering the proposed collusive price path.

The objective of this chapter is to explore the implications of the corporate leniency program in a rich dynamic model that endogenizes the prices that firms charge and allows the probability of detection and penalties to be sensitive to those prices. With this model, we can re-examine the central question thus far explored in the leniency program literature: Do leniency programs make collusion more difficult? In addition, we can also explore a new question: If a leniency program does not prevent cartel formation, what is its impact on the cartel price path?

To engage in this exercise, we draw upon another recent strand of the collusion literature that adapts the classical repeated game model of collusion to allow for a cartel to be discovered and, in that event, penalties being levied (Harrington, 2004, 2005b; Harrington and Chen, 2006). This work allows both the probability of detection and penalties to be endogenous to colluding firms' prices. A cartel is then modeled as choosing a price path to maximize the expected present value of profits while taking into account how this price path impacts the likelihood of paying penalties and satisfying the usual incentive compatibility constraint ensuring the internal stability of the cartel. A cartel then selects a price path that ensures compliance from all firms and which tries to avoid raising suspicions that they are colluding. In that setting, the introduction of a leniency program will impact the price path through its influence on the incentive compatibility constraints. Leniency may influence whether or not collusion is stable and, when it is stable, the properties of the collusive price path.

In sum, this chapter brings together two recent strands in the collusive pricing literature—research that explores the impact of corporate leniency programs and research that explores the impact of antitrust enforcement on cartel formation and the collusive price path. In doing so, we generate two primary findings. First, the optimality of a maximally lenient policy, which has been derived in earlier studies, is shown to be robust when the cartel can adjust its price to the leniency policy and when both the probability of detection and penalties are sensitive to the collusive price path. Second, a policy of partial leniency—which is in effect in the U.S.—can actually make collusion easier and result in a higher cartel price path, relative to a policy of no leniency. After laying out the model in Section 3.2, an optimal collusive price path is defined in Section 3.3. The impact of leniency programs is analyzed in Section 3.4, while Section 3.5 concludes.

3.2. Model

The model is a special case of that in Harrington (2004) with the exception that we allow for a corporate leniency program. As the analysis in this chapter will be numerical, functional forms will be specified. For motivation and elaboration of many assumptions, the reader is referred to Harrington (2005b).

Consider an industry with $n \geq 2$ symmetric firms. To keep matters simple, assume the stage game is the Bertrand price game so that firms offer homogeneous products, make simultaneous price decisions, and have constant marginal cost, denoted $c \geq 0$. Firm i's profit when its price is P_i and all other firms charge a common price of P_{-i} is

$$\pi_i(P_i, P_{-i}) = \begin{cases} (P_i - c)(a - bP_i) & \text{if } P_i < P_{-i}, \\ (P_i - c)(1/n)(a - bP_i) & \text{if } P_i = P_{-i}, \\ 0 & \text{if } P_i > P_{-i}, \end{cases}$$

where $(a - bP)$ is market demand at a price of P and it is assumed $a - bc > 0$. Of course, the stage game equilibrium has all firms price at c with associated profit of $\hat{\pi} = 0$. Finally, let $\pi(P) \equiv (P - c)(1/n)(a - bP)$ denote a firm's profit when all firms charge a common price.

Firms engage in this price game for an infinite number of periods. The setting is one of perfect monitoring which means firms' prices over the preceding $t - 1$ periods are common knowledge in period t. In this chapter, "detection" always refers to a third party, such as buyers, detecting the existence of a cartel. Assume a firm's payoff is the expected discounted sum of its income stream where the common discount factor is $\delta \in (0, 1)$.

If firms form a cartel, they meet to determine price. Assume these meetings, and any associated documentation, provides the "smoking gun" if an investigation is pursued. The cartel is detected with some probability and incurs penalties in that event. Assume, for simplicity, that detection results in the discontinuance of collusion forever. Detection in period t then generates a terminal payoff of $[\hat{\pi}/(1 - \delta)] - X^t - F\ (= -X^t - F)$ where X^t is a firm's damages and F is any (fixed) fines (which may include the monetary equivalent of prison sentences).[2] If not detected, collusion continues on to the next period. It is useful to think of $X^t + F$ as a "hidden liability" for a firm which is incurred only in the event that the cartel is discovered. As we'll be focusing upon symmetric equilibria, all firms will have the same damages so there is a single damage state variable.

Damages are assumed to evolve in the following manner:

$$X^t = \beta X^{t-1} + \gamma x(P^t), \quad \text{where } \beta \in [0, 1) \text{ and } \gamma \geq 0.$$

As time progresses, damages incurred in previous periods become increasingly difficult to document and $1 - \beta$ measures the rate of deterioration of the evidence. $x(P^t)$ is the level of damages incurred by each firm in the current period where γ is the damage multiple applied. While U.S. antitrust law specifies treble damages, γ is often well less than three because of out-of-court settlements. X^t is to be interpreted as that part of antitrust penalties that are sensitive to firms'

[2] One might be bothered that the payoff in the event of detection is negative and thus there is cause for a firm entering into bankruptcy. However, in most price-fixing cases, colluding firms have multiple products and collusion takes places in only a subset of those markets. Thus, the total value of the firm can remain positive even if they are caught colluding in some markets.

prices and how long they've been colluding. Even though buyers cannot collect damages in the European Union, X^t is still relevant as long as E.U. penalties are sensitive to cartel behavior. We will use a specification based on current U.S. antitrust practice:

$$x(P^t) = (P^t - c)D(P^t),$$

where c is the "but for price," that is, the price that would have occurred but for collusion. In the special case when the but for price is unit cost, damages equal the additional profits earned due to collusion.

It is assumed that damages are assessed only in periods of effective collusion. In particular, this means damages are not assessed in the period that a firm deviates. This has the useful implication that, at a symmetric equilibrium, all firms have identical damages and thus there is only one state variable for penalties, X^t. If we instead allowed damages to accumulate in the period that a firm deviated then accumulated damages for the deviator would differ from that of other firms which would require having a separate damage state variable for each firm. Our assumption strikes us a reasonable approximation and serves to reduce the number of state variables.

Successful prosecution of a cartel—by which is meant that penalties are imposed—involves multiple stages. First, detection—the creation of suspicions that a cartel has formed. Some party—for example, buyers—must recognize that, among all of the thousands of industries, this particular one may be plagued by collusion. Second, investigation—in response to a complaint, the antitrust authority must decide that it is worthwhile to pursue a case. Third, prosecution—after conducting such an investigation, the antitrust authority must choose to prosecute the firms (and/or the buyers must decide whether to pursue civil damages litigation). The focus of our modeling is on detection. Detection of a cartel can occur from many sources, some of which are related to price—such as customer complaints—and some of which are unrelated to price—such as internal whistleblowers. Hay and Kelly (1974) find that detection was attributed to a complaint by a customer or a local, state, or federal agency in 13 of 49 price-fixing cases. More recently, an investigation which uncovered the graphite electrodes cartel began with a complaint from a steel manufacturer which is a purchaser of graphite electrodes (Levenstein and Suslow, 2001), and the stainless steel case was launched by buyers complaining to the European Commission about the rapid increase in prices (Levenstein et al., 2004). High prices or price increases or simply anomalous price movements may cause customers to become suspicious and pursue legal action or share their suspicions with the antitrust authorities. Though it isn't important for this model, we do imagine that buyers (in many price-fixing cases, they are industrial buyers) are the ones who may become suspicious about collusion.

To capture these ideas in a tractable manner, an exogenous probability of detection function is specified that depends on the current and previous periods' price vectors. $\phi(\underline{P}^t, \underline{P}^{t-1})$ is the probability of detection when the cartel is active where $\underline{P}^t \equiv (P_1^t, \ldots, P_n^t)$.[3] It is assumed that, in the event of detection, successful prosecution occurs for sure so $\phi(\underline{P}^t, \underline{P}^{t-1})$ also serves as the probability of paying penalties.[4] We will consider a specification in which detection is sensitive to price changes.[5] In light of the environment being stationary, buyers ought to be more surprised by bigger price increases as well as bigger price decreases.

With the Bertrand price game formulation, the transaction price in any period is the lowest price charged. Thus, it is assumed that detection depends on the movement in the lowest price in the market. Let $p^t \equiv \min\{P_1^t, \ldots, P_n^t\}$ denote the minimum price in period t. Making a notational change in the arguments of $\phi(\cdot)$, the probability of detection is specified to be quadratic in the change in the transaction price:

$$\phi(p^t, p^{t-1}) = \begin{cases} \min\{\alpha_0 + \alpha_1^u (p^t - p^{t-1})^2, 1\} & \text{if } p^t \geq p^{t-1}, \\ \min\{\alpha_0 + \alpha_1^d (p^t - p^{t-1})^2, 1\} & \text{if } p^t < p^{t-1}. \end{cases}$$

We then allow for an asymmetric response to price increases and price decreases and consider parameter values such that $0 \leq \alpha_1^d \leq \alpha_1^u$. $\phi(p^t, p^{t-1})$ is assumed to apply to periods in which firms effectively collude. Cartel discovery may also take place after the cartel has collapsed. However, in light of the statute of limitations, this post-cartel window of discovery is bounded. Specifically, we assume, upon discontinuation of collusion, discovery can occur either in the period of collapse (that is, the period in which a firm deviates) or the period afterwards.

In the initial period, firms have the choice of forming a cartel, and risking detection and penalties, or earning non-collusive profit of $\hat{\pi}$. If they choose the former, they can, at any time, choose to discontinue colluding. However, a finitely-lived cartel will cause collusion to unravel so that, in equilibrium, firms either collude forever or not at all (subject to the cartel being exogenously terminated because of detection).

In any period during which firms have a chance of being detected, a firm can apply to the corporate leniency program. This program allows the first firm to come forward to have a reduction in fines. Specifically, a firm awarded amnesty will only have to pay a fraction $\theta \in [0, 1]$ of the penalties levied, $X^t + F$. $\theta = 1$ captures the absence of any leniency program, while $\theta = 0$ provides maximal leniency in that all penalties are avoided. If m firms simultaneously apply for

[3] For an analysis where $\phi(\cdot)$ is derived, see Harrington and Chen (2006).

[4] Alternatively, one can allow the probability of successful prosecution, given detection, to lie between 0 and 1 where this probability is embedded in $\phi(\underline{P}^t, \underline{P}^{t-1})$.

[5] We focus on the dependence of detection on price changes rather than price levels because optimal cartel price paths are more compelling. For this result as well as further motivation for this detection technology, see Harrington (2005b).

leniency, it is assumed that each has an equal chance of receiving it, in which case the expected fraction of penalties to be paid is $\frac{m-1+\theta}{m}$.[6]

Literature review: Collusion and the prospect of cartel detection

An early work integrating the prospect of detection and penalties into the repeated game model of collusion is Cyrenne (1999) who modifies Green and Porter (1984) by assuming that a price war, and the ensuing raising of price after the war, results in detection for sure and with it a fixed fine. The first work to do so while making the probability of detection and penalties endogenous to the price path is Harrington (2005b). There the joint profit maximizing price path is characterized when incentive compatibility constraints are not binding. Assuming that the probability of detection is sensitive to price changes, the cartel is shown to gradually raises price with price converging to a steady-state level. Comparative statics on the steady-state price reveal that it is decreasing in the damage multiple and the probability of detection but is independent of the level of fixed fines. Furthermore, if penalties are independent of the price path then the cartel's steady-state price is the same as in the absence of antitrust laws. Another intriguing result is that a more stringent standard for calculating damages *increases* the steady-state price.

A characterization of the cartel price path when incentive compatibility constraints bind was conducted in Harrington (2004). Depending on the parameter values, two qualitatively distinct cartel price paths emerged. One is qualitatively the same as in Harrington (2005b)—the cartel gradually raises price and it converges to a steady-state level. This establishes that the monotonicity of the price path when incentive compatibility constraints do not bind extends to when they do. The second type of price path has the cartel gradually raise price but then price declines down to the steady-state. Though reducing price lowers profit and cannot make detection less likely, a price decline is required so as to maintain cartel stability. The impact of antitrust laws is also explored and analysis reveals a potentially perverse effect. Though making price-fixing illegal may induce a cartel to initially price lower, in some cases it may allow the cartel to eventually price *higher*; this is due to how antitrust laws affect incentive compatibility constraints. The risk of detection and penalties may deter a firm from cheating, out of fear that a price war may generate suspicions about collusion. Thus, antitrust laws can loosen incentive compatibility constraints and thereby allow the cartel to set higher prices.

---

[6] Initially, we allowed the leniency parameter to vary according to the type of penalty so that a firm receiving amnesty would pay a penalty of $\theta_d X^t + \theta_f F$, where $\theta_d, \theta_f \in [0, 1]$. A motivation for this is that, in the U.S., amnesty means all government fines are waived but a firm is still liable for single (not treble) damages. As the initial results did not reveal any interesting distinctions between θ_d and θ_f, we chose to simplify matters and impose a common leniency parameter applicable to all sources of penalties.

In the previous two papers (and in the current chapter), a reduced form specification was used as the probability of detection was assumed to be increasing in price increases. A more foundational approach is taken in Harrington and Chen (2006) where buyers' beliefs are explicitly modeled and detection occurs when the observed price path is sufficiently unlikely in light of buyers' beliefs. In other words, suspicions emerge when observed prices are anomalous. The cartel price path is shown to be comprised of two phases. During the transitional phase, price is generally rising and relatively unresponsive to cost shocks. During the stationary phase, price responds to cost but is much less sensitive than under non-collusion or simple monopoly. Hence, the variance of price is much lower under collusion; a property consistent with the empirical work of Abrantes-Metz et al. (2005). Furthermore, compared to when firms do not collude, cost shocks take a longer time to pass-through to price and this results in more serial correlation in prices.[7]

3.3. Optimal symmetric subgame perfect equilibrium

The cartel's problem is to choose an infinite price path so as to maximize the expected sum of discounted income subject to the price path being incentive compatible. In determining the set of incentive compatible price paths, the assumption is made that deviation from the collusive path results in the cartel being dissolved and firms behaving according to a Markov Perfect Equilibrium (MPE).

Suppose a firm deviates and the cartel collapses. Since cartel meetings are no longer taking place, the damage variable simply depreciates at the exogenous rate of $1 - \beta$: $X^t = \beta X^{t-1}$.[8] This is still a dynamic problem, however, in that price movements can create suspicions and, while firms are no longer colluding, an investigation could reveal evidence of past collusion. It is assumed that discovery can occur either in the period during which a firm deviates or the period afterwards. The state variables at t are last period's transaction price, denoted p^{t-1}, and (common) damages, X^{t-1}.

Given the Bertrand price formulation, it is easy to argue that a MPE must entail all firms pricing at the stage game equilibrium price of cost.[9] Suppose, to

---

[7] There is earlier work which explores the prospect of detection in a static cartel model. These papers are referenced in Harrington (2005a, 2005b).

[8] Recall that we assume damages stop accumulating once collusion breakdowns which begins with the period in which a firm deviates.

[9] This is not generally true and indeed does not hold under many differentiated products models in which the firm demand function is continuous. In that case, a firm may price above its static best reply function in order to reduce the size of the price decrease (from the collusive price) so as to reduce the chances of detection. This possibility is explored in Harrington (2004). Note that it is then possible that the MPE payoff could be higher than infinite repetition of the stage game equilibrium profit. What is required is that the higher profits (from prices being above the static equilibrium levels) more than compensate for the possibility of paying penalties. Sufficient conditions for that to occur are provided in Harrington (2003).

the contrary, a (symmetric) MPE has all firms pricing at $P' > c$ in the period after a deviation. By the usual argument, a firm could produce an n-fold increase in current profit by pricing just below P'. As the change in the current price vector is arbitrarily small, there is almost no effect on the firm's future payoff since the change in the probability of detection is small and the change in the state variable is small. Since pricing a little below P' significantly raises current profit with almost no effect on future profits, it is not an equilibrium. Therefore, the MPE is infinite repetition of the stage game equilibrium which means the competitive price.

The cartel's problem is represented as a constrained dynamic programming problem:

$$\begin{aligned} V\left(p^{t-1}, X^{t-1}\right) = \max_{P}\, & \pi(P) - \delta\phi\left(P, p^{t-1}\right) \\ & \times \left[\beta X^{t-1} + \gamma x(P) + F\right] \\ & + \delta\left[1 - \phi\left(P, p^{t-1}\right)\right] \\ & \times V\left(P, \beta X^{t-1} + \gamma x(P)\right) \end{aligned} \tag{3.1}$$

subject to

$$\begin{aligned} & \pi(P) - \delta\phi\left(P, p^{t-1}\right)\left[\beta X^{t-1} + \gamma x(P) + F\right] \\ & \quad + \delta\left[1 - \phi\left(P, p^{t-1}\right)\right] V\left(P, \beta X^{t-1} + \gamma x(P)\right) \\ & \geq \max\Big\{ \max_{P' < P} n\pi(P') - \delta\phi\left(P', p^{t-1}\right)\left(\beta X^{t-1} + F\right) \\ & \quad + \delta\left[1 - \phi\left(P', p^{t-1}\right)\right] W\left(P', \beta X^{t-1}\right), \\ & \quad n\pi(P) - \delta\theta\left(\beta X^{t-1} + F\right)\Big\}. \end{aligned} \tag{3.2}$$

A solution to (3.1)–(3.2) is referred to as an Optimal Symmetric Subgame Perfect Equilibrium (OSSPE). W is the expected (non-collusive) payoff after a deviation and is defined by:

$$W = \begin{cases} -\delta\phi(c, P')\left(\beta^2 X^{t-1} + F\right) & \text{if } \theta \geq \phi(c, P'), \\ -\delta\left(\dfrac{n - 1 + \theta}{n}\right)\left(\beta^2 X^{t-1} + F\right) & \text{if } \theta < \phi(c, P'). \end{cases}$$

In the incentive compatibility constraint (3.2), a firm that cheats can choose to apply for amnesty in which case it pays penalties of $\theta(\beta X^{t-1} + F)$. Since detection is no longer an issue, it optimally prices so as to maximize current profit which means slightly undercutting the collusive price of P and earning profit of approximately $n\pi(P)$. This yields a a payoff of $n\pi\ (P) - \delta\theta(\beta X^{t-1} + F)$. Alternatively, it can choose not to use the leniency program when it cheats. In that case, it may want to price differently so as to control the induced series of price decreases. If it deviates by pricing at P' then price will decline by $P' - p^{t-1}$ in the current period and by $P' - c$ in the following period. Note that it faces an expected present value of penalties of

$$\delta\phi(P', p^{t-1})(\beta X^{t-1} + F) + \delta^2[1 - \phi(P', p^{t-1})]\phi(c, P')(\beta^2 X^{t-1} + F).$$

A deviating firm may then want to price lower than just undercutting the collusive price so that the price path falls more gradually and detection is made less likely.

In defining W, note that, as argued above, equilibrium necessarily entails all firms pricing at cost. The only issue is whether they apply for leniency (given the deviator did not already do so). It is always an equilibrium for all firms to apply for leniency. Given that all other firms do so, a firm reduces expected penalties from $\delta(\beta^2 X^{t-1} + F)$ to $\delta(\frac{n-1+\theta}{n})(\beta^2 X^{t-1} + F)$ by doing so itself (where it is assumed that the firm given amnesty is randomly selected). There may also be another equilibrium in which no firm applies for amnesty. This exists if and only if $\phi(c, P') \leq \theta$ so that the probability of detection is weakly less than the fraction of penalties that must be paid if awarded amnesty. If the "no one applies for leniency" equilibrium exists, it is assumed that firms achieve it given it is Pareto superior to the equilibrium in which all firms apply.[10]

For when there is no corporate leniency program (that is, $\theta = 1$), Harrington (2004) proves that an OSSPE price path exists, which may either have a cartel formed with prices above their static equilibrium levels or may involve no cartel formation. It is straightforward to show that the proof still works when $\theta < 1$.

This modeling of detection is stationary and deterministic and thus is similar to that in, for example, Spagnolo (2003). The implication is that, in equilibrium, the leniency program is not used. For if it was used then collusion would end at a known finite date which would destabilize collusion in the initial period. Though the model of this chapter allows the probability of detection to change over time because of its dependence on the price path, the probability moves in a deterministic manner so the same logic applies as in Spagnolo (2003) and thus the leniency program is not used in equilibrium. This property is to be contrasted with the models of Motta and Polo (2003) and Harrington (2005a) where the probability of detection is stochastic. In that case, the leniency program can be used in equilibrium. Though we believe such a stochastic specification is more compelling, tractability prevents that level of richness here.

When colluding firms do not anticipate using the leniency program in equilibrium, leniency operates exclusively through the payoff to cheating in the incentive compatibility constraint. As a deviating firm can receive amnesty from some or all penalties, the standard argument in previous papers is that the payoff to cheating is (weakly) higher, while the payoff to colluding is unaffected (since

---

[10] Note that $\phi(c, P') \leq \theta$ implies:

$$-\delta\phi(c, P')(\beta^2 X^{t-1} + F) > -\delta\left(\frac{n-1+\theta}{n}\right)(\beta^2 X^{t-1} + F).$$

firms do not apply for amnesty in equilibrium).[11] Hence, leniency programs make cheating relatively more profitable and this serves to reduce cartel stability.

It is true in this model as well that the possibility of a deviating firm lowering its penalty through amnesty can raise its payoff and thus make collusion more difficult. However, there are two points to make. First, the effect is more complex here since the price a firm charges when it deviates is endogenous and thus can depend on whether or not it applies for amnesty. If it decides to receive leniency then a deviating firm need not be concerned about a post-deviation price war triggering detection. As a result, it can maximize its profit from cheating by just undercutting the collusive price. With this richer oligopoly model, leniency affects not only the penalties paid by a firm that deviates but also the profits it receives when it does deviate.

Previous models assume that detection can occur only when firms are colluding. We depart from this assumption by allowing detection to occur in the period after the cartel's collapse (that is, the period after which a firm deviates). This leads us to the second point which is that expected penalties can be *higher* when partial leniency is offered, compared to a policy of no leniency. Suppose a firm that deviates finds it optimal not to use the leniency program, perhaps because the probability of detection is relatively low (even for big price decreases). Further suppose that, in the period after the deviation, it is an equilibrium for all firms to apply for leniency. Of course, if that event was anticipated, a deviating firm would generally prefer to apply for leniency when it deviates because, by doing so, it receives amnesty for sure, while if it waits then it only receives it with probability $\frac{1}{n}$. The implication of this argument is that a deviating firm may use the leniency program even though the ensuing payoff is lower than when there is no leniency program. For some values of θ, it is then possible that leniency reduces the payoff to cheating and, therefore, it is not immediate that more leniency (a lower value for θ) reduces cartel stability. This argument, however, only pertains to when $\theta \gg 0$. When $\theta \simeq 0$ then a deviating firm who applies for leniency pays a penalty close to zero and that has to be less than what is paid in the absence of a leniency program. Hence, a policy of maximal leniency necessarily tightens the incentive compatibility constraint relative to having no leniency program. Whether there is a monotonic relationship—waiving a higher fraction of penalties under the leniency program makes collusion more difficult to sustain—is less clear.

---

[11] The latter property is not true when the probability of detection is stochastic as shown in Motta and Polo (2003) and Harrington (2005a). In that colluding firms anticipate that they may use leniency in the future (in the event that the probability of discovery is sufficiently high), the expected collusive payoff depends on the leniency program as well. While more leniency raises the expected collusive payoff in Motta and Polo (2003), it can either raise or lower the expected payoff in Harrington (2005a).

3.4. Numerical analysis

To begin, let us describe the method used to solve (3.1)–(3.2). The price-damage state space is $\Delta \equiv [0, P^m] \times [0, \gamma x(P^m)/(1-\beta)]$, where P^m is the simple monopoly price. Δ^* is a discretized version of Δ which is 30×30 and thus has 900 states. (3.1)–(3.2) is solved through function iteration on Δ^*. The value function is approximated by a linear spline with 30 basis functions and an equal number of interpolation nodes. One specifies an initial value function and then uses (3.1)–(3.2) to produce a new value function for each state in Δ^*. Interpolation using a linear spline then produces a new value function defined on Δ. This process is iterated until convergence is achieved where the criterion is the norm of the difference of the coefficient vectors between iterations and the tolerance level is 5×10^{-10}.[12]

There are a total of 12 parameters. Putting aside the leniency parameter, the benchmark parameter configuration is:

$$a = 100, \quad b = 1, \quad c = 0, \quad \delta = .7, \quad \beta = .9, \quad n = 3$$

$$\gamma = 1, \quad F = 0, \quad \alpha_0 = .05, \quad \alpha_1^u = .0032, \quad \alpha_1^d = .0016.$$

Note that the simple monopoly price is 50 and the non-collusive price is 0. We solved both the unconstrained case, (3.1), and the constrained case, (3.1)–(3.2) for $\theta = .2$. The associated value and policy functions are shown in Figure 3.1. For the unconstrained case (and note that leniency is irrelevant), the policy function is monotonic in the two states. The higher is the previous period's transaction price, the higher the cartel can set price in the current period since the resulting price increase is not as large. As accumulated damages are smaller, the penalty in the event of discovery is smaller which makes the cartel want to raise price more. This reflects the trade-off from a bigger price increase: A higher current profit but a lower future payoff since the probability of detection and accumulated damages are higher.

Turning to the solution to the constrained problem, the policy function is similar except when last period's price is relatively high and damages are relatively low; for those states, the incentive compatibility constraint is violated so firms set the stage game equilibrium price of zero. When price is relatively high, firms have an incentive to cheat in order to earn higher current profit. In order to counteract that incentive, the cartel must lower price significantly. But if that occurs then the probability of detection is high—since there is a large price decrease—in which case the expected future lifetime is short and that induces firms to cheat. As a result, there is no collusive price that is stable and so the policy function prescribes a price equal to cost. However, when damages are high, firms are so concerned about not inducing detection that this stifles the incentive to cheat and thus collusion can be maintained even if the inherited price is rather high. Note that price also tends to be lower near the interface of these two regions—the

---

12 For details on these numerical methods, see Judd (1999) and Miranda and Fackler (2002).

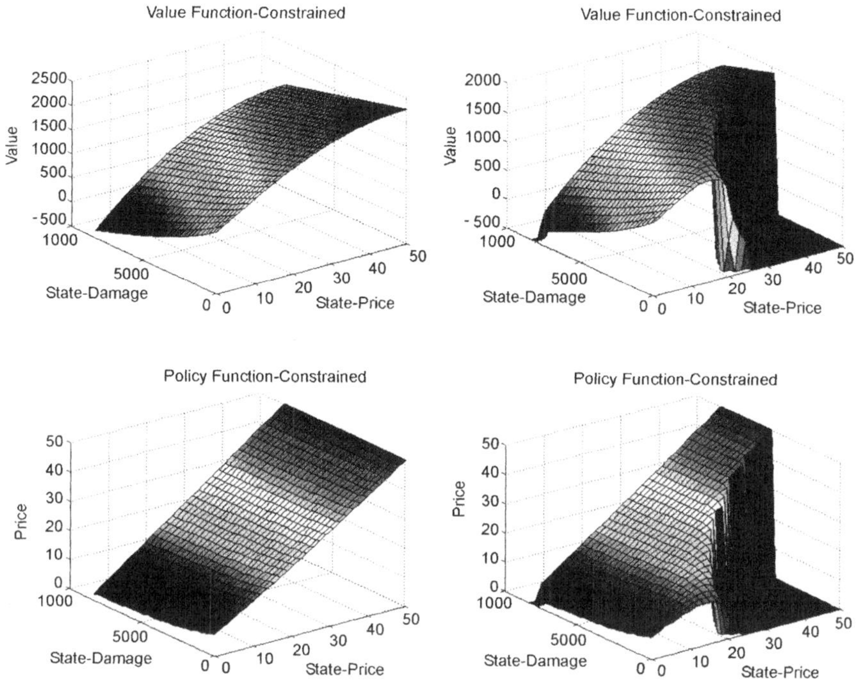

Fig. 3.1: Benchmark parameter specification.

region for which collusion collapses and the region for which the incentive compatibility constraint doesn't bind so the unconstrained solution can be sustained. Around that interface, the incentive compatibility constraint can be satisfied but only by pricing below the unconstrained solution.

To explore the effect of the leniency policy on cartel behavior, (3.1)–(3.2) was solved for all $\theta \in \{0, .1, \ldots, 1\}$. With initial conditions of the cartel's price equalling the non-collusive price and damages equaling zero, we then determined whether cartel formation was optimal and, if it was, the optimal cartel price path. The analysis showed that (3.2) is unaffected by θ when $\theta \geq .3$. We then solved (3.1)–(3.2) for a finer grid: $\theta \in \{0, .01, \ldots, .3\}$. Cartel formation was found to be unsustainable when $\theta < .18$. For $.18 \leq \theta$, firms are able to form a cartel. When $.26 \leq \theta$, firms form a cartel and the resulting cartel price path is very close to the unconstrained optimum so the leniency program is having a minimal effect or perhaps no effect at all as a deviating firm would not use it. Figure 3.2 then focuses on the cartel price path for $\theta \in \{.18, .20, \ldots, .24\}$. The price path steadily rises as firms balance off higher profit and a higher chance of getting caught in determining the rate at which to increase price. Note that it converges to a steady-state level which is below the simple monopoly price

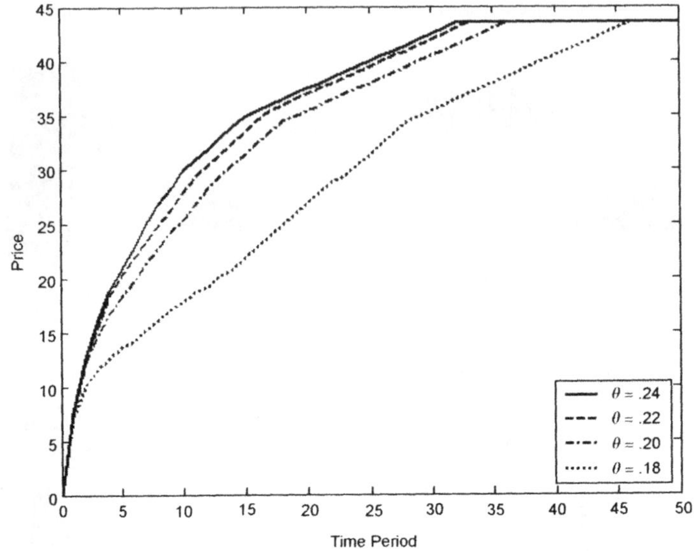

Fig. 3.2: Simulated price paths benchmark parameter specification.

of 50.[13] As the policy becomes more lenient—so that more fines are waived to the first firm to come forward (that is, θ is reduced)—the cartel price path shifts down. Though the steady-state price is left unaffected, it takes a longer time for the cartel to reach it. As θ is lowered, the incentive to cheat becomes stronger—as a firm that cheats can acquire amnesty and avoid a larger portion of penalties—and the cartel must respond by lowering price so as to ensure that cheating is not optimal.

The next exercise characterizes the effect of leniency on cartel formation by deriving the minimum discount factor at which a cartel forms. For both $\theta = .3$ and $\theta = 1$, (3.1)–(3.2) was solved for all $\delta \in \{0, .01, \ldots, .99, 1\}$. For both leniency parameter values, a cartel formed only when $\delta \geq .66$. We inferred that this is true for all $\theta \geq .3$ and then focused on $\theta < .3$. For each $\theta \in \{0, .01, \ldots, .29\}$, (3.1)–(3.2) was solved for a low value of δ and re-solved for a progressively higher value of δ until cartel formation emerged. Figure 3.3 reports the results. The minimum discount factor rises with the extent of leniency until the discount factor has to be at least .86 when there is maximal leniency.

---

[13] As explained in Harrington (2004), this arises for two reasons. First, a cartel will not want to set the monopoly price as long as penalties are sensitive to that price. By marginally lowering price below the monopoly price, there is no first-order effect on current profit but there is a first-order effect in reducing damages. However, if the only penalty is a fixed fine, then this force is not operative so the cartel would indeed want to price at the simple monopoly price. Second, even if the cartel wants to price at the simple monopoly price it may not be able to because the incentive to cheat is too great and thus incentive compatibility constraints are violated. This induces them to set a lower steady-state price.

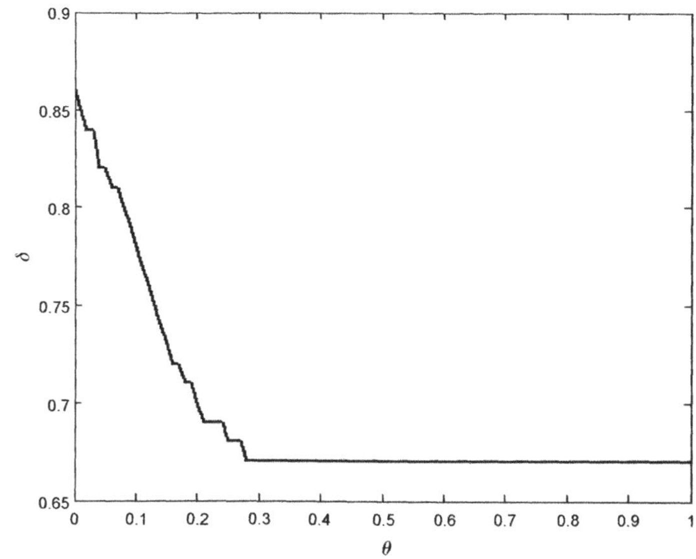

Fig. 3.3: Minimum discount factor for cartel formation.

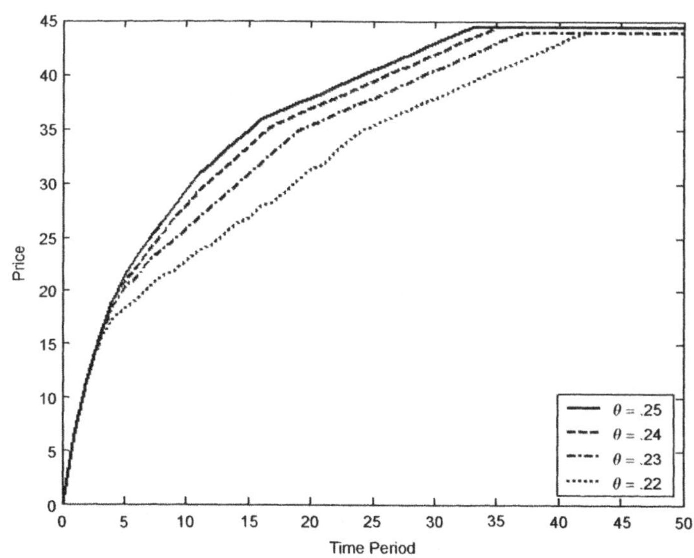

Fig. 3.4: Simulated price paths ($n = 4$, $\delta = .8$).

Waiving a higher fraction of fines makes it more difficult for a cartel to form. These results support earlier theoretical findings, in the context of a Prisoners' Dilemma, that more leniency makes collusion more difficult.

Similar exercises were performed for other parameter configurations. Figure 3.4 reports results for $n = 4$ and $\delta = .8$, Figure 3.5 for $n = 5$ and $\delta = .85$,

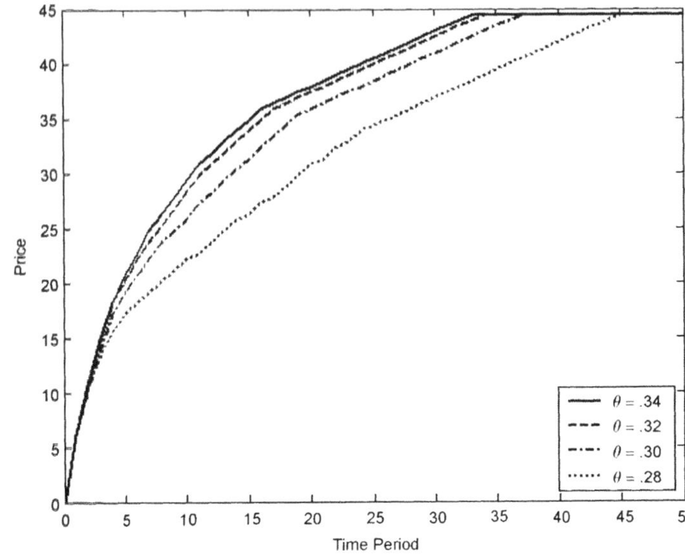

Fig. 3.5: Simulated price paths ($n = 5$, $\delta = .85$).

and Figure 3.6 for $n = 6$ and $\delta = .9$. The same pattern emerges: a more lenient policy (lower θ) causes the cartel price path to shift down. In addition, when θ is sufficiently low then a cartel does not form. Though not reported here, the property in Figure 3.3 also holds: cartel formation is more difficult when there is more leniency. Figures 3.7 and 3.8 report results for a higher damage multiple and a lower minimum value to the probability of detection. Figure 3.7 has $\gamma = 2$ and $\alpha_0 = .04$. while Figure 3.8 has $\gamma = 3$ and $\alpha_0 = .03$. The same qualitative results emerge.

In sum, results thus far show that when leniency is sufficiently great, firms are unable to form a cartel. When it is sufficiently mild, firms cartelize and leniency has no effect since a deviating firm would not use it. For an intermediate range of leniency parameter values, a cartel forms but the price path is shifted down in response to a higher fraction of penalties being waived. It follows from these lower prices that the value to colluding is lower when the leniency program is stronger (that is, the fraction of fines waived is larger). These results are consistent with the cartel-destabilizing effects of leniency programs found, for example, by Motta and Polo (2003) and Spagnolo (2003).

The next set of results tell a different story. When the probability of detection is weak, the provision of partial leniency can serve to *enhance* collusion, though maximal leniency continues to make cartel formation more difficult. For purposes of comparison, let us report the value to forming a cartel under the benchmark parameter configuration. Figure 3.9 shows that value which is the value function evaluated at the initial conditions, that is, the expected present value of the profit stream from forming a cartel. (Keep in mind that the non-collusive value is zero.) Consistent with the price path shifting down when θ

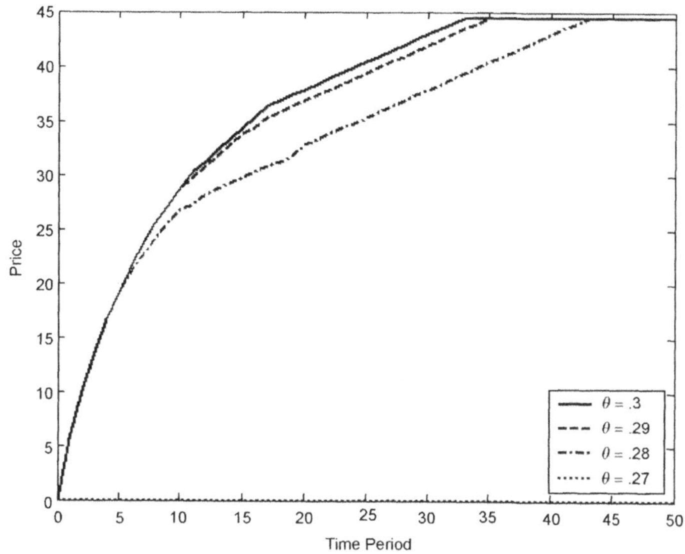

Fig. 3.6: Simulated price paths ($n = 6$, $\delta = .9$).

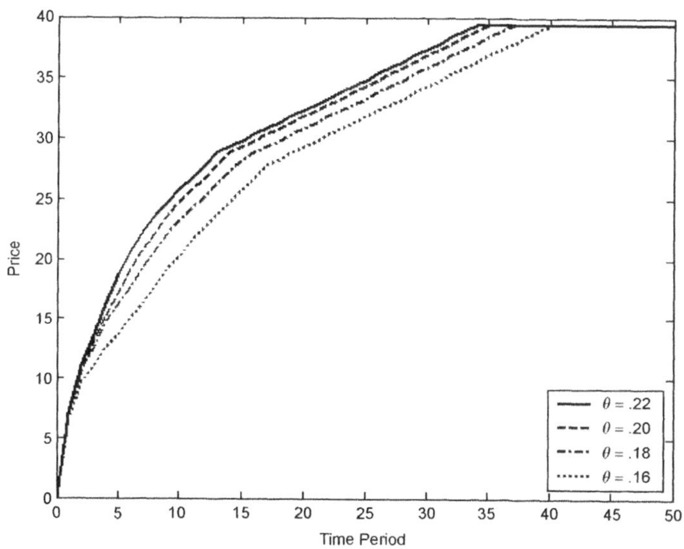

Fig. 3.7: Simulated price paths ($\gamma = 2$, $\alpha_0 = .04$).

is reduced, the collusive value is lower when there is a more generous leniency policy. More leniency is making collusion less profitable. Figure 3.9 also reports the value of forming a cartel when there is no leniency program. Note that the two values—with and without a leniency program—converge when leniency is sufficiently weak which is due to leniency not having an impact as it is not used.

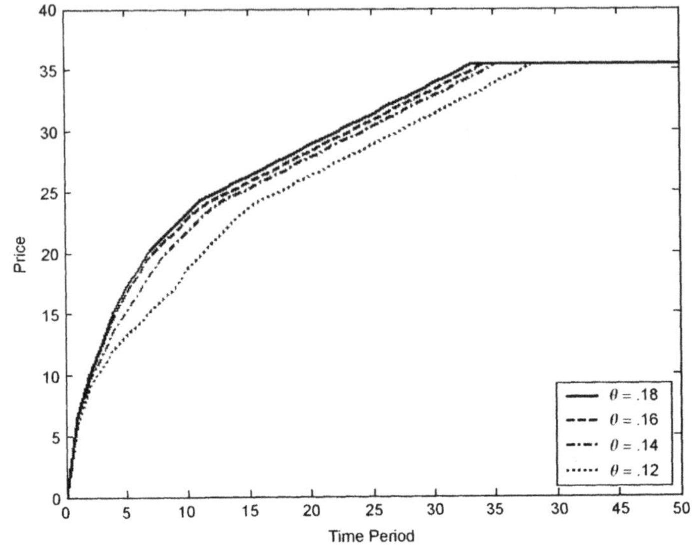

Fig. 3.8: Simulated price paths ($\gamma = 3, \alpha_0 = .03$).

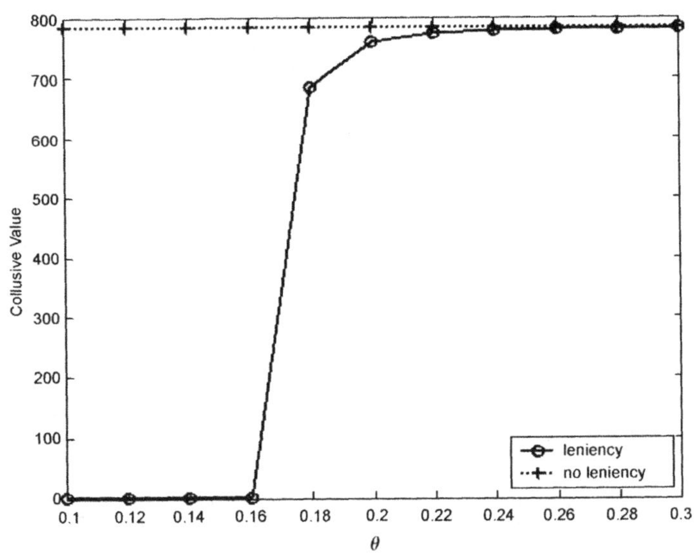

Fig. 3.9: Collusive value: Benchmark parameter specification.

Let us now reduce the probability of detection by setting $(\alpha_1^u, \alpha_1^d) = (.00032, .00016)$, while maintaining all other benchmark parameter values. The resulting value to colluding is reported in Figure 3.10. When $\theta \leq .16$ and thus a sufficiently high fraction of penalties is waived, a leniency program has the desired impact of preventing cartel formation. Notice that the value to colluding

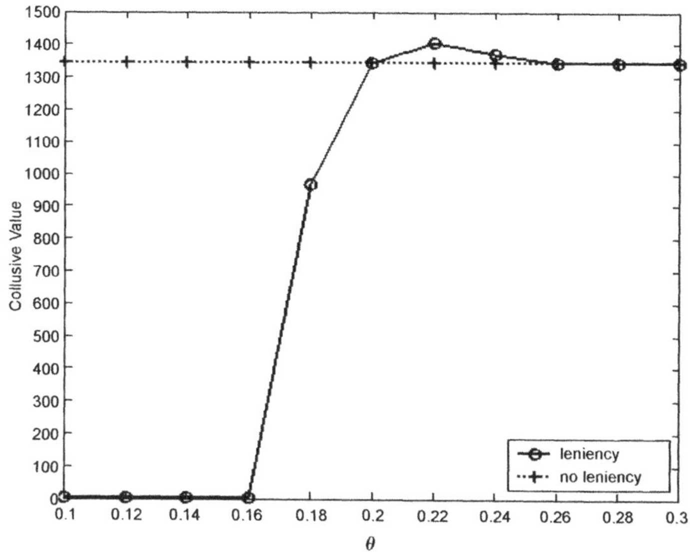

Fig. 3.10: Collusive value: Weak probability of detection.

is positive in the absence of leniency so a cartel would form otherwise. When $\theta = .18$, a cartel forms but the collusive value is around 1000 and thus lower than when there is no leniency when it is over 1300. In that case, partial leniency is making deviation more attractive and this reduces the cartel price path and thus lowers the value to colluding. However, for $\theta \in \{.22, .24\}$, the value to forming a cartel is actually ***higher*** when a leniency program is in place. This must be due to the possibility that firms will apply for leniency after the cartel collapses and this serves to raise expected penalties from cheating.

To see the argument, suppose a firm that deviates would prefer not to apply for amnesty because the probability of detection is relatively low given its optimal deviation price. What is possible, however, is that, in the period after deviation, it is an equilibrium for *all* firms to apply for leniency. The reason is that firms reduce price to marginal cost and this sharp price drop results in a sufficiently large probability of detection so as to make it optimal for a firm to apply for leniency given all other firms do not. Hence, the only equilibrium has all firms applying for leniency after the cartel collapses. Of course, a firm that is contemplating a deviation would anticipate this event and apply for leniency itself when it deviates. By doing so, it receives amnesty for sure, while if it waits then it only receives it with probability $\frac{1}{n}$. The implication of this argument is that a deviating firm may use the leniency program even though its payoff is lower compared to when there is no leniency program. The presence of a leniency program then raises expected penalties when a firm cheats and this reduces the payoff to cheating, loosens the incentive compatibility constraint, and allows the cartel to set higher prices. The resulting higher cartel price path is depicted in Figure 3.11 for $\theta = .22$.

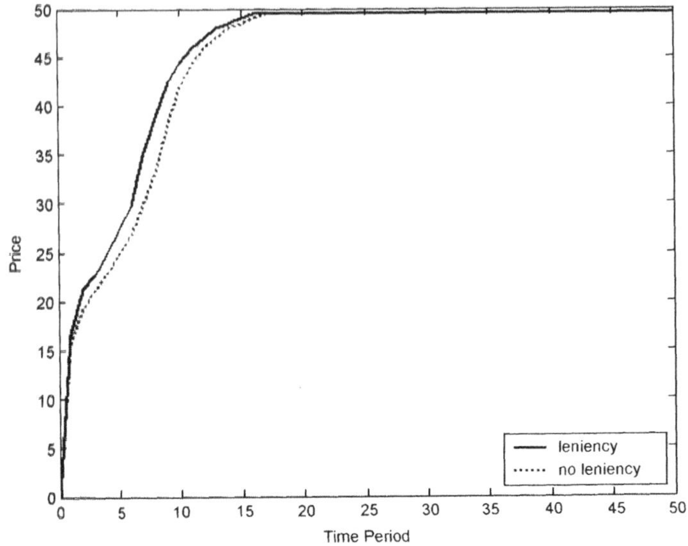

Fig. 3.11: Simulated price paths: Weak probability of detection ($\theta = .22$).

Contrary to our earlier findings and to much of the literature, partial leniency programs—so that some but not all penalties are waived—can *enhance* the attractiveness of forming a cartel. What is robust is that maximal leniency always serves to destabilize cartels. Though the policy of the European Commission is one of maximal leniency to the first firm to come forward, it is only partial leniency in the U.S. The U.S. program waives all government penalties but cartel members are still liable for private customer damages and thus the program is effectively one of partial leniency. Recently, the Antitrust Criminal Penalty Enforcement and Reform Act of 2004 expanded leniency in that a firm is now only liable for single, rather than the usual treble, damages (which corresponds to a lower value for γ for the firm that enters the leniency program). Still, leniency remains partial though is now closer to maximal leniency.

3.5. Summary

A major challenge to stopping cartels is that they are shrouded in secrecy. The corporate leniency program works to break the code of silence among cartel members. Research exploring the effect of such programs grows as more countries adopt them and as more convictions are attributed to the existence of such programs.

This study brings together two recent strands of the collusive pricing literature. One strand explores the impact of corporate leniency programs using a very simple specification in which oligopolistic interaction is modeled as a Prisoners' Dilemma and both the penalty and probability of detection are exogenous to cartel behavior. This simple oligopolistic structure implies that a leniency program can have an impact only by deterring cartel formation; it cannot influence the price path in the event of cartel formation as only one collusive price is presumed feasible. The second strand explores the impact of antitrust enforcement on collusive pricing by modifying the classical repeated game setting so as to allow detection of the cartel—by buyers or authorities—to be sensitive to the price path. Blending these two strands, this paper investigates the impact of a leniency program when the cartel can manipulate the price path so as to influence the likelihood of detection and penalties in the event of detection. Thus, the analysis is able to describe how such programs influence the cartel price path as well cartel formation.

Through numerical analysis, several conclusions are drawn. First, we found that, consistent with earlier results, maximal leniency programs (whereby all penalties are waived to the first firm to come forward) necessarily make collusion more difficult. Second, in most (but not all) cases, the collusive value of cartel is lower when there is a more generous leniency policy (that is, a higher fraction of penalties are waived). A more lenient program provides a stronger incentive for a cartel member to cheat as it can avoid penalties by simultaneously applying for amnesty when it undercuts the collusive price. This tightens the incentive compatibility constraint which induces the cartel to price lower. Hence, even if a leniency program is unsuccessful in deterring cartel formation, it may still be able to cause the cartel to price lower in order to maintain cartel stability. The third result provides a caveat to the result just mentioned in that partial leniency programs (such as is used in the U.S.) can have a perverse effect on antitrust enforcement. When the probability of detection is weak, the collusive value can be higher when a partial leniency program is put in place (compared to offering no leniency program). In response to a firm cheating, firms may excessively use the leniency program and, given that only one firm can receive amnesty, expected penalties can actually be higher with partial leniency. This serves to reduce the payoff to cheating which permits the cartel to sustain a higher price path. Leniency programs can then have subtle perverse effects though, on net, our analysis suggests that they do indeed tend to make collusion more difficult.

Acknowledgements

The authors thank Giancarlo Spagnolo for suggesting this research topic and the comments of two anonymous referees. The first author acknowledges the support of the 21st Century Center of Excellence (COE) Program at the Graduate School of Economics of the University of Tokyo. The second author acknowledges the support of the National Science Foundation under grant SES-0209486.

References

Abrantes-Metz, R.M., Froeb, L.M., Geweke, J.F., Taylor, C.T. (2005), A variance screen for collusion. Federal Trade Commission. March.

Aubert, C., Rey, P., Kovacic, W. (2003), The impact of leniency programs on cartels. University of Toulouse. November.

Cyrenne, P. (1999), On antitrust enforcement and the deterrence of collusive behavior. *Review of Industrial Organization* 14, 257–272.

Feess, E., Walzl, M. (2004), An analysis of corporate leniency programs and lessons to learn for US and EU policies. University of Maastricht. September.

Green, E., Porter, R.H. (1984), Noncooperative collusion under imperfect price information. *Econometrica* 52, 87–100.

Harrington, J.E. Jr. (2003), Some implications of antitrust laws for cartel pricing. *Economics Letters* 79, 377–383.

Harrington, J.E. Jr. (2004), Cartel pricing dynamics in the presence of an antitrust authority. *RAND Journal of Economics* 35, 651–673.

Harrington, J.E. Jr. (2005a), Optimal corporate leniency programs. Johns Hopkins University. March.

Harrington, J.E. Jr. (2005b), Optimal cartel pricing in the presence of an antitrust authority. *International Economic Review* 46, 145–169.

Harrington, J.E. Jr., Chen, J. (2006), Cartel pricing dynamics with cost variability and endogenous buyer detection. Johns Hopkins University. December. (*International Journal of Industrial Organization*, submitted for publication.)

Hay, G., Kelly, D. (1974), An empirical survey of price fixing conspiracies. *Journal of Law and Economics* 17, 13–38.

Hard Core Cartels (2003), OECD Report.

Judd, K.L. (1999), *Numerical Methods in Economics*. MIT Press, Cambridge, MA.

Kobayashi, B.H. (2001), Antitrust, agency and amnesty: An economic analysis of the criminal enforcement of the antitrust laws against corporations. *George Washington Law Review* 69, 715–744.

Levenstein, M., Suslow, V. (2001), Private international cartels and their effect on developing countries. University of Massachusetts, pdf copy.

Levenstein, M.C., Suslow, V.Y., Oswald, L.J. (2004), Contemporary international cartels and developing countries: Economic effects and implications for competition policy. *Antitrust Law Journal* 71, 801–852.

Miranda, M.J., Fackler, P.L. (2002), *Applied Computational Economics and Finance*. MIT Press, Cambridge, MA.

Motchenkova, E. (2004), The effects of leniency programs on the behavior of the firms participating in cartel agreements. Tilburg University.

Motta, M., Polo, M. (2003), Leniency programs and cartel prosecution. *International Journal of Industrial Organization* 21, 347–379.

Spagnolo, G. (2003), *Divide et impera*: Optimal deterrence mechanisms against cartels and organized crime. University of Mannheim. March.

CHAPTER 4

Optimal Fines in the Era of Whistleblowers. Should Price Fixers still Go to Prison?

Paolo Buccirossi[a] and Giancarlo Spagnolo[b]

[a] *Lear—Laboratorio di economia, antitrust, regolamentazione*
E-mail address: paolo.buccirossi@learlab.it
[b] *Stockholm School of Economics, Consip Research Unit, and CEPR*
E-mail address: giancarlo.spagnolo@yahoo.it

Abstract

We review current methods for calculating fines against cartels in the US and EU, and simulate their deterrence effects under different assumptions on the legal and economic environment. It is likely that European fines have not had significant deterrence effects before leniency programs were introduced. Previous simulations of the effects of fines ignore the different type of deterrence that leniency programs bring about, and, therefore, grossly overstate the minimum fine likely to have deterrence effects. With schemes that reward whistleblowers, the minimum fine with deterrence effects falls to extremely low levels (below 10% of the optimal "Beckerian" fine). Strategic judgment-proofness can and should be prevented by suitable regulation or extended liability. Criminal sanctions, in the form of imprisonment, certainly bring benefits (and costs) in terms of cartel deterrence, but the firms' limited ability to pay does not appear any longer such a strong argument for their introduction.

Keywords: antitrust, amnesty, cartels, collusion, corporate crime, debt, deterrence, extended liability, fines, law enforcement, leniency, immunity, imprisonment, judgment proofness, optimal fines, optimal sanctions, optimal liability, organized crime, political economy, rewards, sunk cost bias, whistleblowers

CONTRIBUTIONS TO ECONOMIC ANALYSIS
VOLUME 282 ISSN: 0573-8555
DOI: 10.1016/S0573-8555(06)82004-3

Yet another method of preventing crimes is, to reward virtue. Upon this subject the laws of all nations are silent. If the rewards proposed by academies for the discovery of useful truths have increased our knowledge, and multiplied good books, is it not probable that rewards, distributed by the beneficent hand of a sovereign, would also multiply virtuous actions. (Cesare Beccaria, *Of Crime and Punishment*, Chapter 44: *Of Rewards*)

4.1. Introduction

The recent tendency towards the 'criminalization' of antitrust law in Europe, started with the reforms in Ireland (1996) and UK (1999–2001), and the drastic increase of jail terms for price fixing, introduced by the US Antitrust Criminal Penalty Enhancement and Reform Act in 2004, re-opened the never really settled debate on optimal sanctions against cartels. This paper discusses the issue in the light of two major recent innovations in the theory and practice of law enforcement—leniency programs and reward schemes for whistleblowers—whose novel type of deterrence effects could not have been taken into account in the early debate on optimal antitrust sanctions, and has been largely neglected in the current revival of that debate.[1]

In Section 4.2 we briefly review the evolution of the sanction policy adopted in the EU and the US, and discuss the optimality of current financial fines in the light of normative theory and available data. We simulate optimal financial fines against cartels—the minimal ones that have deterrence effects—according to the standard 'Beckerian' cost–benefit methodology used in previous work, and argue that the sanctions imposed by the European Commission (and by the competition authorities of many European countries) are likely to have been too low, and to have had little deterrence effects before the recent introduction of leniency programs and the parallel increase in fines. We suggest that pretending to enforce cartel prohibitions may have been part of a 'political equilibrium' that pleased everybody, but (dispersed) consumers and tax-payers, and that is no longer sustainable in a globalized world where developed countries that took a tougher stance in favor of competition perform better.

In Section 4.3 we briefly review the main costs and benefits of using imprisonment against price-fixers, and argue that the current debate is based on the wrong premises regarding the minimal size of corporate fines likely to have cartel-deterrence effects on well informed firms. We produce simulations of the minimum fines with cartel deterrence effects that take into account one of the several new deterrence effects well designed and implemented leniency programs bring about, and we find that, by neglecting these effects, previous simulations are likely to have substantially overestimated such minimal fines. We then produce simulations of the optimal fine with schemes that reward whistleblowers with the fines paid by the convicted partners, as proposed by Spagnolo

[1] See Rey (2003) for a brilliant and thorough discussion of the importance of implementation and enforcement issues for competition policy in general and cartel deterrence in particular.

(2000a), Buccirossi and Spagnolo (2001), Kovacic (2001), and Aubert et al. (2005), which have been successfully introduced in the last two decades by the US False Claim Act against government fraud. We show that, with such programs, the optimal fine against cartels lies below firms' normal ability to pay, overcoming a first main concern expressed in support of the introduction of imprisonment for price-fixers (firms' *exogenous* limited ability to pay).

In Section 4.4 we discuss the feasibility of schemes that reward whistleblowers, and argue that with well-designed and well-implemented mechanisms, well informed firms will have no reason to indemnify their managers fined for price-fixing, nor to give them incentives that induce them to fix prices in the first place. Given the change in the attitude of principals and the increased probability of self-reporting these schemes induce, financial sanctions on individual managers are also likely to become effective, alleviating a second main concern in support of imprisonment (indemnification of managers and their limited ability to pay).

We then discuss the possibility that firms strategically exploit bankruptcy law, *endogenously* reducing their ability to pay antitrust fines by issuing large amounts of debt that shield their assets, either because in some jurisdiction debt may be senior to fines, or because in most jurisdictions courts and agencies would not be willing to impose fines that drive firms bankrupt. Because of this strategic judgment-proofness response on the side of firms, policies that reduce fines for firms with lower ability to pay—often followed by courts and agencies and openly suggested by some legal scholars—are likely to be highly socially harmful: they both substantially reduce cartel deterrence, and generate additional inefficiencies (over and above that of non deterred cartels) by inducing colluding firms to distort their capital structure and undertake other cost-increasing activities that increase their judgment-proofness. In the absence of well-designed and well-implemented whistleblower schemes, it may be necessary to limit overborrowing by firms, or to extend liability to other stakeholders,[2] or to let some firms go bankrupt because of the fines, or to fine directly controlling shareholders—waiving all fines on a bankrupt firm to allow new owners to have a "fresh start". Well-designed and well-implemented whistleblower reward schemes would eliminate this problem at the root though, as the optimal fines become so low that no judgment-proofness problem would emerge.

We then discuss how individual liability, leniency programs, and individual rewards are likely to affect optimal fines; and how optimal fines for corporations change if managers are subject to the "Sunk Cost Bias"—as recent experimental evidence suggests—and raise post-conviction competitive prices to try recovering the fine.

Section 4.5 concludes with a brief summary of our main findings, some words of caution, and a suggestion for further, highly needed, theoretical and empirical research.

---

[2] Analogous remedies have been analyzed and proposed for the enforcement of tort law and environmental regulation by Shavell (2004), Che and Spier (2005), and Hiriart and Martimort (2005).

Our chapter can be seen as a contribution to the literature trying to assess the likely cartel deterrence effects of antitrust law enforcement policies with simple or complex simulations, which includes work by Werden and Simon (1987), Gallo et al. (1994), Craycraft et al. (1997), McCoutcheon (1997), UK DTI (2001), Posner (2001), Wils (2003, 2005a), Connor (2004, 2005), and Chen and Harrington (2007, Chapter 3 in this volume).[3]

Together with Chen and Harrington (2007), this chapter presents the first analysis that simulates the likely deterrence effects of cartel enforcement after the introduction of effective leniency programs (1993 in the US, 1996 in the EU) without overlooking the novel, additional deterrence effects these introduce.[4] However, our paper differs from the work by Chen and Harrington, that focuses on the likely effects on cartel prices and formation of different degrees of leniency given the level of fines, because it focuses on the likely change in the optimal fines and the need for incarceration determined by the introduction of effective leniency and whistleblowers schemes. The two chapters can, therefore, be regarded as complementary.

Throughout our chapter we maintain the classic economic perspective on the analysis of efficient law enforcement. Cartels are punished by cease and desist orders and by the imposition of administrative and, in some jurisdictions, criminal sanctions. The primary objective of these sanctions is to ensure deterrence (i.e. prevention) of anticompetitive behavior. This requires the sanction to be set at a level that changes companies' and individuals' incentives so as to discourage them from adopting unlawful conducts. Economic theory provides the analytical tools to address the issue of the optimal sanction policy against cartels. A large body of literature, starting from the seminal work of Becker (1968), has addressed the general question of the optimal public enforcement of law. This literature has taken up a vast array of policy issues, from the optimal amount of resources to be devoted to apprehending violators, to the appropriate form of the sanction between fine and imprisonment, and many many others (see Polinsky and Shavell, 2000, for a rich survey).

Several contributions within this body of literature address specificities of antitrust law enforcement (see, e.g., Landes, 1983), and a lively debate on whether antitrust infringements should be punished only with administrative/pecuniary fines or also with imprisonment took place already in the 70s and 80s (see the many references in Werden and Simon, 1987). Our contribution builds heavily on this literature, and tries to highlight peculiarities of cartels, some of which previously neglected, that suggest the need for some amendments of the prescriptions of the received normative theory. These are:

---

[3] An alternative important way of trying to assess the deterrence effects of antitrust law enforcement policy is that of running laboratory experiments, as done by Apesteguia et al. (2003), Hamaguchi and Kawagoe (2005), and Hinloopen and Soetevent (2005).

[4] If well designed and managed; see Spagnolo (2006) for a survey of economic analyses on the bright and dark sides of leniency programs.

(a) sanctions against cartels must not impair future competition;
(b) cartels are multi-agent infringements;
(c) cartels are carried out by limited liability organizations with internal agency problems.

Features (b) and (c) are particularly important. They can be referred to as the team properties of cartels. Our simulations demonstrate how important it is to consider team properties when designing an optimal sanction policy against cartels, particularly when a well-designed leniency or whistleblower program is in place. These properties impose limits to the set of feasible or desirable sanction policies and provide opportunities to accomplish results that would have been beyond our reach in their absence. These limits and opportunities stem from the existence of a number of implicit and explicit contracts that govern the relationships between team members, both within a firm and among distinct firms. We must recognize that the imposition of sanctions alters not only the incentive of a firm to comply with the law, as if the firm were an individual making isolated rational decisions, but also modifies the way implicit and explicit contracts between agents in each firm are shaped and implemented. Since both illegal and legal (efficient) conducts rely on these contracts, sanctions may achieve their aim by rendering some of these contracts unfeasible.

4.2. Fines without leniency

In this section we review and compare the methods for calculating fines against cartels used in the US and in the EU, with particular focus on the maximum fines that can be imposed. We evaluate whether these fines are consistent with the prescriptions of standard theory and we simulate their deterrence effects according to the standard methodology. We then argue that the EU policy of low fines, not reinforced by the threat of imprisonment, is likely to be the outcome of a no more sustainable political equilibrium.

4.2.1. Fines against cartels: US vs. EU

US sanctions against cartels

In the US cartels are felonies that can be punished with fines on individuals and corporations and imprisonment for individuals. The level of these sanctions is defined by the Antitrust Criminal Penalty Enhancement and Reform Act of 2004. The Act increased the maximum statutory criminal fine for individuals from 350.000 to 1 million US Dollars; the maximum jail term from 3 to 10 years; and the maximum statutory fine against corporations from 10 to 100 million US Dollars or—as before the reform—twice the gain of the violator or the loss of the victim. The US Sentencing Guidelines (USSG) govern the application of these sanctions for antitrust.

According to the USSG, which are now under revision, to determine the appropriate corporate fine it is necessary to calculate a base fine. The base fine is equal to the highest between the pecuniary gain of the violator or the pecuniary loss of the victims. In general this fine is based on the loss because the loss from price-fixing normally exceeds the gain. In addition, since the average gain from price-fixing is estimated to be around 10% of the selling price, the pecuniary loss is assumed to be of the order of 20% of the affected commerce. However, in those cases in which the cartel price appears to include substantially more or less than a 10% overcharge, the fine is adjusted accordingly. This mechanism for assessing the fine, unique to antitrust enforcement, has the purpose of avoiding the time and expense that would be required to determine the actual gain or loss. This base fine is then multiplied by a minimum or maximum multiplier that can range between 0.75 and 4. The multiplier depends on the organization's culpability that can take a score from 0 to 10. This score is determined by adding and subtracting enhancements and reductions from a five-point base score, where enhancements stems from the involvement of high level personnel, prior criminal or civil adjudications for similar conduct, violation of an order and obstruction of justices, and subtractions are granted for an effective program to prevent and detect violations of law, and for self reporting, cooperation and acceptance of responsibility. A culpability score of 10 leads to a minimum multiplier of 2 and a maximum multiplier of 4. A culpability score of 0 results in a minimum multiplier of .05 and a maximum multiplier of 2. However, for cartels the minimum multiplier can never be below .75. Therefore a fine can range from 15 percent of the volume of commerce to a maximum of 80 percent of this volume.[5]

These guidelines are currently subject of an intense debate that may lead to a reform that could substantially increase fines against price-fixers (see, e.g., ABA Section of Antitrust Law 2005). In addition, the "20% of affected commerce" rule of thumb, outlined in the USSG, is "under revision" after the Supreme Court found unconstitutional to base sanctions on a finding that was not subject to a jury decision. Since there is recent evidence that the presumption of a 10% increase in price substantially underestimate the average collusive price overcharges (see, e.g., Connor, 2003, 2004; Connor and Lande, 2004), the change in methodology is likely to increase the baseline fine against cartels. The culpability score is also "under revision", since the US Sentencing Commission has proposed amendments to the Antitrust Recommendations of the USSG that would substantially raise both pecuniary and non-pecuniary baseline sanctions against price-fixers.

In the recent past, US pecuniary sanctions have almost reached the maximum of 80% of US affected commerce (in the *Mitsubishi* case, in 2001, the fine was set to 76% of affected commerce; see Connor, 2003). However, even under current USSG, cartels with a well documented price overcharge could attract higher

[5] For a more detailed description of the US sanctioning policy and some examples see Kobayashi (2002). An in depth comparison of US and EU methods for setting fines is in Ch. 2 of Motchenkova (2005).

fines, since the 10% presumption would be replaced by the real overcharge. A documented 30% overcharge, doubled and multiplied for a culpability factor of 4.5 can lead to a fine equal to 270% of affected commerce. Moreover, US prosecutors could start basing fines on global, rather than US affected commerce, which could more than double pecuniary fines.

Of course, all this applies if the wrongdoer does not negotiate the fine in exchange for pleading guilty, and if he is not eligible for amnesty under the leniency program. As is well known, if a firm is the first to apply for leniency reporting valuable information on a cartel either unknown to the DoJ, or on which the DoJ had little evidence about, it is eligible to full immunity from sanctions under the US Corporate Leniency Program.

Sanctions in the European Union

Pursuant to Article 23(2) of Regulation No. 1/2003, the European Commission (EC) may impose fines on undertakings or association of undertakings that, either intentionally or negligently, infringe Article 81 of the Treaty up to 10% of their total turnover. Article 23 also states that, to this extent, fines shall be computed having regard to the gravity and duration of the infringement (par. 3). In 1998 the EC adopted its first Notice on the method for calculating fines in antitrust cases. This notice has been revised in June 2006 and new Guidelines have been published in September 2006 (O.J. 2006/C 210/02). This document binds the EC to follow a two-step method in setting the amount of the fine. In step one the EC determines the basic amount of the fine. In step two it may adjust the basic amount taking into account: aggravating and mitigating circumstances; the application of the leniency notice; the undertaking's ability to pay; the need to ensure sufficient deterrence; and the legal maximum set in Regulation 1/2003 according to which the fine cannot exceed 10% of the total turnover in the preceding business year of the undertaking concerned.

The revised Guidelines provide that the basic amount (step one) will be determined as a fraction of the company's annual sales to which the infringement relates on a scale from 0% to 30%, depending on the gravity of the infringement. This amount is then multiplied by the number of years of participation in the infringement. For hard-core cartels, the Guidelines state that the proportion of the value of sales taken into account will generally be set at the higher end of the scale. Moreover, irrespective of the duration of the undertaking's participation in the infringement, they will be subject to an "entry fee" as the EC will include in the basic amount a sum of between 15% and 25% of the value of the affected sales.

This basic amount may be increased or decreased (step two) if the EC considers that certain aggravating or mitigating circumstances actually occurred. Particularly, the fine may be increased in case of: (a) Repeated infringement of the same type by the same undertaking; (b) Refusal to cooperate with or attempts to obstruct the EC in carrying out its investigations; (c) Retaliatory measures against other undertakings with a view of enforcing practices which constitute an infringement.

Table 4.1: Fines imposed by US and EU authorities in five global cartel cases (million of dollars).

Cartel	US	EU
Lysine	92.5	97.9
Citric acid	110.4	120.4
Vitamins	906.5	756.9
Sodium gluconate	32.5	51.2
Graphite electrodes	436.0	172.0
Total	1,577.9	1,213.3

On the contrary, the fine will be reduced where attenuating circumstances occurred, such as: (a) An exclusively passive or follow-my-leader role in the infringement; (b) Non-implementation in practice of the offending agreements and practices; (c) Termination of the infringement as soon as the EC intervenes (in particular when it carries out checks); (d) Effective cooperation in the proceedings, outside the scope of the Notice on the non-imposition of fines or reduction of fines in cartel cases. The EC may grant a reduction or even waive the fine if one or more of the undertakings involved in the cartel cooperate in detecting or proving the unlawful behavior. The conditions under which a firm can benefit from this reduction/waive are set out in the so-called leniency program. The EC may further adjust the fine upward or downward, in order to take into consideration any economic or financial benefit derived by the offenders, so as to ensure deterrence. Finally, in exceptional circumstances, the EC takes into account the undertaking's inability to pay and reduce the fine if its full imposition would irretrievably jeopardize the economic viability of the undertaking concerned and cause its assets to lose all their value.

According to Connor (2003) the level of fines for comparable global cartel cases is only slightly higher in the US than in the EU. Table 4.1 reports the total fines imposed on cartel members in five cases prosecuted from 1996 to 2002. With the exception of the *Graphite Electrodes* case, where the overall US fine is substantially higher than the EU one, in all the other cases the magnitude of the fine is roughly the same in the two jurisdictions. Hence, since in EU private antitrust enforcement is negligible and, criminal sanctions are absent, the deterrence effects of the current EU legal regime are clearly lower than in the US. Since many cartels still form and are detected in the US, the level of the sanctions in the EU is likely to be insufficient.[6]

Table 4.2 reports a sample of cartels investigated in the EU and shows the duration of the cartel ascertained by the EC[7] and the fine, before any reduction

---

[6] As pointed out by a referee, an increase in the financial sanctions in the EU may still not suffice to obtain the same level of deterrence of the US antitrust enforcement system, as jail sentences and fines may have intrinsic differences. We do not discuss this point in this chapter although we note some peculiarities of imprisonment in the discussion of its advantages and disadvantages (Section 4.2.4).

[7] The numbers in the table report the minimum and maximum duration of the infringement considering all cartel members. The highest figure is to be considered the life span of the cartel as the

Table 4.2: Fines imposed by the EC in some global cartel cases.

Cartel	**Year of the decision**	**Duration (years)**	**Fine over global turnover**	**Fine over EEA turnover**
Pre-insulated pipes	1998	1–5	n.a.	32.2%
Seamless steel tubes	1999	4–5	12.9%	54.0%
Lysine	2000	3–5	25.8%	99.5%
Citric acid	2001	3–4	40.6%	100.1%
Vitamins	2001	3–9	54.5%	241.2%

Table 4.3: Fines imposed by the EC for each cartel in the *Vitamins* case.

Market (vitamin)	**Duration (years)**	**European sales outside the cartel**	**Fine over EEA turnover**
A	9.5	9%	221.2%
E	8–9.5	8%	175.1%
B2	3.75–4.25	12%	397.9%
B5	8	7%	605.8%
C	4.7	22%	178.5%
D3	4.5	4%	411.6%
Beta-Carotene	6.3	0%	240.0%
Carotinoids	5.7	0%	353.4%

from to the application of the EU Leniency Program, as a percentage of the value of the market in one year in which the cartel was operating, according to the EC's decision, both worldwide or in the European Economic Area (EEA). The last figure does not refer to the sales affected by the cartel as it is computed only with reference to the revenues generated in one year, whereas these cartels lasted for several years.[8]

These data indicate a sharp increase in the severity of the fines imposed on cartels by the EC. Over just four years the fine, from a fraction of the affected commerce (European turnover), became a multiple of it. However, it would be wrong to conclude that the EC has decided to clearly relate fines to the dimension of the market and, therefore, to the likely harm caused by the infringement. The *Vitamins* decision is quite interesting as it concerned several markets and involved distinct cartels. Table 4.3 shows, for each of these cartels, its duration,

lowest figure is mainly due to the fact that some firms entered the market (and joined the cartel) only after some time. The *Vitamins* case concerned several markets and several cartels that had different duration.

[8] Unfortunately, the information reported in this table is limited because most of the data are omitted from the Commission decisions, especially in the most recent ones. It is apparent that the size of the affected commerce is not an important factor as in many decisions we have consulted this information is not reported at all. In some cases, while the original decision contains such information, the published version does not. We do understand that individual firm data (even if generally refers to 4–5 years before) may constitute business secrets, but we do not see any good reason for omitting aggregated values.

the share of the market served by the fringe firms outside the cartel, and the fine imposed on cartel members as a percentage of the value of the European market. It is very difficult to rationalize these figures. Their level (in percentage terms) does not seem to be correlated either to the duration of the cartel or to the share of the market covered by the cartel.[9]

4.2.2. How (in)adequate have been fines before leniency?

4.2.2.1. Theory

The modern economic theory of public enforcement of law which stems from Becker's (1968) seminal paper, focuses, with few exceptions, on a single crime of short duration and a single wrongdoer. The main objective considered is efficient deterrence, i.e. deterring crime only when it is efficient to do so and in the most efficient way (see, e.g., Polinsky and Shavell, 2000). The simple rule it suggests is to deter crime only when the harm it causes, H, is larger than the benefit B accruing to the criminal, and to do it by setting the sanction, S, and the probability of detection, α, so that the expected sanction just equals the harm, i.e.:

$$S\alpha = H.$$

An adaptation of this rule to antitrust violations is provided by Landes (1983). In the case of cartels, B represents the additional collusive profits plus any cost saving or quality improvement the coordinated practice may generate, net of any cartel enforcement expenditure, while H represents the consumer surplus transferred to firms in the form of collusive profits plus the utility of the foregone consumption due to the higher price (H). Some observers think that for 'hard core' cartels the condition $B < H$ is always satisfied and that there are no such infringements that may enhance social welfare.[10] Hence, according to the rule above, the efficient expected fine should be set at a level that deter all possible cartels. If we accept this view and the conventional assumption that fines are socially costless, as they represent mere transfers of money, while imprisonment entails positive social costs, then the only robust principles from the theory of optimal law enforcement left for cartels are:

1. To set fines maximal in order to save on inspection costs.
2. Not to use costly imprisonment before having set fines (and other administrative sanctions) maximal to save on imprisonment costs.

---

9 For a detailed, critical and well document analysis of the EC fining policy see the very rich paper of Geradin and Henry (2005).

10 For example, Werden and Simon (1987) write: "We believe that efficient hard-core price-fixing is no more likely than efficient child molestation." (p. 932) On the other hand, Stiglitz (1989), Fershtman and Pakes (2000), Kranton (2003), and Calzolari and Spagnolo (2005) suggest that in situations where non-contractable quality is very important, restricting price competition may improve the effectiveness of reputational forces, and increase non-contractible quality and consumer welfare.

Risk aversion and legal errors would reduce the optimal fine, but in the case of managers and firms the hypothesis of risk neutrality appears more appropriate, and with risk neutral agents errors do not necessarily change the prescription of maximal fines, and may even imply higher optimal fines than without mistakes (see Polinsky and Shavell, 2000, pp. 60–62). A simple corollary of these statements is that the fines for firms that engage in cartels do not have to be related to their gains, nor to the losses caused to others: they just have to be sufficiently high to deter cartels while keeping to the minimum the cost of investigation and prosecution.

These simple prescriptions appear somewhat in contrast with the actual fining policy in the EU and in the US. In both jurisdictions current legislation (i) sets an exogenous ceiling to the maximum applicable fine; and (ii) *attempts* to relate the fine to a rough measure of the consequences of the cartel either on the colluding firms or on the victims.

Bankruptcy. The existence of caps in terms of a percentage of affected commerce or of overall firm turnover is often justified on the ground that legislators, while interested in deterring collusion, are also interested that firms keep producing (and competing) after conviction. High fines that may jeopardize a firm's financial stability may therefore have been perceived as running against the ultimate goal of antitrust law. This consideration, unique to corporate and antitrust law, is often mentioned in policy debate, where the number of active competitors is used as a proxy for the degree of competition. The same argument may render very high fines not credible, as agencies and judges may autonomously choose not to apply (to reduce) them when they can seriously jeopardize the existence of a firm, with all its "innocent" stakeholders.[11]

This argument, however, has strong limitations. First, no jurisdiction sets fines that could affect firms' survival possibilities. Craycraft et al. (1997), for example, find evidence that courts indeed reduce fines when a firm's ability to pay appears low (which makes caps redundant), and that in the majority of the US cases they analyze, firms could have afforded to pay the optimal cartel-deterring Beckerian fine from their normal cash flow, while they were imposed fines that were only a fraction of the optimal ones.

Second, it is important to remember that antitrust law exists to deter cartels, and thereby to protect and foster competition in all industries, today and tomorrow. If fines became sufficiently high that some convicted cartel members went bankrupt, antitrust enforcement would have decreased the number of firms and (perhaps) competition in the industry of the convicted cartel *for a period* (until bankrupt firms changed hands and became again competitive, or other forms of entry took place), but, at the same time, they could have increased competition through ex ante, general deterrence *in many other industries*. The overall net effect might well be positive.

---

[11] We wrote "innocent" because some stakeholders (like banks or unions) are often at the root of stable cartels. See Spagnolo (2003) and Buccirossi and Spagnolo (2006).

Third, if bankruptcy procedures are efficient (and they could be efficient), the negative effect on that industry's competition may be small, or even absent when the technically bankrupt firm is rapidly sold to new owners who then get a "fresh start" with a complete waiving of all the fine, and who may have more financial resources and a more aggressive attitudes (e.g., less "established connections" with other firms) than the old ones. In addition, if fines are sufficiently high to have robust deterrence effects, possibly leading firms to bankruptcy, and knowledge of this is widespread in the business community, then much fewer cartels will form, and even fewer will be detected and fined, which reduces further the relevance of the above argument.

Finally, as will be further discussed later on, this argument is risky because it may lead to the dangerous idea that—to avoid bankruptcy costs—fines should depend on the financial strength of the firm, i.e. should be higher for firms that have less debt and more cash and lower for financially weaker firms with a lower ability to pay. Such a policy might push cartel members to issue more debt, so that the level of the apparent ability to pay and expected fines fall, adding to the social cost of collusion, that stemming from firms' inefficient financial structure.

We believe that the reasons behind the low fines imposed in the EU, which are well below the level that could deter cartels, are political rather than economic based.

Proportionality. The second feature of the current fining policy, i.e. the principle of proportionality, has a clear economic explanation—even continuing to assume that all cartels are inefficient—once we reject the assumption that fines are socially costless. Indeed, if high fines, coupled with the possibility of legal errors, deter to some extent also socially desirable behavior, increasing the fines behind what is strictly necessary to deter illegal conducts reduces social welfare. If we take into account this social cost of raising fines against cartels, then it may be optimal to set the fine at a lower level, so that the marginal social benefit of deterring cartels equals the marginal social cost of mistakenly deterring efficient conduct. The optimal level of the fine and of deterrence depends then on the extent to which the expected fine is likely to discourage efficient conducts, which may consist either in forms of cooperation with other firms whose object and effects are pro-competitive and may be misjudged as collusive, or in an efficient internal organization that is however less adequate to detect antitrust violations within the firm. Whether these costs are relevant and what is their magnitude is an empirical matter, and is directly linked to the frequency with which courts commit type I errors (false convictions). If these costs are to be taken into consideration, the need to relate the level of the fine to the harm caused or the benefit produced by the illegal behavior is reestablished.

A third feature of the current sanction policy in the US is the recourse to *imprisonment*, which according the to standard economic theory of law enforcement is sound only if, given the existing limits on fines, the level of the expected penalties is too low (see, e.g., Polinsky and Shavell, 2000; for an interesting and quite persuasive alternative view, see Werden and Simon, 1987). Imprisonment will be discussed in depth later on, here we simply observe that, since the level of total expected penalties for similar infringements in the US is higher than in the EU, at least in one of the two jurisdictions the sanction policy against cartels is likely to be suboptimal. We believe that the level of sanctions in the EU is and has always been too low to have strong cartel deterrence effects, and most commentators (at least all those who call for the introduction of criminal sanctions) seem to agree.

4.2.2.2. Old-method simulations

To sustain our claim that it is likely that EU fines have not had significant deterrence effect on cartels, at least not before the introduction of leniency programs, we have run a simple and prudent simulation using a wide set of plausible parameter configurations, following the standard expected costs-expected benefits methodology used in previous studies.[12] In the next section we will explain why this standard methodology is appropriate when there is no effective leniency program in place, but it gives misleading results when such a program is in place, such as in the US after 1993 and in the EU after 1996.

Let us define the following variables:

- c is the constant marginal cost;
- m is the competitive mark-up, i.e. the competitive price is $p = c(1 + m)$;
- q is the individual quantity demanded at the competitive price;
- k is the percentage price increase due to the cartel, i.e. $p^m = p(1 + k)$ is the collusive price;[13]
- ε is the (absolute value of the) demand elasticity at the competitive price;
- α is the probability of detection; and
- f is the fine expressed as a fraction of firm's revenue in the affected market.

In the non-cartelized market profits are $\pi = qcm$.[14] If firms form a cartel and increase the price from p to p^m, each of them sells $q^m = q(1 - \varepsilon k)$ gaining

---

[12] As mentioned in the introduction, analogous 'back of the envelope' calculations for particular parameter constellations are in Werden and Simon (1987) and Gallo et al. (1994, 1997) for environments or periods without effective leniency programs, and in UK Ministry of Trade (2001), Posner (2001), Wils (2003, 2005a), and—with the novel twist of an international cartels perspective—Connor (2003, 2005), for environments or periods where effective leniency programs were already present.

[13] Of course in reality and in oligopoly models this parameter is endogenous, but our simulations encompass many values of this parameter, thereby covering many possible models and real world situation.

[14] In a perfectly competitive market either m is zero or firms have fixed costs such that actual profits are zero. Alternatively, we can imagine that also in the non cartelized market the equilibrium is not perfectly competitive and firms gain positive profits. Which of the above assumptions is true is irrelevant for the following discussion as what matters for the decision of forming a cartel is only the magnitude of the profits variation due to the cartel formation.

collusive profits $\pi^m = qc(1-\varepsilon k)[k(1+m)+m]$. Therefore, a colluding firm increases its profits by:

$$\pi^m - \pi = qkc\big[(1+m)(1-\varepsilon k) - \varepsilon m\big].$$

Revenues in the affected market at the colluding price are:

$$qc(1+m)(1+k)(1-\varepsilon k),$$

and the expected fine is:

$$\alpha f qc(1+m)(1+k)(1-\varepsilon k).$$

Let f^* be the minimum fine with deterrence effects, that is the fine such that the expected gain from participating in the cartel, given by the increase in profits minus the expected fine, is zero. We have:

$$f^*(\alpha, k, \varepsilon, m) = \frac{k[(1+m)(1-\varepsilon k) - \varepsilon m]}{\alpha(1+m)(1+k)(1-\varepsilon k)}. \tag{4.1}$$

If $m = 0$, the minimum fine (4.1) becomes:

$$f^* = \frac{k}{\alpha(1+k)}. \tag{4.2}$$

Note that the minimum fine is defined with respect to the revenues of a firm over the entire period in which the cartel is active and successful.

Levenstein and Suslow (2002) analyze case studies of a sample of cartels discovered in the 1990s in the US, and find that cartels seem to last on average 5 years, and to raise prices from 10 to 100%, with a median collusive mark-up of 25%. John Connor (2004) surveys hundreds of published social-science studies of private, hard-core cartels collecting 674 observations of long-run overcharges. He finds that the median overcharge for all types of cartels over all time periods is 25%: 18% for domestic cartels and 32% for international cartels. Outside the US, data on 62 decisions of competition commissions cited median overcharge of 29% and a mean of 49%.

As for the probability of detection, unfortunately we have no reliable estimate of this parameter, and this is clearly an important topic for future research.[15]

---

[15] The most often quoted and rigorous work on this is Bryant and Eckard (1991). These authors, however, model and estimate a birth–death process for *convicted* cartels between 1961 and 1988. They estimate the probability for a cartel to be convicted *in a given year*, and *conditional on being convicted*, to be between 0.13 and 0.17. Because we do not know the number of non-convicted cartel that were present in that same period, nor whether non-convicted cartels had on average the same characteristics of convicted ones, it is very hard to assess precisely the generic probability of being convicted in a given year faced by a cartel that does not know whether it will be convicted. Their result only estimates that *it cannot be higher than* 0.13–0.17 *per year*. It would be exactly in that interval if all the cartels were convicted with probability one, of about one order of magnitude smaller (about 0.013–0.017 per year) if one out of ten cartels were convicted, of two orders of magnitude smaller if one out of hundred cartels were convicted, and so on. Even less can be said about cartels' perceived probability of detection, which is what really matters.

Table 4.4: Minimum fine expressed as a percentage of the firm's revenue in the affected market for different levels of the competitive mark-up and the demand elasticity.

m	ε								
	.1	**.2**	**.3**	**.5**	**1**	**2**	**3**	**4**	**5**
.01	.605	.605	.604	.603	.599	.591	.580	.566	.546
.03	.604	.602	.601	.597	.586	.562	.530	.488	.430
.05	.603	.600	.597	.591	.574	.534	.482	.414	.317
.07	.602	.598	.594	.585	.562	.507	.436	.342	.210
.09	.601	.596	.591	.580	.550	.481	.392	.272	.106
.11	.600	.594	.587	.574	.539	.456	.349	.206	.005
.13	.599	.592	.584	.569	.529	.432	.307	.141	n.p.
.15	.598	.590	.582	.564	.518	.408	.267	.079	n.p.

Werden and Simon (1987) assume in their calculations that one out of ten cartels is caught by the DoJ, and used in their simulations a probability that a cartel is detected at all—i.e. in its whole lifetime—of 0.10. Given that the DoJ can use tougher investigative methods than the EC, it is likely that the probability of cartels detection is lower for the EU. Moreover, what matters for deterrence is the probability of detection as perceived by the potential wrongdoers, and many agents tend to be overoptimistic regarding their probability of success (see, e.g., Camerer, 2003; Jolls, 2004).

A prudent stance relative to previous simulation would, therefore, be to assume a collusive mark-up (k) equal to .1, as suggested by the USSG, and a perceived probability of detection equal to .15. If we assume that the competitive mark-up (m) is zero this suffices to identify the minimum fine with deterrence effect (Equation (4.2)) that is equal to 61% of firms revenue in the affected market. This value is largely dependent on the magnitude of the collusive mark-up. If we take the value of .29, reported by Connor (2004), as the median overcharge for cartel cases outside the US, to deter the median cartel the fine should be set at 150% of the firms' revenue. *These percentages have to be applied to the revenues of the firm over the entire period of the successful activity of the cartel.*

Table 4.4 reports the results of our simulation and shows the level, expressed as a fraction of the firm's revenue, that the minimum fine would take for a range of values of the competitive mark-up (m) and of the demand elasticity (ε), while holding constant the value of the collusive mark-up ($k = .1$) and of the probability of detection ($\alpha = .15$).

When the competitive mark-up over marginal costs is high (over .13) and the price elasticity is 5 or more a further price increase of 10% is not profitable. The values reported in the table show that when the collusive overcharge is 10% the minimum fine ranges from about 60% to 0.5%, depending on the value of the demand elasticity. With a demand elasticity of 1, the minimum fine with deterrence effects varies between 50% and 60% of the sales in the relevant market. The interested reader can easily compute the value of the minimum fine when the collusive mark-up is higher. For instance if the overcharge is .29 and the elasticity is 1, the minimum fine ranges from 122% to 148%. This shows that it is likely that the current level of the financial penalties imposed in the EU (reported in Table 4.2) has been inadequate to deter cartels that have the ability to raise price by 10% or more and that face a relatively inelastic demand. Note also that a fine below 10% of the firm's turnover in the affected market (over the full period of collusion) is sufficient to deter collusion (if all the other assumptions hold), only if the demand elasticity is at least 4 and if the competitive mark-up is above 10%. Even in these (exceptional) cases the minimum fine may exceed the maximum threshold set in the EU if the conspiracy lasts more than one year and if the affected market generates a substantial fraction of the entire firm's turnover.

4.2.3. A 'Political Economy' interpretation of EU mild sanctions

The simulation presented in the previous section and analogous simulations previously run by other researchers suggest that, both at the EU level and in most European countries sanctions against price-fixing have been too low in the past to have had substantial deterrence effects, particularly in the absence of leniency programs.

EU antitrust enforcement against cartels before leniency programs. Spending public resources in a law enforcement policy that has a small deterrence effect on a crime may be less efficient than having no law enforcement at all. Scarce public money is spent to support agencies, investigations and trials, while private money and effort are spent to try avoid/reduce fines. For a policy to be efficient, law enforcement costs borne by society must be compensated by substantial social benefits in terms of crime deterrence.

Consider three possible worlds: one with sufficiently tough sanctions against cartels such that the costly enforcement of antitrust laws has substantial cartel deterrence effects (say, the US); one without enforcement of antitrust laws (say, China); and one with very mild sanctions against cartels, where the costly enforcement of antitrust laws has little or no cartel deterrence effects. The third one is likely to be the worst, as society bears the cost of antitrust enforcement (cost of public agencies, lawyers, courts) without a valid return in terms of reduced rate of collusion.[16]

Note that our claim is different from that advanced by Crandall and Winston (2003). These authors argue that it is likely that US antitrust law enforcement *in general* has not had large positive effects on consumers, and support their

---

[16] Of course all policies should have a positive net return, and he cost of competition policy are very small compared to other policies. There are so many enormously more expensive policies (just think at agricultural policies in the EU and US) with obvious and large negative returns to society that discussing antitrust policy in this respect is perhaps a bit unfair.

claim with a limited selection of (rather old) cases and an aggregate data analysis. The weaknesses in their analysis have been already pointed out by Baker (2003), Werden (2003), and Kwoka (2003).

Our more narrow claims are, instead, that:

(a) if expected sanctions against a crime are too low to have relevant deterrence effects, then the law enforcement activity is unproductive from an economic point of view and the investigation and prosecution costs are deadweight losses for society (i.e. they do not produce sufficient social benefits that balance them, apart from the compensation of the victims, a pure transfer); and
(b) our and other researchers' simple simulations suggest that expected sanctions against cartels in Europe may have been too low to have substantial deterrence effects on cartels, at least before the introduction of the leniency program.

Competition law with weak enforcement as a 'political equilibrium' in Europe. How did we arrive to a situation of inefficient antitrust enforcement in Europe, which lasted for several decades? Europe is not isolated in this. Gallo et al. (1994, 1997) showed empirically that, even if we include imprisonment and damages, US sanctions before the 90s have fallen short of the level necessary to have deterrence effects. And McCoutcheon (1997) presents a subtle political economy theory of 'low but not too low' antitrust sanctions in the US, which argues that before leniency programs and the increase in sanctions of the recent years, the US legal framework did not deter cartel formation, but instead deterred meetings to renegotiate cartel strategies, thereby increasing the credibility of threats against defectors and stabilizing cartels!

The likely insufficiency of EU sanctions before leniency was introduced was particularly evident because of the absence of imprisonment. We propose a much simpler potential 'political economy' explanation, based as usual on the weak incentives of dispersed consumers to organize themselves to defend their interests, together with a tradition of government-encouraged cooperative/collusive attitudes in most (protected) European industries. In this context, a policy that pretended to enforce cartel prohibitions by an active inspection and prosecution activity, but imposed sanctions with no deterrence effects, satisfied many parties at the same time. Firms could continue avoiding serious competition in the EU and jointly exploit monopoly power by only paying a rather low expected tax on collusive profits called 'antitrust'. Politicians were happy because they could (a) show abroad that they had a competition policy; (b) have profitable firms enjoying a quiet life and willing to pay to support them; (c) avoid confrontations with powerful unions, since lively competition requires a continuous reallocation of workforce (firms striving for cost efficiency shed workers, while more efficient firms grow). The agencies in charge of competition law enforcement and antitrust law firms also gained because sanctions without deterrence effects increase the number of antitrust infringements to prosecute. The unions benefited too from this situation because part of the collusive rents produced by the cartels typically trickled down to the employees (e.g., benefits, job security, etc.). And banks enjoyed financing firms earning a constant, fat collusive stream of profits.

A weak enforcement of competition law made therefore, in the short run, "everybody happy but the consumer". However, lack of competition means less productivity and innovation, which ensures that in an international arena such a political equilibrium cannot last long. The strong differential in economic performance between Europe and the US in the 90s and the loss of power suffered by the unions, linked to the fall of Berlin's wall, may have been two major events leading to the current "European movement" towards more effective antitrust law enforcement.

Of course, as noted by a referee, the difference in the severity of antitrust sanctions between the US and the EU may have more simply been due to sanctions being generally lower in Europe than in the US, most likely because the latter is a multi-racial society with higher mobility and a looser social pattern, therefore with more crime problems requiring tougher sanctions. Another, non-exclusive potential explanation is that Europe is a follower in terms of antitrust law and enforcement, and it requires time to credibly develop the political support for tough enforcement policies. (The US have followed a similar historical pattern, and the US cartel enforcement was also very weak before the 70s.)

4.2.4. Cartels and imprisonment: An old debate reopened

On the basis of the rather negative results of the simulation discussed above, one may be left with the impression that tougher criminal sanctions, in particular jail sentences, are the only credible legal instrument to deter hard-core cartels. Indeed, the new tendency towards criminalization taken by antitrust laws in Europe, as well as the widespread introduction of leniency programs inspired by the one of the US DoJ, appear as a sound—though late—reaction to an inadequate antitrust law enforcement. The EC and *some* governments seem to have recognized that to enforce prohibitions of price fixing, sufficiently strong sanctions are necessary. However, the need for more effective enforcement and tougher sanctions does not automatically imply a compulsory recourse to criminalization and imprisonment. In the remainder of this paper, when writing about criminal sanctions we will mainly refer to imprisonment, as financial criminal sanctions are likely to have some of the drawbacks of imprisonment, but few of its benefits.

Advantages of imprisonment. The US debate of the seventies and eighties, and in particular Werden and Simon (1987) highlighted a number of the benefits of sentencing price-fixers to jail, and the recent revival of this debate, in our view, has added little to the old one.[17] The most important arguments in favor of imprisonment, in our view, remain the following:

---

[17] Wils (2005a) discusses an analogous list of potential benefits of criminal sanctions from an EU competition law perspective, though not of their costs. See also Spagnolo (2005).

(1) Limited liability may protect firm owners from paying the optimal fine, i.e. the *firms' inability to pay* a fine sufficiently large to have a cartel deterrence effect;
(2) Direct targeting of individuals responsible for their unlawful decisions and not of other innocent stakeholders, even when the former have limited wealth (and are therefore shielded from high fines);
(3) Partial solution to the "indemnification problem", i.e. of the possibility that firms reimburse the individual fine to their managers when their unlawful behavior was aimed at increasing shareholder value, as firms cannot easily buy-out a prison sentence against their managers;
(4) Short prison sentences may not be very costly and have a particularly strong psychological and "mediatic" effect as they are imposed on "white collars", while imposing large fines on corporations may instead be quite costly;
(5) More effective investigation tools become available, hence the probability of detection may increase;
(6) Reduction of future collusion through incapacitation (though directors can be disqualified even without criminal sanctions);
(7) Increased effectiveness of leniency programs, as the risk of tougher sanctions implies stronger incentives to apply for amnesty ('protection from punishment effect' through imprisonment strengthen the incentive to report, see Spagnolo, 2004).

In the remainder of this chapter we are going to discuss in depth the first of the benefits listed above, the limited ability to pay, that, in our opinion, is the most relevant. Indirectly, we will also discuss the second, indemnification, as it is strictly related to the first (i.e. if firms expect to pay sufficiently high fines, they would never indemnify any price-fixing manager). The effectiveness of leniency and whistle blowing programs is enhanced whenever the sanction (disutility of conviction) is increased, whatever its nature. Therefore, we can improve the effectiveness of leniency programs also by raising fines and, if the previous remark is correct, this need for stronger sanctions is not a persuasive reason in favor of imprisonment in itself. The relevance of the others, when compared to the costs of imprisonment, is at the end an empirical issue.

Disadvantages of imprisonment. The benefits of prison sanctions should be weighted against their well known drawbacks, which are not often considered in the current debate. These include:

(1) Jurisdictions—i.e. courts and juries instead of public agencies like the DG COMP—hence, typically, longer and more complex and costly procedures;
(2) Much higher standards of proof, hence a lower probability of conviction and deterrence;
(3) Much higher social cost of Type I errors when imprisonment is used (innocents in jail); including the indirect one of deterring people from undertaking socially valuable legal activities that risk being misunderstood/seen as a form of collusive behavior;

(4) High direct cost of imprisonment (both in terms of prison costs and of loss of the activity of the incapacitated managers/entrepreneurs);
(5) Negative externalities when criminal sanctions induce cartel members to adopt "tougher methods" to ensure cartel cohesiveness (see Spagnolo, 2005).

Tougher sanctions against price fixers, and generally a more effective antitrust law enforcement are highly needed in Europe; but it is not clear that this automatically implies criminalization and imprisonment. Some of their benefits would follow also from an increase in the toughness of other sanctions, both criminal or administrative. Since criminal sanctions in the form of imprisonment imply several additional costs, including the ones just mentioned, from an economic point of view it is not efficient to immediately adopt them before adopting all the less costly and potentially more effective administrative mechanisms (e.g., Polinsky and Shavell, 2000, Sections 3.1.3 and 4.1.3). Unfortunately, this has not been done. Given the additional costs of imprisonment, before accepting the conclusion that criminalization is the only feasible way to effectively deter hard-core cartels (or before saying to what extent criminalization is needed to reach this policy objective), we must ask whether we can improve the deterrence properties of pecuniary sanctions. In particular, we need to answer the following questions: How much could we increase the current value of fines without breaking the limit of the firm's ability to pay or impairing the firm's future ability to compete? Can we use financial (dis)incentives in a more efficient way? Do the team properties of cartels change the way we should envisage the sanction policy? We try to answer these questions in the next sections.

4.3. Leniency, whistleblowers, and optimal antitrust fines

Leniency programs for cartels were introduced in 1993 in the US and in 1996 (reinforced in 2002) in the EU.[18] These programs reduce sanctions against the first firm or individual that reports information on a cartel (or other multiagent crime) he took part in, and cooperate with the law enforcers until his former co-conspirators have been convicted. Among those features that are common to the EU and the US programs, there is the rule that only the first party that self reports is eligible to automatic full immunity from the sanctions; the rule that the second parties to self-report can still obtain some reduced forms of leniency;[19] and that the benefits from reporting are higher if it takes place before an investigation has begun, and rapidly falls the later the report it happens during the investigation.

---

[18] The US had a "low power" leniency program since 1978, that had little effects. See Spagnolo (2006) for further details.

[19] In the EU the parties that collaborate second or later may obtain a partial reduction in sanctions if they provide additional information; analogously, in the US firms that did not report first can still obtain substantial reductions in sanctions by collaborating at the prosecution stage and pleading guilty.

The effectiveness of these programs in destabilizing and deterring cartels can be reinforced by the offer of a reward to the wrongdoer (or witness) that first blows the whistle and self-reports turning in former partners (the reward could be financed by part or all the fines imposed on other wrongdoers).[20]

The potential impact of leniency and whistleblower programs on the effectiveness of a fining policy is enormous. The consequence that is probably most noted of adopting a leniency program is a plausible increase in the probability of detection and conviction, α. This has the immediate effect of raising the expected fine and of reducing the minimum optimal fine. Since the expected fine is a linear function of α, any factor that increases α by a proportion β reduces the minimum fine by the same proportion β. Even if this is the most highlighted effect of a leniency program, in our opinion, it is not necessarily the most important. We explain it is so in the next section.

4.3.1. Participation versus incentive constraints

The current debate on the optimal sanction policy is based on the assumption that the sanction should be set so that the participation constraint for would-be conspirators is no longer satisfied. This means that the expected gain from being part of a cartel should not be positive. Our simulation in Section 4.3 is based on the same assumption.

However, the modern theory of oligopoly and collusion, starting from Stigler (1964), teaches us that cartels are successful (i.e. they reduce welfare) only if participants have an incentive to stick to the agreed collusive market conduct, rather than to steal other participants' business by secretly undercutting the agreed cartel price. A cartel is feasible if participants are able to deter unilateral defections (like secret price cuts) by monitoring the members' behavior and by threatening credible sanctions against defectors. As in law enforcement, to achieve cartel enforcement the expected loss from being punished by partner cartel members in the future if detected cheating, must be larger than the gain from cheating/undercutting the cartel today. This condition, necessary for any cartel or illegal agreement to be sustainable, because of the impossibility to use explicit contract, is called "incentive compatibility" or "self-enforcing" constraint. It differs from the "participation" constraint on which the theory of law enforcement focuses, that requires the expected additional profits participants would earn from entering a cartel to be positive.

---

[20] As proposed in Spagnolo (2000, 2004), Buccirossi and Spagnolo (2001), Kovacic (2001), and Aubert et al. (2005), and successfully done for other forms of multiagent crime, like government fraud under the US False Claim Act. We believe that the main efficiency enhancing potential of *well designed and implemented* leniency and whistleblower programs is not in terms of improved prosecution, but in their ability to *directly* deter, prevent cartel formation—avoiding costly prosecution altogether—by "undermining trust" among would be conspirators with the threat that one of them could then cheat on partners and self-report, turning the others in.

Several (old and recent) papers on optimal public law enforcement against cartels or other forms of organized crime—apart from the ones that use a dynamic model that endogenizes the effects of law enforcement variables on the incentive compatibility constraint—completely overlook this crucial aspect, by large the most important aspect when one wants to deters oligopolies and similar forms of multi-agent crime.[21] Both the participation and the incentive constraints must be satisfied simultaneously for all members of a cartel or of another organized criminal activity for this to be viable (so that if at least one of the two is violated for at least one member the cartel is deterred). And, as it turns out, it is much easier for law enforcers to ensure that the *incentive* constraint is violated for at least one of the members, by using leniency and whistleblower programs. Leniency and whistleblower programs can deter cartels by ensuring that the incentive/self-enforcing constraint is not satisfied, even when fines are much below those needed to ensure that the participation constraint of any wrongdoer is violated, i.e. the level that the standard theory of public law enforcement à la Becker considers necessary for a fine to have deterrence effects. To reiterate, a necessary condition for a cartel to be stable is that for each of its members the following inequality is satisfied:

$$
\begin{aligned}
&\text{Present value of expected collusive profits}\\
&\qquad - \text{expected sanction from antitrust conviction } (F)\\
&\quad > \text{Expected profits from secretly deviating/undercutting the cartel price}\\
&\qquad - \text{expected antitrust sanction after deviating } (F^d).
\end{aligned}
$$

We can therefore deter a cartel by increasing individual members' incentives to undercut/betray their cartel: either by increasing the fines on those firms that respect the collusive agreement, F, but not on a firm that "betrayed" its cartel by secretly undercutting the agreed price, F^d; or, by lowering F^d, but not F. In principle, deterrence can therefore be obtained for any F if F^d is low enough (F^d could be negative, in which case it becomes a reward). This novel type of deterrence introduced by leniency programs and whistleblower schemes is not considered in the existing literature on optimal law enforcement, which typically maintains Becker's (1968) static perspective.[22] This more efficient type of deterrence may require fines which are much lower than the optimal "Beckerian" fines on which most of previous work focused. The next section will give an idea of how much smaller optimal fines are when coupled with leniency programs and whistleblower reward schemes.

---

[21] Leniency programs where first formally analyzed within an appropriately dynamic model that endogenizes effects on the self-enforcing incentive constraint by Motta and Polo (2003), who focus mainly on their ability to facilitate prosecution.

[22] So far, this crucial fact, evident from the recent (dynamic) economic analyses of leniency programs, appears not to have been properly understood by legal scholars; the only law and economic work on optimal fines that does not overlook this fundamental point is, as far as we know, Camilli (2005).

4.3.2. Simulations

We will proceed step by step, introducing one aspect at time, to show that deterrence can be greatly improved with a more sophisticated use of financial incentives alone. To validate our claims, we use the simple simulation introduced in Section 4.3, assuming for simplicity that the competitive mark-up, m, is zero. We leave it to the interested reader to compute the levels of the minimum fine in different scenarios.

We start from a benchmark case in which firms are not punished for forming a cartel, even though colluding explicitly remains illegal and, therefore, must form a self-sustained equilibrium. Let π^c denotes the per period collusive profit, $\pi^d = d\pi^c$, with $d > 1$, the profit obtained by deviating from the collusive agreement, and δ the discount factor.[23] We also suppose that both the competitive profit and the profit of a punished deviator are zero. The incentive constraint implies that:

$$\delta \geq \frac{d-1}{d}, \tag{4.3}$$

and we will assume that condition (4.3) always holds.

If the sanction against those firms that enter into the explicit and illegal cartel agreement is the same, irrespective of whether they adhere to the terms of the agreement or deviate, the incentive constraint does not change. In this situation we can only hope to deter cartels by tightening the participation constraint. Can we exploit the incentive compatibility constraint to deter cartels with fines that are below the level that would be required to stop them through the participation constraint? The answer is a big yes. To do so, however, firms that deviate and undercut a collusive agreement should be treated more favorably than those that do not. It is puzzling that, both in the US and in the EU, this factor does not seem to have been taken into consideration in setting fines. In neither of these two jurisdictions defecting from the cartel agreement is deemed an alleviating circumstance.[24]

Let F be, throughout the following discussion, the fine expressed as an absolute financial value rather that as a fraction of the firm's revenue, and F^d the fine imposed on a cartel deviator.[25] The expected profit a firm could derive from

---

[23] The discount factor incorporates the probability of cartel terminating because of an antitrust conviction, i.e. $\delta = \frac{1-\gamma}{1+i}$ where γ is the per-period probability of detection and i is the interest rate.

[24] The situation is possibly even worse than this. Indeed, if the fine is computed as a fraction of the affected commerce, a deviating firm would face a more severe sanction since its revenue increases as a consequence of its deviation. This leads to the unintended consequence of making the cartel more stable by relaxing firms' incentive constraint. See Spagnolo (2004, Prop. 1) for a more general result on the optimality of reducing sanctions against a wrongdoer that betrayed his partners even in the absence of a leniency program.

[25] To simplify the exposition, contrary to what we have done in Section 4.2, here we prefer to use the absolute value, F, rather than the percentage value, f. However, the relation between these two values is straightforward as, when $m = 0$, as assumed in this simulation, $F = fqc(1+k)(1-\varepsilon k)$.

participating in the collusive scheme is:

$$\frac{\pi^c}{1-\delta} - \alpha F,$$

which implies that the minimum fine with deterrence effects (given the participation constraint) is:

$$F^* = \frac{\pi^c}{\alpha(1-\delta)}.$$

We assume that a firm prefers to deviate if, by so doing, it gets a payoff at least equal to the collusive payoff. Therefore, the cartel is stable only if

$$\frac{\pi^c}{1-\delta} - \alpha F > d\pi^c - \alpha F^d.$$

From Equation (4.3) it is apparent that legislators and antitrust authorities can use the fining policy to make cartels unstable by either increasing the fine against firms that do not deviate, or by lowering the fine against the deviator(s), or by doing both. However, since our starting point is that the fine F might be too high, we want to know whether we can deter cartels with a fine F less than F^*. The answer is trivial. In principle, if there is no lower bound to the value that F^d can assume, we can reach our policy objective even with no fines against non-deviating firms, provided that we are willing to reward deviators. At this stage it is not important to discuss whether such policy is politically or morally feasible. What is important is to make clear the simple principle that sanctions and rewards are distinct only from a semantic point of view. They are actually two sides of the same coin and if, for some reasons, we cannot raise the penalty against bad behaviors (the stick), we can always make them less attractive by increasing the reward for acting properly (the carrot). Therefore, the real question is to understand what is the minimum fine that must be imposed on deviating firms. In the absence of a full fledged leniency program that restricts benefits to the first applicant the floor consists of simply waiving the fine to the cartel members that defect.[26] If $F^d = 0$ the minimum fine against non-defecting firms with deterrence effects (given the incentive constraint) becomes:

$$F' = \frac{\pi^c[1 - d(1-\delta)]}{\alpha(1-\delta)}$$

and is clearly less than F^*. The ratio between F' and F^* is:

$$\frac{F'}{F^*} = 1 - d(1-\delta).$$

The assumption that the cartel would be stable without fines (Equation (4.3)), guarantees that $0 < F' < F^*$. The impact of this policy on the minimum value

[26] Giving a reward to defecting firms would be unfeasible because it would make all firms acting in competitive markets eligible.

Table 4.5: Ratio between the minimum fine with and without leniency/whistleblowing programs.

d	$n = 3$	$n = 4$	$n = 5$
1.00	.063	.043	.033
1.50	.059	.040	.031
2.00	.056	.038	.029
2.50	.052	.036	.027
3.00	.049	.033	.025

of the fine with deterrence effects depends on the value of d and δ, and may be significant.[27]

However, there is still some room for more effective policies by combining the principle outlined above with leniency and whistleblowing programs. Following the proposal made in Spagnolo (2000), we could reward the first firm or entrepreneur that applies to the program bringing sufficient hard information to convict a previously undetected cartel by an amount equal to the fines levied on all its former co-conspirators.

Let $r = (n - 1)F$ be the value of the reward. The incentive constraint for a stable cartel becomes:

$$\frac{\pi^c}{1-\delta} - \alpha F > d\pi^c + r.$$

The minimum fine apt to make the cartel no longer viable is:

$$F'' = \frac{\pi^c[1 - d(1-\delta)]}{(1-\delta)(n-1+\alpha)}.$$

The ratio between the minimum fine given the incentive constraint, F'', and the minimum fine given the participation constraint, F^*, is:

$$\frac{F''}{F^*} = \frac{\alpha[1 - d(1-\delta)]}{n-1+\alpha}.$$

Table 4.5 shows the values this ratio can take for different values of n, the number of cartel members and d, the multiplicative factor of profits when a firm deviates, when the probability of detection remains constant ($\alpha = .15$) and that the discount factor (adjusted for the probability of detection) is .9.[28]

---

[27] For instance if a firm can double its profits by deviating ($d = 2$) and if the discount factor is .9 the optimal fine against non deviating firm can be reduced by 20%.

[28] If the probability of detection over the entire duration of the cartel is .15, the stationary per-period probability of detection, γ, is the value that solves the equation $1 - (1-\gamma)^t = .15$, where t is the duration of the cartel. If we assume that a cartel lasts five years, then we have $\gamma = .03198$. It follows that a discount factor of .9 implies an interest rate of 7.5%.

The values in Table 4.5, of course, are not intended to provide a practical guide about how to compute the optimal fine. Their limited goal is to prove that the policy we described would greatly reduce the fine that must be imposed on non-reporting firms to obtain a deterrence effect. The value of the minimum fine falls to about 3% of the "Beckerian" value, F^*, for any cartel with at least five members. This means that, considering our initial simulation ($k = .1$), a cartel with five members in a market whose competitive mark-up, m, is zero could be deterred by imposing a fine on non-reporting firms equal to less than 2% of the firms' affected commerce over the entire duration of the cartel and paying a reward to the whistleblower equal to the total collected fine. If the collusive mark-up is higher, say .29, as the median overcharge found by Connor in non-US cartel cases, the minimum fine becomes 4.5% of the affected commerce over the entire duration of the cartel. It is hard to believe that such fines would cause any firm to go bankrupt.

This massive reduction in the optimal fine is entirely driven by the strong effect fines have on the incentives of individual wrongdoers to "betray" their partners and self-report, if they are used to pay a reward for the first reporting party only. This mechanism maximizes the conflict between the objectives of the individual firm/wrongdoer and the group of firms/wrongdoers, making co-operation in the criminal team impossible to sustain.

Moreover, these values underestimate the reduction of the optimal fine that is brought about by an efficient use of rewarding schemes. Indeed, as noted at the beginning, one of the most publicized effects of leniency programs is the increase (real or perceived) in the probability of getting caught. This will tighten the participation constraint, as already pointed out by many commentators, but will also make the incentive constraint more stringent, further reducing the scope for a viable and successful cartel. If, thanks to the leniency program, the probability of conviction over the entire cartel life becomes $\beta\alpha$, with $\beta > 1$, the ratio between the optimal fine with a leniency program that rewards the whistleblower as described above (F^β) and the optimal fine without the leniency program (F^*), becomes:

$$\frac{F^\beta}{F^*} = \frac{\alpha[1 - d(1 - \delta)]}{n - 1 + \beta\alpha},$$

and is lower than F''/F^* for any value of d and n, although the further reduction is modest. One last effect, that the previous literature on optimal fines has not recognized, is that an increase in the probability of conviction reduces the relevant discount factor, once this incorporates, as it should, the probability that the cartel breaks down as a consequence of an antitrust investigation. This brings a further reduction in the fine that makes collusion unfeasible. Let us denote with F_δ^β the optimal fine that takes into account this effect together with all the other described before, with β the proportional increase in the probability of detection over the entire duration of the cartel and with η the proportional increase in the per-period probability of detection, so that $\delta_\eta = \frac{1-\eta\gamma}{1+i}$ denotes the factor firms use to discount future profits when the leniency program is in place. We have that

$$\frac{F_{\delta}^{\beta}}{F*} = \frac{\alpha[1 - d(1 - \delta_{\eta})](1 - \delta)}{(1 - \delta_{\eta})(n - 1 + \beta\alpha)} \equiv R(\delta_{\eta}).$$

It is immediate to see that

$$\frac{\partial R(\delta_{\eta})}{\partial \delta_{\eta}} = \frac{\alpha(1 - \delta)}{(1 - \delta_{\eta})^2(n - 1 - \beta\alpha)} > 0,$$

so that an increase in η, that reduces the value of the relevant discount factor δ_{η}, determines a reduction in the ratio between the optimal fine with and without a leniency/whistleblowing policy. $R(\delta_{\eta})$ identifies the fraction of the original fine, computed in Section 4.3, that deters the cartel formation through the incentive constraint with a well-designed leniency/whistleblower reward policy, once we consider all the effects of this policy discussed in this section. To give an idea of the overall effect of such a policy, consider a case in which the cartel has five members, the initial probability of detection (α) is .15, the initial discount factor (δ) is .9, the expected duration of the cartel is five years, the deviation profits are two times the collusive profits ($d = 2$), and the probability of detection over the entire duration of the cartel doubles ($\beta = 2$),[29] the minimum fine with deterrence effects is .019 of the original optimal one. This means that if such a cartel allows firms to charge a collusive price 10% higher than the competitive price, a fine of 1.15% of the relevant turnover imposed on non reporting firms is sufficient to prevent its formation, provided firms are aware of the leniency scheme. If the same cartel can apply a collusive mark-up of 29%, the minimum fine on non reporting firms with deterrence effects becomes 2.85% of their sales in the relevant market.

4.3.3. Additional deterrence effects and imperfections

The results from these simulations are striking, and yet this is not the end of the story. Besides the deterrence effects captured by the simulations, the protection from fines and "reward" effects (pointed out in Spagnolo, 2000a, 2000b, 2004) and the direct increase in the probability of conviction (pointed out in Kaplow and Shavell, 1994), recent theory has identified at least four other types of potential deterrence effects brought about by leniency and whistleblower programs that we did not consider in our simulations:

---

[29] To compute η and δ_{η} note that η is the value that solves the following equation $1 - (1 - \eta\gamma)^t = \beta\alpha$, where t is the cartel duration and γ the initial per-period probability of detection. Given the assumption in the text we have that $\gamma = .031981$ and that $\eta = 1.1529$. Then we have that $\delta_{\eta} = \frac{1-\eta\gamma}{1+i}$, where i is the interest rate. Since the other assumptions imply that $i = .075089$, we have that $\delta_{\eta} = .86611$.

- an "improved prosecution effect" (Motta and Polo, 2003), linked to the speeding up of the prosecution generated by the additional information a well-designed and well-implemented leniency program makes available, and the consequent saving in resources which could be reallocated to other inspections, partly captured by the last simulations with increased probability of detection;
- a "protection from punishment effect", which reduces the strength of the market punishment that an undercutting firm faces from its competitors for its defection (see Spagnolo, 2000a, 2004);
- an increase in "the risk of being undercut and denounced" by other firms, linked to the reduction in trust and to the increase in strategic uncertainty determined by the leniency/reward scheme (see Spagnolo, 2004);
- a "rewards for employees effect", which amplifies the incentive and deterrence power of the reward scheme simulated above when each individual employees of a price-fixing firm can cash the reward (see Aubert et al., 2005).

These additional deterrence effects may reinforce the ones included in our simulation exercise, and ensure that its results, in terms of relative reduction of the optimal fine, are far from being unrealistic.

On the other hand, we should not forget that firms, and particularly managers that individually choose to blow the whistle, may face very harsh sanctions from their former business partners, peers, and from the business community in general, that can range from exclusion from the business and social exclusion, to physical harassment. These effects may last for the whole length of the prosecution. This is probably the main reason why, when directed at individuals, only programs with very high expected rewards, like the US False Claim Act, appear to induce informed parties to spontaneously blow the whistle.[30] In addition, wrongdoers may not be well informed about the size of expected fines from being turned in and rewards from self-reporting; and even if they are, they tend to underestimate the probability of being convicted when starting and illegal activity (Camerer, 2003). In the case of international cartels the effect of leniency programs and rewards is also mitigated by the fact that many countries are not subject to antitrust laws (Connor, 2005). All these factors tend—*ceteris paribus*—to reduce cartel deterrence and require fines to be higher than previously calculated, so that direct deterrence is maintained and sufficiently high rewards can be paid to encourage whistleblowing.[31]

---

[30] Korea recently introduced a reward scheme for whistleblowers in antitrust cases, but the maximal rewards are still too small to encourage whistleblowing given the economic and social costs whistleblowers tend to face which are probably higher in a small country with a tightly knit economic and social network.

[31] The rewards paid out should never be above the sum of the fines paid by the co-conspirators, otherwise there would be an opportunity for firms to "milk the system" and make money by pretending to have a cartel, reporting it, paying fines, and then sharing the reward. This is why we are very far from claiming that fines should be reduced with the introduction of reward schemes for whistle-

4.4. Implementing the optimal fine efficiently

According to previous simulations, when well designed leniency programs and whistleblower schemes are in place a substantial increase in the level of financial sanctions that is likely to remain within the firms' *normal* ability to pay should be sufficient to deter cartels without having to introduce imprisonment. This analysis disproves two arguments in favor of imprisonment: the main one, that financial sanctions on their own are insufficient; and the second one that imprisonment makes indemnification more difficult (if fines are such that firms have no incentives to break the law, firms would never indemnify managers that choose to do so).[32] In this section we discuss some issues related to the implementation of the optimal fining policy. The first issue is how to define firms' normal ability to pay (Section 4.4.1). The second issue is whether individual sanctions are needed when firms can adopt an internal monitoring system (Section 4.4.3). The third issue concerns how firms set their prices when they face a sunk cost, such as a fine (Section 4.4.3). We clarify why most of these issues, that may provide reasons in favor of the adoption of criminal sanctions against individuals, can be also addressed by a fining policy that uses efficiently leniency and whistleblowing programs.

4.4.1. Firms' ability to pay and the problem of judgment proofness

The path breaking work of Summers (1983) and Shavell (1986) stressed how limited liability and senior securities may limit the maximal fine a wrongdoer may be subject to, reducing expected sanctions and, hence, the deterrence effect below the levels chosen by the legislator. This problem of "judgment proofness" is well known in antitrust, and is probably the strongest argument put forward for the use of imprisonment by Werden and Simon (1987). Its relevance and limits have been empirically demonstrated by Craycraft et al. (1997), who showed that US courts do tend to reduce financial sanctions against colluding firms with a lower ability to pay. The latter study, however, also shows that the fines actually imposed are about one/fourth of the maximal applicable statutory fines, that almost all firms in their sample could have easily paid the maximal fines, and that contrary to the pessimistic forecast of Werden and Simon, about half of them could also have paid an optimal cartel-deterring "Beckerian" fine without going bankrupt.

---

blowers. Quite the opposite: high monetary fines and rewards are complementary instruments in obtaining efficient deterrence (Spagnolo, 2000a, 2004).

[32] The argument that imprisonment hinders indemnification is anyway rather weak. Mullin and Snyder (2005) elegantly showed that forbidding indemnification costs innocent firms more than guilty ones, reducing deterrence when mistakes are present. The only surviving argument against indemnification is that forbidding it may increase the willingness of firms' employees to cooperate with law enforcement agencies. However, employees' cooperation can also be elicited with rewards, as done by the False Claim Act.

Fines can, and should be substantially increased, both in the EU and in the US, because they are much below the optimal fines, below what most observers regards as firms' maximal ability to pay (the value of total equity), and even below levels that could reduce firms' ability to compete after a conviction.

Fining shareholders to reach "real" ability to pay. There seems to be some confusion about the concept of firms' maximal ability to pay used in the legal and economic literature. A firm's maximal ability to pay is usually taken to be the total "market value" of the firm, measured by the current/normal market price of an individual share times the number of existing shares. This has led many observers to argue (somewhat prematurely) that firms' ability to pay is too low for fines to have any deterrence effect without imprisonment.

However, basic corporate finance teaches us that in public corporations with many shareholders ownership and control are separated, so that dispersed shares incorporate very little 'control rights' on the firm future cash flow, which depresses their price. A firm's market value based on the individual share price times the number of shares—unless the price is picked during a takeover battle for control—is typically a fraction of a firm's *real* market value and, hence, ability to pay, both of which are determined by past, current, and expected future income.

One possible avenue for collecting high fines without causing a firm to become financially insolvent is by forcing it to pay the fine by selling shares with control rights, rather than letting the firm choose how to pay it. The law could establish, for example, that if a firm is convicted for price-fixing, all its shares will be expropriated and sold on the market, and the revenue from this sale used to pay damages and the fine. An analogous way to fine shareholders, less dramatic and possibly easier to implement from a legal point of view, could be to dilute old shareholders' ownership. For example, the law could establish that if a firm is convicted for price fixing (or for another crime), the number of that firm's shares triples, and the new shares—2/3 of total firm shares after the conviction—are sold on the market through a transparent auction. These procedures, aimed at fining shareholders rather than the firm with all its stakeholders, could increase deterrence for at least two reasons:

1. When a firm's shares are sold on the market its control could change hands and a contest analogous to a takeover battle may take place, which may increase share prices and allow the imposition of a fine that is closer to the firm's real ability to pay.
2. Putting a firm's control at stake hits *insiders* (that have control of the firm) much harder than minority shareholders (that have little information and influence on firms' decisions), because insiders risk loosing control on the firm, in addition to the value of their equity stakes. Since insiders that have control are the ultimate decision makers of any corporation, this kind of fine is likely to threaten the right people and induce them to prevent their managers from fixing prices (or committing any other corporate crime).

An additional benefit of a policy of this kind is that, even though the fines are high, it is likely that firms' ability to go on producing and competing is not jeopardized. Firms finance most investment and production through retained earnings and debt, and only in minimal part through equity. A fine on shareholders, of the type described above does not directly affect the firm's earnings, nor its debt capacity, and, hence, has a minimum effect on the firm's ability to invest and produce.

Strategic judgment proofness and extended liability. An apparently less well-known problem in antitrust is that of *strategic* judgment proofing, i.e. of the possibility that cartel members react to an increase in financial fines by issuing more securities senior to the antitrust fines. This problem was raised recently by Che and Spier (2005) in the context of tort law, where damages to victims of accidents are junior claims relative to long term debt, so that long term debt can be used to shield valuable assets from damage claims.

One could think that in antitrust this problem would become relevant, if financial sanction approach firms' current ability to pay, only in those jurisdictions where financial claims senior to administrative fines could be issued.[33] If this was the case, the problem would be of minor importance, as it would be relevant to few jurisdictions, and could be easily solved, for example, by limiting firms' ability to issue senior claims, as suggested by Che and Spier (2005) for tort law. This, however, would be an optimistic stance. First, because there are other, more subtle ways in which the controlling insiders, who are aware of committing a crime and of risking high fines, can hide profits and assets and, thus, reduce their liability (i.e. they can "tunnel" illegal gains out of the liable firm). Second, and most important, because there are "political–reputational" reasons why, even when antitrust fines have priority on other claims, fines that render a convicted firm insolvent towards other stakeholders driving it bankrupt may never be imposed, so that senior fines become effectively junior claims and the judgment-proofness problem may re-emerge. The results of Craycraft et al. (1997), already mentioned, prove that in the US this problem exists. It is plausible to believe that administrative agencies in Europe are even more careful in avoiding to be the source of bankruptcy procedures. We call this additional effect the "political judgment proofness" problem, to distinguish it from the original and the law-induced strategic judgment proofness problem.

Legal and political strategic judgment proofness problems are serious, as colluding firms can avoid harsh fines by appropriately increasing their financial liabilities, distributing all cash flows and financing investment only with debt, or undertaking other inefficient actions. A policy of reducing fines for firms with an apparently lower ability to pay, as followed by US courts, implicit in the EU

[33] In the US antitrust fines are criminal fines, hence according to Chapter 13 they are not dischargeable in bankruptcy. In several European countries administrative fines are equivalent liabilities towards the state (e.g., taxes), and enjoy priority on most other claims.

guidelines, and often implicitly suggested by some legal scholars (e.g., Wils, 2005b), may end up causing *double* welfare losses: those from reduced cartel deterrence due to firms' strategic reduction in their ability to pay and expected fines; and those linked to the direct, real costs of the inefficient financial structure and other costly practices colluding firms may undertake to reduce their ability to pay and expected antitrust fines.

Among the countermeasures currently discussed to reduce problems of judgment proofness in the context of environmental regulation and tort law there are: setting caps on liabilities that have priority on sanctions or damages (e.g., Che and Spier, 2005); extending liability for damages and sanctions to debt-holders (e.g., Hiriart and Martimort, 2005); and imposing a minimal asset requirement as in banking regulation (e.g., Shavell, 2004). All these instruments limit the negative effects of judgment proofness, but generate also some costs. Extended liability and caps to senior securities make external financing more costly, and minimum asset requirements raise barrier to entry and may, thus, reduce competition. Moreover, they are not likely to help with the problem of political judgment proofness, as with this problem it just matters whether bankruptcy is likely to occur once a high fine is imposed.

An alternative potential instrument—to our knowledge not recently discussed, but worth a serious analysis—is reducing/softening shareholders' limited liability constraint in cases where the liabilities derive from proven illegal conducts. Limited liability is essential to ensure a smooth flow of savings/capital from households and financial institutions to firms. However, there is nothing optimal in ensuring a flow of finance to illegal (albeit profitable) enterprises. *Prima facie*, therefore, it appears that it could be desirable to make a distinction between legal and illegal behavior, and to have a somewhat different degree of shareholders' liability protection, stronger when bankrupt is due to a bad outcome of a legal activity, and weaker when it is due to a discovered and sanctioned illegal activity. This possibility must be scrutinized in depth from a number of points of view, but it appears potentially able to provide investors with incentives to prefer firms whose directors select and monitor their managers and write compensation contracts that are unlikely to lead to illegal behavior.[34]

Of course, the issue is very delicate and needs a careful analysis, not least because the shareholders fined when the cartel is detected/convicted may be different from the shareholders that decided the governance structure, and because shareholders may sell and buy shares during the prosecution stage, so that freezing the trade of the shares of the firms under prosecution may be required. Nevertheless, as we mentioned, *a priori* there seems to be no obvious

---

34 With equal limited liability, when facing the choice between a manager known to be good for undertaking very profitable illegal activities without being detected, and a honest manager good at legal but much less profitable projects, profit-maximizing shareholders may well find rational to choose the first option. On the relation between corporate governance arrangements and collusive behavior see Buccirossi and Spagnolo (2006).

justification for granting a perfectly equal degree of protection from liabilities originating from legal and illegal activities.

Not so relevant after all. All these measures entail costs. The latter one could potentially increase the financing costs to all firms, including those that strive to behave legally, given that corporate governance contracts are never perfect and that type I errors (false convictions) cannot be eliminated. The judgment proofness problem, therefore, tends to make imprisonment a relatively more appealing solution. However, one should also take into account that measures that make a firm judgment proof are themselves costly. Overborrowing, for example, distorts the capital structure of a firm, and, therefore, managerial incentives and the firm's cost of financing. Tunneling, i.e. diverting resources out of the firm so that they cannot be reached by law enforcers, entails high transaction costs. This means that high fines, since they induce wrongdoing firms to adopt such behavior and incur such cost, increase the cost of illegal behaviors and, therefore, have partial deterrence effects. Moreover, the costs (and the social cost) of a suboptimal financial structure and other distortions leading to judgment proofness tend to increase at an increasing rate in the "amount" of judgment proofness a firm wants to obtain. This suggests that, when smaller fines are sufficient to deter a crime, as we showed to be the case when well-designed and well-implemented leniency and whistleblower reward schemes are in place, these problems are likely to be of lesser relevance, if any.

4.4.2. Individual sanctions and internal monitoring

Cartels are normally run by top level managers, and appear to be happily tolerated by Board of Directors and large shareholders. Other stakeholders, like minority shareholders, debt-holders or labor unions are typically complacent, if not directly involved in the management of the cartel, as part of the collusive rent tends to "trickle down" in one form or another to all employees and reduce the riskiness of the debtors' claims. This state of affairs should not be surprising. If the expected return of engaging in an unlawful conduct, such as price-fixing, is positive, firms will develop an internal organization that favors this conduct instead of discouraging it. Moreover, as for any rent that accrues to a firm, a collusive rent will be shared among several stakeholders according to their role in the activity or set of activities that give rise to the rent (and their bargaining power). All this is currently reflected in the most common compensation packages for managers—including stock-options—that base pay (and promotion) on short-run profits. Evidence suggests that employees facing these contracts are more likely to commit illegal acts that boost profits in the short and medium term, such as price-fixing, because they gain from the immediate benefit of the act, but do not bear its full cost (see Buccirossi and Spagnolo, 2006).

According to some authors (Werden and Simon, 1987; Polinsky and Shavell, 1993), to remedy this situation, we need sanctions that target directly those in the organization who are responsible for the illegal agreements. The threat of the sanction should be such as to counter the incentives individuals have to commit a crime, when private incentives are not enough. However, this argument, although intuitively appealing, avoids several intertwined questions that need to be fully understood before it can be accepted.

First and foremost, we need to understand why currently the internal organization of many firms is such that top managers are not adequately dissuaded from forming cartels. This may be due to at least two reasons. The first reason is that firms (shareholders) are not able to effectively monitor and punish managers that undertake illegal activities. The second reason is that firms do not have an incentive to do so. If, as we believe, given the current level of expected antitrust sanctions, at least in the EU firms (shareholders) are better off if they participate in hard-core cartels without deviating from the illegal agreement, then the reason that better explains the pro-collusive internal organization of firms is likely to be the second one. Therefore, before interfering with the way incentives are shaped within firms we should try to change the incentives of the organization so to align them to those of society. Our proposals in the previous sections are aimed at this end.

Second, provided that we have been able to make firms (shareholders) fully internalize the social costs of forming cartels, so that firms (shareholders) and public authorities (assuming that the latter pursue the maximization of social welfare) have the same incentives to trail and punish individuals who set up and coordinate cartels, who is in the best position to do it? Is public enforcement against individuals more efficient than an internal system of monitoring and punishment? This question is crucial because, if an internal mechanism is more efficient, then we should focus only on correcting the payoffs of the organization and not those of individuals that work within it. Polinsky and Shavell (1993), in a context of corporate tort, argue that, as the sanction that the firm can impose on managers is limited, shareholders may not be able to provide them with the correct incentive to exert an efficient level of care to avoid harms for which the firm can be held liable. This justifies the adoption of sanctions directly imposed on employees. However, firms can reward employees for good behavior rather than punish bad one, and if we introduce leniency and rewards to whistleblowers as a public law enforcement instrument, firms can always use them to compensate their managers for reporting the cartel, in which case they do not face the constraint identified by Polinsky and Shavell.

Third, sanctioning those agents who are directly responsible for the illegal act changes not only the incentives of these same agents, but also those of their principals that have the task of monitoring them. Individual liability alone may remove incentives for corporations to monitor crime *ex ante*, as principals, who are responsible for deciding the level of internal monitoring, are not directly penalized.[35] However, as shown by Arlen (1994), a regime of strict corporate

[35] See Instefjord et al. (1998) for an elegant formal analysis.

liability creates a problem of credibility of *ex post* policy measures (i.e. of the actions taken after the cartel has been formed and the responsible manager identified). Internal policing measures reduce expected liability insofar as the responsible manager is actually sanctioned *ex post*. Yet, *ex post* measures increase the probability that public law enforcers detect and sanction undeterred illegal conducts, increasing the firm's expected liability. This makes *ex post* sanctions not credible. The problem, though, arises only if the firms that discover a cartel and report it face a sanction. If reporting is rewarded with amnesty or monetary prizes, the credibility problem of *ex post* policy measures does not exist anymore, making internal monitoring a credible and viable policy instrument.

Our proposals aim at improving firms incentives to behave legally, to monitor its employees and to report misconducts. Imposing fines and providing rewards that affect the value of the firm, make shareholders (i.e. the ultimate principals) responsible for setting up an organization that minimizes the risk of antitrust liability. Directors and top managers will then be selected also for their ability to prevent subordinates from acting illegally, envisaging compensation and promotion policies that do not inadvertently encourage wrongdoing. Moreover, an informed and forward looking stock market might reward those firms that adopt effective compliance programs, as they reduce the risk of the corporate crime liability.

4.4.3. The "sunk cost bias" and optimal antitrust fines

All the literature on optimal fines against cartels in law and economics up to now, at least to our knowledge, is based on the standard rational choice paradigm in which economic agents maximize expected payoffs. Behavioral economics has become a lively field of research in recent years because empirical and experimental regularities in non-rational behavior have been shown to be sufficiently robust to be considered reliable primitives for economic reasoning and modeling.[36] In this section we focus on one particular behavioral regularity of economic agents that may have dramatic effects on the definition of an "optimal fine" against cartels, and on the relative convenience to use imprisonment in addition to fines: the so-called "sunk cost bias".

Experimental work shows that sunk costs affect following behavior, and in oligopolistic environments the unexpected effect of sunk costs is that of increasing following prices.[37] It is not clear whether the observed "sunk cost bias" is

---

[36] See Camerer (2003) for both an excellent introduction and an in-depth treatment.

[37] See Offerman and Potters (2005). Their original motivation was the European wave of UMTS spectrum auctions, and some governments' claim that they would prefer to award licenses through a Beauty Contest rather than an auction because the high license fees paid after the auction would lead winning firms to increase prices to recover the license fees, reducing consumer usage and welfare. The argument was readily discharged by many economists, as according to textbook economics sunk costs, like license fees, cannot affect pricing. Under standard forms of competition among profit-maximizing firms, marginal costs determine equilibrium prices and sunk costs do not affect marginal

caused by a form of coordination effects of sunk costs in terms of implicit collusion, to forms of mark up pricing rules used by bounded rational agents, or to a mixture of these effects. Some interpret this finding as agents typically prorating the cost of sunk investment as mark ups on future prices. This bias leads them to price more according to average cost, than to marginal cost. Furthermore, agents do not learn marginal cost pricing through profit and market share losses in repeated competitive situations: Convergence to marginal cost pricing in the long run is obtained only under monopoly, while with oligopolistic competition, agents do not learn "optimal" oligopolistic marginal cost pricing. Al-Najjar et al. (2005) recently developed a theoretical learning model that shows how such a bias may actually persist in an oligopoly, but disappear in a monopoly.[38]

Independently of its roots, this price effect of sunk costs, if really persistent in society, may have important implications for our discussion, and more generally for the theory of corporate law enforcement.

Suppose a cartel is detected, successfully prosecuted and fined by the law enforcement agency, and suppose that, after conviction, a cartel is no longer sustainable—e.g., because the agency and the customers are alerted and sanctions against repeated wrongdoers are higher. After the conviction and the fine payment, the convicted firms, if they are led by profit-maximizing managers, should consider the fine as a sunk cost that does not affect post conviction competitive prices (unless the fine is so high that it affects capital structure of the firms and its marginal cost of financing).

If, instead, convicted firms are led by managers subject to the "sunk cost bias", post conviction competitive prices increase because all managers would simultaneously add a mark up on their costs to recover the fine. If this correctly portrays the firms' behavior after a cartel is convicted, then:

(1) *Ceteris paribus*, fines needed to achieve a given level of cartel deterrence in the absence of leniency or whistleblowers programs would be even higher than those calculated in Section 4.2. This is because the simultaneous increase in competitive prices has a pro-collusive effect that allows firms to recover at least part of the fine. That is, any given fine has a reduced deterrence effect because it helps managers to raise competitive prices and transfer the fine on consumers.

---

costs. In such a profit maximizing environment, if a firm deviates from marginal cost pricing it would lose market share and profits, which should lead it to learn optimal pricing. Offerman and Potters showed that the argument was discharged too early, as in their experiment, when licenses are auctioned, prices increase substantially in the following oligopolistic interaction, all firms do pretty well on average, and do not change strategies.

38 This may seem not at all surprising, given that many business textbooks teach future managers precisely to price according to average cost, and that such a rule may appear intuitively appealing to many unsophisticated agents. Al-Najjar et al. (2005) provide a nice list of business textbooks conveying this message in a number of different and amusing ways.

(2) Higher competitive prices entail lower consumption and the same inefficiency (loss of social surplus) as price fixing. This means that fines are not pure, welfare-neutral, transfers but that they are socially costly to impose, the more the larger they are. This, in turn, implies that Becker's methodology for calculating an optimal fine should *not* be applied to corporations, as it disregards this inefficiency. Taking this inefficiency into account changes the way the optimal fine and the optimal level of fine-driven cartel deterrence should be determined, but it is not clear in which direction. There are at least two conflicting effects. An increase in the level of the fines increases future prices of convicted and prosecuted cartels and the relative inefficiency. This effect points at reducing fines. However, higher fines increases *ex-ante* deterrence, reducing the number of existing, detected and prosecuted cartels and the frequency with which the inefficiency is incurred. This second effect points at increasing the level of the fine.

(3) The sunk cost bias and its consequences, outlined above, is consistent with Sproul's (1993) puzzling and still unexplained empirical finding that colluding firms' prices do not fall after an antitrust conviction. Of course, that finding is also consistent with the hypothesis that the antitrust policy is too mild, and it is not easy to test which of these two explanations is more important.

(4) Because the cost of imposing fines increases while that of imposing non-financial sanctions does not, with the sunk cost bias imprisonment becomes relatively more attractive as a tool to deter cartels and any other corporate wrongdoing.

(5) Leniency and whistleblowers' schemes become even more effective, further reducing the need for high fines and imprisonment. A firm that self-reports first under a leniency program is not fined, while the others are. In the post-conviction competitive interaction, the firm that reported and did not pay a fine will set a lower price than competitors and enjoy an increase in market share and profits. In other words, with the sunk cost bias, leniency determines a post-conviction competitive advantage for the firm that self-reports first. This increases incentives to self-report, and reduces the level of post-conviction competitive prices and the inefficiency linked to higher prices.[39] A reward scheme of the type we have discussed, therefore, could reduce the inefficiency of fines even more. If the first reporting cartel member also enjoys a symmetric "sunk benefit bias" after having received the reward, in the post-conviction phase, it will enjoy or perceive an even stronger competitive advantage and will price even more aggressively than if it had just been granted immunity. This further increases the attractiveness of rewards, their deterrence effects, and lowers the inefficiency generated by the fines

[39] An analogous competitive advantage for cartel members that self-report under a leniency program—caused by the additional costs future rivals face because of remedies linked to antitrust conviction—is considered in a repeated oligopoly model with profit-maximizing firms by Ellis and Wilson (2002).

paid by other firms (who either will have to follow its price downward, or will loose market share so that a smaller fraction of consumers are exposed to inefficiently higher prices). This tends to reduce the need to introduce imprisonment.

(6) Whistleblowers' programs become even more efficient as they further reduce the (costly) financial fine with optimal deterrence properties.

The sunk cost bias, if it is important in the real world as it appears to be from the first experimental evidence available, is likely to have dramatic, but complex, effects on the optimal design of corporate and antitrust law enforcement policy. Understanding in depth these effects and how their interaction affects optimal fines, and the relative cost of fines and imprisonment requires a full-fledged theoretical analysis and more experimental and empirical research, and we must leave it to future work.

4.5. Conclusion

There are four main points the readers should retain after reading this essay. The first one is that past EU fines appear to have been too low to have sufficient deterrence effects. The second is that a different methodology should be used to correctly evaluate the likely deterrence effects of fines when an effective leniency program is in place. In the light of this improved method, current EU fines still appear insufficient, even if the leniency programs was implemented efficiently.[40] The third is that introducing imprisonment is certainly a possible solution to increase deterrence with its costs and benefits, but that well-designed and well-managed whistleblowers schemes could achieve the same result at a lower cost. The fourth is that more empirical and experimental research is needed to understand how to improve the enforcement of antitrust and corporate laws.

Words of caution. Errors cannot be eliminated. Hence, reducing the incentives to act illegally, either with high fines, imprisonment or with a system of fines and rewards, may have the undesired effect of reducing the incentives for firms to behave efficiently if there is a chance that their behavior can be mistakenly judged as illegal.

The legal system is an incentive scheme, and leniency and reward programs for whistleblowers, as well as prison sentences can be seen as "high powered" incentives. Economists are well aware that, if badly designed or badly implemented, high powered incentives can have very negative effects. Hence, leniency and whistleblower programs must be designed and implemented with great care,

---

[40] Recent empirical work by Brenner (2005) and Arlman (2005) suggests that the 1996 version of the EU Leniency program was not well implemented and therefore not helpful in terms of cartel deterrence.

otherwise they could generate counterproductive effects, as any other effective policy instrument.

It has been argued that rewards to whistleblowers could increase law enforcement costs by stimulating information fabrication to cash undue rewards. This claim does not seem to be empirically validated by the US experience under the False Claim Act, where very high rewards are paid to informants, and no serious information fabrication problem has, so far, emerged. The False Claim Act, though, is a very well-designed and well-administered program. Badly designed or badly implemented programs could, of course, lead to problems of information fabrication. Still, as argued in Spagnolo (2004), deterring information fabrication is feasible, and should not impede the introduction of rewards.

Nirvana is not yet here. Dworkin and Near (1997), among others, suggest that rewarding whistleblowers may contribute to an environment of mistrust and uncertainty and have negative effects on organizational efficiency. Kobayashi (2002) suggests that in the US we may be already close to overdeterrence, so that strengthening tools against cartels further could lead to higher internal monitoring costs for firms and higher prices for consumers (the US Congress strongly disagreed though, when it steeply increased sanctions against cartels in 2004). Aubert et al. (2005) analyze formally several situations in which firms may decide to adopt inefficient organizational decisions in order to reduce the risk of being convicted for collusion generated by leniency and whistleblowers' scheme. They point out that reward schemes may deter socially desirable cooperation, and show how these schemes may force colluding firms to reduce turnover in order to retain loyal but inefficient employees, or induce them to overinvest to mimic innocent behavior and avoid raising suspicions. However, these are costs that directly increase deterrence and welfare.

To sum up, the deterrence benefits of *carefully designed and implemented* leniency and reward schemes appear to strongly dominate the additional costs these may bring about, and appear able to solve the main problems that caused many to call for criminal sanctions and imprisonment. However, poorly designed and implemented leniency and whistleblowers' reward programs, as poorly administered criminal sanctions, have the potential to substantially harm welfare.

We conclude with a somewhat obvious statement: empirical research on antitrust law enforcement is highly needed! With so many good empirical economists working on fancy, and often policy irrelevant, subjects, will we manage to get some more of them to address policy relevant questions like these ones?

Acknowledgements

We thank Cecile Aubert, Piero Sabbatini, Michele Grillo, Cristiana Vitale, Paolo Siciliani, two anonymous referees, and participants at the inaugural conference of the Amsterdam Center for Law and Economics (ACLE, February 2005), the first meeting of the Italian Section of the Association of Competition Economics (Italian Antitrust Authority, Rome, October 2005), and the CEPR-European Science Foundation conference on The Effectiveness of Competition Policy: Issues and Methods (Paris, November 2005) for useful comments and stimulating discussions. Usual caveats apply. Spagnolo gratefully acknowledges funding from the Swedish Competition Authority.

References

Al-Najjar, N., Sandeep, B., Besanko, D. (2005), The sunk cost bias and managerial pricing practices. Manuscript, Northestern University.

Apesteguia, J., Dufwenberg, M., Selten, R. (2003), Blowing the whistle. Mimeo. Available from http://ssrn.com/abstract=47328, May 6.

Arlen, J.H. (1994), The potentially perverse effects of corporate criminal liability. *Journal of Legal Studies* 23, 832–867.

Arlman, S. (2005), Crime but no punishment. Master Thesis, University of Amsterdam. Available from http://www.encore.nl/news.htm.

Aubert, C., Kovacic, W., Rey, P. (2005), The impact of leniency and whistleblowers programs on cartels. *International Journal of Industrial Organization*, in press.

Baker, J. (2003), The case for antitrust enforcement. *Journal of Economics Perspectives* 17, 27–50.

Becker, G. (1968), Crime and punishment: An economic approach. *Journal of Political Economy* 76, 169–217.

Brenner, S. (2005), An empirical study of the European Corporate Leniency Program. Manuscript, University of Berlin.

Bryant, P.G., Eckard, E.W. (1991), Price fixing: The probability of getting caught. *The Review of Economics and Statistics* 73, 531–536.

Buccirossi, P., Spagnolo, G. (2001), The effects of leniency on illegal transactions: How (not) to fight corruption. Working Papers in Economics and Finance No. 456, Stockholm School of Economics (available for download at www.swopec.se and http://www.ssrn.com), forthcoming in reduced and revised form in the *Journal of Public Economics*.

Buccirossi, P., Spagnolo, G. (2006), Corporate governance and collusive behavior. In: Collins, W.D. (Ed.), *Issues in Competition Law and Policy*. American Bar Association, Antitrust Section, in press.

Calzolari, G., Spagnolo, G. (2005), Reputation and collusion in procurement. Manuscript, University of Bologna and Stockholm School of Economics.

Camerer, C. (2003), *Behavioral Game Theory: Experiments in Strategic Interaction*. Princeton University Press, New York.

Camilli, E. (2005), Optimal and actual fines in cartel cases: The European challenge. Paper presented at ACLE workshop on Remedies and Sanctions in Competition Policy, Amsterdam, February 2005, http://www.acle.nl/.

Che, Y., Spier, K. (2005), Strategic judgement proofing. Manuscript, University of Michigan.

Chen, J., Harrington, J. (2007), The impact of the corporate leniency program on cartel formation and the cartel price path. In: Ghosal, V., Stennek, J. (Eds.), *The Political Economy of Antitrust*. Elsevier. This volume.

Connor, J.M. (2003), Private international cartels: Effectiveness, welfare, and anticartel enforcement. Purdue Agricultural Economics Working Paper No. 03-12.

Connor, J.M. (2004), Price-fixing overcharges: Legal and economic evidence. American Antitrust Institute, Working Paper No. 04-05.

Connor, J.M. (2005), Optimal deterrence and private antitrust enforcement. Manuscript, Purdue University.

Connor, J.M., Lande, R.H. (2004), How high do cartels raise prices? Implications for reform of sentencing guidelines. American Antitrust Institute, Working Paper No. 04-01.

Crandall, R.W., Winston, C. (2003), Does antitrust policy improve consumer welfare? Assessing the evidence. *Journal of Economic Perspectives* 17, 3–26.

Craycraft, C., Craycraft, J.L., Gallo, J. (1997), Antitrust sanctions and firm ability to pay. *Review of Industrial Organization* 12, 171–183.

Dworkin, T.M., Near, J.P. (1997), A better statutory approach to whistleblowing. *Business Ethics Quarterly* 7, 1–16.

Ellis, C., Wilson, W. (2002), Cartels, price-fixing, and corporate leniency policy: What doesn't kill us makes us stronger. Manuscript, University of Oregon.

Fershtman, C., Pakes, A. (2000), A dynamic game with collusion and price wars. *RAND Journal of Economics* 31, 207–236.

Gallo, J.C., Dau Schmidt, K.G., Craycraft, J.L., Parker, C.J. (1994), Criminal penalties under the Sherman Act: A study of law and economics. *Research in Law and Economics* 16, 25–71.

Geradin, D., Henry, D. (2005), The EC fining policy for violations of competition law: An empirical review of the commission decisional practice and the community courts' judgments. In: Cseres, K.J., Schinkel, M.P., Vogelaar, F.O.W. (Eds.), *Remedies and Sanctions in Competition Policy: Economic and Legal Implications of the Tendency to Criminalize Antitrust Enforcement in the EU Member States*. Edwar Elgar, London, in press.

Hamaguchi, Y., Kawagoe, T. (2005), An experimental study of leniency programs. RIETI Discussion Paper Series 05-E-003.

Hinloopen, J., Soetevent, A.R. (2005), Do corporate leniency programs foster tacit collusion? An experimental study. University of Amsterdam.

Hiriart, Y., Martimort, D. (2005), The benefits of extended liability. Manuscript, IDEI Toulouse.

Instefjord, N., Jackson, P., Perraudin, W. (1998), Securities fraud. *Economic Policy* 27, 525–623.

Jolls, C. (2004), On law enforcement with boundedly rational actors. Olin Center for Law and Economics Discussion Paper 494, Harvard University.

Kaplow, L., Shavell, S. (1994), Optimal law enforcement with self-reporting of behavior. *Journal of Political Economy* 102, 583–606.

Kobayashi, B. (2002), Antitrust, agency and amnesty: An economic analysis of the criminal enforcement of the antitrust laws against corporations. George Mason University School of Law, Working Paper No. 02-04.

Kovacic, W. (2001), Private monitoring and antitrust enforcement: Paying informants to reveal cartels. *George Washington Law Review* 69, 766–797.

Kranton, R. (2003), Competition and the incentive to produce high quality. *Economica* 70, 385–404.

Kwoka, J.E. (2003), The attack on antitrust policy and policy and consumer welfare: A response to Crandall and Winston. Northeastern University, Working Paper.

Landes, W.M. (1983), Optimal sanctions for antitrust violations. *The University of Chicago Law Review* 50, 652–678.

Levenstein, M.C., Suslow, V.Y. (2002), What determines cartel success? University of Michigan Business School Working Paper No. 02-001.

McCoutcheon, B. (1997), Does meeting in smoke-filled rooms facilitate collusion? *Journal of Political Economy* 105, 330–350.

Motchenkova, E. (2005), Optimal enforcement of competition law. Ph.D. Dissertation, Tilburg University.

Motta, M., Polo, M. (2003), Leniency programs and cartel prosecution. *International Journal of Industrial Organization* 21, 347–379.

Mullin, W., Snyder, C. (2005), Targeting employees for corporate crime and forbidding their indemnification. Working Paper, George Washington University.

Offerman, T., Potters, J. (2005), Does auctioning of entry licenses induce collusion? An experimental study. Manuscript, *Review of Economic Studies*.

Polinsky, M., Shavell, S. (1993), Should employees be subject to fines and imprisonment given the existence of corporate liability? *International Review of Law and Economics* 13, 239–257.

Polinsky, M., Shavell, S. (2000), The economic theory of public enforcement of law. *Journal of Economic Literature* 38, 45–76.

Posner, R.A. (2001), *Antitrust Law: An Economic Perspective*, 2nd ed., University of Chicago Press, Chicago.

Rey, P. (2003), Towards a theory of competition policy. In: Dewatripont, M., Hansen, L.P., Turnovsky, S.J. (Eds.), *Advances in Economics and Econometrics: Theory and Applications—Eight World Congress, vol. II, No. 36*. Cambridge University Press, Cambridge, pp. 82–132.

Shavell, S. (1986), The judgement proof problem. *International Review of Law and Economics* 6, 45–58.

Shavell, S. (2004), Minimum asset requirements and compulsory liability insurance as solutions to the judgment proof problem. Harvard, John. M. Olin Center for Law, Economics and Business Discussion Paper No. 456.

Spagnolo, G. (2000a), Optimal leniency programs. F.E.E.M. Nota di Lavoro No. 42.00, Fondazione ENI "Enrico Mattei," Milano, http://www.ssrn.com.

Spagnolo, G. (2000b), Self-defeating antitrust laws: How leniency programs solve Bertrand's paradox and enforce collusion in auctions. F.E.E.M. Nota di Lavoro No. 52.00, Fondazione ENI "Enrico Mattei," Milano, http://www.ssrn.com.

Spagnolo, G. (2003), Banks as collusive devices. Working Paper in Economics and Finance No. 243, Stockholm School of Economics.

Spagnolo, G. (2004), Divide et impera: Optimal leniency programs. CEPR Discussion Paper No. 4840, http://www.ssrn.com.

Spagnolo, G. (2005), Cartels criminalization and their internal organization. In: Cseres, K.J., Schinkel, M.P., Vogelaar, F.O.W. (Eds.), *Remedies and Sanctions in Competition Policy: Economic and Legal Implications of the Tendency to Criminalize Antitrust Enforcement in the EU Member States*. Edwar Elgar, London, in press.

Spagnolo, G. (2006), Leniency and whistleblowers in antitrust. In: Buccirossi, P. (Ed.), *Handbook of Antitrust Economics*. MIT Press, Cambridge, MA, in press.

Sproul, M. (1993), Antitrust and prices. *Journal of Political Economy* 101, 741–754.

Stigler, G.J. (1964), A theory of oligopoly. *The Journal of Political Economy* 72, 44–61.

Stiglitz, J. (1989), Imperfect information in the product market. In: Schmalensee, R., Willig, R. (Eds.), *Handbook of Industrial Organization*, vol. 1. Elsevier Science Publishers, Amsterdam, pp. 771–847.

Summers, J.J. (1983), The case of the disappearing defendant: An economic analysis. *University of Pennsylvania Law Review* 132, 145–185.

UK Department of Trade and Industry (2001), A World Class Competition Regime. The Stationery Office, London.

Werden, G.J. (2003), The effect of antitrust policy on consumer welfare: What Crandall and Winston overlook. U.S. Department of Justice, Antitrust Division Discussion Paper No. EAG 03-2.

Werden, G.J., Simon, M.J. (1987), Why price fixers should go to prison. *The Antitrust Bulletin* 32, 917–937.

Wils, W. (2003), Should private antitrust enforcement be encouraged in Europe? *World Competition* 26, 473–488.

Wils, W. (2005a), Is criminalization of EU competition law the answer? In: Cseres, K.J., Schinkel, M.P., Vogelaar, F.O.W. (Eds.), *Remedies and Sanctions in Competition Policy: Economic and Legal Implications of the Tendency to Criminalize Antitrust Enforcement in the EU Member States*. Edwar Elgar, London, in press.

Wils, W. (2005b), Optimal antitrust fines: Theory and practice. *Journal of Competition Law and Economics*, in press.

CHAPTER 5

Instruments for Cartel Deterrence, and Conflicts of Interests

Cécile Aubert

Université Paris Dauphine (EURIsCO), Dpt. Economie Appliquée, Place de Lattre de Tassigny, 75 016 Paris, France
E-mail address: Cecile.Aubert@dauphine.fr

5.1. Introduction

The different instruments that an antitrust authority can use to deter collusion can have diverse impacts on interest groups. Many of these instruments can be characterized as either a 'stick' (as fines and jail sentences in case of conviction) or a 'carrot' (as a fine exemption in case evidence is provided by the firm to the antitrust intervention). Such carrots help obtain evidence on existing cartels, thereby deterring some potential collusive activities, and are made necessary by the rarity of freely provided information. While some instruments act at the corporate level, others may target individuals. Their effect on taxpayers, shareholders, or employees, can differ strongly, while their effect on consumers can be roughly approximated by their deterrent power. Identifying these effects helps assess the potential adverse effects of some instruments and understand the reluctance to use some that seem quite effective.

This chapter argues that information on existing cartels is unlikely to be often provided for free by economic parties. One should therefore design programs so as to induce the revelation of this information (the 'carrot' component of antitrust intervention), as with Leniency Programs. Leniency Programs aim at increased cartel deterrence by granting corporate and individual amnesty when a firm denounces its participation in an as yet undetected cartel. It has been shown that one could potentially obtain more information with the use of whistleblowing programs, that are less constrained instruments than Leniency Programs since they grant bounties to informants. Individual (rather than corporate) whistleblowing programs allow maximizing revenues compared to a corporate program. They however have more subtle effects with respect to intra-firm agency problems. The issue of incentives for managers and high executives deserves particular attention. Managerial incentives may indeed be affected in an adverse way by otherwise quite effective policies, leading to suboptimal effort choices from managers, as we will see in a simple setting in which the punishments that shareholders can impose on managers are bounded.

CONTRIBUTIONS TO ECONOMIC ANALYSIS
VOLUME 282 ISSN: 0573-8555
DOI: 10.1016/S0573-8555(06)82005-5

Agency problems between shareholders and managers may be exacerbated or lessened according to the instruments used by the antitrust authority. Managers can choose the market conduct of the firm jointly with their (costly) effort to increase profits. A sharp penalty on managers in case of proven collusion obviously makes it more difficult to convince them to collude, while inducing a competitive behavior together with a high effort becomes easier. And a bounty when managers report information on collusive agreements may lead to the break-up of the agreement. Both instruments are therefore a priori effective collusion deterrents. A concern has often been expressed that bounties might give managers incentives to collude (in order to later report information to the antitrust authority) even when shareholders wanted the firm to compete; inducing competition would thus become more costly. The optimal reaction of shareholders should however be taken into account, together with the anticipation by managers that their counterparts in competing firms have similar incentives to their own in equilibrium. We will see that individual and whistleblowing programs directed at managers may give rise to a different type of adverse effects, with respect to *effort incentives*.

This chapter is organized as follows: after summarizing the tools used in different countries to deter cartels, it argues that information will not often be provided freely, which justifies using Leniency and whistleblowing programs to induce reports. The possibility of rewarding individuals, and particularly employees of the concerned firms, raises the issue of potential conflicts between managers' and shareholders' interests. We analyze this issue in a very simple model that highlights that collusion can be used by managers as a way to save on costly effort. Leniency and individual fines are shown to be complementary in this setting. A main concern that has arisen with respect to bounties programs is whether the prospect of bounties can give incentives to the manager to collude in order to later report, when shareholders would have wished the firm to act competitively. We will see that a 'reasonable' bounty does not give rise to such adverse incentives. But the existence of a leniency program can adversely affect incentives, not with respect to market conduct, but with respect to effort choices. It may be that efficient competition, that could be obtained thanks to the threat of individual fines, is no longer feasible. It is then helpful to restrict leniency to the first reporting employee.

Note that the model we use will allow us to get some insights as to the economic efficiency of various instruments, with respect to effort and market conduct incentives. But the choice of instruments by antitrust authorities is likely to also depend on political feasibility.[1] Parties are known to exert forceful lobbying during antitrust investigations as well—the most notable example probably

[1] The literature on the political economy of trade policy (e.g., Mayer, 1984; Grossman and Helpman, 1994; Yang, 1995) has studied how tariffs could be chosen by governments trading off the benefits offered by lobbies and rent-seekers with loss in consumers welfare and potential political costs. The political economy of regulation has also been extensively studied since the seminal works of Stigler (1971), Peltzman (1976) and Becker (1983). Conversely, the role of interest groups in antitrust policy-making has received less attention (McChesney, 1991; McChesney and Shughart,

being the AT&T divestiture in 1984. And the budget allocated to the antitrust authority depends on political factors. We will not investigate these issues here, but will stress in Section 5.3 that some other interest groups than colluding firms may sometimes be reluctant to put an end to collusion.

Stick and carrot instruments

Although fines for price-fixing and other types of cartel behavior have been increased in the United States and the European Union (see Section 5.2), many analysts believe that these fines are still too low to deter cartels. Cartels indeed continue to form and operate in a significant number of industries (Connor, 2004; Levinstein and Suslow, 2004). One of the solutions considered is imposing criminal sanctions on individuals participating in price-fixing agreements (Wils, 2005), as is already done for instance in the United States, or more recently the U.K., Ireland or Estonia (with its first criminal judgment in 2004).

A second direction for increasing cartel deterrence is using a 'carrot', instead of a 'stick'. National competition agencies have achieved notable successes in prosecuting cartels thanks to the adoption, or to the revision, of Leniency Programs. Such programs, as the ones set up in the United States in 1993 and in the European Union in 1996, grant amnesty to the first firm that reports information on a cartel not yet under investigation.[2] The 'stick' and the 'carrot' approaches can of course be complementary: According to Hammond (2000) and Spratling (1999), one of the major reasons of the success of the U.S. Leniency Program is the fear of imprisonment for corporate officials, that complements a 'race to the courtroom' to obtain leniency. And the increase in fines makes leniency more attractive.

Up to now, no Leniency Program offers positive rewards, rather than simply reduced fines. Private parties may obtain treble damages in the United States, but most private actions follow criminal prosecution, and do therefore allow unveiling existing cartels. Offering positive rewards to informants (not only victims of the cartel) is independently suggested by Spagnolo (2003) and Aubert et al. (2005). In a different context, the U.S. Civil False Claims Act rewards individuals who inform the government of fraud in procurement contracts by a substantial share of the fines collected—an amount sufficient to compensate employees for the stream of foregone future wages (Kovacic, 1996; Tokar, 2000).[3]

1995). Rowley and Rathbone (2004) note that the Chicago School, famous for denouncing the costs of a regulation driven by lobbying, has not criticized antitrust policy in the same way. Regulation may indeed be more easily subject to pressure at it is a long-lasting intervention, with better identified winners/losers.

[2] See European Union (1996), Harding and Joshua (2003), Kobayashi (2001), and Spratling (2001).

[3] For a total number of 4,294 cases filed by September 2003, the Department of Defense and the Department of Health and Human Services have respectively recovered \$ 1,592,513,253 (with \$ 291,031,106 for informants), and \$ 5,177,682,597 (with \$ 851,646,391 for informants).

It does not seem to have given rise to large adverse effects. Kovacic (2001) offers a legal perspective on how the Civil False Claims Act approach could be adapted for use by antitrust authorities in prosecuting cartels.

Despite the relative success of the Civil False Claims Act, there exists a reluctance to use similar bounty mechanisms for fighting cartels. This reluctance stems apparently mostly from ethical issues and from a fear of adverse effects on firms' incentives. Managers or other high-level executives are often in a position to take decisions as to the firm's conduct, possibly against the recommendations of shareholders. The latter may be prevented from running a collusive agreement if their managers cannot be induced not to deviate from it. But one may fear that the managers temporarily collude in order to obtain bounties in the future, even though shareholders recommended fair competition. These effects are the object of Sections 5.4 and 5.5.

Literature and modeling issues

In order to assess the impact of antitrust investigation, jail sentences, and leniency and whistleblowing programs on different interest groups, and particularly shareholders and managers, we use a very simple modeling incorporating some elements of the literature on leniency programs, reporting, and managerial compensation.

Cartel deterrence and Leniency Programs

We model collusion and Leniency Programs in a simple dynamic framework as in Motta and Polo (2001), Spagnolo (2003) and Aubert et al. (2005). Communication is taken as a prerequisite for collusion, as in McCutcheon (1997). It allows coordination on a collusive agreement, but firms remain free to implement this agreement or not, as in a standard tacit collusion situation. Communication moreover generates evidence that can be found by the antitrust authority, as well as by firms or individuals.[4]

We do not specify the budget constraint that the antitrust authority may face, and the probability of an antitrust investigation is taken as given. This prevents us from including the benefits of Leniency Programs related to saving on investigation costs. To the contrary, Motta and Polo (2001) specify a budget constraint and show that it can be efficient to grant leniency even after an investigation has started, to save on the costs of finding decisive evidence. Leniency and whistleblowing programs may nonetheless be valuable for other reasons, since they make collusion less substainable.

Spagnolo (2003) argues that positive corporate rewards can help deter collusion at no cost. Aubert et al. (2005) obtain the same result in a slightly different

---

[4] Purely tacit collusion cannot be punished by antitrust authorities since firms act noncooperatively (see Werden, 2004, and the well-known woodpulp case).

model, and show that rewards for individuals can be more effective than corporate leniency, and even than corporate rewards. They may exacerbate agency problems within the firm and may encourage employees and managers to gather and keep evidence.

Collusion and managerial rewards

The impact of the incentive schemes received by managers on the intensity of competition has been studied in games of strategic delegation, especially by Fershtman and Judd (1987), Sklivas (1987), Fershtman et al. (1987) or Aggarwal and Samwick (1999). Committing to a particular incentive scheme can indeed be a way for shareholders to credibly promise to compete more or less than they would have done without delegation. In Fershtman and Judd (1987), for instance, shareholders simultaneously choose the incentive scheme for their own manager before a second stage in which managers compete in an oligopolistic market. The wage scheme being given in this second stage, delegation to the manager solves a commitment issue for the shareholders. Spagnolo (2000) adopts a different perspective by considering stock-related compensation (as stock options) in the infinitely repeated game framework used to model tacit collusion. He shows that this type of compensation, delayed for one period, can lessen short-run incentives to deviate, provided that stock markets anticipate the decline in future profits after a deviation, and correspondingly reduce the stock price. Full collusion becomes possible for any discount factor. In order to introduce antitrust intervention in a coherent way, we prefer to rule out the role of the stock market, and we only briefly discuss the role of stock options when the stock market has imperfect foresight (an issue in our framework is that we need to make assumptions about the revision of belief out of the equilibrium path). We allow the manager to adjust his effort to the conduct she chooses, so as to potentially masks her market conduct choice.

Corporate crime

The literature on corporate crime mostly considers situations in which the manager or employee committing a crime acts in his best interest, but harms shareholders when so doing. Mullin and Snyder (2005) argue that in a number of cases, shareholders benefit from the crime, while the manager undertakes it only because the incentives she receives from shareholders make it optimal to do so. When the manager obtains no gain when committing a crime and the government authority can make mistakes and convict innocent firms, Mullin and Snyder show that imposing penalties on the manager is optimal. They also show that forbidding indemnification may be optimal if the authority seeks to enlist the cooperation of the manager. It can then offer a reduction in fines (as in a Leniency program) in exchange for cooperation, but such a reduction is only attractive to the manager if she is not fully indemnified. The analysis applies to cartels, even though it appears less likely that the antitrust authority mistakes innocent conduct for collusion, than for some other types of corporate crime.

The chapter is organized as follows. Section 5.2 summarizes the enforcement features of various developed countries. Section 5.3 summarizes the incentives that various interest groups have to denounce collusive behavior when aware of it. Sections 5.4 and 5.5 focus on conflicts of interest between shareholders and managers: Section 5.4 sets up a simple model, while Section 5.5 considers the effects of rewards and jail penalties on remuneration schemes and effort choices, and ultimately on shareholders' preference for collusion. Section 5.6 concludes.

5.2. The various instruments used for cartel deterrence in major O.E.C.D. countries

This section sketches the enforcement systems in different O.E.C.D. countries, with respect to the existence of jail sentences, Leniency Programs and other prominent features. We do not describe them in detail as our aim is to underline that these experiences are now sufficiently diverse to allow useful inference a few years from now.[5]

5.2.1. Recent trends towards more severe penalties

Before describing the general features of these systems, let us first stress the recent increase in penalties for price-fixing and other collusive agreements. The U.S. have recently strongly increased the maximum fines for cartel participants in 2001, and then again in 2004 with the Antitrust Criminal Penalty Enhancement Act (Klawiter, 2001; Hammond, 2005). The statutory maximum fine under the Sherman Act for corporations has increased from US $ 10 million in 2001 to ten times this amount, US $ 100 million since 2004, independently of the economic harm generated by the violation. Corporate violators can be assessed fines equal to twice the gain derived by the wrongdoer or twice the injury suffered by victims of the cartel.[6] The monetary maximum indicated for individual fines has increased from US $ 350 000 to US $ 1 million. And jail sentences, that could not exceed three years in 2001, can now reach ten years.

The European Union has followed a similar move towards the imposition of higher penalties. In France, the Conseil de la Concurrence has recently imposed much larger fines than in the past, as for the cartel on mobile telecommunications (256 million euros for Orange France, and 220 million euros for SFR). Japan has decided in April 2005 to double the maximum administrative fine on cartel participants (up to 10% of sales). In addition to the general increase in fines,

---

[5] We will not consider here the various legal restrictions on the modes of intervention, interviewing and searching by antitrust authorities.

[6] The criminal fines paid in 1999 by Hoffmann-LaRoche and BASF for their participation in the vitamins cartel reached US $ 500 million and US $ 225 million respectively. The second largest fine ($ 300 million) has been imposed in October 2005 on Samsung for a cartel in DRAM (Dynamic Random Access Memory).

several countries (most prominently the U.K. and Ireland) have switched to a criminal system and have introduced jail sentences, thereby increasing expected punishments for given fines levels.

5.2.2. The U.S.A.: A criminal system

The Sherman Act (1890) has resulted in antitrust enforcement powers being given to the Antitrust Division within the Department of Justice, thus naturally to a criminal system in which courts ultimately decide after a contradictory procedure. Due to the existence of such contradiction, the evidence provided by the Antitrust Division does not have to be as 'decisive' as in the E.U. (copies of documents and testimonies are accepted, including within the Leniency Program). Another important aspect is that individuals can be sentenced to imprisonment if convicted of collusive behavior. Many U.S. officials insist on the importance of this threat as a deterrent. Since 1999, more than a hundred individuals have served, or are serving, prison sentences related to antitrust enforcement, and the average term has increased from about 8 months by 2000, to 24 months in 2005 (Hammond, 2005). Incarceration is not limited to U.S. nationals as about twenty individuals from other nationalities have been incarcerated. To ensure that staying outside the U.S. is not sufficient to escape the sentence, the Antitrust Division uses since 2001 cooperation via Interpol, for fugitives to be arrested by cooperating polices and later extradited.

In addition to these 'stick' measures, the Leniency Program offers incentives to report existing cartels by providing full amnesty to the first informant. As in other existing Leniency Programs, information obtained from an amnesty applicant is not disclosed to other authorities, except if the applicant agrees to it. Reporting might indeed otherwise be costly to a firm, as it could be pursued by foreign authorities for the information it is revealing. To give firms added incentives, the U.S. are offering an 'Amnesty Plus' Program: A firm that is under an investigation can apply for amnesty in other markets than the one investigated. Even if the firm does not qualify for amnesty on this first market, its cooperation on a second cartel allows it to obtain, not only amnesty for the second offense, but also an additional reduction in fine for the first cartel. This supplementary reduction can be interpreted as a *reward* (rather than a reduced fine) in case of reporting with respect to the second market.

On the other hand, if a firm decides not to report the existence of collusion on a second market, and this collusion is later proved, a 'Penalty Plus' applies: the Antitrust Division 'will urge the sentencing court to consider the company's and any culpable executive's failure to report the conduct voluntarily as an aggravating sentencing factor [. . .] and will pursue a fine or jail sentence at or above the upper end of the Sentencing Guidelines range' (Hammond, 2005).[7]

---

[7] In a 'penalty plus case', Hoechst AG had to pay a fine of roughly 70% of the volume of affected commerce.

The U.S. enforcement system appears quite efficient as there is anecdotal evidence that cartel members avoid meeting, and even operating, in the U.S. for fear of criminal sanctions (an example is the reluctance of participants to the lysine cartel to meet in Hawaii, expressed in a phone call recorded by the U.S. Department of Justice).

5.2.3. The United Kingdom and Ireland: Moving to a criminal system

The Competition Act (1998) in the United Kingdom describes infringements (Chapter I and II) in a similar way to E.C. Articles 81 and 82, and the U.K. Leniency Program follows the general rules of the 1996 version of the European L.P. The Competition Act has been amended on 1 May 2004 to empower the Office of Fair Trading (O.F.T.) to investigate and impose penalties on undertakings breaching the prohibitions on anti-competitive behavior contained in Articles 81 and 82 of the EC Treaty. More importantly for our concern, the U.K. has recently departed from the E.C. model: the Enterprise Act (2002) indeed introduces a cartel offence under which individuals taking part in the most serious types of anti-competitive agreements may be criminally prosecuted. Anyone convicted of the offence could receive a maximum of five years imprisonment and/or an unlimited fine (unless protected by application to the Leniency Program). In addition, as a result of amendments to the Company Directors Disqualification Act (1986) under the Enterprise Act, company directors may be subject to Competition Disqualification Orders, which will prevent them from being concerned in the management of a company for a maximum of 15 years. This criminal system together with directors disqualification[8] are the most noticeable features of antitrust enforcement in the U.K. The move to a criminal system is however very recent and it is not possible to draw any inference from observation at this date.

Ireland has also recently chosen a criminal system under the Competition Act (2002): The maximum fine for corporations is 'whichever of the following amounts is the greater, namely, Euros 4,000,000 or 10 per cent of the turnover of the undertaking in the financial year ending in the 12 months prior to the conviction'. In the case of individuals, the same maximum applies, 'or [...] imprisonment for a term not exceeding 5 years or to both such fine [...] and such imprisonment'. The Competition Authority launched its own Leniency Program, the 'Cartel Immunity Programme' in December 2001. It is explicitly mentioned that 'applications for immunity for an individual employed by an undertaking involved in a cartel will be considered, even where the employer undertaking does not apply or otherwise co-operate under this programme' (Section D). This appears as a useful complement to a criminal system.

As for the United Kingdom, however, the change is too recent to offer valuable insight for now (no jail sentences have been pronounced at this date).

---

[8] Both features are obviously independent, and disqualification may even be viewed as some imperfect substitute for imprisonment.

5.2.4. France and Germany: The E.C. model with some twists

Since May 2001, the French Conseil de la Concurrence offers a Leniency Program ('procédure de clémence', art. L. 464-2 III) for firms that denounce their participation in a cartel. A more original feature is that it also offers a system of plea bargaining inspired by the U.S. and rather unusual for France ('procédure de transaction'): firms that admit their participation and commit to modify their behavior can obtain a reduction in fines (art. L. 464-2 II).

In Germany the Bundeskartellamt set up in 2002 a Special Unit for Combating Cartels (SKK) to increase the quota of uncovered cartel agreements and to speed up proceedings. A Leniency Programme exists since 2000 and follows the 1996 version of the E.C. Leniency Program. The German system is relatively close to the French one. An interesting point is that Germany has expressed a fear that reports be less credible under a Leniency Program: 'The Bundeskartellamt is aware that any statements by cartel members, who expect the fines impending to be considerably reduced as a result of their cooperation, must be treated with caution. Before a statement can serve as the basis of proof of the existence of a cartel and of the extent to which each member was involved, it must always be supported by other evidence.' (Notice No. 68/2000 on the guidelines of the Bundeskartellamt relating to the setting of fines.) This fear of falsified reports with leniency should certainly be addressed for the political acceptability of leniency and rewards to improve.

Other experiences should of course be worth some investigation. Japan, that has a criminal system inspired by the U.S., has introduced with the Antimonopoly Act (2005) a leniency program that grants full amnesty for the first company reporting prior to the commencement of an investigation, and a 30% reduction in the administrative fines for the second leniency applicant. Leniency (even partial) is restricted to the first two informants, a particular feature. Last, one can note that some countries appear relatively behind others with respect to cartel deterrence, as they have not introduced a Leniency Program yet. This is the case of Italy. A few years from now, the comparison of the outcome of these various experiences should allow applied economists to make useful recommendations.

5.3. May we expect freely provided information on collusive practices?

This section investigates to what extent competition policy may rely on information provided by various parties aware of (or strongly suspecting) collusive practices. According to Stigler (1982), 'If you propose an antitrust law, the only people who should be opposed to it are those who hope to become monopolists'. We however argue below that the incentives of various parties to provide information are not as strong as they may seem. This implies that, if a whistle-blowing program is set up, bounties may be needed in excess of litigation costs coverage, in order to compensate for potential costs associated with reporting (like losing one's position for an employee who reports about its firm's misconduct, but also other costs we detail below).

Numerous legal dispositions set up a duty to report particular information and impose higher fines on individuals or firms who did not report it, thus providing external incentives to report. The obligations to report have an obvious legal value and allow imposing fines and requesting closer supervision. We will not discuss them further, despite their practical value and focus below on parties' intrinsic incentives to report.[9]

5.3.1. Final customers

Incentives to provide information

Final consumers are the most obvious victims of collusive practices and clearly loose from collusion. Colluding firms sometimes try to justify their collusive practices by the need to coordinate to invest in new technologies, provide a better quality or to avoid over-use of a particular resource, all positive elements from the point of view of customers. Yet this is widely viewed as a non-valid justification: rather than adding another market imperfection such as collusion, one should try and solve for the first imperfection.[10] Final consumers should therefore always prefer antitrust intervention, possibly together with adequate regulation.

Adverse incentives

Final customers may nevertheless not be good informants due to lack of information as to what the 'normal' price and market conditions should be. In addition, they may also not have good incentives to actively look for collusive practices as, first, they tend not to be organized, and second, they may find it preferable to let antitrust authorities, with their better expertise, investigate on their behalf.[11]

Last, final consumers can sometimes be wary of competition in particular cases, if they fear that it will bring a worsening of quality of service: This appears to be a major concern of the general public when regulated, public utilities

---

[9] In the case of collusive behavior, shareholders and managers can use internal compliance programs, and invoke them to reduce their liability in case collusion is nevertheless proved to have taken place. They must nevertheless show evidence that the program was indeed functioning.

[10] If R&D requires coordination, this should come from a legal agreement, possibly a joint venture. And if pollution, or use of a non-renewable resource, make it preferable to lessen production, this should follow from focused government intervention, like imposing pollution or production quotas, or creating a market for pollution permits.

[11] Antitrust staff may devote more attention to cases involving final customers, as they often benefit from extended media coverage. Lawyers and economists within the authority need to signal their high ability to their future employers, and have therefore incentives to select cases involving large firms, well-known to the general public, or products that are widely consumed, often by end-users—as for instance the cartel on soccer shirts in the UK. Final customers can thus expect antitrust authorities to work well on their behalf.

undergo deregulation and removal of state entry barriers. The treatment by the French media of the promotion by the E.C. of entry in postal services and gas, provides a good example: Its (on average) quite negative tone conveys concerns with public service and USO obligations—that seem to require ongoing state monopoly in the view of the general public. Demonstrations by trade unions against the privatization of Gaz de France go the same way, and prove that political economy aspects may be difficult to seize with a simple cost–benefit analysis.

5.3.2. Downstream and upstream firms

Let us now consider a cartelized industry that produces an input for a second industry, the downstream industry. It also itself uses as an input a good produced by some upstream industry.

Incentives to provide information

Since colluding firms contract output, downstream customers will obtain lower quantities at a higher price, so that their profits can be expected to decrease with collusion. Upstream firms will undergo a reduction in their sales, hence also lowered profits. Collusion can also improve the bargaining power of the firms with respect to their suppliers and retailers. Upstream and downstream firms may therefore learn some information as to the existence of a cartel, and may want to denounce it.

Adverse incentives

Although upstream and downstream firms often suffer from the existence of collusion, there may be situations in which this collusion is profitable to them, in which case they will not want to bring it to term. To avoid raising suspicions, colluding firms tend to avoid large price changes (as analyzed in Harrington, 2004; Harrington and Chen, 2005) and will not react as strongly to economic shocks as competing firms would do. Collusion in the first industry thus imply less risk for the downstream and upstream participants. This facilitates tacit collusion in the vertically related market, as deviations from a collusive agreement downstream (or upstream) will be more noticeable. In a model à la Green and Porter (1984), the reduction in uncertainty allows for more efficient collusion downstream (or upstream). In addition, if the industry to which firms buy or sell their production is also collusive, profits from a unilateral deviation are lower: a deviating firm faces a smaller demand than if its customers were competing.[12]

---

[12] Bernheim and Whinston (1985) have shown how using a common retailer may help firms coordinate and collude. Several recent papers focus on how retail price maintenance can help reduce interbrand competition. Jullien and Rey (2001) base their analysis on the idea that retail price maintenance prevents prices from reacting strongly to demand and cost conditions, hence mak-

Thus collusion in an industry has a direct negative effect on profits in vertically related industries; but by reducing uncertainty and limiting deviation opportunities, it may make it easier for these vertically related markets to collude. Contrary to common beliefs, one may therefore not always expect customers to come forward with information when they discover that their suppliers/retailers are colluding.

5.3.3. Workers' interests

Incentives to provide information

By restricting output, collusion also restricts employment. Workers should therefore oppose collusion, and denounce it when they have information about it.

Adverse incentives

One should note that an employee faces losses when she reports her information to the antitrust authority. If secrecy is difficult to maintain, for instance because few employees had access to sensitive information, a reporting employee faces a high risk of retaliation—at least losing her job, perhaps permanently. If she expects staff reorganization after a cartel decision, she may fear losing her job even if secrecy is maintained. Employees should be compensated for these expected costs. This justifies granting bounties to reporting employees, a possibility we discuss further later.

It may also be the case in some instances that collusion enables one of the firms to survive, or to survive without restructuring, so that current employees may fear redundancy in case their firm is convicted. And colluding firms may be able to exclude outsiders from the market, possibly maintaining local employment at the expense of foreign or non local employment in the firms that are excluded. Local workers may therefore sometimes favor collusion, as they might favor non-competitive practices in large and regulated firms that are major employers in a particular area.

5.3.4. The shareholders

The situation of shareholders is different from that of the other interest groups mentioned above, as shareholders directly benefit from the higher profits obtained by a firm thanks to collusion. This benefit may nevertheless be lessened if

---

ing deviations easier to detect in a tacit collusion setting. Dobson and Waterson (1997) and Rey and Verge (2004) use on the other hand a static model in which two producers can use any of two potential retailers—and possibly both. While Dobson and Waterson restrict the analysis to linear wholesale prices (hence giving rise to a double marginalization issue), Rey and Verge use two-part tariffs (solving for the double marginalization issue) and show that retail price maintenance indeed reduce competition in such a way that the monopoly outcome can be achieved.

the shareholders also possess equity in vertically related markets that are hurt by collusion upstream or downstream. And all shareholders may not wish to foster collusion, even in the absence of antitrust sanctions. Shareholders may indeed have diverging preferences for the present, so that some may prefer deviations to persistent collusion. However, shareholders, who will have to bear the cost of fines if the firm is convicted, can be expected to have very few incentives to provide information about an existing cartel agreement to an antitrust authority.

In the presence of antitrust sanctions, shareholders may also have divergent views as to the desirability of collusion, and of reporting, if they differ in their degree of risk aversion, and in their ability to insure and diversify. It is thus likely that informed[13] shareholders will not hold a unanimous view as to the desirability of a collusive behavior or of an amnesty application.

Allowing a shareholder to apply to a Leniency Program even in the absence of a general agreement of the board may allow for more information disclosure: A Leniency Program does not have to be as generous to be effective if it needs only be attractive to the informed shareholder with the weakest preference for collusion.[14]

5.4. Managerial incentive contracts and collusion

Since shareholders benefit from collusion, the question of their responsibility in inducing collusive agreement arises. Should shareholders be subject to extended liability? In the U.S., shareholders should prove that they have made good use of a compliance program to be exempted from responsibility. Buccirossi and Spagnolo (2006) suggest going further: Since fines cannot be increased above certain bounds for fear of bankruptcy and lessened competitiveness in the industry, they suggest a dilution of shares of convicted firms, thereby penalizing shareholders. Controlling shareholders will then prefer to induce a competitive behavior, provided that the probability of conviction and the extent of share dilution are large enough.

Shareholders may have difficulties inducing the manager to maximize firm's profits while avoiding the occurrence of collusion. Providing incentives to managers and high executives that are very strongly linked with profits (such as a very large share of stock options) can be justified by moral hazard issues within the firm, but it can also induce the choice of more risky options, including collusion. We address this issue with a simple model. This section focuses on the impact of the instruments for cartel deterrence discussed in the introduction, on the cost for shareholders of giving adequate incentives to managers, when these managers can privately choose the type of conduct of the firm, together with their effort level. They can then substitute effort and collusion, since collusion allows obtaining higher profits without exerting much effort.

---

13 Obviously, small shareholders are unlikely to be aware of the collusive conduct of the firm.

14 The effectiveness of such an extension of a Leniency Program may however be restricted by the lack of access of some shareholders to documents constituting evidence of collusion.

5.4.1. The basic model

We follow the general framework of Aubert et al. (2005) with potential collusion between N firms, adding the dichotomy between shareholders and managers. We assume that communication is a prerequisite for collusion, and generates some evidence. Since firms cannot enforce collusive contracts using legal institutions, collusion has to be self-enforcing.

For simplicity, shareholders will be modeled as a homogeneous, controlling, group with the same preferences.

Market conduct

N firms play an infinitely repeated game where, in each period, the following stages take place:

1. In each firm, a shareholder privately meets the manager and offers her a remuneration scheme w together with recommendations as to the market strategy to be followed.
2. Managers from all firms then have an opportunity to communicate before committing to a market strategy for the whole period. Communication between managers only takes place if all managers agree to, and concerns market conduct.
3. Managers privately choose their effort level, e, and (possibly following the recommendations of their shareholder) their market and reporting strategy. If one manager at least has preferred not to communicate, the subsequent market strategy is necessarily competitive. If communication has taken place, on the other hand, a collusive agreement has been reached; each manager can then decide whether to choose a collusive strategy as agreed, or a competitive one (i.e., to 'deviate' from the previous agreement), and simultaneously whether to report information to the antitrust authority.
4. If no information has been reported, the antitrust authority intervenes with probability ρ, in which case it always finds evidence of collusion when communication did take place.

Each shareholder obtains the firm's profit, minus the wage paid to the manager, w. All shareholders have the same discount rate $\delta \in (0, 1)$. We will assume that all managers only remain in their firm for one period, for simplicity. In addition, if a manager reports, shareholders are able to impose a cost R on her, corresponding for instance to a value for reputation.

Shareholders require a return to competition forever after a deviation.[15]

---

[15] If they were using misbehavior by a manager as an excuse allowing to resume collusion, incentives to deviate would be strengthened.

Managerial effort and discretion

In each firm, the (risk neutral) manager chooses her effort level, e. She can either exert a high effort, $e = \bar{e}$, or shirk, $e = \underline{e}$, $\bar{e} > \underline{e}$. Exerting a high effort involves a disutility $\psi > 0$ for the manager, while the cost of shirking is normalized to be zero. Neither effort nor the disutility of effort ψ are observable.

To simplify, we assume that there are two possible levels of profits for each conduct of the firm (collusion, competition, deviation, ...), depending in a certain way on the manager's effort. High profits, corresponding to a high effort level $\bar{e}$, are denoted by an upper bar, while a lower bar indicates that the manager's effort has been low. Superscript C stands for 'competition', M for 'monopolization' (and indicates that the firms collude) and D for 'deviation' (the manager has deviated whereas other firms colluded). In case of a deviation, the non-deviating participants obtain very low profits.

Although profits are linked with effort in a certain way, shareholders may not distinguish between high profits obtained thanks to a competitive behavior and a high effort ($\bar{\pi}^C$), and the same profits obtained with collusion and a low effort ($\underline{\pi}^M$). We assume the following ranking of profits: $\bar{\pi}^D > \underline{\pi}^D = \bar{\pi}^M > \underline{\pi}^M = \bar{\pi}^C > \underline{\pi}^C$. This ranking implies a 'prisoner's dilemma'-type issue as is standard in collusion games, together with a moral hazard aspect: For a given effort by the manager, shareholders gain from collusion, but each benefits at the expense of the others from deviating. The modeling, however simple, allows to consider the possibility for a manager of substituting effort for an illegal market conduct.

We will assume that the socially optimal situation—the most desirable one from the point of view of the antitrust authority—is competition together with a high effort, competition with a low effort coming second.

Shareholders can punish a manager who does not follow their recommendations, but only when the profits observed reveal this misbehavior. In addition, punishment is bounded since the manager can quit the firm at any time, in which case we assume that she gets a zero payoff from exerting her best outside option—hence 'limited liability' constraints, (*LL*). To simplify, we rule out dynamic incentives by assuming that the manager only remains with the firm for one period, as mentioned above, and that deferred payments (for instance via stock options) are not possible.[16]

The incentive scheme received by the manager is assumed to be soft private information, that cannot be credibly communicated to competing firms.[17]

---

[16] This is clearly an important restriction as we will discuss at the end of the section.

[17] We do not consider complex cheap talk games between managers about their own compensation package, and assume that communication between managers only bear on the particular collusive agreement to be adopted.

Evidence and antitrust intervention

The antitrust authority can impose (bounded) fines F on colluding firms, but only if it obtains evidence about current[18] collusion. For simplicity, we assume that the antitrust authority always finds this evidence when it audits a colluding industry. The probability of audit, denoted ρ, is supposed constant,[19] except if a report occurs, in which case the industry is kept under close scrutiny afterwards, so that subsequent collusion is deterred. The assumption that the probability of intervention does not depend on profits can be understood as an assumption about the degree of knowledge of the antitrust authority about the particular market considered: Since it monitors extremely various industries in diverse regions, it is not able to identify collusive and competitive profit levels in each industry, and can only use average values to assess the efficiency of its policy. Obtaining truthful expert advice for each market would be too costly.

It should also be noted that the assumption that the probability of audit is equal to the probability of convicting firms and does not depend on the existence of a Leniency Program is restrictive; it implies that we will *under-estimate* the benefits of such a program. First, reporting by a firm allows obtaining detailed information, making the probability of conviction noticeably higher than in the absence of cooperation. This effect has been highlighted by Motta and Polo (2001), who show that it may be sufficient to make it optimal to grant leniency to cooperating firms even after an investigation has been started by the antitrust authority. Second, this detailed information may enable the disclosure of another violation in a related or independent industry.[20] Any costs of Leniency Programs in our setting should therefore be traded against these potential benefits.

Under our simplifying assumption, the best collusive firm strategies are simple: when collusion is sustainable and profitable, the best strategy consists in colluding in every period, even after a successful audit.

Evidence can also be brought forward by each firm if it chooses to report to the antitrust authority. Some individuals, such as informed employees, also have access to this evidence.

The antitrust authority can impose a maximal fine F that is not large enough to deter collusion if it is imposed with probability ρ only: $\min\{\bar{\pi}^M - \bar{\pi}^C,$

---

[18] We assume to simplify that past behavior cannot be punished.

[19] Harrington (2005) characterizes optimal Leniency Programs when the probability of being detected by the antitrust authority varies over time.

[20] As noted by Hammond (2001) for the U.S., 'over half of these investigations [30 sitting grand juries currently investigating suspected international cartel activity] were initiated as a result of leads generated during an investigation of a completely separate market. What that simply means is that every time the Division opens an international cartel investigation, the chances are better than even that it will also uncover a second, separate conspiracy.' An example is the prosecution of the international citric acid cartel, which led in a chain reaction to the investigation and prosecution of the international sodium gluconate cartel, then of the international sodium erythorbate cartel, and in turn of the maltol cartel.

$\underline{\pi}^M - \underline{\pi}^C\} > \rho F$. Reports to the antitrust authority are assumed to be public, and observed by firms (see Rey, 2003, on leniency with secret reports).[21]

5.4.2. Managers' incentives in the absence of antitrust intervention

When shareholders decide which remuneration scheme to offer the manager, they should offer wages $w(\pi)$ that depends on the profits realized π so as to satisfy incentive compatibility constraints, a participation constraint (P) and limited liability constraints (LL).

As mentioned previously, we make the strong assumption that deferred payments depending on future profits are not feasible, and will later discuss their effect. Suppose that shareholders want to induce a high effort level and collusion, then they should satisfy the following constraints in a symmetric equilibrium, that relate to effort and conduct choice, and participation (P):

$$w(\bar{\pi}^M) - w(\underline{\pi}^D) - \psi \geq 0, \tag{5.1}$$

$$w(\bar{\pi}^M) - w(\underline{\pi}^M) - \psi \geq 0, \tag{5.2}$$

$$w(\bar{\pi}^M) - w(\underline{\pi}^C) - \psi \geq 0, \tag{5.3}$$

$$w(\bar{\pi}^M) - w(\bar{\pi}^C) \geq 0, \tag{5.4}$$

$$w(\bar{\pi}^M) - w(\bar{\pi}^D) \geq 0, \tag{5.5}$$

$$w(\bar{\pi}^M) - w(\bar{\pi}^D) \geq 0, \tag{5.6}$$

$$w(\bar{\pi}^M) - \psi \geq 0, \tag{P}$$

$$w(\bar{\pi}^k) \geq 0, \qquad w(\underline{\pi}^k) \geq 0 \quad \forall k = M, C, D. \tag{LL}$$

Since the corresponding profit levels are not distinguishable, one necessarily has $w(\underline{\pi}^D) = w(\bar{\pi}^M)$ and $w(\bar{\pi}^C) = w(\underline{\pi}^M)$. Thus, (5.1) becomes $0 - \psi \geq 0$. Clearly, the first constraint cannot be satisfied. In this setting, it is impossible to induce collusion together with a high effort level, unless the manager can be given some more complex incentives, for instance a delayed compensation based on profits (as in Spagnolo, 2000). A concern for reputation can also help solve this issue.

If no other incentive device is available, then shareholders will have to decide whether they prefer to induce collusion with a low effort, competition with a high effort, or competition with a low effort. It is easy to see, applying the same type of reasoning, that the manager will never choose to exert a high effort and

---

[21] Note that we abstract from the usual credibility issue related to audit in such a context: In equilibrium, if the tools used by the antitrust authority are effective, collusion is deterred and firms never collude. An investigation is then always a waste of resources. The antitrust authority has thus *ex post* incentives not to audit the industry with the announced probability—but if it does not, firms may prefer collusion. If the antitrust authority cannot credibly commit to a probability of investigation, the equilibrium is in mixed strategies. See Khalil (1997).

compete, when shirking and colluding allows obtaining the same compensation at a lower disutility of effort. There cannot be an equilibrium with competition and a high effort, in the absence of antitrust intervention. The firms will be little efficient, as effort will be lower than if it was observable. The possibility of colluding without being detected and without suffering from the associated drop in profits implies that managers will exert a suboptimal effort.

Here the manager always receives a wage of ψ if she is asked to exert effort, and a wage of zero otherwise. She should always receive a zero wage if the profits realized reveal that she has not been following the recommendations. Shareholders must therefore choose between competition and no effort, hence a zero wage for the manager together with profits of $\underline{\pi}^C$, and collusion and no effort.

Since there is no antitrust intervention, the manager can be given incentives to agree on collusion and then deviate, whether with or without effort, at no other cost than the full information one: $\overline{\pi}^D$ cannot be achieved without effort, and achieving $\underline{\pi}^D = \overline{\pi}^M$ by exerting effort and not deviating is not attractive to the manager.

Since $\frac{1}{1-\delta}\underline{\pi}^M > \frac{1}{1-\delta}\underline{\pi}^C$, shareholders should require a collusive behavior whenever the latter is sustainable, i.e., whenever the excess profits from deviating in the current period do not compensate the losses from the ensuing return to competition:

$$\max\{\underline{\pi}^D, \overline{\pi}^D - \psi\} - \underline{\pi}^M \leq \frac{\delta}{1-\delta}[\underline{\pi}^M - \underline{\pi}^C].$$

Note that the optimal remuneration schemes are implementable with constant bonuses for profits reaching some given threshold level ($\underline{\pi}^C$ or $\underline{\pi}^M$ depending on the conduct they want to induce). But remuneration schemes continuously increasing in profits cannot be used to induce collusion nor competition.

In such a framework, effort can only be induced by auditing the manager's effort, or by offering deferred payments based on future profits. But one should note that the latter solution may not be sufficient, as in practice, effort choices and profit levels are not binary, and shocks in the economy can prevent the stock market from adequately reflecting the value of the firm.

From a methodological point of view, one does not want to assume that stock markets can perfectly infer the market conduct of firms, as antitrust authorities would then find it relatively cheap to obtain the same information. If the stock market bases the value of shares on current profit levels together with the sign of the variation of these profits from the last period, one needs to check that its beliefs are consistent with the actions taken by managers (i.e., a drop in profits can indicate a deviation followed by a return to competition, but can also indicate that the previous manager had been exerting a high effort level, contrary to the current one, which is a priori an out-of-equilibrium occurrence, the best incentive scheme from the point of view of shareholders being the same in all periods in equilibrium. The results obtained would thus depend on the assumptions made on the revision of beliefs after an out-of-equilibrium action.

The setting we are using is too simple to be realistic but it highlights the possibility that the manager substitutes collusion for effort. One may indeed believe that among the benefits of collusion, is 'an easy life' for managers .... The next section introduces antitrust intervention and focuses on its impact on incentives.

5.5. Managers' incentives with antitrust intervention

Let us now add the possibility of antitrust intervention. We assume that the antitrust authority can impose a penalty J on the manager in case of conviction. The compensation to be paid by shareholders was assumed to be subject to a limited liability constraint. Such a constraint clearly does not apply in the case of an antitrust intervention. We do not distinguish in this section between jail sentences and monetary penalties. Jail penalties,[22] available in countries with criminal sentences, such as the U.S. or Ireland, have the advantage of not being bounded by existing wealth; Managers are not likely to lack financial resources, so that large monetary fines are also potentially available despite the limited liability constraints on wages (note that according to many legislative settings, as in the U.K., a conviction for collusion implies director disqualification, hence future foregone profits). We will also consider the possibility of offering leniency, or even bounties B, to managers who report their information.

As previously mentioned, the probability of antitrust intervention, ρ, is independent of the profits realized. In practice, it may be that high profits trigger more scrutiny by antitrust authorities, in which case a high effort would have the drawback of increasing the expected fine. We abstract from this possibility to focus on the basic effects at work when introducing jail sentences, leniency and possibly positive rewards for informants.

Sentences for colluding managers

It may now be the case that a manager can be induced to compete and exert a high effort. She would then obtain in expectation $w(\overline{\pi}^C) - \psi$, to be compared with $w(\overline{\pi}^C) - \rho J$ if she were to collude and shirk. A high enough penalty on managers ($J \geq \frac{\psi}{\rho}$) thus helps shareholders in inducing efficient competition. The cost for shareholders of inducing a high effort is then simply ψ.

On the other hand, inducing collusion becomes more costly since the wage that the manager must receive is now ρJ for collusion without effort. Inducing efficient collusion (with a high effort) is still not possible as long as deviating firms are not punished more than colluding ones—for instance via an increase in the probability of an antitrust intervention.

---

22 Jail sentences can only be interpreted in terms of a constant monetary equivalent if there are no wealth effects. In practice, it is likely that the marginal cost of a jail sentence is larger, the richer the individual.

Collusion with a low effort it thus more profitable than competition with a high effort—i.e., $\frac{1}{1-\delta}(\bar{\pi}^C - \psi) < \frac{1}{1-\delta}(\bar{\pi}^C - \rho J - \rho F)$—only when competition with a high effort is not feasible ($\rho(J + F) < \psi$). In the reverse case, shareholders will prefer to induce competition and a high effort.

If collusion remains more profitable, the shareholders will choose to collude rather than compete with a low effort whenever collusion is sustainable, i.e.,

$$\max\{\underline{\pi}^D, \bar{\pi}^D - \psi\} - \underline{\pi}^M \leq \frac{\delta}{1-\delta}[\underline{\pi}^M - \rho(J + F) - \underline{\pi}^C].$$

The left-hand side is the same as without antitrust intervention, since deviating does not shield the manager from potential sanctions, but the right-hand side is decreased, so that fines on managers indeed reduce the sustainability of collusion.

To summarize,

- An individual fine plays the same role on sustainability as corporate fines, thereby increasing cartel deterrence, via increased wages for managers.
- Individual fines have the added advantage of making it more likely that shareholders can induce a high effort together with competition, hence a better outcome from the point of view of social welfare, of consumers and shareholders.[23]

Individual leniency

Assume now that informants can obtain a full fine exemption. Collusion with a high effort remains impossible to implement. In addition, using the program in case communication has taken place (whether with a deviation or not) allows the manager to save on potential fines, and is always preferable when the cost of lost reputation is small, i.e., when $R < \rho J$. Collusion without effort is then no longer implementable in the sense that, if the shareholders were to offer an incentive scheme inducing collusion, all managers would report in the first round, and firms would compete afterwards. This cannot be an equilibrium.

If only the first reporting manager is eligible for leniency, there still cannot be an equilibrium in which managers do not report when $R < \rho J$: True, the expected loss suffered by managers when all decide to report is $-R - \frac{N-1}{N} J$ to be compared to $-\rho J$ when no one reports. But if a manager anticipates that the other managers will not report (so that she will obtain full leniency with certainty if she does), then it is optimal to report if R is smaller than the expected penalty when not reporting, ρJ. In this case, not reporting cannot be an equilibrium.

Individual leniency is thus a powerful complement to the individual fine J, as inducing collusion is no longer possible in equilibrium whenever J is large

---

[23] Managers do not loose, as they are indifferent in equilibrium between exerting effort and being exactly compensated for it, or not exerting effort.

enough. However, leniency is useless when reputation concerns are strong, or in other terms when the individual penalty J is not sufficiently large.

The next question to consider is the impact of leniency on managerial incentives when shareholders want to induce competition. Assume that the shareholders want to induce a high effort:

- If all reporting managers were allowed to obtain leniency, then the choices of managers would be as follows: if $R < \rho J$, then a manager deciding to shirk and collude rather than exert effort and compete would make use of the program. As long as R is larger than the disutility of effort ψ, the manager would not find such a strategy profitable. But if, on the other hand, reputation concerns were not powerful enough, then inducing a high effort would no longer feasible—although it might have been in the absence of collusion.
- Assume now that only the first reporting manager can obtain leniency. If managers collude, each will prefer to report if she anticipates that others do not: not reporting cannot be an equilibrium. And each manager will find it profitable to report, assuming that others do report as well, if $R + \frac{N-1}{N}J < \rho J$, i.e., $R < (\rho - \frac{N-1}{N})J$. This condition cannot be satisfied for R positive if ρ is smaller than $1/2$, a realistic assumption.[24] Assume nevertheless that the condition is satisfied. Then, when deciding whether to communicate or not, managers must then compare the cost of effort ψ with the expected penalty if they collude and report, $R + \frac{N-1}{N}J$. They will collude, and then report simultaneously, only if the disutility of effort, ψ, is quite large.

In some cases (if $R < \psi < \rho J$ with leniency for all reporting parties, or if $R + \frac{N-1}{N}J < \psi < \rho J$ with leniency only for the first reporting party), leniency destroys the possibility for shareholders of inducing a high effort together will competitive behavior, a possibility that existed in the absence of leniency—when the prospect of a sanction J was powerful enough to induce effort. Note that competition with a low effort level remains unaffected, as the adverse incentives on the side of managers stem from their desire to avoid costly effort.

To summarize,

- Leniency complements a policy of individual fine, by deterring collusion when the expected fine is large enough compared to reputation concern ($\rho J > R$); it is otherwise useless.[25]
- When leniency is useful, it may be the case that competition can no longer be efficient (thanks to a high effort) whereas it would have been so in the absence of a leniency program. There is thus an efficiency cost associated to the use of the program, to be compared to the benefits of increased collusion deterrence.

---

[24] In practice, the probability of antitrust intervention in an industry has been estimated to be around 0.15, up to 0.20.

[25] If we had incorporated the positive effect of reporting on the probability that the antitrust authority convicts cartel offenders, a Leniency Program could still be useful, as shown by Motta and Polo (2001).

- It should nevertheless be noted that restricting leniency to the first reporting party allows to strongly restrict the range of parameters for which this adverse effect arises (while still destroying any equilibrium in which managers who were given incentives to collude, did not report). In particular, it becomes very unrealistic, independently of the size of reputation concerns, when the probability of antitrust intervention is reasonable small (lower than one half).

Individual bounties

Assume now that informants can obtain not only full leniency, but also bounties B.

Then the larger the bounty, the more likely it is that the cost of deviating, R, is smaller than the benefit, $\rho J + B$ when all reporting parties are eligible, or when a manager anticipates that the others will not report. The condition under which an equilibrium in which managers are given incentives to collude and do not report, is thus easier to satisfy. A bounty is clearly more efficient than simple leniency at deterring collusion, and is particularly useful if reputation concerns are assessed as important.

But as leniency, and with more likelihood (whenever $R < \psi < \rho J + B$, when all reporting parties are eligible) bounties may give rise to the adverse effect of preventing efficient competition (competition with effort). Bounties thus increase the range of parameters for which collusion is deterred, but also that for which efficient competition becomes impossible. If leniency is sufficient to obtain collusion deterrence, it is thus better not to use bounties. If leniency is not sufficient, bounties should be restricted to the first reporting party.

One may also be worried that the existence of bounties induce the manager to always choose to collude and then deviate, rather than compete. This reasoning has been frequently mentioned by practitioners with respect to whistleblowing programs. It is not necessarily valid in the case of cartels, as collusion can only occur if other managers participate, and they have the same incentives in equilibrium as the particular manager we are considering. Nevertheless, and contrary to the case of leniency, very large bounties could possibly prevent shareholders from inducing competition, even without effort: Assume that managers are asked to undertake no effort and to compete, and that the bounty is larger than the reputation cost, $B > R$. Then if the whistleblowing program grants a bounty to all reporting parties, managers are better off colluding, and then reporting. This is obviously an absurd setting, and one can expect that if bounties are offered, they only concern the first reporting party. In that case, a manager who anticipates that her counterparts intend to report will never accept to communicate in the first place if the overall gain is negative, i.e., if $\frac{B-(N-1)J}{N} - R < 0$. A 'reasonable' bounty will therefore not give managers incentives to collude and report rather than compete. And given our assumption that the antitrust authority is able to closely monitor the industry after a report—possibly thanks to a better information on the characteristics of the industry—this adverse effect would only take place in a first period.

To summarize,

- Bounties are more effective than individual leniency at deterring collusion when shareholders wanted to induce it.
- As leniency, bounties can give rise to adverse effects and prevent competition from being fully effective.
- In addition, bounties may also prevent an equilibrium with competition altogether, inducing a situation in which all managers would collude and simultaneously report in a fist period. This last setting appears however rather unrealistic.

5.6. Conclusion

We have seen that one may not expect information to be often provided by individuals who are not given explicit incentives to do so. This is indeed strongly confirmed by observation. Mechanisms inducing the revelation of information, such as corporate and individual, Leniency and whistleblowing programs, are therefore potentially quite beneficial.

To summarize, bounties can be quite effective, as already underlined in Spagnolo (2003) and Aubert et al. (2005), and they can maximize the net amount levied as fines when they are used, compared to simple leniency. They may nevertheless give rise to adverse effects in the relationship between shareholders and high executives. It is indeed useful to note that an individual leniency program, despite being a useful complement to individual fines or jail sentences, also entails costs, as it may prevent achieving an efficient type of competitive outcome. Bounties present the same shortcomings. These adverse effects can be lessened by restricting eligibility to the program to the first informant, and have to be traded against the benefits of increased cartel deterrence. If reporting allows increasing the probability of convicting firms, an added benefit should be taken into account. Although bounties are frequently refused on the ground of potential adverse incentives with respect to market conduct, the adverse incentives that appear the most realistic are the ones concerning effort choices in competitive industries. And these incentives are already in existence with an individual leniency program.

A jail sentence is costly, and generally to be avoided on that account, when monetary penalties are available. Yet individuals with a taste for justice may prefer criminal sentences as they are associated with a stronger moral condemnation. In the same line, assume that voters have a preference for fairness and justice, in the sense that they are ready to bear costs for wrong-doers to be punished. Then obviously, a leniency program will have a low political acceptability. Individuals may prefer to bear the costs of imposing jail sentences on convicted wrong-doers, and of possibly lessened cartel deterrence, rather than use a whistleblowing program. A program granting positive rewards may be unacceptable from a political point of view due to individuals' taste for fairness and justice. An individual bounty program fares however better than a corporate one in that respect (and requires smaller bounties[26]).

Both jail sentences and fines for managers of convicted firms are helpful in deterring cartel behavior as they make it more costly for shareholders to induce a collusive behavior from their managers. In more complex settings than the one we have used, and in particular if high profits attract more investigations by the antitrust authority and such investigations are sometimes misleading, it may be the case that in equilibrium, firms compete but in an inefficient way, with managers exerting very little effort so as to maintain profits at a low level.

Note that we have assumed that evidence was 'hard', verifiable by third parties, so that false reports are not possible. A whistleblowing program may have to require the informant to provide sufficiently decisive evidence, since courts may be reluctant to believe a paid informant in a criminal context (as in the U.S. for instance). In a related line of ideas, the literature on economics and psychology (e.g., Benabou and Tirole, 2004) has shown that paying for actions that conveyed a positive message (as giving one's blood, or as here, denouncing illegal activities) may ruin the value attached to executing this action. A very low reward may therefore deter reports by 'moral' individuals who would have reported for free—while not sufficiently covering associated costs (such as losing one's job) for inducing reports by individuals with a lower sense of 'morals'. If a reward is offered, it should therefore be high enough.

Both 'sticks' and 'carrots' being effective but imperfect, the optimal 'policy-mix' is likely to depend on political choices, given the weight among voters of taxpayers relative to consumers (that depend on the share of exports and imports in the economy), and preferences for fairness and moral messages.

Acknowledgements

I thank two anonymous referees for helpful comments and suggestions.

References

Aggarwal, R.K., Samwick, A.A. (1999). Executive compensation, strategic competition, and relative performance evaluation: Theory and evidence. *The Journal of Finance* 54 (6), 1999–2043.

Aubert, C., Rey, P., Kovacic, W. (2005). The impact of leniency and whistle-blowing programs on cartels. *International Journal of Industrial Organization*, in press.

Becker, G.S. (1983). A theory of competition among pressure groups for political influence. *Quarterly Journal of Economics* 98, 371–400.

---

[26] If the antitrust authority offers a bounty B to employees reporting incriminating evidence, colluding firms have to 'bribe' all informed employees to prevent them from reporting their inside knowledge, which reduces collusive profits proportionally to the number of informed employees. Collusion is less sustainable as a consequence. Even if the bounty is paid only to the first employee who denounces collusion, colluding firms must give each informed employee the equivalent of the rewards in each period, hence a 'multiplier effect' (see Aubert et al., 2005).

Benabou, R., Tirole, J. (2004), Incentives and prosocial behavior. Mimeo, IDEI, Toulouse.
Bernheim, D., Whinston, M.D. (1985), Common marketing agency as a device for facilitating collusion. *RAND Journal of Economics* 16 (2), 269–281.
Buccirossi, P., Spagnolo, G. (2006), Optimal fines in the era of whistleblowers. CEPR Discussion Paper No. 5465.
Connor, J.M. (2004), *Global Price Fixing: 'Our Customers Are the Enemy'*. Kluwer Academic Publishers, Boston, MA.
Dobson, P., Waterson, M. (1997), Countervailing power and consumer prices. *Economic Journal* 107, 418–430.
European Union (1996), Notice on the non-imposition or reduction of fines in cartel cases. *Official Journal* 207, 4.
Fershtman, C., Judd, K. (1987), Equilibrium incentives in oligopoly. *The American Economic Review* 77 (5), 927–940.
Fershtman, C., Judd, K., Kalai, E. (1987), Observable contracts: Strategic delegation and cooperation. *International Economic Review* 32 (3), 551–559.
Green, E., Porter, R. (1984), Noncooperative collusion under imperfect price information. *Econometrica* 52, 87–100.
Grossman, G., Helpman, E. (1994), Protection for sale. *American Economic Review* 84 (4), 833–850.
Hammond, S.D. (2000), Detecting and deterring cartel activity through an effective leniency program. International Workshop on Cartels, November 21–22, Brighton, UK.
Hammond, S.D. (2001), When calculating the costs and benefits of applying for corporate amnesty, how do you put a price tag on an individual's freedom? Public Speech, Antitrust Division, U.S. Department of Justice.
Hammond, S.D. (2005), An update of the antitrust division's criminal enforcement program. Public Speech, Antitrust Division, U.S. Department of Justice.
Harding, C., Joshua, J. (2003), *Regulating Cartels in Europe: A Study of Legal Control of Corporate Delinquency*. Oxford University Press, Oxford, UK.
Harrington, J. (2004), Cartel pricing dynamics in the presence of an antitrust authority. *RAND Journal of Economics* 35 (4).
Harrington, J. (2005), Optimal corporate leniency programs. Mimeo, John Hopkins University.
Harrington, J., Chen, J. (2005), Cartel pricing dynamics with cost variability and endogenous buyer detection. *International Journal of Industrial Organization*, in press.
Jullien, B., Rey, P. (2001), Resale price maintenance and collusion. CEPR Discussion Paper 2553.
Khalil, F. (1997), Auditing without commitment. *RAND Journal of Economics* 28 (4), 629–640.
Klawiter, D.C. (2001), After the deluge: The powerful effect of substantial criminal fines, imprisonment, and other penalties in the age of international cartel enforcement. *George Washington Law Review* 69 (5/6), 745–765.
Kobayashi, B.H. (2001), Antitrust, agency, and amnesty: An economic analysis of the criminal enforcement of the antitrust laws against corporations. *George Washington Law Review* 69 (5/6), 715–744.
Kovacic, W.E. (1996), Whistleblower bounty lawsuits as monitoring devices in government contracting. *Loyola of Los Angeles Law Review* 29, 1799–1857.
Kovacic, W.E. (2001), Private monitoring and antitrust enforcement: Paying informants to reveal cartels. *George Washington Law Review* 69 (5/6), 766–797.
Levenstein, M., Suslow, V.Y. (2004), Contemporary international cartels and developing countries: Economic effects and implications for competition policy. *Antitrust Law Journal* 71 (3), 801–852.
Mayer, W. (1984), Endogenous tariff formation. *American Economic Review* 74 (5), 970–985.
McChesney, F.S. (1991), Be true to your school: Chicago's contradictory views of antitrust and regulation. *Cato Journal* 10, 775–798.
McChesney, F.S., Shugart II, W.F. (Eds.) (1995), *The Causes and Consequences of Antitrust—The Public Choice Perspective*. The University of Chicago Press, Chicago, IL.
McCutcheon, B. (1997), Do meetings in smoke-filled rooms facilitate collusion? *Journal of Political Economy* 105 (3), 330–350.

Motta, M., Polo, M. (2001), Leniency programs and cartel prosecution. *International Journal of Industrial Organization* 21, 347–379.

Mullin, W.P., Snyder, C. (2005), Targeting employees for corporate crime and forbidding their indemnification. George Washington University Working Paper, http://ssrn.com/abstract=558341.

Peltzman, S. (1976), Towards a more general theory of regulation. *Journal of Law and Economics* 19, 211–240.

Rey, P. (2003), Towards a theory of competition policy. In: Dewatripont, M., Hansen, L.P., Turnovsky, S.J. (Eds.), *Advances in Economics and Econometrics: Theory and Applications, Eighth World Congress*. Cambridge University Press, Cambridge, UK.

Rey, P., Vergé, T. (2004), Bilateral control with vertical contracts. *RAND Journal of Economics* 35, 728–746.

Rowley, C., Rathbone, A.L. (2004), The political economy of antitrust policy. Mimeo, George Mason University.

Sklivas, S. (1987), The strategic choice of managerial incentives. *RAND Journal of Economics* 18, 452–458.

Spagnolo, G. (2000), Stock-related compensation and product-market competition. *RAND Journal of Economics* 31, 22–42.

Spagnolo, G. (2003), Optimal deterrence mechanisms against cartels and organized crime. Mimeo, Mannheim.

Spratling, G.R. (1999), Making companies an offer they shouldn't refuse. Speech at the Antitrust Division, February 16, Washington, DC.

Spratling, G.R. (2001), Detection and deterrence: Rewarding informants for reporting violations. *George Washington Law Review* 69 (5/6), 798–823.

Stigler, G.J. (1971), The theory of economic regulation. *Bell Journal of Economics* 2, 3–21.

Stigler, G.J. (1982), The economists and the problem of monopoly. In: Stigler, G.J. (Ed.), *The Economist as Preacher and Other Essays*. University of Chicago Press, Chicago, IL.

Tokar, S. (2000), Whistleblowing and corporate crime. Mimeo, The European University Institute.

Werden, G.J. (2004), Economic evidence on the existence of collusion: Reconciling antitrust law with oligopoly theory. *Antitrust Law Journal* 71 (3), 719–800.

Wils, W. (2005), Is criminalization of EU competition law the answer? In: Cseres, K., Schinkel, M.P., Vogelaar, F. (Eds.), *Remedies and Sanctions in Competition Policy*. Edward Elgar Publishing, London.

Yang, C.C. (1995), Endogenous tariff formation under representative democracy: A probabilistic voting model. *American Economic Review* 85 (4), 956–963.

CHAPTER 6

Lessons for Competition Policy from the Vitamins Cartel

William E. Kovacic[a], Robert C. Marshall[b], Leslie M. Marx[c] and Matthew E. Raiff[d]

[a] *U.S. Federal Trade Commission*
[b] *Pennsylvania State University, USA*
[c] *Duke University, USA*
[d] *Bates White, LLC*

Abstract

Mergers have the potential for negative social welfare consequences from increased likelihood or effectiveness of future collusion. This raises the question of whether there are meaningful thresholds for the post-merger industry that should trigger significant scrutiny by the Department of Justice or Federal Trade Commission. This chapter provides empirical analyses relevant to this question using data from the Vitamins Industry, where explicit collusion was admittedly rampant in the 1990s. In analyzing prices in the post-plea period, which is a period of potential tacit collusion, we find that vitamin products with two conspirators continue as if the explicit conspiracy never stopped, while products with three or four conspirators return to pre-conspiracy pricing, or lower, quite quickly. Although it is difficult to extrapolate to other industries, the evidence suggests that, by itself, a proposed reduction in the number of firms manufacturing a given product from four to three via a merger is not problematic in terms of the efficacy of tacit collusion. The danger of a three firm industry is that it is close to duopoly, and the benefits of explicit collusion in a duopoly appear to be sustainable via tacit methods well past intervention by enforcement authorities.

6.1. Introduction

A major social welfare concern regarding a potential merger is the impact of increased concentration on the future suppression of interfirm rivalry within the industry. The Horizontal Merger Guidelines of the Department of Justice (DoJ) and Federal Trade Commission (FTC)[1] implicitly mandate an analysis of the increased chances of future coordination as well as the increased payoffs from any

---

[1] Available at http://www.usdoj.gov/atr/public/guidelines/horiz_book/hmg1.html.

CONTRIBUTIONS TO ECONOMIC ANALYSIS
VOLUME 282 ISSN: 0573-8555
DOI: 10.1016/S0573-8555(06)82006-7

incremental coordination among firms in an industry.[2] Incremental coordination can be explicit collusion or tacit collusion. Although the latter is not illegal, the Guidelines are clear in expressing concern about approving mergers where tacit collusion may become easier and more effective, and thus lead to diminished social welfare.[3]

Any empirical study of an industry that tries to assess the impact of explicit or tacit collusion will confront basic issues. First, prices can vary for a large number of reasons related to demand and cost conditions that are largely unrelated to the nature of interfirm rivalry in the industry. Second, even if controls exist for many of these factors, it can be difficult to separate tacit from explicit collusion. Yet, these are important to disentangle. Suppose that explicit collusion can be profitably sustained with relatively large number of market participants, but the profitability of tacit collusion is highly sensitive to the number of market participants. Specifically, suppose that a duopoly can sustain prices with tacit collusion that are not different from those attainable by an explicit cartel, but a four-firm oligopoly can only sustain tacitly collusive prices that are half of what was possible with explicit collusion. Then it would be sensible for the FTC to devote considerably more resources to challenging "three-to-two" mergers than "five-to-four" mergers.

We argue that there exist some natural experiments in this regard that are commonplace and for which data should be readily available, especially to enforcement agencies.[4] Specifically, when the DoJ discovers explicit collusion, there is typically a plea period, with the conspirators admitting to collusion during that period. In the abstract, the end of the plea period marks the end of the conduct (although there can be substantial lingering effects on price from explicit collusion). Although the explicit collusion has ended, the nature of the agreements that existed between the firms for organizing their illegal conduct,

---

[2] Arguments regarding the change in coordinated effects from a merger have historically consisted of four components. First, if there are a substantial number of firms remaining after the merger, then adverse effects are viewed as relatively unlikely. Second, if the Herfindahl index rises substantially, then the merger is viewed as being worthy of further investigation for adverse social effects through coordinated effects. Third, the Guidelines make special note of "Maverick" firms—if a Maverick is part of a merger, then the merger is viewed as having potentially adverse social effects, but if a Maverick exists in the industry and is not involved with the merger, then the merger is viewed with less concern. Fourth, arguments are made, rooted in the Folk Theorem and economics literature on tacit collusion, about how firms' abilities to monitor each other and punish deviant behavior might change as a result of the merger.

[3] According to the Horizontal Merger Guidelines (at Section 2.1): "A merger may diminish competition by enabling the firms selling in the relevant market more likely, more successfully, or more completely to engage in coordinated interaction that harms consumers. Coordinated interaction is comprised of actions by a group of firms that are profitable for each of them only as a result of the accommodating reactions of the others. This behavior includes tacit or express collusion, and may or may not be lawful in and of itself."

[4] Enforcement agencies should mandate as a condition of merger approval that certain information be made available to them post-merger on an ongoing basis, and they should devote staff resources to the analysis of this data.

Table 6.1: DoJ/FTC merger policy: Litigation threshold for horizontal mergers 1960–2005.

Decade	Threshold of likely litigation challenge
1960s	Merger reduces number of survivors to 12 or fewer firms
1970s	Merger reduces number of survivors to 8 or fewer firms
1980s	Merger reduces number of survivors to 5 or fewer firms
1990s	Merger reduces number of survivors to 3 or fewer firms
2000s	Merger reduces number of survivors to 3 or fewer firms

the processes by which they monitored one another, and the mechanisms used to threaten punishment are not forgotten by the former conspirators. How they organized their conduct to achieve high prices remains well known among them. Thus, these firms should be able to use these lessons, at least in part, to sustain tacit collusion after the end of the plea period.

If data show that after the end of explicit collusion, firms cannot sustain prices close to plea-period levels, this suggests that highly profitable tacit collusion is not easy to sustain in this industry. If data show that prices after the end of explicit collusion are inversely related to the size of the plea-period cartel, this suggests that the number of firms in an industry may affect the potential for profitable and effective tacit collusion as a coordinated effect. Thus, merger policy potentially can be guided based on empirical analyses such as those presented here.

Since the mid-1990s, the DoJ and the FTC ordinarily sued to block horizontal mergers that would have reduced the number of market participants to three or fewer firms. As a rough generalization, over the past decade, antitrust lawyers confidently have been able to advise the parties to proposed mergers that, based on an examination of the agencies' decisions to prosecute, the threshold at which the federal authorities would sue to block deals is "four-to-three."[5] As Table 6.1 indicates, this litigation threshold has shifted significantly over the past half-century.

These adjustments have been the result of two interrelated developments: DoJ and FTC self-assessments driven by changes in the state of research and scholarly commentary, and judicial decisions that retreated from the strong presump-

[5] There have been exceptions to this general proposition. FTC's complaint in its unsuccessful challenge in 2004 to the acquisition by Arch Coal of Triton alleged that the number of firms in one relevant market following the merger would have fallen from five to four. Federal Trade Commission v. Arch Coal Co., 329 F. Supp. 2d 109 (D.D.C. 2004). It is also possible to identify some horizontal transactions (particularly in the aerospace and defense sectors) over the past decade for which the federal antitrust agencies took no action even though the number of surviving firms fell to less than three. Kovacic (2003, 444–47).

tions of illegality adopted by courts in the 1960s and imposed more demanding burdens upon the federal agencies when seeking to block horizontal mergers.[6]

The existing economics literature does not clearly address whether a merger that reduces the number of firms from five to four or from four to three should be viewed as problematic. (For a review of the literature, see Section 6.2.) Thus, empirical studies that can address these numbers could provide a useful guide for enforcement agencies as to where to invest scarce resources in challenging mergers on the basis of coordinated effects.

In this chapter, we analyze price data for thirty vitamin products for which we have observations that span three periods of time: prior to a period of admitted explicit collusion, during a period of admitted explicit collusion, and after a period of admitted explicit collusion. The period of admitted explicit collusion spans much of the 1990s, when many of the manufacturers of vitamins admitted their guilt regarding participation in a worldwide price-fixing conspiracy.[7] Even though we examine data for markets characterized by explicit collusion rather than mergers, we are able to draw implications for merger policy. Note that an explicit cartel can be viewed as an illegal, and possibly temporary, merger of the colluding firms.

There are many different vitamins, and an even greater number of vitamin products. The number and identities of firms that can produce each vitamin product differ across the products, as did the number of cartel participants. Yet, there is no significant heterogeneity in the factor inputs used to produce different vitamin products, and demand fluctuations tend to affect vitamin products in similar ways. Thus, we are able to attribute much of the difference in pricing behavior to the number of firms producing the different vitamin products.

We analyze the price path for these vitamin products after the end of the plea-period. This allows us to examine whether, after the termination of explicit collusion, firms can maintain prices at cartel levels, or whether there is erosion in prices relative to their explicitly collusive levels. We examine whether the price paths following the plea periods for the different vitamin products depend on the number of firms engaged in the previous explicit collusion, controlling for the effects of fringe producers. This analysis allows us to obtain a partial understanding of how market concentration impacts the efficacy of tacit collusion. This understanding can be used to inform merger analysis with respect to concerns about coordinated effects.

Our primary finding is that after the end of explicit conduct, duopolies continue as if the explicit conspiracy never stopped, while markets with three or four cartel firms return to pre-conspiracy pricing, or lower, quite quickly.

---

[6] On the promulgation and revision of merger guidelines by the federal agencies since the 1960, see Greene (2005), Symposium (2003). On the influence of judicial decisions and the change in merger jurisprudence since 1960, see Gavil et al. (2002, 418–558), Leary (2002).

[7] Explicit collusion may have existed prior to the beginning of the period of admitted guilt. In fact, recent work (Marshall et al., 2005) suggests that the collusion may have started in the mid-80's.

6.2. Literature

The early literature in industrial organization discusses how, in industries with small numbers of firms, firms might be expected to recognize their mutual interdependence and that one might expect relatively more collusive outcomes in industries with relatively fewer firms (see Chamberlin, 1933; Bain, 1951; Stigler, 1964). Later work provides experimental and theoretical support for the idea that the competitiveness of an industry with a small number of firm can be expected to be increasing in the number of firms.[8] Selten's (1973) paper argues that "4 are few and 6 are many" (p. 199), so that six firms are sufficiently many that collusive outcomes are unlikely. The empirical work of Kwoka (1979) leads him to conclude that "three-firm coordination problems are so severe as to make a large third firm more likely a rival." (p. 108) Thus, his results suggest that in many cases three firms are sufficiently many to prevent collusive outcomes. The empirical work of Bresnahan and Reiss (1991) lead them to conclude that once there are three to five firms in an industry, a new entrant has little effect on the competitiveness of the industry, suggesting that three to five firms are sufficient to prevent collusive outcomes. Recent experimental work by Huck et al. (2004) suggests competitiveness is monotonic in the number of firms and that four or five firms is sufficient to prevent collusive outcomes.

6.3. Coordinated effects analysis

Concern about post-merger coordinated effects has supplied the main conceptual basis for antitrust scrutiny of horizontal transactions since the Celler–Kefauver Amendment to the Clayton Act's merger control provision in 1950.[9] The views of scholars, enforcement agencies, and courts about the appropriate application of coordinated effects analysis have undergone considerable change over the past half-century. Through the 1960s, merger doctrine and enforcement policy reflected acute apprehension about the oligopoly gap—the zone in which firms in moderately or highly concentrated industries could realize supranormal returns by accounting for their interdependence in ways that did not transgress the Sherman Act's prohibitions on express collusion and abusive single-firm behavior.[10]

---

[8] Dolbear et al. (1968) provide experimental results, and Selten (1973) provides theoretical results. Also, Werden and Baumann (1986) provide theoretical results in which competitiveness is non-monotonic in the number of firms. In their model, damages increase more slowly than the benefits of collusion as the number of firms increases.

[9] The 1950 amendments established the basic substantive framework of today's merger control regime. See Gellhorn et al. (2004, 418–21) (describing rationale for and history of the 1950 amendments to Section 7 of the Clayton Act).

[10] For a representative synthesis of this view, see Kaysen and Turner (1959, 110) (observing that "[t]he principal defect of present antitrust law is its inability to cope with market power created by jointly acting oligopolists"). See also Kovacic and Shapiro (2000, 51–52).

In the 1950s and 1960s, many economists and lawyers endorsed measures to address the oligopoly gap directly by deconcentrating industries with oligopoly market structures.[11] Although many observers regarded deconcentration was the preferred solution, merger policy had a key role to play in ensuring that horizontal combinations did not create new oligopolies or increase the effectiveness of tacit coordination in already concentrated industries. As suggested above, U.S. merger policy in the 1960s and early 1970s aggressively policed horizontal mergers, and Supreme Court decisions establishing powerful (and typically decisive) presumptions of illegality for transactions that resulted in post-acquisition market shares of less than ten percent.[12]

The reliance of merger doctrine and enforcement policy upon structural presumptions fell under heavy scholarly attack. Much of the criticism raised doubts about how effectively oligopolists could coordinate their behavior by tacit means—that is, without resorting to an overt or covert exchange of assurances.[13] From at least the late 1970s to the present, this perspective has influenced courts and enforcement agencies in two basic ways. First, it has dramatically shifted the structural threshold of concern in horizontal merger cases. Decisions of the courts have weakened the power of the structural presumption in coordinated effects cases except at the highest levels of concentration.[14] Second, as reflected in judicial decisions such as *Arch Coal* in the United States and *AirTours* in the European Union, the enforcement agencies have been pressed in coordinated effects cases to explain more fully and convincingly how coordination among the surviving firms will take place in the post-merger period.[15]

In light of these developments, a major challenge for enforcement agencies in future coordinated effects cases is to improve the basis for predicting the competitive consequences of individual cases and, in litigated disputes, to provide a more confident basis for courts to infer that specific consolidations will have

---

[11] See Kovacic (1989, 1136–39) (recounting proposals by economists and lawyers to deconcentrate oligopoly sectors). Congress declined to enact the deconcentration legislation, and efforts by the federal antitrust agencies to use the existing antitrust laws to restructure oligopolies—for example, through the prosecution of "shared monopoly" cases by the FTC—were entirely unsuccessful. See Kellogg Co., 99 F.T.C. 8, 269 (1982) (dismissing shared monopolization complaint against leading U.S. producers of breakfast cereal); Exxon Corp., 98 F.T.C. 453, 461 (1981) (dismissing shared monopolization complaint against leading refiners of petroleum products).

[12] See, e.g., United States v. Pabst Brewing Co., 384 U.S. 546 (1966) (prohibiting merger that yielded a post-acquisition market share of 4.49 percent).

[13] See Baker (1993) (describing evolution of economic thinking about oligopoly and the feasibility and frequency of effective coordination). An important stimulus for this line of inquiry was George Stigler's work (1964) on the difficulties that firms face in achieving effective coordination when they seek to orchestrate their behavior through express, rather than tacit, means.

[14] See, e.g., FTC v. H.J. Heinz Co., 246 F.3d 708 (D.C. Cir. 2001) (condemning acquisition that reduced the number of firms in the relevant market from three to two); see also Baker (2004) (discussing application of structural presumption in Heinz case).

[15] See FTC v. Arch Coal Co., 329 F. Supp. 2d 109 (D.D.C. 2004); AirTours plc v. Commission, Case T-342/99, [2002]ECR II-2585.

anticompetitive effects. One means to this end is for the enforcement community to take steps to strengthen the empirical foundations of merger analysis. In recent years the U.S. agencies have invested additional resources in "competition policy research and development" (Kovacic, 2005). These investments have included ex post assessments of the competitive effects of completed mergers (Muris and Pitofsky, 2005, 827–28) and the review of past merger reviews to identify evidence that most strongly influenced the decision whether to challenge transactions (FTC, 2004)).

A promising additional frontier for empirically-oriented research relevant coordinated effects analysis is for competition agencies to study their experience with the enforcement of antitrust laws against cartels.[16] Government competition authorities have accumulated considerable experience in anti-cartel enforcement programs, and the examination of individual enforcement episodes can yield valuable insights about industry conditions in which tacit coordination is most likely to be effective. The examination of the Vitamins Cartel in the sections that follow illuminate the possibilities of such a research program.

6.4. Data from the vitamins industry

6.4.1. Overview

In this section we provide a brief overview of the Vitamins Industry and collusive behavior by firms in the industry. For more details on the Vitamins Industry, see Bernheim (2002), European Commission (2003), and Marshall et al. (2005).

Vitamins are produced and purchased for both human and animal consumption. Each vitamin has a specific set of beneficial effects. When considering the cost of producing animal feed or human food, the incremental cost of the vitamin additives typically is small. Due to the significant nutritional impact of vitamin supplements, the demand for vitamins is highly inelastic.

Although it is common to think of vitamins as a single entity—such as Vitamin A or Vitamin E—in fact, specific vitamin products are manufactured within each vitamin type. For example, in this section, we consider four different Vitamin A products: A Acetate 500 USP, A Palmitate 250 USP, A Palmitate 500 USP, and A Acetate 650 Feed Grade.

Vitamins are largely produced through processes of chemical synthesis, although there have been recent advances in fermentation technologies for the production of some vitamins. The industry is highly concentrated, and the large capital investments, and especially the production experience, required for the manufacture of vitamins are a barrier to entry. Although the major producers have similar production technologies, the chemical synthesis processes involve substantial "learning by doing." Each producer becomes better, through time, at

---

[16] Some of these possibilities are suggested in Kolasky (2002).

debottlenecking the chemical synthesis process at any given plant. A given vitamin product made by one firm is chemically identical to the same product made by another firm.

In the late 1990s, the DoJ obtained guilty pleas from several major vitamin manufacturers for participating in an international price fixing cartel that extended back to at least January 1990.[17] In addition, the European Community and Canada found that several of the vitamin producers had violated antitrust laws within their jurisdictions. In this report, we refer to the interval of the DoJ plea dates as the "plea period."

Detailed descriptions of the vitamins conspiracy can be found in the European Commission's (2003) decision. In general, the cartel fixed the market shares of the colluding firms, referring to these shares as "budget targets," and monitored the output of the cartel members. The cartel used interfirm output transactions as a mechanism for rectifying any internal issues that arose, whether these were adherence to budgeted market share allocations or other matters regarding the enhancement of cartel profits. For example, "Any company that sold more than its allotted share was required in the following year to purchase the excess from another conspirator that had not reached its volume allocation target."

The cartels in the different vitamin products operated over approximately the same period of time in the 1990s, and possibly prior to 1990. The different vitamins have similar factor inputs and demand for the different vitamins is subject to similar shocks, although on the demand side, there may be some differences between vitamins intended for human use and those intended for use in animals. Because of this, we analyze human and feed vitamins separately. Among human vitamins and among feed grade vitamins, similarities in the environments in which the cartels operated, including the time periods and the supply and demand factors, allow us to make comparisons across vitamins.

6.4.2. Data

Price data on a set of vitamin products is available from the Expert Report of B. Douglas Bernheim, M.D.L. No. 1285, In Re: Vitamins Antitrust Litigation, Misc. No. 99-0197 (TFH), May 24, 2002.[18] Section 12 of Bernheim (2002) provides data for 37 vitamin products, including the monthly weighted average unit price in dollars per kilogram from 1980 to 2002 (shorter time period for some vitamin products), the dates of the plea-period, the identities of the cartel

---

[17] On the abuse by Hoffmann-La Roche of its dominant position in the industry in the 1970s, see Case 85/76, Hoffmann-La Roche v. Commission (Vitamins), 1979 ECR 461, 539-40 (C.J.).

[18] Bernheim (2002) was submitted as exhibit number 243 in In re: Vitamins Antitrust Litigation, case No. 99-0197 (TFH) filed in the District Court of the District of Columbia. We obtained the document through a request to the law clerk to Chief Judge Thomas F. Hogan. The document was made available based on D.C. Local Civil Rule 79.2 and the United States District Court for the District of Columbia's policy of not retaining exhibits that are admitted into evidence at trial in civil cases. The price data used in this paper were reverse engineered from the graphs in the document.

firms, and the identities or locations (e.g., Eastern Europe) of non-cartel firms. In addition, Section 10 of Bernheim (2002) provides data for 2 additional vitamin products, Ascorbic Acid 100% USP and E 50% Adsorbate Feed Grade. For these two vitamin products, prices are broken out by producer, so we used the worldwide production shares for Vitamins C and E, given in Figures 8-1 and 8-7 of Bernheim (2002), to construct a weighted average price.[19]

As an example of the data that is available for each vitamin product in the Bernheim (2002) report, Figure 6.1 shows the data available for Vitamin A Acetate 650 Feed Grade. The information includes a weighted average price for the vitamin product, the plea-era sales value, and a list of the manufacturers, both cartel and non-cartel. As described in the caption of the figure, the price graphs in Bernheim (2002) show the 7-month centered moving average for U.S. "tel quel" price from Roche ROVIS data.[20] The qualifier "tel quel" means that these are prices for vitamin sold in their straight form rather than as part of premix, which is a premixed collection of different vitamin products. Feed vitamins use feed prices, and human vitamins use food, pharma, and cosmetic prices.

According to Bernheim (2002), the price data are derived from the Roche ROVIS database (except Choline Chloride (B4), which we do not include in our data).[21] The vitamin products in Section 12 of Bernheim (2002) are those that satisfy two requirements: the data must be consistently reported throughout the 1980 to 2001 time period (with a few exceptions) and the product must account for at least 1.5 percent of Roche's U.S. sales within the relevant vitamin family between 1980 and 2001 and account for at least $10 million in Roche's sales volume over the same period.

To improve comparability across vitamin products, we focus on vitamin products that are produced by Roche. This eliminates seven vitamin products, including two Choline Chloride products, four Niacin products,[22] and Vitamin B12 Crystals. In addition, we drop the two Biotin products because they are outliers in a number of ways: they are the only two vitamin products with five firms in the cartel (the other Roche vitamins have four or fewer in the cartel); they are small in terms of the dollar amount of sales during the plea period (they have

---

[19] Weights are given by year and are not available after 1998, so for years after 1998, the weights are assumed to be the same as in 1998. Figure 8-7 does not explicitly state BASF's Vitamin C production share for four years. Based on the figure, we judge those shares to be 1980: 2%; 1981: 2%; 1989: 4%; and 1996: 4%.

[20] For Ascorbic Acid 100% USP and Vitamin E 50% Adsorbate Feed Grade the source is listed as "defendant transaction data."

[21] According to Bernheim (2002, p. 23), the ROVIS data were "reviewed and verified" as described in an appendix to the report. Bernheim had access to "documents produced through discovery, litigation-related information including testimony and affidavits, and publicly available documents and data." (p. 24) He also "reviewed testimony, affidavits, written discovery responses, and other litigation-related information." (p. 25)

[22] Although Bernheim's (2002) Figure 12-27 shows Roche as a manufacturer of one Niacin product, Niacinamide (B3) 33 1/3% USP, Figure 8-18 shows that Roche does not produce Niacin, so we do not include this vitamin product in our data.

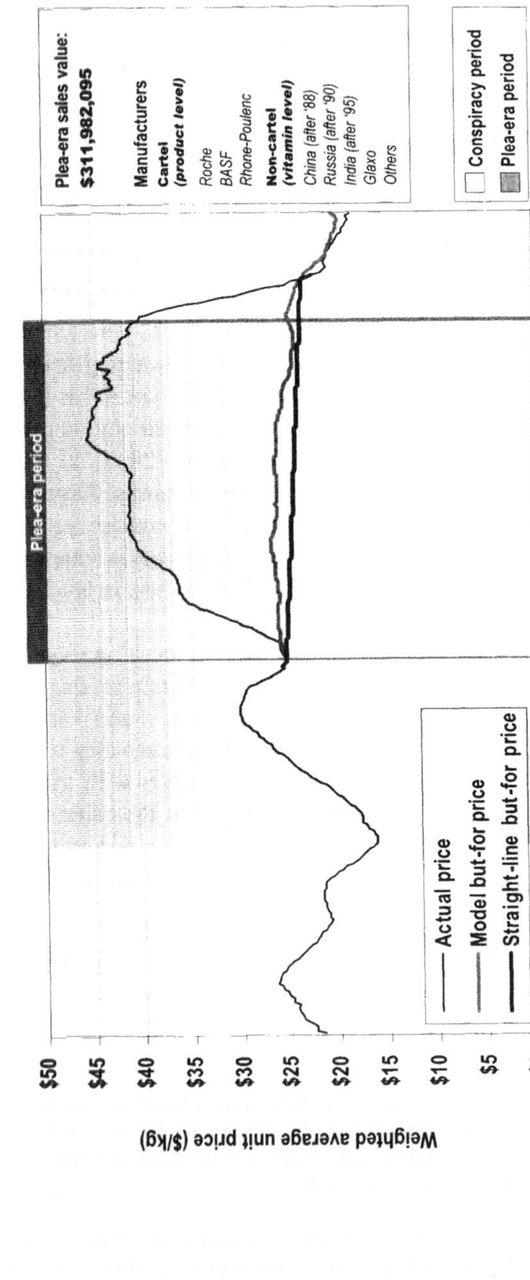

Source: 7-month centered moving average for U.S. "tel quel" feed price from Roche ROVIS data

Fig. 6.1: Data on Vitamin A Acetate 650 Feed Grade as shown in Figure 12-6 of Bernheim (2002, p. 207).

less than $9 million in plea sales, whereas the average plea sales of the other Roche vitamins is over $97 million); and the identities of the cartel firms, although Roche is one, are not consistent with those of the other Roche vitamin products (the Biotin products are the only Roche products that are also produced by Tanabe and Lonza). That leaves us with the thirty vitamin products shown in Table 6.2.

To define the plea period for each vitamin product, we use the U.S. plea period for that product's vitamin type if there is one, and otherwise we use the EC or Canadian plea period as given in Bernheim (2002, Table 6). For vitamin products with both EC and Canadian plea periods, but no U.S. plea period, we use the EC plea period.

To define the non-cartel production shares prior to the plea and at the end of the plea, we use the figures of Section 8 of Bernheim (2002), which show annual world production shares by firm at the vitamin level (not the vitamin product level). We use the shares in the year prior to the beginning of the plea period and in the final year of the plea period.[23]

Note that Table 6.2 shows one vitamin product, Riboflavin (B2) 33 1/3% USP, that had only one firm involved in the conspiracy. For this vitamin product, Roche was the only manufacturer charged with illegal activity. The data for this vitamin product gives us some idea of how a monopolist manufacturer would behave. All other vitamin products had a two, three, or four-firm cartel.

For each vitamin product listed in Table 6.2, we constructed a monthly dataset of prices based on the price graphs in Bernheim (2002).[24] For all but four vitamin products, data are available from January 1980 until December 2001. The exceptions are that the data for Vitamin D3 500 Feed starts in January 1983, the data for Vitamin D3 100 USP starts in January 1985, the data for Ascorbic Acid 100% USP is continuous starting from December 1985, and the data for Vitamin E 50% Adsorbate Feed Grade is continuous starting from January 1986.

Although the plea periods vary for the different vitamin products, data are available for all the vitamin products in our sample for 48 months prior to the beginning of their plea periods and for 31 months after the end of their plea periods.

The data are not useful for examining firms' propensity to engage in explicit collusion. However, the data for the period after the end of the plea period, when it is reasonable to assume that explicit collusion has ended, is useful for examining the efficacy of tacit collusion. Afterall, the lessons of explicit collusion are fresh in the post-plea period. This has implications for merger policy. If prices remain high after the plea period, there is a reasonable chance that firms may

---

[23] Share data is not available for Apocarotenal, so we use the share data for Canthaxanthin for all of the Carotenoids.

[24] The underlying data used to construct the figures in Bernheim (2002) is not in the public domain, so we scanned and digitized the figures using Engauge Digitizer software and then used the software to constructly monthly data by collecting two data points off the graph for each month and then taking the average. Complete details on the procedure used are available from the authors.

Table 6.2: Description of the vitamin products included in the analysis.

	Vitamin type	Vitamin product	Start of plea period	End of plea period	Number in cartel	Non-cartel production share prior to plea	Non-cartel production share at end of plea
1	A	Vitamin A Acetate 500 USP	1/1/1990	2/1/1999	2	1	9
2	A	Vitamin A Acetate 650 Feed Grade	1/1/1990	2/1/1999	3	1	9
3	A	Vitamin A Palmitate 250 USP	1/1/1990	2/1/1999	2	1	9
4	A	Vitamin A Palmitate 500 USP	1/1/1990	2/1/1999	2	1	9
5	B1	Thiamine (B1) Hydrochloride USP	1/1/1991	6/1/1994	3	15	40
6	B1	Thiamine (B1) Mononitrate USP	1/1/1991	6/1/1994	3	15	40
7	B2	Riboflavin (B2) 33 1/3% USP	1/1/1991	9/1/1995	1	10	12
8	B2	Riboflavin (B2) 80%/50% Spray-Dried Feed Grade	1/1/1991	9/1/1995	4	10	12
9	B2	Riboflavin (B2) USP	1/1/1991	9/1/1995	4	10	12
10	B5	Calpan (B5) Spray-Dried Feed Grade	1/1/1991	12/1/1998	3	14	17
11	B5	Calpan (B5) USP	1/1/1991	12/1/1998	3	14	17
12	B6	Pyridoxine (B6) Hydrochloride USP	1/1/1991	6/1/1994	3	10	46
13	Beta Carotene	Beta Carotene 1 0% Cold Water Soluble USP	1/1/1991	12/1/1998	2	0	0
14	Beta Carotene	Beta Carotene 22% HSS USP	1/1/1991	12/1/1998	2	0	0
15	Beta Carotene	Beta Carotene 30% Fluid Soluble USP	1/1/1991	12/1/1998	2	0	0
16	C	Ascorbic Acid 100% USP	1/1/1991	11/1/1995	4	13	38
17	C	Ascorbic Acid Coated Feed Grade	1/1/1991	11/1/1995	4	13	38
18	C	Ascorbic Acid Coated USP	1/1/1991	11/1/1995	4	13	38
19	C	Ascorbic Acid Compressible 90% USP	1/1/1991	11/1/1995	3	13	38

Table 6.2: *(Continued)*

	Vitamin type	Vitamin product	Start of plea period	End of plea period	Number in cartel	Non-cartel production share prior to plea	Non-cartel production share at end of plea
20	C	Sodium Ascorbate USP	1/1/1991	11/1/1995	4	13	38
21	Carotenoids	Apocarotenal 20% USP	5/1/1993	12/1/1998	2	0	0
22	Carotenoids	Canthaxanthin 10% Feed Grade	5/1/1993	12/1/1998	2	0	0
23	Carotenoids	Canthaxanthin 10% USP	5/1/1993	12/1/1998	2	0	0
24	D	Vitamin D3 100 USP	1/1/1994	6/1/1998	3	0	0
25	D	Vitamin D3 500 Feed	1/1/1994	6/1/1998	3	0	0
26	E	Vitamin E 50% Adsorbate Feed Grade	1/1/1990	2/1/1999	4	0	13
27	E	Vitamin E Acetate 50% Spray-Dried Feed Grade	1/1/1990	2/1/1999	3	0	13
28	E	Vitamin E Acetate 50% Spray-Dried USP	1/1/1990	2/1/1999	2	0	13
29	E	Vitamin E Acetate Oil USP	1/1/1990	2/1/1999	3	0	13
30	Folic Acid	FolicAcid (B9)	1/1/1991	6/1/1994	4	4	41

have transferred key components of the profitable conduct of explicit collusion to tacit collusion. And, if there are differences in post-plea prices based on the number of firms in the cartel, this may indicate differences in the ability of firms to sustain tacit collusion after the termination of explicit collusion depending on the number of firms involved.

6.5. Analysis

6.5.1. Graphical analysis

To begin our analysis, we consider the percentage change in price relative to the plea-period maximum for the different vitamin products broken out by the number of firms in the cartel.

Figures 6.2–6.5 provide information on the prices of the different vitamin products included in the analysis. Figure 6.2 shows the product produced by only one conspirator. Figure 6.3 shows the products with a two-firm cartel. Figure 6.4 shows the products with a three-firm cartel. And Figure 6.5 shows the products with a four-firm cartel. On the horizontal axis, we show the number of months prior to the start of the plea period (negative numbers) and the number of months after the end of the plea period (positive numbers), and on the vertical axis the percentage change in price relative to the maximum price achieved during the plea period.[25] Note that we are not claiming that the behavior in the

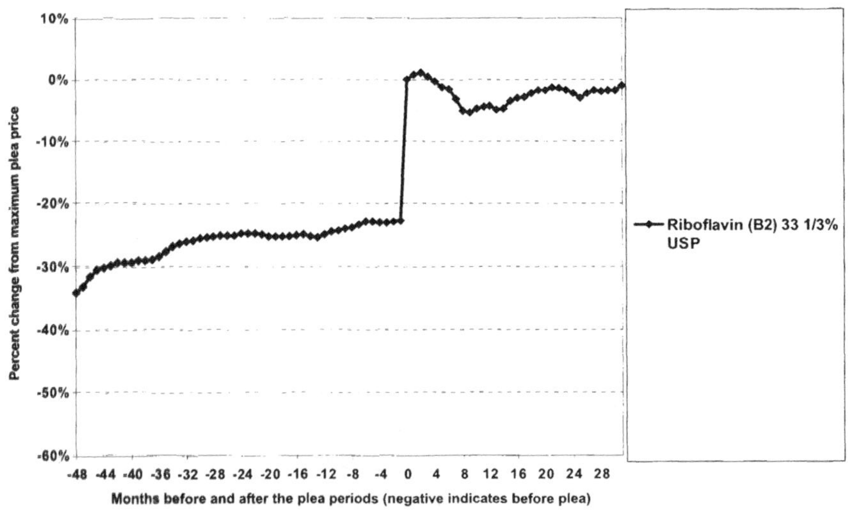

Fig. 6.2: Percentage change in price relative to plea-period maximum for the product produced by only one conspirator.

[25] Note that the prices in Bernheim (2002) are seven-month centered moving averages, so our "maximum plea-period price" is the maximum of these seven-month centered moving averages.

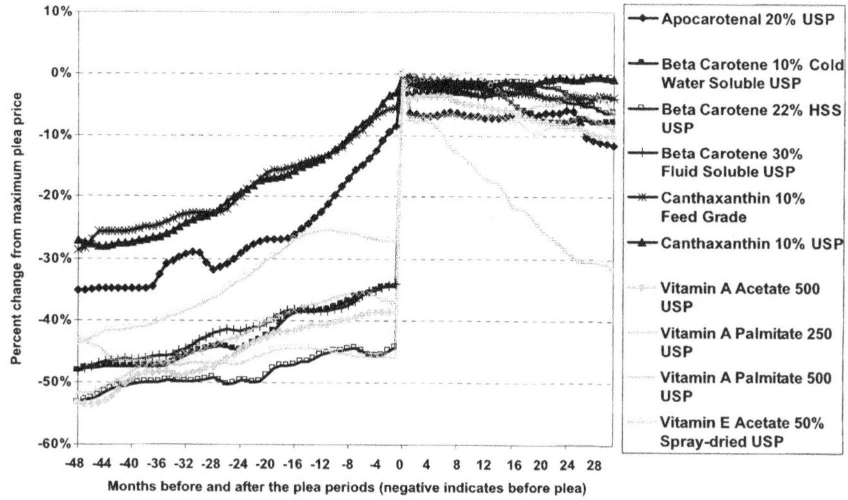

Fig. 6.3: Percentage change in price relative to plea-period maximum by product for products with a two-firm cartel.

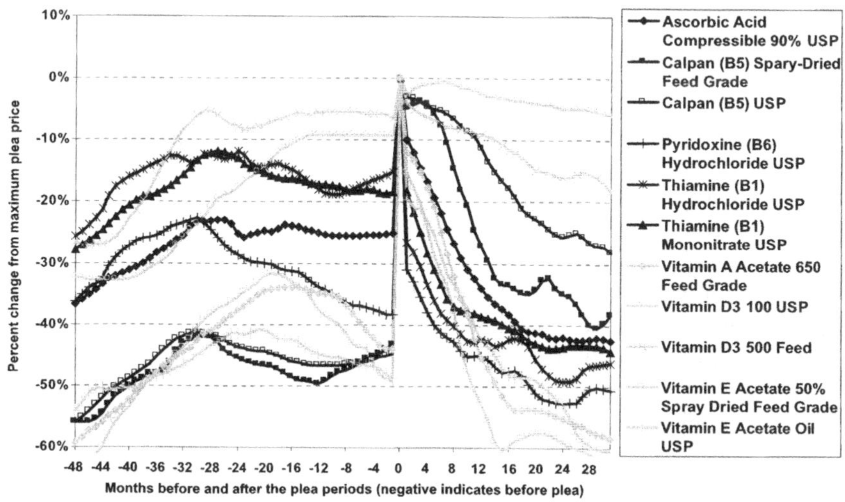

Fig. 6.4: Percentage change in price relative to plea-period maximum by product for products with a three-firm cartel.

Vitamins Industry prior to the plea period was non-collusive. To the contrary, Bernheim (2002) assumes the conspiracy began in January of 1985, an assumption that is supported by the analysis of the vitamin manufacturers' public price announcements in Marshall et al. (2005). We address this more formally in Section 6.5.2.

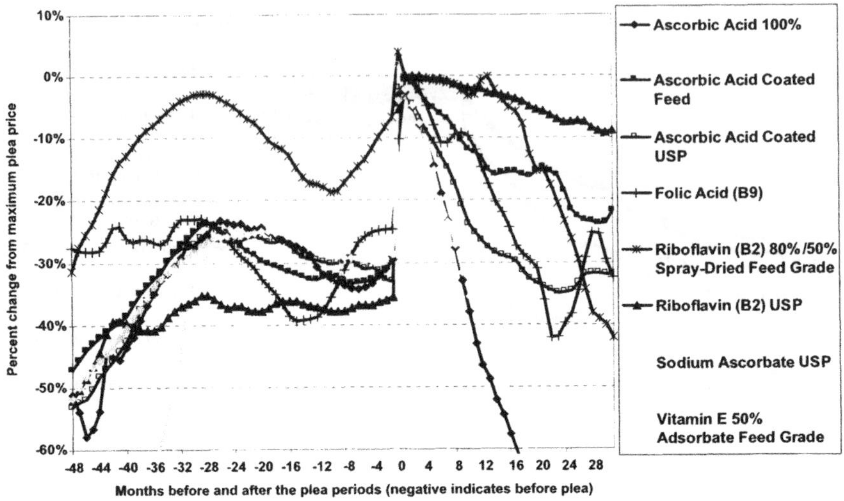

Fig. 6.5: Percentage change in price relative to plea-period maximum by product for products with a four-firm cartel.

We see from Figure 6.2 that for the vitamin product manufactured by only one conspirator, prices remained high after the plea period relative to their pre-plea levels. From Figure 6.3 we see that for all but one of the vitamin products with a two-firm cartel, prices remain close to their plea-period maxima. The price of Vitamin E Acetate 50% Spray-Dried USP falls after the end of the plea period, but after more than two years, remains well above its pre-plea levels. Referring to Figure 6.4, for the cartels involving three firms, the evidence is somewhat mixed.[26] Prices for some products remain above their pre-plea levels, but others drop sharply after the end of the plea period. Finally, referring to Figure 6.5, for four-firm cartels, in all cases, the price eventually ends up below pre-plea nominal levels (for Ascorbic Acid Coated Feed, the price does not drop below pre-plea levels until mid 1999, 41 months after the end of the plea period). The rate of descent varies for these vitamin products, with the prices in coated Vitamin C products descending less rapidly than for many of the other vitamin products.

We now combine the graphs described above, averaging across vitamin products, to obtain the average price changes relative to the plea-period maximum for vitamin products with different numbers of cartel members.

Figure 6.6 shows a dramatic difference between the post-plea prices of products with one conspirator or a two-firm cartel versus products with three or

[26] Bernheim (2002, p. 176) states, "In the case of Riboflavin (B2), the evidence suggests that Roche attempted to re-cartelize the market with Rhone-Poulenc after the end of the conspiracy period. This may have prolonged the effects of the original conspiracy and delayed the onset of non-conspiratorial price dynamics."

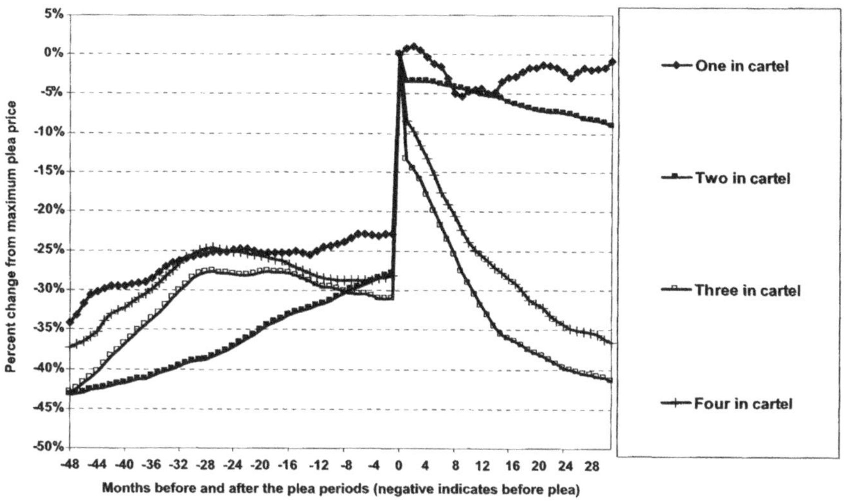

Fig. 6.6: Average percentage change in price relative to the plea-period maxima by number in cartel.

four-firm cartels. When there is one dominant producer or there is a two-firm cartel, firms are able to maintain prices significantly above pre-plea levels. This is despite the fact that for most vitamin products in our sample, there are competing non-cartel producers. The prices for three and four-firm cartels remain elevated above their pre-plea levels for approximately one year after the end of the plea period.

Figure 6.6 also shows that pre-plea prices are 23% to 31% less than the plea-period maxima. It may be surprising that there is any increase at all for a product produced by only one of the conspirators, but it may be that the explicit collusion involved agreements among the larger set of conspiring firms not to enter this market, and that the removal of the threat of entry induced firms to increase prices. It may also be that other vitamin products, although not perfect substitutes, did have some substitutability with the product with only one conspirator, and so the increases in the prices of the other vitamin products due to conspiratorial behavior in those products may have allowed an increase in prices in the product produced by only one conspirator.

To provide an additional way to view the data, we also consider the percentage price change relative to the price one month prior to the beginning of the plea period. This data is shown in Figure 6.7.[27] Note that we only have data for all vitamin products for 31 months after the end of the plea period. Beyond 31 months after the end of the plea period, some vitamin products drop out of our data, resulting in jumps in the price series shown in Figure 6.7.

[27] The price change shown at date zero in Figure 6.7 is the for maximum price during the plea period.

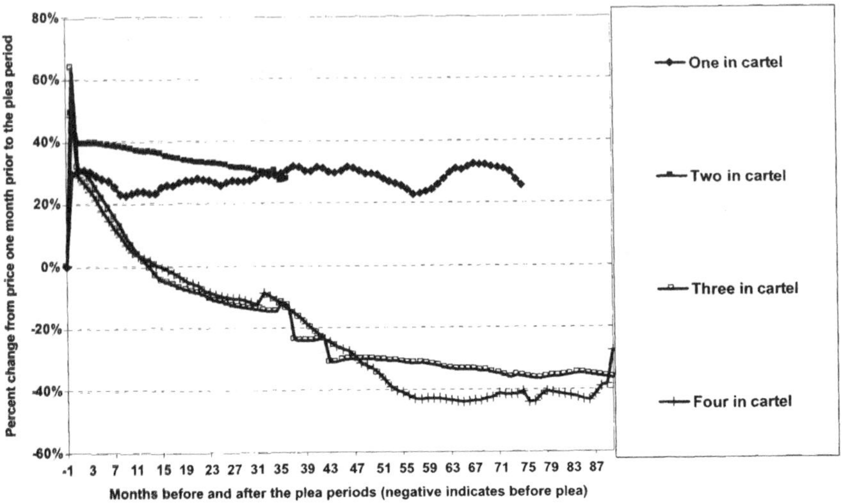

Fig. 6.7: Average percentage change in price relative to one month prior to the beginning of the plea period by number in the cartel.

Figure 6.7 shows that prices for two, three, and four-firm cartels increase between 48% and 64% during the plea period relative to one month prior to the plea period. For products produced by only one of the conspirators, the price increases about 30%. In the months after the plea periods, for products produced by one or two conspiring firms, prices remain well above their pre-plea levels. For products produced by only one conspirator, prices remain close to their plea-period maxima long after the end of the plea period and show no signs of decay. For two-firm cartels there is slight decay, but prices remain more than 20% above their pre-plea levels over three years after the end of the plea period. For three and four-firm cartels, prices fall to their pre-plea levels within fifteen months after the end of the plea period. It is interesting that prices for three and four-firm cartels fall to about 40% below their pre-plea levels within five years after the end of the plea period. This may be due to competition from new entrants whose entry was induced by the high prices during the plea period.

Figure 6.7 also provides information about the sustainability of cartel prices after the end of explicit collusion. One might expect the vitamin manufacturers to be under heightened scrutiny from antitrust authorities in the period after the end of the plea period, and so one might expect especially competitive behavior in that period. However, as shown in Figure 6.7, this does not appear to be the case for products with two-firm cartels. The figure shows that prices for products with one or two conspirators remain steady from the end of the plea period out as far as our data allows. In contrast, the prices for three and four-firm cartels decrease rapidly after the end of the plea period.

The analysis of Marshall et al. (2005) suggests that the collusive period in the Vitamins Industry extended back to 1985. If we use the price on January 1, 1985

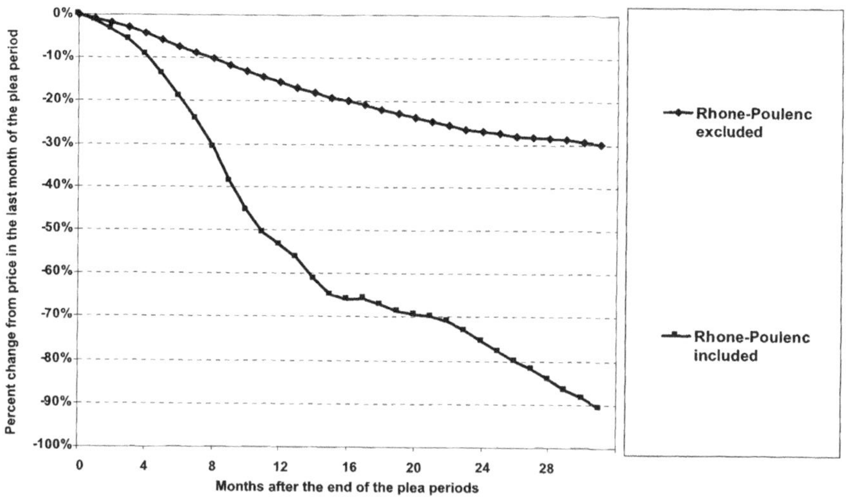

Fig. 6.8: Average percentage change in price relative to the last month of the plea period for vitamin products produced by Rhone-Poulenc and those not produced by Rhone-Poulenc.

as the reference point, we obtain similar results.[28] A general upward trend in prices between month −60 and month zero, and the fact that prices fall below their 1985 levels after the end of the plea period for three and four-firm cartels, provide additional support for a collusive period that predates the beginning of the DoJ plea period.

In the Vitamins Industry, twelve firms paid a total of $911 million in fines related to U.S. antitrust charges; however, Rhone-Poulenc, who is listed in Bernheim (2002) as a cartel producer of Vitamin A 650 Feed Grade, Vitamin E 50% Adsorbate Feed Grade, Vitamin E 50% Spray-Dried Feed Grade, Riboflavin (B2) USP, and Riboflavin (B2) 80%/50% Spray-Dried Feed Grade, received amnesty and did not pay any U.S. fines.[29] The conditions of amnesty may have affected the behavior of Rhone-Poulenc during the post-plea period, as suggested by Figure 6.8.

In summary, the figures in this section suggest that there may be differences in post-plea pricing based on the number of firms in the cartel; however, these differences may be due to factors other than the number of firms, such as the ease of entry and the conditions of DoJ amnesty. In addition, it is not clear from the figures whether the differences are statistically significant. In Section 6.5.2 below, we use regression analysis to control for other factors that may explain

[28] Our data for Ascorbic Acid 100% and Vitamin E 50% Adsorbate Feed Grade does not extend back to January of 1985.

[29] Roche, BASF, Takeda, Eisai, Daiichi, and Merck, which were major manufacturers of the vitamin products in our data, all paid substantial U.S. fines. Besides Rhone-Poulenc, the only cartel firms for vitamin products in our data that did not pay U.S. fines were Solvay (Vitamin D), Kongo (Folic Acid), and Sumika/Sumitomo (Folic Acid).

the differences and to obtain measures of the statistical significance of the effect of the number of cartel firms.

In the Appendix, we review a simple model based on Cournot competition and linear demand, which shows that when there are two firms in an industry, each firm has higher profit if it colludes that if it does not, but if there are more than two firms in an industry, then given any division of the cartel profits, there will be some firm that prefers to be outside the cartel while the remaining firms collude rather than inside the cartel. This model emphasizes that having more than two firms in an industry can be extremely disruptive to firms' attempts to collude.

6.5.2. Regression analysis

The figures in Section 6.5.1 suggest that after the end of a period of explicit collusion, prices may remain above their pre-collusion levels for products with one dominant firm or a two-firm cartel, but not for products with three or four-firm cartels. In addition, the figures suggest that a period of explicit collusion may have a similar effect on post-collusion prices when there are three or four firms in the cartel. In this section, we test these hypotheses using regression analysis to control for factors other than the number of firms that may explain the post-plea differences (or similarities) and to obtain measures of the statistical significance of the effect of the number of cartel firms.

We present results for OLS regressions using as the dependent variable the percentage change in price over different periods of time. In regressions 1–3, we use the percentage change in price 12, 24, and 30 months after the end of the plea period relative to the price one month prior to the beginning of the plea period. In regressions 4–6, we use the percentage change in price 12, 24, and 30 months after the end of the plea period relative to the price during the last month of the plea period. In regressions 7–9, we use the percentage change in price 12, 24, and 30 months after the end of the plea period relative to the price in January of 1985.

As independent variables, we use a dummy that is one if the vitamin product is a feed vitamin, the non-cartel world production share (at the vitamin level) in the last year of the plea, and the change in the non-cartel world production share (at the vitamin level) from the year prior to the plea to the last year of the plea. The size of the non-cartel fringe gives a measure of the competitiveness of a market, and the change in the size of the non-cartel fringe gives a measure of the ease of entry into the vitamin product. To account for any effects of the DoJ's amnesty program, we include a dummy variable for whether Rhone-Poulenc, who received amnesty, was the manufacturer of a vitamin product. For the regressions in Section 6.5.3, we include a dummy that is one if China produces the vitamin product. Finally, we include dummies for whether the cartel for the vitamin product was a two-firm, three-firm, or four-firm cartel, using the product with only one conspirator as the omitted category.

Table 6.3 gives descriptive statistics for the dependent and independent variables used in our regressions.

Table 6.3: Descriptive statistics for variables used in regression analysis.

Variable	Mean	Median	Standard deviation	Kurtosis	Skewness	Min	Max	Count
% change in price from −1 to +12	14.24	6.60	28.17	−0.67	0.44	−32.01	75.79	30
% change in price from −1 to +24	5.23	1.99	29.51	−0.67	0.47	−40.05	74.00	30
% change in price from −1 to +30	2.94	1.40	29.67	−0.89	0.44	−37.90	68.21	30
% change in price from last month of plea to +12	−14.62	−10.00	15.51	−0.13	−0.88	−53.92	0.65	30
% change in price from last month of plea to +24	−21.19	−21.22	18.30	−1.16	−0.39	−57.67	0.38	30
% change in price from last month of plea to +30	−22.71	−23.55	19.07	−1.01	−0.47	−60.94	−0.16	30
% change in price from 1/1985 to +12	57.35	50.92	52.78	5.81	1.80	−7.75	251.95	28
% change in price from 1/1985 to +24	45.84	44.77	54.08	5.38	1.69	−24.29	242.59	28
% change in price from 1/1985 to +30	42.73	43.17	53.60	5.79	1.82	−18.42	240.71	28
Feed	0.27	0	0.45	−0.82	1.11	0	1	30
Non-cartel share	17.17	12.5	15.96	−1.23	0.57	0	46	30
Change in non-cartel share	11.47	8	11.83	−0.75	0.73	0	37	30
Rhone-Poulenc	0.17	0	0.38	1.66	1.88	0	1	30
China	0.73	1	0.45	−0.82	−1.11	0	1	30
2 in cartel	0.33	0	0.48	−1.55	0.74	0	1	30
3 in cartel	0.37	0	0.49	−1.78	0.58	0	1	30
4 in cartel	0.27	0	0.45	−0.82	1.11	0	1	30

Our general functional form is as follows:[30]

$$\begin{aligned}\%\text{ change in price}\\ &= \beta_0 + \beta_1 \cdot \text{feed dummy} + \beta_2 \cdot \text{non-cartel share}\\ &\quad + \beta_3 \cdot \text{change in non-cartel share} + \beta_4 \cdot \text{amnesty dummy}\\ &\quad + \beta_5 \cdot \text{two-firm cartel dummy} + \beta_6 \cdot \text{three-firm cartel dummy}\end{aligned}$$

[30] We also ran the regressions using dummies for different ranges of the non-cartel share rather than the levels themselves and found this made little difference. And we tried dropping the observation with only one conspirator and running the regressions with "2 in cartel" as the omitted category. Again, the change had little effect on the results, although the resulting coefficients on the "3 in cartel" and "4 in cartel" dummies were generally more negative (larger in absolute value) and had somewhat greater statistical significance. The coefficients on the "3 in cartel" and "4 in cartel" dummies were not statistically significantly different from each other in any of the regressions.

$$+ \beta_7 \cdot \text{four-firm cartel dummy.}$$

Regression results are shown in Table 6.4. In regressions 1–3 and 7–9, we focus on price changes relative to dates prior to the beginning of the plea period. The dependent variables used in these regressions provide measures of the lasting impact of explicit collusion on prices. In regressions 4–6, we focus on price changes relative to the last month of the plea period. This dependent variable allows us to focus on the sustainability of the collusive price increase.

In all regressions, the feed dummy appears to be of no consequence. We expect the variables related to the non-cartel production share to capture both entry and competitive effects in regressions 1–3 and 7–9. The high price during the explicitly collusive period would be expected to induce entry, possibly causing the post-plea price to fall below its pre-plea levels (the entry effect), and a larger non-cartel share would be expected to increase the rate at which the price declines after the end of explicit collusion (the competition effect). In regressions 4–6, we expect these variables to capture only competitive effects because in these regressions the percentage change is not measured relative to pre-plea levels. When the coefficients on these variables are statistically significant, they are negative.

The coefficient on the Rhone-Poulenc dummy is negative and large in magnitude in all of the regressions. This suggests that the amnesty program may have affected prices in this industry in the post-plea era.

Focusing on regressions 1–3, the coefficients on the three-firm cartel dummy and the four-firm cartel dummy are generally negative, and in two cases we see statistically significant coefficients for the price decreases of three-firm cartels. The coefficients on the two-firm cartel dummy are positive, indicating that for products with two-firm cartels, post-plea prices remain higher relative to their pre-plea levels than if there were only one conspirator. The coefficient for a two-firm cartel is significantly different from that for a three-firm cartel in regressions 2 and 3, but the coefficients for three and four-firm cartels are not significantly different from one another.

Focusing on regressions 4–6, it is interesting that we see negative and statistically significant coefficients on the Rhone-Poulenc dummy in two cases. The coefficient on the three-firm cartel dummy is negative in all cases and statistically significant in two of the cases. Also in these regressions, the coefficients on the three-firm cartel dummy and four-firm cartel dummy are not significantly different from one another.

The large positive coefficients on the two-firm cartel dummy in regressions 1–3 and 7–9 imply that a two-firm cartel achieves a larger increase in price during the plea-period than when there is a monopoly producer. One might interpret this as occurring because products in which there was a monopoly producer were already priced at monopoly levels. The coefficients on the two-firm cartel dummy are smaller but still positive in regressions 4–6, reflecting the fact that prices are equally persistent relative to a monopoly.

Table 6.4: Regressions 1–9 for the percentage change in price at dates after the plea period relative to dates prior to the plea period and relative to the last month of the plea period.

	1	2	3	4	5	6	7	8	9
Independent var.	**Dependent variable**								
	% change in price from −1 to			**% change in price from last month of plea to**			**% change in price from 1/1985 to**		
	+12	**+24**	**+30**	**+12**	**+24**	**+30**	**+12**	**+24**	**+30**
Constant	21.332**	24.289***	24.852***	−5.912	−3.172	−2.467	69.229**	72.888**	73.512**
	9.353	*6.877*	*7.504*	*5.872*	*5.929*	*7.525*	*28.498*	*30.064*	*31.730*
Feed	−13.914	−12.469	−13.906	−5.373	−4.679	−5.822	−20.224	−20.981	−23.679
	12.018	*12.247*	*11.569*	*5.631*	*7.280*	*8.215*	*24.940*	*25.643*	*25.581*
Non-cartel share	0.485	0.472	0.458	0.323	0.272	0.231	−1.871	−1.944	−1.964
	0.967	*0.709*	*0.782*	*0.606*	*0.595*	*0.752*	*2.663*	*2.808*	*2.973*
Change in	−1.594	−1.658*	−1.474	−1.150	−1.180*	−0.993	−2.233	−2.086	−1.841
Non-cartel share	*1.242*	*0.908*	*1.025*	*0.753*	*0.680*	*0.830*	*1.863*	*1.942*	*2.104*
Rhone-Poulenc	−5.624	−7.940	−8.851	−15.417*	−16.885*	−17.635	−45.098	−50.446	−52.245
	10.634	*10.841*	*11.121*	*8.160*	*8.842*	*10.263*	*33.204*	*33.169*	*32.860*
2 in cartel	20.755	13.883	10.940	7.544	2.557	0.094	22.369	14.165	10.616
	13.518	*11.197*	*11.535*	*6.146*	*5.959*	*7.417*	*25.308*	*25.984*	*27.156*
3 in cartel	−2.233	−16.669*	−21.448**	−3.366	−13.548*	−16.830**	74.902**	54.553	48.410
	13.667	*9.611*	*9.911*	*5.269*	*6.573*	*7.668*	*31.744*	*33.471*	*34.604*
4 in cartel	5.294	−7.581	−13.017	6.163	−3.695	−8.233	82.217**	65.002*	58.153
	12.446	*10.774*	*11.809*	*7.543*	*8.948*	*10.352*	*36.019*	*37.576*	*38.730*
Number of obs.	30	30	30	30	30	30	28	28	28
Adj. R-squared	0.306	0.501	0.497	0.532	0.638	0.557	0.468	0.475	0.435
t-stat 2 in = 3 in	−1.860	−3.250	−3.340	−1.650	−1.830	−1.500	0.990	0.720	0.640
t-stat 3 in = 4 in	0.730	0.950	0.840	1.450	1.530	1.200	0.630	0.880	0.830

Robust standard errors are in italics. Coefficients that are significant at the 90% level are shown with one asterisk, 95% level with two asterisks, and 99% level with three asterisks.

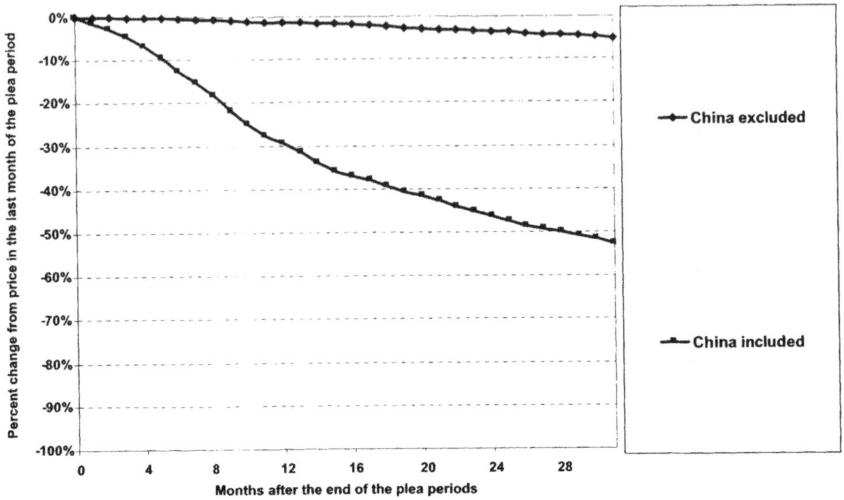

Fig. 6.9: Average percentage change in price relative to the last month of the plea period for vitamin products produced by China and those not produced by China.

The coefficients on the cartel dummies are generally larger in regressions 7–9 than in regressions 1–3, which may reflect collusive behavior prior to the beginning of the plea period as suggested by the results of Marshall et al. (2005).

Overall, our results suggest that prices do not return to pre-plea levels within thirty months after the end of a period of explicit collusion in products with a two-firm cartel, but they do return to pre-plea levels within this time period for products with three-firm or four-firm cartels. In addition, we find a significant difference in pricing behavior based on whether a product had a two-firm cartel versus a larger cartel, but we do not find a significant difference based on whether a product had a three-firm cartel versus a four-firm cartel.

6.5.3. Role of a maverick firm

As suggested by the Horizontal Merger Guidelines, the presence of certain firms, labeled "mavericks," in an industry may reduce the ability of the other firms to maintain prices above their competitive levels. In the Vitamins Industry, the conditions of Rhone-Poulenc's amnesty may have caused Rhone-Poulenc to behave like a maverick firm in this industry during the post-plea period. Consistent with this, we observe large, negative, and sometimes statistically significant coefficients on the Rhone-Poulenc dummy in regressions 1–9. The post-plea behavior of Rhone-Poulenc, which is reasonably conjectured to be induced by the conditions of amnesty, provides a window by analogy to the impact of a maverick firm on pricing behavior in an industry.

One might also consider China to be a maverick in the Vitamins Industry. The Chinese began production of some vitamins in the 1980s and developed a

Table 6.5: Regressions 10–12 for the percentage change in price at dates after the plea period relative to dates prior to the plea period including a control for maverick behavior by China.

	10	11	12
Independent variable	**Dependent variable**		
	% change in price from last month of plea to		
	+12	**+24**	**+30**
Constant	−3.283	2.914	6.343
	6.552	*6.638*	*7.422*
Feed	−5.532	−5.047	−6.355
	5.543	*6.960*	*7.505*
Non-cartel share	0.441	0.545	0.625
	0.612	*0.552*	*0.708*
Change in non-cartel share	−1.177	−1.244*	−1.085
	0.745	*0.609*	*0.730*
Rhone-Poulenc	−12.945	−11.162	−9.350
	8.716	*9.268*	*10.859*
China	−3.985	−9.225	−13.355
	5.027	*6.392*	*7.911*
2 in cartel	6.157	−0.656	−4.557
	6.502	*6.451*	*7.379*
3 in cartel	−5.240	−17.887**	−23.111***
	5.580	*6.269*	*7.447*
4 in cartel	3.799	−9.168	−16.156
	8.267	*9.044*	*10.515*
Number of observations	30	30	30
Adjusted R-squared	0.516	0.647	0.586

Robust standard errors are in italics. Coefficients that are significant at the 90% level are shown with one asterisk, 95% level with two asterisks, and 99% level with three asterisks.

major market presence by the middle of the 1990s in vitamins such as Vitamin C and Thiamine (B1). According to Bernheim (2002), China produced all of the vitamin products in our data except the three Beta Carotene products, the three Carotenoids, and the two Vitamin D products. Figure 6.9 compares prices for vitamin products produced by China with prices for those not produced by China.

To analyze this conjecture, we run three additional regressions, which are the same as regressions 4–6 described in Section 6.5.2 except that we add an additional dummy variable for whether China is a producer of the vitamin product. These regressions allow us to analyze how the presence of China affects the percentage change in price twelve months, twenty-four months, and thirty months after the end of the plea period, relative to the last month of the plea period.

As shown in Table 6.5, the coefficient on the China dummy is negative but is not statistically significant. The point estimate in regression 11 shows that the presence of China as a manufacturer results in a 9.2% decrease in price in the two years after the end of the plea period, all else constant. This effect is comparable to the effect of having Rhone-Poulenc as a manufacturer of the vitamin product.

6.6. Conclusion

Although it is difficult to extrapolate to other industries, the evidence from the Vitamins Industry suggests that a proposed reduction in the number of firms manufacturing a given product from four to three via a merger does not alone pose an incremental threat in terms of tacit coordination. But, this should not be interpreted as suggesting the absence of social harm for mergers in which industry size goes from four to three. The data from the Vitamins Industry suggests that the real social danger after a period of explicit collusion is duopoly, and three is much closer to two than four. Coordinated effects analysis would be required of any merger to assess whether the merger will lead the industry toward effective duopoly through tacit (or explicit) collusion.

Beyond its specific technical findings, our examination of the Vitamins Industry suggests the value of retrospective inquiries as guides to the refinement and application of coordinated effects analysis to the review of mergers. Amid continuing debate about how competition authorities should conduct a coordinated effects analysis and about whether the treatment of coordinated effects in the U.S. merger guidelines requires adjustment, there appears to be broad agreement about the value of using retrospective studies to supplement a careful fact-intensive assessment of proposed transactions and the institutional arrangements that govern the operations of the merging parties (FTC/DoJ Joint Workshop, 2004, 127–195). Merger policy will be well served if enforcement authorities invest resources in research programs to gather and analyze post-merger data as well as post-plea data. The insignificance of many of the coefficients in our statistical analysis speaks to the need for incremental data.

Acknowledgements

We thank Brian McClelland and Scott Lobel for valuable research assistance, and we thank Malcolm Coate, seminar participants at the Federal Communications Commission, and three anonymous referees for helpful comments. Many thanks to Chris Wieman for the reverse engineering of the data displayed in Bernheim (2002). This paper was completed while Marx was visiting the FCC and Marshall was visiting Bates White, LLC. The opinions expressed in this paper are those of the authors and do not necessarily represent the views of the U.S. Federal Trade Commission or its individual members.

Appendix. Review of a simple model

In this appendix we remind readers of a simple model based on Cournot competition and linear demand. This model provides some insights that can be used to understand what appear to be differences in the viability of tacit collusion based on the number of firms in the industry. We do not intend to imply that this model captures all of the relevant features of the Vitamins Industry. In particular, we assume a fixed number of symmetric firms; whereas in the Vitamins Industry, products typically have a small number of dominant firms and entry is possible. The results of the simple model presented here suggest that one might see a discrete difference in the sustainability of tacit collusion in markets with only two firms in contrast to markets with more than two firms.

Assume there are n firms producing a homogenous product with common constant marginal cost c. Assume industry inverse demand is $P = a - bQ$, where $a > c \geq 0$ and $b > 0$. Assuming either Cournot competition or fully collusive behavior, we can calculate the profits for the firms in our model.

Note that when there are two firms in an industry, each firm can increase its profit by colluding. If a firm chooses not to collude, the industry necessarily reverts to non-cooperative play with two firms. However, when there are three firms in an industry, if two firms agree to collude, then the third firm strictly prefers to remain outside the cartel (and play non-cooperatively against the two-firm cartel) rather than join the two firms to form a three-firm cartel. This is apparent from Table A1, which shows that the profit from creating a three-firm cartel is $\frac{(a-c)^2}{12b}$, but the profit from remaining outside while a two-firm cartel operates is $\frac{(a-c)^2}{9b}$.

Table A1: Firm and cartel profits in various environments based on a simple Cournot model with linear demand.

	Cournot profit	All-inclusive cartel profit	All-inclusive cartel profit/firm	Profit if other $n-1$ collude	
				In cartel	Outside cartel
n	$\frac{(a-c)^2}{b(n+1)^2}$	$\frac{(a-c)^2}{4b}$	$\frac{(a-c)^2}{4bn}$	$\frac{(a-c)^2}{(n-1)9b}$	$\frac{(a-c)^2}{9b}$
$n=1$	$\frac{(a-c)^2}{4b}$	$\frac{(a-c)^2}{4b}$	$\frac{(a-c)^2}{4b}$	–	–
$n=2$	$\frac{(a-c)^2}{9b}$	$\frac{(a-c)^2}{4b}$	$\frac{(a-c)^2}{8b}$	–	–
$n=3$	$\frac{(a-c)^2}{16b}$	$\frac{(a-c)^2}{4b}$	$\frac{(a-c)^2}{12b}$	$\frac{(a-c)^2}{18b}$	$\frac{(a-c)^2}{9b}$
$n=4$	$\frac{(a-c)^2}{25b}$	$\frac{(a-c)^2}{4b}$	$\frac{(a-c)^2}{16b}$	$\frac{(a-c)^2}{27b}$	$\frac{(a-c)^2}{9b}$

References

Bain, J.S. (1951), Relation of profit rates to industry concentration. *Quarterly Journal of Economics* 55, 293–324.

Baker, J. (2004), Efficiencies and high concentration: Heinz proposes to acquire Beech-Nut (2001). In: Kwoka, J.E., Jr., White, L.J. (Eds.), *The Antitrust Revolution*, pp. 150–169.

Baker, J.B. (1993), Two Sherman Act Section 1 dilemmas: Parallel pricing, the oligopoly problem, and contemporary economic theory. *Antitrust Bulletin* 38, 143.

Bernheim, B.D. (2002), Expert Report of B. Douglas Bernheim, M.D.L. No. 1285. In Re: Vitamins Antitrust Litigation, Misc. No. 99-0197 (TFH), May 24.

Bresnahan, T.F., Reiss, P.C. (1991), Entry and competition in concentrated markets. *Journal of Political Economy* 99, 977–1009.

Chamberlin, E.H. (1933), *The Theory of Monopolistic Competition*. Harvard University Press, Cambridge, MA.

Dolbear, F.T., Lave, L.B., Bowman, G., Lieberman, A., Prescott, E., Rueter, F., Sherman, R. (1968), Collusion in oligopoly: An experiment on the effect of numbers and information. *Quarterly Journal of Economics* 82, 240–259.

Federal Trade Commission (2004), Horizontal mergers investigation data, fiscal years 1996–2003. Available at http://www.ftc.gov/os/2004/08/040831horizmergersdata96-03.pdf. Feb. 2.

Federal Trade Commission and Department of Justice (2004), Transcript of FTC/DOJ Joint Workshop on Merger Enforcement. Available at http://www.ftc.gov/bc/mergerenforce/040218ftctrans.pdf. Feb. 18.

Gavil, A.I., Kovacic, W.E., Baker, J.B. (2002), *Antitrust Law in Perspective: Cases, Concepts and Problems in Competition Policy*. West Publishing, St. Paul, MN.

Gellhorn, E., Kovacic, W.E., Calkins, S. (2004), *Antitrust Law and Economics in a Nutshell*. West Publishing, St. Paul, MN.

Greene, H. (2005), Agency character and the character of agency guidelines: An historical and institutional perspective. *Antitrust Law Journal* 72, 1039–1056.

Huck, S., Normann, H.-T., Oechssler, J. (2004), Two are few and four are many: Number effects in experimental oligopolies. *Journal of Economic Behavior & Organization* 53, 435–446.

Kaysen, C., Turner, D.F. (1959), *Antitrust Policy: An Economic and Legal Analysis*. Harvard University Press, Cambridge, MA.

Kolasky, W.J. (2002), Coordinated effects in merger review: From dead Frenchmen to beautiful minds to mavericks. Available at http://www.usdoj.gov/atr/public/speeches/11050.htm. Apr. 24.

Kovacic, W.E. (1989), Failed expectations: The troubled past and uncertain future of the Sherman Act as a tool for deconcentration. *Iowa Law Review* 74, 1105–1150.

Kovacic, W.E. (2003), The modern evolution of U.S. competition policy enforcement norms. *Antitrust Law Journal* 71, 377–478.

Kovacic, W.E. (2005), Measuring what matters: The federal trade commission and investments in competition policy research and development. *Antitrust Law Journal* 72, 861–869.

Kovacic, W.E., Shapiro, C. (2000), Antitrust policy: A century of economic and legal thinking. *Journal of Economic Perspectives* 14, 43–60.

Kwoka, J.E. (1979), The effect of market share distribution on industry performance. *Review of Economics and Statistics* 61, 101–109.

Leary, T.B. (2002), The essential stability of merger policy in the United States. *Antitrust Law Journal* 70, 105–142.

Marshall, R.C., Marx, L.M., Raiff, M.E. (2005), Cartel price announcements: The vitamins industry. Working Paper, Duke University.

Muris, T.J., Pitofsky, R. (2005), More than law enforcement: The FTC's many tools—A conversation with Tim Muris and Bob Pitofsky. *Antitrust Law Journal* 72, 773–860.

Selten, R. (1973), A simple model of imperfect competition, where 4 are few and 6 are many. *International Journal of Game Theory* 2, 141–201.

Stigler, G. (1964), A theory of oligopoly. *Journal of Political Economy* 72, 44–61.

Symposium (2003), The 20th Anniversary of the Department of Justice 1982 Merger Guidelines. *Antitrust Law Journal* 71.

Werden, G.J., Baumann, M.G. (1986), A simple model of imperfect competition in which four are few but three are not. *Journal of Industrial Economics* 34, 331–335.

CHAPTER 7

Effectiveness of Antitrust Sanctions on Modern International Cartels

John M. Connor

Purdue University, West Lafayette, IN
E-mail address: jconnor@purdue.edu

Abstract

This chapter assesses the antitrust fines and private penalties imposed on the participants of 260 international cartels discovered during 1990–2003, using four indicators of enforcement effectiveness: investigatory speed and confidentiality and two indexes of the harshness of monetary sanctions. First, the United States is almost always the first to investigate and sanction international cartels, and its investigations are about seven times faster than EU probes. Second, U.S. investigations were more likely to be kept confidential than those in Europe, but the gap nearly disappeared since 2000. Third, median government antitrust fines average less than 10% of affected commerce, but the median ratio rises to about 35% in the case of multi-continental conspiracies. Civil settlements in jurisdictions where they are permitted are typically 6 to 12%. Fourth, fines on cartels that operated in Europe averaged a bit more than half of their estimated overcharges; those prosecuted only in North America paid civil and criminal sanctions of roughly single damages; and global cartels prosecuted in both jurisdictions typically paid less than single damages.

JEL classifications: K21, K14, K33

7.1. Introduction

Twenty years ago the Sentencing Reform Act of 1984 created the U.S. Sentencing Commission, which was charged with devising guidelines for sentencing for the federal judiciary (USSG Advisory Group, 2003). The Commission was established because of Congressional concerns that sentencing was too variable across Circuits and individual judges and that average sentences were too low for certain crimes. Other jurisdictions outside the United States have since adopted similar anticartel sanctions. However, in January 2005, the U.S. Supreme Court declared the Guidelines unconstitutional, virtually guaranteeing that the Congress would pass overriding legislation (Cohen and Fields, 2005).

CONTRIBUTIONS TO ECONOMIC ANALYSIS
VOLUME 282 ISSN: 0573-8555
DOI: 10.1016/S0573-8555(06)82007-9

The Antitrust Modernization Commission is also poised to make recommendations to amend U.S. price-fixing sanctions (AMC, 2004).

The past decade has witnessed an upsurge in prosecutions of international cartels (Connor, 2004). Data collected on these prosecutions offer an opportunity to gain information on the size, duration, and harmfulness of cartel conduct. These data in turn permit the development of indicators of the effectiveness of cross-jurisdictional cartel enforcement policies and sanctions. In this chapter, four quantitative measures of anticartel actions are calculated for a large sample of international cartels punished by several antitrust authorities.

7.1.1. Objective

The purpose of this chapter is to assess the magnitude and pattern of global antitrust sanctions imposed on modern international cartels. Although there is a small literature that examines prosecutions of a few individual cartels, it is believed that this chapter is the first to examine and measure quantitatively all such legal actions. By doing so, this chapter can contribute critical information for the on-going debate about the effectiveness of global antitrust sanctions to deter international price-fixing conduct.

7.1.2. Scope

The focus of this chapter is on all types of monetary and penal antitrust sanctions that have been imposed on participants in private international cartels discovered between January 1990 and August 2005. Monetary sanctions include *fines* imposed by antitrust authorities on both corporations and individuals. Monetary sanctions also include *payments* made by defendants in private suits to both direct and indirect buyers of cartelized products; most often these payments are made as a result of *settlements* made out of court prior to trial, but in a few cases are *litigated judgments* of a trial judge or jury. Sanction amounts do not include the legal fees and costs of defendants, which may be substantial but are almost never revealed.[1] However, payments made by defendants to settle private class-action suits do include the legal fees and costs incurred by plaintiffs in prosecuting their cases.[2]

This chapter analyses only what Evenett et al. (2001) call "Type I" and the OECD calls "hard-core" cartels. A *cartel* is a group of two or more independent sellers who agree to fix or control prices or output in a given market (Dick, 1998). *International* cartels are those that have participants from two or more

---

[1] Other possible sanctions are not measured. These include the money value of prison sentences, stockholders' suits for mismanagement, and reputational losses.

[2] In the United States, among the 23 largest class-action awards for price fixing in 1972–1999, legal fees ranged from 7% to 36% of the net recovery to the plaintiffs (Connor, 2001, 471). This ratio has trended downward over time and by size of the case.

countries[3]; the qualifier does not necessarily refer to the geographic scope of the cartel's agreement, but the two tend to be related. *Hard-core* cartels are those that overtly control prices, limit output, or allocate production among participants.[4] *Private* cartels are those that operate without the protection of national sovereignty; they can be indicted for antitrust violations. Thus, legally registered export cartels are considered private, but not mandatory cartels nor those established by parliamentary statutes or by treaties among nations. Private cartels may contain state-owned or controlled corporations, but if such cartels can be prosecuted under the antitrust laws of any jurisdiction, they are considered private schemes.[5]

Finally, this chapter examines only those international cartels that were "discovered" between January 1990 and August 2005. By *discovered* is meant information that an antitrust authority had opened a formal investigation[6] or had indicted a member of an alleged cartel; was forced to pay a fine by a recognized antitrust authority, was found liable for damages in a private suit pleaded guilty to a criminal indictment, agreed to pay damages in an out-of-court settlement, or agreed to a consent decree.[7] The choice of 1990 is somewhat arbitrary, but is meant to capture the beginning of the current level antitrust sanctions in the United States,[8] the EU,[9] and Canada.[10]

---

[3] The DOJ definition refers to either corporate (ultimate parent) members (nationality determined by location of the headquarters or country of incorporation) or managers' nationalities. In practice, in this paper corporate composition is the key indicator.

[4] Other cartels collude on vertical conduct or such "softer" horizontal practices as patent pooling, R&D, or advertising. The DOJ typically prosecutes non-hard-core collusion as a civil matter.

[5] International comity is a principal ingrained in government antitrust decisions (Waller, 2000).

[6] In the United States this means that a grand jury is empaneled; in most other jurisdictions formal probes are signaled by news of a "raid" by police on a place of business to search for documents or interview managers.

[7] By "prosecuted" I mean to include payments of civil penalties for violations of competition regulations as in the EU, criminal indictments, and announced formal investigations. The latter typically result in fines or guilty pleas.

[8] In 1990, the final increase in the U.S. statutory cap on antitrust fines ($10 million per company) became law. In 1993, the DOJ announced a policy of automatic leniency for the first cartel member to confess that met certain predictable conditions, a policy shift that proved widely-effective.

[9] In Europe, Harding and Joshua (2003) conclude that "... European law has over [1890–1990] caught up with American law" (p. 270) in the sense that cartels are now subject to "categorical censure". Since the 1970s in Europe, "... the classic price-fixing, market-sharing cartel has... been driven underground and become strongly prohibited..." (p. 229). In 1998 the EC issued guidelines for the calculation of price-fixing fines that explained practices being followed during the 1990s (ibid, p. 242). Moreover, in 1996 the EC issued its first leniency notice, which was revised in 2002 in a way that closely mimicked the U.S. policy. Therefore, by the late 1990s, the EU had also developed a set of government Anticartel sanctions for corporations that were similar to those in the United States and Canada (ibid, pp. 216–222).

[10] In 1992, Ontario, Canada passed a major piece of legislation that promulgated rules for private class actions, and other provinces followed soon after (Goldman et al., 2003, 4). A civil remedy was made law in 1976 and affirmed by the Supreme Court of Canada in 1989, but was little used until the 1992 rules change was promulgated (ibid). Passage precipitated a large number of suits against

7.2. Background on the issues

7.2.1. Origin and importance of the 10% presumption

The USSC's cartel fine levels followed from its famous conclusion: "It is estimated that the average gain from price-fixing is 10 percent of the selling price."[11] The Commission explained how it used this estimate to establish cartel fines. After noting that fines should be based on consideration of both the gain to the offender and the losses caused by the offender, the USSC noted that it would double the 10% estimate to account for harms "inflicted upon consumers who are unable or for other reasons do not buy the product at the higher price."[12] That is, the base fine of 20% of affected commerce was designed to exceed both the overcharges imposed on buyers and the dead-weight social loss. To explain why it focused on sales rather than welfare loss, the Commission added: "The purpose for specifying a percent of the volume of commerce is to avoid the time and expense that would be required for the court to determine actual gain or loss."[13]

The Guidelines' approach is consistent with the standard optimal deterrence criterion promulgated by William Landes (1983). Landes convincingly showed that to achieve optimal deterrence the damages from an antitrust violation should be equal to the violation's "net harm to others,"[14] divided by the probability of

---

members of international cartels in Canada. Along with Canada's nearly per se condemnation of price fixing as a criminal act, the addition of feasible compensatory suits brought Canada's legal structure very close to the U.S. model.

[11] U.S. Sentencing Commission Guidelines for the United States Courts, 18 U.S.C. Section 2R1.1, Bid-Rigging, Price Fixing or Market-Allocation Agreements Among Competitors, Application Note 3. The first guidelines were made law in 1989 (Cohen and Scheffman, 1989, 332). It appears that the Commission believed that it had by 1987 sufficient statistical data on price fixing to set penalties at levels that would exceed the financial benefits of price fixing. The USSC appears to have adopted the 10% presumption because its use was advocated by the (then) head of the Antitrust Division of the U.S. Department of Justice (DOJ). In a statement to the Commission, he stated that "the optimal fine for any given act of price-fixing is equal to the damage caused by the violation divided by the probability of conviction ... such a fine would result in the socially optimal level of price-fixing, which in this case is zero" (USSG, 1987, 14). He stated his judgment that "price fixing typically results in price increases that has harmed the consumers in a range of 10 percent of the price..." and that these violations had no more than 10% chance of detection (ibid, p. 15).

[12] Section 8C2.4 (a) (3). It is unclear why the Guidelines doubled the assumed 10% loss, although the explanation in the Guidelines' commentary implies that this could be due to such factors as the allocative inefficiency harms of market power (the deadweight loss), the disruptive effects on victims caused by antitrust violations and/or the umbrella effects of market power. "Umbrella effects" is the name given to higher prices charged by non-cartel members that were permitted or caused by the cartel's supracompetitive prices. The doubling of the 10% presumed overcharge does not, however, given the context, account in any way for the small chances of finding and convicting cartels or the lack of prejudgment interest.

[13] Ibid.

[14] The total of the overcharge paid by direct buyers and the dead-weight loss.

detection[15] and proof (Landes, 1983, 666–68). The base fine (20% of affected revenues) is adjusted by a number of factors, such as whether bid rigging[16] and other aggravating factors were involved, and by mitigating factors as well.[17] This adjustment results in a pair of "culpability multipliers" that are somewhere between 0.75 and 4.0 and are in a 1:2 ratio. The product of the base fine and the culpability multipliers results in the fine range that is to be imposed on a cartel member. Thus, the fine range recommended for convicted cartelists is from 15% to 80% of affected sales. (These fines usually are adjusted downwards for cooperation or as a part of the Division's leniency program.[18]) As the Sixth Circuit noted, the Sentencing Commission "opted for greater administrative convenience" instead of undertaking a specific inquiry into the actual loss in each case."[19]

7.2.2. Critiques of the 10% Guidelines presumption

The USSC's 10% presumption was derided as unreliable and overstated almost as soon as it was issued. For example, Cohen and Scheffman (1989) concluded that "...there is little credible statistical evidence that would justify the Commission's assumptions which underlie the Antitrust Guidelines (p. 333)." Indeed, Cohen and Scheffman state that only three economic evaluations of price-fixing conspiracies were important in shaping the 10% presumption. "At least in price fixing cases involving a substantial volume of commerce, ten percent is almost certainly too high (p. 343)." Moreover, the specific data that the Commission uses was attacked as unreliable: "later research has cast considerable doubt on ... these estimates, concluding that the markups, if they existed, were quite small (p. 345)."

---

[15] In 1986 the Assistant Attorney General for Antitrust, Douglas Ginsburg, estimated that the enforcers catch less than 10% of all cartels. See USSG (1987, 15). If he is correct, optimal damages for cartels should be tenfold! However, the percentage of cartels that are caught and proven probably is much higher today. See Spratling (2001). There is, however, no evidence that it exceeds 1/3, so there is no reason to believe that the treble damage remedy should be lowered. See also the discussion in Landes (1983, 115, fn. 1).

[16] If bid rigging is involved this increases the Base Offense Level by 1, See 18 U.S.C. Section 2R1.1 (b). This indicates the USSC's belief that Bid-rigging is worse than other forms of illegal collusion.

[17] See Section 2R1.1 and Application Note 1.

[18] The USSC's Commentary also notes that "In cases in which the actual monopoly overcharge appears to be either substantially more or substantially less then 10%" they might not employ the 20% assumption. See Application Note 3. But in practice they almost always use the figure of 20% of affected commerce as their starting point in their criminal fine calculations.

[19] See United States v. Hayter Oil Co., 51 F.3d 1265, 1277 (1995). The court noted: "The offense levels are not based directly on the damage caused or profit made by the defendant because damages are difficult and time consuming to establish. The volume of commerce is an acceptable and more readily measurable substitute... We find nothing other than the following commentary language that indicates that the Sentencing Commission adopted the theory of optimal penalties: It is estimated that the average additional profit attributable to price-fixing is 10 percent of the selling price" (ibid).

Recent anticartel sanctions have prompted more criticism of U.S. fine-setting practices. From 1990 to 1999, a series of record corporate fines were imposed for criminal price fixing by U.S. courts; a similar upswing may be noted for fines imposed by the European Commission after 1995 (Connor, 2004; Burnside, 2003). Civil treble-damages cases in the United States have seen a parallel, if lagged response in the size of settlements. Not surprisingly, attorneys involved in such cases have claimed that the Guidelines have resulted in penalties so large that they have resulted in overdeterrence.[20] For example, just as the DOJ's campaign against international cartels was gathering steam, Adler and Laing (1997) assert that "the fines being imposed against corporate members of international cartels are staggering (p. 1)", placing the blame on the "uniquely punitive" requirements of the U.S. Sentencing Guidelines.

> What is... troubling is that the company fines ...have risen astronomically—to levels far higher than the fines for other serious economic crimes and in amounts that can be unrelated to the economic harm caused by the violations. (Adler and Laing, 1999, 1)

More recently, Denger (2003) too decries the prevalence of excessive price-fixing fines and private settlements. He places the blame for excessive fines on the Corporate Guidelines base fine calculation, which is 20% of the volume of affected commerce (p. 3). This approach, he notes, is at odds with fine calculations for all other white-collar federal crimes in that the actual degree of direct harm caused does not have to be proven by prosecutors.[21] Concern about the lack of empirical evidence on the actual harm caused by price fixing extends to antitrust officials as well. Graubert (2003) notes that the controversy over whether antitrust payments are excessive (which on p. 7 he equates with payouts greater than reasonable damage estimates) is largely attributable to the "...difficulty of gathering useful data."

7.2.3. Antitrust fine limits abroad

In the European Union, 10% also plays a key role in setting antitrust fines on international cartels, but it is a different 10%. The maximum amount that the European Commission can impose on a company that violates the EU's competition laws is in principle unrelated to the size of a cartel member's overcharges. Rather, the maximum is 10% of the company's total revenues in the year preceding the EC's decision (Burnside, 2003). The origin of this limit, spelled out

[20] Warnings of over-deterrence often follow from illustrations based on extreme assumptions about the size of overcharges (small), the private costs of antitrust compliance (large), and monetary sanctions or other liabilities (maximal). All too often the gloomy alarms, if not entirely theoretical, are strictly *ex post* analyses of anonymous anecdotes.

[21] Denger appeals primarily to an increase in settlement rates in treble-damage direct-purchaser suits to establish the unfairness of the high fines imposed on corporate price fixers, an increase that, he believes, cannot be explained by increases in overcharge rates. He cites about 8 domestic U.S. law cases that settled for 2 to 4% of sales in the 1970s and one international case in 2001 that settled for 18 to 20% (pp. 3–4). Settlements are inappropriate evidence in this context.

in the EC's Regulation 17, is obscure. If a single-line firm participates in a cartel for only one year, those profits in excess of 10% of revenues will be retained by the violator. Price fixing will be even more profitable if, as is usually the case, the cartel endures for more than a year or if EC fines are less than 10% of revenues.[22] The 10% cap, in force since 1960, has not been seriously considered for amendment.[23]

In Canada, there is no published policy on the imposition of fines. One section of Canada's antitrust law imposes a fine limit of C$10 million, but another section that applies to international conspiracies has no such limit (Low and Wakil, 2004). However, historically since at least the 1980s corporate participants in cartels are fined quite close to 20% of Canadian affected sales. Aggravating and mitigating factors seem to play a minor role in fine setting. Companies that are accepted into Canada's 1994 leniency program pay considerably less. Private follow-on class-action antitrust actions have been permitted since 1992, but for single damages only (Goldman et al., 2003).

Japan's Antimonopoly Law has even more restrictive upper limits on the fines that can be imposed by the Japan Fair Trade Commission (JFTC). For the largest companies in the manufacturing sector, the limit is 6% of sales.[24] For smaller companies in non-manufacturing industries, the limit is far lower. In 2004, the government proposed doubling the upper limit on antitrust fines.[25]

7.2.4. The broader issue of cartel deterrence

Cohen and Scheffman also argue that the Antitrust Guideline, when coupled with civil and marketplace sanctions will cause "a serious problem" (p. 334). That is, they and other critics of the Guidelines believe that there is a disparity between the size of the corporate fines mandated for antitrust violations and the amount of the economic injuries caused by overt price fixing. During recent years this criticism has been repeated with perhaps even more intensity. These attacks could be due to rising levels of corporate antitrust fines in recent years.

Concerns about the inadequacy or excessiveness of antitrust sanctions are part of the larger issue of the effectiveness of antitrust interventions. To make

---

[22] Nearly all cartels sanctioned by the EU are international, and there is abundant research showing that international-cartel duration averages 5 to 7 years. The saving grace for EU fines is the fact that in practice most corporate violators have been large multinational corporations for which the cartelized product is a small share of total company sales. There are, however, many counter examples.

[23] Regulation 17 was amended in 2004 without changing this limit on fines.

[24] In 2006 the limits will rise.

[25] The amendment is supported by the Prime Minister, bar associations, and consumer groups, but is opposed by Japan Business Federation, which may be the country's most powerful lobby. According to a JFTC study, average monopoly profits in Japanese cartels are estimated to average 16.5% (Asahi News Service, April 23, 2004). In 2005, the upper limit was raised to 10% of sales for large manufacturers and lower percentages for small and non-manufacturing firms.

any headway in assessing empirically the adequacy of anticartel enforcement, it is necessary to have reliable information about the degree of harm generated by private cartels. Cartel injuries to purchasers are positively related to three economic factors: the size of the cartel's market, the duration of the conspiracy, and the percentage overcharge. Antitrust sanctions should be calibrated to a cartel's affected sales and overcharges; investigation procedures can reduce the probability of cartel formation or the duration of cartels. Those critical of aggressive antitrust policy have often embraced the comforting notion that cartels are fragile coalitions. When the OPEC cartel began to have an impact on petroleum prices in the early 1970s, several leading economists predicted its imminent demise. Morris Adelman (1972) wrote that

> Every cartel has in time been destroyed by one and then some members chiseling and cheating... (p. 71).

In 1974, in a now infamous news magazine article, Milton Freedman predicted OPEC's collapse. However, research by Eckbo (1976) and Suslow (2001) finds that the mean duration of discovered cartels is around five or six years. The (unknown) duration of undiscovered cartels is likely to be longer. OPEC may be less powerful today than in the 1970s, but its production decisions continued to roil world petroleum markets.

In a provocative essay that quickly drew rebuttals,[26] Crandall and Winston (2003) assert that extant empirical evidence demonstrates that antitrust policy has been ineffective in either raising consumer welfare or in deterring anticompetitive conduct:

> We find little empirical evidence that past [antitrust] interventions have provided much direct benefit to consumers or significantly deterred anticompetitive behavior (p. 4).

The great majority of their criticisms are directed at monopoly and merger enforcement, but remedies in collusion cases also attract their disfavor. To support their view that the prosecution of overt price fixing is misdirected, they cite five empirical studies of overt collusion that find no upward effects on prices of conspiracies convicted in U.S. courts.[27] While Crandall and Winston later admit that there are some "examples" of successful collusion, no studies are cited that

---

[26] See Baker (2003), Werden (2003), and Kwoka (2003). According to Kwoka (2003, note 2), Crandall and Winston's earlier drafts "... endorsed consideration of outright repeal of the antitrust laws."

[27] We should note that space constraints do not appear to be responsible for such a skimpy treatment of this topic, for they list 59 references. The choice of two of the articles is unfortunate, because both are methodologically deeply flawed. Newmark (1988) is discussed later in this chapter; Sproul (1993) is criticized by Werden (2003). Both articles appear in journals managed by University of Chicago economists. Two other studies focus on an odd alleged episode of price fixing, the so-called Overlap group of 23 elite U.S. universities that met regularly to allocate needs-based graduate scholarships; this practice was permitted to continue under a consent decree that limited the degree of detail shared.

support the positive effect on prices.[28] As for deterrence, Crandall and Winston rather grudgingly admit that the large DOJ fines meted out to cartels in recent years possibly deterred the most harmful cartels.[29] This concession is immediately tempered by a citation to an entirely theoretical analysis of the dangers of over deterrence.

In his comment on Kwoka (2003) faults them for their "startlingly selective" body of evidence. He suggests that they should have included "... studies from any source with appropriate evaluation of their credibility" (p. 4). Kwoka is hardly the first specialist to lament the absence of quantitative estimates of the price effects of overtly collusive arrangements.

Despite the evident antitrust successes in sanctioning international cartels in the last decade, skepticism still is expressed about whether current enforcement regimes are capable of serving the aims of antitrust. A narrow construction on the purpose of antitrust laws limits it to maximizing consumer welfare and efficiency; a broader interpretation gives some weight to income redistribution, small business protection, or dispersion of political and economic power. However, under either stance the aims of antitrust are served by competition policies that deter recidivism. While deterrence may have improved marginally in the 1990s, scholars of modern international cartels believe that current competition policies cannot fully deter because they are "...oriented towards addressing harm done in domestic markets... [or] merely prohibit cartels without [sufficiently strong sanctions]" (Evenett et al., 2001, 1222). Moreover, empirical evidence from recent years demonstrates a significant degree of continued cartel formation and multiple corporate convictions for price fixing. It would appear that either greater sanctions ought to be applied or that a multilateral approach implemented in order to approach optimal deterrence of international price fixing.[30]

In sum, there does indeed seem to be a broad consensus among legal and economic writers that the question of the optimality of price-fixing penalties turns mightily on the actual degree of harm caused by cartel conduct, and that we do not know enough about this issue. Moreover, even if the creators of the USSC Guidelines were correct that in the 1980s cartels generally raised prices by 10%, the harsher cartel sanctions imposed more recently could mean that this presumption is no longer justified. This is a gap in the literature that this article attempts to address.

---

[28] They say that the lysine, citric acid, and vitamins cases are "well known". I am aware of only one publication that covers the price effects of all three of these three cases with a degree of depth, viz., Connor (2001).

[29] Their reasoning is obscure. Perhaps they are referring to international cartels, cartels with absolutely large overcharges, or conspiracies with high percentage overcharges. In any case, why they expect the probability of discovery or relative size of expected sanctions to be greater in such cases is not clear.

[30] One way of increasing sanctions without changing the statutes is to extend standing to foreign buyers to permit them to sue for private damages in U.S. courts. On the Empagram case, see Davis (2003) and Bush et al. (2004).

7.3. Literature review

Analyses of the antitrust prosecutions and convictions in single legal jurisdictions are commonplace. Gallo et al. (2000) have reviewed the enforcement of the Sherman Act by the U.S. DOJ for the period 1955–1997. This chapter describes the number antitrust cases by type and outcome over time, but it collects only limited information on the characteristics of the prosecuted cartels. Examining only *per se* horizontal violations during 1955–1989 (a category that corresponds closely to cartels), Gallo et al. find only 34 international cases, which represent merely 2.3% of all such cases. During the Reagan and first Bush administrations, the international rate dropped to 0.4%, but in the late 1990s the rate rose to above 50% (Connor, 2001). Gallo et al. also provide information on the size and duration of U.S.-prosecuted cartels. The average number of defendants was about four, but dropped to less than two in 1980–1997. The average size of affected sales was 870 million 1982 dollars; again, the average size was much smaller during 1980–1994 ($120 million) than before. The average duration of the conspiracies was 5.4 years, with no trend over time. Finally, this study gives summary data on fines and prison sentences imposed in criminal cartels cases. The total fines imposed on 2,908 companies during 1955–1997 was $305 million (approximately 440 million 1995 dollars), two-thirds of which was imposed after 1989. In addition, 1,431 individuals were fined a total of $30 million.

Similar less detailed compilations of prosecution statistics are available for other jurisdictions, but analyses for international cartels are few. Guersent (2004) summarizes the cartels' conduct and sanctions taken against 19 international cartels by the EC from July 2001 to December 2003. This chapter simply collects information previously released by the Commission in its news releases and in-house publication *EC Competition Newsletter*. Perhaps the fullest survey of modern international cartels appears in a lengthy working paper by two of the profession's most active researchers on cartels Levenstein and Suslow (2002). The chapter aims at describing the structure of cartel markets (numbers, concentration, and demand features) and assessing three dimensions of cartel performance: stability, duration and "profitability," the last equivalent to overcharges. Levenstein and Suslow (2002) cite several studies of the interwar period and collect information on 35 international singe-episode cartels prosecuted by the DOJ and EC from 1990 to 2001 (Table 15). While their 2002 monograph employs in part data taken from prosecutors' statements, it does not document the antitrust consequences of the cartels' behavior. A more recent paper by Levenstein et al. (2003) does cite antitrust fines for two modern cartels in Table 2, but it does not aim to analyze cartel sanctions in a cross-sectional manner.

The Organization of Economic Co-Operation and Development (OECD) for several years has had an active program for the consideration of a common policy approach towards international cartels. Its report *Hard Core Cartels* summarizes a unique survey of its member countries' experiences in sanctioning such cartels (OECD, 2003). The EU and 14 members provided data (fines, affected commerce, or harm) on 38 convictions of 27 international cartels; while most of these data are public knowledge, some are unique (ibid, Annex A). These data have been incorporated into the present chapter.[31]

7.4. Description of the sample

The sample consists of 260 private international cartels that were discovered between January 1990 and July 2005 (Table 7.1). Of these 260 cartels, 69 (or 27%) were *global* conspiracies. Global cartels are defined as ones in which price fixing was applied across at least two continents; many operated in as many as six continents, but most fixed prices in the "Triad" of Western Europe, North America, and East Asia. Non-global cartels colluded within only one continent or one nation. The largest number of such cartels were discovered in Europe, of which 52 (20%) were "EU-wide" (active in several countries of the EU), 59 (23%) were confined within the borders of one EU Member State, and six (2.3%) were found in Eastern Europe. Most of the remaining 27 cartels were located in East Asia (Japan, Korea, China, and Philippines), but there were two in Israel, two in Africa, four in Oceania, and four in Latin America. With the exception of Korea and Australia, the small number of cartels discovered outside of North America and Western Europe primarily reflects the fact that the antitrust authorities of those regions are new, understaffed, or simply not aggressive in pursuing or careless about reporting probes of international cartels (Connor, 2004).

7.4.1. Prosecution patterns

Information was found on a total of 387 legal actions, a term that includes the launching of an official investigation, filing of a private antitrust damages suit, or the imposition of one or more legal sanctions. Of the 260 sampled cartels, in about 21 instances the official investigation had been terminated by mid 2005, either because the allegations of illegal activity proved baseless or because the evidence of guilt was insufficient. In a few cases private suits were filed and settlements were made even though a government investigation ended without an indictment.[32] These data demonstrate that antitrust authorities are by and large cautious about opening formal investigations in the sense that 90% to 95% of the cases investigated conclude with sanctions of some sort.

---

[31] Details on more than 1000 overcharges, their methods of calculation, and more than 250 publication sources are contained in Connor (2006) or in Appendix Table 2 of "Price-Fixing Overcharges" http://www.agecon.purdue.edu/staff/connor/papers/PRICE_FIXING_OVERCHARGES_APPENDIX_TABLES_8-05.pdf. The estimates vary considerably in their degree of precision, but no attempt was made to apply a subjective quality filter. In some cases errors have been corrected and reliable additional facts have supplemented the OECD data.

[32] Perhaps the best documented of these cases is the high fructose corn syrup cartel; direct buyers settled for $611 million after the DOJ dropped its investigation as part of a deal to obtain a guilty plea from Archer Daniels Midland Company for its price fixing in a different market (Connor, 2001).

Table 7.1: Private international cartels discovered 1990–2005.

Type	Geographic location of cartel					
	Global scope	NAFTA	EU-wide	Europe nations	Other region	Total actions
	Number					
Antitrust authority prosecuting						
U.S. courts	35 DOJ 34 Private	40 DOJ 18 Private	0	0	1 DOJ	128
Canada courts	24 CBC 13 Private	14 CBC 5 Private	1	0	0	56
European Commission	30	0	27	1	0	58
EU Member State	0	0	0	43	0	43
Other Europe	0	0	0	5	0	5
Oceania	3	0	0	0	2	5
Africa	0	0	0	0	1	1
Asia	4	0	0	0	11 2 Private	17
Latin America	1	0	0	0	1	2
Total cartels	69	47	52	65	27	260
Investigation only[a]	31	18	24	18	11	102
Total convictions	114	77	28	49	17	285
Product type						
Raw material	1	0	1	0	0	2
Intermediate indus. input	56	34	30	18	12	150
Capital input	0	0	2	2	5	9
Generic consumer	0	2	10	7	5	24
Differentiated consumer	2	6	2	16	1	27
Services	10	5	8	22	4	49
Total	69	47	52	65	27	260

Source: Appendix Table.
[a]Still underway (81) or ended in dismissal (21) by mid 2005. Fines, consent decrees, settlement agreements, and warnings are classified as convictions.

Excluding the 21 cartels with closed investigations, 81 (34%) appear to be under investigation as of August 2005.[33] For these cartels, no sanctions are yet

[33] Antitrust authorities do not always announce closure; occasionally the only source of information on termination comes from press releases or financial reports of companies formerly being investigated.

available. The ratio of cartels under investigation is highest for EU-wide cartels (40%), relatively high for global cartels (34%), and lowest for those in North America (24%). However, for 165 (77%) cartels sanctions data are essentially complete, highest for North American (83%) and European national (74%) cartels and about 55 to 65% for those in other locations. In the case of global cartels and those in jurisdiction that permit private suits, sanctions are levied in stages. Some of these cartels are no longer in the purely investigatory stage, but they are not complete either. Therefore, in this chapter a few of the observations will be reported with somewhat incomplete sanctions data.

Consent decrees (only ten unaccompanied by monetary sanctions) are the least common sanction, accounting for only 6% of the sanctioned cartels. Cartel investigations that end with consent decrees only are rare in North America.[34] The EU sometimes uses this sanction also, but it is the favorite sanction of the Japan Fair Trade Commission.

Most cartels that are investigated pay monetary fines or settlements. This study focuses on the 275 instances of monetary cartel sanctions. The vast majority (75%) of such outcomes was imposed in cases prosecuted by government entities; the remaining 25% were the result of private damage suits in the United States and Canada.[35] Global cartels were frequently prosecuted by multiple antitrust authorities and by buyers in North America. The 38 sanctioned global cartels in the sample paid government fines in at least 67 instances and settled suits by purchasers 47 times (Table 7.1). Cartels in the NAFTA area similarly faced multiple legal actions. However, outside North America indicted cartels almost always had to deal with only one antitrust authority.

7.4.2. Industry pattern

Table 7.1 shows the numbers of cartels classified into six general types of goods: raw materials, four kinds of manufactures, and services. The great majority (80%) of the sample cartels sold manufactures. There are only two raw materials cartels, but the number of service-sector groups is high by historical standards. The most prominent services are in construction, transportation, and finance and insurance (Appendix table).

Within manufacturing, producer goods dominate the sample. Cartels in markets for industrial intermediate goods account for 72% of manufacturing cartels and 58% of the total sample. The global and NAFTA cartels were especially concentrated in industrial intermediates. Only nine cartels (3%) sold industrial capital goods. Nearly all the industrial manufactures are homogeneous products. The single most important manufacturing industry group is chemicals (30% of

[34] Most likely the case is handled by the Federal Trade Commission rather than the DOJ.

[35] Two cartels operating in other regions also were subject to compensatory suits. For example, a cartel that rigged bids on water treatment plants built under contracts with USAID funding in Egypt was both fined and paid single damages to the U.S. government.

the cartels), with organic chemicals far more common than inorganic. Other manufactures well represented include food and tobacco (8%), non-metallic minerals (8%), paper (5%), and rubber and plastic (5%). About 20% of the sample consisted of final manufactured consumer products, half standardized and half differentiated goods. Most of the branded consumer goods represented in the sample were sold direct by manufacturers in bulk; for example, most of the pharmaceuticals were sold to national health organizations, not to retailers or consumers; similarly, a number of beer cartels colluded in contract sales of kegs of beer to the foodservice channel.

The industrial distribution of the sampled international cartels differs considerably from samples drawn from the early 20th century. Stocking and Watkins (1946, 469–92) provide a fairly list of 127 international cartels active in the interwar period. Their compilation is relatively heavy in raw agricultural and mining materials (11% of the cartels) but is light in services (3%) compared to the modern cartel sample. However, within manufacturing the interwar cartels had a similar emphasis on producer intermediate inputs and chemicals in particular.

7.5. Measures of effectiveness

The data collected on international cartels for this chapter suggest four indicators of enforcement effectiveness by antitrust authorities. First, the speed with which the agencies investigate, negotiate, and impose sanctions may be analyzed. Generally, long delays in the administration of justice are regarded as bad public policy. One can imagine an investigation that is too short for an adequate judgment about probable cause, but the main complaint of defendants is about excessive length and the consequent period of uncertainty about prosecution or the size of sanctions, especially if the investigation becomes public, as many do. Because of the absence of pre-judgment interest, plaintiffs especially have an interest in quick conclusions to suits, which defendants habitually delay as far as possible (Adams and Metlin, 2002). A peculiar feature of international cartels is that when a probe, fine, or guilty plea is made in one jurisdiction, it may well trigger follow-on investigations in other jurisdictions.[36] Although court trials are rare for either criminal or civil prosecutions, they can add several years to a final determination of guilt. In the EU, appeals about the sizes of cartel fines are common, but as these are by choice of the fined companies, this aspect of speed will not be studied.

A second indicator is the pattern of cartel formation over time. The simple notion underlying this measure of enforcement effectiveness is that as information becomes available to business persons about increases in maximum legal price-fixing penalties, in the probability of detection, or in harshness of actual

[36] Under cooperation agreements among antitrust authorities, information-sharing about allegations of international price fixing is becoming more rapid.

sanctions corporate decision makers will raise their expectations concerning the costs of illegal behavior. Changes in these perceptions are likely to arise from several sources: legal advisors, business and trade publications, and the informal exchange of information between business persons. The lags in learning and in forming expectations may be considerable. For example, the strikingly effective 1993 DOJ Corporate Leniency Program underwent a number of significant amendments for a decade after its implementation, as did the leniency policies of a dozen other antitrust authorities (Spratling and Arp, 2005). Therefore, conclusions about the relationships between milestones in anticartel laws or enforcement actions and decreases in cartel formations will require long periods of analysis.

A third measure of effectiveness is the size of a company's fine relative to its sales during the cartel period; alternatively, the fines on all members of a cartel can be compared to affected sales of the total market. Although these ratios have no direct relationship to economic deterrence, they are the most frequently cited measure of a successful prosecution in legal discussions. Judicial opinions on the fairness of proposed class-action settlements inevitably focus on the recovery/sales ratio proposed relative to the same ratios from other settlements. Class counsel likewise highlight this ratio when defending a settlement from criticisms about a particular deal. Recoveries above 10% or even 5% of sales are cited as successful results for plaintiffs (Spratling and Arp, 2005). Some students of cartels opine that fines as high as 150% of affected sales are necessary for absolute deterrence (Wils, 2001). Despite the absence of a firm economic defense for the fine/sales ratio,[37] this index is broadly computable and is a rough indicator of the rigorousness of anticartel enforcement over time or across jurisdictions.

The fourth measure of enforcement effectiveness is the ratio of monetary sanctions to the cartels overcharge.[38] This index bears directly on the question of economic deterrence. Unfortunately, it is the most difficult to compute, has the smallest sample size, and is the most likely to contain measurement errors.

7.5.1. Rates of international cartel formation

An informal analysis of cartel formation is provided in Figures 7.1–7.4. In every geographic region, the annual rates of cartel formation (the year the cartel began

[37] From a compensation or deterrence standpoint, optimal fines should relate to the antitrust injuries caused by the cartel. While damages in some situations should be based upon lost profits, in U.S. federal law damages are customarily computed from overcharges (Hovenkamp, 1999, 658–659). The size of civil damages is positively related to the overcharge percentage and affected sales. Cartel fines, however, are computed almost solely from affected sales (Connor, 2005). Because of the reluctance of the courts to bankrupt defendants, maximum fines are set relative to profits or liquid assets in order to take into consideration a company's ability to pay.

[38] Of course, the best denominator would the sum of the overcharge and the deadweight loss, but the latter is even more difficult to compute in cartel cases than the overcharge.

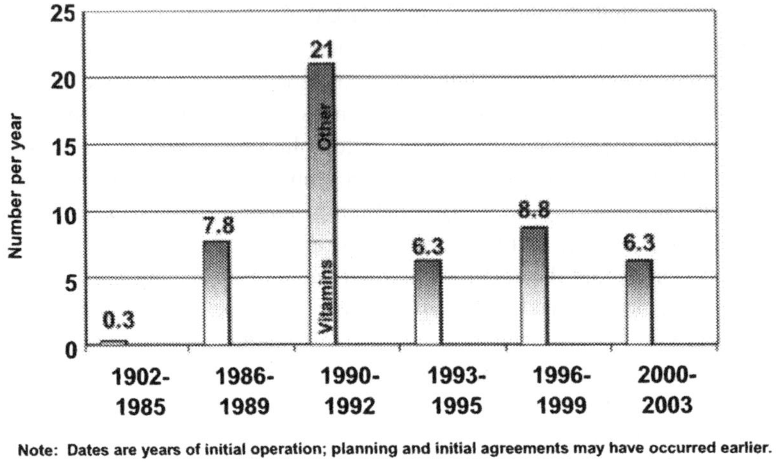

Fig. 7.1: Rates of formation: All international cartel episodes.

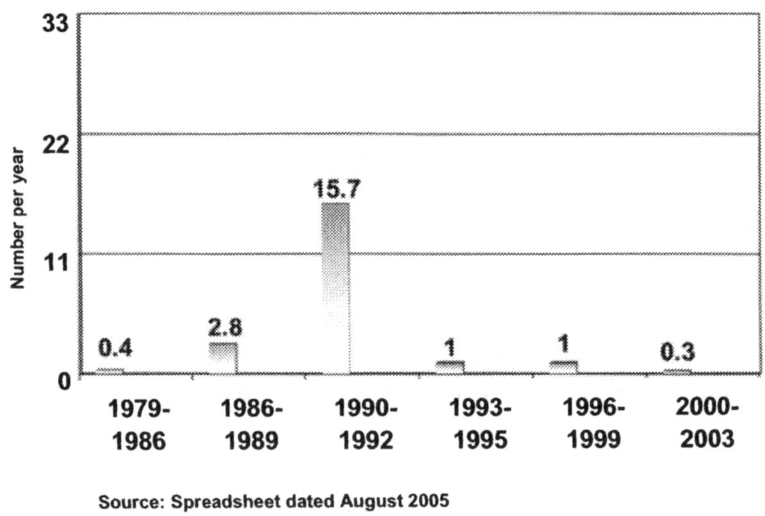

Fig. 7.2: Rates of formation: Global cartel episodes.

fixing prices) peaks in the early 1990s. The increase in formation rates from the 1980s to the 1990s is particularly striking and informative. The acceleration in new cartels is apparent for all types of international cartels, global, European, and North America.

The NAFTA-area cartels began at a slightly earlier time than the other two types (cf. Figure 7.4 with Figures 7.2 and 7.3). During the 1981–1988 Reagan administration, the resources of the U.S. DOJ were directed primarily at small scale bid-rigging conspiracies (Connor, 2001, 67). Attention to interna-

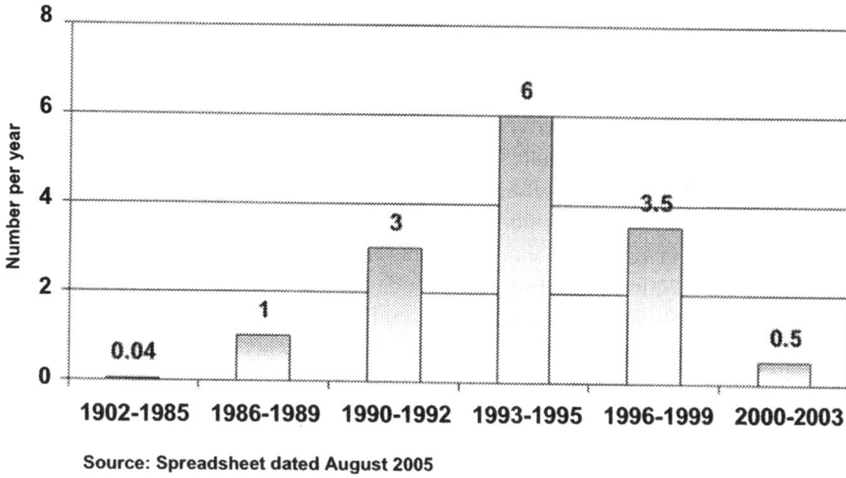

Fig. 7.3: Rates of formation: European cartel episodes.

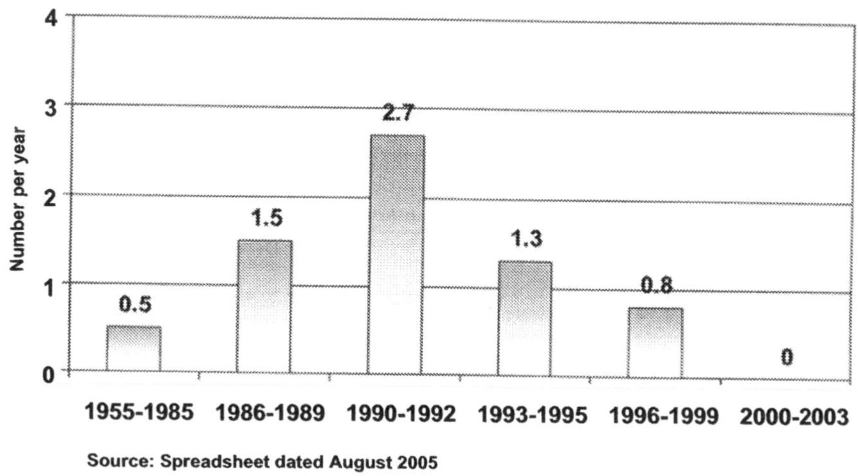

Fig. 7.4: Rates of formation: NAFTA area cartel episodes.

tional cartel enforcement rose slightly during the Bush *pere* administration, but really became a major priority of the DOJ only after 1992. U.S. legal sanctions increased in 1987 when price fixing was made a felony and in 1990 when the statutory corporate fine was raised to $10 million; however, the DOJ seems not to have implemented these new powers until after 1992 or 1993 (Spratling, 1999, 2001). The fall-off on new cartel formations in North America is consistent with the threat of the DOJ's enhanced prosecutorial powers and, after the DOJ's singular victories in the lysine and citric acid cases in 1995–1996, with the demonstrated ability to win in court. The notable decline in new cartel formations after 1997 is suggestive of a deterrence effect, but only a longer time period will allow for a more definitive conclusion.[39]

Europe began successful prosecution of international cartels in 1969, but significantly increased the priority to investigate such cases only from the mid 1990s.[40] Figure 7.1 demonstrates a peak in cartel formation in 1993–1995 and a notable decline after 1995. Again, although time will tell whether the post-1995 decline is just a statistical illusion, the pattern is consistent with increased cartel deterrence after 1995.

Finally, global-cartel initiations also peaked in 1989–1992; those formed prior to 1989 are mostly shipping conferences, which operated in a gray area of the law. Though too early to tell, the successful prosecutions of several high-profile global cartels in the late 1990s may well have had a chilling effect on would-be global cartelists.

7.5.2. Confidentiality and speed of investigations

Table 7.2 summarizes information available on time lags in 301 enforcement actions with respect to international cartels prosecuted from 1990 to 2005. The table shows the percentage of cases for which there were no lags between the first public notice and the announcement of the sanction by the antitrust authority

Table 7.2: Proportion of cartel investigations kept secret by antitrust authorities.

Cartel geographic types	**Location of antitrust authority**				
	U.S.	**Canada**	**EU**	**Other Europe**	**Other**
	Mean percent				
Global scope	33^{49}	20^{26}	40^{43}	50^{2}	5^{8}
NAFTA area	48^{31}	75^{12}	–	–	0^{1}
EU wide	–	–	11^{45}	20^{5}	–
European nations	–	–	0^{3}	36^{59}	–
Africa, Asia & Latin America	–	–	–	–	53^{17}
Total	39^{80}	37^{38}	24^{91}	35^{66}	36^{26}

Note: Superscripts indicate number of investigations; total is 301.
Canada and EU are not independent of U.S. in global-scope cartels.

39 The decline after 1992 is partly attributable to the sample's termination date. Because no data are collected after 2005 there is a ceiling on formations, which tend to lead discoveries by about six years.

40 Competition Commissioner van Miert reorganized DG-4, creating a cartel unit around that time; Commissioner Monti dates the resurgence in anticartel enforcement from 1998. The member states began separate enforcement about 1997.

(guilty plea, indictment, fine, or consent decree). In other words, these percentages are indicators of how frequently investigations are kept secret by various antitrust authorities. The percentages may reflect the investigative procedures of the antitrust authority or the tradition of reporting antitrust matters by various national press organizations. In the United States, grand jury proceedings are secret, but their existence may become known if someone asked to testify voluntarily reveals the fact of their testimony. In the EU the opening of a formal investigation usually is preceded by a raid on the corporate offices of suspected cartel members. If these raids come to the attention of the press, the companies involved or the EC itself may issue press releases confirming the raids. In other cases an EU investigation takes place without raids or other public events.

On average, 33% of the cases were kept secret until the day sanctions were announced. Secrecy was less common in matters being investigated by the European Commission than any other antitrust authority. The U.S. grand jury system is somewhat more effective in maintaining confidentiality, but so are the non-public administrative hearings used by other European antitrust commissions. The frequent use of "dawn raids" by the EC makes most of its investigations public at an early stage of investigation.

Another pattern of note in Table 7.2 is the different degrees of confidentiality accorded suspected members of global cartels compared to more localized cartels. In North America there is a lower proportion of global-cartel investigations kept secret than domestic-cartel probes, whereas in all other jurisdictions the reverse is true. The main reason for this difference is the fact that the DOJ tends to be a first-mover in investigating global cartels.[41] The EC and other national antitrust authorities mostly react to investigations that became public in the United States.

Table 7.3 contains data about the average length of investigations. The DOJ dispatches more localized cartels with amazing alacrity compared with more complex and challenging global-cartel cases. The U.S. DOJ is typically the first mover in global cartel cases, followed first by Canada and second by the EC.[42] In the United States, the average time between "first notice" (generally news accounts of raids or leaks about grand-jury investigations) and the first cartelist to be sanctioned is almost four months for North American cases.[43] Prosecutions of global cartels are more difficult than for other international cartels. The time required by the DOJ is four times longer for global than for more localized

---

[41] The methionine cartel is perhaps the only international cartel in which the EU fined companies without a previous U.S. conviction. The DOJ investigated this cartel for more than three years but closed its investigation without indictments. However, a class-action suit resulted in a large settlement.

[42] In 18 instances, U.S. action on global cartels predated EC action; in 15 cases, Canadian prosecution predated EC fines. In only three cases has the EC completed its work in advance of one of the North American authorities.

[43] News about a grand jury is often revealed at the same time a conviction is announced; these data report only on cases where there are no simultaneous announcements.

Table 7.3: Lags in international cartel enforcement, 1990–2005.

Cartel locational type	U.S.	Canada	EU	Other Europe
	Mean months			
Lag from date of first notice[a]				
Global scope	15.1	10.7	27.1	–
NAFTA area	3.7	10.0	–	–
EU wide	–	0.0	26.3	–
European nations	–	–	53.0	6.7
Asia & Latin America	–	–	–	–
Lag from jurisdiction to jurisdiction				
	U.S. to Canada	**U.S. to EU**	**Canada to EU**	**U.S. govt. to private**
Global scope	9.5	25.2	6.3	17.8[b]
NAFTA area	16.5	–	–	39.8
EU wide	–	–	–	–
European nations	–	–	–	–
Asia & Latin America	–	–	–	–

– = Not applicable or not available.

[a]Measures the time between a raid that is reported publicly and the date the first corporate participant is fined. Cases of no lags are not calculated in these columns.

[b]A mean of 8 cases. In 15 other global cases settlements of private suits preceded U.S. government suits by an average of 12.5 months.

cartels. However, the raid-to-sanction lag is far shorter in the United States than for EC cases, which take slightly more than two years for both global and regional cartels.[44] European national antitrust authorities investigate cartels fairly speedily (less than seven months), which may be related to the smaller size of the cartels prosecuted, greater prosecutorial resources, or the familiarity of agencies' staffs with local markets.[45] Note that the European figures include only the most active phase of cartel investigations. Prior to obtaining search warrants, an antitrust authority may spend many months determining probable cause (as in lysine and vitamins), though a few months is probably more typical.

The final analysis of speed concerns lags between jurisdictions in the case of overlapping prosecutions. In the lysine case, the DOJ began its undercover

44 Time series data are fairly thin, but there is some evidence that the EC is moving its cases through more rapidly in the 2000s than in the 1990s.

45 Since about 2000 the EC has been referring somewhat localized cartel cases to the authorities of its Member States. A few years later a formal EU network was set up to assist the EC and authorities in its Member States in exchanging allegations about cartels.

investigation in November 1992, raided corporate headquarters in June 1995, and negotiated the first guilty pleas in September 1996; EC fines came more than five years later. Are such long leader-follower lags typical?

Table 7.3 shows that the lysine case was atypically long. On average, the lag from the date a guilty plea is made in the United States to the date a cartel fine is imposed by the EC is 25 months. This is a minimum figure, because under cooperative arrangements in force since the 1990s, the EC is informed in advance about U.S. programs in investigations on many cases; the average length of advance notification is unknown. Canada, on the other hand, responds far more quickly to the news of U.S. guilty pleas or indictments. The CCB has had longer and more intimate working arrangements with the U.S. DOJ, has had a corporate leniency program in place long before the EC, and unlike the EC does its work without protracted multi-stage administrative hearings.

Finally, Table 7.3 shows that negotiations that result in private settlements are lengthy, from about 18 to 40 months from the time a first criminal conviction is obtained.

7.5.3. Monetary sanctions relative to sales

From 1974 to 2004, changes in U.S. antitrust laws have permitted notably higher fines.[46] Cohen and Scheffman (1989) provide useful historical benchmark data for U.S. price-fixing fines. From 1955 to 1974 when the statutory maximum fine was set at $50,000, the average fines for corporations and individuals amounted to only 0.4% of the cartel's affected sales. During 1974–1980, when the maximum corporate fine was raised to $1 million, the average price-fixing fines rose to 1.4% of affected commerce. However, mostly as a result of plea bargaining, corporations paid average fines of $140,000, which represents an 86% discount from the maximum fine in 1974–1980. In the late 1970s the U.S. Sentencing Commission adopted guidelines that specified 20% of affected sales as the "base fine," with several aggravating factors allowing fines to rise as high as 80% of affected sales and two mitigating factors permitting downward departures that could drive the recommended fine to as low as 15% of affected sales (Connor and Lande, 2005). A survey of cases in the mid 1980s reported average corporate U.S. price-fixing fines rose slightly to $160,000 per company. In 1987, when price fixing was made a felony, it became possible for U.S. courts to impose fines equal to double the antitrust damages.[47] The "double the harm" standard has seldom been applied in practice. In 1990, the maximum corporate price-fixing fine was raised to $10 million and in April 2004 to $100 million.

In the United States, the DOJ has certainly responded to the demonstrated political will for greater cartel fines. Average antitrust fines, as a proportion of

---

[46] DOJ antitrust officials have requested and testified in favor of these changes.

[47] To be more precise, the fines are to be double the harm or double the illegal profits, whichever is greater. In the context of a particular cartel episode, the overcharge will be greater than or equal to the monopoly profits.

Table 7.4: Cartel sanctions relative to affected sales, 1990–2005.

Regional cartel types	**Origin of sanctions**					
	U.S. DOJ	**CCB**	**EC**	**Other govt.**[b]	**Private**	**Total**[c]
	Median percentage[a]					
Global coverage	13.7^{30}	18.0^{22}	11.2^{24}	0.3^{4}	24.6^{32}	6.2^{44}
EU-wide	–	1.5^{1}	2.2^{25}	–	–	2.1^{25}
European nations	–	–	2.4^{1}	3.1^{24}	6.7^{1}	3.0^{29}
North America	7.0^{14}	13.1^{6}	–	45.2^{1}	5.0^{17}	7.7^{25}
Other regions	–	–	–	1.9^{10}	45.3^{1}	2.1^{10}
Median, all types	11.1^{44}	16.9^{29}	5.9^{50}	2.4^{39}	12.5^{51}	3.5^{133}

Source: Author's spreadsheets of August 2005; superscripts indicate the number of observations.
[a]The median of the sanction/sales ratio. If either is a range, the midpoint of the range is used. The "private" column shows treble-damage suits.
[b]Prosecutions by other national competition authorities include Italy (3.0%, median of 15 cases), Germany (9.5%, 4 cases), the Netherlands (3.4%, 3 cases), Sweden (2.9%, 2 cases), Norway (0.5%, 2 cases), Finland (4.5%, 1 case), Australia (2.4%, 1 case), France (0.4%, 3 cases), Korea (1.6%, 5 cases), Japan (1.25%, 1 case), UK (6.7%, 1 case), Hungary (3.4%, 1 case), Romania (3.0%, 1 case), Czech Republic (0.3%, 1 case), and Israel (0.2%, 1 case).
[c]The number of observations sums vertically but not necessarily horizontally because total sales my refer to affected sales from one or two juridictions or to global geographic markets.

affected sales, meted out to international cartels since 1990 have risen elevenfold since 1970–1980 and forty-fold since 1955–1974.[48] In the EU, Canada, and other national jurisdictions active in sanctioning cartels, there have been few changes in laws permitting harsher fines in the last 20 or 30 years,[49] yet average fines have pushed upward in those jurisdictions as well (Connor, 2004).

There are 346 ratios of sanctions for international price fixing divided by a cartel's affected sales available for approximately half of this study's sample (Table 7.4).[50] In some cases, affected sales are known only for one or two jurisdictions but are unavailable for other parts of the world; these observations are reported under the appropriate jurisdiction(s). However, if reasonably accurate

48 Few of these cases were international (Connor, 2004).

49 The UK, Australia, and New Zealand seem to be the main examples.

50 If a cartel operated in only one of the regions identified, the "total sales" ratio is double counted, but if a cartel fixed prices in two or more regions, then the total-sales ratio is unique. "Affected sales" is frequently provided in the plea agreements, published decisions, or press releases of the prosecuting antitrust authorities. In some cases these sources give cartel sales for only one year of the conspiracy, and the author used the conspiracy dates to calculate a full-period sales figure assuming a 3% or 5% sales growth rate. For about one-quarter of the observations, the author scoured Factiva for trade-press articles that reported conspiracy-period industry sales or quantities of production. These last estimates are less precise than the government announcements.

overcharge or sales figures cannot be found for one region in which a global cartel was known to operate, the total-sales column may not be computable; likewise, in a few cases global sales are known but not regional affected sales. If affected sales are only known as a range, the mid point is used. These ratios are systematically overstated because no adjustments are made for the time value of money.[51]

On average for all types of cartels, the U.S. DOJ and CCB have imposed median[52] corporate fines equal to 11.1% and 16.9% of cartelized sales *in their jurisdictions*. The EC and other national agencies (overwhelmingly located within the EU) assess fines that average 2% to 6% of EU affected sales.[53] In North America, private treble-damage suits against international cartels have won settlements that average 12.5% of affected commerce.[54] Thus, in the United States (and two or three cases in Canada) public fines and private recovery have typically amounted to about 25% of affected commerce—more than quadruple the European rates.

There is some variation in sanction rates by geographic location. Global cartels prosecuted by the U.S. DOJ negotiated fines that averaged 13.7% of U.S. affected sales, almost double the rate imposed on domestic conspiracies.[55] Recall that the guidelines for cartel fines start with a base fine that is 20% of affected U.S. sales, and that fine ranges are supposed to be invariant to whether a cartel is global or national in its reach. This finding suggests that the DOJ and supervising judges are dispensing less generous downward departures from the guidelines' ranges and applying higher culpability scores to global cartels than to domestic conspiracies.[56] Moreover, private plaintiffs in North America that

---

[51] In general, fines and settlements are paid about two to four years after the cessation of overt collusion. The typical cartel successfully raises prices for six to seven years, some much longer. Therefore, on average the profits from price fixing accrue roughly six years earlier than the years the sanctions must be paid. For example, in the frequently studied 1990–1999 global cartels in the bulk vitamins market, Bernheim et al. (2004) estimate that the net present value of the cartels' sales was 2.5 times the value of the money used to pay penalties in 1999–2004.

[52] The distribution of fines/sales ratios is positively skewed. Median fines for all types of cartels are lower than mean fines in every jurisdiction. In addition, while data on government fines are almost always made public, for cartels of all types and sizes, smaller private settlements are often unreported (because they are deemed not newsworthy) or news of them is delayed. In such situations, the median sanction is a better indicator of central tendency than the mean.

[53] This figure is within the range of 2% to 15% suggested as the typical EC practice in the 1990s (Wils, 2001). In most EU cartel cases, affected sales are calculated for the European Economic Area, which consists of the EU proper and those members of the European Free Trade Agreement that did not join the EU.

[54] Canada and the United States are virtually alone in the world in having legal systems that encourage private antitrust suits. Australia had one private damages suit against an international cartel (the vitamins cartel) in 2003, but similar suits are negligible or unknown in the rest of the world.

[55] Recall that although these were cartels that affected prices only in North America, each of the domestic cartels had some foreign members.

[56] Connor (2006) confirms with a much larger data set that throughout history international cartels have displayed significantly higher overcharge rates than domestic price-fixing schemes. Yet, this

sued global cartels extracted payouts were almost *five times* (24.6%) the settlement rates of more localized conspiracies (5%).[57] The same pattern of collecting proportionately higher fines (per euro of EU affected sales) from global cartelists than from intra-EU cartels is observed in EC decisions. However, in Canada the difference in the intensity of fines imposed on global cartels as compared to local conspiracies is not so striking.[58]

The total column of Table 7.4 tells a different story. The size of all monetary sanctions relative to a cartel's sales in every region where it colluded is far lower—the median is only 3.5%. There is a dichotomy between cartels that affected markets in North America and those on all other areas. Cartels that colluded in Canada and the United States—including all the global cartels—paid median penalties of 6% to 8% of their total affected sales. However, cartels that had no operations in North America paid median sanctions of only 2% to 3% of their total affected commerce. Given that overcharges of cartels fixing prices in Europe, Asia, Africa, and Oceania have historically been higher than those in North America, anticartel sanctions are less likely to deter in the Old World than in the New World (Connor, 2006).[59]

Of the 44 global cartels that were sanctioned in at least one jurisdiction, 14 were quadruple-sanctioned: criminally by the United States and Canada, administratively by the EU, and civilly in the USA. These are the "Poster Children" of worldwide anticartel enforcement—the examples cited by defendants' counsel as dreaded examples of excessive prosecutorial zeal (e.g., Denger, 2003, 2005). Despite the geographically broad pattern of sanctions, these cartels paid mean monetary penalties of only 16.3% of the cartels' global sales. An important feature of many global cartels is that they affected commerce in Asia, Australia, Latin America, and Africa (Connor, 2001, 2003). Discovered global cartels were usually sanctioned in North America and the EU, but rarely fined in the other continents.[60] There is, moreover, evidence that global cartels achieve higher overcharges in precisely those countries with weak or nonexistent antitrust regimes (Clarke and Evenett, 2003). These considerations point to a key factor that may explain why the historically high penalties in North America and Europe since 1990 do not yet deter global-cartel formation: even if antitrust

factor is not formally part of the criteria for setting cartel fines. The limited data available also suggests that, adjusted for market share, foreign-owned cartelists are not paying higher fines than participants headquartered in the United States.

57 Class counsel frequently boast of settlements above 5% of affected sales as exceptionally high.

58 This result is driven in part by very high fines in a few national bid-rigging cases where the government was the victim. Moreover, Canada does not, except for leniency applicants, regularly impose higher fines for aggravating circumstances.

59 There is every reason to suspect that the probability of discovery and conviction of cartels activity is lower in the Old World as well, which only reinforces this conclusion.

60 Small fines were imposed by Australia and Korea for three of the 16 vitamins cartels.

detection has improved in the last decade, expected profits net of penalties are still large in the continents with weak anticartel enforcement.[61]

To summarize, multi-continental cartels have generally experienced markedly higher sanctions relative to affected sales than more localized international cartels. Since 1990 the antitrust agencies of North America have levied median fines of 11% to 17% of jurisdictional affected sales; however, in all other jurisdictions government antitrust authorities have imposed median fines of only 2% to 6%. Private treble-damage suits in the United States recovered about 25% of U.S. affected commerce. The intensity of monetary sanctions is higher for global cartels in both North America and the EU. However, international cartels operating in only one country outside North America faced distinctly more lenient treatment: median government fines are only about 2% of national sales and no additional civil liability. The median antitrust outlays from all sources public and private are a modest 3.5% of cartel sales in all the regions where price fixing occurred.[62]

7.5.4. Sanctions relative to injury

Injury is measured by the average monopoly overcharge achieved by a cartel during the entire conspiracy period.[63] These figures fall in a range of degree of precision and are in many cases expressed as fairly wide ranges. Two hundred and seventeen estimates are available (Table 7.5); for some global cartels separate estimates are available for two or more of the continents on which they fixed prices. One or more geographic estimates are available for 79 cartels. *Median* measures of the sanction/overcharge ratios are preferred to the mean because of evident skewness in these ratios.[64]

Before examining the severity of sanctions across types of cartels, an issue must be addressed. It is clear that governments treat bid-rigging against themselves with greater than average severity. Although there are only 35 such observations (17% of the sample), government bid-rigging sanctions averaged two to three times the sanctions inflicted on cartels directed at private buyers.[65]

---

[61] Optimal deterrence principles suggest that with certain prosecution anticipated overcharges above 16% will not deter; alternatively with detection rates of 10% to 33%, expected cartel profits of only 1.6% to 5.3% of sales will motivate cartel formation. The vast majority of international cartels have higher returns (Connor, 2006).

[62] Recall that all these ratios are developed from nominal monetary figures. In net present value terms these ratios should be lowered by one-third to one-half.

[63] Adding the dead-weight or "social" loss due to price fixing would lower these ratios by 10% to 30%. Taking into consideration the unknown effects of umbrella pricing would raise the reported ratios, possibly by similar proportions. Peak overcharge rates (not shown here) are typically 50% to 100% higher than full-period overcharges (Connor, 2006).

[64] The reader should note that the sizes of some of these sub-samples are perilously small to be highly confident about some differences.

[65] Private party bid-rigging cartels are not displayed separately in Table 7.5.

Table 7.5: Cartel penalties relative to cartel overcharge rates, by jurisdiction.

Ratio	Jurisdiction imposing sanctions					
	U.S. DOJ	Canada	EU	Other govt.	Private	Total[a]
	Median percentage					
Penalties/sales	11.1	16.9	5.9	2.4	12.5	3.5
Overcharges/sales	20.3	20.3	42.7	20.1	20.3	24.6
Penalties/overcharges[b]	**55**	**83**	**14**	**12**	**62**	**14**

Sources: Table 7.4 above and median overcharges from Connor (2006, Table 8 and Figure 11).
[a]Overcharge refers to the median of international cartel episodes that ended in 1990–2005.
[b]The ratio of the first row to the second row of this table.

Therefore, Table 7.5 separates these cases from those cartels that sold principally to private buyers. If antitrust prosecutors are disinterested parties in treating cartel violations, this disparity is puzzling.

The median total sanction (government and private) on all types of international cartels is 39.8% of the estimated global overcharges—less than half of single damages. There is considerable variation in the severity of government fines across jurisdictions. Again we see a dichotomy between the antitrust authorities in North America and those elsewhere: Canada has the harshest fines (74%), followed by the United States (44%), the EC (32%), and those of other governments (12%) the lowest. Private settlements in the United States are slightly above single damages,[66] so government and private sanctions together account for almost 150% of U.S. damages. Outside North America, because there are virtually no private antitrust actions, international cartels pay out one-third or less of their overcharges. Less than 20% of the sampled cartels pay penalties in excess of single damages (Table 7.6).

In the previous section global cartels were found to have a relatively high sanctions/affected sales ratios. Global cartels frequently are indicted in three or more jurisdictions, so one might expect their sanctions to be a much higher share of damages than more localized schemes. This turns out to be the case for prosecutions by the United States and the EU. Other European and Canadian sanctions were more lenient for global cartelists than the local ones. Private parties bringing suits against international cartels were more successful in settling with global conspirators than with those engaging in more localized conspiracies. Overall, the sanctions on global cartels as a proportion of damages are not much different than those on other international cartels.

From a historical perspective, cartels are certainly suffering greater absolute monetary costs for antitrust violations than a few decades ago. In part that trend

[66] This point was made about settlements decades ago by Lande (1993). However, this paper does not adjust for other factors that lower the sanctions/damages ratio.

Table 7.6: Size distribution of the severity of cartel sanctions.

Size range	**U.S.**	**Canada**	**EC**	**Other govt.**	**Private suit**	**Total**
Percent	**Percent of column**					
Zero	35	24	25	41	8	4
0.1–9.9	9	0	21	26	11	27
10–49.9	33	27	26	18	13	34
50–99.9	14	24	18	3	16	16
100–149.9	9	17	5	3	32	11
150–199.9	0	3	0	8	13	6
200 plus	0	3	5	3	8	2
Total	100	100	100	100	100	100

may be attributed to fines imposed by the EU and its Member States. European cartel fines were unheard of until the *Quinine* case decided in 1969, but by 2003 the EU's fines on international (including intra-EU) cartels had accumulated to \$3.6 billion (Connor, 2006). Most European national competition authorities have become active in prosecuting cartels only in the last five or ten years, yet these and other national authorities have imposed fines of at least \$1.5 billion on international cartels. For the United States, international-cartel fines from 1990 to 2003 amounted to \$2.3 billion.

The data in Table 7.5 also suggest that international-cartel fines are becoming slightly more severe when gauged against the damages they have created. Longer-term trends in the severity of fines would be desirable, but I have found only one earlier study, an internal U.S. DOJ survey by Sheer and Ho (1989) that found that the average 1988 corporate fine was a mere 0.36% of the overcharges. The data in Table 7.5 show that U.S. fines on international cartels since 1990 have been a hundred times harsher than those in 1988.

These impressive upward trends in themselves imply little about the deterrence power of corporate anticartel sanctions.[67] Indeed, as mentioned in the Introduction, these trends have led several commentators to conclude that current antitrust penalties are over-deterring. Yet, dozens of international cartels continue to be discovered each year, and recidivism is rampant (Connor, 2003). Under U.S. the most extreme application of U.S. laws, an international cartel could in principle be liable for about 1200% of its U.S. price-fixing damages.[68]

[67] Only the United States has applied significant monetary and penal sanctions on individual managers, but incorporating individual penalties into a comprehensive deterrence assessment greatly complicates the analysis.

[68] The DOJ could impose a fine based on double the domestic U.S. harm and then use the cartel's global affected sales, which is typically three to four times domestic sales (see Connor, 2003). Direct purchasers are entitled to treble damages, and indirect buyers to an equal amount in those states with Illinois Brick repealers. The total of the three sets of penalties is 10 to 12 times U.S. damages.

By that measure, actual U.S. cartel fines and settlements of 150% of damages since 1990 are about one-eighth of what is theoretically possible. More importantly, the little that is known about cartel detection implies that to effectively deter, penalties should be three to ten times a cartel's global damages (Connor, 2005). This suggests that under-deterrence may be typical.

Connor and Lande (2005) have attempted to resolve this gulf by confronting U.S. sentencing practices with a massive amount of cartel-overcharge data. A principle conclusion is that international cartels have typically overcharged buyers by 25%.[69] Factoring in the probability of detection[70] suggests that an optimal fine should average 75% to 250% of damages. The data in the bottom of Table 7.5 show that over-deterrence might have occurred in 10% to 35% of the instances. On the other hand, the likelihood of under-deterrence ranges from 65% to 90% of the sample.

7.6. Conclusions

The major objective of anticartel policies should be to lower the expected benefits (profits) or raise the costs (penalties) of price fixing. Other than vigilance in merger control, public policies can do little to change the structural features of markets that make cartels profitable: inelastic demand, large numbers of buyers, economies of scale, product homogeneity, and so forth. Policies can sometimes have salutary effects on exchange conditions, such as the publication of transaction prices in markets characterized by lack of transparency.[71] However, in light of the effectiveness of sanctions noted above the principal role for antitrust is to develop rules, laws, and investigative procedures that make detection surer and punishment harsher than at present.

It is clear from the geographic location of cartel meetings that, as a general rule, United States territory was avoided because of its well-deserved reputation for tough anticartel enforcement. Instead, conspirators met in Switzerland, Mexico, Japan, Hong Kong, and several EU cities that were regarded as less risky. This behavioral pattern is perhaps the best indicator that U.S. anticartel policies are the ones other jurisdictions should emulate.

One investigative technique that has proven especially useful in discovering cartels is the DOJ's 1993 nondiscretionary Corporate Leniency Program

---

[69] This is the median figure over all time periods, types of cartels, and geographic locations. The mean of successful cartels is 43%. The higher mean figure would imply a higher instance of under-deterrence.

[70] Connor (2003, 67–68) found six estimates of cartel-detection rates form U.S. and European sources. The range was 10% to 33%. Many of these estimates are quite dated. For some of the most common felonious property crimes (burglary, auto theft, and arson), U.S. arrest rates in the 1990s vary from 13.8% to 16.5%, well within the range adopted here. Corporate leniency programs may have raised the probability of cartels detection.

[71] Even this policy must be introduced cautiously, avoiding excessively detailed price information (Albaek et al., 1997).

(Delrahim, 2004; Spratling and Arp, 2005).[72] Similar programs were subsequently adopted in several other jurisdictions. Recent refinements are the "Amnesty Plus" program that rewards indicted companies if they inform the DOJ about collusive activity in a market not yet being investigated and the "Penalty Plus" program that promises maximal sanctions if a defendant fails to report under Amnesty Plus. In 2001, more than half of the DOJ's 30 global-cartel investigations were the result of Amnesty Plus leads (ibid, 6). More than three leniency applications per month were received in early 2003 compare wit one *per year* prior to 1993 (Pate, 2003). A trail of connected cartel prosecutions occurred in the graphite-related and carbon-related cartels (Pate, 2003). Kovacic (2001) has suggested extending the corporate leniency program by giving bounties to individuals who provide information about hidden cartels.[73]

The antitrust laws of most nations are extraterritorial. That is, jurisdiction over collusive conduct is determined by the location of the intended impact rather than where the violation occurred. An important issue facing the U.S. courts is the status of wholly foreign purchasers from global cartels under the Sherman Act. In particular, should a foreign (i.e., non-U.S.) entity that buys cartelized products at artificially high prices outside the United States be permitted to seek treble damages in U.S. courts? In the case of global cartels selling tradable goods, such purchases are usually necessary in order to maintain the high U.S. prices; that is foreign injuries are a *sine qua non* for domestic injuries. Therefore, the plain language of the Sherman Act would appear to permit standing by wholly foreign buyers (Bush et al., 2004).

Permitting wholly foreign buyers to use U.S. courts would by itself increase the expected financial losses from global cartels and, thus, increase deterrence (Bush et al., 2004). On the other hand, such suits might strain U.S. judicial resources and would have a negative impact on the number of DOJ leniency applications by international cartelists. Judicial resources could be expanded by charging foreign buyers who pay no U.S. taxes a users' fee, which could fund the employment of court-appointed special masters to deal with such cases. Special masters are quite capable of holding hearings exclusively for foreign buyers because such buyers only have standing if domestic plaintiffs have already filed against the same defendants. Leniency applications might decline in the short run because the DOJ has no authority to intervene in private suits, and permitting wholly foreign plaintiffs to sue for treble damages would increase potential applicants' liability. The net effects on deterrence of these opposing forces is a matter in need of empirical analysis, but Stiglitz and Orszag (2004) conclude from economic principles that standing for wholly foreign buyers in U.S. courts will tend to increase global-cartel deterrence.

---

[72] The 1993 DOJ program replaced a 1978 policy that was highly discretionary and seldom invoked.

[73] In 2005 the Korean FTC recently offered a bounty to an individual with inside information on a cartel.

Other U.S. policies worthy of globalization include: fines based on multiples of overcharges[74] rather than arbitrary sales' percentages, sharply increased penalties for recidivists, encouragement of private damages suits in jurisdictions with no tradition of compensatory suits, and habitual individual criminal indictments for antitrust violations. These policy reforms are especially needed in Japan (which has an arbitrary maximum fine of 6 percent of sales for price fixing by manufacturers) and other industrialized Asian countries (Chemtob, 2000). Criminalization of antitrust violations is especially important for most European and Asian regions because it reduces the number of safe havens for fugitives from U.S. antitrust laws. Similarly, there are enforcement practices abroad that North American antitrust agencies might usefully adopt. For example, the DOJ now calculates fines on the basis of a company's U.S. sales of the cartelized good only, a practice that in effect heightens deterrence of small specialized enterprises. In contrast, the EC practice of basing maximum statutory fines on a company's *global sales* (sales across all product lines in all geographic areas) would enhance the DOJ's negotiating stance vis-à-vis large diversified defendants without requiring legislative changes.

Acknowledgements

Earlier versions of this chapter were presented at the American Agricultural Law Association annual meeting, Indianapolis, IN, October 26, 2002; a Purdue University seminar, September 18, 2002; the 1st International Industrial Organization Conference, Boston, Mass., April, 2003; and a workshop of the International Training Network, "Competition Policy in International Markets," Toulouse, France, October 16, 2003. The author thanks Robert H. Lande and Chris Springman for their help on antitrust issues. Valerie Suslow, Donald Brown, Cindy Alexander, Adair Morse, Jozef Konings, Jan Sand, and other participants in these conferences also provided constructive suggestions.

[74] Since January 2005 the U.S. DOJ has begun setting maximum cartel fines equal to double the cartel's harm if the U.S. Sentencing Guidelines dictate fines above the statutory cap of $100 million per company.

Appendix table: Sample

Appendix table:

Conti-nent	Geog location	Probe active	Probe over	Consent decree	Final	Market
NO	US					Adhesive label stock, U.S.
NO	US			1	1	AIIC (Assn. Intl. Interpretes) U.S.
GLOBAL	GLOBAL	1				Aluminum fluoride [m]
AS	JP	1				Aluminum foil, JP [m]
GLOBAL	GLOBAL		1		1	Aluminum Metal
WE	US				1	Aluminum Phosphide, U.S.
NO	US				1	Anti-anxiety drugs, U.S.
WE	FI				1	Asphalt paving, Finland
WE	SW	1			1	Asphalt, Sweden [m]
WE	IT				1	Auditing services, IT
GLOBAL	GLOBAL	1				Automotive Refinishing Paint [m]
WE	FR				1	Ball & roller bearings, FR
WE	EU	1				Bananas [m]
GLOBAL	GLOBAL	1				Bathroom & kitchen fixtures [m]
AS	KO				1	Batteries manufacturing, auto, Korea
WE	FR				1	Beef, France
WE	EU			1		Beer, Belgian, HORECA channel
WE	EU					Beer, Belgian, Retail Private Label
WE	EU		1		1	Beer, Denmark [n]
WE	EU		1		1	Beer, France, HORECA [f]
WE	EU		1		1	Beer, Italy [n]
AS	KO				1	Beer, Korea
WE	EU				1	Beer, Luxembourg, HORECA
WE	EU	1				Beer, Netherlands, HORECA [m]
WE	EU	1				Beer, Portugal, HORECA [m]
WE	EU		1		1	Beer, Spain, HORECA [n]
GLOBAL	GLOBAL				1	Beta Carotene
WE	NL				1	Bicycles, NL
GLOBAL	GLOBAL				1	Biotin (Vitamin H)
WE	EU	1				Bitumen in NL, BL, and ES [m]
WE	SW				1	Bitumen, Sweden
LA	BR	1				Blood products, Brazil [m]
WE	EU				1	British Sugar
NO	US				1	Bromines, U.S. (possible EU)
WE	DE				1	Cable, high-voltage, Germany
NO	US				1	Cable-stayed bridges, U.S. [n]
WE	EU	1				Calcium carbide[m]
NO	US				1	California bridge, U.S. [n]
GLOBAL	GLOBAL				1	Canthaxanthin
GLOBAL	GLOBAL	1				Carbon Black
GLOBAL	GLOBAL		1			Carbon Cathode Block

(*Continued on next page*)

Appendix table: (*Continued*)

Conti-nent	Geog location	Probe active	Probe over	Consent decree	Final	Market
GLOBAL	GLOBAL	1				Carbon Electrical Products[m]
GLOBAL	GLOBAL		1		1	Carbon Fiber
OC	AU	1				Cardboard boxes, AU + NZ [m]
NO	US			1	1	Cardizem CD hypertension drug, U.S.
WE	EU				1	Cartonboard
WE	IT				1	Cell phones, IT
WE	EU				1	Cement, white & gray
WE	DE				1	Cement I, Germany
WE	DE	1				Cement II, Germany [m]
LA	BR	1				Cement, Brazil [m]
EE	HU				1	Cement, Hungary
WE	IT				1	Cement, Italy (Lombardy)
AS	KO				1	Cement, Korea
NO	CA				1	Cement, Quebec, Canada
EE	RU				1	Cement, Romania
GLOBAL	GLOBAL				1	Choline chloride (Vitamin B4) [f]
WE	IT				1	Cigarettes, Italy
AS	JP			1	1	Circuit plates, printed, Japan
GLOBAL	GLOBAL				1	Citric Acid
EE	CZ				1	Coffee wholesaling, Czech Republic
EE	HU				1	Coffee wholesaling, Hungary
NO	CA				1	Compressed gas, CA
WE	NL				1	Compressed gases, NL
OC	AU				1	Compressors, Australia
WE	DE				1	Concrete, Eastern Germany
WE	NL				1	Construction of athletic tracks, NL
WE	UK	1				Construction, flat roof et al., UK [m]
NO	US				1	Construction, marine, U.S. [n]
WE	NL	1				Construction, Netherlands [m]
GLOBAL	GLOBAL	1				Construction, Nigeria LNG plants [m]
WE	NO	1				Construction, Norway [m]
AF	AF				1	Construction, USAID in Egypt [n]
GLOBAL	GLOBAL		1			Copper Concentrate [m]
WE	EU	1			1	Copper plumbing fittings [m]
WE	EU				1	Copper tubes, industrial
WE	EU				1	Copper tubes, plumbing
NO	US		1		1	Corn Glucose Syrup, U.S.
NO	US				1	Cosmetics, "prestige," U.S.
GLOBAL	GLOBAL	1				Creosote [m]
WE	EU				1	Danish air routes
WE	IT				1	Diabetes testing devices, IT
GLOBAL	GLOBAL				1	Diamonds, Industrial
WE	IT				1	Diesel Fuel, IT
AS	IL		1			Digital switches, Israel
WE	FR				1	Distribution, electrical appliances, FR
GLOBAL	GLOBAL	1				DRAMs[m]

(*Continued on next page*)

Appendix table: (*Continued*)

Conti-nent	Geog location	Probe active	Probe over	Consent decree	Final	Market
NO	US	1				Drugs, over-the-counter, U.S. [m]
GLOBAL	GLOBAL	1				DVD Players, 3C Pool [m]
WE	IT				1	Elevator repairs, IT
WE	EU	1				Elevators [m]
WE	FR	1				Employment services, FR [m]
WE	NL	1				Engineering services, NL [m]
GLOBAL	GLOBAL	1				EPDM, Synthetic Rubber[m]
WE	EU				1	Euro-Zone banks
AS	KO				1	Excavators manufacturing, Korea
NO	US				1	Explosives, commercial, U.S.
NO	US				1	Ferrosilicon, U.S.
WE	EU				1	Ferry services, Adriatic
WE	EU				1	Ferry services, English Channel
WE	EU	1				Ferry services, Nordic [m]
AF	ZA	1				Fertilizer, nitrogen, So. Africa [m]
GLOBAL	GLOBAL				1	Fine Arts (Art Auction Houses)
NO	US				1	Flat glass, U.S.
GLOBAL	GLOBAL				1	Folic Acid (Vitamin B9)
AS	KO				1	Forklift manufacturing, Korea
NO	US		1		1	Foundry resins, U.S.
WE	IT				1	Gas water heaters, IT
LA	MX				1	Gas, liquid propane (LPG), Toluca, Mex.
LA	CL	1	1?			Gasoline, Chile
EE	CZ				1	Gasoline, Czech Republic
WE	FR				1	Gasoline, FR
WE	IT				1	Gasoline, IT
WE	NL				1	Gasoline, NL
WE	ES				1	Gasoline, Spain
WE	SW				1	Gasoline, Sweden
WE	UK	1				Generic drugs, warfarin & penicillin [m], UK
WE	IT				1	Glass (food) containers, IT
NO	US				1	Glass containers, U.S.
WE	EU	1				Glass, flat and auto [m]
GLOBAL	GLOBAL		1			Glyphosate herbicide
NO	NO AM					Glyphosate, North America
GLOBAL	GLOBAL				1	Graphite Electrodes
GLOBAL	GLOBAL				1	Graphite, Extruded
GLOBAL	GLOBAL				1	Graphite, Isostatic Specialty Products
NO	US		1		1	High Fructose Corn Syrup, U.S.
WE	NO				1	Hydro-Electric power equipment, NO
WE	EU	1				Hydrogen peroxide, derivatives II [m]
WE	IT				1	Infant Formula (Episode 1), Italy
WE	IT				1	Infant Formula (Episode 2), Italy
NO	CA				1	Insecticide, BT, CA
NO	CA				1	Insecticides, Syn. Forest, CA
NO	US	1				Insurance brokers, commercial, U.S. [m]

(*Continued on next page*)

Appendix table: (*Continued*)

Conti-nent	Geog location	Probe active	Probe over	Consent decree	Final	Market
WE	DE	1				Insurance, industrial property, DE [m]
WE	NL	1				Insurance, NL [m]
WE	IT				1	Insurance, non-life, Italy
EE	LI	1				Intravenous solutions, Lithuania [m]
NO	CA		1		1	Iron oxide, Canada
NO	CA				1	Iron pipe, Canada
WE	IT	1				Jet fuel, Italy [m]
NO	US				1	Linerboard, U.S.
GLOBAL	GLOBAL				1	Lysine
NO	US				1	Magnetic audio tape, U.S.
GLOBAL	GLOBAL	1				Magnetic Iron Oxide (MIO) [m]
NO	NO AM				1	Maltol, Synthetic, North Am.
WE	IT			1		Matches, IT
GLOBAL	GLOBAL					MCAA
GLOBAL	GLOBAL				1	MCC (microcrystalline cellulose)
GLOBAL	GLOBAL				1	Methionine
GLOBAL	GLOBAL				1	Methylglucamine
WE	EU	1				MMA (methyl methacrylate)[m]
WE	FR	1				Mobile phone operators in FR [m]
WE	NL				1	Mobile phone operators in NL
WE	UK	1				Mobile phone operators in UK [m]
WE	EU	1	1?			Mobile phone roaming fees, UK, DE [m]
NO	US	1				Moving and storage, Germany-U.S.
GLOBAL	GLOBAL				1	MSG
GLOBAL	GLOBAL	1				Naphthalene[m]
WE	DE	1		1		Natural Gas, I, DE [m]
WE	DE	1				Natural Gas, II, DE [m]
GLOBAL	GLOBAL	1				Nitrile Rubber [m]
GLOBAL	GLOBAL					Nucleotides (Nucleic Acid)
GLOBAL	GLOBAL	1				Organic peroxides [m]
WE	EU	1				Oxo-alcohols[m]
NO	CA	1				Paper, Canada [m]
WE	EU				1	Paper, carbonless
WE	EU	1				Paper, cores [m]
WE	NO				1	Paper, corrugated cardboard, Norway
WE	EU		1			Paper, newsprint [p]
WE	EU	1				Paper, procurement of roundwood [m]
GLOBAL	GLOBAL	1				Paper, Publication (a/k/a Magazine) [m]
WE	EU	1				Paper, recovered [m]
GLOBAL	GLOBAL	1				Paper, Release Liner [m]
NO	NO AM				1	Paper, thermal fax, U.S. and CA
GLOBAL	GLOBAL	1				Paraffin wax [m]
GLOBAL	GLOBAL	1				Parcel Tankers, Chemical Shipping[m]
WE	EU			1	1	Pay TV rights [p]
WE	IS	1				Petroleum, Iceland [m]
AS	JP			1?	1	Petroleum, Military fuel, JP

(*Continued on next page*)

Appendix table: (*Continued*)

Conti-nent	Geog location	Probe active	Probe over	Consent decree	Final	Market
AS	KO				1	Petroleum, Military fuels, Korea
WE	IT				1	Pharmaceuticals, cholesterol, IT
WE	IT				1	Pharmaceuticals, obesity, IT
WE	IT				1	Pharmaceuticals, respiratory, IT
AS	US		1		1	Philippines telecom, U.S.
WE	EU				1	Plasterboard
GLOBAL	GLOBAL	1				Plastic Additives: Heat Stabilizers[m]
GLOBAL	GLOBAL	1		1		Plastic Additives: Impact Modifiers[m]
NO	NO AM				1	Plastic dinnerware, U.S. and CA
WE	EU	1				Plastic sacks, industrial [m]
GLOBAL	GLOBAL	1				Polychloroprene synthetic rubber [m]
NO	US	1				Polyester staple, U.S. and CA [m]
WE	EU	1				Polyethylene film [m]
NO	US	1				Polyols, polyester aliphatic, U.S. [m]
WE	EU				1	Polypropylene plastic
AS	JP			1?	1	Polypropylene, Japan
WE	NL				1	Prawns, Netherlands
WE	EU	1	1?		1	Printer ink refill cartridges [m]
NO	US	1	1?			Printing, Holographic, U.S. [m]
WE	EU				1	PVC (polyvinyl-chloride) plastic
WE	IT				1	Radiological media, IT
WE	IT				1	Recorded music, IT
GLOBAL	GLOBAL	1				Rubber Processing Chemicals [m]
NO	US		1		1	Seeds, Genetically Modified, U.S.
WE	EU				1	Sewing needles
GLOBAL	GLOBAL				1	Shipping (Europe/Cent. W. Africa)
GLOBAL	GLOBAL				1	Shipping (Europe/Far East)
GLOBAL	GLOBAL				1	Shipping (French/African)
GLOBAL	GLOBAL			1	1	Shipping conference FEFC
WE	EU				1	Soda ash (sodium carbonate)
NO	NO AM				1	Sodium Erythorbate, North Am.
GLOBAL	GLOBAL				1	Sodium Gluconate
GLOBAL	GLOBAL				1	Sorbates
WE	NL				1	Special concrete foundation eng., NL
NO	US	1				Spun yarn, open end, U.S. [m]
GLOBAL	GLOBAL			1	1	Stamp Auctions (Episode 1)
GLOBAL	GLOBAL	1				Stamp Auctions (Episode 2)
WE	IT				1	Steel bars, concrete reinforcing, IT
WE	EU				1	Steel beams
WE	EU				1	Steel pipes, insulated heating
WE	EU				1	Steel tubes ("oil country tubes")
WE	EU				1	Steel, flat stainless
NO	US	1				Sulfuric acid, U.S. [m]
WE	EU	1				Switchgear, gas insulated [m]
GLOBAL	GLOBAL				1	TACA (Europe/No. Atlantic Shipping)
NO	US				1	Tactile tile, U.S.

(*Continued on next page*)

Appendix table: (*Continued*)

Conti-nent	Geog location	Probe active	Probe over	Consent decree	Final	Market
NO	US				1	Tampico Fiber, U.S.
GLOBAL	GLOBAL					Tar Pitch [m]
AS	KO				1	Telephone services, Korea
GLOBAL	GLOBAL			1	1	Three Tenors CD
AS	JP	1				Tire manufacturing, JP [m]
NO	US				1	Tobacco Leaf, U.S.
WE	EU				1	Tobacco leaf processing, Spain
WE	UK				1	Toys and games, UK
WE	FR	1				Toys, France [m]
OC	AU				1	Transformers, power & distn, E. AU
WE	EU	1				Transport, English Channel [m]
AS	IL				1	Transportation, diamonds, intl., Israel
NO	US				1	Transportation, marine, U.S. [n]
NO	US				1	Tubes, laminated, U.S.
GLOBAL	GLOBAL	1				Urethane Plastics [m]
AS	JP				1	Vinyl food wrap, Japan
GLOBAL	GLOBAL				1	Vitamin A
GLOBAL	GLOBAL				1	Vitamin B1
GLOBAL	GLOBAL				1	Vitamin B12
GLOBAL	GLOBAL				1	Vitamin B2
GLOBAL	GLOBAL				1	Vitamin B3 (Niacin)
WE	EU				1	Vitamin B4 (Choline Chloride) Europe
NO	NO AM				1	Vitamin B4, North America
GLOBAL	GLOBAL				1	Vitamin B5 (Calpan)
GLOBAL	GLOBAL				1	Vitamin B6
GLOBAL	GLOBAL				1	Vitamin C
AS	CN	1				Vitamin C, U.S. imports from China [m]
GLOBAL	GLOBAL				1	Vitamin D
GLOBAL	GLOBAL				1	Vitamin E
GLOBAL	GLOBAL				1	Vitamin Premixes
GLOBAL	GLOBAL				1	Vitamins, total
WE	DE	1				Waste collection, Germany [m]
NO	NO AM	1				Window coverings, PVC, U.S. + CA [m]
GLOBAL	GLOBAL	1?	1		1	Wine Alcohol, EU Auctions [m]
OC	NZ	1				Wood preservatives, NZ [m]
WE	EU				1	Zinc phosphate

Note: The continental abbreviations used are NO = N. America, WE = W. Europe, EE = E. Europe, AS = Asia, AF = Africa, LA = Latin America, OC = Oceania, and GLOBAL = two or more continents. Except GLOBAL, country codes are license-plate or Internet symbols. ? = uncertain classifications. The superscript "m" indicates that an investigation was in progress in mid 2005.

References

Adams, K.L., Metlin, E. (2002), Procedural issues unique to international cartel litigation. Speech, American Bar Association, Antitrust Section, International Forum 2002, New York City, January 31.

Adler, H. Jr., Laing, D.J. (1997), The explosion of international criminal antitrust enforcement. *Business Crimes Bulletin: Compliance & Litigation* 4, 1–5.

Adler, H. Jr., Laing, D.J. (1999), As corporate fines skyrocket. *Business Crimes Bulletin* 6, 1.

Adelman, M.A. (1972), Is the oil shortage real? *Foreign Policy*. Winter 1972–73, 71.

Albaek, S., et al. (1997), Government-assisted oligopoly coordination? A concrete case. *Journal of Industrial Economics* 45, 429–443.

AMC (2004), Criminal Procedure and Remedies Issues Recommended for Commission Study: Memorandum dated December 21. http://www.amc.gov/pdf/meetings/CriminalProcedure.pdf

Baker, J.B. (2003), The case for antitrust enforcement. *Journal of Economic Perspectives* 17, 27–50. Fall.

Bernheim, B.D., et al. (2004), Brief of certain professors of economics as *Amici Curiae* in support of respondents. *F.Hoffmann-LaRoche, et al., Petitioners v. Empagran et al., Respondents, et al.* U.S. Supreme Court 2003 U.S. Briefs 724. March 15.

Burnside, A. (2003), European cartel enforcement and investigations. Paper presented at the spring meeting, Antitrust Section, American Bar Association, April 2–4.

Bush, D., et al. (2004), *Amicus Brief, U.S. Supreme Court, F. Hoffmann-La Roche v. Empagran*. March 15. www.antitrustinstitute.org/recent2/307.pdf.

Chemtob, S.M. (2000), Antitrust deterrence in the United States and Japan. Remarks at a conference, Competition Policy in the Global Trading System, Washington, DC, June 23.

Clarke, J.L., Evenett, S.J. (2003), The deterrent effects of national anticartel laws: Evidence from the international vitamins cartel. *Antitrust Bulletin* 48, 289–726.

Cohen, L.P., Fields, G. (2005), New sentencing battle looms after court decision. *Wall Street Journal*. January 14, 1.

Cohen, M.A., Scheffman, D.T. (1989), The Antitrust Sentencing guideline: Is the punishment worth the cost? *American Criminal Law Review* 27, 331.

Connor, J.M. (2001), *Global Price Fixing: Our Customers Are the Enemy*. Kluwer Academic Publishers, Boston.

Connor, J.M. (2003), Private international cartels: Effectiveness, welfare, and anticartel enforcement. Staff Paper No. 03-12. Department of Agricultural Economics, Purdue University, West Lafayette, IN. November. http://agecon.lib.umn.edu/cgi-bin/detailview.pl?paperid=11506.

Connor, J.M. (2004), Global antitrust prosecutions of modern international cartels. *J. of Industry, Competition, and Trade* 4, 239–267. September.

Connor, J.M. (2005), Optimal deterrence and private international cartels. Paper presented at the Second Biennial Conference of the Food System Research Group, University of Wisconsin-Madison, June 16–17.

Connor, J.M. (2006), Price-fixing overcharges: Legal and economic evidence. In: Kirkwood, J.B. (ed.), *Research in Law and Economics*, vol. 23, Elsevier, Amsterdam and San Diego, in press.

Connor, J.M., Lande, R.H. (2005), How high do cartels raise prices? Implications for optimal cartel fines. *Tulane Law Review* 80, 513–570. December.

Crandall, R.W., Winston, C. (2003), Does antitrust policy improve consumer welfare? Assessing the evidence. *Journal of Economic Perspectives* 17, 1–26. Fall.

Davis, R.W. (2003), U.S. antitrust treatment of international cartels. *Antitrust* 17, 31–35.

Delrahim, M. (2004), The basics of a successful anti-cartel enforcement program. Speech at the Seoul Competition Forum, Seoul, Korea, April 20. www.usdoj.gov/atr/public/speeches/203626.htm.

Denger, M.L. (2003), Too much or too little, a summary of discussion. American Bar Association's Antitrust Remedies Forum, Washington, DC, April.

Denger, M.L. (2005), Prepared statement of Michael L. Denger before the Antitrust Modernization Commission Hearing Panel on "State Indirect Purchaser Actions: Proposals for Reform," Washington, DC, June 27. http://www.amc.gov/commission_hearings/pdf/Denger.pdf.

Dick, A.R. (1998), Cartels. In: Eatwell, J. (Ed.), *The New Palgrave Dictionary of Law and Economics*. Macmillan, London.

Eckbo, P.L. (1976), *The Future of World Oil*. Ballinger Publishing, Cambridge.

Evenett, S.J., Levenstein, M.C., Suslow, V.Y. (2001), International cartel enforcement: Lessons from the 1990s. *The World Economy* 24, 1221–1245.

Gallo, J.C., et al. (2000), Department of Justice Antitrust Enforcement 1955–1997. *Review of Industrial Organization* 17, 75–133.

Goldman, C.S., et al. (2003), Private access to antitrust remedies: The Canadian Experience. Address before the Section of Antitrust Law, American Bar Association, April 2–4.

Graubert, J.D. (2003), Too much or too little, a summary of discussion. American Bar Association's Antitrust Remedies Forum, Washington, DC, April.

Guersent, O. (Ed.) (2004), *The Fight against International Cartels of the European Commission: 19 Decisions in 19 Months between July 2001 and December 2003*. EC Directorate for Competition, Brussels. http://europa.eu.int/comm/competition/antitrust

Harding, C., Joshua, J. (2003), *Regulating Cartels in Europe: A Study of Legal Control of Corporate Delinquency*. Oxford University Press, New York.

Hovenkamp, H. (1999), *Federal Antitrust Policy*, 2nd ed. West Group, St. Paul.

Kovacic, W.E. (2001), Private monitoring and antitrust enforcement: Paying informants to reveal cartels. *George Washington Law Review* 69, 766–797.

Kwoka, J.E. (2003), The attack on antitrust policy and consumer welfare: A response to Crandall and Winston. Working Paper 03-008, Department of Economics, Northeastern University, Boston. March.

Lande, R.H. (1993), Are antitrust "treble" damages really single damages? *Ohio State Law Journal* 54, 117–174.

Landes, W.H. (1983), Optimal sanctions for antitrust violations. *University of Chicago Law Review* 50, 652–678.

Levenstein, M., Suslow, V. (2002), What determines cartel success? Working Paper 02-001, University of Michigan Business School, Ann Arbor, MC. January.

Levenstein, M., Suslow, V., Oswald, L. (2003), International price-fixing cartels and developing countries: A discussion of effects and policy remedies. Working Paper 9511, National Bureau of Economic Research, Cambridge, MA. February.

Low, D.M., Wakil, O. (2004), Cartels/criminal enforcement: Canadian developments. Paper presented at the Fall meeting, Section of Antitrust Law, American Bar Association.

Newmark, C.M. (1988), Does horizontal price fixing raice price? A look at the bakers of Washington. *Journal of Law and Economics* 31, 469–484.

OECD (2003), Report on the Nature and Impact of Hard Core Cartels and Sanctions against Cartels under National Competition Laws (DAFFE/COMP (2002) 7). Organization of Economic Co-Operation and Development, Paris.

Pate, R.H. (2003), The DOJ international antitrust program—Gaining momentum. Speech, American Bar Association, New York City, February 6.

Sheer, A., Ho, C. (1989), Preliminary review of sentences imposed on organizations in 1988. Memorandum to the U.S. Sentencing Commission, August 16.

Spratling, G.R. (1999), International cartels. Speech before the American Conference Institute's 7th National Conference on the Foreign Corrupt Practices Act, Washington, DC, December 9.

Spratling, G.R. (2001), Detection and deterrence: Rewarding informants for reporting violations. *George Washington Law Review* 69, 798–823. December.

Spratling, G.R., Arp, D.J. (2005), The status of international cartel enforcement activity in the U.S. and around the world, address at the fall forum. Section of Antitrust Law, American Bar Association, Washington, DC, November 16.

Sproul, M.F. (1993), Antitrust and prices. *Journal of Political Economics* 101, 741–754.

Stiglitz, J.E., Orszag, P.R. (2004), Brief of Amici Curiae Economists in Support of Respondents. Hoffmann-LaRoche et al., Petitioners v. Empagran et al., Respondents et al., 2003 U.S. Briefs 724. March 15.

Stocking, G.W., Watkins, M.W. (1946), *Cartels in Action*. Twentieth Century Fund, New York.

Suslow, V.Y. (2001), Cartel contract duration: Empirical evidence from international cartels. Unpublished Manuscript that updates a 1988 Hoover Institution Working Paper, University of Michigan Business School, October.

USSG (1987), *Guidelines Manual*. U.S. Sentencing Commission, Washington, DC.

USSG Advisory Group (2003), *Report of the ad hoc Advisory Group on the Organizational Guidelines*. U.S. Sentencing Commission, Washington, DC, October 7.

Waller, S.W. (2000), The twilight of comity. *Columbia Journal of Transnational Law* 38, 563–579.

Werden, G.J. (2003), *The Effect of Antitrust Policy on Consumer Welfare: What Crandall and Winston Overlook, EAG 03-2*. Economic Analysis Group, Antitrust Division, U.S. Department of Justice, Washington, DC. January.

Wils, W.P.J. (2001), The commission's new method for calculating fines in antitrust cases. *European Law Review* 23 , 252–263.

CHAPTER 8

The Economics of Tacit Collusion: Implications for Merger Control[1]

Marc Ivaldi, Bruno Jullien, Patrick Rey, Paul Seabright and Jean Tirole

IDEI, Toulouse, France

8.1. Introduction

Tacit collusion refers to a group of oligopolists' ability to coordinate, even in the absence of explicit agreement,[2] to raise price or more generally increase profit at the detriment of consumers. It has been treated under the notion of collective dominance in a number of important European Court decisions and under the "coordinated effects" label in the US. The present chapter focuses on the economic analysis of the impact of mergers on collusion and its consequences for anti-trust policy.[3]

The legal treatment of collusion depends on the form it takes: explicit, tacit, or any combination of the two. Explicit collusion or cartel agreements are usually banned under antitrust laws, such as Section 8.1 of the US Sherman Act or Article 81 of the European Treaty. The treatment of tacit collusion has however been subject to more controversy than that of cartels, due the absence of a formal agreement or explicit coordination.[4] For this reason the use of the concept of tacit collusion has almost exclusively been used in merger control policy. Moreover the European Commission has relied more heavily on it than the US anti-trust authorities. This can be attributed mostly to the difference in the legal procedures. While the Clayton Act prohibits a merger the effect of which "may substantially lessen competition", until recently, the European merger regulation allowed the Commission to declare incompatible with the EC treaties mergers that "create or strengthen a dominant position as a result of which effective

---

[1] This chapter is based on a report on collective dominance for the European Commission (Ivaldi et al., 2003). We thank Vivek Ghosal and John Martin for comments and references.

[2] "Tacit collusion" need not involve any "collusion" in the legal sense, and in particular need involve no communication between the parties. A better term from a legal perspective might be "tacit coordination".

[3] See our report (Ivaldi et al., 2003) for a more complete analysis.

[4] See in particular the US Supreme Court opinion in Brooke Group, Ltd. v. Brown & Williamson Tobacco Corp (1993) or the appeal decision in Williamson Oil Co. v. Philip Morris USA (Eleventh District, 2003). For the European Community, see the annulment by the Court of Justice of the Commission Decision 85/202/EEC (the *Woodpulp* case).

CONTRIBUTIONS TO ECONOMIC ANALYSIS
VOLUME 282 ISSN: 0573-8555
DOI: 10.1016/S0573-8555(06)82008-0

competition would be significantly impeded", where dominance can be single or collective. While the treatment of mergers in the US has mostly focused on unilateral effects, with a minor role for coordinated effects, due to lack of clarity in the interpretation of collective dominance, the European Commission has in the past preferred to address issues of tacit collusion when dealing with collective dominance with no structural links.[5] Only recently has the new Merger regulation[6] of 2004 allowed the commission to address unilateral effects in a more systematic way, by prohibiting a concentration which would "significantly impede effective competition".[7]

In this chapter, we review the main industry characteristics that affect collusion. We then draw some implications for merger policy. Section 8.2 introduces the concept of tacit collusion, while the factors that are relevant for collusion are discussed in Section 8.3. Section 8.4 proposes a mathematical illustration. Section 8.5 discusses non-price collusion. Finally Section 8.6 focuses on the implications for the practice of merger control.

8.2. The economics of tacit collusion

Tacit collusion can arise when firms interact repeatedly. They may then be able to maintain high prices through the threat that any deviation from the collusive path would trigger some retaliation. To be sustainable, retaliation must be sufficiently likely and costly to outweigh the short-term benefits from "cheating" on the collusive path. These short-term benefits, as well as the magnitude and likelihood of retaliation, depend in turn on the characteristics of the industry.

Retaliation refers to the firms' reaction to a deviation from the collusive path. A simple form of retaliation consists in the breakdown of collusion and the restoration of "normal" competition and profits. Firms anticipate that if one attempts to reap short-term profits, they will be no more collusion in the future. Firms may then abide to the current collusive prices in order to keep the collusion going, in which case collusion is self-sustaining. This form of collusion has a simple interpretation: firms trust each other to maintain collusive prices; but if one of them deviates, trust vanishes and all firms start acting in their short-term interest. However, there may be more sophisticated forms of retaliation that may inflict tougher punishments, thereby allowing sustaining higher collusive prices. Another reason why returning forever to "normal competition" may

[5] Leading cases for EU are Gencor/Lonrho (M.619), Nestlé/Perrier (M.190) or Airtours/First Choice (M.1524). In the US, the FTC has recently and unsuccessfully attempted to challenge a merger on the ground of coordinated effects (FTC v. Arch Coal, 2004).

[6] Council Regulation (EC) No 139/2004 of 20 January 2004 on the control of concentrations between undertakings (the EC Merger Regulation), *Official Journal*, L 24, 29.01.2004, pages 1–22.

[7] Another difference between the US and the EU concerns the proceedings: in the US a merger can only be challenged before a court, whereas in the EU the procedure is internal to the European Commission; the separation between investigation and decision is thus less clear in that case, despite the scrutiny of the member States and the fact that the final decision is made by the Commissioners.

not be a good collusion scheme is the unobservability of rivals' moves. When for example rivals' prices are unobservable, firms must infer aggressive moves by competitors from their own performance on the market; if furthermore demand is random, price wars may then be triggered by low demand rather than deviations.[8] Temporary price wars then make more sense than long-lasting wars. Finally, retaliation may include targeted price wars. For example, in *Compagnie Maritime Belge* (case C-395/96P), it was argued that shipping companies chartered "fighting ships" that were specifically designed to compete head to head against the ships of a targeted company. The common feature of retaliation mechanisms is however that:

(i) The profit loss imposed on a deviant firm by retaliation must be sufficiently large to prevent deviations;
(ii) It must be in the firms' best interest to carry on the retaliation once a deviation has occurred.

The second condition can be difficult to assess, because retaliation is itself an equilibrium phenomenon.

To evaluate the impact of a structural change such as a merger on collusion, it is then necessary to have a clear picture of how industry characteristics affect both the short-term benefits and the retaliation possibilities.

8.3. Relevant factors for collusion

Many characteristics can affect the sustainability of collusion. First, there are some basic structural variables, such as the number of competitors, entry barriers, how frequently firms interact, and market transparency. Second, there are characteristics about the demand side: is the market growing, stagnating, or declining? Are there significant fluctuations or business cycles? Third, there are characteristics about the supply side: Is the market driven by technology and innovation, or is it a mature industry with stable technologies? Are firms in a symmetric situation, with similar costs and production capacities, or are there significant differences across firms? Do firms offer similar products, or is there substantial vertical or horizontal differentiation? This section reviews the impact of these various industry characteristics.[9]

---

[8] See for instance the work of Porter (1983) on the Joint Executive Committee for the rail-roads industry in the 1880s.

[9] While there is little empirical evidence on tacit collusion, there are several studies on cartels, following the initial work of Posner (1970) and Hay and Kelley (1974). Cartels are different due to explicit coordination, exchange of information and greater ability to adjust to specific conditions, but they face many common features since firms must have proper incentives. These studies are surveyed by Levenstein and Suslow (2004) who emphasise their disparity. They however provide support to the importance of some structural factors discussed here, in particular the role of the number of firms, of entry barriers, and of market stability.

8.3.1. Collusion is sustainable if and only if firms put sufficient weight on future profits

As already stressed, collusion arises from dynamic interaction. Collusion emerges when firms conjecture that any attempt to undercut the collusive price will be followed by tough retaliation from competitors. Since retaliation arises in the future while deviations generate immediate profits, the ability to collude depends in turn on the relative importance of current profits compared to future profits in the firms' objective.

8.3.2. Collusion is more difficult when there are more competitors

First, coordination is more difficult, the larger the number of parties involved.[10] Second, and beyond the issue raised by the difficulty of reaching a consensus, deviations from it are more tempting in the presence of many competitors: Since firms must share the collusive profit, as the number of firms increases each firm gets a lower share of the pie. This implies that the short-run gain from deviation increases, while at the same time the long-run benefit of maintaining collusion is reduced. It is thus more difficult to prevent firms from deviating.[11]

8.3.3. Do symmetric market shares facilitate collusion?

It is often asserted that more symmetric market shares facilitate collusion. At first glance, this may seem justified since the firm with the lowest market share has more to gain from a deviation, and less to lose from retaliation. However, market shares are largely endogenous. *While it may not constitute the main relevant factor for a correct analysis of an industry, market share asymmetry may reflect more profound and relevant asymmetries that tend to make collusion more difficult to sustain.* But then, the relevant question becomes the impact of these more profound asymmetries in cost or product range or quality.

8.3.4. Entry barriers facilitate collusion

It should be clear that collusion is difficult to sustain if there are low barriers to entry. First, in the absence of entry barriers any attempt to maintain supra-competitive prices would trigger entry (e.g., short-term or "hit-and-run" entry strategies), which would erode the profitability of collusion. Second, the prospect of future entry tends to reduce the scope for retaliation. This is a well understood factor that is routinely discussed in the cases.

---

[10] The idea that coordination is more difficult in larger groups is intuitive but there is little economic literature on this issue. See nevertheless Compte and Jehiel (2002).

[11] This insight is valid when holding all other factors constant. The number of firms is however endogenous and reflects other structural factors such as barriers to entry and product differentiation.

8.3.5. Frequent interaction and frequent price adjustments facilitate collusion

As already mentioned, there is more scope for collusion when the same firms compete repeatedly. Relatedly, firms find it easier to sustain collusion when they interact more frequently. The reason is that firms can then react more quickly to a deviation by one of them. Therefore, retaliation can come sooner when firms interact more frequently.

To see this clearly, note first that firms could not tacitly collude if they did not anticipate interacting again in the future. Similarly, collusion is unlikely when firms interact only infrequently, since the short-term gains from undercutting a collusive price could then be "punished" only in a far future.[12]

This idea can be illustrated by the US government's practice of buying vaccines in bulk in order to undo collusion.[13] By buying in bulk, the government both increases the stakes of each procurement auction and makes these auctions less frequent, thereby limiting the interaction between the bidders. A similar idea applies to the frequency of price adjustments. When prices adjust more frequently, retaliation will again come sooner; and in addition, a cheating firm will not be able to take advantage for as long a time as before of its cheating behaviour. Both factors contribute to hinder collusion. Examples of frequent interactions include for instance financial security markets (see in particular the NASDAQ Market Makers case), or daily spot markets.

8.3.6. Market transparency facilitates collusion

Quick retaliation when one market participant undercuts the others requires that such deviation be identified by the other participants. As a result, collusion can be difficult to sustain when individual prices are not readily observable and cannot be easily inferred from readily available market data. This observability problem has first been stressed by Stigler (1964)'s classic paper, and formally analysed by Green and Porter (1984) and Abreu et al. (1985). It can be noted that market stability can play a role, since inferring deviations from collusive conduct is easier and requires less market data when the market is stable.[14]

The delay necessary to obtain reliable data on prices and quantities matters, as well as its nature. For example, professional associations sometimes publish information on prices, productions or capacity utilisation rates. It first matters whether this information is about aggregate or individual data, since in the latter case it is easier to identify a deviant firm.[15] The time lag elapsed between

---

[12] Of course, other factors such as market transparency, which is discussed below, also affect the length of time before retaliation effectively occurs. But the point here is that retaliation will not even be feasible in the absence of frequent interaction.

[13] See Scherer (1980).

[14] See for instance the analysis of transparency in UPM-Kymmene/Haindl (M. 2498).

[15] See for example Kühn (2001).

the pricing period and the publication period is also important. Even detailed information may not help to sustain collusion if it is available only after a long delay.

Finally, we should note that there is a link between the circumstances that make collusion difficult to enforce, and those that may make it difficult to coordinate on a collusive outcome in the first place. The harder it is to obtain data on prices and quantities, the harder it may be for the firms to work out, without explicit collusion, what would constitute a monopoly price. However, this equivalence is not precise. For instance, if the technology in the industry is fairly standard and the goods produced fairly homogeneous, the monopoly price may be easy to work out even if there is no transparency about individual production levels. So collusion could be easy to coordinate upon but hard to enforce. Conversely, even in the presence of high transparency about individual production levels, when products are differentiated it may be difficult for the parties to be sure what counts as "not upsetting your competitors": does this just mean "avoiding price cuts" or also "avoiding quality improvements"? Does a Christmas promotion in a consumer goods industry fall within the spirit of tacit collusion? And so on. Thus collusion could be relatively easy to enforce once agreed but hard to coordinate upon. Overall, these considerations suggest that, as with the number of firms in an industry, the lack of transparency that makes collusion hard to enforce *may* also make it hard to agree upon—but this is an intuitive conclusion on which there is little convincing scientific literature.

8.3.7. Demand growth

As stressed above, collusion is easier to sustain when short-term gains from a deviation are small compared with the cost of future retaliation. This implies that:

For a fixed number of market participants, collusion is easier to sustain in growing markets, where today's profits are small compared with tomorrow's ones.

Conversely, collusion is more difficult to sustain in declining markets, where tomorrow's profits (with or without retaliation) will be small anyway.

This conclusion appears somewhat at odds with some case courts and opinions expressed by the European Commission in guidelines. Indeed demand growth is in practice often interpreted as a factor hindering collusion. One possible reason for this apparent discrepancy is that the above reasoning assumes that the number of market participants remains fixed despite market growth, while in practice, entry may be easier in growing markets (see for instance Gencor v Commission, T-102/96).[16] As discussed above, the prospect of future entry then hinders the ability to collude. In this way, *market growth may be associated with market characteristics detrimental to collusion*. However, it may be useful to

[16] Market growth may also be the sign of a lack of maturity, or of a highly innovative market.

disentangle the intrinsic effect of market growth discussed above from the impact of entry and other factors, so as to assess their relative strengths. In markets with low entry barriers, market growth is indeed likely to generate entry, and the overall impact may well be detrimental to collusion. However, in those markets where entry barriers are high (e.g., because of needed patents), the intrinsic impact of market growth may prevail and facilitate collusion.

8.3.8. Business cycles and demand fluctuations hinder collusion

A corollary of the impact of growth and decline is that collusion is less sustainable in markets that are subject to demand fluctuations (see FTC v. Arch Coal). The idea, formally captured by Rotemberg and Saloner (1986) and Haltiwanger and Harrington (1991), is that when the market is at a peak, short-term gains from a deviation are maximal while the potential cost of retaliation is at a minimum. Hence, *demand fluctuations hinder collusion, and more so when fluctuations are deterministic* (*as in the case of seasonal cycles*) *rather than random.*

8.3.9. Collusion is more difficult in innovative markets

Innovation makes collusion on prices less easy to sustain. The reason is that innovation, particularly drastic ones, may allow one firm to gain a significant advantage over its rivals. This prospect reduces both the value of future collusion and the amount of harm that rivals will be able to inflict if the need arises.

Consider for example an industry where, in the absence of any innovative activity, the incumbents would benefit from a secure, stable situation. They would then hesitate before cheating on a collusive conduct, which would trigger a price war and dissipate their future rents. Suppose now that, with some probability, one incumbent makes a drastic innovation, which drives its rival out of the market. If the probability of successful innovation is substantial, the incumbents then anticipate that their market position is short-lived (at least in expected terms); they thus put less emphasis on the cost of future retaliation and are more tempted to cheat on collusion.

8.3.10. Cost asymmetries hinder collusion

The presence of such cost asymmetry has several implications.[17] First, firms may find it difficult to agree to a common pricing policy. Indeed, firms with a lower marginal cost will insist on lower prices than what high-cost firms would wish to sustain. More generally, the heterogeneity in cost structures may rule out any "focal point" in pricing policies and so exacerbate coordination problems.

---

[17] See Bain (1948) for an early discussion and Gertner (1994).

In addition, technical efficiency would require allocating market share to low-cost firms, but this would clearly be difficult to sustain in the absence of explicit agreements and side-transfers.[18]

Second, even if firms agree on a given collusive price, low-cost firms are more difficult to discipline, both because they may gain more from undercutting their rivals and because they have less to fear from a possible retaliation by high-cost firms.[19]

To better induce the low-cost firm to stick to the collusive conduct, firms may tacitly grant a larger share of the market to the low-cost firm. However, *compared to the case of symmetric cost structure, there is less scope for collusion with an asymmetric cost structure, and the most effective collusive conducts induce asymmetric market shares, reflecting firms' costs.*

The intuition that "it is easier to collude among equals" may also explain the informal discussions about the role of so-called "mavericks". A maverick firm can be interpreted as a firm with a drastically different cost structure, which is thus unwilling to participate to a collusive action. Of course, this "asymmetry" can be along other dimensions (see below).

8.3.11. Asymmetries in capacity constraints hinder collusion

The previous reasoning extends to other forms of differences in the cost structure, including differences in production capacities. Capacity constraints potentially affect the sustainability of collusion in two ways. First, a capacity-constrained firm has less to gain from undercutting its rivals. Second, capacity constraints limit firms' retaliatory power. At first glance, capacity constraints thus appear to have an ambiguous effect on collusion, since they reduce both the incentives to deviate and the ability to punish such deviations. And indeed, studies that have focused on symmetric capacities[20] have confirmed this apparent ambiguity.

What is less ambiguous, however, is the impact of an asymmetry in capacities. Compared with a situation where all firms face the same capacity constraints, increasing the capacity of one firm at the expense of the others both increases the first firm's incentive to undercut the others and limits these other firms' retaliatory power. Overall, therefore, introducing such asymmetry hinders collusion. This insight has been hinted at by several studies.[21] It has recently been explored in more detail by Compte et al. (2002), who show that the introduction of asymmetric capacities indeed makes collusion more difficult to sustain when the aggregate capacity is limited, and discuss the Nestlé/Perrier case (M.190).

---

18 Side-transfers need not be monetary, however. For a discussion of these issues, see Osborne and Pitchik (1983) and Schmalensee (1987).

19 Mason et al. (1992) note in experimental duopoly games that cooperation is more likely when players face symmetric production costs.

20 See, e.g., Abreu (1986) for a symmetric Cournot context and Brock and Scheinkman (1985) for a first analysis of a symmetric Bertrand context, later extended by Lambson (1987).

21 Lambson (1994, 1995), Davidson and Deneckere (1984, 1990) and Pénard (1997).

8.3.12. Product differentiation

We have so far assumed that all firms were offering the same product (homogeneous good market). In practice, firms often try to differentiate their offerings, and can do so in different ways.

One possibility is for a firm to develop a "better product"; this is what economists refer to as "vertical differentiation." In essence, firms are then in an asymmetric situation and the analysis is thus similar to that of asymmetric costs of production. A firm that has a better quality (possibly adjusted for the cost) is in a situation somewhat similar to that of a firm that would offer the same quality as the others, but at a lower cost. This firm has more to gain from cheating on a collusive path (put another way, it may favour a different "net" price, even adjusting for the quality differential), and it has less to fear from a possible retaliation from the other firms.

When firms are differentiated in quality, collusion is more difficult, the larger the competitive advantage of the high-quality firm.

Another and quite different form of product differentiation consists for the firms in offering different combinations of characteristics, possibly at comparable prices but targeted at different types of customers; this corresponds to the case of so-called horizontal differentiation. Such differentiation aims at segmenting customers, and at gaining market power over specific customer segments by creating customer loyalty. Indeed, a customer may then be reluctant to switch away from his favourite brand, even if he would benefit from a small price reduction by turning to an alternative brand. This segmentation strategy affects the scope for collusion in two ways. First, it limits the short-term gains from undercutting rivals, since it becomes more difficult to attract their customers. Second, it also limits the severity of price wars and thus the firms' ability to punish a potential deviation.

Overall, the impact of horizontal differentiation appears quite ambiguous.

And indeed, the economics literature on this issue has shown that collusion may become easier or more difficult, depending on the exact nature of the competitive situation (e.g., competition in prices versus competition in quantity).[22] Raith (1996) however notes that *product differentiation may exacerbate informational problems in non-transparent markets.*

8.3.13. Multi-market contact

It is well recognised that firms can sustain collusion more easily when they are present on several markets.[23] First, multi-market contact increases the frequency of the interaction between the firms. Second, it may allow softening asymmetries

---

[22] See for example Ross (1992) and Martin (1993).

[23] The classic reference is Bernheim and Whinston (1990). See also Parker and Röller (1997) and Evans and Kessides (1994) for empirical evidence.

that arise in individual markets. For example, one firm may have a competitive advantage in one market and its rival its own competitive advantage in another market. While a market-level analysis may then suggest that collusion is difficult to sustain, multi-market contact restores in such a case an overall symmetry that facilitates collusion. Third, multi-market contact may allow the firms to sustain collusion in markets where the industry characteristics alone would not allow such collusion.

International cartels such as the vitamins cartel provide good examples of (explicit) collusion with multi-market contacts.

8.3.14. Other factors

We have so far discussed the factors that have been identified in the economics literature as exercising a key influence on sustainability of collusion. In practice, other factors have been considered by competition authorities; demand elasticity, customers' buying power, and so forth. We now briefly discuss these factors.

Demand elasticity

It is often perceived that low demand elasticity should exacerbate collusion concerns. While the above analysis stresses that the elasticity of the demand has no clear impact on the *sustainability* of collusive prices, it is however the case that collusion can be more profitable when demand elasticity is low. *For a given market size, the firms have more to gain from sustaining the monopoly price when demand elasticity is low.* In that sense, demand elasticity may constitute a relevant factor, although of a different nature than the factors listed above.[24] In addition, collusion is a larger concern for consumers when demand is inelastic than when it is elastic. This is both because the potential for a large profitable increase in prices above the "normal" level decreases when demand becomes less elastic, and because consumers are hurt more by a given price increase when they have little alternatives.[25]

Buying power

A related factor concerns the countervailing buying power of the customers. If buyers are powerful, even a complete monopolist may find it difficult to im-

[24] The profitability of collusion can in turn influence the firms' willingness to design and implement practices that facilitate the implementation of a collusive action. It can also induce firms to engage in more explicit collusion, at the risk of being caught by antitrust enforcement. More generally, to the extent that "transactions costs" may affect the ease of identifying and coordinating upon tacitly collusive outcomes, as well as the ease of enforcing them, the profitability of the outcome is likely to increase the probability that the parties will find a way to reach it. Nevertheless, this remains an intuitive argument rather than one for which there exists any formal model.

[25] The potential harm to consumers is thus larger, the less elastic the demand. The impact on total welfare, however, is more ambiguous, since price increases generate less distortion when demand is inelastic (see, e.g., Tirole, 1988, for a discussion of this issue).

pose high prices. The profitability of collusion is similarly reduced. In addition, Snyder (1996) note that large buyers can design procurement schemes that reduce the scope for collusion.[26]

Structural links

Structural links can facilitate collusion among firms. For example, cross-ownership reduces the gains derived from undercutting the other firm. Joint venture agreements can also enlarge the scope for retaliation—a firm can then for example punish a deviating partner by investing less in the venture.[27] For these reasons, collusion is more likely to emerge in markets where competitors are tied through structural links.

Cooperative and other contractual agreements

Even in the absence of structural links, simple cooperative agreements can contribute to foster collusion. As in the case of joint ventures, these cooperative agreements can for example enlarge the scope for retaliation, thereby enhancing the ability to punish deviating partners.

This may be particularly relevant for industries such as the telecommunications industry, where competitors need to reach interconnection agreements in order to offer widespread connectivity. These agreements do not only enlarge the scope for retaliation, they also have a direct impact on the operators' pricing strategies.[28] Competitors may then design these interconnection agreements so as to facilitate collusion.

More generally, firms may alter their contractual agreements, either between themselves or with third parties, so as to facilitate collusion. Marketing agreements can be employed to that effect. Jullien and Rey (2002) show for example that producers of consumer goods can resort to Resale Price Maintenance to impose more uniform prices across local retail markets, thereby making it easier to detect deviations from a collusive price. Record companies have been accused to market their offerings according to simple pricing grids (with only a few categories, instead of personalised prices for each author or title) for a similar purpose.

The existence of a "maverick" firm

It is sometimes asserted that a particular firm acts as a "maverick" that discourages any attempt to sustain collusion. As already mentioned, this is in line

---

[26] A good example is the treatment of Enso/Stora (M. 1225) in which the commission concluded that "Tetra Pak has countervailing buyer power to such an extent that it will neutralise the potential increase in market power of the merger between Stora and Enso."

[27] Martin (1995) provides a detailed analysis of this issue.

[28] For example, telecom operators that compete in linear prices could give each other incentives to maintain high prices, even in the absence of repeated interaction, by agreeing on a high reciprocal access charge—see, e.g., Armstrong (1998) and Laffont et al. (1998).

with the economic intuition according to which "it is easier to collude among equals." The notion of maverick must however be defined properly. Consider for example a firm that has a drastically different cost structure, production capacity or product quality, or that is affected by different factors than the other market participants. Very often such a firm will exhibit a market conduct that differs from others, reflecting its different supply conditions. This firm may then be unwilling to be part to a collusive conduct—put another way, it would do so only under terms that would not be acceptable or sustainable for the other firms. Alternatively, a firm may have a stronger preference for the short-term and be therefore more tempted to undercut the rivals.[29] The existence of such a "maverick" clearly tends to make collusion difficult if not impossible to sustain. It is however necessary to identify carefully the origin of the "maverick" character, in order to determine whether it is an inherent, long-lasting characteristic, or only reflects a transitory situation.

Club and network effects

Some markets are subject to club or network effects, where consumers benefit from being in the same "club": using the same software, typing on the same keyboard pattern, subscribing to the same operator, and so forth.[30] Club effects have several relevant implications. They tilt the market in favour of a single participant, thereby creating a "winner-take-all" type of competition which is not prone to collusion. In addition, club effects create lock-ins effects that reinforce the position of the market leader and thus increase the benefits derived from such a position. Club effects therefore contribute to make collusion less likely.

8.4. A mathematical illustration

We illustrate some effects with a model of Bertrand competition. Suppose that n firms produce the same good with the same unit variable cost c. Short run price competition would then lead these firms to price at cost ($p = c$) and dissipate any profits. When these firms compete repeatedly they are able to sustain a "collusive" price $p^C > c$, sharing the profit $\pi^C = (p^C - c)D(p^C)$ equally, by reaching a tacit understanding that any deviation from this price would lead the firms to revert to the competitive price $p = c$ in all future periods.[31] If the firms have the same discount factor δ, by sticking to the collusive price, each earns

$$\frac{\pi^C}{n} + \delta\frac{\pi^C}{n} + \delta^2\frac{\pi^C}{n} + \cdots = \frac{\pi^C}{n}\left(1 + \delta + \delta^2 + \cdots\right) = \frac{\pi^C}{n}\frac{1}{1-\delta}.$$

---

[29] See Harrington (1989) for an analysis of collusion between firms that have different discount factors, and FTC v. Arch Coal where the court rejected the alleged presence of a maverick.

[30] One important issue concerns the "compatibility" of rival clubs or networks.

[31] See Friedman (1971).

If instead one firm slightly undercuts the other, it captures the entire market and thus the entire collusive profit π^C, but the ensuing price war will eliminate any future profit. Each firm is thus willing to stick to the collusive price if

$$\frac{\pi^C}{n}(1+\delta+\delta^2+\cdots) \leq \pi^C + \delta \times 0,$$

that is, if

$$\delta \geq \delta^*(n) \equiv 1 - \frac{1}{n}.$$

The critical threshold for the discount factor, δ^* depends on the number of firms: the more competitors there are, and the higher this threshold, meaning that collusion is less and less sustainable.

From now on we assume that $n = 2$.

Frequency of interactions

Assume now that firms compete only every T periods. That is, firms compete in periods $1, T+1, 2T+1$, and so forth. Then, collusion is sustainable if

$$\frac{\pi^C}{2}(1+\delta^T+\delta^{2T}+\cdots) \geq \pi^C + \delta^T \times 0,$$

that is, if $\delta \geq \delta^*(T) \equiv \frac{1}{2^{1/T}}$. When firms interact less often, the perceived cost of future retaliation is smaller, and thus collusion is more difficult to sustain.

Price sluggishness

In a similar vein, suppose that firms "compete" in each period but fix their prices for T periods. Collusion is then sustainable if

$$\frac{\pi^C}{2}(1+\delta+\delta^2+\cdots) \geq \pi^C(1+\delta+\delta^2+\cdots+\delta^{T-1}) + \delta^T \times 0,$$

where the right-hand side reflects the fact that a cheating firm can benefit from undercutting its rivals for T periods before they react to its deviation. This condition yields the same threshold as above.

Entry

To illustrate the effects of barriers to entry, suppose that with some probability μ a firm enters the market for one period and charges the competitive price, $p = c$, and then exits.[32] To maximise the scope for collusion, the best scheme consists,

[32] This is a short-cut to reflect the competitive pressure exerted by entrants.

when entry does not occur, in: (i) charging a collusive price p^C and dividing the profit π^C equally, and (ii) reverting to the competitive price after an incumbent deviates. Such collusion is sustainable if

$$\frac{\pi^C}{2} + (1-\mu)\frac{\delta}{1-\delta}\frac{\pi^C}{2} \geq \pi^C + \delta \times 0,$$

that is, if $\delta \geq \delta^*(\mu) \equiv \frac{1}{2-\mu}$. The threshold δ^* thus now increases with μ: the more likely entry is, the more difficult it is to sustain collusion.

Innovation

Similarly, suppose that with probability ρ an outside innovator enters the market and "wipes out" the current incumbents. The incumbents thus survive in each period with probability $1-\rho$. By sustaining a collusive price p^C, as long they survive the two incumbents get an expected rent given by

$$V = \frac{\pi^C}{2} + \delta(1-\rho)\frac{\pi^C}{2} + \delta^2(1-\rho)^2\frac{\pi^C}{2} + \cdots = \frac{1}{1-(1-\rho)\delta}\frac{\pi^C}{2}.$$

Collusion is then sustainable when this rent exceeds the short-term profit from undercutting the rival, π^C, leading to $\delta \geq \delta^*(\rho) = \frac{1}{2(1-\rho)}$, which is more difficult to satisfy when the probability of innovation increases. The same conclusion holds if the innovation is due to one incumbent, provided that the innovation probability is exogenous.

Market growth

Let us consider now the effect of demand. Suppose first that demand "grows" steadily at a rate g. By agreeing on a collusive price p^C, each firm gets in each period t a profit $(1+g)^t\pi^C/2$, with $\pi^C = (p^C - c)D(p^C)$. Collusion is sustainable if

$$\frac{\pi^C}{2} + \delta(1+g)\frac{\pi^C}{2} + \delta^2(1+g)^2\frac{\pi^C}{2} + \cdots \geq \pi^C + \delta(1+g) \times 0,$$

that is, if $\delta \geq \delta^*(g) = \frac{1}{2(1+g)}$. Thus the threshold decreases with the rate of growth.

Demand uncertainty

Suppose now that $g = 0$ but demand is random: with equal probability, demand is either low and given by $(1-\varepsilon)D(p)$, or high and given by $(1+\varepsilon)D(p)$ (Note that the expected monopoly profit is not affected by the demand uncertainty). By sustaining a collusive price p^C, each firm gets an expected discounted profit

$$V = \frac{\pi^C}{2}(1+\delta+\cdots) = \frac{1}{1-\delta}\frac{\pi^C}{2}.$$

Collusion is sustainable when the short-term gain from stealing the rival's market share is lower than the cost of the future price war. The short-term gains from a deviation are clearly higher when demand is high; collusion is therefore sustainable if:

$$\delta V = \frac{\delta}{1-\delta}\frac{\pi^C}{2} \geq (1+\varepsilon)\frac{\pi^C}{2},$$

that is, if $\delta \geq \delta^*(\varepsilon) = \frac{1+\varepsilon}{2+\varepsilon}$. The threshold δ^* increases with the magnitude of demand fluctuations, measured here by ε.

Business cycles

Consider now a "cycle" where demand is alternatively low, given by $(1-\varepsilon)D(p)$, and high, given by $(1+\varepsilon)D(p)$. If firms sustain a collusive price p^C the expected discounted values of profits, evaluated when demand is high and when it is low, are respectively given by

$$V^+ = (1+\varepsilon)\frac{\pi^C}{2} + \delta V^-, \qquad V^- = (1-\varepsilon)\frac{\pi^C}{2} + \delta V^+,$$

which implies $V^+ > V > V^-$. Collusion is again sustainable if it is so when demand is currently high:

$$\delta V^- \geq (1+\varepsilon)\frac{\pi^C}{2}.$$

This condition is more stringent than the condition obtained in the previous example of random fluctuations.

Lack of transparency

Trickier is the effect of imperfect information.[33] Following Tirole (1988) and Green and Porter (1984), suppose that demand is random and can take value $D(p)$ or 0. Suppose moreover that a firm can only observe its sales. Then when observing 0 sales a firm cannot infer whether this is due to a demand shock or to undercutting by the other firm. The equilibrium cannot support a constant price p^C, because this would imply that firms don't react to no sale, which would undermine the incentives not to undercut the collusive price. The collusive price then involves a price war following any instance where one firm doesn't sale:[34]

---

[33] Notice that if firms observe their sales and prices every T periods, then the situation is formally equivalent to the case where prices are fixed for T periods described above. An analysis of imperfect information with patient firms is presented in Fudenberg and Maskin (1986).

[34] With this set-up, both firms agree on when to start a price war. The strategy of each firm is to set a price equal to cost for T periods after a zero sale or after undercutting (implying zero sale of the other firm). With this both firms starts the price war at the same time and end at the same time.

for T periods firms set $p = c$, then they revert to collusion. Denoting by μ the probability of a demand shock, the expected discounted profit V generated by such a conduct is given by:

$$V = (1-\mu)\left(\frac{\pi^C}{2} + \delta V\right) + \mu\delta^{T+1}V = \frac{1-\mu}{1-\delta(1-\mu+\mu\delta^T)}\frac{\pi^C}{2},$$

where the two terms correspond respectively to what happens without and with a shock on demand. Collusion is sustainable if

$$V \geq (1-\mu)\pi^C + \delta^{T+1}V,$$

which is equivalent to $\delta(1-\delta^T)V \geq \frac{\pi^C}{2}$, and thus (since the left-hand side decreases when T increases) requires price wars to be long enough. An infinite price war would effectively "maintain" collusion if $\delta \geq \frac{1}{2(1-\mu)}$.

Cost asymmetry

To illustrate the effect of cost asymmetries, suppose that firms have different marginal costs $c_H > c_L$. If they insist on equal market shares, it is easy to verify that the high-cost firm will sustain collusion if $\delta > \frac{1}{2}$. But the low-cost firm will be willing to sustain collusion if only if

$$(p^C - c_L)\frac{D(p^C)}{2}(1+\delta+\cdots) \geq (p^C - c_L)D(p^C) + \delta P_L,$$

where P_L is the discounted profit of the low-cost firm after a punishment. This condition is clearly more stringent than with symmetric costs whenever $P_L > 0$. More generally, it may be difficult for a high-cost firm to cancel the profit of the low-cost firm without incurring a loss. This is for instance the case if the punishment is to revert to short-run price competition, in which the low cost firm sells at price c_H.[35] Granting a larger market share to the low-cost firm facilitates its participation to the scheme, but it affects negatively the other firm's incentive constraint. The market split that maximises the scope for collusion thus consists in giving "as much as possible" to the low-cost firm while satisfying the other firm's incentive constraint.

Difference in impatience

Suppose there are three firms, the first two with a discount factor $\delta > 2/3$ and the remaining one (the "maverick") with a discount factor $\delta' < 2/3$.[36] Because

---

[35] Note however that the upper bound on possible punishments, the so-called minmax profits, is symmetric and might be achieved through sophisticated strategies. See Thal (2005) for a discussion and a formal analysis.

[36] For expositional commodity, we thus simply posit here that firms rely on different discount factors; this hypothetical scenario can be interpreted as a short-cut for deeper sources of asymmetry,

of the presence of the maverick, a collusive path with equal market shares cannot be sustained: the maverick would deviate and undercut the others, since $\delta' < 2/3$ implies $\pi^C > \frac{1}{3}\frac{\pi^C}{1-\delta'}$. The minimal market share α that can be allocated to the first two firms must satisfy $\alpha\frac{\pi^C}{1-\delta} \geq \pi^C + \delta \times 0$, and is thus $\alpha = 1 - \delta$. The maximal market share that can be granted to the maverick is thus $1 - 2\alpha = 2\delta - 1$, which is higher than $1/3$ but lower than 1. Therefore, collusion cannot be sustained if the maverick is sufficiently short-termist: this is the case when $\pi^C + \delta' \times 0 > (2\delta - 1)\frac{\pi^C}{1-\delta'}$, that is, when the discount factor of the maverick is lower than $2(1 - \delta)$.

8.5. Collusion in other dimensions than prices

Quantity competition

The conclusions derived above apply as well to situations where firms compete in quantity. In this case, retaliation is triggered if one firm attempts at increasing its market share by raising its production. A typical retaliation will have competitors react by raising their outputs.

Under quantity competition there is less temptation to increase one's production level to deviate from a tacitly collusive level, since prices adjust to sell out the competitors' output. On its own this would make collusion easier to sustain. However, retaliation is somewhat more difficult under quantity competition since the firm that is the object of retaliation can always soften the blow (as compared with a situation of price competition) by adjusting its output level. Overall, since deviation is less tempting but the fear of retaliation less strong, it is not easy to compare the scope for collusion under the two forms of competition.

The mechanisms bear strong similarities, however, so that the factors discussed above affect the scope for collusion in the same manner.

Capacity, investment and prices

In some industries such as the chemical industry or in the paper industry,[37] capacity choices are key determinants of the outcome of competition. In such industries, one may be concerned about the potential coordination of firms on

---

such as short-term financial or liquidity constraints, the number of customers interested in the various offerings and the frequency of their purchases, and so forth. A complete analysis should however also consider the various issues (e.g., predation) and solutions raised by these deeper sources of asymmetry.

[37] The chemical industry is investigated by Gilbert and Lieberman (1987) and the newsprint industry is studied by Booth et al. (1991), whereas Christensen and Caves (1997) investigate the pulp and paper industry.

collusive capacity choices. The role of excess capacities in supporting price collusion has been discussed above. Here, we focus instead on situations where firms produce close or up to full capacity utilisation. In this case, a reduction in capacity reduces supply and therefore implies higher prices.[38] Collusion then consists in building less capacity, in order to constrain the subsequent prices. There is a close connection between this type of rivalry in capacity choices and competition in quantity. Thus, to a large extent the analysis of collusion under quantity competition applies to the analysis of collusion in capacities.

In particular, if capacities are short-lived, as for example in the Airtour/FirstChoice case, and if market conditions are indeed such that firms adjust their prices so as to sell up to capacity, a collusion in capacity is formally identical to a collusion on output levels, and thus to collusion with quantity competition. In other cases, though, the nature of capacities and their interplay with price competition introduce some differences.

First, capacity choices are not final production decisions. Once capacities are in place, firms still interact through their pricing decisions. And they need not always reach a full capacity utilisation rate, in particular when demand is uncertain at the time capacity is built. This means that collusion on capacities will usually involve some form of collusion on prices as well.[39] A second aspect is that often capacity choices come in infrequent bursts, at points in time that may differ from one firm to another. The "lumpiness" aspect of capacity building leads to pre-emption phenomena. Last but not least, capacity choices often involve some irreversibility, in contrast with product decisions. Clearly, irreversibility may impede collusion. However irreversibility matters mostly when it is strong and when demand is constant or declining; in this context there is little or no prospect of building new capacities in the future, and thus little scope for repeated interaction. If instead demand is growing fast enough, or if capacities depreciate fast enough, irreversibility matters less because there will be frequent additions of capacities, even on a collusive capacity expansion path, which opens the scope for retaliation. The reader can refer to UPM-Kymmene/Haindl (M. 2498) for a discussion of these issues in the context of the paper industry.

Bidding markets

The principles reviewed above apply to bidding markets as well. For example, collusion is easier when few bidders repeatedly participate in the same bidding markets, when the frequency of these markets is high (e.g., daily markets), and so forth. In addition, bidding markets can be designed in ways that either hinder

---

[38] See Kreps and Scheinkman (1983).

[39] Staiger and Wolak (1992) characterise collusive conducts in the case where capacities are short lived and demand fluctuates in an unpredictable manner. Collusion may emerge, based on coordination on low capacity levels and depending on the realised levels of demand, and so prices may or may not be collusive.

or facilitate collusion. For example, sealed bid auctions generate less information (that is, except if the auctioneer reveals the details of all the bids afterwards) than public descending procurement auctions, where sellers observe at each moment who is still bidding at the current price. Therefore, a close look at the organisation of the bidding markets may be necessary to assess the likelihood of collusion.[40]

Research and Development

Collusion on innovation strategies is subject to the observations already made when discussing the impact of innovation on collusion on prices, and particularly complex to implement. It suffers from substantial transparency problems, making it hard to monitor. The inherent uncertainty attached to R&D projects and the time lags usually involved further contribute to make such collusion difficult. Collusion on R&D is thus unlikely.

8.6. Implications for merger control

The previous section has shown that many factors affect the sustainability of collusion. Most often, a given market will have some characteristics that facilitate collusion, and some that tend to hinder collusion. Predicting on this basis alone the likelihood of collusion can thus be complex.

In addition, the same market situation can give rise to different equilibria. That is, the fact that firms *can* sustain collusion does not mean that they actually succeed in doing so. In particular, the firms may well compete in each period as if it were the last one, even if there exists another equilibrium in which they maintain monopoly pricing in each and every period. It is thus impossible to rely on a theoretical analysis alone to determine whether collusion is *actually* taking place. In an antitrust *ex post* context,[41] the analysis of past history of the industry can help answer that question. In a merger control context, the situation is different. The merger control office must evaluate *ex ante* the future evolution of the industry; the past history may then only provide limited information to that effect.[42]

---

[40] See, e.g., Klemperer (2002).

[41] For a discussion of collective dominance in the context of Article 82 of the European Treaty, see the DG Competition discussion paper on the application of Article 82 of the Treaty to exclusionary abuses.

[42] Past behaviour can however provide some information about specific characteristics of the market participants, which can for example be useful to identify whether firms are prone to collusion or of a "maverick" type (see the new Guidelines on the assessment of horizontal mergers, European Commission, 2004). This was the case for instance in Nestlé/Perrier (case M. 190). Lack of evidence of past collusive conduct can be also used by courts. For instance in FTC v. Arch Coal (District of Columbia, Aug. 16, 2004), the court relied both on lack of evidence of past collusive conduct and on structural factors such as lack of transparency and demand uncertainty to rule that tacit collusion was not likely.

Short of determining whether collusion will indeed occur, a highly difficult if not impossible task, the merger control office can however address a different but still relevant question: will the merger create a situation where collusion becomes more likely, that is, will collusion be significantly easier to sustain in the post-merger situation? This is the basis for a structural approach that assesses the impact of the merger on various factors affecting collusion and uses this to assess whether the change is conducive to collusion. Notice that such an approach is not conflicting with a behavioural approach. Any evidence on conduct can be used in assessing the importance of the structural changes.[43]

A merger often affects many of the factors that are relevant for the sustainability of collusion and it can affect them in ways that tend to off-set each other. For example, a merger reduces the number of competitors, which tends to facilitate collusion, but it can make the remaining competitors more asymmetric, which tends to hinder collusion. The impact of the merger on collusion can thus involve a difficult assessment of possibly conflicting effects. Ideally, this could be done by building a "meta-model" encompassing all the relevant characteristics. However, the previous section makes clear that such a "global model" would probably not be tractable, and thus quite useless. It is therefore necessary to identify the characteristics that are most relevant in each particular industry, and also to prioritise these factors.

While many factors appear relevant when evaluating the impact of a merger on collusion, the above overview highlights natural dividing lines among these factors.

First, some factors that may or may not be affected by the merger have a decisive impact on the firms' ability to sustain tacit collusion. These factors include *entry barriers*, the *frequency of interaction* and the role of *innovation*. Clearly, there is little scope for collusion in the absence of entry barriers, or if firms interact very infrequently, or else in innovation-driven markets. Therefore, whenever an industry presents one of these features, collusion is unlikely to constitute a significant concern.

Second, some factors are both relevant and likely to be directly affected by mergers. These factors include the number of market participants, of course, but also the degree of symmetry among those participants. Other factors in this second group would be the removal of a maverick firm, as well as the existence of structural links or of cooperative agreements.

Third, a series of factors can have an influence on the sustainability of collusion, possibly to a lesser extent, and may or may not be directly affected by mergers. Among these, the degree of market transparency appears to be a key factor. Other factors include product differentiation, the characteristics of demand (demand trend and fluctuations, as well as demand elasticity and buying

[43] A difference between US and EU may come from different weights put on conduct and structure. Casual observation suggests that US courts put more emphasis on conduct in assessing coordinated effects than European courts, but due to the fact that courts acted in a different legal environment (as mentioned in the introduction), this may be misleading.

power), multi-market contact, or the organisation of particular markets such as bidding markets. These dimensions are relevant to assess the plausibility of collusion, particularly when the factors of the first two groups do not suffice to send a clear signal.

The above discussion thus provides some basis for prioritising the relevant factors. But this discussion also calls for a structural analysis. Rather than a pure "check-list" of relevant factors, it seems indeed more appropriate to develop a clear understanding of which dimensions are most relevant, as well as of how they affect collusion—and are affected by a merger. This not only helps prioritise these factors, but also facilitates an overall assessment when several factors are relevant and push in different directions. For example, the above discussion provides an analytical framework for assessing how these conflicting factors affect the effectiveness of retaliation, and thus how these retaliation possibilities are modified by a merger.

Moreover the interplay of the factors may be important. We have for instance pointed out that the effect of demand growth depends on entry barriers. If entry barriers are so large that entry is highly unlikely to occur, demand growth fosters collusion. If instead entry barriers are moderate, demand growth may be sufficient to outweigh them and stimulate entry, which would in turn impede collusion. Similarly, product differentiation may affect market transparency, by affecting what firms can infer from available data. In both instances, it becomes important to undertake a joint assessment of the factors.

References

Abreu, D. (1986), Extremal equilibria of oligopolistic supergames. *Journal of Economic Theory* 39, 191–223.

Abreu, D., Pearce, D., Stachetti, E. (1985), Optimal cartel equilibria with imperfect monitoring. *Journal of Economic Theory* 39, 251–269.

Armstrong, M. (1998), Network interconnection in telecommunications. *The Economic Journal* 108, 545–564.

Bain, J. (1948), Output quotas in imperfect cartels. *Quarterly Journal of Economics* 62, 617–622.

Bernheim, D., Whinston, M. (1990), Multimarket contact collusive behavior. *RAND Journal of Economics* 21, 1–26.

Booth, D.L., Kanetkar, V., Vertinsky, I., Whistler, D. (1991), An empirical model of capacity expansion and pricing in an oligopoly with barometric price leadership: A case study of the newsprint industry in North America. *Journal of Industrial Economics* 3, 255–276.

Brock, W.A., Scheinkman, J. (1985), Price setting supergames with capacity constraints. *Review of Economic Studies* 52, 371–382.

Christensen, L.R., Caves, R. (1997), Cheap talk and investment rivalry in the pulp and paper industry. *Journal of Industrial Economics* 1, 47–73.

Compte, O., Jenny, F., Rey, P. (2002), Capacity constraints, mergers and collusion. *European Economic Review* 46 (1), 1–29.

Compte, O., Jehiel, P. (2002), Multi-party negotiations. Mimeo, CERAS.

Davidson, C., Deneckere, R.J. (1984), Horizontal mergers and collusive behavior. *International Journal of Industrial Organization* 2, 117–132.

Davidson, C., Deneckere, R.J. (1990), Excess capacity and collusion. *International Economic Review* 31, 521–541.

Evans, W.N., Kessides, I.N. (1994), Living by the 'golden rule': Multimarket contact in the U.S. airline industry. *Quarterly Journal of Economics* 109, 341–366.

Friedman, J. (1971), A non-cooperative equilibrium for supergames. *Review of Economic Studies* 28, 1–12.

Fudenberg, D., Maskin, E. (1986), The Folk theorem in repeated games with discounting or with incomplete information. *Econometrica* 54 (3), 533–554.

Gertner, R. (1994), Tacit collusion with immediate responses: The role of asymmetries. Mimeo, University of Chicago.

Gilbert, R., Lieberman, M. (1987), Investment and coordination in oligopolistic industries. *RAND Journal of Economics* 18, 17–33.

Green, E., Porter, R. (1984), Non-cooperative collusion under imperfect price information. *Econometrica* 52, 87–100.

Haltiwanger, J., Harrington, J. (1991), The impact of cyclical demand movements on collusive behavior. *RAND Journal of Economics* 22, 89–106.

Harrington, J. (1989), Collusion among asymmetric firms: The case of different discount factors. *International Journal of Industrial Organization* 7, 289–307.

Hay, G.A., Kelley, D. (1974), An empirical survey of price fixing conspiracies. *Journal of Law and Economics* 17, 13–38.

Ivaldi, M., Jullien, B., Rey, P., Seabright, P., Tirole, J. (2003), The economics of tacit collusion. Report for DG Competition, European Commission.

Jullien, B., Rey, P. (2002), Resale price maintenance and collusion. Mimeo, University of Toulouse.

Klemperer, P. (2002), How (not) to run auctions: The European 3G telecom auctions. *European Economic Review* 46 (4–5), 829–845.

Kreps, D., Scheinkman, J. (1983), Quantity pre-commitment and Bertrand competition yield Cournot outcome. *Bell Journal of Economics* 14, 326–337.

Kühn, K.U. (2001), Fighting collusion by regulating communication between firms. *Economic Policy* 32, 169–204.

Laffont, J.-J., Rey, P., Tirole, J. (1998), Network competition: I. Overview and nondiscriminatory pricing. *RAND Journal of Economics* 29 (1), 1–37.

Lambson, V.E. (1987), Optimal penal codes in price-setting supergames with capacity constraints. *Review of Economic Studies* 54, 385–397.

Lambson, V.E. (1994), Some results on optimal penal codes in asymmetric Bertrand supergames. *Journal of Economic Theory* 62, 444–468.

Lambson, V.E. (1995), Optimal penal codes in nearly symmetric Bertrand supergames with capacity constraints. *Journal of Mathematical Economics* 24, 1–22.

Levenstein, M., Suslow, V.Y. (2004), What determines cartel success? Working Paper, University of Michigan.

Martin, S. (1993), Endogenous firm efficiency in a Cournot principal-agent model. *Journal of Economic Theory* 59, 445–450.

Martin, S. (1995), R&D joint ventures and tacit product market collusion. *European Journal of Political Economy* 24, 357–379.

Mason, C.F., Phillips, O.R., Nowell, C. (1992), Duopoly behavior in asymmetric markets: An experimental evaluation. *Review of Economics and Statistics*, 662–670.

Osborne, M., Pitchik, C. (1983), Price competition in a capacity-constrained duopoly. *Journal of Economic Theory* 38, 238–260.

Parker, P.M., Röller, L.-H. (1997), Oligopoly and the incentive for horizontal merger. *American Economic Review* 75, 219–227.

Pénard, T. (1997), Choix de capacités et comportements stratégiques: une approche par les jeux répétés. *Annales d'Economie et de Statistique* 46, 203–224.

Porter, R. (1983), A study of cartel stability: The Joint executive Committee, 1880–1886. *Bell Journal of Economics* 14, 301–314.

Posner, R.A. (1970), A statistical study of antitrust enforcement. *Journal of Law and Economics* 13 (2), 365–419.

Raith, M. (1996), Product differentiation, uncertainty and the stability of collusion. London School of Economics-STICERD Discussion Paper Series EI/16:49.

Ross, T.W. (1992), Cartel stability and product differentiation. *International Journal of Industrial Organization* 10, 1–13.

Rotemberg, J., Saloner, G. (1986), A supergame-theoretic model of business cycles and price wars during booms. *American Economic Review* 76, 390–407.

Scherer, M. (1980), *Industrial Market Structure and Economic Performance*. RAND-McNally, Chicago.

Schmalensee, R. (1987), Competitive advantage and collusive optima. *International Journal of Industrial Organization* 5, 351–368.

Snyder, C. (1996), A dynamic theory of countervailing power. *RAND Journal of Economics* 27, 747–769.

Staiger, R., Wolak, F. (1992), Collusive pricing with capacity constraints in the presence of demand uncertainty. *RAND Journal of Economics* 23, 203–220.

Stigler, G. (1964), A theory of oligopoly. *Journal of Political Economy* 72, 44–61.

Thal, J. (2005), Optimal collusion under cost asymmetry. Mimeo, University of Toulouse.

Tirole, J. (1988), *The Theory of Industrial Organization*. MIT Press.

CHAPTER 9

The Economics and Politics of International Merger Enforcement: A Case Study of the GE/Honeywell Merger

Jay Pil Choi

Department of Economics, Michigan State University, East Lansing, MI 48824
E-mail address: choijay@msu.edu

"If it appears that the European Commission is unfairly blocking mergers between US companies principally to protect the position of European competitors, then the subcommittee will need to reexamine the open market the US has maintained for those sorts of acquisitions." *Senator Jay Rockefeller IV (D-WV), chairman of the US Senate Aviation Subcommittee.*

"I deplore attempts to misinform the public and to trigger political intervention. This is entirely out of place in an antitrust case and has no impact on the Commission whatsoever. This is a matter of law and economics, not politics." *European Competition Commissioner Mario Monti.*

9.1. Introduction

As the globalization of the world economy entails the growing interdependence among national economies, a nation's competition policies are no longer confined to domestic firms within its jurisdiction. With the prominence of multinational firms, what counts is not the nationalities of firms but the locus of the effects. Antitrust authorities thus are empowered to take actions against foreign firms if they affect competition in their jurisdictions.

The European Commission, for instance, can block or force changes to company mergers and takeovers, even when they do not involve any European firms, if they are deemed to adversely affect the competitive landscape in the European market. The mandate of the European Commission to regulate mergers between non-European companies derives from the EC Merger Control Regulation adopted in 1989, which requires that all companies, regardless of where they are based, notify the Commission about planned mergers if their combined worldwide annual sales exceed five billion euros and at least 250 million euros

CONTRIBUTIONS TO ECONOMIC ANALYSIS
VOLUME 282 ISSN: 0573-8555
DOI: 10.1016/S0573-8555(06)82009-2

worth of their business is done among the 15 EU nations.[1] This means that any US or non-European firms that have a significant presence in the European market that exceeds the threshold above need to clear the Commission's approval. The same applies to the US antitrust authorities such as the Department of Justice and the Federal Trade Commission. They routinely take actions against foreign firms if their actions harm competition and adversely affect consumers in the US market.[2] As of 2001, The United Nations Conference on Trade and Development listed 82 countries that had competition authorities and the American Bar Association identified 46 international merger notification requirements.[3] The current situation naturally raises issues concerning the potential for intergovernmental disagreements about the effects of antitrust actions.

This type of potential conflict finally materialized in a dramatic fashion. On July 3, 2001, in one of its most high-profile antitrust decisions ever, the European Commission blocked the proposed merger (valued at $43 billion) between General Electric (GE) and Honeywell despite intense lobbying by the Republican administration in the U.S.[4] Since it is the first case in which a proposed merger between two U.S. companies that had been approved by Washington has been blocked by European regulators, the decision has been closely scrutinized and has become a focus for intensifying trade disputes between Europe and the United States.[5] This chapter intends to analyze the political economy aspect of international antitrust in light of the European Commission's review of the proposed merger between General Electric and Honeywell.

---

[1] The EC Merger Regulation (Council Regulation (EEC) No 4064/89 of 21 December 1989 on the control of concentrations between undertakings) has been substantially amended. For the new EC Merger Regulation of 20 January 2004, see http://europa.eu.int/comm/competition/mergers/legislation/regulation/.

[2] One such example is the block of a merger between Ciba-Geigy and Sandoz, two Swiss pharmaceutical firms by FTC in 1997.

[3] See Leary (2001).

[4] The GE/Honeywell deal easily met the threshold above. When U.S. lawmakers ask what business it is of the Europeans if two U.S. companies want to merge, part of the answer is that GE alone employs about 85,000 people and collects about $25 billion in annual revenue in Europe.

[5] This incident of divergence in antitrust policy was, however, foreshadowed by the previous merger case in the US between the Boeing Company and the McDonnell Douglas Corporation in 1997. As in the case of GE/Honeywell, this merger was approved by the Federal Trade Commission in the U.S., but the European Commission recommended that the merger to be blocked. Even though this case was eventually approved after Boeing consented to several demands that included elimination of exclusivity clauses in its contracts with three U.S. airlines, it prompted Thomas Boeder (2000), Boeing's council, to "suggest the potential for serious conflicts between U.S. and European merger control regimes in the future," which indeed materialized with the GE/Honeywell case. The direction of divergence is not one-way. For instance, Air Liquide/Air Product/BOC was approved by the European Commission but blocked in the United States.

9.2. A brief history of the GE/Honeywell merger case

GE is a global, diversified conglomerate firm that produces a wide range of products from "jet engines to power generation, financial services to plastics, and medical imaging to news and information"[6] and was ranked as the world's largest company in 2001 (at the time of the merger review) with market capitalization of about $480 billion and 2000 sale of about $130 billion (*Financial Times*, May 9, 2001). In the aerospace sector that concerns the Merger Task Force (MTF), GE produces engines for large commercial aircraft (defined by the Commission as planes with over 100 seats and a range of 2000 to 8000 nautical miles). GE produces engines on its own (GEAE) and through CFMI, a 50–50 joint venture with SNECMA. Other major players in the market for large airplanes are Pratt & Whitney (PW, a subsidiary of UTC) and Rolls Royce (RR). According to the European Commission, GE has a market share of 52.5% whereas PW and RR have market shares of 26.5% and 21%, respectively.[7] With its market share of more than half, GE is considered a dominant producer of engines for large commercial aircraft by EC.[8]

Honeywell is also a diversified advanced technology and manufacturing company with presence in several markets. In the arena of aerospace, Honeywell gained prominence by acquiring Allied Signal. It now produces a variety of products, including not only engines but also avionics (the cockpit electronics that control the plane), Auxiliary Power Units (the generators powering the aircraft when stationary), wheels and brakes, and Environmental Control Systems (the complex air conditioning system used on aircraft). In addition, it has a market share of 50% or above in several of these areas, far higher than its closest competitor(s).[9] In 2001, nearly one-half of Honeywell's $23 billion of revenue came from its aerospace division.

These various aircraft equipment products are 'complements' in the sense that each is of no value to a customer unless used alongside other of the products. The merger between GE and Honeywell would have brought together two major global suppliers of a range of complementary products that are used in the production of large commercial aircraft. GE also has a strong aircraft-leasing arm

---

[6] http://www.ge.com/en/company/index.htm.

[7] In the market share calculations, EC attributes all of the market share of CFMI to GE. PW and RR's market shares also include that of IAE, a joint venture between PW and RR.

[8] Two other major suppliers of engines for large commercial aircraft are Rolly-Royce (RR) and Pratt & Whitney (P&W). These three engine manufacturers have also established joint ventures either among themselves or with other small companies. The most prominent joint ventures are CFMI (a 50/50 joint venture between GE and SNECMA) and IAE (a joint venture between RR, P&W, MTU and Japanese Aero Engines Corp. that manufactures the V2500 engine for narrow bodies). For more details about the structure of aerospace markets, see *Case No COMP/M.2220—General Electric/Honeywell* published by the Commission of the European Communities.

[9] Honeywell's main competitors in avionics are Rockwell-Collins, Thales and Smiths Industries. Their market shares range from 20–30% for Rockwell-Collins, 10–20% for Thales, and 0–10% for Smiths Industries, respectively. In APU, the main competitor is Hamilton Sundstrand.

called GE Capital Aviation Services (GECAS), which is the largest buyer of new aircraft (accounting for around 10% of all large commercial aircraft sales).[10]

Initially, the parties to the merger talk were UTC and Honeywell. However, when Jack Welch, GE's chairman at the time, found out about the UTC' negotiations to acquire Honeywell International Inc. for $40 billion in UTC stock, he personally faxed Honeywell an 11th-hour offer, valued at $45 billion in GE stock. UTC then withdrew from the negotiation in fear of bidding war with GE.[11] On October 22, 2000, GE and Honeywell had a joint press conference to announce their merger.[12]

The U.S. Department of Justice reviewed the merger starting from December 2000. The U.S. Department of Justice essentially considered the merger as a conglomerate one between complementary producers since the product lines of GE and Honeywell directly overlap only in a few areas such as military helicopter engines. With the condition that GE divest Honeywell's helicopter engine business and authorize new maintenance, repair, and overhaul services for certain Honeywell engines and APUs, the Department of Justice approved the merger in May 2001.

Across the Atlantic, EC opened its own investigation on March 1, 2001. The review procedure under the EC Merger Regulation consists of two phases. In Phase I investigations, EC has 25 working days (or in certain circumstances 35 working days) from the formal notification of a concentration to make its initial assessment of the proposed transaction. Within this deadline the Commission must either decide that it does not have jurisdiction, clear the concentration (with or without commitments) or open an in-depth investigation (Phase II).[13] If the European Commission decides to open an in-depth Phase II investigation, it must complete its investigation and reach a conclusion on the concentration within 90 working days or, within 105 working days where commitments have been offered later than 55 working days after the initiation of proceedings. The Commission may clear the merger (with or without commitments) or prohibit it.[14] After the initial review of the GE/Honeywell case, the European Commission certainly saw the case differently from its American counterpart and decided to implement an in-depth Phase II review. After the in-depth review, the Commission issued a 155-page statement of objections to the merger, and a two-day hearing was held on May 29–30, 2001.

On June 14, the legal deadline for the submission of remedies, GE proposed a series of concessions including the divestiture of certain avionics, APUs for small aircraft, and certain *behavioral* undertakings on GECAS and bundling.

---

[10] GECAS's main competitor on the market for aircraft leasing is International Lease Finance Corporation (ILFC) whose fleet size is about half of GECAS.

[11] See Harris (2001).

[12] Welch even delayed his retirement to oversee the integration of GE and Honeywell, which was supposed to be the capstone on his legendary career (Elliott, 2001).

[13] Article 10(1) of the EC Merger Regulation.

[14] Article 10(3) of the EC Merger Regulation.

The Commission, however, considered these concessions as insufficient for addressing the vertical and conglomerate effects of the merger. In particular, the Commission reasoned that some behavioral commitments proposed would have been a mere promise not to abuse the dominant positions and would be extremely difficult to implement in the absence of a *structural* undertaking on GECAS. On June 28, 2001, GE proposed a new set of remedies. However, the proposal was too little and too late (two weeks after the deadline) for the Commission (Giotakos et al., 2001).

In a last ditch effort to revive the merger, Honeywell Chairman Michael Bonsignore contacted Welch by fax and offered to accept a lower price in return for the combined group making more concessions to EC. Welch rejected the offer with a terse statement saying that "[t]he new proposal you propose in response to the Commission, makes no sense for our share owners."[15] Without any further remedies forthcoming by GE that would remove the competitive concerns held by the Commission, it declared the proposed merger incompatible with the European market on July 3, 2001. GE and Honeywell launched separate appeals with European Court of First Instance (CFI). The CFI upheld the Commission's decision on December 14, 2005. It acknowledged that conglomerate mergers may lead to anticompetitive effects in certain circunstances, but cônfirmed the very high standard of proof that the Commission has to meet in order to prohibit such mergers.

9.3. Economic theory behind the EC's decision

EC's rationale to block the merger rested on two main concerns. First, the EC was concerned with the issue of "bundling" that would be made possible by the proposed merger and its likely impact on competition in the markets for jet aircraft engines and avionics. Second, there was a concern that GE's aircraft leasing subsidiary—GECAS—would use its position as a purchaser of aircraft to harm competition in the aircraft equipment supply markets. As mentioned earlier, GE has an aircraft-leasing arm called GE Capital Aviation Services (GECAS), which is the largest buyer of new aircraft (accounting for around 10% of all large commercial aircraft sales). GECAS only buys aircraft with GE engines, whenever they are available. The Commission expected that GECAS would extend this exclusivity to Honeywell products following the merger. In this section, I briefly describe the economic theory behind the Commission's reasoning that concerns the potential anticompetitive effects of bundling.[16] For the theory and evidence regarding the second concern, namely, GE's use of GECAS subsidiary

---

[15] Andrew Hill, "Exchange of Faxes Buries GE Deal," *Financial Times*, June 29, 2001.

[16] See Choi (2003) for more detailed analysis. For a comprehensive review of the effects of vertical and conglomerate mergers on competition, see Church (2004). Martin (1999) provides a related analysis of bundling on welfare.

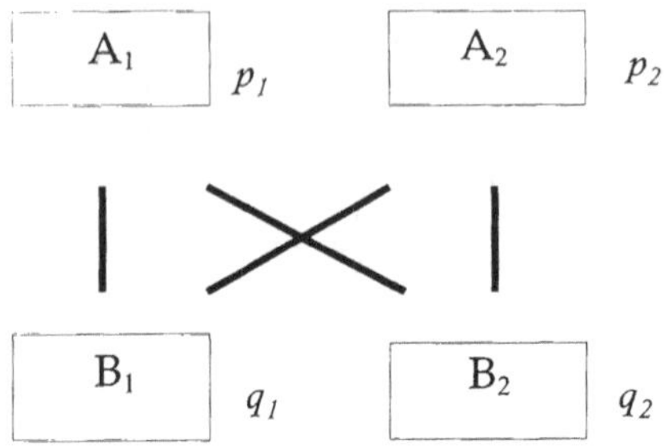

Fig. 9.1: Diagrammatic representation of the pre-merger situation.

to harm competition by foreclosing Honeywell's rivals, I refer to Reynolds and Ordover (2002) and Emch (2004).

To analyze the effects of potential bundling after the merger, consider two *complementary* components, A and B, which are valuable only when used together. Customers combine A and B in fixed proportions on a one to one basis to form a final product. In the proposed GE–Honeywell merger, for instance, A and B can be thought of as engines and avionics, respectively, to form an aircraft. Assume that there are two differentiated brands of each of the two components A (A_1 and A_2) and B (B_1 and B_2). That is, there are four ways to form a composite product, A_1B_1, A_1B_2, A_2B_1, A_2B_2. Let the price of brand A_i be p_i and the price of brand B_j be q_j, where $i = 1, 2$ and $j = 1, 2$. Then, the composite product A_iB_j is available at the total price of $s_{ij} = p_i + q_j$. Let D^{ij} denote demand for the composite product A_iB_j. The combinations of products and suppliers in this stylized model amount to four possible systems, as shown in Figure 9.1.

As in Economides and Salop (1992), we can assume that the four potential composite goods are substitutes for one another: D^{ij} is decreasing in its own price and increasing in the prices of the three substitute composite goods. For instance, D^{11} is decreasing in s_{11} and increasing in s_{12}, s_{21}, and s_{22}. We can derive the demand functions for the components from the demand functions for the composite goods. For instance, component A_i is sold as a part of composite goods A_iB_1 and A_iB_2. The demand for component A_i thus is given by

$$D^{A_i} = D^{i1} + D^{i2}$$

Similarly, the demand for component B_j is given by

$$D^{B_j} = D^{1j} + D^{2j}$$

Now suppose that A_1 and B_1 merge. It is assumed that the firms after merger engage in '*mixed bundling*', in which the firms sell the individual components separately as well as selling the bundle (but the bundle is offered at a discount to the sum of the stand-alone prices). The reason for this assumption is that at least for *existing generations* of products, the potential for the merged firm to engage in *pure* bundling may be limited, considering that the two products were sold

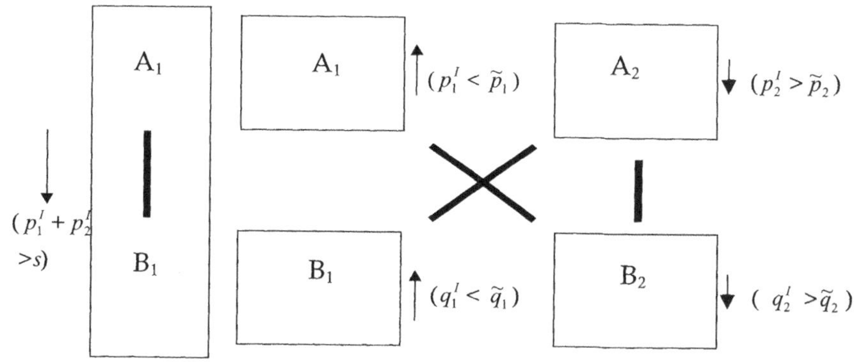

Fig. 9.2: Diagrammatic representation of post-merger with mixed bundling.

independently by separate firms prior to the merger. As a merged entity, A_1–B_1 now can offer three prices: s for the bundled product (A_1B_1), and $\tilde{p}_1$ and $\tilde{q}_1$ for individual components A_1 and B_1, respectively. A_2 and B_2 remain independent and charge prices $\tilde{p}_2$ and $\tilde{q}_2$, respectively. Figure 9.2 describes the post-merger situation with mixed bundling.

To get closed-form solutions, assume that system demand functions are linear and the demand system is symmetric:

$$D^{11}(s_{11}, s_{12}, s_{21}, s_{22}) = a - bs_{11} + cs_{12} + ds_{21} + es_{22},$$
$$D^{12}(s_{12}, s_{11}, s_{22}, s_{21}) = a - bs_{12} + cs_{11} + ds_{22} + es_{21},$$
$$D^{21}(s_{21}, s_{22}, s_{11}, s_{12}) = a - bs_{21} + cs_{22} + ds_{11} + es_{12},$$
$$D^{22}(s_{22}, s_{21}, s_{12}, s_{11}) = a - bs_{22} + cs_{21} + ds_{12} + es_{11},$$

where $a, b, c, d, e > 0$.

To illustrate the effects of the merger, further simplify the analysis by assuming that all four composite products are equally substitutable, that is, $c = d = e$. It can then be shown that when the merging firms were to bundle its complementary products, foreclosure could result from the following effects[17]:

1. The merged firm will reduce the price of its bundled system and expand market share, relative to the situation prior to the merger. Prior to the merger, any price cut by one of the merging firms will tend to benefit the other's sales. In the absence of the merger, neither party will take account of this benefit of a price cut on the other's sales. Following the merger, however, the merged entity can "internalize" these "pricing externalities" arising from the complementarity of their components by reducing the price of the bundle to

[17] The discussion below follows Choi (2003). See Choi (2003) for explicit expressions for the equilibrium market prices under different market structures.

below the level the two players would choose if acting independently. This will expand the merged firm's sales and market share.
2. The merged firm will raise the prices of its stand-alone components, relative to their levels prior to the merger. The merged firm has less to lose from raising its stand-alone prices than prior to the merger, because a proportion of those customers that switch away from the stand-alone components as a result of the price rise will simply switch to the bundle offered by the merged firm, rather than to the competing system. As such, the merged party will have an increased incentive to set high prices for its components. This raises the price of "mix-and-match" systems (i.e. systems including a GE/Honeywell component of the merged firm alongside a competitor's component) and makes them less attractive to buyers.
3. Independent rivals selling single components reduce their prices in response, but fail to recapture all market shares. In response to the price cut by the merged firm for their bundled system, and the price increase for the 'mix-and-match' systems, the independent rivals will cut price in order to retain some market share. However, they will not cut their prices as much as the merged firm (i.e. their system will remain more expensive than the bundled system of the merged firm), since—in the absence of counter-merger—they cannot internalize the externality arising from the complementarity of their components. As a result, they will fail to recapture all market shares.[18]

The merger would therefore reduce the profits of the merged firm's competitors. This reduction in profits follows directly from the combination of a loss of market share and the need to cut prices. The profits of the merged firm can be shown to increase, which provides an incentive to merge and engage in mixed bundling.

To illustrate the points above, consider an example where $a = b = 1$ and $c = d = e = 1/4$. Then it can be shown that with the independent ownership (pre-merger) structure, $p_1^I = p_2^I = q_1^I = q_2^I = 4/5$. The total price of each system good is 8/5 and each firm gets profits of 24/25. After the merger between A_1 and B_1, the merged entity (A_1–B_1) charges $\tilde{s} = 11/8$ for the bundle and $\tilde{p}_1 = \tilde{q}_1 = 1$ for separate components. Thus, it offers discount for the bundle ($11/8 < 1 + 1 = 2$). Independent producers, A_2 and B_2, charge $\tilde{p}_2 = \tilde{q}_2 = 3/4$ for their component products. Thus, the prices for system goods, A_1B_1, A_1B_2, A_2B_1, and A_2B_2 are given by $11/8, 7/4, 7/4$, and $3/2$, respectively, where $7/4 > 3/2 > 11/8$. After the merger A_1–B_1 receives the profits of $129/64$ ($> 24/25+24/25$), whereas independent producers get $27/32$ ($< 24/25$). This implies that A_1 and B_1 together increase their combined profits after merging while independent producers' profits decrease.

---

[18] Even though these results were derived from a linear demand model, they seem to be robust. For instance, the same qualitative results can be derived from a Matutes-Regibeau (1988) type mix-and-match model that extends the original Hotelling spatial competition model to system goods markets.

Economic theory explains how bundling may have both anti-competitive effects and efficiency benefits. The welfare effects of merger with mixed bundling in the model above depend on the extent to which systems are substitutes. Simulation results in Choi (2003) suggest that when the systems are close substitutes it is possible for total surplus to fall even without any foreclosure effects.[19] In the case of GE/Honeywell, the anti-competitive effects could also arise in the form of market foreclosure, over either the short or the medium term. If the financial impact of bundling on GE/Honeywell's rivals were such that they would be unable to cover their ongoing avoidable fixed costs of production, then their short-term exit could be expected.[20] Alternatively, even if the post-merger profitability of rivals were sufficient for them to remain in the market over the short-term, it might not be sufficient to justify new R&D investment or capital expenditure.[21] This would have serious consequences for their viability over the medium term. EC's concern was that the detrimental impact on welfare of such foreclosure arising from the GE/Honeywell merger might outweigh any efficiency benefits associated with bundling.

9.4. The American criticism and "politicization" of the case

The EC's decision to block the merger between GE and Honeywell was immediately met with harsh criticism by U.S. antitrust authorities, as well as some academics, for the alleged lack of sound economic models that support the decision.[22] Unfortunately, the case has also been politicized and portrayed as an attempt to shield European firms from competition without any hard evidence.

From the perspective of top ranking government officials and politicians, it was after all a purely American merger with full blessings from U.S. antitrust authority that was frustrated by EC for its alleged adverse impact on European markets. For instance, in a letter sent to Loyola de Palacio, European Union transport commissioner, Senator Jay Rockefeller IV (D-WV), chairman of the U.S. Senate Aviation Subcommittee said that he was "deeply disturbed" and

---

[19] When systems are sufficiently differentiated and become almost independent, the model will converge to the original situation considered by Cournot (1927) with total surplus increasing as a result of merger.

[20] If one of the two outside firms exits from the market, it could potentially have a *ripple effect* in terms of threatening the viability of the other outside firm in the complementary segments. From the demand system we have, we can derive the inverse demand for the system consisting of the merging firms' components as $s_{11}(D^{11}, D^{12}, D^{21}, D^{22}) = (\beta+\gamma)a-(\beta-2\gamma)D^{11}-\gamma D^{12}-\gamma D^{21}-\gamma D^{22}$, where $\beta = \frac{b}{(b-3c)(b+c)}$ and $\gamma = \frac{c}{(b-3c)(b+c)}$. When there is foreclosure of outside firms with $D^{12} = D^{21} = D^{22} = 0$, it can be easily verified that the system price by the merging firms becomes 2, which is higher than the pre-merger system price of $8/5$. Consumers also lose from the lack of variety.

[21] See Choi (2003) for an analysis of merger with bundling that accounts for R&D incentives.

[22] See Kolasky (2001) and Nalebuff (2002). In this chapter, I focus on the political economy aspect of the merger and the detailed discussion of the merit of economic analysis is beyond the scope of the current chapter.

warned that such a decision "could have a chilling effect on future transatlantic aviation and aerospace co-operation." Even President George W. Bush weighed in on the deal, saying that America "has a strong interest in fair treatment" of GE and Honeywell.[23]

Despite the political portrayal of the case as a protectionist measure, the case seems to be remarkable for the lack of political considerations in the decision. As Evans (2002) points out, perhaps "Monti deserves much credit for keeping European politics out of the decision making and pushing hard for competitive European markets."

There are several reasons to suspect that seemingly dramatic differences between the United States and the EC in their deliberations on the case are driven by any political considerations. First, as within the United States, antitrust policy of the EC has been increasingly based on welfare-oriented economic analysis. It might have been true that the level of sophistication in economic analysis at the EC was not up to the levels conducted by US antitrust agencies due to the lack of personnel at the time of the GE/Honeywell merger decision. Nonetheless, there seemed to have been clear consensus over what the core standards of antitrust should be across the Atlantic. An often-heard American critique of the European Commission, "You protect competitors; we protect competition" seems to be out of place in this case and at least such a rhetoric can be counterproductive.[24]

Second, if the EC's decision was driven by political considerations, the right question to ask is, "Would the merger have been approved if GE and Honeywell were European firms?" Considering many blocked cases by the EC that involve only European firms, the answer seems to be in the negative.[25] Thus, the criticism of the decision as mercantilistic trade policy seems to be unfounded and the threat of retaliation on the part of American politicians is unfortunate. In addition, it needs to be noted that some of the most ardent opposition parties to the merger were American firms that include UTC and Rockwell.

Finally, it should be acknowledged that reasonable people can disagree even if they assess with the same facts. This is especially so in antitrust enforcement because it is a highly imprecise enterprise despite significant recent advances in the analytical tools available to enforcement agencies. Thus, the differences in decisions should not be automatically attributed to political considerations or subject to a criticism that one agent's regulation is informed by sophisticated economic reasoning while the other's is not. Disagreements between agencies are often overstated. This is due to the fact that an assessment can be considered

---

[23] Other high ranking government officials and politicians who commented publicly on the case include Secretary of Commerce Donald Evans, Trade Representative Robert Zoellick, and Republican Senator Phil Gramm among others.

[24] In fact, Duso et al. (2003) find that the EC's decisions are not sensitive to firms' interests in their study of EU merger control decisions using stock market data.

[25] One such a case is a merger between Volvo and Scania, Sweden's two big truck manufacturers in 2000.

as a point in a continuum of spectrum whereas the decision to be made is essentially dichotomous, that is, either approval or disapproval of the merger.[26] For instance, we can envision a line segment of length 1 as in Hotelling product line. The left extreme point ($d = 0$) can be considered as the disapproval decision and the right extreme point ($d = 1$) can be considered as the approval decision. An antitrust agency's assessment can be indexed by $z \in [0, 1]$. Suppose that the agencies adopt the following rule: $d = 0$, if $z < 0.5$ and $d = 1$, if $z \geq 0.5$. Suppose that two agents' assessment points are clustered around 0.5, but one being slightly higher than 0.5 and the other slightly below 0.5. In such a case, two agents will reach divergent conclusions even though both agents assess the effects of a proposed merger in a very similar way. As a result, a small difference in opinions can be exposed with magnification.

In a recent article, Heyer (2005) also points out the possibility that the observed cross-jurisdictional differences in the GE/Honeywell case "stem less from contradictory views as to either the relevance of economics or the ultimate goals of antitrust, and more from the uncertainty inherent in antitrust decision making and enforcement." He further points out that "[D]ifferent antitrust analysis can, in good conscience and using the exact same analytical apparatus (i.e., good old microeconomic and industrial organization theory), reach different conclusions" if one of the following conditions holds true:

(1) They have differing estimates of the probability that the conduct is harmful;
(2) They have differing estimates of the magnitudes of the harms and benefits;
(3) They have differing levels of confidence in the ability of antitrust authorities to mete out and enforce remedies that will enhance welfare; or
(4) They have different levels of tolerance towards risk.

For instance, European competition law has no provisions for structural remedies that would dissolve merger *ex post*. This implies that the cost of type II error (where a merger is not blocked even though it should be) is higher for the EC, which naturally leads to more conservative approach in approving mergers.

If the differences in the decisions across the Atlantic were not driven by political considerations and were due to differences in honest opinions, we are inevitably led to the question of who was right. A short answer to the question is that nobody knows. Given the uncertainty inherent in antitrust enforcement, the decision is in essence an optimal statistical one that weighs the potential costs of type I error (where an efficient merger is not approved) against type II error. Antitrust authorities make their merger enforcement decisions based on counterfactual analysis that relies on many assumptions that are typically satisfied only imperfectly. In addition, documents or other evidence gathered in the

---

[26] Merger approvals with conditions of divestiture and other behavioral restrictions can make the decision less dichotomous and make it more aligned with the assessment. However, if the conditions are not accepted by the merging parties, it will be an all or nothing decision. In fact, it was ultimately a GE's decision not to pursue the merger rather than to concede more to the EC.

process of investigations can be subject to conflicting interpretation.[27] Thus, we can make only probabilistic assessments.[28] However, the agnostic answer given above does not mean that the current system is acceptable and nothing can be done when the differences arise from genuinely honest opinions.

9.5. Looking forward with a silver lining

The GE/Honeywell case rather demonstrated the need for consistent simple rules and better coordination by harmonizing antitrust controls across antitrust enforcement agencies in different jurisdictions, especially between Europe and the United States.[29] There are several reasons for this.

First, it is important not to impose any additional burden on businesses with unnecessary regulatory uncertainty. Different substantive and procedural regimes make mergers with international locus of effects complex, time consuming, and expensive process. Clear and consistent standards across jurisdictions will facilitate global businesses and eliminate any bureaucratic burden associated with uncertainty.

Second, in the current set-up where a merger needs to get approval in each jurisdiction where the firms operate, each agency has a veto power. As a result, the enforcement decision on a merger does not reflect the majority view and any international merger will be essentially determined by the least permissive agency. This decision rule is likely to be inefficient, and the degree of inefficiency will be exacerbated as more agencies are involved since the view reflected in the decision would be the one most extreme. This is true even if all antitrust agencies pursue the same economic goal (either social or consumer welfare maximization) without any political considerations and the effects of mergers are uniform across jurisdictions. If we consider the outcome of each investigation as an independent estimate of the effects of the proposed merger, the best estimate in the statistical sense would be the *average* view unless there is any systematic bias in the evaluation process. With the current system, however, the merger enforcement would be driven by the *first-order statistic*. The problem can be exacerbated if political considerations are also at play. For competitors opposed to the merger, there will be a tendency to appeal to the most sympathetic ear, which can marginalize all other agencies. This tendency could have serious consequences if any of the agencies are run by political-minded populist bureaucrats and standing up against big corporations can be seen as an act of

---

[27] See Heyer (2005) for a discussion of how to deal with uncertainty effectively in antitrust enforcements.

[28] According to Leary (2001), "we are ultimately attempting to weigh somewhat uncertain present effects against even more uncertain future effects."

[29] See Francois and Horn (2006) for a different perspective on the issue of the scope for an international agreement. Their model adopts a general equilibrium approach in the tradition of international trade theory in which the conflict is not between the "surpluses" of consumers and producers, but between the real incomes of different factor owners.

Table 9.1: Payoff matrix of the simultaneous merger approval game.

	Block	**Approve**
Block	C, C	C, 0
Approve	0, C	W, W

protecting wellbeing of consumers. There could be a race to be the toughest in an attempt to be a relevant player, which can preclude many pro-competitive mergers.

Third, even if there is no uncertainty in the evaluation of the effects of mergers, there could be conflicts if the effects of mergers are not uniform across jurisdictions. Suppose that there is a proposed merger that affects two countries, 1 and 2. The welfare impacts of the merger on each country are given by W_1 and W_2. The merger is globally efficient if and only if $W_1 + W_2 \geq 0$. However, the merger will be approved if and only if $W_1 \geq 0$ and $W_2 \geq 0$ under the current system.[30] Certainly, the latter condition is more stringent than the former condition, which implies that efficient mergers can be blocked since each agent ignores *external* effects. The scope of this type of inefficiency certainly increases as more agencies are involved. Cabral (2003) suggests that such a problem can be mitigated if international merger policy is considered as a repeated game. The idea is that each agency compromises and approves efficient mergers even though they decrease the country's welfare, with tacit coordination that the partner country will reciprocate the favor in the future. However, the efficacy of this framework is suspect since it crucially depends on the assumption that the policy-makers are infinitely lived long-run players and are sufficiently patient.

Finally, type I error (where an efficient merger is not approved) is not the only problem associated with the veto power of each agency. The existence of multiple jurisdictions can also lead to a free-rider problem that results in type II errors (where a merger is not blocked even though it should be) when resource constraints are considered. To illustrate the main intuition, consider the following merger approval game. There are two antitrust agencies who must decide whether or not to block the proposed merger. For simplicity, let me assume that the welfare effect of the merger is the same across jurisdictions and given by $W < 0$ in each country. Thus, it should be blocked. The block of the merger, however, entails enforcement costs C. The game can be described by the following matrix (Table 9.1). We assume that the merger can be blocked by either

---

[30] The European Commission has jurisdiction only over actions that distort trade in the Common Market; arguably, if they were to approve a merger with $W_{U.S.} + W_{EU} > 0$ and $W_{EU} < 0$, they would be in violation of their mandate. By the same token, U.S. antitrust authorities seek to maximize U.S. welfare, not world welfare. One such example is Webb-Pomerene Act of 1918, U.S. Federal legislation exempting certain exporters' associations from certain antitrust regulations. I thank an anonymous referee for pointing out this.

country with the veto power, and the welfare in each country without merger is normalized to zero. We further assume that $W < C < 0$, which implies that the merger would be banned in each country if there is no other agency to block it.

There are multiple equilibria in this game, with two asymmetric pure strategy equilibria and one symmetric mixed strategy equilibrium. In the two asymmetric pure strategy equilibria, one agency chooses 'Block' while the other chooses 'Approve,' and the resulting equilibrium is efficient. However, the most natural equilibrium may be the symmetric mixed strategy equilibrium since both agencies are symmetric in this game. Without any coordination, the unique, symmetric equilibrium is that each agency blocks with probability $p = \frac{W-R}{W}$. With the symmetric mixed strategy equilibrium, however, we have a coordination failure and the merger can be approved with the probability of $(1-p)^2$. Another source of inefficiency with independent investigations is the possibility of duplicative efforts in the event that both agencies decide to block, which occurs with the probability of p^2. In this stylized situation, it would certainly be beneficial for both parties to consider the designation of a "lead agency" to eliminate duplication and streamline the process. All the reasons listed above suggest a more integrated approach in the enforcement of international mergers.

On the positive side, the enormous media attention to the GE/Honeywell case revealed some of the problems inherent in the European merger control and played as a catalyst in the discussion of reforming the merger review process.[31] The reform will certainly contribute to harmonization and convergence of transatlantic merger enforcements.

One of the criticisms levied on the EC was a procedural one. In contrast to the U.S. system in which antitrust agencies have to go to court to block mergers and hence are "exposed to the crucible of cross-examination before an independent fact-finder," the European merger review lacks such a mechanism of checks and balances.[32] Investigation in the shadow of independent court certainly requires more disciplined analysis. In contrast, Directorate General (DG) Competition of the EC is sometimes said to act as investigator, prosecutor, judge, and jury. To appeal for a judicial review, firms must petition the Court of First Instance (CFI) in Luxembourg. The review process, however, is slow and the Court has been considered as an ally of the commission.[33] The lack of built-in checks and bal-

---

[31] See Kuhn (2002) for an excellent discussion of priorities for the reform of European merger policy. See also Lyons (2004).

[32] Kolasky (2001). However, it can be also argued that a plaintiff before the European Commission is in a situation which is not fundamentally different from the situation of a plaintiff before the U.S. FTC. Appeals of FTC decisions to the U.S. courts can take just as long as appeals of Commission decisions to the European courts. I am grateful to an anonymous referee for this observation.

[33] This perception (especially in the U.S.) that the Court is highly deferential to the Commission's factual determinations is changing with a series of reversal of the Commission's decisions in recent years. For instance, the European Court in a landmark case overturned the Commission's ban on the merger of Airtours and First Choice in 2002 (Airtours/First Choice v. Commission, Case T-342/99). Other overturned cases include Schneider/Legrand and Tetra Lavel/Sidel. These reversals provided another impetus in hastening the reform process that was set in motion with a Green Paper on merger

ances through the merger proceedings can lead to serious incentive problems.[34] Without any external constraint, there is a danger that the Merger Task Force team in charge of a specific merger case may have difficulties in correcting itself out of any initial prejudices that they might have held. Pulling the plug without anything to show would be especially difficult if they have already spent a significant amount of time and resources on the case.

As pointed out by Kuhn (2002), it may be asking too much to adopt the US style court system since such a move would require a radical change in the overall organizational structure of the European Union or the European legal system. As a partial remedy to this problem, the EC now employs so-called "devil's advocate" panels to provide an internal critique of the arguments put forth by case teams. In addition, a fast track procedure has been introduced for certain cases in the appeal process. In fact, this expedited procedure was used in the two recent cases (Schneider/Legrand and Tetra Lavel/Sidel) that were reversed by CFI. Even though these changes are certainly piecemeal measures and do not adequately address the underlying problem, at least they constitute an improvement over the previous regime and hopefully signals the beginning of more changes to come within the framework of current administrative proceedings.[35]

Another problem identified was resource constraints at the EC. In particular, there was a serious lack of qualified economic staff. This is largely due to the legacy of Merger Task Force (MTF) that mostly recruited personnel with training in law. Despite the Commission's recent efforts to hire economists and strengthen the MTF's capacity in economic expertise, the resource availability of qualified economists falls short of the level needed to carry out increasingly complex merger cases considering the increase in the caseload over the years. This is in sharp contrast to the US antitrust agencies such as Department of Justice or Federal Trade Commission, with each agency having about 50–60 professional economists, headed by Chief Economists who are usually respected academics brought from outside universities. The lack of personnel is said to lead them to rely on information by rivals. This practice has the potential to give the impression that the interested parties exert too much influence on the outcome of the merger review.[36]

In response, a new post of Chief Economist has been created, which was filled by a respected academic economist, Lars-Hendrik Roller, with a three-year term.

---

reform in December 2001. However, some people argue that there is a long history, going back to the first decision of the European Court of Justice under the European Coal and Steel Community, of the ECJ reversing Commission decisions. I thank an anonymous referee for this counterpoint.

[34] Kuhn (2002) considers this as the most serious problem and a priority for reform.

[35] Kuhn (2002), for instance, suggests splitting the Merger Task Force into an investigative and a decision making branch or leave decision making power to another entity in DG Competition.

[36] Mr. Monti, however, dismisses the notion that the commission's approach drives it to block deals unfairly on behalf of rivals. According to Monti's address delivered at the American Bar Association in March 2001, "We are sufficiently non-naïve as to be able to discount the elements provided by competitors for their vested interests. Competitors are a rather powerful source of overall assessment of mergers and potentially for the identification of remedies."

He was empowered to hire a team of Ph.D. level economists who support him in high profile cases that require sophisticated economic analysis. This is indeed a long overdue, but very welcome, development that would certainly upgrade the capability for advanced economic analysis.

On a more global scale, a notable and welcome new development is the formation of the International Competition Network (ICN). It was founded in by the U.S. Department of Justice, Federal Trade Commission and 13 other jurisdictions and has since grown to approximately 90 members from 80 jurisdictions. It is a member-driven virtual network that works as a platform to achieve global antitrust convergence with the understanding that "[c]onsistency in enforcement policy and elimination of unnecessary or duplicative procedural burdens stands to benefit consumers and businesses around the globe."[37] In the area of merger enforcement, they promote the adoption of best practices in the design and operation of merger review regimes in order to: (i) enhance the effectiveness of each jurisdiction's merger review mechanisms; (ii) facilitate procedural and substantive convergence; and (iii) reduce the public and private time and cost of multijurisdictional merger reviews. In particular, ICN members have adopted 8 Guiding Principles for Merger Notification and Review Procedures around which a merger regime should be built, and 13 Recommended Practices for Merger Notification and Review Procedures that have been identified as the most important to facilitating convergence toward best practices in merger review. Even though these Principles and Recommended Practices are non-binding, many governments and agencies have already made changes to their laws, practices, and procedures to conform with the ICN practices or are in the process of developing or amending them.[38]

9.6. Concluding remarks

The increasingly global nature of business transactions has resulted in a growing number of mergers falling under the purvey of multiple jurisdictions with multiple corresponding competition authorities. This inevitably invites potential conflicts among competition authorities. This chapter considered one such incidence as a case study, namely, the proposed GE/Honeywell merger which was cleared by the Department of Justice in the U.S. but blocked by the EC. The case revealed potential problems that can arise when multiple antitrust agencies independently pursue their own goals, and it calls for international coordination in the merger enforcement.

At the same time, the case needs to be put in a broader perspective. It should be recognized that the divergent conclusions reached in the GE/Honeywell case is the exception rather than the rule. The competition authorities in the US and the European Union maintain close antitrust cooperation and agree far more

---

[37] http://www.internationalcompetitionnetwork.org/.

[38] See Delrahim (2004).

often than they disagree. We only hear about divergent cases, which tend to underestimate the extent to which the competition authorities promote convergence on substantive issues between them. The GE/Honeywell case will serve as a catalyst for more cooperation and hopefully contribute to speeding up the process of convergence among antitrust authorities in different jurisdictions.

Acknowledgements

I am grateful to an anonymous referee for helpful and constructive comments. The author served as a consultant for one of the interested parties opposed to the transaction. However, the opinions expressed in this chapter are solely those of the author and should not be attributed to any other parties. The chapter is based only on publicly available information.

References

Boeder, T.L. (2000), The Boeing–McDonnell Douglas merger. In: Evenett, S.J., Lehmann, A., Steil, B. (Eds.), *Antitrust Goes Global: What Future for Transatlantic Cooperation?* Royal Institute of International Affairs, London.

Cabral, L.M.B. (2003), International merger policy coordination. *Japan and the World Economy*, pp. 21–30.

Choi, J.P. (2003), Mergers with bundling in complementary markets. Unpublished Manuscript.

Church, J. (2004), The impact of vertical and conglomerate mergers on competition. Report for DG Competition, European Commission, September.

Cournot, A. (1927), *Researches into the Mathematical Principles of the Theory of Wealth*. Macmillan, New York. Originally published in French (1838), translated by Nathaniel Bacon.

Delrahim, M. (2004), Antitrust enforcement priorities and efforts towards international cooperation at the U.S. Department of Justice. Available at http://www.usdoj.gov/atr/public/speeches/208479.htm.

Duso, T., Neven, D.J., Roller, L.-H. (2003), The political economy of European merger control: Evidence using stock market data. Unpublished Manuscript.

Economides, N., Salop, S.C. (1992), Competition and integration among complements, and network market structure. *Journal of Industrial Economics* XL, 105–123.

Elliott, M. (2001), The anatomy of the GE–Honeywell disaster. *Time*, July 08.

Emch, E. (2004), GECAS and the GE/Honeywell merger: A response to Reynolds and Ordover. *Antitrust Law Journal* 72 (1), 233–266.

Evans, D.S. (2002), The new trustbusters: Brussels and Washington may part ways. *NERA Economic Journal*, 71–80. Spring.

Francois, J., Horn, H. (2006), Antitrust in open economies. In: Ghosal, V., Stennek, J. (Eds.), *The Political Economy of Antitrust*. Elsevier, Amsterdam. This volume, Chapter 18.

Giotakos, D., Petit, L., Garnier, G., De Luyck, P. (2001), General Electric/Honeywell—An insight into the Commission's investigation and decision. *EC Competition Policy Newsletter*, 5–13.

Harris, R. (2001), Playing take-away: With its 11th-hour acquisition of Honeywell, General Electric is engaging in M&A's most dangerous game. *CFO Magazine*, February 1.

Heyer, K. (2005), A world of uncertainty: Economics and the globalization of antitrust. *Antitrust Law Journal*, 375–422.

Kolasky, W.J. (2001), Conglomerate mergers and range effects: It's a long way from Chicago to Brussels. Address before the George Mason University Symposium, Washington, DC, November 9, 2001. Available at http://www.usdoj.gov/atr/public/speeches/9536.htm.

Kuhn, K.-U. (2002), Reforming European merger review: Targeting problem areas in policy outcomes. *Journal of Industry, Competition, and Trade* 2 (4), 311–364.

Leary, T.B. (2001), A comment on merger enforcement in the united states and in the European Union. Address before the Transatlantic business Dialogue Principals Meeting, Washington, DC, October 11. Available at http://www.ftc.gov/speeches/leary/tabd010111.htm.

Lyons, B.R. (2004), Reform of European merger policy. *Review of International Economics*, 246–261.

Martin, S. (1999), Strategic and welfare implications of bundling. *Economics Letters*, 371–376.

Matutes, C., Regibeau, P. (1988), Mix and match: Product compatibility without network externalities. *RAND Journal of Economics*, 221–234.

Nalebuff, B. (2002), Bundling and the GE–Honeywell merger. Yale SOM Working Paper No. ES-22.

Reynolds, R.J., Ordover, J.A. (2002), Archimedean leveraging and the GE/Honeywell transaction. *Antitrust Law Journal* 70 (1), 171–198.

CHAPTER 10

The Political Economy of EU Merger Control: Small vs. Large Member States

Henrik Horn and Johan Stennek

Research Institute of Industrial Economics, Stockholm, and CEPR, London

10.1. Introduction

The European Commission has recently intervened against a number of mergers and acquisitions in small Member States arguing that the mergers would reduce competition in nationally defined markets within the Union. For instance, in March 2000, the Commission prohibited Volvo's acquisition of Scania, arguing that Volvo/Scania would have an adverse effect in e.g. Sweden and Finland.[1]

These interventions triggered a political debate about EU merger control and market definitions in several Member States. Representatives of smaller countries have declared that, in effect, EU merger policy makes it impossible for companies in small countries to merge and obtain a leading global position. Following the Volvo/Scania decision, there was almost complete consensus among the political parties in Sweden on this view, with only the Liberal party expressing support for the Commission's decision.

These claims have been rebutted by EU officials, who argue that companies in smaller countries can expand by merging with companies operating in other countries. According to this line of reasoning, the Volvo/Renault operation and the strategic partnership concluded by Scania/Volkswagen, following the prohibition of the Volvo/Scania merger, clearly showed that there were alternative ways for these companies to merge.[2]

There are several possible interpretations of this critique against EU merger control. It could be seen as a "national champion"-type argument, based on the notion that competition authorities should allow mergers that hurt domestic consumers if domestic firms thus gain a sufficient competitive advantage over foreign firms in foreign markets. The argument against this from EU officials would be that the purpose of merger control is only to protect European consumers.

---

[1] *COMP/M.1672 Volvo/Scania.*

[2] It is also maintained that several other alternatives are open to firms from small member states in addition to international mergers, for example internal growth and the possibility of adequate remedies (e.g. selling off parts of the assets to reduce concerns for competition). Although these possibilities are important strategies for the firms, these issues are not addressed in the present analysis.

CONTRIBUTIONS TO ECONOMIC ANALYSIS
VOLUME 282 ISSN: 0573-8555
DOI: 10.1016/S0573-8555(06)82010-9

And, while there may be efficiency gains related to firm size and therefore to mergers, those gains can be achieved with less impediments to competition, for example through international mergers. Moreover, experience shows that companies that are successful abroad are, in most cases, those facing a competitive environment back home.

But the critique has also taken other forms. It has been acknowledged that international mergers may indeed constitute alternatives to domestic mergers. The problem is instead that international mergers may be less advantageous from the point of view of smaller countries. These worries seem to be at least partly based on the possible effect of international mergers on employment and the location of R&D units and head quarters. In response to these worries, EU officials only concede that EU merger control does not take into account a possible move of firms abroad.

It is evident from this discussion that the issues involved are highly complex. Therefore, it is natural to seek guidance in the economic literature on the merits of the arguments put forth in the policy debate. To the best of our knowledge, there does not exist any research that can be directly applied to this end. Nevertheless, the economic literature has provided us with a number of useful analytical tools, and the purpose of this chapter is to employ these, to discuss the validity of some of the main claims in this debate on EU merger control rules.

The structure of the chapter is as follows. In next two sections, we demonstrate why and how EU merger control treats companies from small and large states differently and discuss whether the whole idea of merger control is well founded: Do we really need to control mergers? The rest of the chapter discusses various proposals suggested to reduce this asymmetry. These ideas include fighting market segmentation (Proposal 1), or that the Commission should change its principles for geographical market delineations (Proposal 2). Still others argue that the root of the problem is the "skewed" goals of competition policy, i.e. that only consumer welfare is considered (Proposal 3). Such issues as the appropriate goal for competition policy, whether efficiency defenses should be allowed, etc., have of course been intensively discussed before. The distinguishing feature of the discussion here is that we reexamine these questions from the point of view of the debate about the alleged asymmetry in EU merger control.

Most of the space, however, will be devoted to two related claims, which we feel to be more central to the policy discussion (referred to as Proposals 4 and 5). One is a refutation of the argument that firms in smaller countries are at a disadvantage, even if treated asymmetrically, since they can instead choose to merge internationally. Implicitly, this thus suggests that the Commission should take into account the possibility for alternative mergers. The second claim, which is a counter-argument to the first, is that international mergers may be worse than for Member States domestic mergers, due to adverse implications for the location of production following international mergers, and that the Commission should take these effects into account in its assessment. The chapter ends with a section summarizing the main findings.

10.2. The asymmetric treatment of small and large countries

This section will explain the sense in which EU merger control can be said to treat mergers in small and large member states asymmetrically. To this end, it starts by very briefly laying out core features of EU merger control.

10.2.1. Salient features of EU merger control

EU merger policy is enshrined in the so-called Merger Regulation.[3] The main purpose of EU merger control is usually seen as the protection of competition. The latter goal is, in turn, often motivated by consumer protection (Monti, 2001).[4] The Merger Regulation prohibits a merger if, and only if, it "... would significantly impede effective competition, in the common market or in a substantial part of it, in particular as a result of the creation or strengthening of a dominant position ...".

In the original Merger Regulation, adopted in 1990, the substantive test put an even larger emphasis on the concept of *dominance*, which is defined in the case law under Article 82 as "... a position of economic strength enjoyed by an undertaking ... affording it the power to behave to an appreciable extent independently of its competitors, customers and ultimately of its consumers".[5] Market shares play important roles in the assessment of dominance. But many other factors believed to indicate dominance are also considered, such as legal protection, superior technology, strong financial status, economies of scale and scope, extensive vertical integration, and a degree of product differentiation.

Firms' market shares obviously depend on the definition of the extent of the market, and the delineation of the "relevant market" is consequently a key aspect of merger control. The definition of the relevant market consists of two parts, namely the relevant product market and the relevant geographical market.[6] Interestingly, adjudicating bodies have applied rather different approaches to determinate these two aspects of market delineation.

The key criterion for judging whether two goods are competing on the same product market is if they are *interchangeable*. The primary aspect is if customers consider the goods to be substitutable. Demand side substitutability may be measured by the cross-price elasticity of demand, or assessed using the physical

---

[3] Council Regulation No 139/2004 of 20 January 2004 on the control of concentrations between undertakings, which entered into force on May 1, 2004.

[4] Sometimes other goals are also mentioned. For instance, the Commission (1980) refers to economic integration of Member States, as well as "fairness", as such objectives. It is unclear to us whether and to what extent these goals actually influence merger policy. More elaborate discussions of the goals of EU merger control may be found in Martin (1994) and Fridolfsson (2002).

[5] *United Brands v Commission*, Case 27/76 [1978] ECR 207, [1978] 1 CMLR 429.

[6] See the Commission's Notice on the definition of the relevant market for the purpose of community competition law, OJC 372 (1997).

characteristics of the products, or their prices or intended use. Supply side substitution plays a less important role. A certain firm is considered to be part of the relevant market, even if it is not active on that market at present, but can quickly start to supply the market if prices are slightly increased. If this were to take longer, the firm would not be considered to be in the market. Still, it may influence the dominance assessments by being considered as a potential entrant.

The relevant geographical market is defined as a geographical area where the product is marketed and "...where the conditions are sufficiently homogenous for the effect of the economic power of the undertaking concerned to be able to be evaluated".[7] Our interpretation of this definition is that customers in different locations are considered to be in the same geographical market if the merger affects them in a very similar way. To define the geographical market, the Commission may, among other things, consider whether products are expensive to transport in relation to their value or two areas are separated due to market-sharing agreements.[8]

When the Merger Regulation was reformed in 2004 the substantive test was changed from 'the creation or strengthening of a dominant position' to a 'significant impediment to effective competition'. The new test is intended to emphasize that unilateral effects (to use U.S. terminology) are included: a merger may be prohibited also where the fear is that the merged entity could raise prices even though it will not become the largest player (single dominance) and without the need of for tacit coordination with other players (joint dominance).

Finally, for a merger to be blocked, it does not suffice that anticompetitive effects are found in a particular geographical market. It must also be the case that this market constitutes a *substantial part of the common market*. Thus, it is important to note that determining the relevant market is different from determining the limits of what constitutes a substantial part of the common market. The former is basically an analytical aid in the positive assessment of the consequences of the merger. The normative criterion largely lies in determining how geographically widespread the negative effects must be to be deemed undesirable. Further, this requirement prevents mergers of minor importance from being caught. It seems clear that large Member State may be considered as substantial parts of the common market. In some cases, it has even been established that parts of Member States can be substantial parts. However, the lower bound on the size of a substantial part is as yet unclear.

10.2.2. The asymmetry identified

It is clear that if the whole common market were found to be the relevant market, it would be immaterial to the assessment of a notified merger whether it took

---

[7] *United Brands v Commission*, Case 27/76 [1978] ECR 207, [1978] 1 CMLR 429 at paras 10 and 11.

[8] Additional types of evidence that may be used are exemplified in the Commission's notice.

place in a small or large Member State. However, as will be more fully argued below, it is likely that the boundaries of relevant markets sometimes coincide with national borders. In that situation, an asymmetry arises between larger and smaller Member States in the sense that the relevant markets are smaller in the smaller states.

This conclusion hinges on two facts. For most products, the servicing of a market is associated with fixed costs. There is therefore a tendency for smaller markets to support fewer firms, and the competitive pressure is consequently likely to be weaker in such markets. There is also a strong tendency for firms to primarily serve the markets in which they are located—there is typically a "home market bias". A merger between firms of a given magnitude in terms of turnover is thus more likely to lead to a dominance finding in a smaller than in a larger Member State (still assuming that relevant market delineation and national boundaries coincide). An inescapable consequence of this is that *large companies active in small countries are treated differently from equally large companies in large countries, in the sense that their possibilities to merge domestically* (*that is, with other firms in the same market*) *are more limited, due to the merger policy being pursued.*

It is not clear to us to what extent this asymmetry actually constitutes a problem, even for small Member States. Nevertheless, some observers perceive it as a problem and have made a number of proposals in the policy debate for how this asymmetry can be removed. The rest of the chapter will seek to shed some light on situations where the asymmetry may cause problems, and discuss the pros and cons of the different proposals for reform that have a bearing on the asymmetry.

10.3. Proposal 1: Reduce market segmentation

The notion of geographical "market segmentation" is central for the discussion of EU merger control and smaller country interests. Roughly speaking, it refers to barriers to the transportation of goods and services. The essential consequence of such barriers is that they provide shelter from outside competition for firms inside the barriers.

Segmentation is what makes it necessary for the Commission to delineate relevant geographical markets smaller than the Common market. It is also due to segmentation that the anti-competitive effects of mergers of a given size are worse in small that in large countries. Therefore, it seems reasonable to believe that reducing market segmentation is the best way of reducing the asymmetric treatment of companies from small and large Member States, in addition to other more direct benefits such policies may have.

10.3.1. Sources of segmentation

There are a couple of distinctions that need to be made. First, one should distinguish between segmentation on the consumer and the producer side of the market. Consumers typically face much higher costs of importing products from other markets than do firms, so that markets are often more strictly segmented on the consumer than on the producer side. Hence, from a competition point of view, the hope often rests with the ability of firms and middlemen to reduce price divergences between different markets.

Another distinction is between *variable trade costs* barriers and *sunk cost* barriers as sources of partial or complete segmentation on the side of the firms. The most obvious example of the former is the cost of physically moving a good from one location to another. For instance, if the value to weight ratio is very low, it is not economically viable to transport the product very far, and there is a tendency that local producers do not face any external competition. If, in addition, there are pronounced economies of scale, there is a strong tendency for local monopolies to arise.

But there are also other costs affecting the transportation of products in a common market. These often arise when passing national borders, and stem from differences across countries in terms of legislation, culture, language, etc. Much of the EC 1992 Internal Market program was directed at the removal of government-induced barriers of this type, such as differences in product standards, customs red tape, etc. These barriers are sometimes in the firm of sunk costs, but a significant component often depends directly on the traded volume, making them "variable trade costs."

Sunk cost barriers are of a different nature. They may arise in situations where certain firms have already incurred costs from investments in e.g. distribution networks, while others have not. These investments are "sunk" in the sense that they cannot be recovered should the incumbent firms decide to leave the market. In situations where incumbents firms have already made sunk cost investments, it may not be profitable for outside firms to enter, if entry requires a significant investment in building up distribution and maintenance networks, and they would face intense competition from incumbent firms after the entry. The asymmetry between the firms thus shelters the incumbent firms from competition from outside.

It is clear that market segmentation is still important in the EU, despite the attempts to reduce it. This is evidenced by the significant price differences that still exist across countries for a large number of products. In particular, it seems as if the Nordic Member States are segmented from the other Member Countries. Such geographical segmentation may have important implications for the effects of mergers, as can be illustrated by a few simple examples.

10.3.2. Implications of segmentation for merger control

A central aspect of a common market is that normally, it does not comprise one homogenous market, but rather a set of markets partly segmented from each other. The assessment of pro- and anti-competitive effects of mergers becomes much more complicated when done at the level of the common market, than for a national, homogeneous market.

The consequences of a merger in a common market partly depend on the extent to which the markets involved are segmented, and partly on whether a merger is domestic or international. Large trade barriers between different countries imply that the anti-competitive effects of a domestic merger are worse than when these barriers are low, since foreign firms are less able to discipline the merged entity when barriers are high. The anti-competitive effect of an international merger, on the other hand, may even be smaller when barriers are high as compared to when they are low, the reason being that in the former case, the firms were not engaged in very intense competition before the merger in any event. This argument is especially important for small countries, where the markets sustain fewer active firms. In particular, in small markets international mergers may be preferred to domestic mergers from a competition point of view.

10.3.3. Can segmentation be reduced?

Some barriers such as national product safety standards are the result of public policies, and may be changed, while some are the result of the firms' own activities, such as exclusive dealing arrangements, and can be battled using other areas of competition policy. Yet other barriers are the result of factors outside the reach of political influence, for example the costs of transporting goods, or barriers created by linguistic or cultural differences. Furthermore, some barriers are unavoidable negative side-consequences of policies with positive net effects and should not be changed for that reason.

10.3.4. Conclusions

Market segmentation is the root of the problem of asymmetric treatment of companies from small and large Member States. The most obvious strategy for curbing the problem would therefore be to hit against the barriers to competition between different countries within Europe, as well as between Europe and the rest of the world. But while there may still be scope for reforms to reduce intra-EU market segmentation, segmentation is likely to remain in the foreseeable future. Reduced market segmentation is thus not likely to be a manageable way of eliminating all asymmetric treatment in EU merger control in large and small countries.

10.4. Proposal 2: Change geographical market delineations

It has also been argued that the method of geographical market delineation is the cause of the asymmetry between small and large Member States. Thus, it has been suggested that the Commission should define the geographical market to be union-wide rather than national. We are not convinced by this idea, however. As already argued, geographical market delineations should only be viewed as an administrative technique used to assess the pattern of market segmentation. The Commission defines markets as narrowly as is appropriate to estimate the effect on price in all possible locations. This procedure is necessary to correctly assess the effects of a merger on competition and consumer welfare.

It is important to point out that it does not necessarily follow that a merger should be prohibited if competition is impeded in one or more of these geographical markets. The regulation requires that competition is impeded in a substantial part of the common market and, depending on the degree of segmentation of the markets, the latter may be a more encompassing concept than the individual relevant geographical markets. In principle, one could thus imagine that a merger is allowed even if it hurts consumers in a certain relevant market, if other consumers gain. Hence, if anything, it must be the conclusions for merger policy drawn from the information obtained through the relevant market definitions that should be changed, rather than the method of obtaining the information itself.

10.5. Proposal 3: Change the objective of EU merger control

Many economists would argue that mergers should be permitted even if directly harming consumers, if they result in cost savings that more than compensate the direct loss to consumers, from an aggregate point of view. Such a change in the *goals* of merger control, away from consumer protection to the protection of some notion of national welfare, would also tend to reduce the asymmetric treatment of domestic mergers in countries of different size.

Fridolfsson (Chapter 11 in this volume) discusses these issues much more fully, and we will therefore just very briefly mention some of the basic arguments in favor of changing the goals of merger control.

10.5.1. The consumer surplus standard—a means of affecting distribution?

The most obvious reason why competition policy would focus more on consumer welfare than on firms' profits is that the policy maker cares for the distribution of wealth between different individuals in the economy, combined with the idea that firm owners are typically wealthier than consumers. The facts are more complicated, however.

Many "ordinary" consumers are also shareholders, at least indirectly through pension funds. Likewise, owners of firms are also consumers (if they are large in terms of shares they are probably also large in terms of consumption). It is therefore not obvious that a consumer welfare approach will have substantial positive effects on distribution. If that is the case, one may question the idea of forbidding mergers that would increase national income by generating substantial fixed cost savings (which are typically not passed to consumers).

Yet another reason why including the implications for profits in the assessment of mergers might be reasonable is that a significant proportion of the profits made by firms goes to employees. While these types of estimates should be viewed with considerable skepticism, it can still be noted that a main textbook on Industrial Organization estimates that about 2/3 of oligopoly profits actually end up with employees.

One may also add that there probably exist more efficient policy tools to affect distribution, in particular progressive taxation, public financing of different services and transfers.

We should emphasize, however, that all these arguments are "common sense" arguments and that there exists no research measuring the relative efficiency of competition policy in affecting distribution.

10.5.2. The national champions argument

A somewhat stronger version of the same type of argument builds on variable cost synergies reaped through mergers. According to this "national champion" argument, a merger should be permitted even if it is detrimental to domestic consumer interests through its market power implications, if it reduces the variable costs sufficiently for the increase in profits reaped abroad to be large enough to increase national income. From a national income point of view, there may thus arise a conflict between the increased profits the domestic firms can earn on international markets and the loss for domestic consumers. This type of argument, even though not put as bluntly as done here, has been important in e.g. Sweden in most of the post-World War II period, when many Swedish firms were allowed to dominate the domestic market, while successfully competing in export markets.[9] It is not clear to what extent this underlies the current criticism of the EU merger control, even though it appears to lurk in the background.

In principle, there is nothing wrong with the notion that profits in foreign markets may more than compensate for consumer surplus losses in domestic markets. However, for this reasoning to be an argument in favor of allowing such mergers, it must be verified why the same cost reducing effects cannot be obtained through international mergers, or if they can, why the share of the profits from these mergers accruing to domestic firms does not suffice to make them a better alternative.

10.5.3. The consumer surplus standard—a solution to information problems?

The focus on consumer welfare does not seem to be well motivated by distributional concerns. One may therefore conclude that a total surplus standard would

---

[9] The national champion argument is also raised by large countries, as was for instance the French case *Schneider/Legrand* in 2001.

be more appropriate—that is, to take into account both the effects on consumers and those on the firms' stakeholders. However, recent work on informational problems (Besanko and Spulber, 1993; Fridolfsson, this volume; Lyons, 2002) and lobbying (Neven and Röller, 2005) in merger control suggests that there may be good reasons for competition authorities to use consumer surplus as a "tactical goal", even though the true objective is a more encompassing measure of social welfare. These issues are discussed in more detail in Fridolfsson (this volume).

10.5.4. The substantiality criterion and the "give-and-take" problem

Many EU markets are geographically segmented, and mergers in such markets may affect consumers in different countries differently. There may thus be a need for some trade-offs between different consumers. In Europe, the solution to this problem is rather extreme, however. A merger is prohibited if it hurts consumers in *any* significant part of the Common Market, independent of the effects of the merger in other parts of Europe.

At first sight, it appears that the main beneficiaries of the Volvo/Scania decision, for example, were the customers in Sweden and other small countries where the two companies have large market shares. However, to evaluate this claim, it is necessary to remember that the merger control system as a whole and not only single decisions should be evaluated.

For simplicity, assume that the competition authority must evaluate two mergers and that each merger affects consumers in different markets differently. Merger A reduces consumer welfare in region 1 and increases consumer welfare in region 2. Merger B reduces consumer welfare in region 2 and increases consumer welfare in region 1. Assuming that both regions constitute a substantial part of the Common Market, the Commission would have to prohibit both mergers. It is entirely possible, however, that consumers in both regions would be better off if both mergers were allowed, that is, it may pay for all consumers to "give" in some markets if simultaneously allowed to "take" in others.

10.5.5. Conclusions

Standard arguments suggest that competition policy should not be used as a tool for redistribution, but to enhance efficient allocations. This would suggest a change in the goals of merger control away from a consumer surplus standard toward a total surplus standard. However, an inherent problem facing merger regulation is lack of information, and there are arguments to suggest that one should give the competition authorities more consumer oriented goals, even if the ultimate objective is total surplus. The state of the art of research on this issue is not yet sufficiently well developed to allow for more definite conclusions. For this reason, and due to the fact that EU merger control is unlikely to be changed in any more dramatic fashion, we believe that a solution to the alleged asymmetry problem must be sought elsewhere than through changes in the current objectives of EU merger control. We do believe, however, that consumer interests in different geographical markets should be aggregated.

10.6. Proposals 4–5: Take alternative mergers and location into account

We will now turn to the core of the policy debate, which can be seen as consisting of two separate ideas/proposals. One is based on the notion that the asymmetry in EU merger control is really not to the disadvantage of firms from smaller countries, if the fact that they can instead merge with competitors from larger countries is taken into account, thus achieving the necessary size for competing in the global markets.[10] More generally, this argument suggests that the Commission should *take alternative mergers into account* when assessing a notified merger. The other argument is based on the notion that the interests of smaller countries may be systematically disadvantaged in certain merger structures, since they may lead to a relocation of production from smaller to larger markets. The argument is thus that the Commission should *take locational implications of mergers into account.*

In this section, we will discuss these proposals within a common framework, since the pros and cons of one of them may depend on whether the other is adopted. Further, discussing these proposals jointly we capture the idea that the Commission should take both alternative merger structures, and their different locational consequences into consideration in its assessments. This would be a unique European element of merger policy, possibly motivated by the fact that Europe consists of several segmented markets.

There are many reasons why the location of firms' head-quarters and production may be of concern to countries. For instance, this may have beneficial effects on employment, and may yield spillovers of various forms of know-how. However, these aspects are of little relevance for merger control, as long as its goal is consumer protection. It may thus be considered that the idea to take locational implications of mergers into account in merger assessments is completely unfounded. One of the main purposes of this section is to show how the relevance of locational effects for merger policy can be expected to depend on the *type* of frictions to trade that exists between different markets.

The analysis is meant to capture salient features of mature or even declining markets where there exists a fixed initial distribution of plants and the choice of location is essentially a choice of plant closure. This focus is motivated by the fact that mergers often occur in declining markets, sometimes even as a response

[10] There are actually two possible interpretations of this suggestion. One is that international mergers are favored since they reduce competition and hurt consumers less. Another is that international mergers are favored, since they lead to increased economic integration of the member states.

to reductions in demand. It may also be suspected that the anti-competitive effects of mergers are more problematic in declining than in expanding markets where new investments and new entry are important and locational choice is more related to greenfield investment decisions.

The analysis is complicated by the fact that, to the best of our knowledge, the relationship between mergers and choice of location has not received any attention in the literature. The discussion must therefore be based on preliminary research (see Horn and Stennek, 2002). Note that the intention is *not* to provide a full-fledged analysis of this question—which would require a much more solid basis in research than what currently exists.[11] The idea is rather to point to some issues that would arise in case the Commission were to take possible alternative merger structures, and the resulting locational choices, into account in its decision-making, or conversely, some of the problems that might result if it does not.

In the next section, we will discuss possible outcomes of the interaction between mergers and locational decisions. Policy implications are dealt with in the ensuing subsection.

10.6.1. Location and mergers: An analytical framework

As an analytical aid, we will employ a simple economic model of an oligopolistic industry. To allow for a role for the location of production, we assume that the output of this industry is sold in two markets, "Small" and "Large". These markets differ in size, as measured by the number of buyers in the respective market, and possibly also in the degree of competition, but they are identical in all other respects. The two markets are completely segmented from each other on the buyers' side—buyers' trade costs are thus such that they will never find it profitable to buy abroad. With regard to producers, we will consider two alternative scenarios. In one, there are variable trade costs: when a firm located in one market exports to the other market, it incurs a cost for each unit delivered. These costs include those of transportation, but should be considered as including all variable costs associated with servicing a market from a foreign location, including difficulties due to different languages and tastes. The increase in delivery time may also be a disadvantage in the era of just-in-time production. The alternative scenario is where fixed cost investments in distribution and service networks are required in order to sell in a market and when some, but not all, firms have undertaken this expenditure. There is thus an asymmetry between firms having already incurred this cost, and those that have not. We start with the variable cost scenario, and return to the other scenario later.

[11] One important issue from which we abstract in our analysis is the fact that mergers may trigger new entry, which reduces the anticompetitive effects of mergers, a factor acknowledged in merger control.

It should be stressed that we are not arguing that variable trade costs, or fixed cost of entry, are in practice important in each industry, or even that they are important in some average sense. But it is quite clear that such costs are important determinants of location of production in some industries. Basically, we have drawn on the fields of International Economics/Industrial Organization to construct a simple analytical framework that is rich enough to rationalize the argument that the asymmetry in merger control may have undesirable effects for consumer interests in smaller Member States. But theory also suggests other determinants of location. For instance, as highlighted in the literature on economic geography, location may be determined by the balance between various forms of positive externalities in production (i.e., Silicon Valley-type phenomena) that make location in certain areas attractive (including knowledge spill-over and skilled subcontractors) and, on the other hand, high costs of land, labor, etc., in these locations. The choice of which model to apply should obviously depend on the particulars of the market to be analyzed.

In order to capture possible differences between domestic and international mergers in as simple a fashion as possible, let there be four main firms in this market, two in each region, and each operating one production plant. This will allow us to discuss the implications of both a structure where firms merge with domestic counterparts, and where they undertake international mergers. There is also a group of "outside" firms in Large. These firms compete with the other firms in delivering to Large, but as outsiders they face sufficiently large trade costs to make it unprofitable for them to serve Small. The reason for including these firms is to allow for the possibility that competition is fiercer in Large. In order to substantially simplify the analysis of the incentives for mergers, outside firms are not allowed to merge.

The firms first decide whether to merge into two international firms—in this case each firm has a plant in each region—or into two domestic firms, where each firm owns two plants in the same region. The incentive to merge is partly to enhance market power, but it is also to achieve marginal cost synergies (*that is, to lower marginal production costs*), *or reduce duplication in fixed plant costs through the closing of one of the plants in the merged entity.*

10.6.2. Choice of location

The advantage of closing a plant is that it saves on fixed costs. Following *domestic* mergers, there is no disadvantage for a firm of reducing the number of plants in the same region since it has enough production capacity, and domestic merger will hence definitely induce firms to shut down one plant each.

After an *international* merger, the decision is more complex, however. When closing the plant in one region, this region must be served from the other market, which has the disadvantage of forcing the firm to bear trade costs that would be avoided if producing locally. Whether a firm finds it profitable to close the plant in Large or in Small, or in neither region, thus depends on the balance

Table 10.1: Locational implications of domestic and international mergers.

	Weak "outside" competition in Large	**Intense "outside" competition in Large**
Domestic mergers	Each firm has one plant only, located in its home country	
International mergers	Each firm has one plant only, located in Large	Each firm has one plant only, located in Small

between fixed cost savings and increases in trade costs, as well as on market power considerations—being alone in a market sheltered by large trade costs has a significant value to a firm.

The locational decision after international mergers is substantially complicated by the fact that the balance between cost savings, market power effects, etc., depends on the competitor's actions. However, it can be shown that *under certain circumstances, including a sufficiently weak competitive pressure from the outside firms in Large, both international firms will shut down the plant in the small market, regardless of the locational choice of the other firm.*[12] On the other hand, *when the outside firms are sufficiently competitive, both firms will locate in the small region*. This pattern is summarized in Table 10.1.

10.6.2.1. Domestic or international mergers?

The process of merger formation is likely to differ from that of choosing location in the sense that when choosing location, firms can be expected to act rather independently. Indeed, overt coordination among firms on decisions about location is likely to violate the prohibition of agreements between firms that restrict competition.[13] The merger process, on the other hand, is characterized by (legal) communication between firms, in the form of negotiations, and the possibility of transferring wealth between the parties. In such a negotiation, the participating firms must take into account how their future production structure would be affected by a merger, and how other firms would act with regard to mergers and location. But they must also consider in what *other* mergers they might instead engage, as well as the outside opportunities of their counterparts. Thus, it is a rather complicated strategic interaction that leads to a pattern of mergers in a concentrated industry, such as the one we are portraying here.

---

[12] For both firms to locate in the large region, independent of the other firm's choice, it is necessary that the size difference between the regions is large and that the variable trade cost is relatively small so that the location in the small market does not provide too much shelter from competition.

[13] Naturally, this does not imply that such collusion does not occur. Still, one may suspect it to be relatively inefficient (from the firms' point of view) since the firms must enforce the agreements themselves without the help of the legal system and since there is always a risk of being caught and fined. As this is the first attempt to analyze the issue of location and merger, we abstract from these issues for the sake of simplicity.

The obvious question is then: which firms are likely to merge in the example we have in mind? A fair amount of research has gone into this question over the years, employing a large variety of different analytical tools.[14]

Due to the complexity of the strategic interaction in such situations, the literature has not come up with any clear-cut predictions. However, some recent research on merger formation suggests that if mergers to duopoly are permitted, the merger pattern will be such as to maximize *industry* profits. Intuitively, whenever a market structure is about to be realized mergers that would not maximize industry profits, firms have incentives to rearrange the merger pattern, and will be able to do so, since they are free to communicate with whomever they wish in the industry (see Horn and Persson, 2001a, 2001b). This might be viewed as an instance of the much more general Coase theorem.[15]

There are caveats to the idea of global maximization. A careful analysis of the bilateral and interdependent negotiations, which are probably the norm in a merger context, shows that the result may be suboptimal, as a result of conflicts over the distribution of the surplus from mergers (see Section 10.6.2.3). Since these complications do not concern the core of the political debate on EU merger control and the interests of small Member States, we will simply abstract from them here, and *assume* that as long as both a pattern of domestic and a pattern of international mergers are allowed, absent any policy intervention, the resulting duopoly structure will maximize the industry profits.[16]

Then, what is the implication of this assumption for the predicted merger structure? Generally speaking, the firms' choices between domestic and international mergers depend on the balance between the magnitude of trade costs, market characteristics such as the intensity of competition in Large, and the relative magnitude of the two regions.[17] When trade costs are very substantial, it becomes very difficult to compete effectively from a foreign location. Under such circumstances, there is a tendency toward domestic mergers, since the merged firm in Small will essentially be a local monopoly. Each of the merged

[14] The so-called theory of endogenous merger aims at predicting which merger will occur when there are many alternatives, using different economic models of bargaining and/or stock market interaction, but it is still in its infancy. The first traces of this kind of reasoning can be found in Stigler (1950) who noted that horizontal mergers may be hard to arrange, since it may pay more for a firm to stand outside the merger than to participate. This free-rider problem was later formalized by Kamien and Zang (1990, 1991, 1993). For an empirical test of the free-rider problem, see Lindqvist and Stennek (2005).

[15] According to the Coase theorem, independent of the initial allocation of certain assets within a group of agents, and despite the externalities inflicted by one agent's use of the assets on other agents in the group, the final allocation of the assets between agents is efficient (from the point of view of the group), if there are no transaction costs in transferring ownership between members of the group.

[16] In our example, we assume that a merger to monopoly would not be allowed by the "Commission".

[17] We will focus on those determinants of merger patterns that are of special relevance for the debate on whether EU Merger Control disfavors small Member States. This should not be taken as a denial of the existence of other determinants, such as differences in fiscal policies between countries.

Table 10.2: Merger and location patterns.

	Weak outside competition in Large	**Intense outside competition in Large**
Variable trade costs Large	Domestic mergers; production in both regions	
Variable trade costs Small	International mergers; production in Large only	International mergers; production in Small only

firms will then close one of its local plants to save on fixed costs, as explained above. In this case, when trade costs are high, the merger pattern is essentially driven by *market power* aspirations.

On the other hand, when the variable trade costs are relatively small, there will be international mergers. Firms then know that the future pattern of location will be determined by the degree of competition in Large. When there is little competition from outside firms, locating production to Large will be attractive for both firms, since this will limit the trade cost expenditures. But, when competition is quite intense, it is very hard to make any profit at all in this market, and it is then better to locate in Small, since this minimizes trade costs. Hence, in these cases, *reduced trade cost expenditures* is the main factor driving mergers.[18]

The above outcomes are summarized in Table 10.2.

10.6.2.2. Distribution networks

The Volvo/Scania case suggests that in some markets, the segmentation of different regional markets may rather be connected to differences in sales and maintenance networks, and differing technical standards, than to variable trade costs. To capture this, let us assume that the variable trade costs are small, but that investments of a certain magnitude are necessary in order to serve a region. The two local firms in Small have already made such investments both in Small and in Large, but the two main firms in Large have only invested in such infrastructure in their domestic market. Hence, in order to serve the Small region, it is necessary to have access to one of the two firms in this region, whereas all firms can serve the Large region.

Following *domestic* mergers, each firm closes one plant if the fixed cost saving is large enough. The merged entity in Large only serves its home market, if (as is assumed here) the investment cost required to serve Small is too large relative to the limited size of this market. The firm in the small region will thus have a local monopoly in this market, but it will also sell in Large, where there may be more intense competition. Following *international* mergers, on the other

[18] Note the dual role of trade costs. On the one hand, trade costs provide shelter from competition. On the other hand, they must be incurred by the firms. When trade costs are high, the former effect is more important for the firms' merger decisions, while the latter effect dominates in markets with low variable trade costs.

hand, both firms have access to distribution networks for both markets. Absent variable trade costs, the firms are indifferent between the two locations, independent of the other firm's choice. But, presuming that there are some smaller variable trade costs and that competition in Large is not too intense, both firms will locate in Large. In the merger negotiations, the firms foresee the different choices of locations resulting from domestic and international mergers. The only difference between the two cases is that there will be competition in the small country following international mergers. As a result, the firms will always choose domestic over international mergers.

Thus, in the case where segmentation is partly supported by distribution networks, and where firms from the smaller region have invested in networks for this region, the simple framework we have employed here suggests that market power driven mergers will be proposed in the smaller region.

10.6.2.3. Appendix: Why the merger process may be biased against international mergers

The analysis in this chapter builds on the presumption that the firms (through some unexplained process) will be induced to merge domestically or internationally depending on which pattern leads to the highest industry profit. There are reasons, however, why nationality differences may obstruct international mergers and instead force firms into less efficient domestic alliances. These "frictions" in the merger process may arise as a result of differences in opinions over how the surpluses from mergers should be shared between the merging parties. Such disputes may hinder international mergers more than they hinder domestic mergers, at least when the primary source of difference between firms is nationality. As a result, the firms may merge with domestic partners, even when international mergers would lead to a higher aggregate profit in the industry.[19]

To illustrate this claim, consider a situation in which a domestic merger in the large country only has a small impact on the merging firms' profits, for example as a result of a high remaining competitive pressure in that country. In contrast, a domestic merger in the small country may reduce competition more and lead to a substantial increase in profits. In such an asymmetric situation it may well be that the profit of a merged international firm is lower than the profit of a domestically merged firm in the small country, even though international mergers increase

[19] In case firms are different between countries and similar within countries, there are also other reasons why domestic mergers may be more prevalent than international mergers. Differences in culture may, for instance, mean that international mergers are less profitable. However, any such considerations which affect profits are captured by the previous analysis, and need not be further elaborated here. Nationality differences may also add to the perceived uncertainty about the outcome of international mergers. Such risk differences should also have been captured in the previous analysis. Yet another reason why international mergers may be more difficult is that nationality differences may be associated with asymmetric information between parties. Standard bargaining theory may then be taken to suggest that such mergers will be less easily agreed upon.

the aggregate profit more than domestic mergers. Will the firms then agree to international mergers and, if so, how will the surpluses be split?

Standard bargaining theory suggests that the two parties to e.g. an international merger will both receive whatever they would have earned in status quo (the so-called inside option), and that they will split the surplus—which is the increase in the sum of their profits relative to the status quo—equally between themselves. The so-called outside option, which in this case is to merge domestically instead, will not affect the bargaining strength of the parties. The irrelevance of the outside option is unfavorable to the firms from the small country, and favorable to the firms from the large country. As a result, the stock market values of the firms from the small country may be lower if the stock market expected international mergers, than if the stock market were to expect domestic mergers. The opposite is true for the firms from the large country.[20]

However, further analysis suggests that the story doesn't end here. The firms can choose if they want to bid for a domestic or an international partner. Then, if the stock market values of the firms from the small country are low, they may start to bid for each other, rather than for international partners. This bidding means that the "outside option" becomes a realistic alternative to the international merger. The firms from the large country will thus have to consider the possibility that they will be left to merge with each other. They will therefore be prepared to offer more to the firms from the small country. There will, in short, be bidding competition for the firms from the small country. It can be shown that the stock market values of the firms will adjust to balance the firms' bidding strategies in such a way that there is a positive probability for both domestic and international mergers to occur. That is to say, the firms' stock market values will adjust to make firms indifferent between the different merger options, and the final outcome will be determined by circumstances of second-order importance from an efficiency point of view.

This "bias" of the merger formation process towards domestic mergers raises the theoretical possibility that the desired policy should be designed to assist the firms to avoid such strategic behavior. Such a conclusion is premature, however, since the gains from such intervention will accrue differently between the two countries. Moreover, these considerations have rather little to do with consumer protection which, at least today, is the major goal of merger control. In Europe, of course, competition policy is also to some extent viewed as an instrument to promote further European integration. Then, the obstacles raised by nationality differences may be seen as an argument for biasing the control system against domestic mergers.

Since these considerations, though related, do not concern the core of the political debate on EU merger control and the interests of small Member States, we will simply abstract from them here.

---

20 This transformation of the issue of surplus-sharing into an issue about firms' stock market values is built on the endogenous merger model by Fridolfsson and Stennek (2005a, 2005b).

10.6.3. Implications for merger control

So far, we have highlighted some determinants behind mergers and location patterns. Against this background, we will now discuss some aspects of EU merger control.

The basic idea behind EU merger control is to protect consumer interests. In practice, the legal criteria described above fall short of a full cost–benefit analysis. Thus, even if the legal test set up in the Merger Regulation may be a useful tool, perhaps even producing accurate information in some average sense, it is still probably an imperfect predictor of the effect of a merger on consumer welfare in individual cases. As a starter, however, we give the Commission the benefit of the doubt and simply assume that the legal criteria correctly assess the effect of mergers on consumer welfare.

We assume that the two regions are both sufficiently segmented to be considered as separate geographical markets and sufficiently large to be considered as substantial parts of the common market.

10.6.3.1. Should location be of importance?

In the above framework, there is a special case of interest for the policy debate, which arises when competition in the large market is not too intense, and the trade cost is of an intermediate magnitude. We may then have a situation where firms will seek to undertake domestic mergers entailing local production but where, at the same time, they will both choose to locate in Large if domestic mergers are prevented. This case roughly reflects the notion put forth in the debate that the Commission's blocking of domestic mergers in small countries will induce international mergers that will eventually lead firms to concentrate their production to large regions only, to the detriment of small Members states.

In our view, this possibility is less obvious than it might first appear. After all, if firms seek to merge domestically, which is when the asymmetry is mainly of importance, they seem to prefer to be located in their respective home countries, yielding a geographically dispersed pattern of production. One may then reasonably believe that the firms would also choose to locate in separate countries following international mergers. If so, the asymmetry in the merger control would not be of any significant importance for the actual outcome.

The reason for this somewhat counter-intuitive result is the difference in the nature of the merger game and the location game. Following an international merger, the firms will find themselves engaged in a non-cooperative location game where the outcome is inefficient from the point of view of the firms. Both firms may locate in the large region, since they do not take into account the negative externality (a business-stealing effect) that their choice of location will imply for the competitor. In the merger game, however, the possibility for firms to negotiate with each other and transfer wealth, actually makes them internalize these externalities. Thus, they merge domestically to ensure location in different regions, which maximizes the aggregate profit.

There are many reasons why loss of production hurts the small country. It reduces the demand for the types of labor used in the affected industry, which will cause lower wages or increased unemployment or both. From a regional perspective, the reduction in demand may be large, even if only one or a few firms in the small country are affected. The negative effects of the relocation of production may also be multiplied by the negative repercussions for other firms in the economy, such as subcontractors. At the same time, the loss of production hurts the public finances in the small country by reducing the tax base. Our interpretation of the debate in e.g. Sweden is that it is primarily the fear of such negative effects on the factor markets that is the cause of the critique of EU merger policy. Our analysis shows, however, that blocking domestic mergers in favor of international mergers may also hurt consumers in the small country.

Suppose that the competition authority effectively chooses whether to accept international or domestic mergers *without* taking plant closures into account. Firms do not relocate after domestic mergers, and the resulting prices are thus those predicted by the Commission. With international mergers, however, the evaluation of the anti-competitive effects is erroneously based on the assumption that the two merged entities will maintain their production in both markets. In practice, however, firms will locate in Large, serving Small from a foreign base and with higher variable costs than they would have had, had they maintained the local plants. Hence, in this example, *by disregarding locational implications, the competition authority underestimates the negative impact of the international merger on competition in Small.* It may thus prohibit domestic mergers, believing that international mergers better serve small country consumer interests, thereby hurting the very same consumers. More generally, not taking locational consequences into account tends to bias the assessment against the country that does not attract investment.

This example highlights conditions under which the above-mentioned critique of the Commission's policy may be valid. But it can be noted that the conditions identified by this example are rather special: On the one hand, there must be substantial segmentation, otherwise, the firms' first choice would be to merge internationally to save on transportation costs. A negative attitude toward domestic mergers has no consequences. On the other hand, the regions must not be too segmented, otherwise firms would choose different locations following international mergers in order to benefit from local monopoly power.

Our analysis also shows that the "small-country critique" also crucially hinges on the intensity of competition in the two markets. If there is much more competition in the large than in the small market, more and not less production may be located in the small country following international mergers than following domestic ones. In this case, the Commission's skepticism against domestic mergers may be beneficial for the small region.

It is also important to emphasize that the negative effect on consumers builds on variable trade costs being a source of trade friction, and does not work with investment in distribution and service networks as barriers between markets. Since many trade costs are fixed rather than variable, and since many of the variable trade costs have been reduced in Europe as a result of the creation of the common market, it is questionable whether this effect is actually quantitatively important.

Finally, it is far from clear how a competition authority would predict changes in the location of production as a result of mergers, and how, in turn, the incomes, the unemployment rates and so on would be affected in different regions. There doesn't exist any readily available analytical framework for these issues, and the informational requirements would most likely be enormous. Given the importance of relatively strict time limits, such a policy is probably not feasible. Moreover, there may exist other and better suited policy measures for combating regional imbalances.

10.6.3.2. Should alternative mergers be of importance?

When regional markets are sufficiently segmented, they are treated as different relevant geographical markets, and the effect of a merger is assessed separately in each region. As we have seen, it is possible that international mergers may give rise to the same cost savings as domestic mergers, but with less distortion of competition. It thus seems reasonable that the Commission takes into consideration alternative merger structures that might arise as a consequence of blocking a proposed merger.

Attractive at it seems, such a merger policy may face serious problems. *First*, as we saw in the example above, consumers may be affected differently by different merger structures because of relocation of production in certain structures. A merger policy which considers these latter structures as alternatives to other proposed structures, but does not take into account locational implications, will be based on erroneous premises, and will tend to be biased against the countries losing the production.

A *second*, and potentially serious, problem stems from the fact that each "substantial part of the common market" has "*veto power*", in the sense that it suffices to find negative effects in one of these substantial parts for a merger to be blocked. This decision criterion may work well as long as a merger affects consumers in different substantial parts of the common market, either in the same direction, or not at all. But it might run into problems when consumers are affected differently, which is possible when mergers have locational implications,[21] as we have seen above.

To highlight the potential severity of these problems, consider what may appear to be the "ideal" merger policy, a policy that (i) compares notified mergers with their relevant alternatives, (ii) requires that consumers must be made better off (compared to the relevant alternative) in all regions, and (iii) that takes the implications of location into account. By requiring that consumers in *each*

---

[21] Another example is that a merger which both reduces competition and marginal costs may benefit consumers in regions where competition is intense while harming consumers in regions with little competition.

substantial part of the common market prefer a proposed merger *to the situation at the outset*, the "veto power" criterion is a rather stringent condition generally speaking. However, with this type of policy, which compares *more than one merger structure*, the criterion becomes even more conservative. To see why, consider a proposed domestic merger. When international mergers are taken into account, not only must the proposed merger be better for consumers in each substantial part of the market as compared to the outset, *in addition, there must not be any such group of consumers who would prefer the international structure.* The inclusion of alternative merger structures in the assessment may thus make it very unlikely that a merger is accepted, even if it were to improve the situation for *all* consumers relative to the outset.

For instance, in our framework above, suppose that an international merger would lead to a relocation of production to Large, and that consumers in Small would therefore prefer domestic mergers to international mergers, while consumers in Large would prefer international mergers to domestic mergers. However, both groups would prefer any of the mergers to the outset. The Commission would now conclude that a proposed domestic merger cannot be accepted, since when ranking the proposed merger against an international structure, consumers in one substantial part of the common market—Large—would prefer the latter. On the other hand, if an international merger were proposed, consumers in Small would object, and the merger would thus be blocked. Consequently, *neither merger structure would be accepted, despite the fact that both are preferred to the outset by both groups of consumers.*

Then, what is the source of this problem, and how generic is it? The problem arises due to a combination of two factors. First, the Commission in our example takes into account more than one alternative to the proposed merger structure, and second, the locational implications of mergers, tend to make consumer interest diverge in the two regions. Hence, in any situation where there is such a divergence and alternative structures are taken into account, this problem is likely to arise.

A *third* and important objection to the idea of letting merger policy take alternative mergers into account, is that such a policy would face considerable practical difficulties as a result of informational limitations. A first problem is to correctly predict the alternative mergers that will be proposed if the one under scrutiny is rejected. Here, the Commission would largely have to rely on *fingerspitzgefühl*, since economic theory provides very little guidance. A second problem is how to evaluate the implications of the alternative mergers. The Commission can obtain information about a notified merger from participating firms, but this is not possible for mergers that are not yet notified. A third aspect is the possibility of informational leakage caused by the investigation process itself.[22] Firms often have an interest in keeping merger plans confidential, but

---

22 We are grateful to a referee for bringing this, in practice probably very important, aspect to our attention.

since the competition authority would need to contact competitors to obtain sufficient information to evaluate alternative mergers, the process of investigation could alert competitors about their rivals' plans.

Yet another issue is whether the Merger Regulation, in fact, does allow the Commission to take alternative mergers into account. The wording of the Regulation itself does not give explicit support for either conclusion, but the more common interpretation is probably that the statutes speak of a change in the competitive situation vis-à-vis the status quo. Moreover, the Commission's guidelines seem to suggest such an interpretation, at least for most cases.[23] Nevertheless, statements by Commission officials following the *Volvo/Scania* decision indicate that alternatives may have played a role in that decision.

The main conclusion is hence that taking alternative mergers into account is likely to be associated with serious problems. Unfortunately, disregarding alternative mergers also comes at a cost, in terms of foregone benefits from socially more attractive mergers.[24]

10.7. Summary and concluding discussion

The chapter has discussed a number of issues that arise when evaluating the criticism of EU merger control from the point of view of smaller Member States. The main conclusions can be summarized as follows:

1. Are there systematic differences in the treatment of mergers in small and large Member States?

Yes, in a certain sense. Since geographical markets sometimes coincide with national borders, and since smaller markets often support fewer firms, it follows that domestic mergers between large companies in small countries may reduce competition in their home-market more than domestic mergers between companies of similar size in large countries.

Moreover, since also smaller EU Member States are interpreted to constitute "substantial parts of the common market", and since a merger must not impede competition in any such part, large companies in small countries have more limited possibilities to merge domestically.

2. Does the asymmetry in merger control have implications for firms' choices of location?

---

[23] According to the guidelines, the competitive conditions existing at the time of the merger constitute the relevant comparison for evaluating the effects of a merger, in most cases. However, in some circumstances, the Commission may take into account future changes to the market that can reasonably be predicted. See the Commission's Guidelines on the assessment of horizontal mergers under the Council Regulation on the control of concentrations between undertakings (2004/C 31/03).

[24] Fridolfsson and Stennek (2005b) provide an example of a situation where a merger policy that maximizes social welfare on a case-by-case basis, but that does not take alternative mergers into account, may be worse than a laissez-faire regime.

The answer to this question is less obvious than it might appear. After all, if firms seek to merge domestically, which is when the asymmetry is of main importance, they seem to prefer to be located in their respective home countries, yielding a geographically dispersed pattern of production. It may then reasonably be believed that the firms would also choose to locate in different countries following international mergers. If so, the asymmetry in the merger control would not be of any great importance for the actual outcome.

In order to identify circumstances under which firms would actually locate in the larger region following international mergers, we investigated a simple framework. In the model, three forces determine locational choice following an international merger. First, firms tend to prefer to locate in the large region in order to avoid trade costs in servicing the large market. Second, they tend to prefer to locate in the small region since competition may be more intense in the larger region. Finally, there is also an advantage from locating in different regions (as they would following domestic mergers), by limiting competition.

In this framework, firms locate in the larger region following international mergers under certain circumstances, but prefer domestic mergers entailing local production to international mergers. The reason is that the firms in the location game do not take into account the externalities of their choices on their opponents. They may well locate in the same region (e.g. the large one) despite the fact that this entails a reduction in aggregate profits, due to a "business stealing" effect. In the merger game, however, the firms may transfer wealth between themselves, thereby enabling them to better internalize such effects.

Hence, scenarios can be constructed where the claim that the asymmetry is important for firms' choice of location is validated. However, the conditions under which this occurs are rather restrictive, at least in this framework.

3. Are smaller Member States adversely affected by the asymmetry?

Yes, this is possible, at least in theory. Much of the policy discussion has focused on the effects of mergers on factor markets. In particular, there is a widespread fear that relocation of production to larger regions may reduce employment in smaller regions. EU merger control, on the other hand, is mainly concerned with consumer welfare and, in this sense the critique may at the same time appear relevant to smaller country governments, and irrelevant from the point of view of the Commission. But as we have shown, location may also be of importance for consumers. In particular, if competition authorities block domestic mergers (entailing local production), hereby promoting international mergers (entailing concentration of production to the large region), consumers in the small region may be hurt, since they must pay the higher prices associated with the higher variable trading costs.

More generally, if the assessment of the effects of mergers does not take locational consequences into account, the procedure tends to underestimate the negative impact on competition in the regions from which the firms relocate.

4. Should the Commission take alternative mergers into account when assessing notified mergers?

We made several observations concerning the role of alternative mergers in merger control:

- Taking alternative mergers into account has positive consequences under certain conditions.
- Taking alternative mergers into account without also considering location may harm consumers in small countries.[25]
- Taking alternative mergers into account may lead to an overly restrictive merger policy when markets are segmented, as long as mergers are blocked if they impede competition in any significant part of the common market.
- It would be exceedingly difficult in practice to take alternative mergers into account in a systematic fashion.

We thus believe that at the current state of affairs in economic research, the Commission should not take into account alternative mergers, in particular not if the current interpretation of the "substantial part of the common market"-criterion is employed. The Commission should evaluate each notified merger as if the alternative to accepting the merger is no merger at all.[26] This is an imperfect solution, however, dictated by the insurmountable problems of information. The foregone benefits from socially more attractive mergers and industry structures may be substantial.

5. Should the Commission Take Location into Account when Assessing Mergers?

Our findings with regard to location are the following:

- The claim that international mergers may lead to different patterns of location than domestic mergers can be supported by theory in a plausible fashion.
- International mergers *may* be detrimental to consumer interests in smaller Member States. However, it is unclear how likely this is. In the analytical framework we have relied on, this claim is only true for a limited set of parameters, and it relies on the existence of variable trade costs.
- Although, it would not involve any fundamental problem if the Commission were to take locational implications of mergers into account, the practical difficulties in reliably predicting location choices would probably be overwhelming.

Where does this leave us then; should we accept the asymmetry? It should first be noted that the empirical magnitude of this problem is unclear. We would therefore be reluctant to propose any changes in current practices solely to solve

---

[25] Not taking location into account may lead to problems also if the Commission does not consider alternative mergers. However, if the Commission considers alternative mergers, the problems can be expected to be worse, since this will tend to favor international mergers over domestic mergers in segmented markets.

[26] It is also not clear whether the Merger Regulation in fact allows the Commission such a broad evaluation of mergers.

this alleged problem, before it has convincingly been shown that the problem is real. But, in our view, if one were nevertheless to seek to remove the asymmetry, several of the remedies suggested in the debate should be avoided, including changes in relevant market definitions. The most natural change to current procedure would be to explicitly weigh consumer interests in different substantial parts of the market, and make a judgment on the aggregate effects. It may also be natural to take locational implications of mergers into account. It is not clear, however, that such a reform would be quantitatively important, due to the difficulties in predicting location and since it is questionable to what extent location actually affects consumer prices. In the longer run, the problem will hopefully be resolved by reduced market segmentation.

Acknowledgements

We are grateful for very extensive and helpful comments on an earlier version by Damien J. Neven, and for useful discussions with officials at the Swedish Competition Authority, as well as for comments from two anonymous referees.

Horn gratefully acknowledges financial support from the Marianne and Marcus Wallenberg Foundation, and Stennek from the Jan Wallander and Tom Hedelius Research Foundations, and from Swedish Competition Authority.

References

Besanko, D., Spulber, D.F. (1993), Contested mergers and equilibrium antitrust policy. *Journal of Law, Economics and Organization* 9 (1), 1–29. April.

Fridolfsson, S.-O. (2002), En ekonomisk analys av olika målsättningar för förvärvskontrollen. (Roughly: Economic analysis of the goals of merger control). Submitted for publication *Konkurrensen i Sverige 2002*, Konkurrensverket, Stockholm.

Fridolfsson, S.-O., Stennek, J. (2005a), Why mergers reduce profits, and raise share prices—A theory of preemptive mergers. *Journal of the European Economic Association* 3 (5), 1083–1104. September.

Fridolfsson, S.-O., Stennek, J. (2005b), Holdup of anticompetitive mergers. *International Journal of Industrial Organization*, in press.

Horn, H., Persson, L. (2001a), Endogenous mergers in concentrated markets. *International Journal of Industrial Organization* 53 (2), 307–333. April.

Horn, H., Persson, L. (2001b), The equilibrium ownership of an international oligopoly. *Journal of International Economics* 53 (2), 307–333. April.

Horn, H., Stennek, J. (2002), Mergers and location: Does EU merger control hurt smaller Member State interests? Mimeo.

Kamien, M.I., Zang, I. (1990), The limits of monopolization through acquisition. *Quarterly Journal of Economics* 105 (2), 465–499. May.

Kamien, M.I., Zang, I. (1991), Competitively cost advantageous mergers and monopolization. *Games and Economic Behavior* 3 (3), 323–338. August.

Kamien, M.I., Zang, I. (1993), Monopolization by sequential acquisition. *Journal of Law, Economics and Organization* 9 (2), 205–229. October.

Lindqvist, T., Stennek, J. (2005), The insider's dilemma: An experiment on merger formation. *Experimental Economics* 8.

Lyons, B. (2002), Could politicians be more right than economists? Norwich UEA.

Martin, S. (1994), *Industrial Economics—Economic Analysis and Public Policy*, 2nd ed. Prentice-Hall, New Jersey.

Monti, M. (2001), Market definition as a cornerstone of EU Competition Policy. Speech by Commissioner Mario Monti, Workshop on Market Definition, Helsinki Fair Centre, Helsinki, 5 October.

Neven, D.J., Röller, L.-H. (2005), Consumer surplus versus welfare standard in a political economy model of merger control. *International Journal of Industrial Organization* 23, 829–848.

Stigler, G.J. (1950), Monopoly and oligopoly by merger. *American Economic Review, Papers and Proceedings* 40, 23–34.

CHAPTER 11

A Consumer Surplus Defense in Merger Control

Sven-Olof Fridolfsson

Research Institute of Industrial Economics, Stockholm, Sweden
E-mail address: sof@industrialeconomics.se

Abstract

A government wanting to promote an efficient allocation of resources as measured by the total surplus, should strategically delegate to its competition authority a welfare standard with a bias in favor of consumers. A consumer bias means that some welfare increasing mergers will be blocked. This is optimal, if the relevant alternative to the merger is another change in market structure that will even further increase the total surplus. Furthermore, a consumer bias is shown to enhance welfare even though it blocks some welfare increasing mergers when the relevant alternative is the status quo.

Keywords: merger control, competition policy, consumer surplus

JEL classifications: L11, L13, L41

11.1. Introduction

The main task of Merger Control is to evaluate mergers in light of their welfare effects on different interest groups and to take a decision based on this evaluation. This task requires that the Merger Control system specifies the interest groups—consumers, shareholders, workers, competitors, suppliers and so on—to be included in the evaluation. In case of conflicting interests, the Merger Control system must also trade-off the different groups' interests against each other. The purpose of so-called welfare standards is to clarify how these trade-offs are made by explicitly stating which interests groups ought to be included in the evaluation and by assigning specific weights to each group.

The actual welfare standards used in different jurisdictions are characterized by two particularly striking regularities. First, many welfare standards tend to be strongly biased in favor of the consumers' interests. In the US, a merger that increases market concentration might be challenged unless it is expected to deliver such cost-savings that it is also beneficial to consumers (US Horizontal Merger Guidelines, 1997). In the EU, the EC Merger Regulation (2004) stipulates that concentrations are allowed unless they significantly impede effective

CONTRIBUTIONS TO ECONOMIC ANALYSIS
VOLUME 282 ISSN: 0573-8555
DOI: 10.1016/S0573-8555(06)82011-0

competition. Furthermore, competition is significantly impeded if the concentration harms consumers' interests. Thus the world's two largest economies apply a pure consumer welfare standard (henceforth referred to as a consumer surplus standard). Second, if a jurisdiction does not apply a consumer surplus standard, the producers (i.e. the merging firms and competitors) tend to be the additional interest group represented in the welfare standards. In Canada, for example, Section 96 of the Competition Act directs the Tribunal not to issue an order ... if it finds that the merger ... is likely to bring about efficiency gains that will be greater than, and will offset, the effects of any prevention or lessening of competition .... The 1991 Canadian Merger Enforcement Guidelines interprets these wordings as a welfare standard giving the same weight to consumers and producers (henceforth referred to as a total surplus standard). However, in Hillsdown this interpretation was questioned by the court; a reasonable reinterpretation of the court's decision suggests a standard, which in effect gives a larger weight to consumers than to producers (see McFetridge, 1998).

The two above regularities raises at least two questions. What is the motive behind the strong focus on consumers' interests and why are the interests of some groups, for example workers, so unlikely to be taken into account? When faced with policy objectives in favor of a specific interest group, a natural reaction is to look after an explanation based on distributional considerations. A tempting answer to the first question is therefore that the focus on consumers' interests is driven by a concern for the distribution of wealth, combined with a belief that consumers are, on average, less wealthy than firm owners. This view, however, has been criticized on at least two grounds (see, e.g., Williamson, 1968). First, it has been questioned whether consumers are poor; for sure, many luxurious goods are primarily purchased by rich consumers. Second, even if the focus on consumers' interests has some distributional effects, there are other instruments such as taxes and transfers that seem more appropriate for affecting distribution. On these grounds, many economists argue that competition policy ought to promote allocative efficiency only (see, e.g., Crampton, 1994; Jenny, 1994).

Any reasonable answer to the second question seems even more unlikely to incorporate a distributional dimension. Indeed, among all the interest groups affected by mergers, the one group that may perhaps motivate a distributional concern, namely workers,[1] is excluded from most welfare standards[2] or at least is not given a large weight. Note also that because workers probably would merit a larger weight than consumers if welfare standards were primarily designed for the purpose of affecting distribution, the actual focus on consumers' interests is all the more puzzling.

---

[1] If merger induced rationalizations primarily take place through a process of skill biased technological change, one may at least hypothesize that mergers tend to hurt low skilled workers with low wages.

[2] Interestingly, in Sweden, a country which is widely perceived as one of the most pro-egalitarian ones in the world, it is explicitly stated that the workers' interests should not be taken into account (see Röller et al., 2001).

Table 11.1:

	M^1	M^0	M^2
Π	++	0	+
S	–	0	+
T	+	0	++

The present chapter shows in the context of merger control that the choice of welfare standard can have an impact on which mergers are proposed by firms. As a result, a government whose aim is to promote an efficient allocation of resources as measured by the total surplus—the sum of the consumer and producer surpluses—should strategically delegate a welfare standard with a consumer bias. This result thus indicates that the current practice of protecting the consumers' interests need not be understood as a concern for the distribution of wealth; rather it may be motivated on the sole ground of promoting allocative efficiency.

The underlying mechanism behind this result is simple. In terms of the total surplus it may be optimal to block a merger, even though it enhances the total surplus relative to the initial market structure, if the relevant alternative is another merger. To see this, consider the example described in Table 11.1. For simplicity, there are only three possible market structures, the initial one, M^0, and market structures M^1 and M^2. A change in market structure, for example achieved by means of a merger, induces changes in the producer (Π), the consumer (S) and the total (T) surpluses. The producer surplus is largest in market structure M^1, followed by M^2 while it is smallest in the initial market structure. Similarly, Table 11.1 ranks the different market structures in terms of the other two surpluses.

Assume that any change in market structure is initiated by the firms and that they maximize the producer surplus. Furthermore, assume that the competition authority can assess the consequences of a proposed change in market structure relative to the initial one, but not the consequences of the alternative change in market structure. Delegating a consumer surplus standard to the competition authority is then, in the example of Table 11.1, optimal in terms of the total surplus. Indeed, such a welfare standard forbids market structure M^1, since it reduces the consumer surplus relative to the initial market structure, M^0. Thereby, it instead induces market structure M^2 which maximizes the total surplus. In contrast, the total surplus standard is not optimal, since it induces market structure M^1.

The crucial assumption underlying the above argument is that the competition authority can perfectly assess the consequences of a *proposed* change in market structure, but not the consequences of *alternative* changes. Clearly, the former assumption overestimates the ability of competition authorities to assess the consequences of a proposed change in market structure. The latter assumption, on the other hand, possibly underestimates the ability of competition authorities to assess the consequences of alternative changes in market structure.[3] For instance, the US Horizontal Merger Guidelines (1997) prescribe that US competition authorities should assess whether alleged cost savings are specific to the proposed merger. Thus some competition authorities at least attempt to evaluate the consequences of alternatives to a proposed merger, possibly other changes in market structure. While the above assumption abstracts from these important issues, it captures in the simplest possible way the following realistic feature of merger control. Assessing the consequences of all possible changes in market structure is clearly much more difficult for a competition authority than assessing the consequences of a proposed one only. For example, it may be possible to perform the latter task while pursuing the former is too costly due to time constraints. Furthermore, it may be easier for a competition authority to require firms to disclose information regarding a proposed change in market structure as opposed to disclose information about some other hypothetical change in market structure. The present chapter may thus be viewed as a first attempt to analyze the implications of the differences in how difficult it is for a competition authority to perform these different tasks.

Due to the above information problem, the competition authority cannot pursue a first-best policy. The reason is that different welfare standards yield different errors. By applying a total surplus standard, the competition authority may allow a market structure increasing the total surplus, even though the relevant alternative is a market structure increasing the total surplus even further (as in the example of Table 11.1). By applying a consumer surplus standard, on the other hand, the competition authority may forbid market structures that increase the total surplus even though the relevant alternative to the proposed market structure is the status quo. The choice of welfare standard ought to take into account that both these types of errors may occur. Due to the first type of error, however, distorting the competition authority's objective function, that is delegating an operational goal that differs from the total surplus, turns out to be optimal in expected terms. This result is best understood by considering a small distortion in favor of the consumers. The foregone surplus due to the second type of error must be small, since the consumer bias is small. In contrast, the gain in terms of total surplus generated by avoiding the first type of error is potentially large. Therefore the total surplus standard cannot be optimal in expected terms even though the objective of Merger Control is assumed to be to maximize the total surplus.

This result is derived in Sections 11.3 and 11.4 using a simple model where two firms can merge to form a monopoly or can undertake an alternative change in market structure. In this model, the changes in surpluses resulting from the different changes in market structure are taken as the model's exogenous variables. It should be emphasized, however, that these changes in surpluses ought

[3] Note that this latter assumption is implicit in most policy analyses related to merger control (see, for example, Williamson, 1968; Farrell and Shapiro, 1990; Besanko and Spulber, 1993; Neven and Röller, 2005).

to be viewed as the outcome of some oligopolistic interaction before and after the possible changes in market structure. I postpone to Section 11.5 the discussion of how these changes in surpluses may be generated so as to focus on the important insight of this chapter—that alternatives to a proposed change in market structure matter for the choice of welfare standard. The paper ends by some concluding remarks in Section 11.6. Before introducing the model, I discuss the related literature in the next section.

11.2. Related literature

The present chapter constitutes an application of the concept of strategic delegation whereby a principal (the government) distorts the objective function of its agent (the competition authority) so as to affect the interaction between the agent and a third party (the merging firms) in a manner that benefits the principal. Strategic delegation has been applied in many different areas of economics, in particular for the purpose of designing economic policy. A classical application in this vein is due to Rogoff (1985) in the context of monetary policy. Monetary policy typically exhibits a time-inconsistency problem when wage setters have rational expectations. As a result, delegating monetary policy to a "too conservative" central banker—a central banker whose weight on inflation relative to unemployment is higher than what is socially optimal—may be optimal. Rogoff considers an economy where the natural rate of unemployment is higher than what is socially optimal (for example due to labor market imperfections) and where wage negotiations determine nominal wages for a fixed period of time. In such a framework, and provided that inflation is not too high, an "unbiased" central banker is tempted to inflate the economy by issuing money so as to reduce real wages and thereby reduce unemployment below its natural rate. Under rational expectations, however, wage setters foresee this opportunistic behavior, and negotiate *ex ante* high nominal wages associated with high inflation. Thereby it becomes too costly for the central banker to reduce unemployment at the expense of a further increase in inflation. That is, under rational expectations, an unbiased central banker's only time-consistent policy is one where both unemployment and inflation is fairly high. Delegating monetary policy to a conservative banker mitigates the time-inconsistency problem. Intuitively, the temptation of a conservative central banker to inflate the economy so as to reduce unemployment is removed at lower levels of inflation.

Needless to say, there exist many other applications of strategic delegation.[4] Three of them are of particular interest for the present chapter, since they also constitute defenses for a consumer bias in merger control, which are not based

[4] Strategic delegation has for instance been applied to positive analyses. For example, Fershtman and Judd (1987) have proposed strategic delegation as an explanation for managerial incentive schemes, which differ from profit maximization.

on distributional considerations. Besanko's and Spulber's (1993) consumer surplus defense is driven by two important assumptions: merger induced marginal cost savings are private information to the merging firms and the merging firms incur a fixed cost when they propose a merger. These assumptions turn out to imply that an "unbiased" competition authority lacks the ability to credibly commit to an optimal policy as captured by an optimal probability of challenging mergers. The reason is that the mere decision to propose a merger conveys information to the competition authority—in fact, it conveys good news. To see why, note that mergers are more profitable, and enhance welfare more, the larger the cost-savings. Therefore, taking the challenging probability as given, a merger proposal is profitable in expectation if and only if the cost savings are sufficiently large. This means that the competition authority, when faced with a merger proposal, will update its beliefs in favor of the proposed merger. In fact, if the unbiased competition authority could commit to the optimal challenging probability thanks to some exogenous commitment technology, its updated beliefs would be so favorable to the proposed merger that the competition authority would strictly prefer not to challenge it. The problem is that the competition authority does not have access to an exogenous commitment technology and, as an immediate consequence, the unbiased authority cannot credibly commit to challenge the merger with the optimal probability. Besanko and Spulber show that delegating a welfare standard with a consumer bias mitigates the commitment problem, since it implies that competition authorities' assessments of a proposed merger become less favorable.

More recently, Neven and Röller (2005) compare a total surplus standard with a consumer surplus standard in a lobbying model where the firms can influence the competition authority's decision through perks. The competition authority's objective function is assumed to consist both of the delegated welfare standard and the perks. Due to the presence of the welfare standard in the objective function, competition authorities are tougher under a consumer surplus standard implying also that under such a standard, they are less sensitive to perks. Thereby a consumer surplus standard reduces the extent of type 2 errors—to allow welfare reducing mergers due to perks. Of course, the disadvantage of a consumer surplus standard is that it increases the extent of type 1 errors—to forbid welfare enhancing mergers on the ground that they reduce the consumer surplus.[5]

Finally, Lyons (2002) has recently proposed in independent work a consumer surplus defense, which is driven by the same insight as in the current chapter:

---

[5] Neven and Röller argue informally that the perks' weight in competition authorities' objective function depend on the institutional framework: they conjecture that less transparent legal frameworks are likely to increase authorities' ability to take decisions in conflict with the delegated welfare standard. If this conjecture is correct, their analysis suggests that a consumer surplus standard is better suited in jurisdictions where the legal framework is less transparent. On this ground, Neven and Röller argue that a consumer surplus standard probably fits better to the EU than to the US, since the legal framework in the latter jurisdiction is commonly viewed as more transparent than in the EU.

there are alternatives to proposed changes in market structure. The main differences between his work and mine are twofold. First, he models a merger formation game where the potential alternative to a proposed merger is another merger. In contrast, I only consider a model with two firms. The main advantage with my model is its simplicity. In particular, the restriction to two firms makes it unproblematic to assume that the firms choose the market structure maximizing the producer surplus. Thereby I avoid dealing with the tedious details involved in the modeling of endogenous merger formation games. Second, Lyons only compares the performance of the consumer surplus standard with the total surplus standard. As a result, he finds that depending on the situation, either the consumer or the total surplus standard is optimal. In contrast, I consider all possible welfare standards. Thereby I clarify why, in expected terms, the optimal welfare standard must have a consumer bias.

The above mentioned studies and the present chapter are all applications of strategic delegation and as such they share the following feature: a consumer bias renders the competition authority tougher and thereby affects the firms' merger decisions. It is striking, however, that the underlying mechanisms are very different in nature. Equally striking is that the studies nevertheless point in the same direction and, as such, should be viewed as complementary. The fact that the different mechanisms point in the same direction suggests that a more general principle may be at work. Consumers typically have difficulties to organize themselves so as to promote their common interests—they suffer from a collective action problem. As a result, they end up in a weak position relative to the merging firms. The above studies suggest that the collective action problem is important for at least two reasons. First, by its very nature, consumers become unable to counteract lobbying activities by the firms. Second, consumers have little incentives to gather information about for example cost-savings or potential alternatives to proposed mergers and thus are particularly poorly informed. In turn, the firms exploit the consumers' collective action problem and this give rise to inefficiencies. The more general principle suggested by the above studies is thus that organizing an agency whose objective is to defend the interests' of a weak party reduces inefficiencies.

11.3. A simple model

Consider a market with two competing firms, which may alter the market structure in two different ways: the two firms may merge to monopoly or they may undertake an alternative change in market structure. In Section 11.5, I give several possible interpretations of the alternative market structure.

Time is divided into four periods. In period 0, a policy objective, a so-called welfare standard, is delegated to a competition authority. In period 1, the firms decide which change in market structure to propose to the competition authority. In period 2, the competition authority either accepts or rejects the notified proposal. In period 3, the firms earn the profits in the resulting market structure.

Note that the firms' interests perfectly coincide at the time of the proposal. In period 1, the firms are therefore assumed to propose the market structure, which maximizes aggregate profits in period 3, subject to the approval of the authority in period 2.

Let the changes in producer surplus following the merger to monopoly and the alternative change in market structure be denoted Π_m and Π_a respectively. Throughout the paper it is assumed that the monopoly maximizes the producer surplus, i.e. $\Pi_m > \max\{0, \Pi_a\}$. The alternative change in market structure is either profitable ($\Pi_a \geq 0$) or unprofitable ($\Pi_a < 0$). The relevant alternative to the monopoly is thus the alternative market structure in the former case while it is the original market structure in the latter.

Changes in market structure typically alter firms' price and output decisions and thereby affect consumers' welfare. Let S_m (S_a) denote the change in consumer surplus relative to the original market structure following the merger to monopoly (the alternative change in market structure). A change in market structure may have an adverse effect on consumers ($S < 0$) for example by increasing the firms' market power, but may also have a positive effect ($S > 0$) if it reduces market power or if it allows the firms to exploit synergies.

As discussed in the Introduction, I assume that the competition authority has the ability to perfectly assess the consequences of a proposed change in market structure relative to the original market structure, but not the consequences of the alternative change. Therefore, I restrict the attention to the class of policies approving a transfer of assets if and only if it increases a weighted average of the consumer and producer surpluses relative to the initial market structure, i.e. $\Pi + \alpha S \geq 0$. An element of this class of policies will be referred to as an α-standard and is characterized by the parameter $\alpha \in [0, +\infty)$. Note that the competition authority is delegated a total surplus standard (henceforth referred to as a T-standard) when $\alpha = 1$ and a consumer surplus standard (referred to as a S-standard) when $\alpha \to \infty$.

Before presenting the equilibrium market structure, I make two additional assumptions, namely that $S_m < 0$ and $S_a \geq 0$. The first assumption is not important, since all standards are equivalent when $S_m \geq 0$. Indeed, any welfare standard induces the merger to monopoly when $S_m \geq 0$, since $\Pi_m > 0$ and thus $\Pi_m + \alpha S_m \geq 0$. The second assumption simplifies the exposition by making it redundant to state the conditions under which the alternative market structure is allowed. Indeed, $\Pi_a + \alpha S_a \geq 0$ under the assumption whenever the alternative market structure is proposed ($\Pi_a \geq 0$). It should be emphasized, however, that the assumption is not innocuous, since it implies that the alternative market structure always raises the total surplus. I discuss how the assumption affects my main result after its derivation.

Recall that in period 1, the firms can either propose the monopoly, propose the alternative market structure or choose to remain in the status quo. The firms equilibrium strategies are the following. (i) Propose the monopoly whenever it is allowed ($\Pi_m + \alpha S_m \geq 0$), since the monopoly maximizes the producer surplus ($\Pi_m > \max\{0, \Pi_a\}$). (ii) Propose the alternative market structure whenever the monopoly is blocked ($\Pi_m + \alpha S_m < 0$) and the alternative market structure is profitable ($\Pi_a \geq 0$). (iii) Remain in the status quo whenever the monopoly is blocked ($\Pi_m + \alpha S_m < 0$) and the alternative market structure is unprofitable ($\Pi_a < 0$). Taking the α-standard as given, the unique equilibrium market structures are thus given by

$$\begin{cases} \text{The monopoly if and only if } \Pi_m + \alpha S_m \geq 0, \\ \text{The alternative if and only if } \Pi_m + \alpha S_m < 0 \text{ and } \Pi_a \geq 0, \\ \text{The status quo if and only if } \Pi_m + \alpha S_m < 0 \text{ and } \Pi_a < 0. \end{cases} \tag{11.1}$$

11.4. A consumer surplus defense

Throughout the chapter it is assumed that the overall objective of competition policy is to maximize total welfare as measured by the total surplus, i.e. the sum of the consumer and producer surpluses. Nevertheless, delegating a T-standard to the competition authority needs not be optimal. To see why, consider an example where the monopoly increases the total surplus so that the T-standard approves the merger to monopoly. This is suboptimal if the relevant alternative to the monopoly is the alternative market structure ($\Pi_a > 0$) and if this market structure increases the total surplus by even more ($\Pi_a + S_a > \Pi_m + S_m$). Note also that the S-standard would be optimal, since it would block the consumer harming merger to monopoly and thereby induce the alternative market structure. This example thus shows that the S- but not the T-standard may be optimal. There are, however, other examples where the reverse is true. For instance, assume that the alternative market structure is unprofitable. Then the S-standard will block mergers to monopoly that increases the total surplus even though the original market structure is the relevant alternative. Clearly, the T-standard does not suffer form this drawback.

Taken together, the two above examples suggest that there is no single welfare standard, which is optimal for all possible parameter configurations. A natural extension is therefore to analyze different welfare standards in terms of their performance in expected terms. For this purpose, let the probability density function $f(\Pi_a, S_a, \Pi_m, S_m)$ (in short, $f(\cdot)$) describe the distribution of the exogenous parameters. The expected change in total surplus as a function of the welfare standard can then be written as

$$\begin{aligned} W(\alpha) = & \int_{-\infty}^{0}\int_{-\alpha S_m}^{\infty}\int_{0}^{\infty}\int_{-\infty}^{\Pi_m} (\Pi_m + S_m) f(\cdot)\,\mathrm{d}\Pi_a\,\mathrm{d}S_a\,\mathrm{d}\Pi_m\,\mathrm{d}S_m \\ & + \int_{-\infty}^{0}\int_{0}^{-\alpha S_m}\int_{0}^{\infty}\int_{0}^{\Pi_m} (\Pi_a + S_a) f(\cdot)\,\mathrm{d}\Pi_a\,\mathrm{d}S_a\,\mathrm{d}\Pi_m\,\mathrm{d}S_m \\ & + \int_{-\infty}^{0}\int_{0}^{-\alpha S_m}\int_{0}^{\infty}\int_{-\infty}^{0} 0 f(\cdot)\,\mathrm{d}\Pi_a\,\mathrm{d}S_a\,\mathrm{d}\Pi_m\,\mathrm{d}S_m. \end{aligned} \tag{11.2}$$

The first line corresponds to those parameters when the merger to monopoly arises in equilibrium. (By inspection of the integration limits, $\Pi_m + \alpha S_m \geq 0$ and thus the monopoly is approved.) The second line corresponds to those parameters when the alternative market structure arises in equilibrium. (By inspection of the integration limits, $\Pi_m + \alpha S_m < 0$ and $\Pi_a \geq 0$ and thus the monopoly is forbidden when the relevant alternative is the alternative market structure.) The third line corresponds to those parameters when the status quo is an equilibrium. (By inspection of the integration limits, $\Pi_m + \alpha S_m < 0$ and $\Pi_a < 0$ and thus the monopoly is forbidden when the relevant alternative is status quo.) Note that this line equals 0, since the status quo generates no change in total surplus.

So as to discuss the pros and cons of different welfare standards, consider the difference in expected total surplus from using an arbitrary α-standard relative to the T-standard, i.e. $W(\alpha) - W(1)$. Note that

$$\begin{aligned} W(\alpha) - W(1) &= \int_{-\infty}^{0}\int_{-S_m}^{-\alpha S_m}\int_{0}^{\infty}\int_{0}^{\Pi_m} \left[\Pi_a + S_a - (\Pi_m + S_m)\right] f(\cdot)\,\mathrm{d}\Pi_a\,\mathrm{d}S_a\,\mathrm{d}\Pi_m\,\mathrm{d}S_m \\ &\quad - \int_{-\infty}^{0}\int_{-S_m}^{-\alpha S_m}\int_{0}^{\infty}\int_{-\infty}^{0} (\Pi_m + S_m) f(\cdot)\,d\Pi_a\,\mathrm{d}S_a\,\mathrm{d}\Pi_m\,\mathrm{d}S_m. \end{aligned} \tag{11.3}$$

To interpret this expression, consider a welfare standard with a consumer bias ($\alpha > 1$). The difference $W(\alpha) - W(1)$ is determined by those parameter configurations when the monopoly is approved under the T-standard ($\Pi_m + S_m \geq 0$) but not under the α-standard ($\Pi_m + \alpha S_m < 0$).[6] The second line corresponds to those parameter configurations when the relevant alternative to the merger to monopoly is status quo, since $\Pi_a < 0$. This line is negative if and only if $\alpha > 1$. Intuitively, a welfare standard with a consumer bias blocks mergers to monopoly even though these mergers increase the total surplus. This is costly in terms of total surplus, since the relevant alternative to the merger to monopoly is the status quo. By contrast, the first line corresponds to parameter configurations when the relevant alternative to the merger to monopoly is the alternative market structure, since $\Pi_a \geq 0$. The sign of this line is ambiguous, since the total surplus may be largest both in the monopoly and in the alternative market structure ($\Pi_a + S_a \gtreqless \Pi_m + S_m$). What is important to note for the purpose of this chapter, however, is that there are cases where the total surplus is maximized in the alternative market structure. It is those cases that provide a reason for delegating a welfare standard with a consumer bias. As in the example where the S-standard was optimal, the α-standard blocks a merger to monopoly, which would increase the total surplus. This is optimal, since it thereby induces the alternative market structure, which increases the total surplus by even more.

Equation (11.3) thus highlights the costs and benefits of distorting the competition authority's welfare standard in favor of consumers. A closer inspection of Equation (11.3) also suggests why such a distortion can serve the purpose of maximizing the expected total surplus. Recall that the (potential) cost of a

[6] Otherwise the two standards induce the same market structure and are thus equivalent.

welfare standard with a consumer bias is that such a welfare standard will block some mergers to monopoly, which increase the total surplus. Thereby, society foregoes an increase in total surplus of $\Pi_m + S_m$. By inspection of the upper integration limit of Π_m, note however that this cost is incurred if and only if Π_m is sufficiently low, namely lower than $-\alpha S_m$. (Otherwise the merger to monopoly would be allowed also under the α-standard.) Thus the foregone increase in total surplus will be bounded from above by $-\alpha S_m + S_m$ and will thus be negligible if α is close (although larger) to one. By contrast, the (potential) benefit, $\Pi_a + S_a$, is strictly positive. Expressed differently, by raising α marginally above 1, the competition authority will block mergers to monopoly, which yield 0 in total surplus. In exchange, the alternative market structure arises with strictly positive probability and is associated with a strictly positive change in expected total surplus, since $\Pi_a > 0$ whenever the merger to monopoly arises in equilibrium and since $S_a > 0$ by assumption. (I discuss this assumption at the end of this section.) For this reason, it is at least optimal to distort the welfare standard in favor of consumers by a small amount. Formally, this is shown by evaluating the derivative of $W(\alpha)$ at $\alpha = 1$. By Equation (11.2), $W'(\alpha)$ is given by

$$
\begin{aligned}
W'(\alpha) = & \int_{-\infty}^{0}\int_{0}^{\infty}\int_{-\infty}^{-\alpha S_m} (1-\alpha) S_m^2 f(\Pi_a, S_a, -\alpha S_m, S_m)\, \mathrm{d}\Pi_a\, \mathrm{d}S_a\, \mathrm{d}S_m \\
& - \int_{-\infty}^{0}\int_{0}^{\infty}\int_{0}^{-\alpha S_m} (\Pi_a + S_a) S_m f(\Pi_a, S_a, -\alpha S_m, S_m)\, \mathrm{d}\Pi_a\, \mathrm{d}S_a\, \mathrm{d}S_m.
\end{aligned} \tag{11.4}
$$

The second line is the benefit of marginally increasing the weight α: by blocking mergers to monopoly, it induces the alternative market structure, which has the value $\Pi_a + S_a$. The first line is the cost of marginally increasing the weight α, since the competition authority, after the marginal increase, blocks mergers to monopoly with value $-\alpha S_m + S_m$.[7] Clearly this cost equals 0 when $\alpha = 1$ so that $W'(1) > 0$. Thus the T-standard must in expected terms be dominated by some welfare standard with a consumer bias.[8]

While the above analysis shows that the optimal welfare standard must have a consumer bias, it does not tell which welfare standard is the optimal one. That depends on the shape of the distribution $f(\cdot)$, i.e. on the likelihood of making the different mistakes. The fact that the potential benefit of distorting α in favor of the consumers may be very large suggests, however, that the distribution $f(\cdot)$ must be very skewed in favor of the T-standard for that standard to be a good approximation of the optimal welfare standard.

---

[7] The potential gain and cost (i.e. $\Pi_a + S_a$ and $-\alpha S_m + S_m$), are multiplied by $-S_m$, since we are considering a marginal increase in α and α is the standard's weight on the consumer surplus.

[8] To complete the proof of the present consumer surplus defense, it actually remains to show that a welfare standard with a producer bias ($\alpha < 1$) cannot be optimal. Intuitively, a welfare standard with a producer bias is suboptimal, since it allows some mergers to monopoly, which reduce the total surplus. This intuition can be verified through an inspection of Equation (11.3) and is proved by noting that $W(\alpha) - W(1) < 0$ if $\alpha < 1$.

Finally, I discuss how the above result must be qualified if the assumption $S_a \geq 0$ is relaxed. For this purpose, make the distinction between those alternative changes in market structure that must be notified to the competition authority and those that must not. In the former case, the assumption is innocuous. The reason is that the alternative change in market structure must satisfy the welfare standard, that is $\Pi_a + \alpha S_a \geq 0$, implying that the alternative market structure will increase the total surplus if $\alpha > 1$.[9] The assumption is not innocuous in the latter case, however, since then the alternative change in market structure may well take place and reduce the total surplus. The critical condition for a small consumer bias to increase the expected total surplus is then that

$$E[\Pi_a + S_a \mid \Pi_a > 0 \text{ and } \Pi_m + S_m = 0] > 0.$$

That is, the expected change in total surplus from the alternative market structure is positive, given that the merger to monopoly yields no change in total surplus and the firms would choose the alternative change in market structure in case the monopoly is blocked.[10]

11.5. Underlying market interactions

So far I have abstracted away from how the changes in surpluses can be generated as outcomes of market interactions. In this section, I give several possible interpretations of the model with an emphasis on how alternative changes in market structure may arise.

In the original version of this chapter (Fridolfsson, 2001b), the changes in surpluses were modeled formally using a two firm Cournot model where the firms are endowed with transferable physical assets. By merging their assets, the firms can form a monopoly. Because the production technology exhibits long run increasing returns to scale, the merger gives rise to cost-savings. Therefore the merger to monopoly does not only maximize the producer surplus ($\Pi_m > \max\{0, \Pi_a\}$); it may also increase the total surplus ($\Pi_m + S_m > 0$) even though it increases market concentration and thereby harms the consumers ($S_m < 0$).[11] The model also exhibits a more surprising feature, which gives rise to the alternative market structure. A transfer of assets from the largest to the smallest firm may yield so large cost-savings in the small firm that the transfer increases the two firms' aggregate profits ($\Pi_a > 0$). Furthermore, such a

---

[9] To see this, assume that $\Pi_a + S_a < 0$ due to the fact that $S_a < 0$. Such a market structure will not be approved by a competition authority with a consumer bias, since $\Pi_a + \alpha S_a < \Pi_a + S_a < 0$ if $\alpha > 1$.

[10] I thank the referee of this chapter for pointing out this qualification.

[11] The model thus captures the important welfare trade-off that increased concentration can reduce production costs, but at the expense of an increase in market power. As such it provides an example where an efficiency defense as outlined by the US Horizontal Merger Guidelines (1997) or the EC Merger Regulation (2004) could be applied.

transfer of assets also benefits the consumers, since it reduces market concentration ($S_a > 0$). Because this alternative transfer of assets both gives rise to cost savings and reduce market concentration, it also maximizes the total surplus ($\Pi_a + S_a > \Pi_m + S_m > 0$). As a result, a consumer bias may be optimal by blocking the merger to monopoly and thereby induce the alternative transfer of assets, which maximizes the total surplus.

A partial merger, whereby the two firms merge but divest a subset of their assets (for example, some of their brands) to a new entrant, constitute a second example of an alternative to a full-fledged merger. Due to the entrant, the merger's anti-competitive effects are mitigated and still at least some of the merger induced cost savings are likely to materialize. Also in this example, a consumer bias may be optimal by blocking the full-fledged merger and thereby induce the alternative in the form of the partial merger with divestiture.[12]

The third example of an alternative change in market structure is an alternative merger. This interpretation of the model is straightforward if we are willing to accept the following assumption: the process of endogenous merger formation—the process by which firms choose a specific merger(s) when there are alternative mergers—selects the merger that maximizes the producer surplus. In this case the merger to monopoly should be reinterpreted as the merger, which, among all allowed mergers, maximizes the producer surplus. In such a setting, anti-competitive mergers may preempt pro-competitive ones[13] and, as a result, a welfare standard with a consumer bias may be optimal. In general, however, the literature on endogenous mergers suggests that it is difficult to motivate the above assumption.[14] Nevertheless, the assumption is not crucial for the chapter's main result, namely that a consumer bias is optimal in expected terms. What is important to note is that the result may need to be qualified if firms propose mergers which benefit consumers but at the expense of an even higher

---

[12] Of course the divestiture has the same qualitative effects as a remedy ordered by a competition authority. The notable difference is that here, it is the merging firms who propose the divestiture without any initial proposal or suggestion by the competition authority. Note that initial merger proposals, which include a divestiture proposal for the purpose of reducing market concentration, is not only a theoretical construct; in the 1992 merger between Nestlé and Perrier, the merging firms proposed to divest Pierrier's subsidiary Volvic to the competitor BSN (see Compte et al., 2002 for an in-depth discussion of this merger).

[13] Fridolfsson (2001a) makes this point in a model of endogenous merger formation with asymmetric firms.

[14] Horn and Persson (2001) provide some foundation for efficient outcomes from the firms' point of view in a game theoretical cooperative model of merger formation. Lyons' (2002) merger formation game suggests that the firms select the merger maximizing the producer surplus. To obtain this result, however, he makes sufficient assumptions on the underlying parameters of his oligopoly model and does not solve his merger game for the remaining parameters. In contrast, Kamien and Zang (1990, 1993) show in a non-cooperative model that the monopoly may not arise even though it maximizes the producer surplus. Fridolfsson and Stennek (2005a) highlight yet another inefficiency from the firms' point of view: profitable mergers may be delayed if it is even more profitable to remain as an outsider to mergers.

reduction in the producer surplus.[15] In such cases, a merger may not only be required to increase a weighted surplus with a consumer bias; it may also be required to increase the total surplus. This additional criterion in effect means that a competition authority could block a merger on the ground that it harms the firms themselves, possibly including the merging firms. Extending the powers of competition authorities in this direction may be perceived as delegating tasks to competition authorities, which go beyond the role of competition policy. The additional criterion should therefore be scrutinized with care before considering implementation.

The above examples share the common feature that the alternatives must be approved by the competition authority. Of course it is conceivable that the firms undertake an alternative course of action, which has not to be scrutinized by competition authorities. For example, internal reorganization or investment in new machinery may for each firm work as an imperfect substitute to the merger. They may also choose other forms of cooperation than mergers such as the establishment of for example a R&D joint venture. Such alternatives may also imply cost reductions without the negative side effects associated with merger induced increases in market concentration. These examples thereby suggest that a welfare standard with a consumer bias may be optimal. It should be emphasized, however, that the qualification discussed at the end of Section 11.4 applies in those cases.

11.6. Concluding remarks

The critical assumption behind the present consumer surplus defense in merger control is worth a final emphasis: the competition authority is assumed to perfectly assess the consequences of a *proposed* change in market structure, but not the consequences of *alternative* ones. It is widely recognized that the former assumption overestimates the ability of competition authorities. Given this wide consensus, the latter assumption seems much less problematic to accept. Yet it is striking that most competition authorities seem to be acutely aware of alternatives' relevance. The efficiency defenses as outlined by the US Horizontal Merger Guidelines (1997) and the EC Merger Regulation (2004) both stress that the efficiencies should be merger specific. The US failing firm defense constitutes one instance where competition authorities actively look for alternatives (to the status quo). Furthermore, the vast majority of problematic mergers are eventually cleared subject to the use of remedies. The proposed merger between the two Swedish truck manufacturers Volvo and Scania even suggests that the decision by the European Commission may have been influenced by the possibility

---

15 Such a scenario cannot be disregarded. Indeed, Fridolfsson and Stennek (2005b) show in a non-cooperative model of endogenous mergers that unprofitable mergers may occur if they harm competitors. Furthermore, mergers that harm competitors typically benefit consumers (see for example Farrell and Shapiro, 1990). Thus firms may well propose mergers, which benefit consumers while they reduce the producer surplus.

of alternative mergers.[16] All these observations suggest that real world competition authorities are more sophisticated with respect to alternatives than what has been assumed here. It should be emphasized, however, that even if competition authorities may sometimes identify alternatives and perhaps even evaluate their welfare effects accurately, these alternatives are not necessarily the ones maximizing welfare. If so, the argument underlying the present consumer surplus defense is still valid.

Finally, it should be emphasized that the main result is qualitative only. Absent some knowledge about the likelihood of alternatives and about the magnitude of the additional surplus generated, it is impossible to say something about the optimal weight on consumers. In fact, the optimal weight may even correspond to a pure consumer surplus standard if the distribution of the exogenous variables is sufficiently skewed in favor of the alternative.

Acknowledgements

This work has been significantly improved through numerous discussions with Johan Stennek. Comments from Mats Bergman, Jonas Björnestedt, Raymond Deneckere, Vivek Ghosal, Lars Persson, Susanna Sällström, from an anonymous referee and from participants in seminars and conference presentations at the Research Istitute of Industrial Economics, the Stockholm University, the Stockholm School of Economics, EARIE2002 in Madrid and IIOC2005 in Atlanta are also gratefully acknowledged. The author thanks Konkurrensverket for financial support.

References

Besanko, D., Spulber, D.F. (1993), Contested mergers and equilibrium antitrust policy. *The Journal of Law, Economics & Organization* 9 (1), 1–29.

Compte, O., Jenny, F., Rey, P. (2002), Capacity constraints, mergers and collusion. *European Economic Review* 46 (1), 1–29.

Crampton, P.S. (1994), Alternative approaches to competition law: Consumers' surplus, total surplus, total welfare and non-efficiency goals. *World Competition* 17, 55–86.

EC Merger Regulation (2004), Council Regulation (EC) No 139/2004 on the Control of Concentrations between Undertakings.

Farrell, J., Shapiro, C. (1990), Horizontal mergers: An equilibrium analysis. *American Economic Review* 80 (1), 107–126.

---

[16] When the two firms announced their intention to merge, there were plenty of rumors in the Swedish business press suggesting that the main motive was to preempt alternative mergers. The merger was subsequently blocked by the European Commission on the ground that it was deemed anti-competitive, and, within a few weeks, Volvo acquired the French truck manufacturer RVI. This latter merger was subsequently cleared, since the merger partners were judged to be more distant competitors. After the clearance, a few Swedish newspapers raised the concern that the European Commission was pursuing an active industrial policy.

Fershtman, C., Judd, K.L. (1987). Equilibrium incentives in oligopoly. *American Economic Review* 77 (5), 927–940.

Fridolfsson, S.-O. (2001a). Anti-competitive versus pro-competitive mergers. In: *Essays on Endogenous Merger Theory*. Dissertations in Economics, Stockholm University, Chapter 4, pp. 75–108.

Fridolfsson, S.-O. (2001b). A consumers' surplus defense in merger control. In: *Essays on Endogenous Merger Theory*. Dissertations in Economics, Stockholm University, Chapter 5, pp. 109–141.

Fridolfsson, S.-O., Stennek, J. (2005a). Hold-up of anticompetitive mergers. *International Journal of Industrial Organization* 23 (9–10), 753–775.

Fridolfsson, S.-O., Stennek, J. (2005b). Why mergers reduce profits and raise share prices—A theory of preemptive mergers. *Journal of the European Economic Association* 3 (5), 1083–1104.

Horn, H., Persson, L. (2001). Endogenous mergers in concentrated markets. *International Journal of Industrial Organization* 19 (8), 1213–1244.

Jenny, F. (1994). Competition and efficiency. In: Hawk, B.E. (Ed.), *Antitrust in a Global Economy*. Kluwer Law International, Fordham Corporate Law Institute, Chapter 10, pp. 185–220.

Kamien, M.I., Zang, I. (1990). The limits of monopolization through acquisition. *Quarterly Journal of Economics* 105 (2), 465–499.

Kamien, M.I., Zang, I. (1993). Monopolization by sequential acquisition. *Journal of Law, Economics & Organization* 9 (2), 205–229.

Lyons, B. (2002). Could politicians be more right than economists? A theory of merger standards. Centre for Competition and Regulation, Working Paper 02-1.

McFetridge, D.G. (1998). Merger enforcement under the competition act after 10 years. *Review of Industrial Organization* 13, 25–56.

Neven, D.J., Röller, L.-H. (2005). Consumer surplus versus welfare standard in a political economy model of merger control. *International Journal of Industrial Organization* 23 (9–10), 829–848.

Rogoff, K. (1985). The optimal degree of commitment to an intermediate monetary target. *Quarterly Journal of Economics* 100 (4), 1169–1189.

Röller, L.-H., Stennek, J., Verboven, F. (2001). Efficiency gains from mergers. *European Economy* 5, 31–128.

US Horizontal Merger Guidelines (1997). Department of Justice and Federal Trade Commission, Washington, United States.

Williamson, O.E. (1968). Economies as an antitrust defense: The welfare trade-offs. *American Economic Review* 58, 18–36.

CHAPTER 12

EU Merger Remedies: An Empirical Assessment

Tomaso Duso[a], Klaus Gugler[b] and Burcin Yurtoglu[b]

[a]*Humboldt University, Berlin, and WZB, Germany*
E-mail address: duso@wz-berlin.de
[b]*University of Vienna, Austria*
E-mail addresses: klaus.gugler@univie.ac.at; burcin.yurtoglu@univie.ac.at

Abstract
Mergers that substantially lessen competition are challenged by antitrust authorities. Instead of blocking anticompetitive transitions straight away, authorities might choose to negotiate with the merging parties and allow the transactions to proceed with modifications that restore or preserve the competition in the involved markets. We study a sample of 167 mergers that were under the European Commission's scrutiny from 1990 to 2002. We use an event study methodology to identify the potential anticompetitive effects of mergers as well as the remedial provisions on these transactions. Stock market reactions around the day of the merger's announcement provide information on the first question, whereas the stock market reactions around the commission's final decision day convey information about the outcome of the bargaining process between the authority and the merging parties. We first classify mergers according to their effects on competition and then we develop hypotheses on the effects that remedies are supposed to achieve depending on the merger's competitive outcome. We isolate several stylized facts. First, we find that remedies were not always appropriately imposed. Second, the market seems to be able to predict remedies' effectiveness when applied in phase I. Third, the market also seems able to produce a good prior to phase II's clearances and prohibitions, but not to remedies. This can be due either to a measurement problem or related to the increased merging firms' bargaining power during the second phase of the merger review.

Keywords: merger control, remedies, European Commission, event studies

JEL classifications: L4, K21, C12, C13

12.1. Introduction

Few major mergers are completed without some conditions being imposed by an antitrust authority such as divestitures, provision of access, termination of agree-

CONTRIBUTIONS TO ECONOMIC ANALYSIS
VOLUME 282 ISSN: 0573-8555
DOI: 10.1016/S0573-8555(06)82012-2

ments or other behavioral requirements. These conditions that seek to remedy the competition concerns caused by the merger are an important instrument in merger control, yet an under-researched topic in the economic literature. Looking at the European experience (see Table 12.1), the economic importance of merger remedies is evidenced by the fact that 191 of the 2,592 merger cases (around 7%) notified to the European Commission (EC) until the end of 2004 have been decided as being compatible with the common market only with commitments (either article 6.2 or 8.2).[1] More than *half* of phase II decisions (72 out of 121—59%) are compatible only with commitments, yet only 19 mergers have been blocked since 1990. What is more, mergers that are cleared with commitments are apparently the most important ones in terms of competition policy concerns, since market power is most likely to increase due to the merger.

The situation is quite analogous in the USA. In its 1998 and 1999 fiscal years, the Federal Trade Commission (FTC) challenged 63 mergers; of these 41 (65%) involved negotiated restructuring, 18 (29%) were abandoned, and only four (6%) were litigated.

Despite their economic importance, remedies are an under-researched topic as far as their economic effects are concerned. In particular, there is no systematic econometric evidence on the question of whether ordered remedies achieve what they are supposed to achieve, namely to assure that proposed mergers do not lead to an increase in the firms' market power net of any efficiency gains. We review the existing evidence in the next section.

This chapter answers these questions by analyzing the effects of remedies in a sample of 167 mergers analyzed by the European Commission between 1990 and 2002. We use an event study methodology to identify the potential anticompetitive effects of mergers as well as the remedial provisions on these transactions. Stock market reactions around the day of the merger's announcement provide information on the first question, whereas the stock market reactions around the day of the commission's final decision convey information about the outcome of the bargaining process between the authority and the merging parties.

We isolate several stylized facts. First, we find that remedies were not always appropriately imposed. That is, sometimes remedies were unduly imposed in mergers that we found being efficiency increasing (type I errors), while some other times remedies were not imposed in mergers that we found to increase market power (type II errors). Second, judging from our results on abnormal returns the market seems to believe that remedies are effective when applied in phase I, since positive abnormal returns for rivals are decreased when remedies are announced. Third, it appears that the market is able to produce a good prior to phase II's clearances and prohibitions, but not for remedies in phase II. We suggest that information leakage between phase I and phase II decisions plays an

---

[1] See http://www.europa.eu.int/comm/competition/mergers/cases/stats.html for statistics on EU merger control.

Table 12.1: Merger cases and European Commission's decisions.

Article, kind of decision	**90**	**91**	**92**	**93**	**94**	**95**	**96**	**97**	**98**	**99**	**00**	**01**	**02**	**03**	**04**	**All**
6.1.a	2	5	9	4	5	9	6	4	6	1	1	1	1	0	0	**54**
6.1.b	5	47	43	49	78	90	109	118	207	236	293	299	240	203	220	**2237**
6.1.b remedies (6.2)	0	3	4	0	2	3	0	2	12	19	28	13	10	11	12	**119**
9.3	0		1	1	1	0	3	7	4	4	6	7	13	9	3	**59**
Tot. Phase I	7	55	57	54	86	102	118	131	229	260	328	320	264	151	235	**2469**
8.2	0	1	1	1	2	2	1	1	3	0	3	5	2	2	2	**26**
8.2. remedies	0	3	3	2	2	3	3	7	4	8	12	10	5	6	4	**72**
8.3	0	1	0	0	1	2	3	1	2	1	2	5	0	0	1	**19**
8.4	0	0	0	0	0	0	0	2	0	0	0	0	2	0	0	**4**
Tot. Phase II		5	4	3	5	7	7	11	9	10	17	20	9	6	7	**121**
Total final decisions	7	60	61	57	91	109	125	142	238	270	345	340	273	157	242	**2590**

Source: European Commission, Directorate Competition.
Note: 6.1.a: Out of scope of merger legislation; 6.1.b: compatible; 6.1.b remedies (6.2): compatible with commitments; 9.3: referral to member states; 8.2: compatible; 8.2 remedies: compatible with commitments; 8.3: prohibition; 8.4: restore effective competition.

important role in explaining these results. An additional explanation would be due to the merging firms' increased bargaining power vis-à-vis the commission during the phase II investigation, in those cases where a prohibition is politically unfeasible.

The chapter proceeds as follows. In Section 12.2 we describe the existing literature on remedies as well as event studies that have been used to assess antitrust decisions. In Section 12.3 we present the institutional background of the European Union (EU) merger control, while Section 12.4 discusses the policy issues related with the use of remedies and presents an international comparison. In Section 12.5 we discuss our approach, describe the event study methodology that we use to assess mergers' competitiveness as well as remedies effectiveness, and formulate hypotheses concerning the use and the effects of remedies. In Section 12.6 we introduce the data, present the results of the event studies and, accordingly, give taxonomy of mergers. The results of our empirical analysis are presented in Section 12.7, while Section 12.8 sums up and concludes with some remarks and directions for further research.

12.2. The evidence on merger remedies

12.2.1. General

Elzinga (1969) is perhaps the first study, which tried to evaluate the *ex post* effectiveness of ordered remedies in challenged mergers. Using a random sample of 39 antimerger cases, he analyzes the effectiveness of remedies under the Celler-Kefauver Amendment of 1950, which revitalized the antimerger statute contained in Section 7 of the Clayton Act. He rates remedies using a four category ranking system: successful, sufficient, deficient, or unsuccessful. The cases are also measured by the time required to achieve the remedy. Elzinga's results suggest that only one out of ten cases can be classified as successful or sufficient. These two categories correspond to cases where a full or partial divestiture was achieved and where these assets created viable competitors in less than two years time.

Rogowsky (1986) extends Elzinga's analysis to 104 merger cases brought by the FTC or DOJ from 1968 to 1980. His case by case evaluation shows that in less than half of the cases only a full or partial divestiture was achieved. Once the timeliness of remedies is taken into account, he concludes that only two out of five cases remain successful or sufficient, because the ordered assets were divested more than two years after the acquisition.[2]

Ellert (1976) is the first study that analyzes the valuation effects of antimerger complaints. He studies the abnormal returns of 205 acquirers challenged under Section 7 of the Clayton Act from 1950 to 1972 and shows that acquirers' returns

---

[2] Pfunder et al. (1972) offer a similar analysis of US divestiture orders.

increase substantially over a long period before the antitrust complaint. The cumulative abnormal returns average 23% (7%) over 100 (48) months before the complaint. In 123 mergers where defendants were ordered to divest acquired assets, the cumulative abnormal returns are much higher, reaching 31% (13%) over 100 (48) months leading to the complaint. In the month of the complaint, both types of companies experienced negative abnormal returns of almost 2%.[3] Since the decrease in returns during the complaint and settlement periods is much smaller than the increase over the period that led to the complaint, Ellert argues that antimerger law has been largely unsuccessful in reversing the discounted monopoly gains achieved by these mergers.

More recently, Baer (1999) reviewed FTC divestiture orders entered during the agency's fiscal years 1990 through 1994. He examined 35 orders involving 50 divestitures from a broad set of industries by interviewing 37 buyers, eight respondents and two third parties. The divestiture study reached three overall conclusions. First, most divestitures appear to have created viable competitors in the market of concern (28 out of 37), whereas a higher percentage (19 out of 22) of divestitures were successful when they involved the sale of an entire ongoing business. Second, respondents tended to look for marginally acceptable buyers (those least likely to become serious competitors) and engage in strategic conduct intended to impede the success of these buyers (e.g. late and poor supply of indispensable inputs). Third, most buyers of divested assets did not have access to sufficient information to prevent mistakes in the course of their acquisitions and/or had incentives that differed from those of the FTC. Despite its novelty, however, the divestiture study suffers from severe drawbacks, namely that only qualitative information (interviews) has been used to assess the effects of a limited number (35) of divestiture orders.

Motta et al. (2003) present a descriptive analysis of the use of remedies in EU merger control and enumerate the most important pros and cons of the different provisions used by the European Commission. One can group merger remedies in two categories. (1) Structural remedies modify the allocation of property rights and possibly create new firms. The most important structural remedy is divestitures of entire ongoing businesses. Others involve the disposing of shareholdings or the break up of other structural links such as interlocking directorates. (2) Non-structural remedies or behavioral remedies constrain the merging firms' property rights. They might consist of contractual arrangements such as compulsory licensing or access to intellectual or infra-structural property. Also, many merger decisions involve a package of different remedies. The most important advantage of structural remedies is that they are supposed to fully and timely solve the competition concerns and need no (or not much) further monitoring by antitrust authorities. However, while Motta et al. (2003) in

---

[3] According to Ellert, the magnitude of this effect is consistent with the direct legal costs, loss of executive time, and uncertainty affecting business decision-making introduced by the antitrust challenge.

principle favor the use of structural remedies to clear problematic mergers, they point to information asymmetry and incentive problems as well as to the increased possibility of pro-collusive effects of divestitures. Thus, they suggest the same double test that the EC uses to assess mergers also for structural remedies, namely that both single firm and joint dominance will not likely arise after divestiture (unilateral and pro-collusive effects).

Moreover, as mentioned by Farrell (2003), the effectiveness of structural remedies may suffer from inadequate buyers, "over" (or miss-) fixing and the discounting of merger efficiencies. Cabral (2003) also qualifies the superiority of structural remedies, in his case asset sales. Assuming a "free entry" equilibrium before and after the merger in a spatially differentiated oligopoly, the author shows that by selling assets (e.g. stores) to potential rivals, merging firms effectively "buy them off", that is, dissuade them from opening new stores, which may be detrimental to consumers. The crucial assumption is the "free-entry" assumption: If the two firms merge and there is no entry, then a monopoly with two stores arises; whereas if merging firms sell assets (stores) to a third firm, then duopoly competition is maintained. This rationale highlights the importance of assessing the counterfactual to the remedy decision, i.e. would entry occur in the absence of imposing (structural) remedies or not.

12.2.2. Evidence using event study methodologies

One common prediction of some prevalent models in Industrial Organization, e.g. the Cournot model, the Bertrand model with differentiated products and the dominant firm model, is that horizontal mergers, *ceteris paribus*, result in higher product prices in equilibrium.[4] While profit increases for the merging (insider) firms can be due to two effects—the market power effect but also (desirable) efficiency gains—profit increases of rival firms unambiguously must result from the post merger increase in market power.

This latter effect may stem from several sources. First, in the logic of the aforementioned papers, firms in an oligopolistic setting have a unilateral incentive to raise prices after the merger if there are no efficiency gains. Second, an increased possibility for collusive behavior post merger might also arise, because for instance the number of firms has gone down.[5]

Under the market power hypothesis, the merging firms' combined stock prices should increase at the time of the merger announcement. Any antitrust complaint that decreases the likelihood of this event or reduces its market power related impact (such as an ordered divestiture) is expected to have a negative impact on stock prices. The same pattern of abnormal stock price reaction is expected for firms that are merging to achieve efficiency gains.

---

[4] See for instance Salant et al. (1983) and Farrell and Shapiro (1990).

[5] These are called "unilateral" and "coordinated" effects in the EU merger regulation's guidelines.

Since effective collusion generates monopoly rents, the collusion hypothesis implies that the merging firms' rivals in a horizontal merger will earn higher profits after the merger and, hence, experience positive abnormal returns around the merger announcement. Any antitrust complaint that decreases the likelihood of this event is again expected to decrease the rival firms' market value. Thus, a direct test of the collusion hypothesis, which relies on the efficient capital market hypothesis, is based on the abnormal stock returns of rivals that are observed around the date of the merger's announcement and around the announcement date of the antitrust complaint. The fact that positive abnormal returns around the merger's announcement for both the merging firms and their rivals are reversed around the time of the announcement of the antitrust complaint, suggests that the proposed merger is anticompetitive and the remedy is effective.

If the new firm resulting form a merger is more efficient than the merging companies, the product market competition is intensified and consequently there will be an increase in output and lower prices. Merging firms are expected to have higher profits due to their enhanced efficiency and this change should be reflected in an abnormal stock price reaction of companies announcing such mergers. The horizontal rivals of the merging companies have to cope with lower prices in the product market and, hence, they are expected to have lower profits compared to the pre-merger market structure. This product market effect implies a negative abnormal return for the rival firms' shares around the time of the merger announcement. Any event that decreases the likelihood of such an efficiency increasing merger to go through should be good news for the rivals. Consequently, the efficiency hypothesis predicts that rivals in an efficiency increasing merger exhibit positive abnormal returns upon the announcement of an antitrust complaint or an ordered remedy that reduces the efficiency effect of the merger.

A complicating factor concerning efficiency increasing mergers is the possibility that the merger announcement signals some additional information that might reverse the rivals' expected profitability. Eckbo (1983) and Eckbo and Wier (1985) argue that if the production technologies of competitors are related, then the proposed efficiency increasing merger can also signal opportunities for the rivals to increase their productivity. Under this scenario, the merger announcement is good news from the rival firms' perspective, because it makes them (or the market) aware of real profit opportunities that were so far unknown. The potential magnitude of this "information effect" can be, according to Eckbo and Eckbo and Wier, so large that it might offset the product market effect. Hence, they make unambiguous prediction with respect to the rivals' abnormal returns around the merger announcement and around the announcement of the antitrust complaint. They analyze a sample of 259 horizontal and vertical mergers in mining and manufacturing industries of which 76 were challenged by government agencies. Though they find significantly positive abnormal returns to shareholders of the rival firms, they explain that the positive valuation effect may be due to positive information released by the merger. To separate the market power effect from the information effect, they also estimate abnormal returns to rival firms around the time of an antitrust challenge to the merger. They find no statistically significant abnormal decreases in the stock prices of rival firms and they claim that this is inconsistent with the market power hypothesis. In a similar paper, Stillman (1983) analyzes 11 horizontal mergers attempted between 1964 and 1972 that were challenged by antitrust enforcement authorities. Instead of looking at the portfolio of rivals, he studies the valuation effects for each of the 11 mergers. His findings suggest that only for one merger the market power hypothesis cannot be rejected.

The second complicating factor concerning the rivals' stock price is the possibility that the merger announcement signals that a rival is more likely to become a merger target. The sign pattern of the rivals' abnormal returns would then generally be the same as under the collusion hypothesis. If the proposed merger increases the likelihood that a rival will become an acquirer, then the implied sign pattern would be the same as for the collusion or efficiency hypotheses, depending on whether the market predicted higher or lower profits as a result of the expected acquisition (McGuckin et al., 1992).[6]

Schumann (1993) argues that the impact of antitrust complaints on the value of rival firms will also depend on the relative size of the rivals. For example, an antitrust complaint to an efficiency increasing merger between the larger firms in an industry, will increase the probability that small rivals will be subsequently acquired (the "small firm in play" hypothesis). Alternatively, if the merger with a small rival (by either a large or small rival) cannot create the efficiencies achievable through a combination of large firms (because of different technologies), the antitrust complaint benefits smaller rivals at the expense of larger ones by protecting them from the efficiency gains that their larger rivals might otherwise have achieved (the "disadvantaged small rival" hypothesis). Schumann (1993) conducts an event study analysis of 37 acquisitions that were challenged by the FTC over the period 1981–1987 and comes up with the same pattern of abnormal returns as in Eckbo (1983) and Eckbo and Wier (1985). Consistent with his arguments, he also finds that rivals' abnormal returns around the time of the antitrust complaint are positive and larger for rivals with smaller market shares.

In an analysis of trust formation during the first U.S. merger wave (1897–1903), Banerjee and Eckard (1998) find that merging companies exhibit value gains of about 12% to 18%. They conclude that these gains are due to the enhanced operational efficiency, because the trust competitors suffer an economically and statistically significant value loss (ranging from 3.5% to 9.5%).

[6] A recent test of the acquisition probability hypothesis (Song and Walkling, 2000) suggests that rivals earn significantly positive abnormal returns and rivals that become targets in the subsequent year earn significantly larger abnormal returns at the initial merger announcement than untargeted rivals. The sample of rivals in this study is, however, based on Value Line classifications and not on some type of relevant market based on antitrust considerations. Hence, their results are also consistent with the argument that acquisitions have a disciplining effect in an industry and lead to a reduction in agency costs of the rival firms (Servaes and Tamayo, 2005).

Simpson (2001) employs the same methodology to test the collusion and efficiency hypothesis in a merger of department stores in Denver and Southern California. He finds positive abnormal returns for merging firms and their rivals consistent with an increased concentration due to this merger. He also reports that rivals that operate in areas more likely to be affected by the merger experience much higher abnormal returns. To discriminate between the collusion and acquisition probability hypothesis, Simpson looks at the abnormal returns of likely targets among all rivals and finds that these had returns, which were 2.3% higher than other rivals. The rivals which are most likely to gain from the collusion have, however, still substantial (7.7%) abnormal returns.

McAfee and Williams (1988) criticized the Eckbo–Stillman methodology on two grounds. First, the failure to detect market power may be due to the fact that rivals were large conglomerates, which received only a small portion of their profits from the relevant market. Second, the existence of an anti-merger policy may have had a deterrent effect on the types of mergers that were attempted.[7]

Mullin et al. (1995) do find evidence for the market power hypothesis. They investigate the U.S. Steel consolidation and incorporate an examination of downstream firms in addition to merging and rival firms. They find reaction patterns that imply dissolution of U.S. Steel lowers steel prices and raises output. Slovin et al. (1991) analyze whether airline consolidation post-deregulation generates monopoly profits. They find insignificant abnormal returns for the acquiring firms, but significantly positive abnormal returns to airline target firms and argue that there is no evidence of monopoly gains from carrier consolidations after deregulation. In contrast, Singal (1996) documents both significantly positive abnormal returns to airline bidding firms and their target in a sample of mergers from the airline industry during 1985–1988. His tests show that mergers have enhanced both the market power and the efficiency of merging firms.[8] It is worth noting that Singal's results are confirmed by an analysis of product prices and profit changes from mergers.

More recent evidence is also inconclusive. Fee and Shaw (2004) find only slightly supportive evidence consistent with collusion. They look at the upstream and downstream product market effects of horizontal mergers and acquisitions and identify the customers, suppliers, and rivals of the merging firms. In their sample of 554 U.S. mergers, the net effect of a merger on a particular supplier depends largely on the supplier's ability to retain its product market relationship with the merged entity. Consistent with previous studies, Fee and Shaw (2004) also report positive abnormal returns to rivals of merging firms around announcements which range from 0.67% to 2.61%. An antitrust challenge to

---

[7] However, Eckbo (1992) comparing US and Canadian experiences rejects this conjecture. Song and Walking (2000) propose an alternative explanation to the market power hypothesis when finding positive abnormal returns for rivals, namely that these positive returns are due to the investors' anticipation of further M&A activity in the same industry.

[8] Kim and Singal (1993) show that the impact of efficiency gains on airfares is more than offset by the post merger increased market power.

such mergers, however, does not lead to negative abnormal returns for rivals. These findings concerning the rival firms' stock price reaction is corroborated by those presented by Shahrur (2005) in a more recent study using a sample of 463 US mergers and takeovers. His results suggest that the average merger in his sample is driven by efficiency considerations rather than collusion and buyer-power motives. The evidence provided by Bittlingmayer and Hazlett (2000) on the antitrust action against Microsoft also rejects the joint hypothesis that (a) Microsoft's conduct was anticompetitive and (b) antitrust policy enforcement produced net efficiency gains.[9]

In contrast to this fairly long list of event studies on the merger activity in the US and partly in Canada, there are only a few studies of mergers that were analyzed by the European Commission.[10] Duso et al. (2006a), using the same sample and, partly, the same methodology as utilized in this chapter, find evidence in favor of the market power hypothesis for a sub-sample of EU mergers. Yet they look only at the reactions around the time of the merger's announcement. By contrasting the markets' reactions with the actual commission's decisions, they define type I (i.e. procompetitive mergers blocked or modified by the authority) and type II errors (anticompetitive mergers that were unconditionally cleared). In a second step, they use regression analysis to study the determinants of such mistakes. They show that procedural issues, market definition, as well as the merging firms' country and industry of origin play a crucial role in predicting both kinds of errors. However, they do not find any evidence of lobbying by firms to be effective.

Aktas et al. (2004a) provides another notable exception. They look at 602 decisions by the EU Commission involving 1070 firms. Consistent with the rest of literature they document significant abnormal returns for the target firms and smaller and less significant bidder abnormal returns. They also estimate the abnormal price reaction to phase I and phase II decisions and show that outright prohibitions are associated with negative abnormal returns and approvals subject to conditions are relatively good news. In another paper the same authors (Aktas et al., 2004b) suggest that European merger control is protectionist. They reach this conclusion by showing that the likelihood of an intervention by the EU Commission is higher, whenever the merger is proposed by a bidder from outside the EU and has a negative effect on European rivals.

12.3. Institutional background

There are four stages in the application of merger policy (Lyons, 2004): (1) The review (investigation) decision, (2) Review, (3) Decision to prohibit or require remedies, and (4) Appeal.

---

[9] Carstensen (1999) offers a less favorable conclusion on the Microsoft case. See also Comanor (2001), who discusses the problem of remedy in the specific Microsoft case.

[10] Brady and Feinberg (2000) used event studies to evaluate the impact of the introduction of the EU merger regulation. They focus on merging firms and do not consider the effect on competitors.

The first stage, which corresponds to phase I in the EU Merger control, selects the cases that might raise a competitive concern. The second stage (phase II investigation) leads to an assessment of the transaction's competitive effects.[11] The third stage (phase II decision) either leads to a prohibition decision or to the choice of remedies that are aimed to remove the competitive issues detected in stage 2. The fourth and final stage constitutes an important disciplining mechanism for the soundness of decisions taken in the earlier stages.

In the US, stages 1 and 2 are concentrated in the hands of the two competition agencies (FTC and DOJ). They then present their analysis to the court for a preliminary injunction which corresponds to stage 3. While most of the cases are resolved before the agency goes to the court, the immediacy of the courts has an important disciplining effect (Lyons, 2004).

In the EU, however, stages 1, 2 and 3 are concentrated in the hands of the Directorate General Competition (DG Comp).[12] A single team conducts the entire investigation and an appeal system takes a period of several years.[13] The role of the courts in Europe is limited to a formal and not substantial control of the commission's decision. However, in the last years some very controversial cases (prohibitions) were overturned by the Court of First Instance and, in second instance, by the European Court of Justice.[14] This is considered one major factor that triggered a substantial review of the merger regulation as well as some fundamental changes in the institutional details such as the creation of the Chief Economist Office.

12.3.1. The EU merger regulation

Merger control in the EU began in 1989 with the European Communities Merger Regulation (ECMR), which came into force in September 21st 1990. The regulation was amended on May 1, 2004 after a 3-year review process.[15] Since 1990 more than 2,500 mergers were under the scrutiny of the European Commission.

---

[11] Eventually, remedies can also be imposed in Phase I. For details see the next section.

[12] Every DG in the European Commission is headed by a politically appointed Commissioner. In our sample period Karel Van Miert and Mario Monti were the DG Comp commissioners. Currently, Neelie Kroes is the head of DG Comp.

[13] In the Kali+Salz/MDK/Treuhand merger (M.308) of December 1993 the Court annulled the Commission's remedies on the basis of insufficient evidence to support collective dominance. The Court's decision (C-68/94 & C-30/95) came in March 1998.

[14] The cases were Airtours/First Choice (M.1524), Tetra Laval/Sidel (M.2416), Schneider/Legrand (M.2283), and General Electric/Honeywell (M.2022). Interestingly, according to our analysis, three out of four of these cases were type I errors, i.e. procompetitive mergers that were unduly blocked by the Commission.

[15] Council Regulation (EEC) No. 4064/89 was amended by Council Regulation (EC) No. 139/2004 on the control of concentrations between undertakings that entered into force on January 20, 2004. Commission Regulation (EC) No. 802/2004 implements the Council Regulation (EC) No. 139/2004. See http://europa.eu.int/comm/competition/mergers/review/ for a description of the review process.

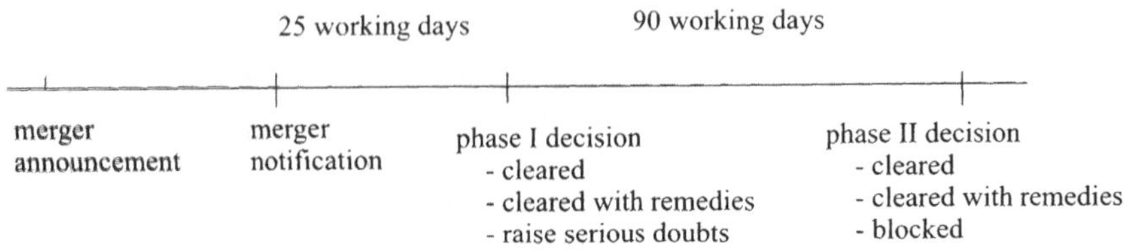

Fig. 12.1: The EU merger control.

According to the ECMR, a merger has community dimension if it takes place between firms with a combined worldwide turnover of at least 5 billion Euros and a turnover within the European Economic Area of more than 250 million Euros for each of at least two of the undertakings. This definition also includes mergers between firms that produce outside of Europe and sell into Europe. If necessary, a merger can be referred back to the member states for review.

Art. 2(3) of the ECMR states that "A concentration, which creates or strengthens a dominant position as a result of which effective competition would be significantly impeded in the common market or in a substantial part of it, shall be declared incompatible with the common market." This is commonly referred to as the dominance test (DT). DT constitutes an important difference to the SLC (Substantial lessening of competition) test, which is used by the US competition authorities. Some observers (e.g., Lyons, 2004) argue that the DT puts unnecessary weight on the concept of dominance in cases where the more important issue concerns the *significant impediment of effective competition.*[16]

The regulation defines the legal steps, which serve to control concentrations between undertakings (see Figure 12.1). Merging parties are obliged to notify their intentions to merge to the commission when the deal has a community dimension. After receiving notification of the concentration, the commission has 25 working days to asses whether the concentration is compatible with the common market (the so-called phase I).

After this short period of time, the commission can either clear the proposed concentration unconditionally (Art. 6.1.b), it can decide to let it go through after verifying that the commitments and obligations proposed by the undertakings can effectively restore competition (Art. 6.2), or it can decide that the proposed concentrations raise serious doubts as to its compatibility with the common market (Art. 6.1c) and, therefore, a more in depth analysis is needed. In this case, the commission opens the so-called phase II, which consists of 90 working days. During this period of time, an in depth investigation is carried out. Generally, the commission makes use of the entire available time, given the problematic nature of these cases, after which it has to come to a final decision: either to block the merger (Art. 8.3) or to let it through unconditionally or with commitments and obligations (Art. 8.2).

[16] The new merger regulation, which is applicable from May 1, 2004, focuses on the impact of a merger on competition.

Looking at Figure 12.1, there are three events, which are important for our empirical analysis. The first one is the merger announcement, which we define as the first rumor appearing in the press about the proposed merger, and should help us identify the market assessment of the competitive effects of the merger. The other two relevant events are the phase I and the phase II decision dates, which should help us identify the effect of remedial action, as we will discuss in Section 12.5.

12.4. Merger remedies

Before describing how different jurisdictions deal with the use of remedies in merger control, we shall illustrate several commonly accepted principles guiding most antitrust authorities.[17] Largely, these principles were stated in the FTC's Remedies Guidelines, which were issued at the end of 1999 and were strongly influenced by Baer's (1999) study mentioned earlier.[18]

First of all, the use of remedies should be considered only if they are demonstrably necessary, i.e. the competition authority has the burden to prove that the mergers might impede or reduce competition. In this case, the merging parties have to come up with proposed solutions to the competitive concerns raised by the deal.

Structural remedies, in particular divestitures, should be preferred to behavioral remedies—such as termination of exclusive agreements, obligations on licensing and access to essential infrastructures or technology, use of patents, etc.—because they are supposed to fully and timely solve the competitive harm caused by the merger. Moreover, they need not much further monitoring by antitrust authorities. Conduct remedies are, however, not prohibited and might be used, mostly in a remedies-package proposed by the merging parties.

The divestiture should be a demonstrably autonomous on-going business unit comprising the entire business of one of the merging parties. This preference for "as is" divestitures is supported by the higher success rate of such divestitures as compared to a limited divestiture in the FTC's divestitures study (Baer, 1999). In some cases (mostly in retail markets) the agencies require the divestiture of overlapping assets to ensure that there is no increase in concentration.

A second aspect of the preferred divestitures is the increasing use of up-front buyers, which has been considered as the "most vital tool in assuring a successful divestiture" (Parker and Balto, 2000).[19] An up-front buyer is less commonly

---

[17] See the study on merger remedies by the OECD (2004) on this issue.

[18] The EU guidelines were very much affected by this study as well. Former EU competition commissioner Mario Monti (2003) stated: "The Commission's approach to remedies as set out in the notice was influenced by the FTC's previous study on the divestiture process [. . .]. Furthermore, the EU and US antitrust authorities discussed their respective approaches to remedies within the framework of a working group on merger control. The exchange of expertise in this group proved invaluable to the drafting of the Notice on Remedies."

[19] Unlike the FTC, the DOJ generally does not insist that the parties identify the buyer upfront, and is amenable to divestitures arranged independently by the parties that do not require entry of a

required when the divested assets constitute a standalone business. The agencies are also using crown jewel provisions, which require the divestiture of additional highly marketable assets, if the merging firms fail to divest the original asset package as required by the consent decree. Finally, a divestiture trustee shall oversee the implementation of the commitments.

12.4.1. The use of remedies in the EU

At the end of 2001, the European Commission issued the Commission Notice (2001/C68/03) on remedies acceptable under Council Regulation (EEC) No. 4096/89 and under Commission Regulation (EC) No. 447/89, which gives guidelines on the use of remedial action in merger control. These guidelines were an important step in making the process of using remedies more transparent, to increase legal certainty, as well as to achieve convergence towards the American antitrust procedure.[20]

The notice on remedies clearly states that the commission is required to demonstrate that the proposed concentration raises competition concerns. However, it is then the responsibility of the parties to prove that the proposed remedies fully eliminate such concerns (see Monti, 2003). Moreover, the parties must provide specific details and procedures, called in the EU antitrust jargon "obligations", relating to the commitments' implementation.

The preferred remedy is the divestiture of viable standalone businesses, i.e. structural remedies, but other remedies are possible such as exclusive agreements, licensing, and access to the necessary infrastructure or technology. The divested activities must be preferably an already existing business unit that can operate on a standalone basis. The purchaser must be suitable and has to be approved by the commission.

Parallel to the introduction of the remedies guidelines a Remedies Enforcement Unit was established within the DG Comp with the aim of developing and ensuring a consistent policy for remedies in merger cases. The unit is expected to follow the implementation of remedies and their revision, as well as monitor their effectiveness. Therefore, it is supposed to develop over time best practice guidelines and enhance transparency in the remedies' policy.

The implementation of the commitments is an equally delicate step, which involves the monitoring of accepted divestitures, the approval of mandates to trustees and, finally, the approval of proposed buyers for the divested assets. The role and powers of trustees have been reinforced by the remedies notice. The

---

formal consent decree (the "fix-it-first" approach). Halverson and Ewing (2005) argue that the DOJ believes that it has no power to review and block a different transaction from the one, which the parties have not already agreed to ("post-fix"). The EU Commission, instead, seem to follow the FTC approach and requires the merging parties to propose the buyer.

[20] The FTC had already issued remedies guidelines in 1999. The Antitrust Division of the DOJ, instead, issued its remedies guidelines in 2004.

trustee should ensure that no competitive harm comes to the assets by the divestiture during the period between the implementation of the original operation and the sale.

12.4.2. The use of remedies in the USA and other jurisdictions[21]

USA

Section 12.7 of the Clayton Act (*15 USC §8*) prohibits mergers that have the likely effect of substantially lessening competition (SLC) or tending to create a monopoly in the relevant market. Merger remedies have received little attention until Congress enacted the Hart-Scott-Rodino Antitrust Improvements Act in 1976 (*15 USC §18a*) (HSR Act).[22] Subject to certain exemptions, the HSR Act requires merging parties in transactions above certain thresholds to file a notification form with the FTC and the Antitrust Division of the DOJ before closing the transaction. The two agencies have 30 days to investigate the merger and, if their competitive concerns are not resolved, they may issue a second request for additional significant information.[23] The waiting period is then extended by a further 30 days after the parties declare themselves in substantial compliance with the second request, at which time the parties are allowed to proceed with the deal unless the government has initiated proceedings to block the transaction. The pre-closing notification guarantees the agencies timely knowledge of potentially anticompetitive mergers. The HSR filing and second request processes provide them with information to analyze the competition issues, to prepare for a preliminary injunction hearing, and to evaluate any proposed remedy. Accordingly, the average number of FTC merger enforcement actions after the HSR Act increased significantly.[24]

Both the FTC and the DOJ prefer to resolve concerns about anticompetitive effects by using structural remedies that require the parties to divest business lines or assets to restore the competition reduced by the merger.[25] In general, such remedies are negotiated by the parties with the agency staff and then incorporated into a binding consent order issued by the FTC; or a binding consent decree issued by a federal court at the request of the DOJ.

---

[21] We will not discuss the remedies' policy for the UK and Germany in this section, since the key authority in Europe is the European Commission. However, German antitrust principles and tradition have very strongly influenced the European approach to competition policy since its beginning. See Motta (2004) for a historical perspective on European vs. US antitrust policy.

[22] Baer and Redcay (2003).

[23] "Second Request" refers to the official "Request for Additional Information and Documentary Material," which the agencies may issue pursuant to 15. USC §18(a)e.

[24] Baer and Redcay (2003) report that between 1983 and 1989 HSR filings averaged 1877 per year. Over the same period the FTC averaged 11 merger enforcement actions annually. For the period between 1993 and 1999, those figures were 3090 and 30, respectively. The workload statistics of the Antitrust Division of the DOJ for the fiscal years 2000 and 2003 show that these numbers are 2375 and 10, respectively.

[25] See http://www.ftc.gov/bc/mergerfaq.htm.

Behavioral remedies are considered to be a less satisfactory solution than a divestiture, since they often involve some form of ongoing regulation (Parker and Balto, 2000). On the other hand, structural remedies are "relatively clean and certain" (McDavid and Breed, 2005). In some cases the FTC has used behavioral remedies such as firewalls and nondiscrimination provisions in vertical mergers.

Japan

The Japan Fair Trade Commission (JFTC) is responsible for the initiation of an investigation of conduct that may violate the Antimonopoly Act (Act Concerning Prohibition of Private Monopolization and Maintenance of Fair Trade—Act No. 54, 1947). The Act prohibits mergers or acquisitions where the effect may be to substantially restrain competition or where such a transaction is implemented through an unfair trade practice. The Act has been clarified by guidelines published by the JFTC in 1998. Recently, JFTC (2004) has published a new set of guidelines, which also devote some space on potential remedies.

The JFTC guidelines consider the divestitures as the most effective means to restore competition. The divestitures aim to establish new competitors or strengthen the existing competitors of the merging parties. Besides the usual divestitures, such measures include the reduction in the voting rights or cancellation of interlocking directorates in another company.

If a divestiture is not a viable option, then JFTC considers promotions of imports or entry as remedial measures as well. Behavioral remedies include the prohibition of discriminatory treatment of competitors with respect to essential facilities for business and regulatory policies by fixing some aspects of the behavior of the merging parties.[26]

Australia

The Australian Competition and Consumer Commission's (ACCC) Guidelines (1999) outline the merger review process under the Trade Practices Act 1974. The ACCC considers divestitures as a more viable remedy than behavioral undertakings such as price, output, quality or service guarantees and obligations. In practice, very few mergers attract ACCC concern and of those a vast majority goes forward after slight changes to their structure. For example, in 1996–97 147 mergers were considered by the ACCC, of these 140 were not opposed and of the remaining seven, two proceeded with remedies and the other five were withdrawn.

---

[26] Besides a reduction of their turnaround slots, the remedy package in the merger between Japanese Airlines Co. Ltd. (JAL) and Japan Airsystem Co. Ltd. (JAS) included remedial measures in favor of new airlines as well as regulatory measures such as a reduction of 10% on normal fares and the requirement that fares would not be raised during a period of 3 years (Arai, 2004).

Canada

In Canada, the Commissioner of Competition oversees the Competition Bureau, which is part of the Federal Department of Industry. Under the Competition Act, the commissioner commences an inquiry and, in case of a presumed violation, a formal recourse is taken by applying to the Competition Tribunal for an order. The tribunal exercises no investigative functions and is purely a body to make findings and issue remedial orders. The Tribunal has a wide range of remedies available when it finds that the Competition Act has been violated. In case of mergers, these include orders of divestiture assets and/or shares, the dissolution of the transaction or orders regulating conduct. Out of 215 (267 in 2002/2003) merger cases concluded in 2003/2004, 6 (6) cases were agreed with remedies and 6 (3) were abandoned either as a direct result of the commissioner's position or for other reasons.[27]

While divestitures have traditionally been the favorite remedy, behavioral remedies have been used very frequently (Neylan, 2002). Campbell and Halladay (2002) analyze a number of merger cases reviewed by the commissioner and suggest that the bureau has in fact been willing to use diverse and innovative remedies in a considerable number of mergers.

12.5. Approach and hypotheses

The evaluation of remedies' effectiveness is intrinsically an empirical question. The first task is to identify those mergers that are most likely to lead to an increase in market power and where remedies should theoretically be applied. In particular, we classify mergers according to the likely net effects of market power versus efficiency gains. We shall assume that the antitrust authority follows a consumers' surplus standard, which is the adopted welfare measure in the U.S. as well as EU merger control.[28] An anticompetitive merger is then defined as such to reduce consumers' surplus. We look at the profit change of the rival firms at the merger's announcement date to assess the merger's competitiveness, since there exists a correspondence between the decrease in consumers' surplus and the increase of competitors' profits following a merger, as long as the considered merger is profitable for the merging firms. This correspondence between the sign of the rivals' profit change and the change in consumers' surplus holds in a large class of static oligopolistic models such as homogenous good Cournot competition and differentiated goods price competition (see Neven and Röller, 2005; Duso et al., 2006a on this point).

---

[27] See the Annual report of the Commissioner of Competition (Competition Bureau Canada, 2003, 2004).

[28] Actually, the old EU merger regulation did not explicitly state the use of a consumer surplus standard. However, Commissioner Monti stated several times that the ultimate scope of European competition policy is to serve consumers' interest.

Table 12.2: Possible effects of mergers on merging (M) and rival (R) firms' profits and the optimal incidence of remedies.

	$\Delta\Pi_M > 0$	$\Delta\Pi_M < 0$
$\Delta\Pi_R > 0$	Market power increase; remedies	Efficiency reduction; possibly remedies (if $\Delta\Pi_I > 0$)
$\Delta\Pi_R < 0$	Efficiency increase; no remedies	Efficiency reduction; no remedies

In principle, a merger might have four possible effects on the merging and rival firms' profits. Table 12.2 lists these four possibilities as well as the optimal incidence of remedies. If the merger generates positive profits for both the merging and the rival firms ($\Delta\Pi_M > 0$ and $\Delta\Pi_R > 0$), the market power effect following from the merger is likely to outweigh any efficiency gains (the "umbrella effect"). In this case appropriate remedies should be imposed on the merging parties, which reduce the market power effect (at least) until the point where the two effects neutralize each other on consumer or total welfare (depending on which standard the competition authority chooses).

If the merger generates positive profits for the merging firms but has a negative effect on rival firms' profits ($\Delta\Pi_M > 0$ and $\Delta\Pi_R < 0$), the efficiency effect of the merger is likely to outweigh the market power effect, since only merging firms enjoy the positive effect of increased efficiency. There should be no remedies in this case, at least none that (also) reduce the efficiency gains from the merger.[29]

The fact that mergers, which reduce the efficiency and profits of merging firms, happen cannot be well explained by standard industrial organization models.[30] Nevertheless, there is overwhelming evidence that many of such mergers do take place. For example, Gugler et al. (2003) find several of these mergers taking place around the world and attribute them to managerial motives, such as growth and size maximization.[31] Within this category, two cases can be distinguished: mergers that reduce the profits of the merging firms but increase the profits of the rival firms and mergers that reduce profitability of both parties.

---

[29] Remember that, according to the merger regulation, efficiencies should be "merger specific" and should "benefit consumers". See Röller et al. (2001) on considerations about the role of efficiency gains in merger control.

[30] One exception is the literature on pre-emptive mergers (see Fridolfsson and Stennek, 2005; Molnar, 2003). In these models, profit maximizing firms rationally do unprofitable mergers in order to pre-empt rivals, in those cases where being an insider is more profitable than being an outsider. Of course, another simple possibility is that they happen just because managers make evaluation mistakes in a world with imperfect information.

[31] Molnar (2003) uses a sample of all horizontal mergers that resulted in 100% ownership of the target between 1981 and 1998 where both the acquiring and the target firms were quoted in the NYSE, AMEX, or NASDAQ stock exchanges. He claims that, in his sample, pre-emptive motives for mergers find stronger support than hubris and agency theories.

If a merger decreases insider profits but increases rival firm profits ($\Delta\Pi_M < 0$ and $\Delta\Pi_R > 0$), the net effect of the merger on welfare depends on the relative magnitudes of the profit effects. If industry profits go up ($\Delta\Pi_I > 0$), the merger may be considered as being predominantly anticompetitive since rival firms react to the reduced efficiency of the merging firms by increasing their prices. Here remedies may be considered, although the source of the problem is not one of competition policy but one of inadequate corporate governance. If industry profits go down, nothing can be said about the anticompetitive effects and necessary remedies.

The same holds true in the last case, where both merging and rival firms' profits decrease ($\Delta\Pi_M < 0$ and $\Delta\Pi_R < 0$). One possible interpretation of this cell is that the merger not only reduced the efficiency of the merging firms, but at the same time had an effect on industry conduct. That is, the strategic interaction between firms has changed and reduced the collusiveness in the industry. Alternatively, the merger led to an increase in competition in the market, e.g. in technology markets leading to unambiguous improvements in consumer welfare.

12.5.1. Measuring the effects of mergers and remedial actions: The event study methodology

The first aim of this chapter is to provide a taxonomy of mergers by empirically estimating their effects on merging firms' as well as rivals' profitability (also see Duso et al., 2006a on this point). Therefore, the question is how to measure profitability. There are two strands of literature that look at the effects of mergers and propose empirical methodologies to quantify them.[32] One possibility consists of using balance sheet data and following the performance of the involved firms several years after the merger (see Gugler et al., 2003 as a recent example). The other strand of literature, which we discussed in Section 12.2, looks at stock market reactions to mergers' announcements, under the assumptions that markets are able to efficiently process information about the mergers. We follow this second approach and run event studies on the firms' stock prices to measure the merger's profitability effects. Duso et al. (2006a) discuss more thoroughly the advantages (and disadvantages) of using stock prices to assess merger and antitrust decision. A part of the obvious motivations that stock prices are more

[32] A third methodology for the measurement of mergers' effects is the structural modeling approach developed in the last decade by the empirical industrial economic literature (see for instance Nevo, 2000; Pinske and Slade, 2004; Ivaldi and Verboven, 2005) and recently used in antitrust cases. By estimating a full equilibrium model of oligopolistic interactions, the researcher is able to recover parameter estimates of the primitives of the model, which allow simulating the future industry outcomes under different market structure scenarios such as a merger. While this method allows a much more precise modeling of the underlying industry structure than the two mentioned in the text as well as a more precise quantification of the merger's effects, it is clearly unfeasible when doing a study based on a large sample of mergers, since the data and computational requirements cannot be met.

easily available and the this approach implicitly deal with dynamic issues that are more difficult to model using accounting data, is worth to note that stock prices are available at a much higher frequency and almost instantly allowing us to assess both the short and the longer run movements. In contrast profitability measure can typically be constructed at a much lower frequency and at a future period thus making it harder to gauge the impact at the time of the announcement.

Under the assumptions of efficient markets and rational expectations, the market model predicts that firm j's stock return at time t ($R_{j,t}$) is proportional to a market return:

$$R_{j,t} = \alpha + \beta R_{m,t} + \varepsilon_{j,t}.$$

To study the stock price reaction to the mergers' announcements, we estimate the market model over 240 trading days, starting 20 days prior to the announcement day and using the Scholes–Williams (1977) method.[33] We obtain estimated values for the model's parameters α and β, which we can use to predict what firm j's stock price would have been, had the merger not been announced or, more in general, had the event under consideration not occurred ($\widehat{R}_{j,t}$). For firm j, we calculate then the abnormal return around the mergers' announcement day t ($AR_{j,t}$) as:

$$AR_{j,t} = R_{j,t} - \widehat{R}_{j,t} = R_{j,t} - \hat{\alpha} - \hat{\beta} R_{m,t}.$$

We then calculate a cumulative abnormal return over an event window of $2x + 1$ days ($x = 0, 1, 2$, etc.):

$$CAR_{j,t+2x} = \sum_{\tau=t-x}^{t+x} AR_{j,\tau}.$$

We calculate these measures for merging firms and all rivals for each merger. In order to obtain the aggregate effects on merging firms and on rivals ($\Delta\Pi_i^d$, $i = M, R, d =$ Announcement, Decision), we took the weighted average of the cumulative abnormal returns of all firms in each of the two groups

[33] The choice of the estimation window to has always been problematic in the event study literature. Some studies use an estimation window which is very close to the event date, some others use windows that end as far as 6 months from the event date. If the estimation period is close to the event date, the estimated parameters from the market model will incorporate recent changes in systematic risk, which is a desirable property for our purposes. On the other hand a close estimation window has the disadvantage of being potentially influenced by the event, which is not desirable. There is some empirical evidence that such differences in the choice of the estimation window do not produce biased abnormal returns. For example, Goergen and Renneboog (2004) analyze the short-term wealth effects of large European takeover bids over the 1993–2000 period using an event study methodology. Both the choice of the sample and sample period is very similar to ours. They make use of 6 different ways of estimating α's and β's and argue that not only the choice of the estimation window but also differences in the estimation method do not result in economically significant differences in the abnormal returns.

($i = M, R$), the weight being firm j's market value (MV_j^d):

$$\Delta\Pi_i^d = \frac{\sum_{i=1}^{N_i} CAR_j^d MV_j^d}{\sum_{i=1}^{N_i} MV_j^d}, \quad j = 1, \ldots, N_i, \ i = M, R, \ d = A, D.$$

These give us a measure of the merger's and remedies' profitability effects.

We use the above explained methodology to quantify two effects. First, we asses the merger's competitive effect by looking at the reaction of merging and rival firms' share prices around the deal's announcement date. This allows us to measure the merger's profitability effects on merging (M) and rival (R) firms, which we label $\Delta\Pi_M^A$ and $\Delta\Pi_R^A$, and thus classify mergers as problematic and not so problematic according to Table 12.2. Second, we look at the different merger review's decision dates and try to infer information about the effectiveness of antitrust intervention from the stock market reactions to these events.

12.5.2. Measurement issues

There are some measurement problems in doing this exercise, since one has to understand how much the market predicts, or can predict, about the antitrust action around each event date as well as how much information was disclosed to the market and when it happened.

We start with the merger's announcement reactions. This measure is an unbiased measure of the merger's effects if the market assumed clearance without later commitments at the announcement day. Indeed, the observed abnormal return around the announcement day is equal to the real value of the merger ($\Delta\Pi_i^*$) minus the expected value of the remedies ($E[R_i|I_A]$) given the information available in the market at that time about remedies:[34]

$$\Delta\Pi_i^A = \Delta\Pi_i^* - E[R_i|I_A].$$

As long as the expected value of remedies is low, one should expect the observed abnormal return ($\Delta\Pi_i^A$) to have the same sign as the real value of the merger ($\Delta\Pi_i^*$).[35] Therefore, even though we might wrongly measure the real merger value with our event study, we still should be able to have an accurate prediction of the sign of this effect. This is what we are mostly interested in for the first step of our analysis, since we need to know whether profits from the merger are positive or negative in order to categorize mergers according to Table 12.2.

To measure remedies' effectiveness we look at the stock market's reactions around the date when the information about the commission's decision was disclosed. The main problem is to understand how much the market knows about,

---

[34] This formulation allows us to include clearances (remedies = 0) and prohibitions (the strongest form of remedies).

[35] Indeed, we would not expect a benevolent agency to impose remedies, which are higher than the value of the merger for merging firms.

or how good the market can predict, the outcome of the bargaining process between the commission and the merging parties, which results in the imposed remedies.

The first important date is the phase I decision. After the first four weeks of investigation, the commission has different possible choices—as discussed in Section 12.3. If the merger does not raise serious market power concerns, the commission clears the merger either unconditionally or with conditions and obligations. In this case, our event study should capture the effect of this decision, under the assumption of no information leakage during this first investigation period. Hence, for these cases, the phase I decision effect is the difference between the remedies' real effect (R_i) and the market expectation about remedies, given the information available around the announcement date.[36]

The worst decision from the merging firms' perspective—and therefore the decision that should trigger strongest price reactions—is when market power concerns are substantial and the commission decides to open a phase II investigation. In this case, the market reaction corresponds to the update of the market's beliefs about remedies. Indeed, when a case goes into phase II, the probability of a commission's intervention increases sharply.[37] Therefore, the abnormal returns around the day of the phase I decision for mergers that go into a phase II investigation should simply be the update of the market expectation about remedies, given the newer information set available at this point in time (I_{P1}).[38]

Summarizing, the phase I effect can be summarized as follow:

$$\Delta\Pi_i^{P1} = \begin{cases} R_i - E[R_i|I_A] & \text{if cleared,} \\ E[R_i|I_A] - E[R_i|I_{P1}] & \text{if phase II,} \end{cases} \quad i = M, R.$$

Similarly, around the day of the phase II decision, the abnormal return should measure the difference between the real value of phase II remedies (prohibitions are the extreme case of remedy) and the expectation that the market built given the information available on the phase I decision:

$$\Delta\Pi_i^{P2} = R_i - E[R_i|I_{P1}], \quad i = M, R.$$

Only under the assumption that not all relevant information about remedies is available on the announcement date, other events such as the commission's decision should trigger significant stock price reactions even in presence of efficient markets. Therefore, we will measure only the unexpected component of these announcements. Yet, there are several reasons why it might be difficult for the

---

[36] Notice that, by comparing the abnormal returns around the announcement day and those around the phase I decision it might be possible to identify the ex ante market assessment of an antitrust clearance.

[37] Table 12.1 shows that the incidence of remedies in phase I is 4%, while it increases to over 60% in phase II. Moreover, a merger can be prohibited only after a phase II investigation.

[38] Actually at the beginning of a phase II investigation, the market could also value the cost of such a procedure. Therefore the abnormal return around the phase I decision for those mergers that went into a phase II investigation might also reflect the high costs these firms are expected to pay.

market to know a priori the real effects of remedies. First and most importantly, remedies are the outcome of a (secret) bargaining process between the merging parties and the commission. Second, during the sample period the commission still did not have any kinds of official guidelines for the use of remedies, which made the policy process not perfectly predictable.

As in all event studies, there is a final problem regarding information leakages. It might be possible that some information about the final decision was disclosed to the market during the investigation period. Hence, around the day of the decision, we would only measure the market updates with respect to the already revealed information. While this can be a major problem during the phase II investigation, since it is a long process and the probability of information disclosure might be high, we do not think that this should be particularly relevant during the phase I investigation, which is conducted over a very short period of time.[39] Abnormal returns around the day of the phase I decision should therefore be a quite accurate measure of the effects of phase I decision and of the market's priors about the phase II procedure.

12.5.3. Hypotheses

A comparison of the incidence of mergers and remedies allows us to formulate our first hypothesis: Are remedies targeted at the *right* mergers (i.e., mergers that increase market power)? Or, put another way, did the commission make type I errors (impose remedies in procompetitive mergers) and type II errors (not impose remedies in anticompetitive mergers) when compared to the counterfactual given by the market merger's assessment?

We can then further evaluate the effectiveness of remedies by looking at the profitability effects around the various decision dates. In general, we expect remedies that effectively reduce market power to shrink rivals profitability in anticompetitive mergers. Analogously, we expect remedies to reduce merging firms' profitability in these mergers. However, if remedial action works in the right way, it should not completely destroy profits stemming from the increase of merging firms' productive efficiency. Hence, the reduction of merging firms' profitability should not be drastic, at least where the merger produces some efficiency gains.

In procompetitive mergers one should not observe remedies. If, however, the commission mistakenly applied them in such cases (type I errors), the remedies should not have a strong impact on both firms' profitability otherwise the commission's action would be detrimental to efficiency.[40]

---

[39] Indeed, we also estimate abnormal returns for an 11-day window, which would cover one fourth of the phase I investigation period.

[40] One potential problem of our analysis is that we look at the "average competitiveness" of a merger. In many cases, however, there are several product/geographical markets involved. Hence, there might be cases, which are on average procompetitive but where competitive concerns are

12.6. The data, the estimated abnormal returns, and mergers taxonomy

Our sample consists of 167 concentrations that have been analyzed by the European Commission from the period 1990–2002. Our starting database was developed in Duso et al. (2006a). Our sample includes almost all phase II mergers completed by the EU till the end of 2001, and a randomly matched sample of phase I cases, which run up to June 2002. Because of difficulties in identifying competitors or their stock, we end up with 78 phase II cases and 89 phase I cases for which we have complete information.[41] We identify 880 different firms involved in several mergers either as merging parties or as rivals.

Table 12.3 presents a short description of relevant variables that illustrate some of the main characteristics of the mergers in our sample. These variables are mostly derived from the commission's decision files.

The market value of the merging firms is on average 45 billion US dollars. The aggregate market value of rivals is of course much larger (385 billion US dollars on average) since we have several competitors involved in one merger, whose values are summed up.[42] The merger's average number or rivals for which we have data is 3.66, since we are not able to identify all competitors listed in the commission's reports and varies between 1 and 14.

The majority of the concentrations in our sample (56.9%) were full mergers, 24% joint ventures, 13.1% partial acquisitions, 11.4% were tender offers, and only 6% consisted of asset acquisition.

In 41.3% of cases the geographical market definition is the European Economic Area, in 34.7% it was defined to be national, and for the rest (21%) it was worldwide.

Remedies have been imposed in 35.3% of the mergers (6.6% in phase I and 28.7% in phase II).[43] Only 12 mergers in our sample (7.1%) were blocked. Considering these prohibitions as an extreme type of remedies, we have 43.1% of cases where the commission intervened to modify the merger in order to restore effective competition. We will use these cases to identify the effect of remedies by contrasting them to the rest of the sample, which consists of mergers that were cleared outright.

---

present in some, but not in all of the relevant markets. In such a situation, it would then be right for the Commission to intervene in order to solve these problems in the specific markets. Yet, with our methodology, we would define such a case as a type I error, since the deal was on average procompetitive. In Duso et al. (2006b), by using regression analysis, we can control for the merger characteristics (such as the number of product markets involved), which should help us to control for these considerations.

[41] In the sample period, information about roughly 1840 mergers was available. Of course phase I decisions are underrepresented in our sample. We choose however to randomly select some cases from the universe of all phase I mergers (around 1800 cases) in order to avoid any problem of endogenous selection.

[42] This information comes from our calculations on Datastream data and might therefore diverge from the (mostly censored) figures reported in the Commission's files.

[43] Note that mergers where remedies were imposed in phase I are a little overrepresented in our sample (6.6%) in comparison to the entire population (4.6% of cases).

Table 12.3: Variables definition and summary statistics.

Variable	Description	Mean	Std. Dev.
mvd_mer_a	Market value of the merging firm in million US $	44416	84507
mvd_com_a	Market value of the rivals in million US $	385498	3858280
competitors	Average number of competitors	3.6687	2.5216
full	Full acquisition	0.5689	0.4967
partial	Partial acquisition	0.1317	0.3392
jv	Joint Venture	0.2395	0.4281
assetacq	Asset acquisition	0.0599	0.2380
tender	Tender offer	0.1138	0.3185
phase1	The merger was cleared in phase I	0.5329	0.5004
phase2	The merger was cleared in phase II	0.4671	0.5004
national	The geographical market is national	0.3473	0.4775
EEA	The geographical market is the European Economic Area	0.4132	0.4939
world	The geographical market is worldwide	0.2096	0.4082
remedies	Remedies have been applied	0.3533	0.4794
prohibitions	The merger was prohibited	0.0719	0.2590
sremedies	Strong remedies: prohibitions are strongest type of remedy	0.4251	0.4959
structural	Structural remedies have been imposed	0.2909	0.4556
behavioral	Behavioral remedies have been imposed	0.2121	0.4101
remed_mix	A remedies mix (structural and behavioral) was imposed	0.1557	0.3637
p_structural	Only structural remedies have been imposed	0.1317	0.3392
p_behav	Only behavioral remedies have been imposed	0.0539	0.2265
divestiture	The remedy consisted in a divestiture	0.2364	0.4261
shares_sell	The remedy consisted in selling shares	0.1030	0.3049
interlocking	The remedy consisted in dissolving interlocking directorates	0.0364	0.1878
exclusive_agree	The remedy consisted in eliminating exclusive agreements	0.0727	0.2605
licensing	Merging firms must license some products/processes	0.1152	0.3202
access	Merging firms must guarantee access to an essential technology/facility	0.0970	0.2968

All variables excluding the market values and the average number of rivals are dummy variables.

Remedies are categorized as structural or behavioral using the information contained in the commission's decision. In 15.6% of the mergers, the commission adopted a "remedies mix" consisting of structural and behavioral remedies together. In only 13.2% of the cases, pure structural remedies have been imposed, while behavioral remedies have been adopted alone in only 5.4% of the mergers in our sample.

The most adopted kinds of remedies are divestitures, which were imposed in 23.6% of the cases. This corresponds to 67% of the mergers where remedies have been applied. The selling of shares was imposed in 10.3% of cases, licensing agreements in 11.5%, the access to essential technologies or facilities in 9.7%, the dismissing of exclusive agreements in 7.3%, and the dissolution of interlocking directorates only in 3.6% of the mergers in our sample.

For each case, merging firms and competitors have been identified from the published commission's decisions.[44] The mergers' announcement date was collected from the financial press by using the Dow Jones Interactive database.[45] For each firm j (merging and rival firms), we have computed the abnormal return around the merger's announcement day, as well as phase I and phase II decision dates. We then calculated the cumulative 3-day, 5-day, and 11-day abnormal returns for each firm. In order to obtain the aggregate effects on merging firms' and on competitors ($\Delta\Pi_i^d$, $i = M, R$), we took the weighted average of the abnormal returns of all firms in each of the two groups ($i = M, R$), the weight being the firms j's market value (MV_j^d), as we described in paragraph 2.

Table 12.4 reports the preliminary statistics of the various measures of estimated aggregated abnormal returns for merging firms and competitors around various points in time and using different event windows.

According to our estimates, the mergers in our sample were on average profitable since the average aggregated cumulative abnormal returns for the merging firms around the announcement date ($\Delta\Pi_M^A$) are positive and statistically significant at the 1% level for all used windows. The size of the profitability effect ranges from 1.1% (1 day window) to 2.07% (5-day window).

This result seems however to be in line with the literature.[46] The cumulative abnormal returns for the rivals around the announcement date ($\Delta\Pi_R^A$) are, instead, not statistically significantly different from zero and very small in size.[47]

---

44 This is a big advantage of our data set, since we can rely on the Commission's analysis concerning the market definition (the relevant competitors). However, this has also the disadvantage that we might have picked the wrong competitors because the Commission made mistakes in defining the relevant market.

45 This is a customizable business news and research product that integrates contents from newspapers, newswires, journals, research reports, and web sites. The peculiarity of our approach is that we looked at the first rumors about the merger, i.e. the first time a discussion of the mergers appeared in the international press, and not necessarily the official merger's announcement by the involved parties. This has the advantage of reducing the noise in identifying the "right" event. On the other hand, our measure of abnormal returns might be downward biased by the fact that the market might still not be sure whether the merger will take place or not. What we observe is, therefore, the value that the market attaches to a particular merger times the expected probability that this merger will really be consumed.

46 See for instance Andrade et al. (2001). In fact, $\Delta\Pi_i^d$ is the weighted sum of the acquiring and of the target firms' abnormal returns. Depending on the event window, we estimate average abnormal returns for acquirers in the range between −0.54% and 0.12% (not statistically significantly different from zero) and for the targets in the range between 3.4% and 6.2% (statistically significantly greater than zero at the 1% level). These results are quite similar to those reported by Aktas et al. (2004a) using a comparable sample of mergers analyzed by the EU Commission. Note however that in their sample the phase II cases are much more underrepresented than in ours.

47 The abnormal returns for rivals are measured with errors, since we lost part of them due to the fact that they are small—not quoted—firms. Because we have mostly the biggest competitors in our

Table 12.4: Estimated abnormal returns.

Variable	1 day	3 days	5 days	11 days
Announcement day				
$\Delta\Pi_M^A$	**0.0114****	**0.0157*****	**0.0207*****	**0.0191*****
	(0.0049)	(0.0059)	(0.0065)	(0.0072)
$\Delta\Pi_R^A$	0.0038	0.0029	0.0005	0.0056
	(0.0041)	(0.0023)	(0.0031)	(0.0075)
Notification day				
$\Delta\Pi_M^N$	0.0028	**0.0072****	0.0044	**0.0081***
	(0.0028)	(0.0032)	(0.0035)	(0.0058)
$\Delta\Pi_R^N$	0.0041	0.0030	0.0024	0.0050
	(0.0063)	(0.0045)	(0.0034)	(0.0136)
Phase I decision				
$\Delta\Pi_M^{p1}$	**−0.0034****	**−0.0112****	**−0.0115****	**−0.0143****
	(0.0016)	(0.0058)	(0.0061)	(0.0075)
$\Delta\Pi_R^{p1}$	**−0.0026***	**−0.0033***	**−0.0050***	0.0098
	(0.0019)	(0.0025)	(0.0036)	(0.0145)
Phase II decision				
$\Delta\Pi_M^{p2}$	0.0022	**0.0068***	0.0033	0.0068
	(0.0018)	(0.0029)	(0.0038)	(0.0087)
$\Delta\Pi_R^{p2}$	−0.0002	−0.0039	−0.0054	−0.0043
	(0.0025)	(0.0043)	(0.0057)	(0.0081)
Final decision[a]				
$\Delta\Pi_M^D$	**−0.0024***	**−0.0082***	**−0.0101***	**−0.0112***
	(0.0017)	(0.0059)	(0.0062)	(0.0085)
$\Delta\Pi_R^D$	−0.0027	**−0.0052***	**−0.0076***	0.0078
	(0.0022)	(0.0033)	(0.0047)	(0.0151)
Sum				
$\Delta\Pi_M^A + \Delta\Pi_M^D$	**0.0093***	0.0075	0.0104	0.0074
	(0.0054)	(0.0085)	(0.0089)	(0.0112)
$\Delta\Pi_R^A + \Delta\Pi_R^D$	0.0012	−0.0023	−0.0071	0.0134
	(0.0031)	(0.0035)	(0.0059)	(0.0209)

We report the mean and standard errors (in parentheses) of the different abnormal returns. We use a one tailed t-test to test whether the abnormal returns are significantly positive or negative, and report significance.

*10% significance level.

**5% significance level.

***1% significance level.

[a]This variable is defined as the abnormal return around the phase I decision date for cases cleared (with or without remedies) in phase I and as the sum of the abnormal returns around the phase I and phase II decision dates for the cases that went through the phase II procedure.

On average, these mergers seem to be welfare-neutral, in the sense that neither they increase nor decrease the average rivals' profits.

The notification date effects are for both merging and rival firms very small and almost always insignificantly positive. Under the assumption of efficient markets, we would expect exactly these kinds of effects. The notification, in fact, is a required act by the parties and should not convey any relevant information to the market since it is common knowledge that merging firms must notify the transaction.

Looking at phase I decisions, we observe negative and statistically significant abnormal returns for the merging firms as well as for the competitors for almost all event windows. This suggests that the phase I decision is on average bad news for both merging firms (around −1%) and competitors (−0.5%). Especially, the negative effect on merging firms' stocks is relatively big, since it comes close in absolute value to the average positive effect observed around the announcement date. This would mean that, on average, around the phase I decision already almost the entire average profitability effect for the merging firms disappears. The interesting question is then to look whether this average negative effect is driven by the cases where conditions and obligations have been imposed by the commission, or whether it is a pure "decision effect" independent of the use of remedies. We will turn to this question later on.

In the case of phase II decisions, almost all measures of abnormal returns are statistically insignificant. The only exception is the measure of the cumulative 3-day abnormal returns for the merging firms, which is positive (0.68%) and statistically significant at the 5% level. The effect for the merging firms is on average positive, even though small, while the rivals' abnormal return is on average negative, and also very small.

As we pointed out before, we are interested in the stock market reactions around the final decision date, since at this point in time all information about the outcome of the antitrust legacy is provided to the market. First of all we have to define this event and which measure of abnormal returns we consider. For mergers cleared in phase I, this is an easy task: the final decision effect is simply the abnormal return around the phase I decision date. For cases that go to phase II, we chose to use the sum of the phase I and phase II abnormal returns as the final decision effect, since around the phase I decision the market updates its beliefs about the final outcome. In fact, the probability that the merger will be blocked or cleared with remedies sharply increases when a merger goes into a phase II investigation. Looking at this event, we observe negative and significant abnormal returns for merging firms as well as competitors. The size of this

---

sample we possibly have another bias towards "no significance": big firms derive probably only a small fraction of their revenues from the market under consideration and are, therefore, only partially affected by the merger.

Table 12.5: Mergers taxonomy based on profitability of merging and rival firms and the incidence of remedies: Frequencies.

	$\Delta\Pi_M > 0$	$\Delta\Pi_M < 0$	Tot.
$\Delta\Pi_R > 0$	55 (32.9%)	32 (19.1%)	87 (52.0%)
With remedies[a]	24	13	37
Prohibitions	3	6	9
$\Delta\Pi_R < 0$	43 (25.8%)	37 (22.2%)	80 (48.0%)
With remedies[a]	17	17	34
Prohibitions	1	2	3
Tot.	98 (58.7%)	69 (41.3%)	167
With remedies[a]	41	30	71
Prohibitions	4	8	12

[a]Prohibitions are considered as an extreme case of remedies.

effect ranges from −0.24 to −1.1% for the merging firms and from −0.27% to −0.78% for the rivals.[48]

Now we use the result of our event studies to fill our merger taxonomy with frequencies based on the estimated 3-day abnormal returns (Table 12.5). According to our estimates, 52% of the mergers in our sample were on average anticompetitive in the sense that they increased the profitability of rivals. Almost 33% increased profits of competitors as well as merging firms.[49]

Almost 59% of the mergers in our sample were profitable, which is consistent with our previous findings of average positive and significant abnormal returns for the merging firms around the announcement day. Only 25.8% of the mergers were efficiency increasing—meaning that the merging firms had a positive abnormal return and the rivals had a negative one—while 41.3% were efficiency decreasing mergers in the sense that the merging firms' profitability effect was negative. Among the latter, 22% were mergers with all involved parties registering some losses.

The second row in Table 12.5 reports the number of cases where remedies were applied, while the third row reports the number of blocked mergers. We should only observe remedies (and prohibitions) in anticompetitive mergers. Yet, this is clearly not the case.[50] Remedies (and prohibitions) have also been

[48] Just to give an idea, using the average market values, these effects amount to a loss of between 106 and 489 million dollars for the merging parties and between 1 and 3 billion dollars for the rivals.

[49] Results based on the 1-day and 5-day abnormal returns are almost identical. Small differences can be obtained when using the 11-day window.

[50] This is a kind of strong statement, which is based on the assumption that the markets on average do not make mistakes because they efficiently process information. Indeed, one might wonder whether in a situation with strong information asymmetry where the antitrust authority might have private information about the transaction under scrutiny, perhaps the mistakes are made by the markets rather than by the commission. By using accounting data together with our stock market reactions one could try to test efficient market hypothesis.

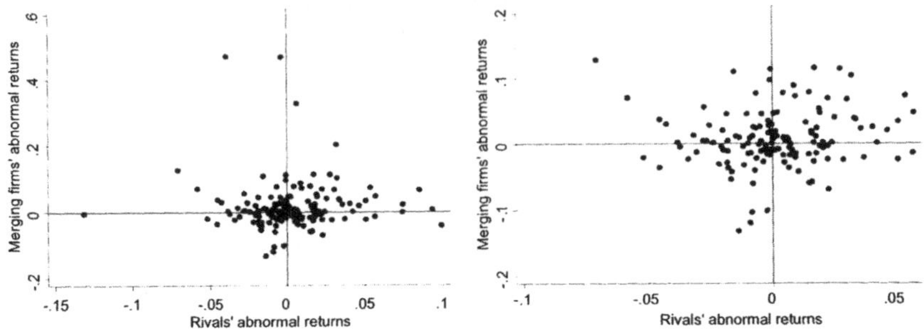

a. with outliers **b. without outliers**

Fig. 12.2: The distribution of merging firms' and rivals' abnormal returns.

applied in all kinds of mergers, suggesting that the commission made type I errors. Out of the 80 procompetitive mergers, it unduly imposed restrictions in 37 cases and, even worse, blocked three mergers. The incidence of type I errors is therefore 20.36% (or 46.25% of the procompetitive mergers).[51]

Moreover, the commission also made type II errors by not imposing remedies in some of the mergers that were anticompetitive. Out of the 87 anticompetitive mergers in our sample, the commission imposed remedies only in 37 cases (among which 9 prohibitions), which means that the incidence of type II errors is as high as 29.94% of all cases (57.47% of the anticompetitive ones). [52] This was the first question we wanted to answer. Yet, before moving to the testing of the previously developed hypotheses, we want to take a closer look at the data.

Figure 12.2 gives a graphical representation of the joint distribution of merging and rival firms' abnormal returns around the announcement date. A quite strong concentration around the origin (no abnormal returns for either group of firms) can be observed. However, the dispersion is also evident and generates the variation that is a prerequisite for our empirical tests.

It is also interesting to look at the size of the abnormal returns in the different sub-samples and test hypotheses about their sign. Table 12.6 reports the average abnormal returns and their standard errors along with a one-tailed t-test whether these are positive or negative.

The 3-day average abnormal return for merging firms is around 5% in profitable mergers and around −2.7% in non-profitable mergers (both figures significant at the 1% significance level). In these two sub-samples, the rivals have a positive abnormal return of 0.5% (significant at the 5% level) and a negative abnormal return of −0.03% (not statistically different form zero) respectively.

In anticompetitive mergers rivals have a positive and significant return of 2.3% and merging firms an average positive abnormal return of 1.76%. In the

---

[51] Note that this figure is an upper bound for the type I errors' probability because of the problems concerning the merging firms being involved in several product markets. See footnote 37.

[52] Duso et al. (2006a) provide evidence on the determinants of type I and type II errors.

Table 12.6: Mergers taxonomy, abnormal returns around the announcement date, and hypotheses testing.

		$\Delta\Pi_M^A > 0$	$\Delta\Pi_M^A < 0$	Tot.
$\Delta\Pi_R^A > 0$	$\Delta\Pi_M^A$	0.0454***	−0.0240***	0.0176***
		(0.0083)	(0.0034)	(0.0064)
	$\Delta\Pi_R^A$	0.0246***	0.0203***	0.0230***
		(0.0033)	(0.0042)	(0.0026)
$\Delta\Pi_R^A < 0$	$\Delta\Pi_M^A$	0.0564***	−0.0302***	0.0137***
		(0.0169)	(0.0056)	(0.0102)
	$\Delta\Pi_R^A$	−0.0174***	−0.0171***	−0.0172***
		(0.0026)	(0.0038)	(0.0022)
Tot.	$\Delta\Pi_M^A$	0.0502***	−0.0273***	0.0157***
		(0.0087)	(0.0034)	(0.0059)
	$\Delta\Pi_R^A$	0.0052**	−0.0003	0.0029
		(0.0031)	(0.0036)	(0.0023)

The mean values of the 3-day cumulative abnormal returns in each sub-sample are reported; standard errors are reported in parentheses. Significance refers to one sided t-tests for positive or negative abnormal returns.
**Significance at 5%.
***Significance at 1%.

sub-sample of mergers where both the merging and the rival firms' abnormal returns are positive, the profitability effect for merging firms rises to 4.54%. In procompetitive mergers, merging firms still gain on average 1.37% (significant at the 10% level) while rivals lose on average −1.72%.

One possible objection to the methodology that we used so far is that in many cases in our sample both merging firms and rivals' abnormal returns are nearly zero. A less crude categorization should take this into account. Hence, we define as positive only those abnormal returns that, according to our sample, are bigger than the considered abnormal return's standard error and as negative those which are smaller than the standard error. We can then generate a third category of mergers having a "neutral" profit effect either for the merging or the rival firms. Table 12.7 reports this extended mergers' taxonomy.

The main message remains similar to what was observed before: the commission still made type I errors (imposed strong remedies in 30 out of 57 procompetitive cases equal to 52.63% of these cases) with an incidence of 17.96%, and type II errors (did not impose due remedies in 39 of 66 anticompetitive mergers, equal to 59.1% of these cases) with an incidence of 23.35%. Of course, the incidence of errors decreases when we consider this restricted sample.

We can now move to the analysis of the effects of remedies and answer the second question of interest for our study: did remedies, when rightly applied, restore effective competition? Moreover, we can look at whether remedies that were incorrectly applied caused a further competitive damage.

Table 12.7: Mergers taxonomy, abnormal returns around the announcement date, and hypotheses testing considering statistical significance.[a]

	$\Delta\Pi^A_M > 0$	$\Delta\Pi^A_M = 0$	$\Delta\Pi^A_M < 0$	Tot.
$\Delta\Pi^A_R > 0$	41	10	25	76
Remedies	18	5	9	32
$\Delta\Pi^A_R = 0$	16	1	7	25
Remedies	4	0	6	10
$\Delta\Pi^A_R < 0$	28	14	25	57
Remedies	16	4	10	30
Tot.	85	25	57	167
	38	9	25	72

[a]We consider to be zero all observations for which either the abnormal returns of the merging firms or those of the rivals are inside a symmetric confidence interval around zero and with a size equal totwice the standard error of the considered abnormal returns.

12.7. Results and discussion

In this section we shall look at the abnormal returns for merging and rival firms in different sub-samples and around different decisions dates, in order to infer how the commission's decision was valued by the market and hence to assess its effectiveness. We first analyze how stock markets reacted around the final decision date and look at the differences between pro- and anticompetitive mergers as well as whether the use of remedies had significant effects. Then we focus on the market's reaction to phase I decisions, since around this date the most important information is conveyed to the market. We claim that from this event we shall get the best prediction about the market's assessment of the commission's decision. Finally, we look at the phase II abnormal returns.

As we discussed in the previous section, the "final decision" abnormal return ($\Delta\Pi^D_i, i = M, R$) is equal to the phase I decision's abnormal return for cases that were cleared (with or without remedies) in phase I, and to the sum of the abnormal returns around the phase I and phase II decisions for those mergers, which went through a phase II investigation. Table 12.8 reports the mean values and the standard errors of these measures in three different samples: the entire sample, that of anticompetitive mergers, and the procompetitive mergers' sample.[53]

The first striking result is that around the decision date all firms involved in the merger lost value: our measures of abnormal returns are negative independently of the sub-sample as well as of whether remedies were imposed or the case was unconditionally cleared.

[53] In this section we will define as anticompetitive all those mergers where rivals' abnormal returns at the announcement date were positive. This allows us to work with bigger samples.

Table 12.8: Final decision abnormal returns in different sub-samples and remedies effects.

	Entire sample		**Anticompetitive**		**Procompetitive**	
	Remedies	**No remedies**	**Remedies**	**No remedies**	**Remedies**	**No remedies**
$\Delta\Pi_M^D$	−0.0132	**−0.0046***	−0.0198	**−0.0083***	−0.0060	−0.0009
	(0.0134)	(0.0034)	(0.0239)	(0.0052)	(0.0067)	(0.0042)
$\Delta\Pi_R^D$	−0.0024	**−0.0087****	−0.0037	**−0.0148***	−0.0012	−0.0024
	(0.0054)	(0.0049)	(0.0068)	(0.0091)	(0.0034)	(0.0034)
Obs	71	97	40	51	31	46

The "final decision date abnormal return" is defined as the abnormal return around the phase I decision date for cases cleared (with or without remedies) in phase I and as the sum of the abnormal returns around the phase I and phase II decision dates for the cases that went through the phase II procedure. Remedies also include prohibitions. The mean values of the 3-days cumulative abnormal returns in each sub-sample are reported; standard errors are reported in parentheses. Significance refers to one sided t-tests for negative abnormal returns. Anticompetitive are those mergers where the rivals' profitability increased; procompetitive are those where it decreased.

*Significance at 10%.

**Significance at 5%.

The second compelling finding is that the market does not seem to significantly react to the announcement of remedies (prohibitions) in any of the different kinds of mergers, since the average final decision abnormal returns are never significantly different form zero neither for the merging firms nor for the competitors when remedies have been imposed. Note however that these are average effects for phase 1 and phase 2 decisions.

On the other hand, the effects on merging firms' profitability are on average economically more relevant when remedies have been imposed, though this is not true for rivals. While merging firms have more negative abnormal returns in anticompetitive mergers (−1.98%) than in procompetitive ones (−0.83%)—which is consistent with the hypothesis of remedies reducing the market power effect—exactly the opposite happens for the rivals' abnormal returns. We test whether average abnormal returns in cases with remedies are statistically different from those in mergers cleared without remedies. We cannot reject the null hypothesis of equal means. Therefore, we conclude that, on average, remedies do not seem to have a significantly different impact than unconditional clearance on merging firms' and rivals' profitability.

Interestingly, we observe more statistical significance looking at the cases where remedies have not been applied. In particular, the average abnormal return around the decision date is negative and significant in anticompetitive mergers (rivals gain) both for merging firms (−0.83%) and for rivals (−1.48%). A similar result can be observed in the entire sample. Also in this case, the reaction around the final decision date is negative both for merging firms and competitors when no remedies were used, though only the rivals' abnormal return is significantly different from zero (−0.73%). This finding is quite puzzling. In order to more carefully interpret this finding, however, one should consider that the remedies' choice might be endogenous to the abnormal returns around the decision date. Regression analysis, which accounts for this endogeneity problem, could help to more cleanly measure the real effect of remedies.[54]

As we already stressed, the event that seems to trigger most of the market reactions is the phase I decision. It is well known that merging firms are very unwilling to go through a phase II investigation, since this is an extremely costly and risky process. Moreover, a commission's intervention in phase II is very likely, therefore the beginning of a phase II investigation should have a significant impact on firms' profitability.[55]

Table 12.9 reports abnormal returns for merging and rival firms depending on the nature of the phase I decision and looking at the entire sample and the sub-samples of anticompetitive and procompetitive mergers. Figure 12.3 gives a graphical representation of these findings.

At the end of phase I, if the merger does not seem to be problematic in the sense that market power concerns are low or nonexistent, the commission applies Art. 6.1.b and clears the merger unconditionally. In the entire sample, this event has a slightly negative but not statistically significant impact on both merging firms and rivals. However, if we divide the sample into anti- and procompetitive mergers, we observe significantly different results. We find that the average abnormal returns in case of anticompetitive mergers are significantly lower than in the case of procompetitive mergers at the 5% significance level. Merging firms significantly lose almost 1% in anticompetitive mergers and have almost zero abnormal returns (0.3% not significant) in procompetitive mergers.

This result is quite surprising, since we would have expected the market to positively evaluate the future profitability of merging firms for anticompetitive mergers that are approved without conditions. We cannot explain this result as being a pure update of the market beliefs, since merging firms in this sub-sample had an average abnormal return of 1.5% around the announcement day, which was significantly positive at the 10% level. Rivals' abnormal returns show a similar pattern, even though they are not statistically significantly different from zero, nor statistically significantly different from each other in the two sub-samples.

When the commission has concerns about the anticompetitive nature of a merger but it thinks that these problems can be easily fixed, it might choose to impose remedies in phase I. In our sample this happened in a limited number of cases (11 mergers), which reflects the relatively seldom use of remedies

54 See Duso et al. (2006b) on this issue.

55 Note also that, even though information leakage problems might also bias the abnormal return around the phase I decision, we do believe that this problem is less relevant than, say, for phase II decisions. Phase I is indeed a quite short period of time (3 weeks) and the commission's economic analysis is limited to some days, while a large fraction of the time being used for bureaucratic and administrative procedures. Therefore, we think that the information disclosure during the phase I is limited and hence important news are revealed to the market around the decision day that could not be clearly anticipated by the analysts.

Table 12.9: Abnormal returns around the phase 1 decision date for different phase 1 decisions.

Decision		Entire sample	Anticompetitive	Procompetitive
Art. 6.1.b	Merging	−0.0031	**−0.0094****	0.0030
Clearance	Firms	(0.0038)	(0.0056)	(0.0049)
	Rivals	−0.0070	−0.0129	−0.0013
		(0.0055)	(0.0104)	(0.0036)
	Obs.	79	41	38
Art. 6.2	Merging	−0.0022	−0.0030	0.0012
Remedies	Firms	(0.0059)	(0.0067)	(0.0175)
	Rivals	**−0.0182*****	**−0.0214****	**−0.0118***
		(0.0062)	(0.0098)	(0.0058)
	Obs.	11	7	4
Art. 6.1.c	Merging	**−0.0210****	**−0.0318***	**−0.0102****
Phase II	Firms	(0.0121)	(0.0233)	(0.0066)
	Rivals	0.0003	0.0007	-0.0002
		(0.0026)	(0.0033)	(0.0040)
	Obs.	78	43	35

The mean values of the 3-days cumulative abnormal returns in each sub-sample are reported; standard errors are reported in parentheses. Significance refers to one sided t-tests for negative abnormal returns. Anticompetitive are those mergers where the rivals' profitability increased, procompetitive those where it decreased.
*Significance at 10%.
**Significance at 5%.
***Significance at 1%.

in phase I observed.in the entire population of mergers analyzed by the commission. Also this event has a negative impact on both merging and rival firms' profitability. Yet, the effect of the former is small (−0.2%) and not significantly different from zero. For rivals, however, the abnormal loss is substantial, it is significant at the 1% level, and it ranges from—1.2% in procompetitive mergers to −2.13% in anticompetitive ones. This result is consistent with remedies effectively resolving the competitive problems. Indeed, if the market power concerns are solved by remedial actions, then rivals should be losing the most, since merging firms still might have the beneficial effect of efficiency gains. Moreover, the effect seems to be stronger in anticompetitive mergers, which is also expected. Finally, if remedies are (wrongly) applied in phase I in procompetitive mergers, they negatively impact rivals but not the merging firms: it is bad news for rivals and good news for merging parties, when an efficiency increasing merger goes through even with remedies.

When mergers raise serious competition concerns, the commission decides to open up a phase II investigation. This is the event that triggered the largest, negative and strongly significant, reaction for merging firms in our sample. On average the abnormal return is equal to −2.1%, rising to −3.18% for those mergers that the market valued to be anticompetitive, and sinking to −1.02% for the procompetitive ones. This is however not the case for competitors. Since the

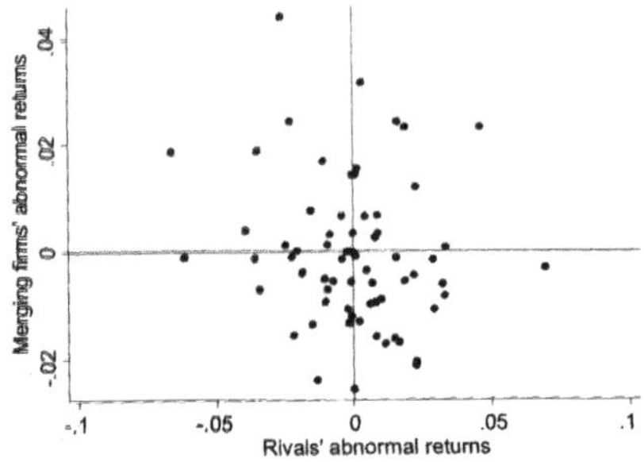

Art. 6.1b

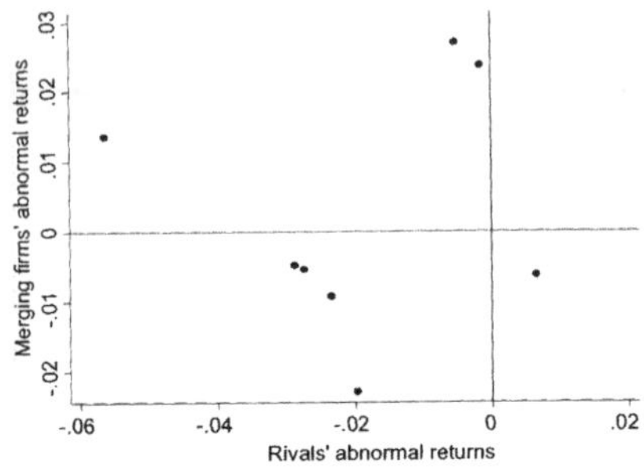

Art. 6.2

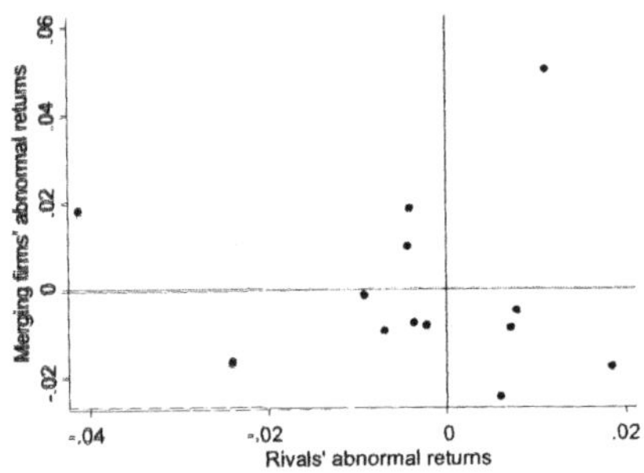

Art. 8.1.

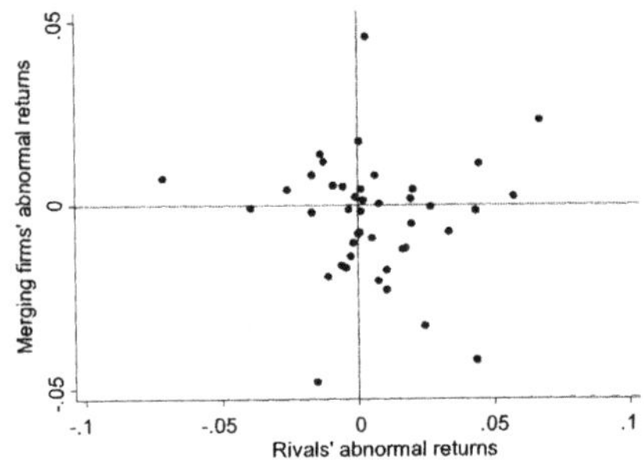

Art. 8.2.

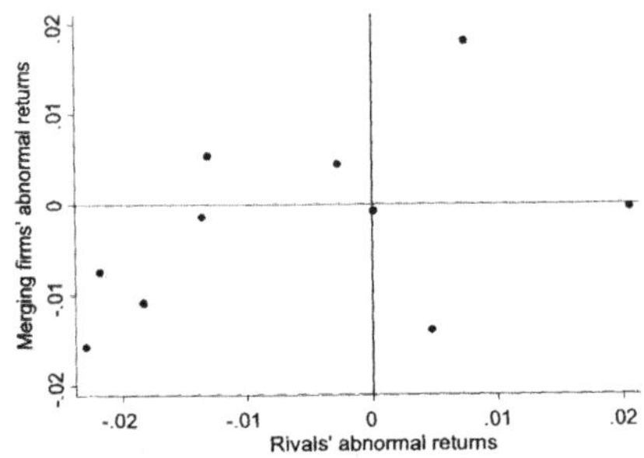

Art. 8.3

Fig. 12.3: The distribution of merging firms and rivals' abnormal returns around the phase I decision date for different decisions.

variability is quite large, rivals face negligible average reactions when the commission announces the opening of a phase II investigation. The abnormal returns are around 0.01% and are not statistically significant different from zero.

From these last results, especially from the comparison between merging and rival firms' different reactions around the phase I decision, we make our first inference of what the market thought about remedies and about the occurrence of a phase II investigation.

First of all, it seems that the market values remedies to be successful in reducing the market power effect in phase I. In fact, rivals' profitability is reduced by the remedies but this is not true for the merging firms. And this is even more evident in anticompetitive mergers where the negative effect is almost double if compared to that in procompetitive mergers.[56]

Much more difficult to interpret are the results concerning the decision to open up a phase II investigation. For merging firms, the market might react to two different kinds of news. The first is related to the antitrust procedure. The market might value that the probability of remedies and, in the worst case, of prohibitions is now extremely high. Since remedies hurt the merging parties, the market reduces its predictions of the future value of these companies. The size of the abnormal return should then represent the value of the remedies times the probability that they will be imposed, given that the investigation is in the second phase.

The other kind of negative information that comes to the market at this point in time is that the merging parties will be involved in a long and costly process: phase II. If this is the main explanation, then the abnormal returns only represent the expected cost for the merging companies and, eventually, the cost of the delay with which the merger will be consumed.

Information about the competitors' reactions is particularly helpful in trying to identify which of the two explanations better fits the data. Rivals do not have to pay the costs of the antitrust procedure; therefore this explanation cannot be used to rationalize their abnormal returns. However, their profitability is influenced by the phase II decision. The fact that the rivals' abnormal returns are essentially equal to zero might suggest that the market does not think that the phase II investigation will end with a decision that indeed solves the competitive problem recognized by the commission in the investigation's first phase.

We can look even more in depth at the profitability effects around the phase I decision and try to asses what the market predicted about phase II. In Table 12.10, we report the abnormal returns *around the phase I decision* date for those mergers that went to phase II and divide them according to the commission's final decision. This is essentially a breakup of the last line of Table 12.9 and should allow us to test how well the market predicted a phase II decision given the information available around the end of phase I. Again, we look at three sub-samples: the entire sample, anticompetitive mergers, and procompetitive mergers.

On average, the abnormal returns for merging firms are negative (−1.15%) and significant at the 10% level for cases that were cleared. Yet, they are significantly lower (at the 5% level) than the average merging firms' abnormal return for all cases that went to phase II (−2.1%, see Table 12.9 Art. 6.1.c). We do not observe significant differences between anticompetitive and procompetitive

---

[56] Note however that, given the limited size of the sample, the difference between the two values is not statistically significant.

Table 12.10: Abnormal returns around the phase 1 decision date for different phase II decisions in different sub-samples.

		Entire sample	Anticompetitive	Procompetitive
Art. 8.1	Merging firms	**−0.0105***	−0.0094	−0.0119
Clearance		(0.0071)	(0.0097)	(0.0113)
	Rivals	−0.0035	0.0021	−0.0088
		(0.0039)	(0.0031)	(0.0067)
	Obs.	17	10	7
Art. 8.2 with	Merging firms	−0.0031	−0.0029	−0.0032
Remedies		(0.0036)	(0.0055)	(0.0048)
	Rivals	0.0047	0.0038	0.0056
		(0.0036)	(0.0037)	(0.0061)
	Obs.	48	20	28
Art. 8.3	Merging firms	**−0.0967***	−0.1018	−0.0814
Prohibitions		(0.0667)	(0.0891)	(0.0511)
	Rivals	**−0.0111****	**−0.0089****	−0.0176
		(0.0046)	(0.0045)	(0.0139)
	Obs.	13	10	3

The mean values of the 3-day cumulative abnormal returns in each sub-sample are reported; standard errors are reported in parentheses. Significance refers to one sided t-tests for negative abnormal returns. Anticompetitive are those mergers where the rivals' profitability increased, procompetitive those where it decreased.
*Significance at 10%.
**Significance at 5%.

mergers. Essentially, the negative effect of going to phase II is small and almost not significant for cases that were lately cleared. This would mean that the market has a much less negative prior for these cases, as if the market was predicting lower costs for these mergers. This is consistent with the idea of remedies/prohibitions being the cause for large negative abnormal returns around the decision date. One can also read the negative abnormal returns in these cases by measuring the (opportunity) cost of the phase II investigation, which is higher for procompetitive mergers.

Rivals' abnormal returns, which are on average very small in size (−0.35%), do not appear to be significantly different from zero. The clearance of procompetitive mergers has, however, a larger negative, even if insignificant, effect on rivals' profitability: it is bad news for competitors that an efficiency increasing merger went through without remedies. This finding is consistent with our explanation as well.

A puzzling result is that the market does not have any significant prediction for those mergers that were cleared with remedies in phase II. In this sub-sample, the abnormal returns of both merging and rival firms are very small and not statistically significantly different from zero, as if the market would not give a negative valuation to the forthcoming remedies.

Interestingly, the merging firms' average abnormal return around the phase I decision in mergers that were blocked by the commission in phase II is extremely negative and very significant. These firms lose on average 9.67% of their value around the announcement that a phase II investigation will start. The effect is even stronger for mergers valued to be anticompetitive, where the abnormal return is −10.18%, though not significant given the small sample size and the high standard error.[57] This result suggests that the market was able to build a good prior about prohibitions. Also rivals involved in mergers that were lately blocked significantly lose 1% of their value around the phase I decision date. This is also in line with the interpretation that prohibitions indeed solve the market power concerns, since otherwise there would not be any reason for rivals to lose value when the merger was not allowed.

One possible reading of the discussed results is that the market is indeed not able to predict remedies in phase II, while it is able to predict prohibitions. Alternatively, one might think that the market does predict the use of remedies but it does not believe that remedies will have any kind of significant effect.

Finally, another possible explanation is as follows. Some firms know that the commission will experience political pressure not to block a merger in phase II, since they are "national champions" or firms in strategic industries. Since firms are, nevertheless, reluctant to go through the lengthy phase II investigation, they are willing to accept tougher remedies in phase I in order to avoid going into phase II (because it is probably more costly than the imposed remedies). The commission on the other hand might be willing to clear the case in phase I without a deeper investigation in order to avoid a situation where they have less bargaining power. In circumstances in which this does not happen and a phase II investigation is opened, the commission lost its threat because everybody knows that the merger cannot be blocked and must, thus, accept conditions, which are not very severe.

The second question we want to answer is whether the various types of remedies had different effects on future firms' profitability. As we extensively discussed, both in the U.S. and in the EU remedies guidelines the use of structural remedies is strongly privileged. Table 12.11 reports results, which answer this question.

We saw that remedies reduce rivals' profitability when applied in phase I. However, according to Table 12.11, only structural remedies *significantly* produce negative abnormal returns for competitors of −1.35%.[58] Pure behavioral remedies also have an average negative impact, which is even more pronounced (twice as big!) than in the case of structural remedies (−2.76%), yet the very small number of observations makes this figure not statistically significant.

---

57 Note that the average abnormal return and its variability in case of a procompetitive merger are much lower than in anticompetitive mergers.

58 We consider remedies-mix as being primarily structural remedies.

Table 12.11: Abnormal returns around the phase 1 decision date for different decisions and depending on the remedies' types.

Kind of decision		**Structural remedies**	**Pure behavioral**	**P-values of the difference**
Art. 6.2. Remedies	Merging firms	0.0020	−0.0119	0.1518
		(0.0056)	(0.0154)	
	Rivals	**−0.0135****	−0.0276	0.9742
		(0.0063)	(0.0167)	
	Obs.	8	4	
Art. 8.2 with remedies	Merging firms	−0.0041	−0.0009	0.6876
		(0.0038)	(0.0078)	
	Rivals	0.0048	0.0047	0.8183
		(0.0042)	(0.0060)	
	Obs.	42	6	

Remedies also include prohibitions. We consider as structural remedies also remedies-mix, since the "structural" part of the mix is usually the most important. The mean values of the 3-day cumulative abnormal returns in each sub-sample are reported; standard errors are reported in parentheses. Significance refers to one sided t-tests for negative abnormal returns. Anticompetitive are those mergers where the rivals' profitability increased, procompetitive those where it decreased.
**Significance at 5%.

The sample of mergers cleared with remedies in phase II is much larger. However, when we divide it into the various sub-samples according to the kind of remedies, we again have very few observations to conduct statistical tests.

At the phase I decision date the market predicts that all types of remedies will on average have a negative effect on merging firms' profitability. This effect though is not statistically significant. For rivals, the effect of remedies is positive and around 0.4% independently of the different remedies' types and, also in this case, not statistically significantly different from zero. All together these results seem to suggest that there are no significant differences between the different types of remedies, even though they might strongly depend on the small sample size.

The final question we can answer is how the market reacts to phase II decisions. Table 12.12 reports results for the abnormal return around this date. Again, we look at three sub-samples: the entire sample, the sample of anticompetitive mergers, and the sample of procompetitive mergers. If it is true that the market can build a good prior of the effect of the commission's intervention, as it seems to be according to the previous result, the market's reaction around the final decision date should only reflect the presence of "surprises" in the decision that could not be anticipated by the market.

In the entire sample, each decision has a positive impact on merging firms' profitability. That is, the market probably expected even more severe measures and, on average, positively updates its beliefs. Especially for mergers that were

Table 12.12: Abnormal returns around the phase II decision date for different phase II decisions.

Decision		Entire sample	Anticompetitive	Procompetitive
Art. 8.1.	Merging firms	0.0022	0.0112	**−0.0068****
Clearance		(0.0056)	(0.0097)	(0.0037)
	Rivals	−0.0123	−0.0182	−0.0046
		(0.0111)	(0.0180)	(0.0114)
	Obs.	17	10	7
Art. 8.2.	Merging firms	**0.0047***	**0.0104****	0.0006
Remedies		(0.0033)	(0.0051)	(0.0042)
	Rivals	−0.0004	−0.0034	0.0017
		(0.0054)	(0.0062)	(0.0082)
	Obs.	48	24	24
Art. 8.3.	Merging firms	**0.0197****	**0.0185***	**0.0232***
Prohibition		(0.0094)	(0.0121)	(0.0126)
	Rivals	−0.0067	−0.0003	**−0.0261***
		(0.0078)	(0.0090)	(0.0109)
	Obs.	13	9	4

The mean values of the 3-days cumulative abnormal returns in each sub-sample are reported; standard errors are reported in parentheses. Significance refers to one sided t-tests for negative abnormal returns. Anticompetitive are those mergers where the rivals' profitability increased, procompetitive those where it decreased.
*Significance at 10%.
**Significance at 5%.

blocked, the abnormal return for merging firms is quite substantial (1.97%) and largely significant. Remember, however, that the market reaction when a phase II investigation was announced was a reduction of the stock prices by 10% on average for merging firms. This result stays true in both the sub-samples of anticompetitive (1.85%) and procompetitive mergers (2.32%). Also the announcement of remedies has a significant impact on merging firms' abnormal return, 0.47% in the entire sample, 1.04% in the sample of anticompetitive mergers, but only 0.06% (and not significant) in the sample of procompetitive mergers. Clearance has a positive but not significant impact on merging firms' profitability in the entire sample and when the market valued the deal to be anticompetitive. Instead, the effect is negative and significant (−0.68%) in procompetitive mergers.

The effects for rivals are negligible, in the sense that they are not significantly different from zero independently of the decision type and the kind of merger. There are however two exceptions. When the merger was cleared without remedies, abnormal returns for rivals have been on average substantial and negative (−1.23% in the entire sample, −1.82 for anticompetitive mergers, and −0.68% in procompetitive mergers). Yet, given the low number of observations and the high standard errors, these figures are not significant. A very strong and significant negative reaction on competitors' stock prices can be observed when the merger was blocked and the market had valued this deal as being procompetitive.

Results for phase II decisions are very difficult to interpret since they not only do not fit our predictions but also the common sense. We think that information leakage problems might play a crucial role during a phase II investigation given its length. Therefore, the phase II abnormal returns might be a bad proxy for the commission's decision effect since they just reflect an update to reactions that we did not observe and happened between the phase I and phase II decisions. In order to more cleanly answer this question, one should look at the development patterns of abnormal returns during the period of time between phase I and phase II decisions and try to capture how much information was disclosed to the market before the final decision.

12.8. Conclusions

Merger control is an important and widely discussed policy instrument. Its proponents claim that it is necessary to maintain effective competition in markets subject to consolidations and at the same time ensures that efficiencies produced by merger activity are not lost. Antagonists claim that it is a costly process, subject to political capture, most likely used to reach other goals than protecting consumers, and therefore essentially useless. Which of the two ideas is more plausible is essentially an empirical question. Moreover, an *ex-post* policy evaluation might per se be useful to improve the quality of the policy intervention based on the available evidence on its effectiveness in the past.

This chapter pursues several aims. First, we want to provide an extensive overview of the existing literature on the effectiveness of remedial actions. Particularly, we appraise the literature on the use of event studies that have quite extensively been applied in the past to assess antitrust decisions. In doing so, we specifically tackle some issues related to the interpretation of such methodology that diverges in different disciplines (finance vs. IO).

Second, we provide an international comparison of institutional arrangements and regulatory approaches to deal with remedies in merger control. We conclude that there is a clear convergence on some shared principles that guide competition authorities in the application of remedies.

Finally, we present our own study based on an event study methodology of the European Commission's decisions by examining a sample of 167 concentrations analyzed between 1990 and 2002. In particular, we aim at answering two interrelated questions: First, were remedies correctly applied? Second, did remedies reach their goal of restoring competition and solve the market power problem when applied?

Our empirical analysis reaches some first conclusions. We provide evidence that the commission made some mistakes in its evaluation when contrasted to the market's assessment of the merger competitive effects. Not only did the commission unduly impose remedies in mergers that were valued by the market to be procompetitive (type I errors), but also it unconditionally cleared some mergers where the market recognized the existence of market power concerns (type II errors).

We further look at stock price movements around the commission's decision date in order to infer how the market evaluated the commission's decision. We observe that the market seems to regard remedies as effective when adopted in phase I, since rivals mostly loose when remedies are applied, especially in anti-competitive mergers. This corresponds to our expectations based on a standard model of oligopolistic competition. Moreover, it seems that the market is able to generate a good prior for some types of phase II decisions, when information about the opening of an in depth investigation is provided. Particularly, the market predicts very clearly the negative impact of prohibitions and the less severe impact of clearance without conditions and obligations. Instead, the market seems not to be able to build a good prior about phase II remedies. Our results suggest that the period between the phase I and phase II decisions deserves special attention to assess the market's evaluation of remedies in phase II, since it is difficult to predict the outcome of the bargaining process between the authority and the merging parties. Moreover, we suggest that one possible explanation for the apparently lower effectiveness of remedies in phase II might be explained by the shift in bargaining power from the commission to the firms when moving into phase II in cases where to prohibit a merger is politically difficult.

To understand the robustness of our approach, we discussed its several drawbacks and suggest improvements and lines of further research. In particular, in Duso et al. (2006b), we tackle three essential issues. Most fundamentally, we point out the implicit difficulty to evaluate the remedies' effectiveness by looking at the impact of the commission's decisions on stock markets, since the policy choice might be endogenous to the market outcome (see Duso and Röller, 2003). Regression analysis might be a helpful development of the proposed methodology, since it allows for correcting this endogeneity problem, testing causal relationships, and controls for the influence of other factors.

Second, the importance of information leakage during phase II investigation is highlighted by the difficulties the market had to predict remedies. The findings about market reactions around the phase II decision date seem to confirm this prediction. We propose to look at the long run abnormal returns or, even better, at the evolution of stock prices during the in depth investigation period in order to answer this question.

Finally, we suggest matching our sample with information about firms' performance after the merger based on balance sheet data as a robustness test of the adopted methodology. This would allow us to create an alternative measure of the merger's competitive effects.

Acknowledgements

We would like to thank Mats Bergmann and Lars-Hendrik Röller for very valuable comments. We also thank Vivek Ghosal, Paul Heidhues, Giancarlo Spagnolo, two anonymous referees, and participants at the IIOC 2005 Conference in Atlanta, the Conference "Remedies and Sanction in Competition Policy 2005" in

Amsterdam, the EARIE Conference 2005 in Porto, the CEPR conference "The Effectiveness of Competition Policy: Issues and Methods" in Paris, and seminar participants at the University of Vienna and University of Innsbruck for helpful discussions. Cinzia Alcidi provided excellent research assistance. Tomaso Duso gratefully acknowledges financial support from the Deutsche Forschungsgemeinschaft through SFB/TR 15.

References

Aktas, N., de Bodt, E., Roll, R. (2004a), Market response to European regulation of business combinations. *Journal of Financial and Quantitative Analysis* 39 (4), 731–757.

Aktas, N., de Bodt, E., Roll, R. (2004b), European M&A regulation is protectionist. Mimeo.

Andrade, G., Mitchell, M., Stafford, E. (2001), New evidence and perspectives on mergers. *Journal of Economic Perspectives* 15, 103–120.

Arai, K. (2004), An airline merger in Japan: A case study revealing principles of Japanese merger control. *Journal of Industry, Competition and Trade* 4 (3), 207–222.

Baer, W.J. (1999), *A Study of the Commission's Divestiture Process*. FTC.

Baer, W.J., Redcay, R.C. (2003), Solving competition problems in merger control: The requirements for an effective divestiture remedy. In: Leveque, F., Shelanski, H. (Eds.), *Merger Remedies in American and European Union Competition Law*. Edward Elgar Publishing, Northampton, MA.

Banerjee, A., Eckard, E.W. (1998), Are mega-mergers anticompetitive? Evidence from the first great merger wave. *RAND Journal of Economics* 29 (4), 803–827.

Bittlingmayer, G., Hazlett, T.W (2000), DOS kapital: Has antitrust action against Microsoft created value in the computer industry? *Journal of Financial Economics* 55 (3), 329–359.

Brady, U., Feinberg, R. (2000), An examination of stock-price effects of EU merger control policy. *International Journal of Industrial Organization* 18, 885–900.

Cabral, L.M.B. (2003), Horizontal mergers with free-entry: Why cost efficiencies may be a weak defense and asset sales a poor remedy. *International Journal of Industrial Organization* 21, 607–623.

Campbell, A.N., Halladay, C.W. (2002), The use of behavioural remedies in Canadian merger law. Paper delivered at the Canadian Bar Association Fall Conference on Competition Law (Panel on Remedies in Competition Law: October 3rd and 4th).

Carstensen, P.C. (1999), Remedying the Microsoft monopoly: Monopoly law, the rights of buyers, and the enclosure movement in intellectual property. *The Antitrust Bulletin* 44 (3), 577–617. Fall.

Comanor, W.S. (2001), The problem of remedy in monopolization cases: The Microsoft case as an example. *The Antitrust Bulletin* 46 (1), 115–133. Spring.

Competition Bureau Canada (2003), Annual Report of the Commissioner of Competition.

Competition Bureau Canada (2004), Annual Report of the Commissioner of Competition.

Duso, T., Röller, L.-H. (2003), Endogenous deregulation: Evidence from OECD countries. *Economics Letters* 81 (1), 67–71.

Duso, T., Neven, D., Röller, L.-H. (2006a), The political economy of European merger control: Evidence using stock market data. *The Journal of Law and Economics*, in press.

Duso, T., Gugler, K., Yurtoglu, B.B. (2006b), How effective is EU merger control? WZB Discussion Paper SP II 2006-12.

Eckbo, B.E., Wier, P. (1985), Antimerger policy under the Hart-Scott-Rodino Act: A re-examination of the market power hypothesis. *The Journal of Law and Economics* 28, 119–149.

Eckbo, B.E. (1983), Horizontal mergers, collusion, and stockholder wealth. *Journal of Financial Economics* 11, 241–273.

Eckbo, B.E. (1992), Mergers and the value of antitrust deterrence. *Journal of Finance* 47 (3), 1005–1029.

Ellert, J. (1976), Mergers, antitrust law enforcement and stockholder returns. *Journal of Finance* 31 (2), 715–732.

Elzinga, K. (1969), The antimerger law: Pyrrhic victories? *Journal of Law and Economics* 43, 52.

Farell, J. (2003), Negotiation and merger remedies: Some problems. In: Leveque, F., Shelanski, H. (Eds.), *Merger Remedies in American and European Union Competition Law*. Edward Elgar Publishing, Northampton, MA.

Farrell, J., Shapiro, C. (1990), Horizontal mergers: An equilibrium analysis. *American Economic Review*, 107–126. March.

Fee, E.C., Shawn, T. (2004), Sources of gains in horizontal mergers: Evidence from customer, supplier, and rival firms. *Journal of Financial Economics* 74, 423–460.

Fridolfsson, S.O., Stennek, J. (2005), Why mergers reduce profits and raise share prices. *Journal of the European Economic Association*, in press.

Goergen, M., Renneboog, L. (2004), Shareholder wealth effects of European domestic and cross-border takeover bids. *European Financial Management* 10 (1), 9–45.

Gugler, K., Mueller, D.C., Yurtoglu, B.B., Zulehner, C. (2003), The effects of mergers: An international comparison. *International Journal of Industrial Organization* 21 (5), 625–653.

Halverson, J., Ewing, K. (2005), Recent developments in EU and US merger remedies. *Competition Law*.

Kim, E.H., Singal, V. (1993), Mergers and market power: Evidence from the airline industry. *American Economic Review* 83 (3), 549–569.

Ivaldi, M., Verboven, F. (2005), Quantifying the effects from horizontal mergers in European competition policy. *International Journal of Industrial Organization*, in press.

Lyons, B. (2004), Reform of European merger policy. *Review of International Economics* 12 (2), 246–261.

McAfee, R.P., Williams, M.A. (1988), Can event studies detect anticompetitive mergers? *Economics Letters* 28, 199–203.

McDavid, J., Breed, L. (2005), Merger remedies. *The National Law Journal*, January 17.

McGuckin, R., Warren-Boulton, F.R., Waldstein, P. (1992), The use of stock market returns in antitrust analysis of mergers. *Review of Industrial Organization* 7, 1–11.

Molnar, J. (2003), Preemptive horizontal mergers: Theory and evidence. Mimeo, London.

Monti, M. (2003), The Commission's notice on merger remedies. In: Leveque, F., Shelanski, H. (Eds.), *Merger Remedies in American and European Union Competition Law*. Edward Elgar Publishing, Northampton, MA.

Motta, M. (2004), *Competition Policy. Theory and Practice*. Cambridge University Press.

Motta, M., Polo, M., Vasconcelos, H. (2003), Merger remedies in the European Union: An overview. In: Leveque, F., Shelanski, H. (Eds.), *Merger Remedies in American and European Union Competition Law*. Edward Elgar Publishing, Northampton, MA.

Mullin, L., Mullin, J., Mullin, W. (1995), The competitive effects of mergers: Stock market evidence from the U.S. Steel dissolution suit. *RAND Journal of Economics* 26, 314–330.

Neven, D., Röller, L.-H. (2005), Consumer surplus vs. welfare standard in a political economy model of merger control. *International Journal of Industrial Organization*, in press.

Nevo, A. (2000), Mergers with differentiated products: The case of the ready-to-eat cereal industry. *RAND Journal of Economics* 31, 395–421.

Neylan, S.C.D. (2002), Quantification and design of merger remedies under the competition act. Paper delivered at the Canadian Bar Association Fall Conference on Competition Law (October 3 and 4, as part of the Panel on Remedies in Competition Law).

Organisation for Economic Co-operation and Development (2004), Merger remedies. DAF/COMP(2004)21.

Parker, R.G., Balto, D.A. (2000), The evolving approach to merger remedies. Antitrust Report (Lexis Publishing), 2–28 May.

Pfunder, M.R., Plaine, D.J., Whittemore, A.M. (1972), Compliance with divestiture orders under Section 7 of the Clayton Act. *Antitrust Bulletin* 17 (1), 19–180.

Pinske, J., Slade, M. (2004), Mergers, brand competition, and the price of a pint. *European Economic Review* 48 (3), 617–643.

Rogowsky, R.A. (1986), The economic effectiveness of Section 7 relief. *Antitrust Bulletin*, 187–233. Spring.

Röller, L.-H., Stennek, J., Verboven, F. (2001), Efficiency gains from mergers. *European Economy* 5, 31–128.

Salant, S.W., Switzer, S., Reynolds, R.J. (1983), Losses from horizontal merger: The effects of an exogenous change in industry structure on Cournot–Nash equilibrium. *Quarterly Journal of Economics* 98, 185–199.

Scholes, M., Williams, J. (1977), Estimating beta from non-synchronous data. *Journal of Financial Economics* 5, 309–327.

Schumann, L. (1993), Patterns of abnormal returns and the competitive effects of horizontal mergers. *Review of Industrial Organization* 8, 679–696.

Servaes, H., Tamayo, A. (2005), The response of industry rivals to control threats. Working Paper, London Business School.

Shahrur, H. (2005), Industry structure and horizontal takeovers: Analysis of wealth effect on rivals, suppliers, and corporate customers. *Journal of Financial Economics* 76, 61–98.

Simpson, H.D. (2001), Did May company's acquisition of associated dry goods corporation reduce competition? An event study analysis. *Review of Industrial Organization* 18, 351–362.

Singal, V. (1996), Airline mergers and competition: An integration of stock and product price effects. *Journal of Business* 69 (2), 233–268.

Slovin, M.B., Sushka, M.E., Hudson, C.D. (1991), Deregulation, contestability, and airline acquisitions. *Journal of Financial Economics* 30 (2), 231–251.

Song, M.H., Walkling, R.A. (2000), Abnormal returns to rivals of acquisition targets: A test of the 'acquisitions probability' hypothesis. *Journal of Financial Economics* 55 (2), 143–171.

Stillman, R. (1983), Examining antitrust policy towards horizontal mergers. *Journal of Financial Economics* 11, 225–240.

CHAPTER 13

The Significant Impediment of Effective Competition Test in the New European Merger Regulation: In Theory and Practice[1]

Jérôme Foncel[a], Marc Ivaldi[b] and Valérie Rabassa[c]

[a]*GREMARS, University of Lille 3*
[b]*University of Toulouse, EHESS and IDEI, Toulouse, France*
[c]*European Commission, Chief Economist Office, Directorate General for Competition*

Abstract

In recent years, the EC competition authorities have increased their interest for empirical methodology in particular to study potential anti-competitive harms arising from mergers. These developments have been shaped by a higher interest dedicated to unilateral effects. The new EC Merger Regulation (2004) has incorporated the *"significant impediment of effective competition"* test which gives more weights to the competitive effects of a transaction. The recent highlighted media case *Lagardère/Editis (2004)* can be considered as the first empirical illustration of this new test.

13.1. Introduction

The new EC Merger Regulation (2004) incorporates a new test to check whether a concentration or a merger between undertakings would constitute a *"Significant Impediment of Effective Competition, in particular as a result of the creation or strengthening of a dominant position."*[2] This test, the SIEC test herein, is aimed to be an instrument to analyse potential anti-competitive harms like unilateral effects conducts arising from mergers. The recent highlighted media case *Lagardère/Editis* (*2004*) could be considered as the first case where this

---

[1] The views expressed in this article are exclusively the views of the authors and not necessarily those of the European Commission. Valérie Rabassa is member of the Chief Economist Office. She was representing the Chief Economist in *Lagardère/Editis*.

[2] EC Merger Regulation (ECMR) 139/2004.

CONTRIBUTIONS TO ECONOMIC ANALYSIS
VOLUME 282 ISSN: 0573-8555
DOI: 10.1016/S0573-8555(06)82013-4

test has been implemented by means of an empirical illustration.[3,4,5] It is also an example of the application of empirical analysis in a standard investigation.

The objective of this chapter is to present the SIEC test in the context of the new merger regulation and guidelines, to show how it is implemented in the *Lagardère/Editis* case, and from this illustration to understand the scope of the SIEC test with respect to more traditional tests like the dominance test. Section 13.2 discusses the new EC regulatory framework. Section 13.3 examines the role of the empirical methodology. Section 13.4 present the *Lagardère/Editis* case and the empirical analysis developed in the curse of the investigation of this case. Section 13.5 concludes.

13.2. The EC merger regulation

Since the beginning of the EC Merger Control in September 1990 up to December 2004, 2648 cases have been notified to the Commission.[6] Eighty-four percent of all cases have been cleared without any conditions after a phase I investigation. Figure 13.1 illustrates the statistics of the EC Merger Control over

Phase I[7]		Phase II[8]			Total
Clearance	Clearance with Remedies	Clearance	Clearance with Remedies	Prohibition	
2237	119	26	72	19	2648
84.44%	4.49%	0.98%	2.71%	0.71%	100%

[7] 6.1(b) decision.
[8] 8.2 compatible decision and 8.3 prohibition decision.

Fig. 13.1: Final decisions merger control.

[3] Case COMP/M.2978.

[4] On March 2000, the Commission, for the first time, has included in a final merger decision—see case *COMP/M.1672 Volvo/Scania*—a reference to unilateral conducts. In this case, the Commission requested an econometric study from Professors Ivaldi and Verboven in order to attempt to measure directly what the effects of the merger could be on the prices charged by heavy truck producers in various national markets. However, given the novelty of the approach, the Commission did not base its assessment on the results of the study, but rather based its analysis on its traditional dominance test.

[5] In a companion paper (Foncel et al., 2005) we provide a detailed presentation of the econometric analysis.

[6] Note that, on the 2648 notified cases to the Commission, a certain number of cases are out of scope of the Merger Regulation like 6.1(a) decisions; others (86 cases) have been withdrawn in Phase I and Phase II (3.24 percent of the total of the notified cases), some cases (3.5 percent of the total of notified cases) were also refer partially or fully to the member States (9.3 decision), some of them were also declared compatible because they restore effective competition (8.4 decision). These statistics are computed by us from data on mergers published on the website of the Directorate General for Competition of the European Commission.

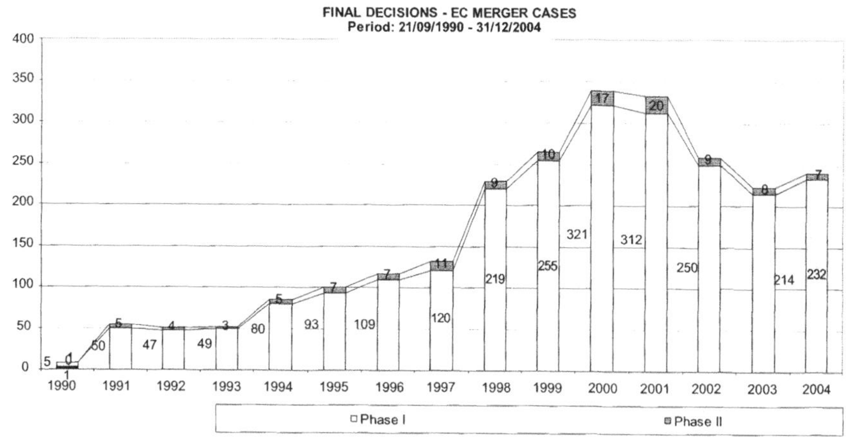

Fig. 13.2: Phase I and II decisions in merger control.

the last years. Since 1990, the Commission has prohibited only 19 deals (with a pick of 5 prohibitions in 2001), less than one percent of the total number of notified cases.

However, the system put in place in 1990 has shown some signs of strain. The growth in workload has significantly increased overtime since the introduction of the Merger Regulation. Thus, the number of final decisions has risen from 5 in 1990 to 239 in 2004.[9] Figure 13.2 illustrates this evolution. Larger and more complex mergers have also required greater care in the economic analysis contained in the Commission decisions, and those decisions have been subject to increasingly close scrutiny by the European courts. In particular, recent judgements delivered by the European Court of First Instance ('CFI') (i.e., Airtours/First Choice,[10] Schneider/Legrand[11] and Tetra Laval/Sidel[12]) raised important issues concerning the functioning of the EC merger review process. The CFI has imposed to the Commission a high standard of proof, which has important implications for the way in which the Commission conducts its investigations. As a result, on December 2003, the Commission adopted a reform of its system of merger control. The reform package consists in particular of the following elements: A new test introduced by Regulation 139/2004 which replaces the dominance test laid down in Regulation 4064/89[13]

---

[9] Cases out of scope of the Merger Regulation (6.1(a) decision) have been excluded from this dataset.

[10] Case T-342/99 *Airtours plc v Commission* [2002] ECR II-2585.

[11] Case T-310/01 *Schneider Electric v Commission* [2002] ECR II-4071.

[12] Case T-5/02 *Tetra Laval v Commission* [2002] ECR II-4381.

[13] Regulation 139/2004 has entered into force on May 1, 2004. See http://europa.eu.int/eur-lex/pri/en/oj/dat/2004/l_024/l_02420040129en00010022.pdf

and a Commission Guidelines with guidance on the assessment of horizontal mergers.[14]

13.2.1. The new test

The previous test was based on the notion of dominance. In particular, it analysed whether a merger *"creates or strengthens a dominant position as a result of which effective competition would be significantly impeded in all or a substantial part of the European Union."* (See EC Merger Regulation 4064/89.) This test was perceived by commentators as not covering all mergers that produce anti-competitive effects. This would refer to cases where, in oligopolistic markets, the merging firms would not be in a position to become the "clearly largest company" in the market. In other words, the merging firms would be in a position to raise prices exercising thus market power, without leading to co-ordination and without necessarily holding the largest market share in the market. This uncertainty as to the treatment of unilateral effects in oligopolistic markets has become known as "the gap." The dominance test was also perceived as being a static test. Its fundamental problem was mainly associated with its inability to take into account the rival's responses and the corresponding appropriated new equilibrium. Therefore, the dominance test went under a range of critics from economists.

A compromise solution finally adopted in the form of a new SIEC test is whether a merger *"would significantly impede effective competition, in particular as a result of the creation or strengthening of a dominant position."* As a result, a merger may significantly impede effective competition by removing competitive constraints due to the loss of competition between merging firms. The new test considers dominance as only one possible cause of a significant impediment to effective competition. Indeed, it is likely to be wider in scope than the dominance test as it applies clearly to situations where a merger results in "unilateral effects" in situations of non-collusive oligopoly. Indeed, it could be viewed as a compromise solution which removes the uncertainty which is surrounding the potential "gap" in the scope of the dominance test. The new test is also close to the so-called "substantial lessening of competition" test or SLC test used in several other jurisdictions like the US, the UK (since June 2003) and Ireland.

Overall, the new test has a number of benefits. In particular, it is a better instrument to deal with the full range and complexity of competition issues raised by mergers; it clearly focuses on the change in competition and takes into account the equilibrium effect of mergers. It would encompass the dominance concept and consequently all the jurisprudence would remain relevant; By allowing to

---

[14] See the Commission Guidelines on the assessment of horizontal mergers: http://europa.eu.int/eur-lex/pri/en/oj/dat/2004/c_031/c_03120040205en00050018.pdf

investigate mergers even when they involve relatively low levels of concentration, it should enlarge the scope of investigation closing thus the "gap;" finally, it is aimed to make consumer welfare as the objective of the new European merger regulation.

13.2.2. The EC horizontal merger guidelines

The Guidelines have been drafted with the view to provide a sound economic framework for the assessment of mergers under the Merger Regulation. The document is structured as following. After a short introductory section and an overview section (Section II), Section III of the Notice describes the market shares and the concentration levels considered as useful indicators of the market structure. Then the central question is raised: Do mergers enhance the level of market power? Section IV of the Notice describes the appropriate analysis of the various possible types of competitive harm from horizontal mergers: Unilateral—called "non-co-ordinated"—effects and co-ordinated effects. The subsequent sections deal with particular countervailing factors that could mitigate the initial finding: Buyer power (Section V), entry analysis (Section VI), efficiencies (Section VII), failing firm defence (Section VIII).

Market indicators

In assessing mergers, market indicators like market shares and concentration thresholds may give useful preliminary information about the competitive situation in a market. Market share indicators are very established by case law as the interpretation of the dominance concept. According to the Notice, large market shares—50 percent and above—may in themselves be evidence of the existence of a dominant market position. Limited market shares may also lead to presumption of compatibility—for instance a market share below 25 percent. Indeed, the Commission has clearly adopted a "soft safe harbour" approach. As a second screening device, the Commission's Notice proposes to apply the Herfindahl–Hirschman Index (HHI).[15] In particular, the Commission is "unlikely to identify competition concerns" when: (i) $HHI < 1000$; (ii) $1000 < HHI < 2000$ and $\Delta HHI < 250$; (iii) $HHI > 2000$ and $\Delta HHI < 150$.[16]

Scenarios of competitive harms

According to the Notice two scenarios of competitive harms may happen: unilateral ("non-coordinated") effects and co-ordinated effects.

---

[15] The HHI is equal to the sum of the squares of market shares of the firms in the relevant market. Note that the HHI is less informative when a transaction involves a potential entrant or when the merging parties are important innovators in ways not reflected in market shares.

[16] ΔHHI is the difference between post and pre merger level of concentration.

Unilateral effects A merger may remove important competitive constraints on one or more sellers, who consequently have increased market power. Indeed, unilateral effects refer to a situation where the merging parties decide to charge a higher price (or to decrease the quantity/capacity produced or the quality of the products) *post-merger*. Before the merger, one of the merging firms decided to increase prices unilaterally; part of their final consumers would turn to other competing firms, among which the other merging firm. As a result of the concentration, the merging parties can absorb some of these competitive pressures, and can thus recover some of the customers that left. Unilateral effects may arise, in particular, when the merger leads to a dominant position. In such cases, single firm dominance "typically" associated with the new entity having an appreciably larger market share than the next competitor post-merger.

The following factors may also influence whether significant unilateral effects are likely to result from mergers:

- Merging firms are close competitors: The incentive to increase prices is strongly related to the degree of substitution between the merging firms and the other competitors' products. First the Commission focuses on the degree of substitution between the merging firms. The higher the degree of substitution between the merging firms' products, the stronger would be the incentive for the merging firms to raise prices and the higher the likely post-merger price increase. Second the Commission evaluates the degree of product differentiation between the merging firms and their competitors' products. The merging firms' incentive to raise prices is more constrained when rival firms produce close substitutes than when they offer distant substitutes;
- Customers have limited possibilities from switching to another supplier;
- Competitors are unlikely to increase supply if prices increase (capacity constraints of competitors);
- The merged entity is able to hinder expansion by competitors: control or influence over the supply of inputs, or distribution possibilities;
- The merger eliminates an important competitive force, recent or potential competitive entrant, or merger between the only two major providers of innovations.

Indeed, one of the crucial issues of the new EC Guidelines is to assess closeness of competition in practice in order to predict unilateral effects. The *Lagardère/Editis* case is a perfect illustration of this concern. As explained later, books are typically differentiated products; in this industry, publishing groups can be recomposed *post-merger* and price discrimination occurs over time.

Coordinated effects A merger may create or reinforce a situation where competition is constrained by a co-ordination among market players. Co-ordination is more likely to emerge in markets where it is fairly easier to establish it and where co-ordination is sustainable over time. Sustainability requires that:

- The companies involved can monitor each other's market behaviour (market transparency);

- There is a credible "deterrence mechanism" (disciplining mechanism) to ensure adherence to the terms of co-ordination;
- Outsiders and customers cannot undermine the co-ordination.

Countervailing factors

According to the Notice, buyer power is an important element of countervailing power as well as entry. For entry, the relevant criterion is whether decreased competitive pressure would make entry sufficiently profitable to make it likely. In particular, entry has to be likely, timely and sufficient to deter or defeat any potential anti-competitive effects of the merger.

Efficiencies The section on efficiencies clarifies the way in which the Commission explicitly considers efficiency claims. According to the Guidelines, the burden of the proof would be on the parties. Efficiencies may take various forms: cost savings in production or in distribution leading to lower prices; synergies leading to new or improved products. Furthermore, variable and marginal costs are "more likely to be relevant" to the assessment than fixed costs. Three (cumulative) conditions are also required for efficiencies:

- Benefit to consumers timely, and substantial, likely to be realised. In other words, efficiencies should be passed on to consumers;[17]
- Merger-specificity: efficiencies are relevant to the competitive assessment when they are a direct consequence of the notified merger;
- Verifiability: the parties must provide all the relevant information demonstrating the claimed efficiencies are merger-specific and likely to be realised, and must show to what extent the efficiencies are likely to benefit consumers.

13.3. The role of the empirical analysis

Over recent years, the use of empirical and quantitative methods in merger investigation has developed for at least three factors: The growing call for of economists by the EC authorities for expertise, the development of fairly and friendly reliable software, the availability of more and better data. One could expect that the introduction of the new EC Merger Regulation should prolong this trend.

13.3.1. The recent use of empirical methods

The traditional EC merger investigation is mainly conducted in the form of written requests for investigation.[18] However, some recent EC merger decisions

---

[17] According to the Notice, the relevant benchmarking in assessing efficiency claims is that "consumers will not be worse off as a result of the merger."

[18] Examples of request are: requests pursuant Article 11 of the Merger Regulation (questionnaires to suppliers, customers, competitors and other relevant parties); Requests for information from the

have paid more attention to empirical evidence provided by the use of quantitative techniques. The empirical methodology is traditionally used as a support to delineate relevant product and geographic markets.[19] More recently empirical analysis has also been more extensively applied in parallel with the development of the technique of merger simulations. Merger simulations attempt to predict the effects that a merger might have on prices of the merging and the rival firms.

Simulation models could thus be defined as the formal use of game theoretic models and structural assumptions to make quantitative predictions of unilateral effects. The *Volvo/Scania (2000)* decision is one of the pioneering cases where a simulation model is applied in the analysis of the impact of a merger in the European truck market. It anticipates on the Commission's new test and by Guidelines on the assessment of horizontal mergers. The *Lagardère/Editis (2004)* case, where a simulation analysis similar to the one implemented in the *Volvo/Scania* case is developed, is certainly the first case concomitant to the new Merger regulation.[20]

The role of the empirical methods is also reinforced by the recent appointment of a Chief Economist[21] and the creation of the Chief Economist Team in September 2002 at the Directorate General for Competition of the European Commission. Furthermore, the EC "Best Practices," by providing a useful tool for interaction between the parties and the Commission's economists, also contributes to this move.[22] This co-operative conduct in terms of empirical methodology is also present in the *Lagardère/Editis* case.

---

parties (internal documents, business plans, etc....); industry reports, trade press, experts studies, etc.

[19] For instance, in *CVC/Lenzing (2001)*—Case COMP/M.2187—the Commission has conducted its own price correlation analysis to define whether the different fibres, viscose, polyester and cotton, were substitute products. The Commission has also examined whether correlation was spurious. In *Rexam/ANC (2001)*—Case COMP/M.1939—the Commission has checked whether aluminium and steel beverage cans are substitutable products also using a price correlation analysis. In *Blackstone/Acetex (2005)*—Case COMP/M.3625—the Chief Economist Team, in order to delineate the relevant geographic market, has performed a so-called "shock analysis," in order to examine the affect on unexpected plant outage on prices and trade flows.

[20] The Commission has also recently developed simulation techniques in other cases, for instance: *GE/Instrumentarium (2003)*—Case COMP/M.3083—where the Commission has analysed bidding data and price impact of the merger; *Oracle/PeopleSoft (2004)*—Case COMP/M.3216—where the Commission has calibrated its own model of the software industry to analyse the impact of the merger. Both simulations were performed by the Chief Economist team.

[21] Professor Lars-Hendrik Röller.

[22] "Best Practices" may provide helpful guidance at both the pre-notification and the notification stages. At a pre-notification level, contacts and discussions between the economists advising the Commission and the parties could enhance transparency on methodological issues. Once the case has been notified, in the interest of an efficient investigation, the Commission could consult the parties or third-parties on empirical methodology regarding data and information gathering in the relevant economic sector. See the EC Commission "Best Practices" on the conduct of EC merger control proceedings: http://europa.eu.int/comm/competition/mergers/legislation/regulation/best_practices.pdf

13.3.2. Pitfalls and benefits

At least three different sources of errors could affect the robustness of results in the course of an empirical investigation: Data collection, choice of functional forms and specifications, structural assumptions on firms' conduct.

Data issues are keys in the econometric modelling process. Data should be representative in order to reduce measurement errors. Hence, there exists a heavy burden of data collection. However, the level of data requirement is strongly related to the simulation method used. Calibration techniques require much less information than statistical estimation. When calibrating a model, one just need a few set of data to adjust (calibrate) plausible values for the parameters of interest of the economic model. When estimating a model, one makes use of a statistical technique to find (estimate) the parameter value so that the model fits a series of data.

Empirical methodology requires also the economist to specify functional and parametric forms for the equations that form the model. For instance, a demand equation parametrically specifies the relationship between prices charged and quantities sold in the relevant market. The choice of functional forms has major implications for the magnitude of predictions drawn from a model as different functional forms may produce substantially different outcomes. However, statistical tests can help the analyst to measure the severity of this type of errors or the quality and the robustness of predictions.

Structural assumptions on firms' conduct could also impact the magnitude of effects measured with a merger simulation model. Here the solution to limit the scope for such errors is either to statistically compared the realism of different firms' conduct or to rely on outside expertise in a Bayesian type of approach.

However, empirical methods also provide benefits as a complementary tool for traditional methods of investigation in competition policy. They highlight critical assumptions and factors, to improve the accuracy by putting numbers on the issues, to provide a persuasive set of arguments by making them more concrete and better grounded on facts and theory. With regard to merger analysis, they can provide quantitative predictions of unilateral effects, tests of different assumptions of market equilibria, estimations of the impact of efficiencies and evaluations of the effects of potential remedies. Hence, empirical methodology is helpful in the decision-making process as far as they can be applied in a constrained period of time.[23] Of course they incur costs which depend on the features of investigated cases. Nonetheless cost reduction in collecting data and

---

[23] For Phase I merger investigation, the timetable, under the new regulation, is the following: (i) 25 working days starting the day which follows the receipt of notification; (ii) Extended to 35 working days if undertakings are offered or a referral request is received. In phase II, the timing becomes: (i) 90 working days from the day that follows the decision to carry out an in-depth inquiry; (ii) +20 working days if requested by the notifying parties or by the Commission with the agreement of the notifying parties; (iii) +15 working days if companies offered remedies after the 54th working day that followed the initiation of the in-depth inquiry.

software development have probably contributed to facilitate the application of empirical methods.

13.4. An empirical illustration: The Lagardère/Editis case

13.4.1. Motivation

The *Lagardère/Editis* case was one of the leading 2003 European mergers in the book industry. The book industry is characterised by a high degree of market concentration along the "book vertical chain." Publishers could be spitted between different tiers depending on their scale and degree of vertical integration. The first tier is made of Hachette (Lagardère) and Editis (former VUP). They both act along the book vertical chain from the upstream segment of the publishing rights to the downstream segment of the distribution and the retailing. The second tier is composed of four medium sized groups (Gallimard, Flamarion, Le Seuil, and Albin Michel). Both are also vertically integrated publishers with the exception of Albin Michel partly dependent of Hachette for marketing. The six major French publishers—Editis, Hachette, Gallimard, Flammarion, Albin Michel and Le Seuil—control more than two thirds of the market measured by sales. The third tier is made of small non-vertically-integrated publishers.

Indeed, the combination of Hachette and Editis raises competition concerns not only because it involves the two leading market players of the book industry but also because it combines two entities with a high degree of vertical integration. In particular, the Commission considered that the merger would have lead to dominant positions along the vertical book chain and notably at the downstream level for the sale of book to resellers.[24] Hence, on the markets for the sale of general literature title in large and pocket formats by publishers to retailers, the merging entity would reach a market share of around [20–40%] for general literature titles in large format and a market share of around [55–65%] for pocket formats.[25] The merger also increases significantly the level of the industry concentration.[26] In the market for the sale of general literature in large format to wholesalers, the HHI, considered here as another screening device, indicates that after the transaction the degree of concentration would be relatively high, at 1714 points, and that the increase would be significant, at 782 points. In the pocket market, the HHI was already at 2212 points before the transaction, indicating a very high level of concentration, and would increase after the transaction by 1890 points to 4102.

---

[24] In particular creation or strengthening of a dominant position were found in the following markets: (i) Textbooks for schools in France; (ii) educational supporting materials; (iii) dictionaries and smaller general encyclopedia; (iv) general literature books in hardcover and paperback formats; (v) children's books; (vi) guides and manuals.

[25] According to the findings of the Commission's investigation.

[26] See the EC Horizontal Guidelines defined in Section 13.2.2.

Given the high importance of this merger for the book industry,[27] and in order to complement its traditional dominance analysis, the Commission has carried out an econometric study to measure unilateral effects on these markets. The case is a good illustration of the empirical implementation of the new SIEC test. The measure of unilateral effects is also a complementary tool to estimate concretely the market power of the new merging entity. Note that the focus of our present analysis is on the horizontal aspects of the case.

Interactions between Commission's and parties' economists

The *Lagardère/Editis* case is also a good example for the implementation of empirical methodology in a day to day investigation. This case has contributed to an extensive level of discussion between the economists of both the Commission and the notifying parties. Thus, since the pre-notification stage, the economists have developed an exchange of information through formal meetings or conference calls. These meetings were very helpful at different stages of the procedure, in particular to better understand the functioning of the book industry. The economists on both sides agreed that the book industry is highly differentiated and that Bertrand competition in prices is the most likely conduct. These features of the industry have in part motivated the econometric analysis. At the gathering data stage, exchanges between both parties have helped identifying the relevant databases. Once the econometric study carried out by the Commission was done, meetings between the parties and the Commission on the methodological issues were also constructive. In particular, the Commission's invited the economists of the parties to react to the econometric study.[28]

The quality and the usefulness of these have certainly contributed to the inclusion of the econometric study into the final decision.

---

[27] The four most significant segments of the book market—general literature titles including books in pocket format, children's books, guides and manuals and educational books—account on their own for more than half of all sales and for the highest growth rates since 1994. Source: the parties' form CO.

[28] The economists of the parties found that the results of the econometric decisions were robust to alternative model specifications; all estimations and simulations exercises confirmed the results presented by the econometric study of the Commission. They filtered the dataset to eliminate reporting errors and outliers and generated all control and instrumental variables to be used in the empirical model. They also proceeded to various checks aimed at verifying that the results were not biased due to potential omitted variables or weak instruments. Indeed, to the four instruments used by Foncel and Ivaldi—sum of surface of books of other editors, sum of the surface of books in other nests, number of editors in the same category, book surface multiplied bu number of pages—they used the number of editors of all other firms, the number of pages divided by surface, the share of titles in each nest over the total number of titles, the share of titles of other firms, the share of pocket titles of the firm over all titles in the nest, the share of grand format titles of the firm over all titles in the nest, and the sum of the age of all books in the nest and the sum of all pages in the nest. They obtained similar results than the Professor Ivaldi and Foncel's study, in particular they obtained similar elasticity estimates and thus similar post-merger price increases when additional exogenous variables were included and a larger set of instrumental variables was used.

13.4.2. The econometric study

Before merging, given the features of the book industry, if Hachette have decided to increase prices unilaterally, some of their final consumers would have turned to other competing publishers, among which Editis, because of significant but not necessarily high substitution effects. After merging Editis, Hachette would have been able to absorb a part of these competitive pressures, i.e., have been able to recover a part of the lost customers due to the initial price increase, conducing to a higher market power. However this effect can be partly or totally offset by potential but merger specific efficiency gains.

The econometric study is aimed to test this conjecture, i.e., to measure the impact of the merger on the public selling prices in the market of the sale of hardcover and paperback books of general literature.[29]

Data

The data set used for the econometric study is drawn from an annual survey conducted by the marketing institute IPSOS on the top 1500 hardcover books and the top 5000 paperback books, covering respectively 44 percent and 96 percent of the total sales of hardcovers and paperbacks in year 2002. The database contains information, for each title, the name of the author, the number of pages, the format (length and width), the volume sold and the price.[30,31] The final dataset contains 3267 products (titles) representing a total of 42.98 millions books sold. At the distribution level, three channels are considered: bookstores, specialised bookstores, large distribution stores. As a product in the model is defined to be a title sold in one of the three channels of distribution, the total sample of observations is finally 9566 books.

Relevant markets

Based on different arguments, in particular on the fact that the distributions of prices of paperbacks and hardcovers do not coincide (i.e., their difference of means are significantly different from zero, see Figure 13.3) the Commission concluded that there were two separate markets for harcovers and paperbacks. From an economic point of view, this could be criticised on the ground that at the microeconomic level (i.e., the consumer), these differences in the distribution of prices does not preclude substitution. Moreover, it is known that prices

---

29 The econometric has been performed by two of us, J. Foncel and M. Ivaldi, who acted as experts to the Commission.

30 Physical characteristics (length, width, number of pages) have been added from ELECTRE, a database that contains information on all books published so far in French. Note that the model assumes linear prices and does not account for the discounts granted to the retailers. How non-linear prices impact the measure of market power is discussed in Miravete and Röller (2003).

31 Note that the date of first edition of a specific title does not seem to play a role. Clearly the life cycle of a book is not summarised by the age of the book.

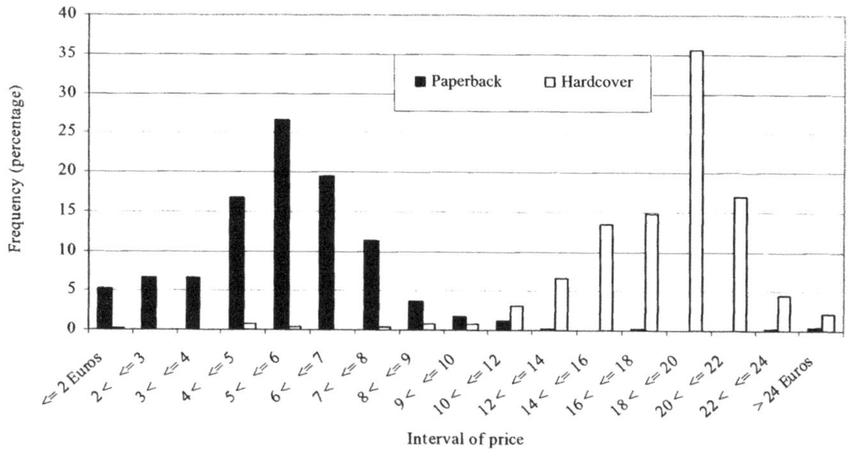

Fig. 13.3: Distributions of prices of paperbacks and hardcovers.

drops after a book's release date. Indeed a book is first published under a hardcover, aimed to hit the population of "first adopters." Then it is published under the paperback format, while the hardcover format is removed from the shelves. Depending on the unobserved tastes of individuals and unobserved characteristics of books, a customer may well buy a hardcover and a paperback at the same date.

In the econometric study below, it was decided not to separate the two markets and to look at all books in the same time. Proceeding in that way allows us not only to have more degrees of freedom from a statistical point of view, but also to have the chance to test whether the differentiation in terms of format matters on this market. In addition, by considering all the books under the two formats, one enlarges the market and we adopt a conservative attitude, a priori more favourable for the parties. It is where a test entirely based on dominance criteria and a measure of unilateral effects involves different perspectives. Under a test based on a dominance criterion, defining the markets beforehand is a crucial step in the investigation, while the definition of markets can be almost ignored when the question is to measure market power and how a merger affects market power.

Model[32]

To approximate market demand in the market of general literature books, the nested logit was chosen. The nested logit model is of particularly significant interest in differentiated markets like the book industry as it is parsimonious in

---

[32] The model is based on Verboven (1996), Ivaldi and Verboven (2005) and Foncel and Ivaldi (2005).

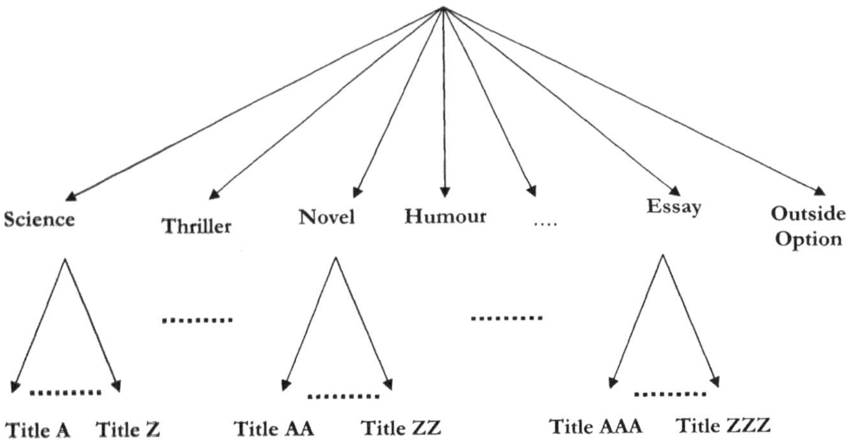

Fig. 13.4: Choices of the representative consumer.

parameters.[33] There are $i = 1, \ldots, N$ potential consumers. Consumer i makes first a discrete choice among a set of different $g = 1, \ldots, G$ alternatives corresponding to different types/categories of literature like novel, detective, science fiction, romantic. At this level an alternative is called a nest. The consumer can also choose not to buy a book in a certain category, or to buy an used book. This type of choices is gathered under the term of outside alternative. After having made a choice at this level, the consumer may choose a title j in the concerned nest. Figure 13.4 represents the consumer choices in a tree form.

The utility of consumer i utility of buying book j is given by

$$u_{ij} = \delta_j + \zeta_{ig} + (1 - \sigma)\varepsilon_{ij},$$

where the first term, δ_j, represents to the mean valuation for book j common to all consumer. The second term, ζ_{ig}, and the last term, ε_{ij}, are random variables reflecting individual i's deviation from the mean valuation. The term ζ_{ig} is consumer i's utility, common to all products belonging to group g, whereas the term ε_{ij} is consumer i's utility, specific to product j. The parameter σ lies between 0 and 1 and measures the correlation of the consumers' utility across products belonging to the same group. If $\sigma = 1$, there is a perfect correlation of preferences for products within the same group; so these products are perceived as perfect substitutes. As σ decreases, the correlation of preferences for products within same group decreases. If $\sigma = 0$, there is no correlation of preferences: consumers are equally likely to switch to products in a different group as to products in the same group in response to a price increase. In this case, we have the standard logit model in which products compete symmetrically.

[33] It would be extremely cumbersome to estimate flexible demand systems or to use simulation package like PCAIDS.

The term δ_j is a function of the price of book j, p_j, a vector of characteristics of book j, x_j, and a random term, ξ_j, representing the non-observable characteristics of book j. It is defined as:

$$\delta_j = x_j\beta - \alpha p_j + \xi_j, \tag{13.1}$$

where α and β are parameters to be estimated. Parameter α measures the sensitivity of utility to prices.

Demand equation Market demand is derived from the aggregation of individual consumer choices. Indeed, the demand equation is given by

$$\ln\left(\frac{q_i}{N - \sum_{j=1}^{J} q_j}\right) = \delta_j + \sigma \ln s_{j/g},$$

where the left-hand side represents the quantity of products j, over the overall quantity of the outside goods; the right-hand side corresponds to the mean valuation of book j plus a term corresponding to market differentiation.

Pricing equation The market for the sales of general literature books operates as a Bertrand competing market. Equilibrium prices are endogenously determined by price-setting publishers. In equilibrium, prices equal to marginal costs plus a margin that depends on elasticities, substitution effects, and differentiation. The price–cost margin is given by

$$\frac{p_j - c_j}{p_j} = \frac{1-\sigma}{\alpha(1 - \sigma s_{f/g} - (1-\sigma)s_f)p_j},$$

where the left-hand side is the Lerner index which here equals to the inverse of a sort of super elasticity that depends on the parameters of interest α and β and the market shares, s_f and $s_{f/g}$, of firm f over the whole market and within the nest g. In practice, marginal costs c_j are approximated by observable and empirically measurable variables. In our present case, marginal cost of product j is approximated by

$$c_j = \exp(\gamma w_j + \omega_j),$$

where w_j is a vector of product j's characteristics, ω_j is a random element representing non-observable characteristics of product j, and γ is a vector to estimate.

Market size The market size is a crucial element of the model. Indeed, choosing a market size is equivalent to choose the market share of the outside alternative. This outside alternative should include all the outflow possibilities, either future book purchases, purchases of other types of books, renewals purchases or purchases of complements. The data set used for calibrating the market size is drawn from the marketing institute SOFRES. Indeed, according to SOFRES, the sale of general literature title in large and pocket formats by publishers to retailers represents some 100 millions units. Overall, the market size is negatively correlated with the *post-merger* price increase. Hence, the higher the market size, the lower the market shares and the lower the market power of the merged entity.

Estimation and simulation Demand and price equations are simultaneously estimated using a non-linear three-stage least squares (NL3SLS) method, implemented through the MODEL procedure of the SAS software.[34] The parameters of interest are well estimated. Moreover several variables like dummies specific to publishers or even to famous authors (Agatha Christie, Barbara Cartland, Conan Doyle—three Anglo-saxon writers!—etc.) are strongly significant showing the model speaks about the industry.

The impact of the merger, the effects of efficiency measure and possible remedies are simulated by means of a simulation programme which solves the different Nash equilibria associated with the different modified industry structures.

Results

The econometric study provides, among others, the following results:

- On the retail markets of all general literature books (paperbacks and hardcovers) by retailers to the final consumer, the study indicates that, for a market size of 100 million units of books sold,[35] post-merger average prices would increase by 4.82 percent even without taking account of the vertical aspects of the concentration. On the retail market of paperbacks, the average price would increase by 5.51 percent.[36] Note that, on this latter market, and given the high level of market shares and the high degree of market concentration, the *post-merger* price increase is much lower than the change in the HHI.[37] The price increase is also inversely correlated with the market size. (See Figure 13.5.) Consumers' surplus would also fall significantly (by 6.04 percent) which is equivalent to 1.5 percent of the turnover of industry in the field of general literature;
- A "Bootstrap" methodology was used to derive a confidence interval for the average price increase due to the merger.[38] At 95 percent confidence level,

---

[34] For a discussion on the instruments see footnote 27 and also Foncel et al. (2005).

[35] Given the available data, the size for the market of general literature books is estimated to 100 millions of books which corresponds to an outside alternative of 57 percent.

[36] Note that there are few differences from one channel of distribution to another. However, the price increase is higher in large distribution stores (i.e., 4.99 percent) than in bookstores (i.e., 4.67 percent) or specialised bookstores (i.e., 4.77 percent).

[37] The *post-merger* HHI is equal to 4102 points whether the ΔHHI is equal to 1890 points. This corresponds to an increase of 46 percent.

[38] Indeed, a sample of 1000 values of σ and α was drawn from the asymptotic distribution of the estimated parameters of the model, i.e., the normal distribution whose mean and covariance matrixes are those obtained at the estimation stage. The new Nash equilibrium and the average value

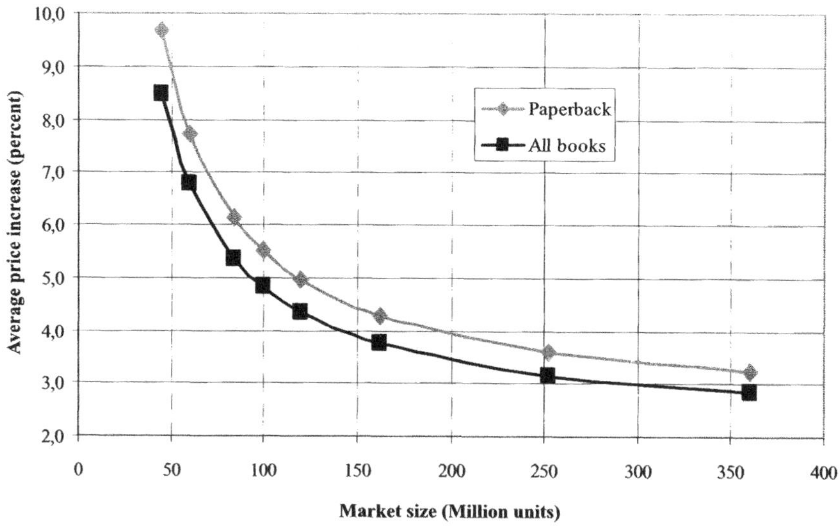

Fig. 13.5: Unilateral effects and market size.

the price increase due to the concentration is included in an interval of 3.74 percent and 5.54 percent. (See Figure 13.6.)

- In addition to the Bootstrap method, different elements speak for the robustness of the model: The very high number of observations, different statistical tests of significance and robustness which say that the estimated model captures nuances of the book industry, and the stability of the main parameters. Overall, the model employed is robust and is in line with the state of the heart of empirical analysis in such a market.

In reply to the Commission's concerns, Lagardère has undertaken to sell Editis with the exception of the some assets,[39] which make up around 40 percent of the total turnover of the company: On the basis of these undertakings, the transaction no longer presented any competition problems to the eyes of the Commission and has been authorised.

---

of the price increase have been simulated 1000 times. The distribution of these increases in price is presented in Figure 13.6.

[39] The divestiture involves the Larousse publishing house and all of its business and its publisher's lists; the Dalloz publishing house and all of its business and its publisher's lists; the Dunod publishing house and all of its business and its publisher's lists; the academic lists made up of the publishers' lists of Armand Colin, Sedes and Nathan Université and the academic journals; the Spanish group Anaya and all of its business and its publisher's lists; the Ivry distribution centre.

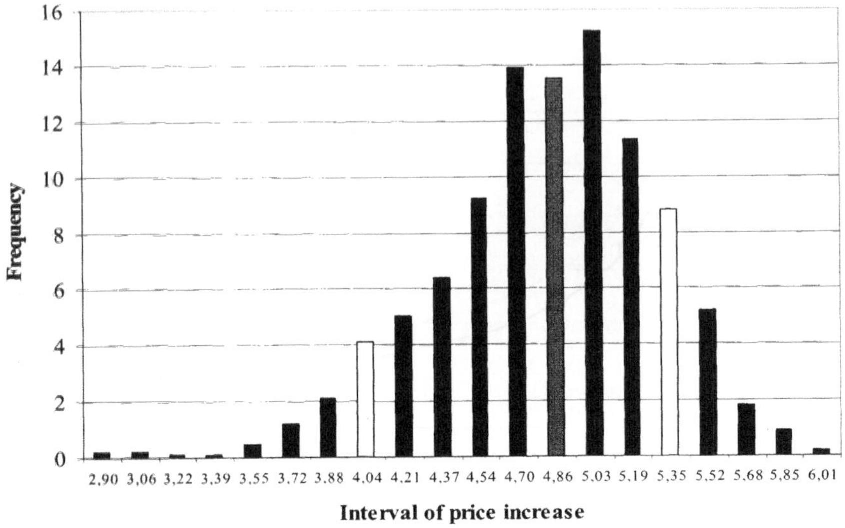

Fig. 13.6: The Bootstrap method.

13.5. Conclusion

Several conclusions can be derived from the results obtained through the econometric study.

First, the Lagardère/Editis case is a good empirical illustration of the new SIEC test. From the EC decision on this case, the dominance criteria remains at the core of the theory of harms. However, the econometric model, by providing some significant empirical measures on unilateral price increases and consumers' surplus losses, clarifies and complements the traditional dominance approach. Note that the method applied to evaluate unilateral effects is not the only possible empirical implementation of the new test. To our point of view it is certainly one of the most appropriate and operational.

Second, the econometric model has shown that unilateral effects are significant without paying attention to market definition. As a result, the definition of the relevant markets and by extension the notion of dominance matter much less when we focus on the measure of anti-competitive affects. Hence, in particular when quantitative techniques are available, market definition may be not the starting point, but rather the conclusion of a merger investigation.

References

Foncel, J., Ivaldi, M. (2005). Operating system prices in the home PC market. *Journal of Industrial Economics* 53 (2), 265–298.

Foncel, J., Ivaldi, M., Rabassa, V. (2005). The case for econometrics under the new European merger regulation: Hachette/Editis. Mimeo.

Ivaldi, M., Verboven, F. (2005), Quantifying the effects from horizontal mergers in European competition policy. *International Journal of Industrial Organization* 23 (9), 669–691.
Miravete, E.J., Roeller, L.-H. (2003), Competitive non-linear pricing in duopoly equilibrium: The early US cellular telephone industry. CEPR Discussion Paper 4069.
Verboven, F. (1996), International price discrimination in the European car market. *RAND Journal of Economics* 27, 240–268.

CHAPTER 14

Vertical Restraints and the Effects of Upstream Horizontal Mergers[1]

Luke Froeb[a,*], Steven Tschantz[b] and Gregory J. Werden[c]

[a] *Owen Graduate School of Management, Vanderbilt University, Nashville, TN 37203*
E-mail address: luke.froeb@vanderbilt.edu
[b] *Department of Mathematics, Vanderbilt University, Nashville, TN 37203*
E-mail address: tschantz@math.vanderbilt.edu
[c] *U.S. Department of Justice, Washington, DC 20530*
E-mail address: gregory.werden@usdoj.gov

Abstract

The downstream effects of mergers between manufacturers of differentiated consumer products are partly determined by the relationship between the merging manufacturers and retailers. The relationship may be such that the retail price effects of the merger are exactly those if the manufacturers sold directly to consumers, and that relationship may be such that the merger produces similar effects with subtle differences, including the possibility of price decreases for non-merging products. Alternatively, that relationship may be such that consumer prices do not change following a merger.

Keywords: vertical restraints, pass-through, mergers, retailing

JEL classifications: L41, L44

14.1. Introduction

Formal modeling of merger price effects has become a standard tool of analysis. A conventional oligopoly model, calibrated to fit the particular industry under review, is often used to assess the likely price effects of proposed mergers. As applied to mergers involving differentiated consumer products, this tool was endorsed by the court in the *Oracle* case (2004, p. 1122). To analyze competition among differentiated consumer products, economists generally use a Bertrand model, in which equilibrium is reached when all competitors are happy with

---

[1] Support for this project was provided by the Dean's fund for faculty research. The views expressed in this chapter are not purported to represent those of the U.S. Department of Justice.
* Corresponding author.

CONTRIBUTIONS TO ECONOMIC ANALYSIS
VOLUME 282 ISSN: 0573-8555
DOI: 10.1016/S0573-8555(06)82014-6

their prices, given rivals' prices. A merger internalizes the competition among substitutes brought together by the merger, causing the merged firm to prefer higher prices. Non-merging rivals may prefer higher prices as well when the prices of the merging products rise.

Although the conventional Bertrand model assumes that competing manufacturers sell directly to final consumers, manufacturers normally sell to retailers, which then resell to final consumers. In litigated cases, that scenario most often has arisen with products sold primarily through supermarkets, as in the *Coca-Cola* (1986), *Heinz* (2001), *Kraft* (1995), and *Swedish Match* (2000) cases. The Federal Trade Commission challenged Coca-Cola's proposed acquisition of Dr Pepper involving carbonated beverages, Swedish Match's proposed acquisition of National Tobacco Co. involving snuff, and H.J. Heinz's proposed acquisition of the baby food division (Beech-Nut) of Milnot Holding Corp. The State of New York challenged Kraft's acquisition of Nabisco involving breakfast cereal. A larger number of uncontested merger challenges have presented much the same scenario, including the Justice Department's challenge to a merger involving white bread, details from which are presented by Werden (2000) and are used below in an illustrative example. Of course, a supermarket is just one type of retailer that sells products manufactured by others, and the Justice Department's challenge to the merger of leading manufacturers of fountain pens, in the *Gillette* (1993) case, involved specialized pen stores.

Werden et al. (2004) argue at length that the use of a Bertrand model to assess the price effects of differentiated products mergers is warranted only if the model can be said to fit the industry. As Werden (2005) explains, this does not mean that the model must accurately capture all of the institutional details of an industry, but rather that the model explains well for the recent past whatever it is being relied on to predict for the future. Hence, it is important to ask whether a Bertrand model without a retail sector can satisfactorily explain the pricing of differentiated consumer products sold through retailers independent of the manufacturers in the model. Ignoring the retail sector in analyzing a manufacturer merger obviously presents no problem if retailers apply a fixed percentage markup to wholesale prices. In that event, the demand elasticities at the wholesale level are the same as those at the retail level, so a Bertrand model explains wholesale and retail prices without any explicit consideration of the retail sector. Evidence of fixed percentage retail margins justified reliance on a Bertrand model in the bread merger discussed by Werden (2000).

Fixed percentage margins may accurately describe the facts in some cases, but economic theory does not suggest that retailers normally behave in such a manner, and we consider the implications of alternative behavior. In particular, we examine three game theoretic models of the wholesaler and retailer relationship, and to avoid the enormous complexity that can arise in models of the retail sector, we consider only the case of a monopoly retailer. O'Brien and Shaffer (2005) consider two of the same models in analyzing other issues associated with mergers between manufacturers. These models provide an intuitive understanding of how the nature of the game played between manufacturers and a retailer influences the price effects of manufacturer mergers.

In one game the retail sector is "transparent"—manufactures' mergers have exactly the effects they would have if there were no retail sector separating merging manufacturers from final consumers. Thus, a Bertrand model without any consideration of the intervening retail section explains pricing perfectly. For another of these games, the retail sector matters, but ignoring the retail sector may not result in a significantly misleading analysis of a merger's effects. For the remaining game, however, ignoring the retail sector results in a highly misleading analysis. The retail sector in that game is "opaque"—consumers see no change in retail prices following the manufacturers' merger. Rather, the merger results in a lump-sum profit transfer from the retailer to the manufacturer. This transfer may present much the same antitrust concerns as retail price increases, and the court of appeals found unlawful the proposed merger of baby food manufacturers in the *Heinz* case (2001) primarily because the court concluded that the merger was likely to produce such a transfer.

Our analysis shows that careful consideration of the retail sector is important in assessing the likely affects of mergers of manufacturers selling differentiated products through retailers. Stronger conclusions are unwarranted on the basis of our analysis because real-world retailers are rarely monopolists, as assumed here, but rather compete on selection, price, and convenience. It is an open question how our results extend to an oligopoly retail sector. What is clear is that the implications of a merger are apt to be quite different when the relationship between manufacturers and retailers resembles the game with the opaque retail sector than when it resembles either of the other games.

14.2. Game I: Transparent retail sector

We assume that Bertrand competitors manufacture differentiated products subject to constant marginal costs. Our exposition of the model considers just two products, but the analysis is easily extended, which we do in a numerical example. Manufactured products are marketed to final consumers through a monopoly retailer, which incurs no costs apart from payments to the manufacturers. Consumer demand is a function of retail prices. Wholesale and retail prices are the outcome of a noncooperative bargaining game played by the retailer and the manufacturers, with full knowledge of all demand and cost functions. Villas-Boas (2006) and Sudhir (2001) consider similar models in empirical attempts to determine which model best fits particular industries.

We denote the retail prices of products 1 and 2 as p_1 and p_2, and the consumer demand functions as $q_1(p_1, p_2)$ and $q_2(p_1, p_2)$. Manufacturers present the retailers with a (differentiable and increasing) function, $W_i(q_i)$ $(i = 1, 2)$, which gives the retailer's total cost for any given quantity purchased. The marginal wholesale price to the retailer purchasing q_i is $W_i'(q_i) \equiv w_i$.

The retailer maximizes its profit

$$\pi_r = p_1q_1 - W_1(q_1) + p_2q_2 - W_2(q_2) \tag{14.1}$$

by setting retail prices to satisfy the first-order conditions

$$0 = \frac{\partial \pi_r}{\partial p_1} = q_1 + (p_1 - w_1)\frac{\partial q_1}{\partial p_1} + (p_2 - w_2)\frac{\partial q_2}{\partial p_1}, \tag{14.2}$$

$$0 = \frac{\partial \pi_r}{\partial p_2} = q_2 + (p_1 - w_1)\frac{\partial q_1}{\partial p_2} + (p_2 - w_2)\frac{\partial q_2}{\partial p_2}. \tag{14.3}$$

The retailer's pricing decision depends only on final demand and the marginal wholesale prices at the equilibrium quantities, which the manufacturers can set arbitrarily.

The bargaining game between manufacturers and the retailer over the division of the profits is indeterminant without additional assumptions. We assume that: (i) the retailer does not carry a product on which it loses money, and (ii) the retailer must carry a product on which it does not lose money. The second assumption implies that the retailer has no bargaining power. Together, these assumptions imply that $W_i(q_i) = p_i q_i$, i.e., in equilibrium, the retailer passes all profit back to the manufacturers. Under these assumptions, perfect competition among retailers would produce essentially the same result as with a monopoly retailer.

Manufacturer $i = 1, 2$ has marginal cost c_i and sets its marginal wholesale price to maximize

$$\pi_i = W_i(q_i) - c_i q_i. \tag{14.4}$$

With all profit going to the manufacturers, $W_i(q_i) = p_i q_i$ in equilibrium, and the first-order conditions are

$$0 = q_i + (p_i - c_i)\frac{\partial q_i}{\partial p_i}. \tag{14.5}$$

These are the usual first-order profit-maximization conditions in a Bertrand model: The manufacturers choose marginal wholesale prices that induce the retailer to set its prices at the levels that would prevail if the manufacturers sold directly to final consumers. The manufacturers also set fixed fees to extract all of the retailer's profit.

Subtracting Equation (14.5) for manufacturer 1 from Equation (14.2), and Equation (14.5) for manufacturer 2 from Equation (14.3), yields the equilibrium conditions

$$0 = (c_1 - w_1)\frac{\partial q_1}{\partial p_1} + (p_2 - w_2)\frac{\partial q_2}{\partial p_1}, \tag{14.6}$$

$$0 = (p_1 - w_1)\frac{\partial q_1}{\partial p_2} + (c_2 - w_2)\frac{\partial q_2}{\partial p_2}. \tag{14.7}$$

If products 1 and 2 are substitutes, the cross-price derivatives of the demand functions are positive, while the own-price derivatives are negative. Since retail prices are greater than wholesale prices, the wholesale marginal prices to the retailer must be less than the manufacturers' marginal costs. The marginal wholesale prices may need to be negative if the cross-price demand derivatives are large enough. (Of course, there may be legal or practical limits on wholesale pricing schemes.) The equilibrium wholesale marginal prices can be computed by solving Equations (14.6) and (14.7) simultaneously for w_1 and w_2.

When the manufacturers merge, they internalize price competition between their products. The merged manufacturer sets marginal wholesale prices equal to its marginal costs to induce the retailer to set retail prices that maximize total profit on both products. The resulting effect on prices paid by consumers is the same as would occur if the manufacturers sold directly to consumers (e.g., Werden and Froeb, 2007). The manufacturers capture this entire profit by setting $W_i(q_i)$ at the equilibrium quantities equal to the total revenue.

14.3. Game II: Opaque retail sector

In Game II, the retailer may carry both products 1 and 2, carry just product 1, carry just product 2, or carry neither product. The first option is "joint dealing," and middle two options are "exclusive dealing." The possibility of exclusive dealing gives the retailer some bargaining power and allows it to earn positive profits. Because this game has been analyzed by Shafer (1991), O'Brien and Shaffer (1997), and Bernheim and Whinston (1998), we only sketch the equilibrium.

Crucial to this equilibrium is the assumption that manufacturers can offer contingent contracts to the retailer, i.e., each manufacturer can offer two different wholesale price functions—one with, and one without exclusivity. Because exclusive dealing in product i likely results in a higher equilibrium quantity for product i than would joint dealing, a single continuous wholesale price function may effectively serve as a contingent contract.

The retailer selects the offer providing the greatest profit. If marginal costs and consumer demand are known, the competitive process operates somewhat like a private-values English auction: Either manufacturer may obtain an exclusive arrangement with the retailer by offering slightly more profit than the other manufacturer can afford to offer. This competition, however, is more complex than a simple auction for exclusivity because the retailer can engage in joint dealing and collect payments from both manufacturers.

What matters to the retailer in setting retail prices is the marginal wholesale price, so without loss of generality, we limit consideration to linear contingent contracts. Let $W_i^J(q_i) = a_i^J + b_i^J q_i$ be the offer by wholesaler i for quantity q_i with joint dealing, and let $W_i^E(q_i) = a_i^E + b_i^E q_i$ be its offer with exclusive dealing. The a coefficients determine how the retailer and manufacturer split profits and the b coefficients are the marginal wholesale prices, which determine the retailer's prices. Let the q_i^J be the demand for each product with joint dealing, while the q_i^E are the demands with exclusive dealing. The total profits available in the three scenarios are: $T_{E1} = (p_1^E - c_1)q_1^E$, $T_{E2} = (p_2^E - c_2)q_2^E$, and $T_J = (p_1^J - c_1)q_1^J + (p_2^J - c_2)q_2^J$.

In equilibrium, each manufacturer sets its marginal wholesale price equal to its marginal cost, and adjusts the price of initial units (essentially a fixed fee) to extract as much profit as possible. Retail prices and quantities depend on which of its four options the retailer selects. With exclusive dealing, the equilibrium yields the single-product monopoly price and quantity, while with joint dealing, the equilibrium yields the two-product monopoly prices and quantities.

If the total profits from exclusivity were higher than those from joint dealing, one manufacturer would outbid the other for exclusivity. As in an auction, this manufacturer would "pay" the retailer a price equal to the profits the retailer could have earned from an exclusive deal with the other manufacturer. Because products 1 and 2 are substitutes, however, joint dealing must be more profitable to the retailer than exclusive dealing, and the joint dealing profit is likely to be less than the sum of the two exclusive dealing profits. Each manufacturer must "outbid" the retailer's option of exclusive dealing with the other, so in equilibrium, each earns a profit equal to its marginal contribution to total profits. If T_J is greater than T_{E1} and T_{E2} but less than $T_{E1} + T_{E2}$, the retailer sells both products, manufacturer 1 realizes $T_J - T_{E2}$, and manufacturer 2 realizes $T_J - T_{E1}$, leaving $T_{E1} + T_{E2} - T_J$ for the retailer.

In the forgoing scenarios, retail prices always maximize total profits. Since the retailer continues to maximize total profits after a merger of the manufacturers, the effects of such a merger are not seen by consumers, so we say that the retailing sector is "opaque." Manufacturers' mergers do not affect retail prices but instead shift rents from the retailer to the merging manufacturers as a consequence of the fact that the manufacturers' joint marginal contribution to total profits is greater than the sum of their individual marginal contributions. This is essentially what the court of appeals found would be the effect of the proposed merger of baby food manufacturers in the *Heinz* case (2001, pp. 712, 718–19).

14.4. Game III: Double marginalization

If the manufacturers are constrained (e.g., by law) to offer a wholesale price independent of quantity supplied, the familiar double marginalization problem arises. The retailer acts as a monopolist with marginal costs equal to the wholesale prices set by the manufacturers. The retailer maximizes profit by setting retail prices satisfying the first-order conditions in Equations (14.2) and (14.3). The manufacturers perceive a derived wholesale demand function based on the reaction of the retailer to their wholesale prices, and in Bertrand equilibrium, they price above their marginal costs of production.

Let $p_1^*(w_1, w_2)$ and $p_2^*(w_1, w_2)$ be the retailer's optimal prices as functions of wholesale prices in accord with the retailer's first-order conditions, and let $q_1^*(w_1, w_2) = q_1(p_1^*, p_2^*)$ and $q_2^*(w_1, w_2) = q_2(p_1^*, p_2^*)$ be the quantities sold to consumers at these prices. The manufacturers maximize profits, $\pi_i = (w_i - c_i)q_1^*$, by setting wholesale prices satisfying the first-order conditions

$$0 = \frac{\partial \pi_i}{\partial w_i} = q_i^* + (w_i - c_i)\frac{\partial q_i^*}{\partial w_i}. \tag{14.8}$$

In equilibrium

$$\frac{w_i - c_i}{w_i} = \frac{-1}{\eta_{ii}}, \tag{14.9}$$

where

$$\eta_{ij} = \frac{\partial q_i^*}{\partial w_j}\frac{w_j}{q_i^*} \tag{14.10}$$

are the wholesale price elasticities for the manufacturers' derived demands. The pass-through rates from wholesale to retail prices,

$$\mu_{ij} = \frac{\partial p_i^*}{\partial w_j}, \tag{14.11}$$

are derived by differentiating the retailer's first-order conditions with respect to w_j. Equilibrium can be computed by simultaneously solving the resulting four equations for μ_{1j} and μ_{2j}.

The retail price elasticities of demand are

$$\varepsilon_{ij} = \frac{\partial q_i}{\partial p_j}\frac{p_j}{q_i}. \tag{14.12}$$

The wholesale price elasticities of demand are functions of these retail elasticities, the pass-through rates, and relative wholesale and retail prices:

$$\eta_{ij} = \varepsilon_{i1}\mu_{1j}w_j/p_1 + \varepsilon_{i2}\mu_{2j}w_j/p_2. \tag{14.13}$$

The retailer's equilibrium conditions can be rewritten

$$0 = s_1 + m_1^r s_1 \varepsilon_{11} + m_2^r s_2 \varepsilon_{21} p_1/p_2, \tag{14.14}$$

$$0 = s_2 + m_1^r s_1 \varepsilon_{12} p_2/p_1 + m_2^r s_2 \varepsilon_{22}, \tag{14.15}$$

where $s_i = q_i/(q_1 + q_2)$ and $m_i^r = (p_i - w_i)/p_i$ is the retail price-cost margin. These are a form of the usual first-order conditions for a two-product monopolist. If the two manufacturers merge, their first-order conditions become the two-product analog to Equation (14.5):

$$0 = s_1 + m_1^w s_1 \eta_{11} + m_2^w s_2 \eta_{21} w_1/w_2, \tag{14.16}$$

$$0 = s_2 + m_1^w s_1 \eta_{12} w_2/w_1 + m_2^w s_2 \eta_{22}, \tag{14.17}$$

where $m_i^w = (w_i - c_i)/w_i$ is the wholesale price-cost margin. This is easily generalized to more than two manufacturers and to mergers involving any group of manufacturers.

To evaluate the effect of a merger of manufacturers, Equations (14.14)–(14.17) are solved for the new equilibrium. A useful approximation is provided by computing the retailer's pass-through rates at the pre-merger equilibrium, assuming these are constant, specifying the elasticities of derived wholesale demand and wholesale quantities as functions of wholesale prices, solving Equations (14.16) and (14.17) for the post-merger wholesale prices, and then solving

(14.14) and (14.15) for the retail prices. The post-merger retail pass-through rates may not equal the rates pre-merger, so the retail prices and quantities from a solution to Equations (14.16) and (14.17) may not equal those from a solution to Equations (14.14) and (14.15). If the inequality is significant, the process can be repeated with the new pass-through rates to iterate to a solution.

In this model, the retailer acts as a monopolist in setting retail prices, and manufacturers also exercise market power, so consumers lose twice. The retail margins are determined essentially by the aggregate elasticity of demand for the two products together, although the share weighting of elasticities may shift as retail prices change. The derived wholesale demand can be significantly less elastic than retail demand because retail prices significantly exceed wholesale prices, and for some functional forms (e.g., linear and logit), pass-through rates are less than one. With relatively inelastic demand at wholesale, prices are likely to increase significantly following a merger. Retail prices increase by a smaller absolute amount if the pass-through rate is less than one. The retail price increase expressed in percentage terms is especially likely to be less that the that at wholesale, because retail prices were already significantly higher than those at wholesale. We analyze only the case of a monopoly retailer, but we conjecture that with substantial retail competition, Game III produces an outcome very similar to that from Game I.

14.5. An illustrative example

We illustrate the differing retail effects of mergers in Games I–III with an example based on the facts of a proposed merger involving leading manufactures of white bread, as described by Werden (2000). To simplify, we normalize all retail prices to $ 1, and we initially assume logit final demand. The existence of equilibrium consistent with Game III requires that the wholesale own-price elasticity of demand be less than -1 for each brand, and to assure that with logit demand, we must assume that retail demand is more elastic than reported by Werden (2000). At retail, we assume that the aggregate elasticity of demand for premium white bread was -1.5 and that the price coefficient in the indirect utility function was 4.5.

Retail own-price and cross-price elasticities of demand for various brands (each with a separate manufacturer) are as indicated in Table 14.1. The rows correspond to the quantities of the various brands, and columns correspond to their prices. In the "Row" column is the demand elasticity when all retail prices are raised proportionately, which is the aggregate elasticity of demand for all the brands. In the "Column" row are the effects on aggregate demand of a change in the retail price of any single brand.

For each of the brands and each of the three games, Table 14.2 presents the wholesale marginal costs and margins consistent with the observed elasticities and logit demand. For all three games, the retailer marks up the marginal wholesale prices to internalize competition among brands and sets the joint profit

Table 14.1: Retail elasticity matrix.

	Brand 1	**Brand 2**	**Brand 3**	**Brand 4**	**Brand 5**	**Others**	**Row**
Brand 1	−3.87	1.08	0.89	0.18	0.11	0.11	−1.50
Brand 2	0.63	−3.42	0.89	0.18	0.11	0.11	−1.50
Brand 3	0.63	1.08	−3.61	0.18	0.11	0.11	−1.50
Brand 4	0.63	1.08	0.89	−4.32	0.11	0.11	−1.50
Brand 5	0.63	1.08	0.89	0.18	−4.39	0.11	−1.50
Others	0.63	1.08	0.89	0.18	0.11	−4.39	−1.50
Column	−0.31	−0.54	−0.45	−0.09	−0.06	−0.06	−1.50

Table 14.2: Calibration to upstream premerger equilibrium.

	Brand share	**Game I**		**Game II**		**Game III**	
		c	m^w	c	m^w	c	m^w
Brand 1	20.9	\$0.742	−1.23	$\$0.33\bar{3}$	0.0	\$0.060	0.82
Brand 2	36.0	\$0.708	−1.12	$\$0.33\bar{3}$	0.0	\$0.006	0.98
Brand 3	29.8	\$0.723	−1.17	$\$0.33\bar{3}$	0.0	\$0.031	0.91
Brand 4	6.0	\$0.768	−1.31	$\$0.33\bar{3}$	0.0	\$0.098	0.70
Brand 5	3.7	\$0.772	−1.32	$\$0.33\bar{3}$	0.0	\$0.104	0.69
Others	3.7	\$0.772	−1.32	$\$0.33\bar{3}$	0.0	\$0.104	0.69

maximizing prices. With −1.5 as the aggregate elasticity of demand, the retailer prices to achieve a price-cost margin of $.66\bar{6}$. And since the retail price is assumed to be \$ 1 in all three games, the marginal wholesale prices must be $\$0.33\bar{3}$ in all three. The games differ with respect to the manufacturing marginal costs necessary to yield this common marginal wholesale price.

In Game I manufacturers set wholesale prices far below marginal costs to induce the retailer to set the prices manufacturers would set if they sold directly to consumers. Wholesale price-cost margins, m^w, less than −1 imply that marginal wholesale prices are less than half of marginal costs.

In Game II manufacturers set wholesale prices at marginal costs to induce the retailer to set jointly profit maximizing retail prices. All of the marginal cost are the same because we assume equal prices, and with logit demand, the multi-product monopoly first-order conditions require that the difference between price and marginal cost be the same for all products.

In Game III manufacturers set wholesale prices above marginal costs to maximize profits given the derived wholesale demand. The inferred marginal costs are low because the derived wholesale demands are relatively inelastic. This is largely a consequence of the fact that the pass-through rates with logit demand are less than 1 (see Werden et al., 2005), while the retail prices are three times wholesale prices.

Table 14.3 presents the wholesale and retail price effects of the merger of Brands 1 and 2. In Game I retail prices increase as they would if the manufactur-

Table 14.3: Simulated percentage price changes from the proposed merger.

	Game I		Game II		Game III	
	Wholesale	Retail	Wholesale	Retail	Wholesale	Retail
Brand 1	38.2	7.28	0.0	0.0	35.2	8.50
Brand 2	27.9	3.87	0.0	0.0	19.0	3.13
Brand 3	17.7	0.46	0.0	0.0	4.9	−1.60
Brand 4	16.6	0.08	0.0	0.0	0.9	−2.93
Brand 5	16.5	0.05	0.0	0.0	0.5	−3.04
Others	16.5	0.05	0.0	0.0	0.5	−3.04
Average	25.5	3.06	0.0	0.0	15.7	2.03

ers sold directly to consumers. For the merging brands, the difference between the wholesale and retail price increases is largely due to the fact that pre-merger retail prices are triple those at wholesale and the logit own pass-through rates are less than 1. For the non-merging brands, the enormous difference between the wholesale and retail price increases is largely due to the fact that logit demand implies negative cross pass-through rates. That is, the wholesale price increases for the merging brands cause the retailer to reduce the prices of non-merging brands. To keep the retail prices of non-merging brands roughly at pre-merger levels, their wholesale prices must significantly increase to offset the effects of the wholesale price increases for the merging brands.

In Game II both pre and post merger, manufacturers set wholesale prices at marginal cost to induce the retailer to set joint profit maximizing retail prices. Thus, the merger has no effect on prices. However, the merger does affect the profit split between the manufacturer and retailer. Since the joint marginal contribution of the merging products to the total profit is higher than the sum of their individual marginal contributions, the merger transfers rents from the retailer to the merging manufacturers. In this case, the merging manufacturers' profits increase by 19.9% while the retailer's profit decreases by 7.1%.

In Game III the wholesale and retail price effects of the merger are similar to those in Game I with respect to the merging brands. The most important differences are in the prices changes of the non-merging brands. The negative cross pass-through rates with logit demand actually cause the prices of non-merging brand to decline as a result of the merger.

Since the foregoing results depend on the logit demand assumption, we perform a second experiment with a different assumption. We continue to calibrate the pre-merger demand elasticities using the logit assumption; hence, the elasticities in Table 14.1 are also those for this experiment. Now, however, we assume that quantity effects of price changes are determined by a SAIDS model (i.e., AIDS demand without income effects). For Games I and II, changing the demand assumption does not affect the pre-merger manufacturing marginal costs, because they are uniquely determined by the retail prices and demand elasticities, which remain the same in this second experiment. For Game III, however, the different demand assumption affects wholesale demand elastici-

Table 14.4: Simulated percentage price changes with SAIDS demand.

	Game I		Game II		Game III	
	Wholesale	**Retail**	**Wholesale**	**Retail**	**Wholesale**	**Retail**
Brand 1	15.2	9.6	0.0	0.0	17.7	11.4
Brand 2	9.9	6.8	0.0	0.0	12.7	8.7
Brand 3	1.7	2.2	0.0	0.0	3.8	3.8
Brand 4	1.4	2.0	0.0	0.0	3.6	3.7
Brand 5	1.3	2.0	0.0	0.0	3.6	3.7
Others	1.3	2.0	0.0	0.0	3.6	3.7
Average	7.5	5.4	0.0	0.0	9.8	7.1

ties and hence the inferred manufacturing marginal costs. With SAIDS demand, marginal costs are far higher, and wholesale price-cost margins are in the neighborhood of .5–.6.

Table 14.4 presents the wholesale and retail price effects of the merger of Brands 1 and 2 under this alternative demand assumption. The results for Games I and III differ in important respects from those with logit demand. The wholesale and retail price increases for the merging brands are far closer because the own pass-through rates are roughly twice as high with SAIDS demand as with logit demand. The wholesale and retail price increases for the non-merging brands are much closer with SAIDS demand than with logit demand largely because cross pass-through rates are positive with SAIDS demand, while they are negative with logit demand.

14.6. Conclusions

We examine three game theoretic models of wholesaler and retailer interaction. These models determine profit-maximizing price-setting strategies, and consequently the price effects of manufacturers' mergers. Just as the literature on vertical restraints demonstrates that effects depend on details in the specification of the strategic games being played, we find that the explicit introduction of the vertical dimension of horizontal mergers makes the impact of the mergers dependent on the particular game played between the merging manufacturers and their retailers. Consideration of the retail sector, therefore, is important in assessing the likely affects of mergers of manufacturers selling differentiated products through retailers.

If the game actually being played among retailers and manufacturers were known to be one of the three we consider, a cursory examination of wholesale margins would suffice to indicate which game was being played and hence to indicate how properly to analyze the effects of manufacturers' mergers. With a transparent retail sector, wholesale margins are negative; with an opaque retail sector, they are zero; and with double marginalization, they are positive. With the substantial positive wholesale margins as typically are observed, only the double marginalization case is possible. Villas-Boas (2006) and Sudhir (2001) attempt to infer the game being played by manufacturers and retailers in essentially this way.

Of course, the real world is not nearly as simple as any of these games, but an examination of margins nevertheless is apt to be useful in determining whether any particular model satisfactorily explains industry pricing. Also useful is an examination of the actual practices of retailers in their dealings manufacturers and in setting their prices. At noted at the outset, retailers applied fixed percentage mark-ups in the bread case, thus eliminating any need for explicit modeling of the retail sector.

A major limitation of our analysis is the assumption of a monopoly retailer. Retailers may have market power, but we cannot recall observing retail margins as high as those in our example. Real-world competition among retailers also is extremely complex, featuring spatial and brand differentiation, and competition for shelf space both within and across product categories. Considerable further efforts are required to gain a better understanding of this process. It would not surprise us to find that fixed percentage margins is a boundedly rational retailing strategy. In addition, the absence of significant retailing market power in a particular case may cause the retail sector to have little impact on the effects of an upstream merger.

References

Bernheim, B.D., Whinston, M.D. (1998), Exclusive dealing. *Journal of Political Economy* 106 (1), 64–103.

Federal Trade Commission v. Coca-Cola Co. (1986), 641 F. Supp. 1128 (D.D.C.).

Federal Trade Commission v. H.J. Heinz Co. (2001), 246 F. 3d 708 (D.C. Cir.).

Federal Trade Commission v. Swedish Match (2000), 131 F. Supp. 2d 151 (D.D.C.).

New York v. Kraft General Foods, Inc. (1995), 926 F. Supp. 321 (S.D.N.Y.).

O'Brien, D.P., Shaffer, G. (1997), Nonlinear supply contracts, exclusive dealing, and equilibrium market foreclosure. *Journal of Economics and Management Strategy* 6 (4), 755–785.

O'Brien, D.P., Shaffer, G. (2005), Bargaining, bundling, and clout: The portfolio effects of horizontal mergers. *RAND Journal of Economics* 36 (3), 573–595.

Shaffer, G. (1991), Capturing strategic rent: Full-line forcing, brand discounts, aggregate rebates, and maximum resale price maintenance. *Journal of Industrial Economics* 39 (5), 557–575.

Sudhir, K. (2001), Structural analysis of manufacturer pricing in the presence of a strategic retailer. *Marketing Science* 20 (3), 244–264.

United States v. Oracle, Inc. (2004), 331 F. Supp. 2d 1098 (N.D. Cal.).

Villas-Boas, S.B. (2006), Vertical contracts between manufacturers and retailers: Inference with limited data. Unpublished Paper, University of California, Berkeley, July.

Werden, G.J. (2000), Expert report in *United States v. Interstate Baking Corp. and Continental Baking Co. International Journal of the Economics of Business* 7 (2), 133–137. July.

Werden, G.J. (2005), Merger simulation: Potentials and pitfalls. In: van Bergeijk, P., Kloosterhuis, E. (Eds.), *Modelling European Mergers: Theory, Competition Policy and Cases*. Edward Elgar, Cheltenham, UK, pp. 37–52.

Werden, G.J., Froeb, L.M. (2007), Unilateral competitive effects of horizontal mergers. In: Buccirossi, P. (Ed.), *Advances in the Economics of Competition Law*. MIT Press, Cambridge, Mass., in press.

Werden, G.J., Froeb, L.M., Scheffman, D.T. (2004), A *Daubert* discipline for merger simulation. *Antitrust*, 89–95. Summer.
Werden, G.J., Froeb, L.M., Tschantz, S.T. (2005), The effects of merger efficiencies on consumers of differentiated products. *European Competition Journal* 1 (2), 245–264.
United States v. Gillette Co. (1993), 828 F. Supp. 78 (D.D.C.).

CHAPTER 15

Political Stabilization by an Independent Regulator

Antoine Faure-Grimaud[a] and David Martimort[b]

[a] *London School of Economics, FMG and CEPR*
[b] *Université de Toulouse, and IUF*

Abstract
This chapter analyzes the relationship between elected partisan political principals with partisan objectives and their regulators when those regulators can be captured by an interest group, namely the firm they are supposed to regulate. Independence of the regulator stabilizes regulatory policies and avoids much of the fluctuations induced by an exogenous political uncertainty on the electoral outcomes: a *stabilization effect*. However, independence also increases the cost of preventing regulatory capture: an *agency cost effect*. Even when both effects are taken into account, regulatory independence still increases *ex ante* social welfare. We also investigate how the independence of the bureaucracy affects electoral outcomes when political uncertainty is endogenized by modeling the decision of forward-looking voters who compare the policy platforms offered by competing political principals. Endogenizing political uncertainty reinforces the stabilization effect.

Keywords: regulation, bureaucracy, organization of the government, partisan politics

JEL classifications: D82, L51

15.1. Introduction

There seems to be a consensus, not only amongst political scientists but also between politicians and the electorate, to recognize that economic policies remain relatively stable even though political parties alternate in power. This phenomenon also appears to be more pronounced in areas where political powers engage in substantial delegation to more or less independent agencies. Delegation is indeed prevalent in many countries for a wide range of economic decisions. A large body of empirical literature focusing on the American case has documented extensive delegation from Congress to administrative non-elected

CONTRIBUTIONS TO ECONOMIC ANALYSIS
VOLUME 282 ISSN: 0573-8555
DOI: 10.1016/S0573-8555(06)82015-8

agencies.[1] Out of a data set of 257 important pieces of legislation between 1947 and 1990, which on average comprehend 45 major provisions, Epstein and O'Halloran (1997) computed for instance delegation ratios by counting the percentage of provisions of these bills which one way or the other involved delegation of authority by Congress. Eighty-one percent of all laws delegated authority to at least one cabinet department, thirty-eight percent to independent regulatory agencies, sixteen percent to independent commissions. Fifty-two percent of the laws in their sample created at least one new agency, board or commission to whom substantial authority was delegated. If the European Central Bank remains the most spectacular example of delegation to a new European institution, the European Union has also created a dozen of independent agencies over the last thirty years or so. Those agencies differ greatly in terms of the procedural requirements, the membership of their management board and the role of member states in the nomination of directors. For instance, in the field of merger control, the European Commission was delegated the competence to regulate mergers under the 1989 Merger Control Regulation.[2]

This chapter provides an explanation for a possible link between the degree of independence of a regulatory agency and policy stabilization. The first key-ingredient of our model is the possibility of capture of these agencies by the interest groups they regulate. Indeed, in a world of informational asymmetries, regulators accumulate information about the welfare effect of different policies and they can be bribed for manipulating information. The second ingredient is political uncertainty. The extent to which an agency is affiliated to a political party affects the likelihood that this particular regulator remains in place as political powers alternate in office. The status of the regulatory agency changes thus significantly the collusive opportunities between this regulator and the industry.

In a nutshell, we argue below that regulatory independence, although it stabilizes policies and avoids unnecessary fluctuations due to pressures by politically elected principals, also increases the scope for regulatory capture. Nevertheless we can identify circumstances where the first effect dominates, justifying the constitutional choice of this institutional mode.

Interestingly, this set of results might shed new light on one of the most documented episode of merger regulation in Europe: the *De Haviland* case. After a complete two-stage investigation, the Merger Task Force recommended in September 1991 that the merger between the Franco-Italian ATR and De Haviland

---

[1] See Kiewert and McCubbins (1991).

[2] Another well-known example of delegation is given by environmental policy. When passing the *Clean Air Act*, the U.S. Congress did not establish exactly what concentrations of harmful substances are permissible in the air but, instead, delegated to the Environmental Protection Agency the authority to do so. In the U.S., other examples of independent agencies include The Interstate Commerce Commission made independent in 1889, the Federal Trade Commission (1914), the Federal Communication Commission (1934), the Securities and Exchange Commission (1972), the Consumer Product Safety Commission (1972) and the Nuclear Regulatory Commission (1974).

be rejected on grounds that it would create a dominant position for the combined firm in the relevant market. Even though this stance was heavily criticized at the time by both the French and Italian governments, the mechanisms available to these countries to control bureaucratic drift[3] were weak and Commissioner Leon Brittan could argue that "*nobody wanted a system that only served the interests of the countries that shout loudest*"[4] signifying thereby the degree of formal independence of the Merger Task Force vis-à-vis member states and advocating de facto its depolitization. However and beyond the *De Haviland* case, other critics of the European Union merger control have also documented the lack of transparency of its decisions and its lax enforcement,[5] two ingredients which clearly point at the possible capture of this agency.

In our model, we examine two possible status for regulatory agencies, capturing stylized views of real life institutions. First, the regulator may be *affiliated* to his political principals and be removed from office each time a new political principal is elected. Second, the regulator may be *independent* and keeps office whoever political principal gets elected.[6] This difference in the independence degree of an agency affects the set of collusive agreements which can be signed between the interest group and his regulator. In the first case, collusion can only occur *ex post*, once political principals have been elected. In the second case, collusion can also occur *ex ante*, before the political principals get elected. This latter possibility enlarges the set of collusive agreements and thus increases the agency cost of capture.

In this context, our main result is that an independent regulator plays a stabilizing role in the political process. When collusive side-contracting suffers from some *transaction costs* which are *convex* with the size of the bribe exchanged,[7,8] the independent agency wants to smooth the possible bribes it may receive over the possible electoral outcomes. The agency cost of capture depends now on *an average* between the regulatory stakes that either principal would like to implement. To react to the threat of capture of this independent regulator, political

---

3 On this issue see Weingast and Moran (1983) and McCubbins et al. (1987, 1989).

4 Quotation taken from Pollack (1996, p. 294).

5 See Wilks and McGowan (1995).

6 Most of the time, in the real world, the board of regulatory agencies is made of a fixed number of members with staggered terms who are removed by the elected government once those terms are finished. Our dichotomy can also correspond to policy implementation by different types of agencies. As documented before, there is some variance in the delegation ratios according to the type of agency to whom policies are delegated. For instance, there is no doubt that the cabinet departments are less independent from political powers than the Federal Trade Commission.

7 For instance, these transaction costs can be viewed as a reduced form for the possibility that collusion may be detected which could result in collusive partners facing heavy penalties. Our assumption is then that the probability of detection increases with the size of the bribes exchanged. Implicit in this formulation is the idea that bigger frauds are more easily detected by the principal.

8 In Faure-Grimaud and Martimort (2001), we offer microfoundations for this assumption. Here, we take as given the technology of side-contracting and do not derive it from more fundamental assumptions. This short-cut turns out to be necessary to introduce political uncertainty in a simple way.

principals with different preferences *ex ante* offer regulatory policies which are close to each other. In comparison to the affiliated case, bureaucratic independence has thus two main consequences:

- Because *ex ante* collusion enlarges the set of feasible collusive agreements between the regulator and the interest group, the agency cost of capture unambiguously increases: an *agency cost effect.*
- Political parties anticipate this new feature of the agency cost and adjust their political platforms accordingly. When a political principal gets elected, he tends to implement policies which look closer to what the other political principal would like to implement: a *stabilization effect.*

To derive those effects, we model a government as a three tier regulatory hierarchy with the regulator being an intermediary between partisan political principals and the interest group. Following the partisan politics literature,[9] two political principals having different preferences over the optimal rent-efficiency trade-off may alternate in office. Under asymmetric information about the industry they are supposed to regulate, different partisans political principals implement second best regulations reaching different balances between allocative efficiency and the extraction of costly information rents which accrue to the regulated industry.[10] A "rightist" (resp. "leftist") party puts a relatively high (resp. low) weight on these rents. Thus, the policies implemented definitely fluctuate with the identity of the elected political principal. The choice of the agency legal status balances a *higher bureaucratic bias* coming from the possibility for an independent regulator to increase the scope for capture and a *stronger political bias* as parties implement more biased policies when regulators are affiliated. An independent regulator acts as a safeguard against excessive political fluctuations and as such improves *ex ante* social welfare. We provide some comparative statics suggesting that the gains of independence are greater when society is more polarized, when political variance is large and when asymmetric information distortions increase.

Despite the importance of the concept of agency independence in administrative law,[11] theories justifying it are scarce. In complete information models, Spulber and Besanko (1992) for environmental policies and Rogoff (1985) for monetary policies argue that a social planner may get more credibility by delegating, or more exactly giving up, policy-making to a bureaucrat with biased preferences. Like in these papers, the starting point of our model is the recognition that delegation entails some loss of control. We depart from previous studies

[9] See Alesina (1987) among others.

[10] Both partisan political principals would implement the same first best policy under complete information. Fluctuations in regulatory policy would not exist in a first best world.

[11] Kahn (1988, Vol. 2, p. 93) argues that the main question raised by this literature is "*whether the administrative commissions sought to retain as much as their traditional formal independence or whether they ought not, instead, be more closely integrated into the executive branch of the government and subjected more directly to the control and responsability of the presidency.*" This is precisely the issue of this chapter.

in that we do not take delegation to lead to a total absence of control on the bureaucracy.[12] We look instead at changes in the agency cost of delegation coming from variations in the legal status of the agency. We view asymmetric information, political uncertainty and capture as the three important motivations behind independence. To do so, our chapter merges into an integrated framework two strands of the literature dealing with the impact of informational issues on politically oriented regulatory outcomes. On the one hand, Laffont and Tirole (1993), Laffont and Martimort (1999) and Martimort (1999) analyze how a bureaucracy endowed with discretionary power can use its information advantage to foster its own interests under the threat of capture by interest groups. These papers emphasize control of this captured bureaucracy by a social planner and are thus purely normative. On the other hand, Baron (1989), Laffont (1995), Boyer and Laffont (1999) and Martimort (2001) analyze how biased political principals induce fluctuations in regulatory or taxation policies under asymmetric information. These papers are nevertheless silent on the relationship between these political principals and their bureaucracy. Unifying the two approaches highlights how the agency cost of capture changes in a world of political uncertainty. Faure-Grimaud and Martimort (2003) analyzed such relationships in a dynamic model. The model are obviously close enough but the present chapter addresses issues related to the impact of this relationship on the political game which were not addressed in our previous paper.

Section 15.2 presents the model. Section 15.3 derives the cost of capture with affiliated regulators and shows that both political principal can implement their most preferred policy. Section 15.4 analyzes the case of an independent regulator and in particular the difference between *ex post* and *ex ante* side-contracting. We characterize the different contractual equilibria of the game. Section 15.5 derive several comparative statics concerning equilibrium outputs. Section 15.6 highlights the costs and benefits of granting political independence to the regulator. For most of our analysis, political uncertainty is exogenous. Section 15.7 nevertheless discusses what is the impact of the agency's status in the case of endogenous political uncertainty, i.e., when political principals choose policy platforms affecting their probability of being elected. Our previous results might now be reinforced by an electoral effect. Section 15.8 concludes. All proofs are relegated to an Appendix.

15.2. The model

We model the relationship between elected political principals, a regulator and a regulated firm. The political principal can be thought of as the Legislative branch of the government. In the case of merger control in the European Union, political principal can be viewed as the member states delegating the day to day control of merger policy to the Merger Task Force.

---

[12] Typically, the Congress will still choose the agency's budget or suggest some broad guidelines for policy-making.

15.2.1. Information

The firm has some private information about its marginal cost. This efficiency parameter θ is drawn from a common knowledge distribution on $\Theta = \{\underline{\theta}, \bar{\theta}\}$ ($\Delta\theta = \bar{\theta} - \underline{\theta} > 0$) with respective probabilities ν and $1 - \nu$. The firm is efficient (resp. inefficient) when $\theta = \underline{\theta}$ (resp. $\theta = \bar{\theta}$).

The political principal is supposed to be too far away from the day-to-day control of the firm which is left to a regulator. This regulator acquires information relevant to design regulatory policies. This regulator (affiliated or not) bridges the information gap on θ. We denote by σ the hard information signal received by the regulator on θ and also learned by the firm. The monitoring technology is such that, conditionally on the firm being efficient, the regulator observes with probability ε the firm's type. Otherwise, he observes nothing. Hence, $\sigma = \underline{\theta}$ with probability $\nu\varepsilon$ and $\sigma = \emptyset$ with probability $1 - \nu\varepsilon$.

15.2.2. Preferences

• *Political principals*: Asymmetric information between the uninformed government and the informed firm at the time of contracting introduces a well-known trade-off between efficiency and the extraction of the regulated firm's information rent.[13] Political principals have different preferences regarding this trade-off depending on whether they defend a "leftist" or a "rightist" constituency.[14] Political principal P_i's objective function writes as:

$$SW_i = S(q_i) - s_i - t_i + \alpha_i u_i, \tag{15.1}$$

where $S(\cdot)$ ($S'(\cdot) > 0$, $S''(\cdot) < 0$) is the consumers surplus.[15] t_i (resp. s_i) is the transfer given to the firm (resp. regulator) and u_i its information rent. $\alpha_i < 1$ is the weight that the principal puts on the firm's profit.[16] As $\alpha_i < 1$, both political principals dislike giving up rents to firms. However, α_i changes with the identity of the elected political principal. We denote by $\Delta\alpha = \alpha_R - \alpha_L > 0$ the degree of polarization of this society. The rightist (resp. the leftist) government gets elected with an exogenous probability β (resp. $1 - \beta$).[17] For further references,

---

[13] See Baron and Myerson (1982).

[14] One can view the political principal as the median voter in Congress as in Baron (1989). In this case, political fluctuations come from change in the identity of this median.

[15] $|S''(\cdot)|$ is sufficiently large to ensure strict concavity of the political principal's objective function in all circumstances.

[16] The agency has no weight in the principal' objective function, capturing the fact that redistributing wealth to bureaucrats as such is not part of the government's objective. Alternatively, civil servants represent a group with a negligible social weight. The main insights of our analysis are robust to the case where parties' objective functions give the same positive (but less than one) weight to the regulator's utility.

[17] Section 15.7 endogenizes this probability.

we define also a measure of aggregate social welfare as:

$$SW = S(q) - s - t + \hat{\alpha} u,$$

where $\hat{\alpha} = \beta\alpha_R + (1 - \beta)\alpha_L$.

• *Firm*: The firm is risk-neutral. The regulated firm's expected profit writes as

$$u = \beta u_R + (1 - \beta)u_L,$$

where $u_i = t_i - \theta q_i$ (resp. q_i) is profit when principal P_i gets elected.

• *Regulator*: An independent regulator R, receives a budget s_i from P_i to perform the regulatory control. The regulator's expected utility writes thus as:

$$s = \beta s_R + (1 - \beta)s_L.$$

If the regulator, say R_i, is affiliated to P_i and comes to office only when P_i gets elected he receives only a budget s_i following this event.

15.2.3. Regulatory contracts

The *grand-contract* GC_i between the political principal P_i, the regulator and the firm consists of a budget for the regulator, a transfer and an output target for the firm. Without loss of generality, grand-contracts are direct mechanisms of the form: $GC_i = \{q_i(\hat{\sigma}_i, \hat{\theta}_i); t_i(\hat{\sigma}_i, \hat{\theta}_i); s_i(\hat{\sigma}_i, \hat{\theta}_i)\}$ where $\hat{\sigma}_i$ and $\hat{\theta}_i$ are respectively the regulator and the firm's date i reports on their respective information. Note that σ_i being hard information, the firm's report is useful when $\hat{\sigma}_i = \emptyset$.

15.2.4. Collusion technology and side-contracts

The *side-contract* between the agency and the firm consists of secret side-transfers τ_i paid by the efficient firm to the informed regulator. These bribes are offered when P_i is elected to prevent the regulator from reporting he has learned an informative signal $\sigma = \underline{\theta}$. For simplicity, we assume that the regulator has all the bargaining power in designing side-contracts.

• *Affiliated regulators*: These regulators come in power if the party they are affiliated to gets elected. Informative signals are learned by R_i only after P_i has been elected and GC_i has been offered. A secret side-contract can only be offered *ex post*, i.e., once $\sigma = \underline{\theta}$ has been learned.

• *Independent regulator*: This regulator is in power regardless of the election outcome. He can still mimic the behavior of affiliated regulators and ask for a bribe τ_i once the P_i has been elected and has subsequently offered his own contract. We will denote by *Ex Post Collusion* this possibility. However, there is now also the possibility of an *Ex Ante Collusion* with the firm since the regulator may find optimal to commit to hide information to both principals before the election outcome is known.

We suppose that the side-contract is enforceable. This is a standard simplifying assumption that allows us to study collusion without providing a fully fledged analysis of the exact game that would sustain it (possibly in a repeated setting similar to the one in Martimort, 1999).[18]

Crucially, we suppose that there exist some transaction costs of side-contracting meant to capture the fact that side-contracts are not perfectly enforceable. The exchange of τ units of bribes only yields to the regulator a private benefits from holding office $k(\tau) = k\tau - \frac{r}{2}\tau^2$ where $r > 0$. The existence of such costs has already been recognized.[19] The specificity of our model comes from the fact that those transaction costs $(\tau - k(\tau))$ are convex. There are several reasons to think that this may be so. Intuitively, one could argue that there is some technology to detect collusion in the background, and that convexity of transaction costs of collusion simply means that the detection probability, say $p(\tau)$, is sufficiently increasing in the size of the bribes exchanged: bribe exchanges suffer from some expected loss equal to $p(\tau)\tau$ and we assume that $p''\tau + 2p' > 0$. But the convexity of those costs can also be justified from first principles. Faure-Grimaud and Martimort (2001) consider a setting where a risk averse supervisor can extract a rent from his ability to sub-contract with a productive agent. The supervisor has to be induced to offer the best possible delegated contract from the principal's point of view, a problem akin to a moral hazard situation. If the supervisor is risk averse, some rents have to be given up to induce proper behavior and those rents are proportional to those the productive agent can guarantee for himself (the collusive stake). Risk aversion implies that when the collusive stake is higher, the supervisor obtains higher rents but at a decreasing rate, as collusion (understood as not offering the contract that the principal wishes) is then a more profitable, but riskier, activity. Therefore convex transaction costs of collusion can result from the risk aversion of (some of) the colluding parties.[20]

---

[18] We assume that the enforceability of a collusive agreement between the firm and its regulator is not affected by the agency status. In particular we should be careful in appealing to reputational incentives as a way to sustain collusion because presumably the alternation of regulators in the case of affiliation would make collusion more difficult (e.g. sustainability could require a higher discount factor than with an independent regulator as shown in Martimort, 1999). This would not go against our results though, as in our model it is already the case that an independent regulator has greater opportunities to collude than an affiliated one. Another justification for our reduced form could also be that collusion is enforced through the pressure imposed by some social norms and that those are unrelated to agency status.

[19] See Tirole (1992) for a first discussion of the origins of these transaction costs.

[20] This is related to the argument proposed in Spagnolo (1999) who studies collusion between firms that interact in a multi-market set up. He shows that collusion is easier when firms are risk averse. A risk averse firms' evaluation of profits in one market depends on profits in other markets. The threat of retaliation after a deviation from a collusive strategy has therefore more bite than in the risk neutral case.

Values of the various parameters of the model are such that possible bribes remain on the increasing part of $k(\cdot)$.[21] To justify the use of the regulator in the first place, we assume that using the regulator is less costly than asking the firm directly for its type against some information rent. A sufficient condition for this is that $k < 1 - \alpha_R = \min_i(1 - \alpha_i)$.

Finally, note that as the transaction costs $\tau - k(\tau) = \frac{r}{2}\tau^2$ are convex in bribes, an independent regulator facing changing political conditions wants to smooth the bribes he receives to save on the dead-weight loss of collusion.[22]

15.2.5. Benevolent regulators

The first best policy obtained in the absence of any information constraint requires the firm to produce $\underline{q}^{FB}$ and $\bar{q}^{FB}$ such that respectively $S'(\underline{q}^{FB}) = \underline{\theta}$, and $S'(\bar{q}^{FB}) = \bar{\theta}$. Whatever the type of the firm and the majority in power, the firm obtains no rents. Even though principals put different weights $\alpha_i < 1$ on the firm's utility, they both dislike giving up rents.

Following Baron and Myerson (1982), let us now consider the second best regulatory policies which are implemented by a political principal P_i in the absence of any political uncertainty. For ease of notations, we denote thereafter by $\underline{t}_i = t_i(\emptyset, \underline{\theta})$, $\bar{t}_i = t_i(\emptyset, \bar{\theta})$ the regulatory transfers and $\underline{q}_i = q_i(\emptyset, \underline{\theta})$, $\bar{q}_i = q_i(\emptyset, \bar{\theta})$ the output targets for both types of firm when the regulator has observed nothing. The efficient (resp. inefficient) firm's information rent is accordingly $\underline{u}_i = \underline{t}_i - \underline{\theta}\underline{q}_i$ (resp. $\bar{u}_i = \bar{t}_i - \bar{\theta}\bar{q}_i$).

We shall simplify presentation by observing that there is no need to pay the regulator if he claims having reported nothing. Instead, let $s_i = s_i(\underline{\theta})$ be the regulator's wage when he reports an informative signal $\hat{\sigma}_i = \underline{\theta}$. In that case, since its type is perfectly known, the firm's profit is then zero and its output is necessarily first-best $\underline{q}^{FB}$.[23]

---

[21] The lessons of this quadratic model still hold in the general case if the uncertainty $\Delta\theta$ is small. Indeed, for any functional forms, the costs and benefits of independence can be derived with Taylor expansions which take quadratic expressions similar to the present ones.

[22] Note that transaction costs are independent of the agency legal status. It is a priori as easy to capture an independent regulator as an affiliated one. What will change with the institutional setting is the set of collusive side-contracts between the firm and the regulator.

[23] There is here a slight loss of generality in our formulation. Indeed, the firm and the (independent) regulator accept contracts before the outcome of an election. All that matters to write participation constraint are the firm's expected rent of that firm which must remain non-negative conditionally on the information available to (affiliated or not) regulators and the expected wage of an independent regulator. The presentation is simplified by focusing on the case where, *ex post*, i.e., once the identity of the elected principal is known, participation constraints of both the firm and the independent regulator are still satisfied. This amounts indeed to assuming that the firm and the supervisor have a positive albeit very small degree of risk-aversion and must be insured against political fluctuations.

As it is standard in two-type adverse selection models, the following constraints are of a particular importance when the regulator reports an uninformative signal $\hat{\sigma}_i = \emptyset$:[24]

- Incentive compatibility constraints for an efficient firm:

$$\underline{u}_i \geq \bar{u}_i + \Delta\theta\bar{q}_i. \tag{15.2}$$

- Participation constraints for an inefficient firm:

$$\bar{u}_i \geq 0. \tag{15.3}$$

- Participation constraint for the informed regulator:

$$s_i \geq 0. \tag{15.4}$$

The characterization of the optimal grand-contract offered by P_i is standard. There is no need to pay a benevolent regulator whether he gets informed or not. Optimal outputs are respectively equal to the first best when the firm is efficient, $\underline{q}_i^{SB} = \underline{q}^{FB}$, and downward distorted below the first best when the firm is inefficient, $\bar{q}_i^{SB} < \bar{q}^{FB}$ where:

$$S'(\bar{q}_i^{SB}) = \bar{\theta} + \frac{\nu}{1-\nu}\Delta\theta(1-\alpha_i)(1-\varepsilon). \tag{15.5}$$

At the optimum, only the efficient firm gets a strictly positive information rent $\underline{u}_i^{SB} = \Delta\theta\bar{q}_i^{SB}$ when the regulator has not observed its cost. The inefficient firm's output is downward distorted to limit this information rent. However, rent extraction is less a concern for a principal with a high α_i and the firm's rent is larger with α_i. Under asymmetric information, second best policies depend now on the identity of the principal in power.

Finally, the policy chosen by a unbiased social planner is obtained by just substituting in (15.5) α_i by $\hat{\alpha}$. A simple inspection of the formula reveals that a rightist (resp. leftist) government chooses too high (resp. too low) a production level.

15.2.6. Timing

The timing of the regulatory game with affiliated regulators is as follows:

- $T = 1$. The regulated firm learns his productivity parameter θ and σ. The regulators learn σ.[25]

---

24 When the two constraints below are binding, it is easy to show that the incentive compatibility constraint of an inefficient firm and the participation constraint of an efficient one are also strictly satisfied.

25 The assumption that affiliated regulators learn also information on the industry before being in office makes sense when those regulators are specialists coming from the industry.

- $T = 2$. Both political candidates propose non-cooperatively their respective electoral platforms, i.e., commit to a grand-contract for their affiliated regulators and the firm. The firm accepts both or none of the contracts. The affiliated regulators accept or refuse only the contract offered by their own principal.
- $T = 3$. Political uncertainty is resolved. The preferences of the elected political principal are revealed.
- $T = 4$. *Ex post collusion stage*: The regulator offers a side-contract to the firm. The firm accepts or refuses this side-contract.
- $T = 5$. Production and transfers (both official and possibly hidden) take place. Importantly, with affiliated regulators the regulator and the firm cannot agree on a side-contract before political uncertainty is resolved. With an independent regulator, the timing of the game is almost as above. However, an independent regulator and the firm can now also agree on an *ex ante side-contract*. To model this issue, we introduce an intermediate stage between dates 2 and 3. The timing of the game is otherwise exactly the same as previously from date 3 on. In particular, the independent regulator learns σ at date 1 and accepts now both or none of the contracts at date 2.
- $T = 2{,}5$. *Ex ante collusion stage*: The independent regulator offers a menu of side-contracts to the firm. These contracts consist of side-transfers contingent on the identity of the principal who will be elected. The firm accepts or refuses this *ex ante* collusion.[26]

15.3. Affiliated regulators

When the regulator is affiliated to one particular political principal, he holds office if and only if this principal gets elected. Suppose then that the second best grand-contract without collusion is offered by P_i. An efficient firm is willing to bribe a regulator who has learned $\sigma = \underline{\theta}$ up to the level of its rent $\underline{u}_i = \Delta\theta\bar{q}_i$. Since the regulator has all the bargaining power at the side-contracting stage, the private benefits he draws from colluding with the firm are worth the regulatory stake minus the transaction costs dissipated in the course of side-contracting, i.e., $k(\Delta\theta\bar{q}_i)$.

---

[26] If bribes can only be paid to the empowered regulator, *ex ante* collusion for affiliated regulators cannot improve on *ex post* collusion and our focus on this timing for coalition formation in the case of affiliated regulators is warranted. This is particularly relevant if the identity of the affiliated regulator is not known before the election of the corresponding political principal. Note also that, even if his identity was known and bribes could be credibly promised to the un-elected regulator, firms might find it too onerous to engage in *ex ante* collusion with *both* regulators if the value of smoothing bribes was not too large. Indeed, this form of *ex ante* collusion with affiliated regulators would require colluding with both regulators while only one is elected. The total amount of bribes that those two regulators could extract would be limited by incurring twice the, admittedly smaller, transaction costs of collusion. If the reduction in transaction costs coming from the ability to smooth bribes is not too large, *ex ante* collusion for affiliated regulators remains a dominated strategy.

The Collusion-Proofness Principle holds in this context.[27] There is no loss of generality in having political principal P_i offering direct revelation mechanisms which are immune to the formation of the coalition between R_i and the firm. Indeed, because $\frac{k(\tau)}{\tau} = k - \frac{r}{2}\tau \leq 1 - \alpha_R$, it is always socially cheaper to pay the regulator to induce him to report an informative signal rather than obtaining this information directly from the firm. Therefore any contractual offer that would possibly induce collusion along the equilibrium path could be replicated at a cheaper cost for the principal by a contract that would deter collusion. From the Collusion-Proofness Principle, we only need to focus on contracts such that the following collusion-proofness constraint hold:

$$s_i \geq k(\Delta\theta\bar{q}_i). \tag{15.6}$$

Note that the collusion-proofness constraints that each principal considers are not linked in the case of affiliated regulators.

With respect to the benchmark analyzed in Section 15.2.5, the equilibrium platforms offered by the political principals are obtained as best responses to each other given the set of incentive and participation constraints.[28]

PROPOSITION 15.1. *All Nash equilibria with affiliated agencies entail:*

- *The collusion-proofness constraint* (15.6) *are binding.*
- *The optimal output of the efficient firm is always equal to its first best value:* $\underline{q}_i^{A*} = \underline{q}_i^A = \underline{q}^{FB}$.
- *The optimal output of the inefficient firm is downwards distorted with respect to its second best value:* $\bar{q}_i^A < \bar{q}_i^{SB} < \bar{q}^{FB}$ *with:*

$$S'(\bar{q}_i^A) = \bar{\theta} + \frac{\nu}{1-\nu}\Delta\theta\big((1-\alpha_i)(1-\varepsilon) + \varepsilon k'(\Delta\theta\bar{q}_i^A)\big). \tag{15.7}$$

- *The leftist government implements a greater distortion of output:* $\bar{q}_L^A < \bar{q}_R^A$.

Since the right-hand side of (15.6) is increasing with output, it is more costly to satisfy the collusion-proofness constraint as the regulatory stake $\bar{u}_i = \Delta\theta\bar{q}_i$ increases. Each principal wants to reduce the wage given to his affiliated regulator and does so by reducing output below its second best value. The optimal contracts move towards simpler bureaucratic rules leaving less discretion to the affiliated regulators as supervisory information is more informative.

With affiliated regulators, there is no linkage between the regulatory policies proposed by different parties. Whoever gets elected implements a policy reflecting only his own preferences and the cost of preventing capture with an affiliated regulator.

---

27 See Laffont and Tirole (1993, Chapter 11) for a proof in the case of a constant returns to scale technology of side-contracting. Changing this assumption has no consequence for this result.

28 See the Appendix for details.

15.4. Stabilization with an independent regulator

15.4.1. *Ex ante* collusion

An independent regulator who has learned $\sigma = \underline{\theta}$ can always mimic the behavior of the affiliated regulators and propose side-contracts SC_i once GC_i has already been offered. Again, preventing this sort of collusions requires that the *ex post* collusion-proofness constraints (15.6) for $i \in \{R, L\}$ are both satisfied. On top of these possibilities, the independent regulator can now also commit to an *ex ante side-contract* before political uncertainty resolves. With such a side-contract, the regulator promises to hide informative reports whoever gets elected against a pair of contingent bribes (τ_R, τ_L) which extract all the efficient firm's expected information rent:

$$\beta\tau_R + (1-\beta)\tau_L = \beta\underline{u}_R + (1-\beta)\underline{u}_L. \tag{15.8}$$

From the binding incentive compatibility and participation constraints, the right-hand side above is $\Delta\theta(\beta\bar{q}_R + (1-\beta)\bar{q}_L)$.

To minimize the expected transaction costs of side-contracting which are convex functions of bribes, the optimal *ex ante* side-contract should smooth bribes over the realization of political uncertainty. This requires a constant bribe

$$\tau^* = \Delta\theta\big(\beta\bar{q}_R + (1-\beta)\bar{q}_L\big).$$

Because the efficient firm is risk-neutral, it accepts this *ex ante* side-contract even if it may correspond to a loss when the left gets elected and offers a regulatory stake $\Delta\theta\bar{q}_L$ smaller than the bribe τ^*. This loss is, on average, covered by the gain obtained when the right comes to power and offers an information rent $\Delta\theta\bar{q}_R$ larger than τ^*.[29]

The optimal *ex ante* side-contract consists thus in a commitment to the following bribing and reporting strategies:

- The regulator reports $\hat{\sigma}_R = \hat{\sigma}_L = \emptyset$ when

  $$\beta s_R + (1-\beta)s_L < k\big(\Delta\theta\big(\beta\bar{q}_R + (1-\beta)\bar{q}_L\big)\big)$$

  and receives bribes τ^* whoever gets elected.
- The regulator reports $\hat{\sigma}_R = \hat{\sigma}_L = \underline{\theta}$ when

  $$\beta s_R + (1-\beta)s_L \geq k\big(\Delta\theta\big(\beta\bar{q}_R + (1-\beta)\bar{q}_L\big)\big)$$

  and gets wages s_i if P_i gets elected. He receives no bribe.

---

[29] Of course, the possibility that the firm would be risk-averse would undermine bribe smoothing but it would not completely destroy its benefits. As long as the firm is relatively not too risk-averse, it would agree to smooth bribes exchanges with the regulator.

To avoid *ex ante* collusion, the following *ex ante collusion-proofness* constraint must be satisfied:

$$\beta s_R + (1-\beta)s_L \geq k\big(\Delta\theta\big(\beta\bar{q}_R + (1-\beta)\bar{q}_L\big)\big). \tag{15.9}$$

Due to the ability of the independent regulator to smooth bribes, the collusion-proofness constraint (15.9) depends now on the *expected* information rent of a good firm $\beta\underline{u}_R + (1-\beta)\underline{u}_L = \Delta\theta(\beta\bar{q}_R + (1-\beta)\bar{q}_L)$. The independent regulator still extracts a private benefit from being captured on an *ex ante* basis. However, the relevant regulatory stake which matters to evaluate this benefit is now averaged over political outcomes. The ability of the independent regulator to commit to an *ex ante* side-contract implies that both political principals assess now in the same way the agency costs of capture as a function of the *average* output of a high cost firm.

15.4.2. Equilibria

The independent regulator accepts now both political platforms before the electoral outcome.

That the Collusion-Proofness Principle still holds in this context with a non-cooperative implementation of contracts is not a priori clear. Indeed, it could be that paying the regulator a wage s_i high enough so that, on top of (15.6), (15.9) is also satisfied is more costly for principal P_i than giving up to the efficient firm a rent $\Delta\theta\bar{q}_i$ necessary to induce the revelation of its type. Nevertheless, next proposition shows that this is always true for a class of so-called *interior equilibria*.

The next step is to find out whether the *ex post* (15.6) and/or the *ex ante* (15.9) collusion-proofness constraints are binding in equilibrium. Indeed, three sorts of equilibria are a priori feasible depending on whose principal bears the greatest cost of preventing the *ex ante* collusion-proofness constraint. *Interior equilibria* are such that only (15.9) is binding in equilibrium. *Corner equilibria* are such that an *ex post* and the *ex ante* collusion-proofness constraints are both binding. The latters may not always exist and when they exist, they yield a lower expected social welfare as we show in the Appendix. Hence, in what follows, we focus on interior equilibria. For those equilibria, both principals find optimal to satisfy only (15.9), (15.6) being slack for both principals.

PROPOSITION 15.2. *There exists a set of interior Nash Equilibria of the contractual game (Class 1) such that:*

- *The efficient firm produces the first best output:* $\underline{q}_i^I = \underline{q}^{FB}$ *for all* $i \in \{R, L\}$.
- *The inefficient firm is asked to produce either* $\bar{q}_R^I$ *or* $\bar{q}_L^I$ *(depending on the outcome of the election), jointly defined as the solutions to:*

$$S'(\bar{q}_R^I) = \bar{\theta} + \frac{\nu}{1-\nu}\Delta\theta \times \big((1-\alpha_R)(1-\varepsilon) + \varepsilon k'\big(\Delta\theta\big(\beta\bar{q}_R^I + (1-\beta)\bar{q}_L^I\big)\big)\big), \tag{15.10}$$

$$S'(\bar{q}_L^I) = \bar{\theta} + \frac{\nu}{1-\nu}\Delta\theta \times \left((1-\alpha_L)(1-\varepsilon) + \varepsilon k'\left(\Delta\theta\left(\beta\bar{q}_R^I + (1-\beta)\bar{q}_L^I\right)\right)\right). \quad (15.11)$$

- *These interior equilibria differ with respect to the wages offered by both principals. Any equilibrium pair of wages* (s_R^I, s_L^I) *satisfy the ex ante collusion-proofness constraint* (15.9) *with equality and both ex post collusion-proofness constraints* (15.6) *are slack.*
- *Collusion-proofness is obtained in equilibrium for a non-empty set of wages* (s_R^I, s_L^I) *such that* (15.9) *is binding and*

$$s_R^I < \min\left((1-\alpha_R)\Delta\theta\bar{q}_R^I, \frac{k(\Delta\theta(\beta\bar{q}_R^I + (1-\beta)\bar{q}_L^I)) - (1-\beta)k(\Delta\theta\bar{q}_R^I)}{\beta}\right), \quad (15.12)$$

$$s_L^I < \min\left((1-\alpha_L)\Delta\theta\bar{q}_L^I, \frac{k(\Delta\theta(\beta\bar{q}_R^I + (1-\beta)\bar{q}_L^I)) - \beta k(\Delta\theta\bar{q}_R^I)}{1-\beta}\right). \quad (15.13)$$

All those equilibria correspond to the same allocative distortions but differ with respect to the payoff distribution between the principals. More exactly, this distribution depends on their respective contributions to satisfy the *ex ante* collusion-proofness constraint (15.9) provided that those contributions themselves are smaller than the cost of giving up information rents to the firm, i.e., we must have $s_i^I < (1-\alpha_i)\Delta\theta\bar{q}_i^I$ to still insure that both principals want to offer collusion-proofness contracts.

Let us focus on the worst payoff distribution from the point of view of P_R. This equilibrium is obtained when (15.12) is binding. Consider first the behavior of P_L, taking as given s_R and $\bar{q}_R^I$. To deter collusion, P_L offers a wage s_L which just makes the *ex ante* collusion-proofness constraint binding and leaves his *ex post* collusion-proofness constraint slack (at least weakly). Reducing such a wage would automatically trigger collusion *ex post* if P_L gets elected. This wage depends of course on the output that P_L wants to implement. Maximizing with respect to output yields $\bar{q}_L^I$ as the best level of output offered by P_L when only (15.9) is binding. Now, a best response of P_R to the contract offered by P_L is, for P_R, to offer a relatively high wage s_R which just makes the *ex ante* collusion-proofness constraint binding, and leaves P_R's *ex post* collusion-proofness constraint strictly satisfied as long as it is less costly than giving to the firm some informational rent. The optimal output is then also $\bar{q}_R^I$.

Only the *average* wage of the regulator and the equilibrium outputs are fully determined for an interior equilibrium. Indeed, when only the *ex ante* collusion-proofness is binding for *both* principals, those principals consider the average collusion stake as the relevant one, independently of the exact wages offered by each principal to their common regulator. The possibility of collusion still leads both principals to downward distort production below the outcome they would implement with a benevolent regulator. This downward distortion is now needed to reduce the *average* regulatory stake which becomes relevant to assess the independent regulator's benefits of capture.

15.5. Comparative statics

PROPOSITION 15.3. *Politically induced output fluctuations are reduced with an independent regulator. With respect to the case of affiliated regulators, the leftist (resp. rightist) government asks for a higher (reps. lower) output level when the firm is inefficient*:

$$\bar{q}_R^A \geq \bar{q}_R^I \geq \bar{q}_L^I \geq \bar{q}_L^A.$$

As previously discussed, the cost of ensuring *ex ante* collusion-proofness depends now on the average output which obviously lies between the outputs implemented by a leftist government and a rightist one. Consider first the point of view of a leftist government. Given the policy included in the rightist electoral platform which typically stipulates a higher output than what the left would like, the leftist government has now to consider the average collusion stake which is typically higher than if he wins for sure the election. Compared to the affiliated case, the convexity of transaction costs imply that *at the margin*, the leftist party finds now relatively less costly to increase production than in the case of affiliated regulators. Conversely, the rightist party regards as given the leftist policy, which from its point of view calls for too low an output level. This means that the rightist government faces a cost of preventing *ex ante* collusion which increases relatively more quickly with output than in the affiliated case. Compared to the case of affiliated regulators where parties would simply ignore the platform of their defeated rival, there is now *less polarization* in economic policy. Granting independence to the bureaucracy induces some *convergence* in the platforms. The independent regulator stabilizes the implemented policy making it less sensitive to the actual preferences of elected principals.

To get further insights, we now assume that $S(\cdot)$ is quadratic, i.e., $S(q) = \lambda q - \frac{\mu}{2}q^2$ for $\mu > \frac{\varepsilon r\nu\Delta\theta^2}{1-\nu}$ to insure concavity of the principal's problem in all circumstances and λ sufficiently large with respect to $\bar{\theta}$ and $\Delta\theta$ so that equilibrium outputs remain always positive.

It is easy to rewrite the outputs emerging with affiliated regulators as:

$$\left(\mu - \frac{\varepsilon r\nu\Delta\theta^2}{1-\nu}\right)\bar{q}_i^A = \lambda - \bar{\theta} - \frac{\nu}{1-\nu}\Delta\theta\big((1-\varepsilon)(1-\alpha_i) + \varepsilon k\big). \tag{15.14}$$

With an independent regulator, we get instead:

$$\left(\mu - \frac{\varepsilon r\nu\Delta\theta^2}{1-\nu}\right)\bar{q}_i^I = \lambda - \bar{\theta} - \frac{\nu}{1-\nu}\Delta\theta\big((1-\varepsilon)(1-\tilde{\alpha}_i) + \varepsilon k\big), \tag{15.15}$$

where $\tilde{\alpha}_R = \alpha_R - \frac{(1-\beta)\nu(1-\varepsilon)}{\mu(1-\nu)}\Delta\alpha\Delta\theta$ and $\tilde{\alpha}_L = \alpha_L + \frac{\beta\nu(1-\varepsilon)}{\mu(1-\nu)}\Delta\alpha\Delta\theta$. Direct observations of these formula yields:

PROPOSITION 15.4. *Assume that $S(\cdot)$ and $k(\cdot)$ are both quadratic, then we have:*

- *The average output of an inefficient firm under independence is the same than with affiliated regulators:*

$$\beta\bar{q}_R^I + (1-\beta)\bar{q}_L^I = \beta\bar{q}_R^A + (1-\beta)\bar{q}_L^A.$$

- *The average output of an inefficient firm with an independent regulator is just equal to the optimal output level, $\bar{q}_{\hat{\alpha}}$, that a benevolent social planner would choose:*

$$\beta\bar{q}_R^I + (1-\beta)\bar{q}_L^I = \bar{q}_{\hat{\alpha}}.$$

- *The variance of output diminishes under independence:*

$$\bar{q}_R^I - \bar{q}_L^I = \frac{\nu(1-\varepsilon)}{\mu(1-\nu)}\Delta\alpha\Delta\theta < \bar{q}_R^A - \bar{q}_L^A = \frac{\nu(1-\varepsilon)}{(\mu - \frac{\varepsilon r \nu \Delta\theta^2}{1-\nu})(1-\nu)}\Delta\alpha\Delta\theta.$$

The rightist government (resp. leftist) decreases (resp. increases) the production of a high cost firm compared to the case of an affiliated bureaucracy. Everything happens as if the trade-off between rent and efficiency that is reached by either principal is modified with the status of the regulator. The elected political principal shifts his own preferences towards the non-elected minority. Even if a political principal does not get elected, he has some impact on the policy implemented by the winner of the elections, however this influence diminishes with the probability that he does not get elected. Hence, an independent bureaucracy also allows the preferences of the minorities to be incorporated into actual policies in a way which reflects the "stochastic" political influence of these minorities.

The new welfare weights $\tilde{\alpha}_i$ that principals give to the regulated sector capture this phenomenon. Those new weights depend now also on the degree of polarization of the society ($\Delta\alpha$) and on the probability that the corresponding party *does not* get elected. With more polarization, the independent regulator's desire to insure himself against political uncertainty becomes greater and correcting terms are more important. When the probability that a given political principal loses the election increases, the regulation he implements is shifted more significantly towards that offered by his rival.

Interestingly, in this quadratic case, the average equilibrium output under bureaucratic independence is just *equal* to the optimal output that would be chosen by a benevolent social planner having to rely on a bureaucracy to implement his regulatory policy. As such, the cost of ensuring collusion-proofness under partisanship but political independence is equal to its value for a social planner. Both principals modify their policies towards the socially optimal middle-road policy. This convergence towards the socially optimal outcome will turn out to have important welfare implications.

15.6. Constitutional design

So far, we have shown that independence allows the regulator to enlarge the set of collusive agreements with the interest group but also that the variance of output diminishes, keeping a constant average. To further assess the consequences of the regulator's legal status on *ex ante* social welfare, first note that the efficient firm's production is always equal to the first best whatever the institution and the principal in charge. Thus, we can omit the terms depending on $\underline{q}^{FB}$ in the expression of social welfare and focus our analysis on the consequences of changes in the output $\bar{q}$ of an inefficient firm. Let us thus consider:

$$SW_{\hat{\alpha}}(\bar{q}) = (1-\nu)\big(S(\bar{q}) - \bar{\theta}\bar{q}\big) - \nu(1-\hat{\alpha})(1-\varepsilon)\Delta\theta\bar{q} - \nu\varepsilon k(\Delta\theta\bar{q}).$$

$SW_{\hat{\alpha}}$ is thus the part of expected social welfare which is a function of $\bar{q}$ only. Let us also denote by $SW^I_{\hat{\alpha}}$ (resp. $SW^A_{\hat{\alpha}}$) the expected value of this function in the case of an independent (resp. affiliated) regulators. We have:

$$SW^I_{\hat{\alpha}} = \beta SW_{\hat{\alpha}}\big(\bar{q}^I_R\big) + (1-\beta)SW_{\hat{\alpha}}\big(\bar{q}^I_L\big)$$

and

$$SW^A_{\hat{\alpha}} = \beta SW_{\hat{\alpha}}\big(\bar{q}^A_R\big) + (1-\beta)SW_{\hat{\alpha}}\big(\bar{q}^A_L\big).$$

These expressions are useful to compare both institutions. Indeed, the social welfare difference between the cases of independence and non-independence writes as:

$$\Delta SW_{\hat{\alpha}} = \underbrace{\big(SW^I_{\hat{\alpha}} - SW^A_{\hat{\alpha}}\big)}_{A\,=\,\text{Stabilization effect}} \\ \underbrace{+\,\nu\varepsilon\big(\beta k\big(\Delta\theta\bar{q}^I_R\big) + (1-\beta)k\big(\Delta\theta\bar{q}^I_L\big) - k\big(\Delta\theta\big(\beta\bar{q}^I_R + (1-\beta)\bar{q}^I_L\big)\big)\big)}_{B\,=\,\text{Agency cost effect}}.$$

• *The stabilization effect*: The first bracketed term (A) represents the difference in social welfare which would be obtained if the cost of ensuring collusion-proofness under independence was computed as with affiliated regulators *but* with the equilibrium outputs of the independent case. The second bracketed term (B) represents thus the difference between the cost of ensuring collusion-proofness with an independent regulator and that with affiliated ones when that cost has been computed with the outputs implemented by an independent regulator. We observe that:

$$A = \beta\big(SW_{\hat{\alpha}}\big(\bar{q}^I_R\big) - SW_{\hat{\alpha}}\big(\bar{q}^A_R\big)\big) + (1-\beta)\big(SW_{\hat{\alpha}}\big(\bar{q}^I_L\big) - SW_{\hat{\alpha}}\big(\bar{q}^A_L\big)\big).$$

This first term is positive since $SW_{\hat{\alpha}}(\bar{q})$ is a concave function of $\bar{q}$ which is maximum for $\bar{q}_{\hat{\alpha}}$ in the quadratic case and outputs converge towards this socially optimal target with an independent regulator. This *stabilization effect* yields therefore some *benefits* from an *ex ante* welfare point of view. The nature of this benefit is clear. Indeed, incentive constraints convexify the set of payoffs that can be achieved by both political principals. With affiliated regulators, outputs fluctuate quite a lot and the expected social welfare corresponds to a point of this utility space which lies in the interior of this set. With an independent regulator, outputs are better stabilized and less sensitive to political fluctuations. Expected social welfare moves closer to the Pareto frontier of the set of implementable utility levels.

• *The agency cost effect*: For a given pair of policies, the cost of preventing collusion with an independent regulator is nevertheless greater than with affiliated ones:

$$B = \nu\varepsilon\big(\beta k\big(\Delta\theta\bar{q}_R^I\big) + (1-\beta)k\big(\Delta\theta\bar{q}_L^I\big) - k\big(\Delta\theta\big(\beta\bar{q}_R^I + (1-\beta)\bar{q}_L^I\big)\big)\big) < 0$$

from the *strict concavity* of $k(\cdot)$. Stabilization of output is achieved at the cost of an increase in the agency's budget needed to satisfy the *ex ante* collusion-proofness constraint. Comparing with the case of affiliated regulators, an independent regulator benefits from greater slacks. As a whole, political principals lose some control over an independent regulator.

15.6.1. *Ex ante* social welfare

Combining the stabilization and the agency cost effects, we find that:

PROPOSITION 15.5. *Assume that $S(\cdot)$ and $k(\cdot)$ are both quadratic, then expected social welfare is greater with an independent regulator*:

$$\Delta SW_{\hat{\alpha}} = \frac{r\beta(1-\beta)\nu^3\varepsilon(1-\varepsilon)^2(\Delta\alpha)^2(\Delta\theta)^4}{2(1-\nu)^2\mu(\mu - \frac{\varepsilon r\nu\Delta\theta^2}{1-\nu})} > 0. \tag{15.16}$$

$\Delta SW_{\hat{\alpha}}$ is thus increasing in the convexity of transaction costs of side-contracting r, the political variance $\beta(1-\beta)$, the degree of polarization $\Delta\alpha$, and the incentive distortion $\frac{\nu}{1-\nu}\Delta\theta$.

The reduction in output fluctuations improves expected social welfare. Less political control of the administrative branch of the government is better when the information rents given up both to the firm and the regulator (these terms being increasing in $\Delta\theta$) are relatively large. When rent extraction becomes more of a concern, policies fluctuate more and society is better off with an independent bureaucracy.

Using (15.16), we observe that the welfare gain of independence depends monotonically on a number of parameters. When $k(\cdot)$ becomes more concave, the bureaucrat's demand for bribes smoothing increases and the stabilization effect is reinforced. Similarly, more political variance ($\beta(1-\beta)$ greater) increases the attractiveness of this smoothing strategy. More polarization ($\Delta\alpha$ greater) means also a larger difference between the regulatory policies implemented by a rightist and a leftist government. This justifies to further stabilize output by using regulatory independence. Lastly, when $\frac{\nu}{1-\nu}\Delta\theta$—a measure of the second best distortion due to asymmetric information—increases, output fluctuations have a greater amplitude and this information motive reinforces also the desire for stabilization.

15.6.2. The political principals' gains from stabilization

Once elected, both principals dislike independence. Even though delegation to an independent regulator is individually costly for political principals since it induces further agency costs with respect to a more politicized regulation, the independent regulator significantly stabilizes policies and makes these policies less sensitive to the identity of who gets elected. This stabilization is good from an *ex ante* social welfare point of view as we have seen above. To some extent it may even be desirable for biased principals at the *ex ante* stage, i.e., *before* the election takes place. Indeed, if a given political principal loses the elections, his rival will implement a policy less different from what he would have done himself. Moreover, if political principals can exchange lump sum transfers at the *ex ante* constitutional stage, they can certainly both benefit from the increase in expected welfare associated to regulatory independence. Of course, the relative gain of each of these principals may depend on the bargaining power of each constituency at this *ex ante* stage when the legal status of the agency is chosen.

COROLLARY 15.1. *Assume that $S(\cdot)$ and $k(\cdot)$ are both quadratic, then both political principals prefer an independent regulator from an ex ante point of view.*

Let us now assume that the bargaining power of one of the principal, say the rightist one, at this *ex ante* stage is null so that this constituency should bear all the increase in the agency cost of capture in case the regulator is independent. We show below that this principal would nevertheless prefer to let the regulator be independent. Let us also denote by $SW^I_{\alpha_R}$ (resp. $SW^A_{\alpha_R}$) the expected value of the rightist political principal's objective function in the case of an independent (resp. affiliated) regulators. We have:

$$SW^I_{\alpha_R} = \beta SW_{\alpha_R}(\bar{q}^I_R) + (1-\beta)SW_{\alpha_R}(\bar{q}^I_L)$$

and

$$SW^A_{\alpha_R} = \beta SW_{\alpha_R}(\bar{q}^A_R) + (1-\beta)SW_{\alpha_R}(\bar{q}^A_L),$$

where $SW_{\alpha_R}(\bar{q})$ has a definition which is similar to that of $SW_{\hat{\alpha}}(\bar{q})$ with α_R replacing $\hat{\alpha}$. With this definition, the social welfare difference between the cases of independence and non-independence writes as:

$$\begin{aligned}\Delta SW_{\alpha_R} &= \Delta SW_{\hat{\alpha}} + (1-\beta)\nu\Delta\alpha(1-\varepsilon)\\ &\quad\times \Delta\theta\big(\beta\bar{q}^I_R + (1-\beta)\bar{q}^I_L - (\beta\bar{q}^A_R + (1-\beta)\bar{q}^A_L)\big),\end{aligned}$$

where the last term represents the conflict of interest between the rightist political principal and the social planner in evaluating the firm's expected information rent. In fact, thanks to Proposition 15.4, this latter term is zero under the assumption of quadratic functional forms and with this *ex ante* criterion, the rightist constituency also favors the choice of an independent regulator since it measures the difference in welfare levels corresponding to both institutions just as a social planner does.

15.6.3. Impact on the regulated firm

From Proposition 15.4, independence stabilizes output at the same average level than with affiliated regulators. Since the firm's information rent is proportional to output, the next corollary immediately follows:

COROLLARY 15.2. *Assume that $S(\cdot)$ and $k(\cdot)$ are both quadratic, then the regulated firm's expected rent does not depend on the legal status of the agency.*

The interest group is unlikely to lobby for a particular design of the agency. This design remains just an issue concerning only the political principals and the bureaucracy. The firm is neutral with respect to the choice of the regulator's legal status.[30]

15.6.4. The agency cost of independence

We have already observed that the agency cost under independence is *greater* than its expected value with affiliated regulators *if equilibrium outputs were taken as fixed*. Hence, the independent regulator's ability to commit to a side-contract increases a priori the agency cost of delegation. Of course, optimal outputs differ across regimes and one might want to know if the bureaucracy as a whole is also better off in equilibrium. The next result shows that, at least in the quadratic case, the agency prefers being independent from political principals.

COROLLARY 15.3. *Assume that $S(\cdot)$ and $k(\cdot)$ are both quadratic, then the expected wage of the independent regulator is strictly greater than the expected wages given to affiliated regulators.*

An independent agency is better able to push its own interest than affiliated agencies. Moreover, since an independent regulator implements partisan policies closer to the socially optimal one, he becomes a representative of the general

---

[30] Had the firm been risk-averse, its own demand for insurance may favor the choice of the institutions with the lower variance in output and information rent but risk aversion also weakens the ability of the regulator and the firm to smooth their bribe exchanges and thus would certainly undermine the stabilization effect.

interest even though part of the benefit of stabilization is immediately pocketed by the regulator himself.

15.7. Endogenous political uncertainty

Let us now endogenize political uncertainty by assuming that forward-looking voters decide of their ballot by comparing the expected payoffs they obtain with each party. Voters are ideologically differentiated with respect to the trade-off they would like to implement between efficiency and rent extraction, i.e., with respect to their α.[31] The distribution of those α over $[0, 1]$ varies with a distribution of its median α_m having a cdf $F(\cdot)$ with density $f(\cdot)$.

• *Affiliated regulators*: Let us first consider the case of affiliated regulators. The agent α^A being indifferent between a rightist policy $\bar{q}_R$ and a leftist policy implementing $\bar{q}_L$ must get the same expected payoff with both policies. α^A is thus such that

$$SW_{\alpha^A}(\bar{q}_R) = SW_{\alpha^A}(\bar{q}_L).$$

Using the quadratic specification yields:

$$\frac{\nu(1-\varepsilon)(1-\alpha^A)\Delta\theta}{1-\nu} = \lambda - \bar{\theta} - \frac{\nu\varepsilon k\Delta\theta}{1-\nu} - \frac{1}{2}\left(\mu - \frac{r\nu\varepsilon\Delta\theta^2}{1-\nu}\right)(\bar{q}_R + \bar{q}_L).$$

α^A is finally a function of $\bar{q}_R + \bar{q}_L$ only. The probability that the right gets elected is thus $\beta^A = 1 - F(\alpha^A(\bar{q}_R + \bar{q}_L))$. For further references, note that $\frac{\nu(1-\varepsilon)(1-\alpha^A)\Delta\theta}{1-\nu}\frac{\partial\alpha^A}{\partial q_R} = \frac{1}{2}(\mu - \frac{r\nu\varepsilon\Delta\theta^2}{1-\nu}) > 0$. As outputs increase, the swing voter moves up, increasing the probability that the left gets elected. Indeed, as the output proposed by the right and the left increase by the same amount, the payoff of a given voter with the right increases slower than with the left: $\bar{q}_R$ is always greater than $\bar{q}_L$ and the result obtains by concavity of his objective function. This makes more likely to have this voter prefer the left.

In a Nash equilibrium of the choice of platforms, P_R chooses $\bar{q}_R$ so that it maximizes

$$\left(1 - F\left(\alpha^A(\bar{q}_R + \bar{q}_L)\right)\right)SW_{\alpha_R}(\bar{q}_R) + F\left(\alpha^A(\bar{q}_R + \bar{q}_L)\right)SW_{\alpha_R}(\bar{q}_L).$$

P_R takes now into account the impact of its policy choice on the probability of getting elected. The corresponding first-order condition writes now as:

$$\left(\mu - \frac{\varepsilon r\nu\Delta\theta^2}{1-\nu}\right)\bar{q}_R^A = \lambda - \bar{\theta} - \frac{\nu}{1-\nu}\Delta\theta\left((1-\varepsilon)(1-\alpha_R) + \varepsilon k\right)$$
$$\underbrace{- \frac{\nu(1-\varepsilon)\Delta\theta f(\alpha^A)}{(1-\nu)(1-F(\alpha^A))}\frac{\partial\alpha^A}{\partial q_R}\left(\bar{q}_R^A - \bar{q}_L^A\right)\left(\alpha_R - \alpha^A\right)}_{\text{Electoral effect} < 0}, \tag{15.17}$$

---

[31] This may capture differences in ideologies.

where $\alpha_R > \alpha^A$ since the swing voter has preferences within the interval $[\alpha_L, \alpha_R]$. A similar equation would be obtained by permuting indices for the leftist party.

Direct observations show that the electoral effect is negative with the right and positive with the left. Indeed, reducing (resp. increasing) output increases now the probability that the right (resp. left) gets elected and, for this reason, the right offers a platform shifted downwards.

• *Independent regulator*: The agent α^I being indifferent between a rightist policy $\bar{q}_R$ and a leftist policy $\bar{q}_L$ must get the same expected payoff with both policies. To simplify, we focus on the case where both parties pay the same wage $k(\Delta\theta(\beta\bar{q}_R + (1-\beta)\bar{q}_L))$ to the independent regulator in an interior equilibrium, i.e., we posit a particular distribution of the gains from dealing with a common bureaucrat. The identity of the swing voter α^I is now such that

$$SW_{\alpha^A}(\bar{q}_R) + \nu\varepsilon k(\Delta\theta\bar{q}_R) = SW_{\alpha^A}(\bar{q}_L) + \nu\varepsilon k(\Delta\theta\bar{q}_L).$$

Using the quadratic specifications again yields:

$$\frac{\nu(1-\varepsilon)(1-\alpha^I)\Delta\theta}{1-\nu} = \lambda - \bar{\theta} - \frac{\nu\varepsilon}{1-\nu}k\Delta\theta - \frac{1}{2}\mu(\bar{q}_R + \bar{q}_L).$$

α^I is still a function of $\bar{q}_R + \bar{q}_L$ only. The probability that the right gets elected is now $\beta^I = 1 - F(\alpha^I(\bar{q}_R + \bar{q}_L))$. Nevertheless, we have now $\frac{\partial\alpha^I}{\partial q_R} > \frac{\partial\alpha^A}{\partial q_R}$. Hence, the swing voter becomes more sensible to changes in the regulatory policy with an independent bureaucrat than with affiliated regulators. Indeed, both parties fight collusion in the same way with an independent agency and the swing voter is only determined by the difference in their preferences over the pure trade-off between efficiency and the firm's rent. The swing voter is the same as if the bureaucracy was not corrupted at all. In this case, the voter's objective function would be less concave and more sensitive to output variations.

In a Nash equilibrium, P_R chooses $\bar{q}_R$ so that it maximizes

$$\begin{aligned}&\big(1 - F\big(\alpha^I(\bar{q}_R + \bar{q}_L)\big)\big)\big(SW_{\alpha_R}(\bar{q}_R) + \nu\varepsilon k(\Delta\theta\bar{q}_R)\big)\\&\quad + F\big(\alpha^I(\bar{q}_R + \bar{q}_L)\big)\big(SW_{\alpha_R}(\bar{q}_L) + \nu\varepsilon\big(k(\Delta\theta\bar{q}_L)\big)\big)\\&\quad - \nu\varepsilon k\big(\Delta\theta\big(\big(1 - F\big(\alpha^I(\bar{q}_R + \bar{q}_L)\big)\big)\bar{q}_R + F\big(\alpha^I(\bar{q}_R + \bar{q}_L)\big)\bar{q}_L\big)\big).\end{aligned}$$

The corresponding first-order condition becomes:

$$\begin{aligned}&\left(\mu - \frac{\varepsilon r\nu\Delta\theta^2}{1-\nu}\right)\bar{q}_R^I\\&\quad = \lambda - \bar{\theta} - \frac{\nu}{1-\nu}\Delta\theta\big((1-\varepsilon)(1-\alpha_R) + \varepsilon\big(k + r\Delta\theta(1-\beta)\big(\bar{q}_R^I - \bar{q}_L^A\big)\big)\big)\end{aligned}$$

$$
\underbrace{-\frac{\nu(1-\varepsilon)\Delta\theta f(\alpha^{I})}{(1-\nu)(1-F(\alpha^{I}))}\frac{\partial\alpha^{I}}{\partial q_R}(\bar{q}_R^{I}-\bar{q}_L^{I})(\alpha_R-\alpha^{I})}_{\text{Previous electoral effect} < 0}
$$

$$
\underbrace{+\frac{\nu\varepsilon\Delta\theta f(\alpha^{I})}{(1-\nu)(1-F(\alpha^{I}))}\frac{\partial\alpha^{I}}{\partial q_R}(\bar{q}_R^{I}-\bar{q}_L^{I})k'(\Delta\theta(\beta^{I}\bar{q}_R+(1-\beta^{I})\bar{q}_L))}_{\text{New electoral effect} > 0}. \qquad (15.18)
$$

For both parties, the electoral effect still includes a term having the same form as with affiliated regulators. However, a new term appears which captures the impact of the choice of the platform on the agency cost of delegation to the independent agency. Since the agency cost depends only on the average output, both parties have an incentive to affect the probabilities of winning in such a way that the leftist party wins more often to have a low average output and reduce agency cost. This creates a motive for both principals to raise outputs. This favors the election of the leftist party. However, when the marginal efficiency of side-contracting $k'(\cdot)$ is small relative to the polarization $\alpha_R - \alpha^I$, this effect is unlikely to introduce any significant change in the analysis. More importantly, the greater sensitivity of the swing voter to output variations under independence might increase the convergence of the platforms towards middle-road policies. This would reinforce our previous findings that the independent bureaucracy makes policies converge further one towards the other.

15.8. Concluding remarks

Regulatory independence increases the agency cost between political principals and this bureaucracy. It makes thus any change in policy less easily implementable. Political principals must concede more freedom to the independent regulator who becomes a better representative of the general interest. An independent bureaucracy becomes then an institutional check against expropriation of the minority by the elected majority.

This research could be pursued along several lines. First, our view of the government and the election system is quite simplistic. We could, for instance, introduce divided governments or coalitional behavior in multi-parti systems. It has often been argued that those features may increase political uncertainty. This suggests that the benefits of independence are greater with parliamentary systems, a fact which should be assessed both on the theory and on the empirical sides. Second, our model could be extended to a dynamic environment with elections taking place at different dates. In a companion paper, Faure-Grimaud and Martimort (2003), we take a first step towards such an analysis and develop a two period model having a regime switching taking place for sure. The regulator's desire for bribes smoothing over the results of political uncertainty is then replaced by the desire for bribes smoothing over time. We then investigate the conditions under which a party may want to enact an independent agency to strategically commit to affect future policies. Of course, the value of commitment will be affected by political uncertainty as well. Finally, with the quadratic specifications used in this chapter, it appears that the interest group is indifferent with respect to the kind of agency it is facing. Generalizing our findings is likely to give insights on the conditions under which an interest group prefers to be controlled by an independent agency and will thus lobby for it at the constitutional level stage.

Acknowledgements

We thank Vivek Ghosal, Jean-Jacques Laffont, Johan Stenneck and a referee for useful comments on an earlier version of this chapter. We have also benefited from participants' comments at seminars at LSE and Université de Montreal. All errors are ours.

Appendix A15.

Benchmark: Benevolent regulators. For further references, we define the expected welfare of P_i when the grand-contract GC_i is offered as:

$$\begin{aligned} SW(GC_i, \alpha_i) = {} & \nu\varepsilon\big(S(\underline{q}^{FB}) - \underline{\theta}\underline{q}^{FB}\big) + \nu(1-\varepsilon)\big(S(\underline{q}_i) - \underline{\theta}\underline{q}_i\big) \\ & + (1-\nu)\big(S(\bar{q}_i) - \bar{\theta}\bar{q}_i\big) - \nu\varepsilon s_i \\ & - (1-\alpha)\big(\nu(1-\varepsilon)\underline{u}_i + (1-\nu)\bar{u}_i\big). \end{aligned}$$

The optimal contract solves the following problem:

$$\max_{GC_i} SW(GC_i, \alpha_i)$$

subject to (15.2)–(15.3) and (15.4).

The solution to this problem is described in the text.

PROOF OF PROPOSITION 15.1. The grand-contract offered by P_R must solve the following problem:[32]

$$\max_{GC_R} \beta SW(GC_R, \alpha_R) + (1-\beta) SW(GC_L, \alpha_R)$$

subject to (15.2)–(15.3) and now (15.6).

Similarly, we could define the programme (P_L) by simply permuting indices.

Inserting the values of the transfers from all those binding constraints into P_i's objective function and optimizing with respect to outputs gives (15.7). Finally, the fact that q_i^A is monotonic in α_i is derived from the concavity of $S(\cdot)$.

---

[32] The fact that (15.6) is binding (as it is the case at the optimum) may introduce some non-concavity in the principal's objective function with respect to output. To avoid these uninteresting technicalities, we assume that $|S''(\cdot)|$ is sufficiently large, typically, greater than $\frac{r\nu\varepsilon\Delta\theta^2}{1-\nu}$.

PROOF OF PROPOSITIONS 15.2 AND A15.1. For a given contract offered by P_L, P_R wants to find a best response which solves the following problem (denoted thereafter by (P_R)):

$$\max_{GC_R} \beta SW(GC_R, \alpha_R) + (1-\beta)SW(GC_L, \alpha_R)$$
$$\text{subject to} \quad (15.2)\text{–}(15.3)\text{–}(15.6) \text{ and } (15.9).$$

One can already see that P_L's contract has distributive consequences on P_R's payoff through its impact on (15.9).

Then the proof proceeds through several stages. First, we construct the best responses of both political principals to the other's contract under the condition that each principal prefers to offer a collusion-proof contract than letting collusion occur between the independent regulator and the firm. We analyze there *monotonic equilibria* where, as in the case of affiliated regulators, the leftist principal implements a lower output than the rightist one. Second, we construct the three different classes of equilibria. Third, we check that both principals find optimal to offer a collusion-proof contract.

Best responses: For further reference, we also denote by $\bar{q}_i^*(\bar{q}_j)$ the unique solution to:

$$S'\big(\bar{q}_i^*(\bar{q}_j)\big) = \bar{\theta} + \frac{\nu}{1-\nu}\Delta\theta\big((1-\alpha_i)(1-\varepsilon) + \varepsilon k'\big(\Delta\theta\big(\beta\bar{q}_j + (1-\beta)q_i^*(\bar{q}_j)\big)\big)\big). \tag{A15.1}$$

Let us also define $\hat{\bar{q}}_i(s_j, \bar{q}_j)$ as the output solution to

$$\beta s_j + (1-\beta)k(\Delta\theta\bar{q}_i) = k\big(\Delta\theta\big(\beta\bar{q}_j + (1-\beta)\bar{q}_i\big)\big)$$

for $i \neq j$. For a given pair $(s_j, \bar{q}_j)$, $\hat{\bar{q}}_i(s_j, \bar{q}_j)$ is the value of output for which both the *ex post* and the *ex ante* collusion proofness constraints are binding in (P_i).

• *Leftist principal*: Observe that $\phi(x) = (1-\beta)k(\Delta\theta x) - k(\Delta\theta(\beta\bar{q}_R + (1-\beta)x)) + \beta s_R$ is such that $\phi'(x) = (1-\beta)\Delta\theta(k'(\Delta\theta x) - k'(\Delta\theta(\beta\bar{q}_R + (1-\beta)x)))$ and, from the concavity of $k(\cdot)$, $\phi(\cdot)$ is thus increasing over the interval $[0, \bar{q}_R]$. Note that $\phi(\hat{\bar{q}}_L(s_R, \bar{q}_R)) = 0$.

Hence, when $\bar{q}_L \geq \hat{\bar{q}}_L(s_R, \bar{q}_R)$ and $\bar{q}_L \leq \bar{q}_R$, (15.6) for $i = L$ implies (15.9) and (15.6) is thus the harder collusion-proofness constraint to satisfy in (P_L). For those outputs, (15.6) for $i = L$ is in fact binding in (P_L) since collusion-proofness must be implemented at minimal cost by this principal. Inserting the corresponding value of s_L into P_L's concave objective function and optimizing with respect to the inefficient firm's output over the set of relevant outputs yields the following best response for $\bar{q}_L \geq \hat{\bar{q}}_L(s_R, \bar{q}_R)$ and $\bar{q}_L < \bar{q}_R$:

$$\bar{q}_L = \max\big(\hat{\bar{q}}_L(s_R, \bar{q}_R), \bar{q}_L^A\big).$$

Similarly, observe also that, when $\bar{q}_L \leq \hat{\bar{q}}_L(s_R, \bar{q}_R)$, (15.9) implies now (15.6) for $i = L$ and (15.9) is thus the harder collusion-proofness constraint to satisfy in (P_L). (15.9) is then binding if collusion-proofness is implemented at minimal cost by this principal. Inserting the corresponding value of s_L into P_L's objective function and optimizing with respect to the inefficient firm's output over the set of relevant outputs yields now the following best response for $\bar{q}_L \leq \hat{\bar{q}}_L(s_R, \bar{q}_R)$:

$$\bar{q}_L = \min\left(\hat{\bar{q}}_L(s_R, \bar{q}_R), \bar{q}_L^*(\bar{q}_R)\right).$$

- *Rightist principal*: Similarly, observe that

$$\psi(x) = \beta k(\Delta\theta x) - k\left(\Delta\theta\left(\beta x + (1-\beta)\bar{q}_L\right)\right) + (1-\beta)s_L$$

is such that

$$\psi'(x) = \beta\Delta\theta\left(k'(\Delta\theta x) - k'\left(\Delta\theta\left(\beta x + (1-\beta)\bar{q}_L\right)\right)\right)$$

and, from the concavity of $k(\cdot)$, $\psi(\cdot)$ is thus decreasing over the interval $[\bar{q}_L, \infty]$. Note that $\psi(\hat{\bar{q}}_R(s_L, \bar{q}_L)) = 0$.

Hence, when $\bar{q}_R \leq \hat{\bar{q}}_R(s_L, \bar{q}_L)$ and $\bar{q}_R \geq \bar{q}_L$, (15.6) for $i = R$ implies (15.9) and (15.6) is thus the harder collusion-proofness constraint to satisfy in (P_R). For those outputs, (15.6) for $i = R$ is in fact binding in (P_R) since collusion-proofness must be implemented at minimal cost by this principal. Inserting the corresponding value of s_R into P_R's concave objective function and optimizing with respect to the inefficient firm's output over the set of relevant outputs yields the following best response for $\bar{q}_R \leq \hat{\bar{q}}_R(s_L, \bar{q}_L)$ and $\bar{q}_R \geq \bar{q}_L$:

$$\bar{q}_R = \min\left(\hat{\bar{q}}_R(s_L, \bar{q}_L), \bar{q}_R^A\right).$$

Similarly, observe also that, when $\bar{q}_R \geq \hat{\bar{q}}_R(s_L, \bar{q}_L)$, (15.6) for $i = R$ is implied by (15.9) and (15.9) is thus the harder collusion-proofness constraint to satisfy in programme (P_R). Inserting the corresponding value of s_R into P_R's objective function and optimizing with respect to inefficient firm's output over the set of relevant outputs yields now the following best response for $\bar{q}_R \geq \hat{\bar{q}}_R(s_L, \bar{q}_L)$:

$$\bar{q}_R = \max\left(\hat{\bar{q}}_R(s_L, \bar{q}_L), \bar{q}_R^*(\bar{q}_L)\right).$$

Of course, for both the leftist and the leftist principals, the optimization of their objective functions still results in the first best output being always offered to the efficient firm.

- *Three different equilibria classes*:
  First note that

$$\bar{q}_L^A < \bar{q}_L^I < \bar{q}_R^I < \bar{q}_R^A$$

as we show in the proof of Proposition 15.3 below.

Interior equilibria: Consider first the case where the equilibrium wages s_L and s_R are such that:

$$\bar{q}_L^A \leq \bar{q}_L^I \leq \hat{\bar{q}}_L(s_R, \bar{q}_R^I) \tag{A15.2}$$

and simultaneously

$$\bar{q}_R^A \geq \bar{q}_R^I \geq \hat{\bar{q}}_R(s_L, \bar{q}_L^I). \tag{A15.3}$$

These two inequalities imply respectively that

$$\begin{aligned}\phi(\bar{q}_L^I) = (1-\beta)k(\Delta\theta\bar{q}_L^I) - k(\Delta\theta(\beta\bar{q}_R^I + (1-\beta)\bar{q}_L^I)) \\ + \beta s_R < 0\end{aligned} \tag{A15.4}$$

and

$$\begin{aligned}\psi(\bar{q}_L^I) = \beta k(\Delta\theta\bar{q}_R^I) - k(\Delta\theta(\beta\bar{q}_R^I + (1-\beta)\bar{q}_L^I)) \\ + (1-\beta)s_L < 0.\end{aligned} \tag{A15.5}$$

When conditions (A15.4) and (A15.5) are both satisfied by a pair of wages (s_R, s_L), each principal finds optimal to offer wages such that only the *ex ante* collusion-proofness constraint (15.9) is binding and both *ex post* collusion-proofness constraints (15.6) for $i = L, R$ are slack. The equilibrium outputs are thus given as fixed points of (15.10) and (15.11).

The last point to show to prove that there exist interior equilibria is that there exist equilibrium wages s_R and s_L such that both *ex post* collusion-proofness constraints (15.6) for $i = L, R$ hold and such that the inequalities (A15.4) and (A15.5) also hold simultaneously. Summing those latter two inequalities and taking into account that (15.9) is binding in Class 1 equilibria, we obtain:

$$\beta k(\Delta\theta\bar{q}_R^I) + (1-\beta)k(\Delta\theta\bar{q}_L^I) - k(\Delta\theta(\beta\bar{q}_R^I + (1-\beta)\bar{q}_L^I)) < 0. \tag{A15.6}$$

But from concavity of $k(\cdot)$, the latter inequality holds. Finally, there exist wages s_R (resp. s_L) such that (A15.4) and (15.6) for $i = R$ (resp. (A15.5) and (15.6) for $i = L$) hold since the concavity of $k(\cdot)$ ensures that the following inequalities define a non-empty set for s_R^I and s_L^I:

$$-(1-\beta)k(\Delta\theta\bar{q}_L^I) + k(\Delta\theta(\beta\bar{q}_R^I + (1-\beta)\bar{q}_L^I)) > \beta s_R^I > \beta k(\Delta\theta\bar{q}_R^I)$$

and

$$-\beta k(\Delta\theta\bar{q}_R^I) + k(\Delta\theta(\beta\bar{q}_R^I + (1-\beta)\bar{q}_L^I)) > (1-\beta)s_L^I > (1-\beta)k(\Delta\theta\bar{q}_L^I).$$

Note that the latter two left-hand side inequalities characterize a priori also some upper bounds for the equilibrium values of s_R^I and s_L^I in an interior equilibrium. However, since (A15.6) holds, it is easy to check that all pairs (s_R^I, s_L^I) such that both (15.9) is binding and (15.6) for $i = R, L$ are slack can be part of an equilibrium.

Consider now the case where the wages s_L and s_R are such that each principal optimizes his objective function at a kink respectively $\bar{q}_L = \hat{\bar{q}}_L(s_R, \bar{q}_R)$ for the leftist principal and $\bar{q}_R = \hat{\bar{q}}_R(s_L, \bar{q}_L)$ for the rightist one. In this case, we should have

$$\bar{q}_L^A \leq \hat{\bar{q}}_L(s_R, \bar{q}_R) \leq \bar{q}_L^I \tag{A15.7}$$

and simultaneously

$$\bar{q}_R^I \geq \hat{\bar{q}}_R(s_L, \bar{q}_L) \geq \bar{q}_R^A. \tag{A15.8}$$

If each principal is at a kink of his objective function, both (15.9) and (15.6) are binding for each principal. In particular, since (15.6) are both binding for $i = R, L$, the equilibrium wages must thus satisfy:

$$\begin{aligned} \beta s_R + (1-\beta)s_L &= \beta k(\Delta\theta\bar{q}_R) + (1-\beta)k(\Delta\theta\bar{q}_L) \\ &< k\big(\Delta\theta\big(\beta\bar{q}_R + (1-\beta)\bar{q}_L\big)\big) \end{aligned} \tag{A15.9}$$

from the concavity of $k(\cdot)$ if $\bar{q}_R > \bar{q}_l$. Hence, (15.9) is not satisfied and it cannot be that both (15.6) are binding for each principal. Therefore, there does not exist an equilibrium where each principal is at a kink of his objective function and they offer different policies.

Corner equilibria:

PROPOSITION A15.1. *When $\Delta\theta$ is small enough, there exist two other classes of corner Nash Equilibria of the game such that*:

- *In the first class of equilibria* (*Class* 2)*, both* (15.6) *and* (15.9) *are binding in P_L's programme and only* (15.9) *is binding in P_R's programme. The optimal output of the inefficient firm $\bar{q}_L^I$ implemented by P_L belongs to $[\bar{q}_L^A, \bar{q}_L^I]$ and is equal to $\bar{q}_L^I = \hat{\bar{q}}_L(s_R, \bar{q}_R^I)$. The output of the inefficient firm implemented by P_R is $\bar{q}^R =^I \bar{q}_R^*(\bar{q}_L^I)$.*
- *Collusion-proofness is obtained in equilibrium when $\Delta\theta$ is small enough.*
- *Class* 3 *of corner equilibria is obtained by permuting the roles of P_L and P_R. The output of the inefficient firm $\bar{q}_R^I$ implemented by P_R belongs to $[\bar{q}_R^I, \bar{q}_R^A]$.*

Consider the case where the equilibrium wages s_R is such that the leftist principal optimizes his objective function at a kink $\bar{q}_L = \hat{\bar{q}}_L(s_R, \bar{q}_R)$. For that to be a best response we must have:

$$\bar{q}_L^A \leq \hat{\bar{q}}_L(s_R, \bar{q}_R) \leq \bar{q}_L^I. \tag{A15.10}$$

In this case, s_L is such that both (15.9) and (15.6) for $i = L$ are binding. From the concavity of $k(\cdot)$, (15.6) for $i = R$ is necessarily slack and P_R optimizes his objective function with s_R given by the binding collusion-proofness constraint (15.9). Inserting this value of the regulatory wage into P_R's objective function and optimizing, we find that this latter principal offers an optimal output to the inefficient firm which is $\bar{q}_R = \bar{q}_R^*(\bar{q}_L)$ where $\bar{q}_L = \hat{\bar{q}}_L(s_R, \bar{q}_R)$.

A last condition is needed to be sure that P_R optimizes his objective function with s_R given by the binding collusion-proofness constraint (15.9): deviations by P_R such that (15.6) for $i = R$ is binding should not be profitable. A sufficient condition for this to be the case is that:

$$\hat{\bar{q}}_R(s_L, \bar{q}_L) \leq \bar{q}_R^*(\bar{q}_L) \leq \bar{q}_R^A. \tag{A15.11}$$

But the first inequality above is satisfied when $\psi(\bar{q}_R^*(\bar{q}_L)) < 0$, i.e., when:

$$\beta k\big(\Delta\theta\bar{q}_R^*(\bar{q}_L)\big) - k\big(\Delta\theta\big(\beta\bar{q}_R^*(\bar{q}_L) + (1-\beta)\bar{q}_L\big)\big) + (1-\beta)s_L < 0$$

but (15.6) for $i = L$ being binding $s_L = k(\Delta\theta\bar{q}_L)$ and the latter inequality follows from the concavity of $k(\cdot)$.

A last class of corner equilibria (Class 3) is obtained by permuting the roles of P_R and P_L.

• *Collusion-proofness:* So far, we have derived the equilibria above under the assumption that both principals find optimal to pay the independent regulator for his information rather than to ask the firm directly for its type against some information rent. For an interior equilibrium, these conditions amount respectively to:

$$s_L^I < (1-\alpha_L)\Delta\theta\bar{q}_L^I \tag{A15.12}$$

and

$$s_R^I < (1-\alpha_R)\Delta\theta\bar{q}_R^I \tag{A15.13}$$

for all equilibrium values of (s_R^I, s_L^I) satisfying (15.9) with equality and both (15.6) constraints. These latter inequalities are automatically satisfied for a non-empty subset of (s_R^I, s_L^I) when

$$\beta(1-\alpha_R)\Delta\theta\bar{q}_R^I + (1-\beta)(1-\alpha_L)\Delta\theta\bar{q}_L^I > k\big(\Delta\theta\big(\beta\bar{q}_R^I + (1-\beta)\bar{q}_L^I\big)\big)$$

but this inequality is true because the left-hand side above is bounded below by $(1-\alpha_R)\Delta\theta(\beta\bar{q}_R^I + (1-\beta)\bar{q}_L^I)$ and, by our assumption on the technology of side-contracting, this term is greater than $k(\Delta\theta(\beta\bar{q}_R^I + (1-\beta)\bar{q}_L^I))$.

Let us now consider corner equilibria in Class 2. First, P_L finds optimal to offer a collusion-proof allocation. Since (15.6) for $i = L$ is binding, we have indeed:

$$s_L = k(\Delta\theta\bar{q}_L) < (1-\alpha_L)\Delta\theta\bar{q}_L$$

by assumptions made on $k(\cdot)$. Second, P_R finds optimal to offer a collusion-proof allocation when:

$$s_R = \frac{k(\Delta\theta(\beta\bar{q}_R^*(\bar{q}_L) + (1-\beta)\bar{q}_L) - (1-\beta)k(\Delta\theta\bar{q}_L)}{\beta}$$
$$< (1-\alpha_R)\Delta\theta\bar{q}_R^*(\bar{q}_L)$$

for the equilibrium output $\bar{q}_L \in [\bar{q}_L^A, \bar{q}_L^I]$. This latter inequality holds when $\Delta\theta$ small enough since then $\bar{q}_R^*(\bar{q}_L)$ and $\bar{q}_L$ are then close one from the other.

• *Equilibrium selection*: In any equilibrium with an independent regulator, (15.9) is binding and expected welfare differs only with respect to the various equilibrium outputs which are implemented. Moreover, in Class 1 and Class 2, those outputs describe a whole interval $\bar{q}_L \in [\bar{q}_L^A, \bar{q}_L^I]$. Expected welfare can be written as follows (up to terms which are the same for both principals):

$$\begin{aligned} SW_{\hat{\alpha}}(\bar{q}_L) = {} & (1-\nu)\big(\beta\big(S(\bar{q}_R^*(\bar{q}_L)) - \bar{\theta}\bar{q}_R^*(\bar{q}_L)\big)\big) + (1-\beta)\big(S(\bar{q}_L) - \bar{\theta}\bar{q}_L\big)\big) \\ & - \nu(1-\varepsilon)(1-\hat{\alpha})\Delta\theta\big(\beta\bar{q}_R^*(\bar{q}_L) + (1-\beta)\bar{q}_L\big) \\ & - \nu\varepsilon k'\big(\Delta\theta\big(\beta\bar{q}_R^*(\bar{q}_L) + (1-\beta)\bar{q}_L\big)\big). \end{aligned}$$

Computing the derivative with respect to $\bar{q}_L$ of this expression and using the envelope theorem yields:

$$\begin{aligned} SW'_{\hat{\alpha}}(\bar{q}_L) = {} & -\beta(1-\beta)\nu(1-\varepsilon)\Delta\theta\left(\frac{\partial q_R^*}{\partial q_L}\right) \\ & + (1-\beta)\big((1-\nu)\big(S'(\bar{q}_L) - \bar{\theta}\big)\big) - \nu(1-\varepsilon)(1-\hat{\alpha})\Delta\theta \\ & - \nu\varepsilon k'\big(\Delta\theta\big(\beta\bar{q}_R^*(\bar{q}_L) + (1-\beta)\bar{q}_L\big)\big). \end{aligned}$$

For a quadratic surplus function, we have:

$$\begin{aligned} & \left(\mu - \frac{\varepsilon r\beta\nu\Delta\theta^2}{1-\nu}\right)\bar{q}_R^*(\bar{q}_L) \\ & \quad = \lambda - \bar{\theta} - \frac{\nu}{1-\nu}\Delta\theta\big((1-\varepsilon)(1-\alpha_R) + \varepsilon\big(k - r\Delta\theta(1-\beta)\bar{q}_L\big)\big). \end{aligned}$$

Hence, $\bar{q}_R^*(\bar{q}_L)$ is linear in $\bar{q}_L$ with $0 < \frac{\partial q_R^*}{\partial q_L} = \frac{\frac{\varepsilon r(1-\beta)\nu\Delta\theta^2}{1-\nu}}{\mu - \frac{\varepsilon r\beta\nu\Delta\theta^2}{1-\nu}} < 1$. Moreover, $SW'_{\hat{\alpha}}(\bar{q}_L)$ is linear in $\bar{q}_L$ with a positive derivative for $\bar{q}_L^I$ which is worth $\beta(1-\beta)\Delta\alpha(1 - \frac{\partial q_R^*}{\partial q_L}) > 0$. Hence, the optimal output is found at $\bar{q}_L = \bar{q}_L^I$, i.e., for interior equilibria.

PROOF OF PROPOSITIONS 15.3 AND 15.4. From the definitions of $\bar{q}_R^I$ and $\bar{q}_L^I$:

$$-S'(\bar{q}_R^I) + S'(\bar{q}_L^I) = \frac{\nu(1-\varepsilon)}{1-\nu}\Delta\theta\,\Delta\alpha > 0. \tag{A15.14}$$

Hence, $\bar{q}_R^I > \bar{q}_L^I$. This latter inequality implies also that: $k'(\Delta\theta\bar{q}_L^I) > k'(\Delta\theta(\beta\bar{q}_R^I + (1-\beta)\bar{q}_L^I)) > k'(\Delta\theta\bar{q}_R^I)$. This yields:

$$S'(\bar{q}_L^I) < \bar{\theta} + \frac{\nu}{1-\nu}\Delta\theta\big((1-\alpha_L)(1-\varepsilon) + \varepsilon k'\big(\Delta\theta\bar{q}_L^I\big)\big)$$

and

$$S'(\bar{q}_R^I) > \bar{\theta} + \frac{\nu}{1-\nu}\Delta\theta\big((1-\alpha_R)(1-\varepsilon) + \varepsilon k'\big(\Delta\theta\bar{q}_R^I\big)\big).$$

Using the concavity of $S(\cdot)$, we obtain immediately that $\bar{q}_R^I < \bar{q}_R^A$ and $\bar{q}_L^I > \bar{q}_L^A$.

• We observe that:

$$\beta S'(\bar{q}_R^I) + (1-\beta)S'(\bar{q}_L^I)$$
$$= \bar{\theta} + \frac{\nu}{1-\nu}\Delta\theta\big((1-\hat{\alpha})(1-\varepsilon) + \varepsilon k'\big(\Delta\theta\big(\beta\bar{q}_R^I + (1-\beta)\bar{q}_L^I\big)\big)\big).$$

Similarly, we have:

$$\beta S'(\bar{q}_R^A) + (1-\beta)S'(\bar{q}_L^A)$$
$$= \bar{\theta} + \frac{\nu}{1-\nu}\Delta\theta\big((1-\hat{\alpha})(1-\varepsilon) + \varepsilon\big(\beta k'(\Delta\theta\bar{q}_R^A) + (1-\beta)k'(\Delta\theta\bar{q}_L^A)\big)\big).$$

When $S'(\cdot)$ and $k'(\cdot)$ are both linear, we have thus:

$$\beta\bar{q}_R^I + (1-\beta)\bar{q}_L^I = \beta\bar{q}_R^A + (1-\beta)\bar{q}_L^A = \bar{q}_{\hat{\alpha}},$$

where

$$\lambda - \mu\bar{q}_{\hat{\alpha}} = \bar{\theta} + \frac{\nu}{1-\nu}\Delta\theta\big((1-\hat{\alpha})(1-\varepsilon) + \varepsilon(k - r\Delta\theta\bar{q}_{\hat{\alpha}})\big).$$

PROOF OF PROPOSITION 15.5.

• Since $\bar{q}_{\hat{\alpha}}$ maximizes $SW_{\hat{\alpha}}(q)$ which is quadratic in q, we have:

$$A = \frac{(1-\nu)}{2}\left(\mu - \frac{r\nu\varepsilon\Delta\theta^2}{1-\nu}\right)\big(\beta\big((\bar{q}_R^A - \bar{q}_{\hat{\alpha}})^2 - (\bar{q}_R^I - \bar{q}_{\hat{\alpha}})^2\big)$$
$$+ (1-\beta)\big((\bar{q}_L^A - \bar{q}_{\hat{\alpha}})^2 - (\bar{q}_L^I - \bar{q}_{\hat{\alpha}})^2\big)\big).$$

But using the quadratic specifications, we have also: $(\mu - \frac{r\nu\varepsilon\Delta\theta^2}{1-\nu})(\bar{q}_R^A - \bar{q}_{\hat{\alpha}}) = \frac{(1-\beta)\nu\Delta\theta\Delta\alpha(1-\varepsilon)}{1-\nu}$ and $\mu(\bar{q}_R^I - \bar{q}_{\hat{\alpha}}) = \frac{(1-\beta)\nu\Delta\theta\Delta\alpha(1-\varepsilon)}{1-\nu}$. Hence, we get:

$$A = \frac{(1-\nu)}{2}\left(\mu - \frac{r\nu\varepsilon\Delta\theta^2}{1-\nu}\right)\beta(1-\beta)\frac{\nu^2}{(1-\nu)^2}$$
$$\times (1-\varepsilon)^2\Delta\theta^2\Delta\alpha^2\left(\frac{1}{(\mu - \frac{r\nu\varepsilon\Delta\theta^2}{1-\nu})^2} - \frac{1}{\mu^2}\right). \tag{A15.15}$$

• Using that $k(\cdot)$ is quadratic, we can also express:

$$B = \nu\varepsilon\frac{r}{2}\Delta\theta^2\big((\beta\bar{q}_R^I + (1-\beta)\bar{q}_L^I)^2 - \beta(\bar{q}_R^I)^2 - (1-\beta)(\bar{q}_L^I)^2\big)$$
$$= -\frac{\nu\varepsilon r}{2}\Delta\theta^2\big[\beta(\bar{q}_R^I - \bar{q}_\alpha)^2 + (1-\beta)(\bar{q}_L^I - \bar{q}_\alpha)^2\big].$$

Simplifying, we get:

$$B = -\frac{r\nu\varepsilon\beta(1-\beta)\Delta\theta^2}{2}(\bar{q}_R^I - \bar{q}_L^I)^2$$
$$= -\frac{r\nu^3\varepsilon(1-\varepsilon)^2\Delta\theta^4\beta(1-\beta)\Delta\alpha^2}{2\mu^2(1-\nu)^2}. \tag{A15.16}$$

Adding up (A15.15) and (A15.16) yields (15.16).

PROOF OF COROLLARY 15.3. First, with quadratic functional forms, note that $\beta \bar{q}_R^I + (1-\beta)\bar{q}_L^I = \beta \bar{q}_R^A + (1-\beta)\bar{q}_L^A = \bar{q}_{\hat{\alpha}}$. Hence, the expected cost of the regulator's wage under independence is worth $k(\bar{q}_{\hat{\alpha}})$ which is greater than $\beta k(\bar{q}_R^A) + (1-\beta)k(\bar{q}_L^A)$ from the concavity of $k(\cdot)$.

References

Alesina, A. (1987), Macroeconomic policy in a two-party system as a repeated game. *Quarterly Journal of Economics* 102, 651–678.

Baron, D., Myerson, R. (1982), Regulating a monopolist with unknown costs. *Econometrica* 50, 911–930.

Baron, D. (1989), Regulation and legislative choice. *RAND Journal of Economics* 20, 467–477.

Boyer, M., Laffont, J.J. (1999), Towards a political theory of the emergence of environmental incentive regulation. *RAND Journal of Economics* 30, 137–157.

Epstein, D., O'Halloran, S. (1997), *Delegating Powers: A Transaction Cost Politics Approach to Policy Making Under Separate Powers.*

Faure-Grimaud, A., Martimort, D. (2001), On some agency costs of delegated contracting. *Economic Letters* 71, 75–82.

Faure-Grimaud, A., Martimort, D. (2003), Regulatory inertia. *RAND Journal of Economics* 34, 413–437.

Kahn, A. (1988), *The Economics of Regulation: Principles and Institutions.* MIT Press.

Kiewert, D., McCubbins, M. (1991), *The Logic of Delegation: Congressional Parties and the Appropriations Process.* Chicago University Press, Chicago.

Laffont, J.J. (1995), Industrial policy and politics. *International Journal of Industrial Organization* 14, 1–27.

Laffont, J.J., Martimort, D. (1999), Separation of regulators against collusive behavior. *RAND Journal of Economics* 107, 1089–1127.

Laffont, J.J., Tirole, J. (1993), *A Theory of Incentives in Regulation and Procurement.* MIT Press.

Martimort, D. (1999), The life cycle of regulatory agencies: Dynamic capture and transaction costs. *Review of Economic Studies* 66, 929–948.

Martimort, D. (2001), Optimal strategic budget deficit under political regime switching. *Review of Economic Studies* 68, 573–593.

McCubbins, M., Noll, R., Weingast, B. (1987), Administrative procedures as instruments of political control. *Journal of Law, Economics and Organization* 3, 243–277.

McCubbins, M., Noll, R., Weingast, B. (1989), Structure and process, politics and policy: Administrative arrangements and the political control of agencies. *Virginia Law Review* 75, 431–482.

Pollack, M. (1996), *The Engines of European Integration: Delegation, Agency, and Agenda Setting in the E.U.* Oxford University Press.

Rogoff, K. (1985), The optimal degree of commitment to an intermediate monetary target. *Quarterly Journal of Economics* 100, 1169–1189.

Spagnolo, G. (1999), On interdependent supergames: multimarket contact, concavity and collusion. *Journal of Economic Theory* 89, 127–139.

Spulber, D., Besanko, D. (1992), Delegation, commitment, and the regulatory mandate. *Journal of Law, Economics and Organization* 8, 126–154.

Tirole, J. (1992), Collusion and the theory of organizations. In: Laffont, J.J. (Ed.), *Advances in Economic Theory, vol. 2.* Cambridge University Press, Cambridge, pp. 151–206.

Weingast, B., Moran, M. (1983), Bureaucratic discretion or congressional control? Regulatory policy-making by the federal commission. *Journal of Political Economy* 91, 765–800.

Wilks, S., McGowan, L. (1995), Disarming the commission: The debate over a European cartel office. *Journal of Common Market Studies* 32, 259–273.

CHAPTER 16

Saving Section 2: Reframing U.S. Monopolization Law

Timothy J. Brennan

Professor of Public Policy and Economics, University of Maryland Baltimore County; Senior Fellow, Resources for the Future
E-mail address: brennan@umbc.edu

16.1. Section 2's unfortunate distinctiveness

Antitrust policy famously divides into three categories: collusion, monopolization, and mergers. In the United States, three very long-standing statutes initially set out these categories, respectively Sections 1 and 2 of the Sherman Act (1890) and Section 7 of the Clayton Act (1914).[1] These statutes, known in antitrust by their section numbers, are notoriously short. Section 1 proscribes "every contract, combination ... or conspiracy in restraint of trade;" Section 2 finds guilty "every person who shall monopolize, attempt to monopolize, or ... combine or conspire to monopolize;" and Section 7 prohibits asset acquisitions that "may be substantially to lessen competition or to tend to create a monopoly." The operational content of these brief statutes is defined by the case law arising from the public and private enforcement actions brought under them. Their ability to remain a vital part of U.S. economic policy rests in their brevity and the ability of case law to adapt them to changed circumstances and advances in knowledge.

Relatively speaking, collusion and merger law as set out in Section 1 and Section 7 cases is uncontroversial within fairly broad margins, primarily because their focus, not necessarily exclusive, is on horizontal dealings among competitors that suppress competition. Collusion cases under Section 1, particularly the *per se* violations of fixing prices and allocating markets, present the clearest examples (Shenefield and Stelzer, 1998, pp. 43–50). Apart from libertarian critiques based on freedom of contract (Armentano, 1982) and what might be regarded as a generous view of the ability of free entry to cure all ills (Dewey, 1979), there is little dispute that horizontal collusion should be deterred. Investigations tend to focus more on factual questions such as whether there was a conspiracy and by how much did it raise price than on theoretical analyses of whether practices are harmful.

---

[1] 15 U.S.C. §§1, 2, 18.

CONTRIBUTIONS TO ECONOMIC ANALYSIS
VOLUME 282 ISSN: 0573-8555
DOI: 10.1016/S0573-8555(06)82016-X

There are margins of dispute, to be sure. "Rule of reason" Section 1 cases often require delicate judgments about whether a nominally restrictive practice is necessary to achieve greater benefits,[2] but those inquiries again tend to rest more on the factual strength of an efficiency defense than on a fundamental policy dispute.[3] Non-horizontal agreements, such as resale price maintenance and tie-ins, are more problematic. For our purposes, we treat those here as variants of monopolization.[4]

A similar rough consensus surrounds mergers, particular horizontal mergers. The consensus on why such mergers are problematic, and how to analyze them, constitutes the Department of Justice (DOJ) and Federal Trade Commission (FTC) Horizontal Merger Guidelines (HMGs) (DOJ, 1997). The underlying consensus is reflected in the incorporation of these guidelines in merger analyses taken throughout the government, e.g., in the FERC Merger Policy Statement (FERC, 1996). This is not to suggest that merger cases are uncontroversial, but that the root of the controversial is largely factual rather than on the principle of how and perhaps whether cases should be brought (Eckbo and Weir, 1985; Crandall and Winston, 2003; Baker, 2003; Werden, 2004). Disputes fundamentally involve market delineation—the determination of who competes with whom, and whether entry is likely to mitigate any problems created by otherwise undue concentration.

Surrounding this question are other difficult issues involving the identification of the mechanism of competitive harm (unilateral or coordinated effects) (DOJ, 1997 at 2.1, 2.2),[5] the construction and relevance of differentiated product simulation models (Froeb and Werden, 1996; Baker and Rubinfeld, 1999), and other methods for estimating propensity of merged firms to reduce output (Harris and Simons, 1989; Katz and Shapiro, 2003; O'Brien and Wickelgren, 2003). A more fundamental dispute is perhaps whether the appropriate measure of welfare is total or just consumer welfare (Lande, 1982; Ross and Winter, 2004; Competition Bureau, 2004, §§8.5, 8.25–28, 8.31–35). But as with collusion, there is relatively little conceptual (as opposed to empirical) dispute except perhaps for mergers going beyond the market of the involved parties (Brennan, 2004b). Those, too, fall for our purposes here within the monopolization category.

Monopolization cases, primarily but not exclusively brought under Section 2, differ from both collusion and merger cases in being controversial at the more

---

2 Broadcast Music Inc., et al., v. Columbia Broadcasting System et al., 441 U.S. 1 (1979).

3 One could apply efficiency defenses even in *per se* cases (Clyde and Reitzes, 2004), but we do not typically do so (Baker, 1991; Brennan, 2000).

4 Exclusionary practices may be addressed under Section 1 and Section 2, and sometimes may be found illegal under the latter yet legal under the former. U.S. et al. v. Microsoft Corp. ("*Microsoft*"), 87 F. Supp. 2d. 30 (D.C.D.C. 2000), *direct appeal to the Supreme Court denied*, 530 U.S. 1301 (2000); *aff'd in part, r'vsd in part and remanded*, 253 F. 3d. 34 (D.C. Circ. 2001); *final judgment entered*, 2002 U.S. Dist. LEXIS 22864 (2002).

5 Mergers leading to a less competitive oligopoly are included in the "unilateral" category (Scheffman and Coleman, 2003, p. 323).

fundamental level of whether such cases should even be considered. Monopolization typically involves foreclosure or exclusion, the idea that actual or potential rivals are precluded from competing in some market. These cases typically take the form of "abuse of dominance,"[6] where input or complementary product suppliers (e.g., retailers) are threatened by a firm with market power that its product will not be available, or only available at high prices, unless those supplier sign exclusive contracts, accept tied products, or adopt similar practices that keep out other entrants by "raising rivals' costs" (RRC).[7] A traditional monopolization concern has been when vertical mergers or restraints would restrict competition. A focus of some recent Section 2 cases has been the use of discounts, particularly involving bundles of products, as a way to discourage buyers from turning to competitors.[8]

Unlike collusion and (horizontal) mergers, monopolization has been a persistently controversial practice, for reasons familiar to those engaged in antitrust policy debates over the last twenty-five years. Normally, firms cut prices without taking into account the adverse effects on competitors' profits. Increasing price involves inhibition of independent action among competitors, i.e., sellers in the same market. Vertical dealings or other relationships between firms in separate markets should be largely irrelevant. Vertical integration and restraints have to do with the internal organization of production; they do not expand coverage over a market.

The "Chicago" critique pointed out that forcing buyers to do certain things, such as accept tied goods or use only selected retailers, reduces demand for the product, implying a justification based on cutting costs, raising quality, or improving the marketing of the product. Penalizing firms, even monopolies, for bundling, discounting, or charging low prices is to penalize them for doing what competitive firms are supposed to do. Central to all of these concerns is that if competition is also about beating rivals in a market, monopolization law may protect competitors at the expense of competition, harming the public that competition is nominally supposed to benefit.

An initial goal is to understand why monopolization law differs from collusion and merger law in the quality and level of controversy. For example, is

---

[6] 2002 O.J. (C325) 65 (2002). Facey and Assaf (2002) provide a useful review of monopolization law in the U.S., the European Union, and Canada.

[7] U.S. v. Dentsply (*"Dentsply"*) 277 F. Supp. 2d 387 (D.C. Del. 2003), r'vsd and remanded, 399 F.3d 181 (3rd Circ. 2005); *Microsoft*, supra note 4; European Commission, Case Comp/C-3/37.792 Microsoft, Mar. 3, 2004. http://europa.eu.int/comm/competition/antitrust/cases/decisions/37792/en.pdf. For more on raising rivals' costs, *see* Krattenmaker and Salop (1986).

[8] Concord Boat Corp. v. Brunswick Corp., 207 F.3d 1039 (8th Cir. 2000), cert. denied, 531 U.S. 979 (2000) (Brunswick's purchase share and absolute volume discounts for purchases of motor boat engines were found legal as above cost, with no implicit tying in the sales of different types of engines); LePage's, Inc. v. 3M (*"LePage's"*), 324 F.3d 141 (3d Cir. Pa., 2003), *cert. denied* 124 S. Ct. 2932 (2004) (3M's discounting of bundled wholesale sales of trademarked (Scotch) and store-brand tape excluded LePages from retail outlets).

monopolization about economic welfare or some other effect, e.g., competitor protection? Perhaps monopolization is not so much about effect as intention, whether a firm is culpable because it wants to harm competitors. These distinctions of principle between monopolization and the other prongs of antitrust policy have practical implications. They may support screens for monopolization that better fit conceptions of competitor protection and intent to harm rather than economic efficiency.

The goal is not merely to lament the disharmony of Section 2 with Section 1 and 7, but to correct it. A different method of looking at monopolization cases, what we call here "complement market monopolization" (CMM), focuses instead on how and whether exclusionary conduct ties up a previously competitive complement market in an upstream production input or downstream distribution and retailing.[9] CMM is both necessary to make it more difficult for firms to compete, but will generally be sufficient on its own, absent an efficiency defense, to infer antitrust liability. CMM allows the application of the tools and perspectives of collusion and horizontal merger analysis, particularly the latter, to assessments of monopolization. This will suggest a different set of screens involving increased concentration or control of input or complement markets that can apply to most monopolization cases, relying on the methods for delineating markets and identifying competitive effects that have become commonplace for mergers. Vertical considerations remain germane, but primarily in the same way that buyer preferences ultimately determine relevant markets.

We conclude by proposing a simple method to reconcile monopolization doctrine with its collusion and merger cousins, deleting only two words, "or maintain," from the canon of Section 2 law. In doing so, the purpose is not to dispute the appropriate strictness of antitrust or define away monopolization. In part, the analysis here arises out of a traditional criticism that monopolization law and other vertical antitrust doctrines are used to attack inconsequential or beneficial practices by preventing organization efficiencies and assuming that multiple monopolies along a production chain are significantly worse than having one in the middle. However, the primary objective is to save Section 2 by bringing monopolization analysis within the generally successful paradigms used in the rest of antitrust. Monopolization doctrines can exempt harmful practices because the perpetrators or their conduct fails to pass screens based on economically dubious anti-rival views of monopolization, rather than on whether the practice in question created a monopoly where none would have existed otherwise.

---

[9] Earlier versions and presentations of this chapter referred to this method as "input market monopolization" or IMM. Some commentors suggested that such a definition might be taken to exclude exclusionary contracting that affects markets normally though of as downstream, e.g., retailing. Although one can interpret retailing as an input even though the retailer buys the product at wholesale and resells it, the CMM appellation may avoid the impression that the approach is restrictive to "inputs." It applies to any relevant complementary market that, prior to exclusive contracting, was competitive and not subject to effective monopoly control.

16.2. The fallacious syllogism

The following syllogism highlights the nature of the controversy regarding Section 2 cases and points the way toward the solution:

- *Premise 1*: Section 2 cases are about actions taken by a firm that bring undue harm to rivals.
- *Premise 2*: Because competition hurts rivals, the burden of proof in cases based on rival injury should be very high, if not insurmountable.
- *Conclusion*: Section 2 cases should bear a very high if not insurmountable burden.

Both sides in the present controversy accept the first premise on the defining primacy of harm to rivals. A leading textbook described Section 2 cases as "actions [that] exclude or harm rivals and thereby either help to maintain or create a monopoly to the disadvantage of consumers" (Carlton and Perloff, 1990, p. 759). The "Chicago" perspective, taking a dim view of monopolization cases, accepts the second premise as well, and hence the conclusion (Posner, 1976, pp. 214–215; Easterbrook, 1984, pp. 8–9). Those with a more activist bent, often utilizing the so-called "post-Chicago" approach (Antitrust Law Journal, 1995) reject the conclusion by rejecting the second premise. Experts, prosecutors, and judges on this view either (at best) can use game theoretic tools to distinguish rival harms due to competition from those due to monopolization, or (at worst) take protection of competitors as a primary goal (Coate and Fischer, 2001). A recent example of the tension between these views is the recently adopted "Positive Comity Agreement" on competition enforcement between the U.S. and Canada.[10] Article II.1, defines "adverse effects" first as "harm caused by anticompetitive activities to"

> the ability of persons, either natural or legal, in the territory of a Party to export to, invest in, or otherwise compete in the territory of the other Party

and only afterwards as

> competition in a Party's domestic or import markets.

One might read this as placing "protecting competitors" ahead of "protecting competition."

Implicit construal of the fallacious syllogism, starting from the first premise that monopolization is about harm to rivals, is that it drives debate to extreme positions rather than encouraging arrival at a balanced and clear policy. It has led to spurious screens requiring prior monopoly or market dominance and that the monopolization practice requires a profit sacrifice. We will observe that such tests suit both sides in the debate, in that they play into the "harm competitors"

---

[10] Agreement Between the Government of the United States of America and the Government of Canada on the Application of Positive Comity Principles to the Enforcement of their Competition Laws, signed Oct. 5, 2004, available at http://www.ftc.gov/os/2004/10/0410comityagreeenglish.pdf, accessed Feb 5, 2005.

concern of the activist school, yet from a more narrowly economic perspective may be designed to subvert monopolization cases.

The expansion of perspective from focusing on agreements among those in the same market to agreements across markets leads to definitional contradictions, including oxymoronic turns of phrase as the "vertical market power" framework used by the Federal Energy Regulatory Commission (Brennan, 2004b) and the focus on the "rivals" rather than the "costs" aspect to "raising rivals' costs" (Brennan, 1988). The need to rely on game theoretic principles has led to the use of non-robust theories, relying on situation-specific assumptions and inferences that courts would likely have a difficult time verifying (Brennan, 2001). With clever economists able to offer analyses on either side, the possibility of harm in some instance supposedly provides support for the claim that the practice is harmful in a particular case (Coate and Fischer, 2001; Brennan, 2004a).[11]

The crucial flaw is that both sides in the decades-old debate about monopolization law focus only on the second premise and do not question the first—that monopolization law is concerned with harm to rivals. Our proposal is not to reject or accept the second premise, but to reject the first. We should reconstrue monopolization law as not about rivalry in a primary and previously dominated market, but on the cornering of a separate previously competitive market. This market will generally be a complement, most often an input that is used to supply firms in the market of the nominal monopolist in Section 2 cases, hence we refer to the alternative reformulation as "complement market monopolization" (CMM).

A common, if not the standard, crucial piece of anticompetitive conduct in monopolization cases involves acquiring monopoly control over an input or complement (e.g., distribution outlets) through exclusive contracts (e.g., where the distributor agrees to distribute only a single manufacturer's product). This allows the use of horizontal screens used in standard merger cases—market delineation, concentration, entry conditions—to be employed in monopolization cases. We will also see how one may use horizontal screens to analyze monopolization cases based on bundled discounting. These cases involve discounts to intermediaries in the production chain rather than final consumers. Hence, foregoing discounts creates a disincentive to deal with others similar to penalties for breach of exclusive dealing contracts.

Vertical stories remain, but these can and should be recast in ways to illustrate how horizontal control is being enhanced. For example, so-called "convergence" mergers between electricity generators and natural gas suppliers seem vertical but present competitive harms only to the degree that the generator acquires control over the output of competing generators through control over gas sup-

[11] Canceling expert witnesses becomes a litigation tax, which perhaps is a good idea if litigation is excessive.

plies to them (Brennan, 2004b).[12] Other notable vertical cases involve mergers or practices that enhance incentives to exploit opportunistically commitments that buyers have made to a particular seller's product.[13] However, these should be viewed as breaches of (implicit) contracts that normally would accompany buyers being "locked-in," rather than treated as antitrust cases at all.

One vertical monopolization story with some appeal to critics of Section 2 law was when regulated monopolists entered other markets to exploit their market power through non-price discrimination or cross-subsidization (Brennan, 1987, pp. 750–764). Although such theories were the basis for the 1984 break-up of AT&T[14] and restrictions on vertical control of regulated transmission operating companies,[15] the Supreme Court's recent decision in *Verizon v. Trinko*[16] calls their continued antitrust relevance into question. Part of the difficulty is that the fallacious syllogism led the Court to employ screens such as profit sacrifice and prior dealing that are of dubious relevance even outside regulated industries. Moreover, the *Trinko* decision reversed the presumption that regulation creates the potential for antitrust violations, instead finding that the presence of a regulator diminishes the need for antitrust oversight.

The complement market monopolization approach to Section 2 cases works most clearly in what one might call "static" monopolization settings, in which the effect of cornering control over the supply of an input or complement is most direct. Based on the survey of cases looked at here, most cases appear to be static. However, some may genuinely be dynamic, in which the putative monopolization works only through changing the strategic positions in a market evolving over time. A review of the Microsoft case suggests that, contrary to widespread belief, a dynamic case requires substantially different market delineations, evidence, and remedies than those appropriate for a static case (Brennan, 2004a). Profit sacrifice screens may not be appropriate even in apparently dynamic predatory pricing cases, specifically whether predation requires short-term pricing below cost (Edlin, 2002).[17] As noted earlier, a simple recommendation to change prevailing monopolization doctrine should counter the

---

[12] Enova Corp., 79 F.E.R.C. ¶61,372 (June 25, 1997); Dominion Res., Inc., 89 F.E.R.C. ¶61,162 (November 10, 1999).

[13] Examples include AT&T's acquisition of McCaw cellular (prior to AT&T having extensive dealings in the cellular market) and Kodak's decision to restrict copier service to its own maintenance personnel by denying parts to independent repair companies. AT&T Corp., 59 Fed. Reg. 44,158, 44,166 (D.O.J. Aug. 26, 1994) (proposed final judgment and competitive impact statement); Eastman Kodak Co. v. Image Technical. Services, Inc. et al. ("*Kodak*"), 504 U.S. 451 (1992). *Kodak* does not seem to be having much of an influence on that analysis of competition in intrabrand "aftermarkets" (Goldfine and Vorrasi, 2004).

[14] U.S. v. AT&T ("*AT&T*"), 552 F. Supp. 131 (D.C.D.C. 1982).

[15] Federal Energy Regulatory Commission, Regional Transmission Organizations, Order No. 2000 ("FERC Order 2000"), 65 FR 810 (Jan. 6, 2000).

[16] Verizon v. Trinko ("*Trinko*"), 540 U.S. 398 (2004).

[17] See Elhauge (2003) for a restatement of the standard profit sacrifice requirement for predation.

fallacious syllogism and bring Section 2 analysis more in line with its less problematic Section 1 and 7 cousins.

16.3. Spurious screen #1: Dominance in primary market

One of the screens for monopolization, arising from the fallacious syllogism's presumption that monopolization involves injury to rivals, is that prior dominance in a market be a requirement for Section 2 liability. The implication is that monopolization involves the big guy beating up on its smaller, defenseless competitors.

Examples abound. As Shenefield and Stelzer put it in their overview of the antitrust laws, "monopoly itself is [only] a threshold requirement for Section 2 application" (Shenefield and Stelzer, 1998, p. 36). The plaintiffs in *U.S. v. Microsoft* believed themselves to be required to prove that Microsoft had an existing monopoly in some relevant market, there "Intel-based PC operating systems."[18] Citing *U.S. v. Grinnell*,[19] Edlin and Rubinfeld (2004, pp. 119–157, 139) state that a Section 2 monopoly maintenance claim requires "the possession of monopoly power in the relevant market." That screen, however, is at best irrelevant and at worst counterproductive.

16.3.1. Prior dominance looks at what the perpetrator was, rather than what it is doing

The problem with "abuse of dominance" is not dominance; it is abuse. The archetypal abuse of dominance story is that a monopolist forces intermediate good producers (e.g., retailers) to take tied or bundled products or to sign exclusionary contracts, using the threat of withholding sales of the monopoly product as the lever. A prior dominance screen diverts attention away from the harm to the characteristics of the perpetrator. Whatever the Chicago school's limitations, it effectively showed that dominance is not a sufficient condition for harm from exclusionary conduct or other foreclosing activities (Telser, 1960).[20] However, the dominance screen may be too restrictive, contrary to the U.S. legal position that treats dominance as necessary. Requiring prior dominance excuses actions by firms that happened not to have a prior monopoly, yet acquired the ability to create such a monopoly, e.g., by cornering an input market through exclusive contracts.

Empirically, it may well be that large firms in primary markets may be the most likely entities to undertake such a scheme, and threatened withholding may

---

[18] Brennan (2001, p. 1059), citing the plaintiffs' complaint filed in *Microsoft*, No. 98-1232, (D.D.C. Aug. 1998), ¶54.

[19] U.S. v. Grinnell Corp. ("*Grinnell*"), 384 U.S. 563 (1966).

[20] This sufficiency perspective is implied in the European Commission's Article 82 on abuse of dominance, *supra* note 6.

be the tactic chosen (Rasmusen et al., 1991). However, requiring prior dominance prioritizes tactics over harm. It is as if one decided that since large people are more able to inflict harm than small people that one has to weigh at least 100 kilograms before one is guilty of battery. Who obtains control over an intermediate market and how they did it is essentially immaterial; it is the monopolization of that market that matters. One should not need to condition the identification of harm on prior dominance of a primary market. To continue the battery metaphor, the criterion for a crime is the injury, not the size of the injurer.

Anticompetitive harm through obtaining exclusive control over distribution channels, retail outlets or other needed inputs could come about from threats from a preexisting monopolist. But it could also come about by payments from an aspiring monopolist, or someone outside the sector who realizes that acquiring control would be valuable because of its value to potential competitors in that primary market.[21] The problem is in the effect, not the cause. One gets the same anticompetitive effect whether it is obtained reluctantly via threat or cooperatively via sharing of the monopoly profits obtainable through the acquisition of control over the relevant complement.

16.3.2. The inherent contradiction

The requirement of prior dominance forces a contradiction into the core of Section 2 litigation. To establish that the defendant already has a prior monopoly in its primary market, plaintiffs will provide all arguments necessary to meet the legal burden of proof and to leave as little doubt as possible that entry barriers into the primary market are inordinately high. The recent Microsoft case provides an example. The plaintiffs invoked the high costs of developing operating systems, network externalities that lead most consumers to want the same operating system as most everyone else, and the potential cost of porting applications to explain why Microsoft has an operating system monopoly (Brennan, 2001, p. 1072).

But after having done so, one is left with a conundrum. If entry barriers are as high as plaintiffs assert, what difference can the specific conduct at issue in a Section 2 case make? The stronger the case that the defendant has market power, the weaker is the case that the defendant is guilty of monopolization through the alleged exclusionary conduct. Monopolization cases would be stronger to the extent that one would show either that the defendant lacked market power or that its monopoly would disappear but for the monopolizing conduct.[22] The issue should not be whether a firm has a monopoly at present, but whether the conduct in question is creating a monopoly where there would not be one otherwise.

---

[21] One example of a previously small firm potentially engaging in monopolization involved accusations by Stroh's brewing that Miller, prior to becoming a large entity, tied up the market for television advertising and thus positioned itself to obtain a large share for its "Lite" brand (Brennan, 1988).

[22] Posner (2004) has recently stated that exclusion cases are most plausible when the monopoly is "fragile."

16.3.3. Prior dominance a defense, not condition of guilt

Prior dominance may be more than an indirect rationale for these practices; it supports affirmative defenses that efficiency is a likely motive for the challenged practice. A firm that is large in one market is likely to have a large involvement in upstream markets commensurate with its size. A firm that manufactures 80% of the volume of a particular type of product is likely to have 80% of the distribution capacity or retail space used to sell that product. If so, one might expect such a nominally dominant firm to want to engage in practices that improve coordination, to the extent such coordination is valuable, with a similar fraction of the market for distributing its product.[23] Disproportionate exclusionary conduct by small firms, on the other hand, would be more suspicious. For example, exclusive contracts by a small firm with a large fraction of the relevant retailers, would warrant more concern, as such contracting would seem beyond any apparent efficiency justification.

Moreover, the marginal harm from exclusionary conduct, e.g., from tying up a distribution system so competitors cannot survive, will be lower the bigger is a prior monopoly in the primary market. Many analysts have properly taken exception to the "single monopoly profit" theory, which is that there can be no additional harm in a vertical chain when a monopoly sits in the middle.[24] Rationales for exceptions may be consistent with increasing welfare by increasing the scope of monopoly, e.g., by facilitating price discrimination or correcting for input market distortions. But even if the single monopoly profit theory does not exactly hold, the more surplus is extracted at one stage, the less is available to be taken at others. Hence, a firm with a secure monopoly could argue that fact alone reduces the likely harm from the practice in question.

One can put this in terms used for statistical error. The Type I error would be rejecting a monopolization claim when it is true; the Type II error would be accepting a monopolization claim when it is false. The above suggests that the Type I error would be smaller for a dominant firm than for a smaller firm. If a dominant firm is let go, the added costs of monopolization are small. If a non-dominant firm monopolizes by excluding competitors from a market, however, the monopoly harm would be greater. Conversely, accepting a monopolization claim when it is false is likely to be more costly when a dominant firm is involved, since vertical efficiencies rather than added monopoly profits are more likely to be the rationale for a challenged practice for a firm that already is extracting significant monopoly profits from the market. Consequently, Type I and

---

[23] Sometimes, of course, the complement market extends far beyond sales to a buyer dominant in a downstream market. The supply of generic retail capacity for some products may be substantially larger than the retail capacity devoted to the sale of a particular product. If so, exclusive contracts will not have an anticompetitive effect because downstream competitors can easily switch to others in the larger market.

[24] Bork (1978, pp. 228–229) provides the essential statement; for critical views, see the sources cited at Brennan (2004b, pp. 897–900).

Type II error are likely to be greater if decision rules tend to immunize non-dominant firms and increase the likelihood of prosecution for dominant firms.

When there is market power at multiple levels in a vertical chain, an additional justification for exclusionary conduct is preventing double marginalization. A firm with market power at one level might increase welfare by creating a monopoly it controls at another level via exclusive contracts or vertical integration. While competitors might be foreclosed from such conduct, it also eliminates the inefficiency when separate monopolists in a vertical chain raise price without recognizing the negative effects on complement suppliers.

16.3.4. Crafting careful remedies

The prior dominance screen persists because it follows from the perspective, reflected in the fallacious syllogism, that Section 2 cases are about harm to rivals. It seems intuitively less plausible that small firms can hurt big firms rather than *vice versa*.[25] A second reason for persistence may be that non-dominant firms would seem more vulnerable to excessive prosecution otherwise.[26] This may be understandable, particularly in the U.S. where private parties are free to bring cases against each other, claiming that harms to them are the result of monopolistic conduct, even when the net economic effect is positive (Baumol and Ordover, 1985).

However, a concern may also arise from the typical all-or-nothing nature of antitrust remedies in monopolization cases. If the concern is that a particular practice is exclusionary, the usual proposed remedy is to halt the practice altogether. For example, in the Microsoft case a concern was that contracts with personal computer manufacturers that discouraged them from displaying competing Internet browsers; the eventual remedy was to ban any such contracts.[27] In a more recent monopolization case, the Justice Department sought to ban a dominant manufacturer of artificial teeth from engaging in exclusive dealing arrangements with dental laboratories that manufactured dentures.[28]

Such all-or-nothing remedies may seem reasonable when placed on dominant firms, although as noted above, a market-wide practice, even if exclusionary, may be less harmful if instituted by a firm without prior monopoly power. But if placed on smaller firms, the remedy may seem excessive, in that exclusive dealing, bundling, tying, or other potentially monopolistic practices would not be harmful if done on a scale proportional to the size of a small firm. A complete ban would be excessive. But the solution to the problem here is not to restrict

---

[25] *But see* Gelman and Salop (1983), for a discussion of how small firms can hurt big firms, albeit not in the monopolization context. Also, if minimum efficient scale is relatively small, dominant incumbents will be more vulnerable to entry than if large size is required to enter (Spence, 1977).

[26] I owe this observation to participants at a seminar on this topic at the Federal Trade Commission.

[27] *Microsoft*, *supra* note 4, particularly the final judgment decision.

[28] *Dentsply*, *supra* note 7. This case is discussed in more detail *infra* in Section 16.6.1.

focus to dominant firms, but to fashion appropriate remedies that allow a practice to some extent, but not to the extent that it creates monopoly control over a distribution channel, retail outlets, or other inputs or complements needed to compete. For example, one could allow firms to contract exclusively with some distributors or retailers, but below a percentage necessary to give it the power to directly or indirectly raise the price of distribution or retailing.

The analogy to mergers is obvious. One does not ban all mergers in a sector, even those involving firms with significant shares. Mergers below some market share may be acceptable in a market while mergers above that share would be prohibited. With respect to monopolistic exclusion, one could in principle delineate a complement market (production input, distribution, retailing), informed by conventional criteria,[29] and a share that constitutes a threat of monopoly control, and ban exclusive dealing or other relevant practices only when that share is exceeded. Remedies in monopolization cases should not involve halting such arrangements absolutely, but only down to a non-threatening level. Remedies based on shares of relevant complement markets would reduce the concern that focusing on monopolization by non-dominant firms would lead to market-wide bans of potentially efficient practices. Small firms, in particular, would be free to match such contracting with the scale of their operations.

16.4. Spurious screen #2: Profit sacrifice

16.4.1. Practical and theoretical shortcomings

A hallmark of recent monopolization practice has been that an act must involve a sacrifice of profits or make no business sense if it is to be deemed anticompetitive.[30] For the screen to be meaningful, the test cannot simply be that the tactic

---

[29] Issues in delineating complementary markets are discussed at more length *infra* at Section 16.5.3. Market delineation for this purpose is not as direct as in merger cases, because it will typically be done *ex post* (after the exclusive contracts or arrangements are instituted) rather than *ex ante* (before the merger is consummated). However, it is less problematic than when one is forced to begin with dominant firms, because under CMM one will typically be dealing with a setting where suppliers of the complement, e.g., retail outlets or distribution channels, will have previously been independent. Thus, one will have prior evidence that the effective price of the complementary product had been lower until the operations were effectively "merged" under the coverage of the exclusionary agreements.

[30] Aspen Skiing Co. v. Aspen Highlands Skiing Corp., 472 U.S. 585 (1985); cited in *Trinko, supra* note 16. Although I have heard antitrust practitioners attempt to parse out differences, I assume that "make no business sense" and "profit sacrifice" have the same economic meaning. If firms are profit maximizers, a practice that that makes business sense and that leaves no profits on the table are one and the same.

This criterion is presumably derived from the below cost criterion for predatory pricing (Areeda and Turner, 1975; Brooke Group Ltd. v. Brown and Williamson Tobacco Corp. ("*Brooke Group*"), 509 U.S. 209 (1993)). We discuss in part 16.7.2 whether rejecting the profit sacrifice test for exclusionary monopolization suggests that the *Brooke Group* standard is inappropriate for predation cases.

is costly. Any practice that involves future returns will have a positive economic cost, so the idea of a profit sacrifice needs to bear some relevance to competition itself. So interpreted, that idea is that the practice needs to have been unprofitable "but for" gains from a subsequent anticompetitive outcome.[31] But as with the "prior dominance" criterion, the "profit sacrifice" criterion misdirects attention from competitive effects and thus runs the risk of letting harmful conduct be excused. Looking at profit sacrifice, ironically, gives primacy to the welfare of the alleged perpetrator, as if one determined whether a crime had been committed by seeing how much effort the criminal made rather than whether a victim had suffered a loss.[32]

In effect, a profit sacrifice test leads us to ask whether the price paid by the alleged monopolist to carry out a particular tactic was too high. But if monopolization takes place, why should the price paid matter? The price speaks only to the ability of those who participate in monopolization—for example, by signing exclusive contracts with a monopolist—to extract rents up front. The adverse welfare effects are identical. The positive and important contribution of the otherwise troublesome "raising rivals' cost" doctrine is that it correctly observes that when monopolization takes place through acquisition of market power over an input, no up-front loss is necessary (Salop and Scheffman, 1983).[33]

Theoretical analysis has confirmed these doubts about the profit sacrifice test. Using a simple duopoly model, Schwartz (1989) has shown that the profit sacrifice test leads to error in both directions. A cost-reducing innovation that is free to one firm, hence involves no profit sacrifice, may reduce welfare if it those reduced costs lead to a duopoly equilibrium under which the profits of the second firm become negative, inducing its exit and leading the remaining firm to raise price. Hence welfare falls without a profit sacrifice. In the other direction, an innovation may be profitable to one firm only if the other one leaves, but welfare could go up if the firm that exits was less efficient than the firm that remains.[34]

A more concrete example of the failure of the profit sacrifice test arises in Section 2 cases based on regulatory evasion, particularly where there are network externalities.[35] In the canonical regulatory evasion case, e.g., *U.S. v. AT&T*,[36] a regulated monopolist vertically integrated into a related market profits by creating an artificial competitive advantage for subsidiaries or affiliates in unregulated

---

[31] The "but for" test came to widespread notice following Ordover and Willig (1981).

[32] Salop (2005) provides a more extensive discussion of the problems with a profit sacrifice test from a consumer welfare perspective.

[33] An early formulation of RRC was "non-price predation," specifically to highlight the lack of need for having to spend now in the hope of subsequent recoupment (Salop, 2005).

[34] A variation on the profit sacrifice theme that also is not supported by theory is a rule that allows practices that exclude only equally efficient competitors. An inefficient competitor can still increase welfare by causing overall market prices to fall. Hence, a practice that excludes an inefficient competitor may still reduce welfare.

[35] Regulatory evasion cases may no longer be considered Section 2 violations. *Trinko, supra* note 16.

[36] *AT&T, supra* note 14.

markets. One method is to discriminate against competitors of the unregulated affiliate in terms of the access they get to the regulated sector, e.g., denying competing electricity generators access to a utility's distribution grid.[37] A second is to cross-subsidize unregulated affiliates by misallocating unregulated sector costs to the regulated side, inducing regulators to raise regulated rates, effectively having the regulated firm's customers cover the unregulated affiliate's costs. In neither case does the tactic entail a short-run sacrifice; discrimination or cross-subsidization will be profitable even if competitors only shrink but do not exit.

With network externalities, e.g., in a telephone network, a dominant incumbent may find it profitable to refuse to deal with new entrants. If the customers of those new entrants cannot access the customer base of the incumbent, the new entrants may not be able to compete effectively.[38] Again, this refusal is immediately profitable, especially if interconnection itself entails its own costs. Insistence on a profit sacrifice test will lead to the wrong conclusion.[39]

16.4.2. Sinking Section 2?

With the theoretical and practical difficulties of the profit sacrifice or business sense test, one may wonder what purpose it serves. One might pose the question of what would happen if we used the profit sacrifice test for Section 7 cases. If the test is such a good idea in monopolization cases, perhaps we could use it to block only mergers that would be unprofitable but for an increase in market power. If that were the rule, mergers that would be profitable without a price increase would be permitted, no matter how much market power the merger would create. I suspect that so few mergers are unprofitable but for a market power test that such a rule would end most Section 7 enforcement.[40]

---

[37] Such concerns rationalize policies to promote the independent operation of transmission grids from the interests of generation companies (FERC Order 2000, *supra* note 15).

[38] This type of case appears to require prior dominance, but not in the provision of the service directly but in controlling access to customers needed for other firms to compete. The two are separable, at least in principle. Mandatory interconnection, e.g., as set out in Sections 251 and 252 of the 1996 Telecommunications Act (Pub. L. No. 104-104, §§251–252 (1996)), exists so that a dominant share of the service market does not translate into dominance over the ability to realize network externalities. Moreover, interconnection has to be regulated, otherwise consumers could be harmed even if interconnection is mandatory, but at a monopoly price. Inter-competitor interconnection agreements may also generate similar competitive harm (Brennan, 1997). Part of the problem with *Trinko* (*supra* note 16) is that it treated mandatory interconnection to realize network externalities as an order to deal with a competitor, when in fact it is forcing the incumbent to provide an input—access to its customers—so that other firms can offer telephone service to *their* customers as well as compete for each other's.

[39] As it did in *Trinko, id.*

[40] Many mergers end up unprofitable, of course, but that either has nothing to do with market power or occurs in spite of any market power that the merger may have created.

Similar arguments would apply if the profit sacrifice test were applied to collusion cases. If one were to block only price fixing or market allocation agreements that were unprofitable in and of themselves, most would fail. "Rule of reason" cases, in which the benefits of a competition-reducing agreement are weighed against the competitive costs, would disappear. Agreements and other practices would fail to involve a profit sacrifice necessary to conclude that an agreement were anticompetitive.

These analogies make it clear that a profit sacrifice test is tantamount to an absolute efficiencies defense. If a practice produces a penny's worth of net benefit above its opportunity cost, thus involving no sacrifice of profits, it would be permitted even if it led to many dollars of welfare loss. Thus, and perhaps paradoxically, the profit sacrifice test plays to both sides in the fallacious syllogism. Those who accept the second premise, that the burden should be very high in monopolization cases because they are directed at rivals, have a test that essentially guts Section 2 by allowing an absolute efficiencies defense. Those with a more activist perspective who reject the second premise, however, would see in the profit sacrifice test not an issue of economic efficiency, but a measure of the lengths to which an alleged monopolist would go to harm rivals. For this group, the profit sacrifice test shows that Section 2 is about intent to harm, and not economic welfare.

16.5. The "complement market monopolization" alternative

16.5.1. Focus on the complement market, as if its providers had merged

To avoid the fallacious syllogism and the spurious screens it has spawned, we can adopt a method for analysis in many if not most monopolization cases that begins not by focusing directly on rivals, but on the market for an input or complement that rivals may need in order to compete. We begin with a truism, that to exclude a rival or raise its cost of production, one has to raise the effective price of necessary complements (Brennan, 1988). Examples of such complements include production inputs, distribution and retail outlets, or sales to other manufacturers who produce their own goods or services using the rivals' products. This level of control over the effective price of the complements requires the *acquisition* of market power over their supply. Hence, the necessary condition for anticompetitive effect is that the market for the complement has been monopolized through acquisition of control over it. The standard means would be through excusive dealing contracts with input suppliers that allow the alleged monopolist to decide who gets how much of that input.

"Exclusion," "foreclosure," and "raising rivals' costs" can thus be thought of in horizontal terms—what I call here "complement market monopolization." Not only is CMM a necessary condition for monopolization as construed, it is sufficient to constitute a violation under conventional horizontal terms. The anticompetitive acquisition of control over a market is a problem whether the entity acquiring that control is a dominant firm in a market targeting rivals (as present monopolization doctrine would have it) or a non-dominant firm acquiring the ability to target rivals (as might make more sense if dominance already implies monopoly power).

Moreover, CMM is anticompetitive even if done by someone not in the market at all, who could capture the monopoly value of that complement by raising its price or offering it on an exclusive basis to one or a handful of downstream buyers. For example, I am not in the soda business, but suppose I signed exclusive contracts with a monopoly share of grocery stores and convenience stores that said that they could sell soda that only I delivered. I could then sell the rights to that capacity to soda companies at a monopoly price, which is passed on to soda consumers. Under CMM, such a case would not be dismissed because the alleged monopolizer is too small in the primary market or not in it at all. In addition, whether such control was acquired profitably or unprofitably is, as it should be, immaterial to an analysis of competitive effects.

Acquisition of control over a set of suppliers of a complement, e.g., through exclusive dealing contracts, is economically equivalent to a horizontal merger of the set of suppliers of that complement. For that reason, prior dominance and profit sacrifice screens can be replaced by the familiar screens used to analyze horizontal mergers (DOJ, 1997). One begins by delineating a relevant input or complement market using the "hypothetical monopolist" test of identifying the set of firms necessary to raise price a significant amount for a reasonable length of time. The inquiry would proceed to the familiar questions of what share of that market has been controlled through exclusionary contracts or practices, and whether that market is easy to enter. Such questions arise only indirectly in monopolization cases; CMM makes them central.

16.5.2. Vertical irrelevance and relevance

One of the advantages of the CMM approach to monopolization is that it places priority on the monopolizing act—cornering a market for a complement—and appropriately ignores the irrelevant question of who the monopolizer happens to be. Complement market power is both necessary and sufficient for competition concerns; prior market dominance and profit sacrifice are neither.

Vertical considerations remain relevant, but primarily to provide the type of information on buyer characteristics that pertain in any horizontal analysis. For example, to determine if a properly delineated relevant input market has been monopolized, one needs to know what sets of inputs downstream firms view as substitutes. For example, in the 1980s a beer company was accused of, in CMM terms, acquiring via exclusive contracts control over the ability to advertise during nationally televised sports contests (Brennan, 1988, pp. 108–110). The crucial market is not specifically the market for beer, but the market for advertising beer. The competitive effects of the practice depend on degree to which beer companies view advertising over different television broadcasts or other media as sufficiently close substitutes for advertising over sports. Putting it bluntly, if yes, there's no problem; if no, there would be.

A second aspect in which vertical information matters to this essentially horizontal story involving the complement market is in describing the competitive effects. In most if not all monopolization cases amenable to CMM analysis, the story is unlikely to involve the prospect of enhanced collusion between input suppliers controlled by exclusive contracts and other input suppliers.[41] Consequently, the likely story will involve unilateral rather than coordinated effects. One would want to know whether a complement market monopolist with the share of the market controlled through exclusive contracts or other means would be able to raise price.

The second issue would be the effects of such a price increase. Intermediate good markets behave differently than final product markets because buyer demands in the former are interdependent; the price one buyer pays affects the willingness of other buyers to pay (Ordover and Panzar, 1982; Katz, 1987). A small downward difference in input prices can create a significant competitive advantage that, depending on the downstream strategic game, could cause downstream firms to exit.[42] While the complement market should be the central focus, a model of unilateral effects that recognizes interdependence of buyers' demands may be central in deciding whether a particular degree of exclusionary control would be anticompetitive.

16.5.3. Clarify (in part) market delineation

A potential practical advantage of the CMM approach is that it partially finesses a thorny question in Section 2 cases—how to define the relevant market in which the firm has a prior monopoly (Nelson and White, 2003).[43] Since almost every product has some differential characteristics, prices are rarely going to just equal marginal cost. As the famous "Cellophane fallacy" illustrates,[44] observed demand elasticity facing a firm is unlikely to be indicative, because any monopolist

---

[41] Such a story might be somewhat more plausible if the other input suppliers were controlled by other firms in the putative monopolist's market.

[42] This fact explains why regulators spend considerable if not most of their effort in many input markets on ensuring that prices are not discriminatory, as opposed to their level. High but uniform input prices create no competitive disadvantage, and the higher costs will be passed on to final consumers. Discriminatory prices, on the other hand, can cause some sellers to lose profits and perhaps exit. Hence, risk-averse buyers in intermediate goods markets will be far more interested in preventing differential pricing than in preventing high prices.

[43] An indication of the complexity and difficulty in identifying whether a single firm has market power is that much of *Microsoft*, *supra* note 4 was about whether Microsoft had a monopoly in personal computer operating systems, even if the universe of personal computers is restricted to those running Intel-based processors (Brennan, 2001, pp. 1059–1063).

[44] The term (in)famously comes from U.S. v. E.I. du Pont de Nemours and Co., 351 U.S. 377 (1956), in which the Supreme Court erroneously concluded that du Pont had no monopoly in Cellophane because people turned to inferior substitutes (e.g., paper bags) at the prices du Pont was charging (Carlton and Perloff, 1990, p. 740).

will raise price up to the point where it begins to lose customers to other suppliers. Price-cost margins may not be a good test if firms are close to capacity and average variable costs are used as proxies for marginal cost (Brennan, 2003).[45] Profits are not a good test, in that high profits are consistent with competitive behavior and inframarginal rents, and low observed profits at any time may be consistent with expenses made today by a monopolist to invest in serving a growing market (Fisher and McGowan, 1983). Overall cost coverage requires lifetime data for a firm, and since market conditions may change over that lifetime, high profits *ex post* may be consistent with competitive behavior *ex ante*.

The CMM approach can avoid these difficulties by looking at exclusive contracting as a succession of events like a merger among input suppliers. Market delineation in mergers is less problematic than in monopolization cases as conventionally construed, because it asks not whether a firm has market power, but whether a merger between or among firms will increase market power. Under CMM, as noted above, one can apply standard Horizontal Merger Guidelines tests to that ascertain whether exclusionary conduct makes matters worse than if the exclusion had not taken place.

To do this, one needs to begin with the premise that a single exclusionary contract between a downstream firm and a complement supplier is unproblematic. Such a contract does not increase market power at either level of the market. It is the additional contracts with multiple complement suppliers that create the pricing power in the complement market that would not have been there otherwise. But one can look at those additional contracts as one would look at a merger between the initial complement supplier and those additional suppliers, and thus use the less problematic "make it worse" horizontal merger tools rather than address the highly problematic "market power or not" question.[46]

While market delineation under CMM is less problematic compared to when one is trying to show that a single firm has sufficient market power to pass a "prior dominance" screen, it has disadvantages and advantages relative to market delineation with mergers. Unless exclusive arrangements will be subject to the same kind of prior review as mergers, the antitrust evaluation will take place after the fact, rather than before. Hence, the question will be not, as in a merger, whether the exclusivity will make matters worse, but whether it made matters worse. This precludes direct application of forward-looking tests as in the Merger Guidelines, where one looks at whether a merger would produce a

---

[45] The distinction between marginal cost of increasing output beyond the present level and the potentially much lower marginal cost of producing output up to that level is a proposed rationale for why mergers that may seem anticompetitive may nonetheless not result in significantly reduced output (Harris and Simons, 1989).

[46] Identifying firms with stand-alone market power remains a necessary policy question, but primarily for regulation, not antitrust. Regulation is concerned with the need to hold down prices of firms with market power when such control can be implemented effectively. Antitrust deals with preventing practices, including growth in a market through merger or contract, which impedes the competitive process.

small but significant non-transitory increase in price. However, because exclusion involves the acquisition of control over previously independent complement suppliers, one need not look at hypothetical price increase but actual ones. For example, one could ask whether exclusive arrangements with a set of retail outlets, for example, actually increased the price of retailing. One might be able to use actual data on price increases, rather than attempt to predict price increases yet to happen. [47]

16.6. CMM applications

The key idea in any CMM case is to identify the relevant complement market that is being controlled in such a way to create market power that may be used to foreclose competition. We looked at the example of a soda company that contracts with grocers and convenience stores to obtain exclusive rights to prime shelf space, perhaps in sufficient quantity to preclude entry or effective competition from other soda companies. The relevant market being monopolized here is not soda, however, but shelf space. It is entry conditions into that market, and not soda *per se*, that speak to whether such contracting leads to anticompetitive effects. We illustrate how this should operate with three recent prominent monopolization cases, two from the U.S. and one from Canada, that very closely match the soda example. We then see how CMM may help deal with the recent spate of cases involving bundled discounts.

16.6.1. U.S. v. Dentsply[48]

Dentsply is the dominant supplier of artificial teeth in the U.S., with an approximately 80% share of the market. These artificial teeth are supplied to dental laboratories either directly by the manufacturer or through dealers. Dental labs, in turn, fabricate dentures ordered by dentists for their patients. Labs generally decide which firm's teeth will go in the dentures they fabricate; dentists prescribe a particular brand only about 10% of the time.

The Department of Justice's Antitrust Division accused Dentsply of Section 2 monopolization of the market for artificial teeth through exclusive contracts with dealers, which prohibited them from carrying other manufacturers' teeth if they

---

[47] When monopolization involves exclusion, the complement suppliers will no longer be making their goods or services available to rivals of the excluder. However, a price comparison is still available, in which one can ask whether the price of the complement available outside the exclusive agreement has risen. Such an inquiry is necessarily part of a Section 2 case under the fallacious syllogism, in that such a finding is necessary to know if the alleged monopolization in fact harmed the rivals.

[48] *Dentsply*, *supra* note 7. The description of the case comes from that trial court decision.

carried Dentsply's.[49] DOJ initially lost at trial. Agreeing with DOJ that the relevant market is artificial teeth, the court found that Dentsply lacked market power, despite a large market share, because competitors were not excluded. The judge found that hundreds of dealers outside the 23 Dentsply uses are available and that teeth makers can and do sell directly to labs, bypassing dealers. Moreover, even Dentsply's dealers were free to switch to carrying competing brands at any time, although "in the recent past" none had done so.

The Third Circuit Court of Appeals reversed the trial court, finding that Dentsply had market power in the "relevant market[,] the total sales of artificial teeth to the laboratories and dealers"[50] and "has held its dominant share for more than ten years."[51] While it agreed with the court regarding the definition of the relevant market, it claimed that Dentsply did have power to exclude by threatening to withhold its teeth from dealers that carried others. The Court of Appeals also found that dealers provided important benefits that could not be reproduced through direct sales from teeth manufacturers to dental laboratories.

The case and decision were predicated upon the relevant monopoly being that for artificial teeth; however, the relevant market is that in *dealers* for artificial teeth. If Dentsply did not acquire power in the market for dealing artificial teeth, it would have acquired no ability to exclude other teeth manufacturers from the market or undertake other actions equivalent to exploiting a market in dealing. Notably, the Court of Appeals in its description of exclusion said that the "paltry" success of the rivals was brought about by "the blocking of access to the key dealers. This is part of the *real market* that is denied to the rivals" [emphasis added].

This is the very point of CMM—the "real market" is the complement market, here dealers. The main flaw in the reasoning is the insistence on defining the relevant market as "artificial teeth" and in requiring prior dominance in the primary market. Dentsply's alleged dominance over artificial teeth manufacturing is neither necessary nor sufficient for competitive harm. If such dominance were the result of Dentsply's exclusionary practices, then that dominance would be relevant as an *effect* of monopolization, not as a condition for *causing* it. The economic welfare losses from Dentsply's contracts would likely be just as great if not greater if Dentsply had offered use of its dealer network to its rivals (and, in an opportunity cost sense, to itself) at a monopoly price for dealer services.

The trial court and Court of Appeals decisions did attend to the market for dealing, including barriers to entry or expansion and the ability of manufacturers and labs to bypass dealers. These are just the questions one would ask

---

[49] DOJ also cited as evidence of intent instances in which Dentsply solicited and signed up dealers it had previously not used or rejected, with contracts including the exclusionary restriction, only after Dentsply's competitors had shown interest in these dealers. DOJ also claimed that Dentsply's restrictive dealer contracts were unreasonable restraints of trade, violating Sherman Section 1, and that the probable effect would be to reduce competition, violating Section 3 of the Clayton Act. Neither of these aspects of the case are discussed here.

[50] *Dentsply*, 399 F.3d. at 188.

[51] *Id.*

under the HMGs were one attempting to see whether Dentsply's dealers constituted a large share of a relevant market for purposes of market delineation in merger cases. Because the court took teeth manufacturing rather than dealing to be the relevant market, it did not express its analysis and conclusions in this way. Rather, "market power in dealing" and other market delineation issues were expressed in terms of ability to exclude other teeth manufacturers from that market. Looking at the wrong market also means that both courts gave no indication of what share of the relevant dealer market Dentsply obtained through its practices. Were courts encouraged to look at the complement market in these cases (dental dealers) rather than the nominal market (teeth manufacturing), litigants would produce information that more accurately characterizes the competitive issues at stake.

The trial court found that Dentsply's contracts were not exclusionary because the dealers could opt out at any time.[52] As the Court of Appeals noted, opting-out contracts could still be exclusionary.[53] If there are scale economies in the manufacturer market, a single dealer would not leave because it would not be able get enough business from other manufacturers to survive (Rasmusen et al., 1991). In addition, Dentsply may have left rents on the table that a dealer would lose were it switch to another supplier. This need not imply a sacrifice of profits on Dentsply's part. The dealers could be sharing in the monopoly profits generated by Dentsply's exclusion, and each might lose some of its share of that profit were it to leave.

16.6.2. U.S. v. Microsoft, parts I and II

The long history of the Microsoft antitrust cases brings out two instances of how a monopolization claim could be clarified if viewed through the CMM lens. The first of the cases, settled by a consent decree in 1995, alleged that Microsoft monopolized the operating system market during the 1980s and early 1990s by licensing MS-DOS installation rights to personal computer (PC) companies (OEMs, for "original equipment manufacturers") on a "per processor" (i.e., per PC) rather than per copy basis.[54] Such licenses implied that the marginal cost to an OEM of selling an additional PC with or without MS-DOS was greater by the per-processor license fee, but the marginal cost to the OEM of installing MS-DOS on that PC was zero, once the PC was produced.

Although the alleged monopolization was over MS-DOS like operating systems, the actual market monopolized by the practice was the means for distributing the operating system—personal computers. The relevant facts would be

---

[52] The *Dentsply* trial judge cited a 1984 7th Circuit decision, *Roland Machinery Co. v. Dresser Industries Inc.*, 749 F.2d 380 (1984), for the proposition that "exclusive dealing contracts terminable in less than a year are presumptively lawful under [Clayton] §3." *Dentsply*, 277 F. Supp. 2d 450.

[53] *Dentsply*, 399 F.3d. at 193-94.

[54] Brennan (2001, pp. 1056–1058); United States v. Microsoft Corp., 1995-2 Trade Cas. (CCH) ¶71,096 (D.D.C, 1995).

whether (a) the per-processor contracts were sufficiently exclusionary to give Microsoft control over access to OEMs, (b) Microsoft had acquired control over a sufficiently large share of the OEMs to control operating system distribution, and (c) it is hard to enter the OEM market to carry other operating systems. These conditions together are necessary and sufficient for per-processor contracting to have raised the price of distributing software through PCs.

The degree to which these conditions were satisfied remains unclear. For the first, a per processor contract has the same effect as an exclusive dealing contract, with damages for breach requiring compensating Microsoft for its lost profits from lost sales to other operating system companies.[55] If exclusive dealing is the test for control, these contracts would satisfy it. However, in part because complement market delineation and entry conditions are not a part of monopolization cases, and because the case was settled by the litigants, we do not have a court determination as to whether these contracts spanned enough of the relevant OEM market to create monopoly power and whether new OEMs to carry the new operating system could enter. The agreed-upon remedy was to eliminate per-processor contracting entirely, and not to restrict it to a share of the OEM market that would not have market power in operating system distribution.

Three years later, the second Microsoft case turned out to be concerned at its root with the distribution of middleware (browsers, e-mail, audio and video streaming), initially Web browsers.[56] The alleged monopolization was "Intel-based PC operating systems," indirectly through monopolization of the browsers. Unfortunately, this case confused a static case of acquiring power to exclude browsers with a dynamic case involving the creation of strategic advantage in future competition in the application platform market (Brennan, 2001).[57] With respect to the static case, the complement market monopolized was browser distribution, through exclusionary contracts Microsoft had with OEMs and Internet service providers. The central competitive question is whether this control caused the cost of distribution to increase, as indicated by whether Netscape could still distribute its browser effectively. If the browser *distribution* market was not affected by Microsoft's practices, Netscape could not have been excluded by them. The eventual remedy in the U.S. was a settlement consistent with an CMM-founded case: The plaintiffs and Microsoft essentially agreed to eliminate exclusionary contracts.

Both cases offer lessons for the advantages of CMM. They were each subject to the inherent contradiction in having to show prior monopoly. As noted above, after establishing market power in operating systems by showing significant scale economies, network externalities (file sharing, using multiple computers), and customers "locked in" in order to continue to be able to run legacy applications, it seemed difficult to argue that per processor contracting or browser

55 The "efficient breach payment" standard is used below to assess bundled discounts.

56 *Microsoft, supra* note 4.

57 *See infra* Section 16.7.1 for the contrast between the static and dynamic monopolization theories, particularly with regard to relevant market delineation and remedy.

monopolization would have much effect on the market. Arguably, prior dominance should be a defense, in that given an operating system monopoly, vertical integration into middleware markets would increase development incentives by facilitating capture of inframarginal rents. To the extent that middleware markets are themselves subject to the scale economies, network externalities, and lock-in of operating systems, they will also tend toward monopoly, and vertical integration would avoid double marginalization.

16.6.3. The Canadian *Heinz* case

In 2000, the Canadian Competition Bureau (Bureau) announced that it had settled a case against Heinz Canada (Competition Bureau, 2001). Heinz Canada was the only supplier of baby food in jars and infant cereal. According to the Bureau, Heinz had maintained that monopoly by long-term exclusive dealing contracts with food retailers. The Bureau noted that Heinz paid substantial up-front fixed fees to retailers for them to sign the contracts, and provided discounts as long as they complied. The remedy obtained by the Bureau in settling with Heinz was primarily to not enforce existing exclusive supply agreements or enter into new ones, including ceasing volume discounts and generally limiting any supply arrangement to one year.

The remedy in the case may well have been appropriate from an CMM perspective, but the description of the case suggests that Canadian law shares many of the same flaws of U.S. practice. The emphasis on Heinz's current monopolies in these segments of the baby food sector suggests a prior dominance requirement, although the press release does not indicate that the Bureau had engaged in the contradictory exercise of showing dominance aside from the exclusionary practice at issue.[58] The press release also emphasizes the terms of the exclusionary deals, e.g., the up-front payment. This hints at attention to a profit sacrifice standard, although perhaps more as a matter of revealing intention to monopolize baby food retail outlets rather than reflecting losses necessary for antitrust liability. Whether volume or other discounts are relevant for inferring exclusion is the subject of the following section.

16.6.4. CMM perspectives on bundle discounts

Some recent cases have featured claims that offering discounts across product lines, also referred to as bundled discounts, is exclusionary.[59] *LePage's v. 3M*[60]

---

[58] It would not appear that there are enormous scale economies or network externalities in baby food, although long-term quality or safety reputations may be difficult to establish.

[59] For a description of these cases and a different analysis of this practice, see Greenlee et al. (2004). Their model essentially has a monopolist in one market charging high prices for another as a device for charging a lump-sum up front fee for the monopoly service. The welfare effects, as with many price discrimination models, are ambiguous.

[60] *LePage's*, supra note 8. LePage's won at a divided Third Circuit Court of Appeals. The Supreme Court denied hearing the case after an *amicus brief* filed jointly Department of Justice and Fed-

involved discounts that 3M offered to retailers for carrying its version of unbranded (house brand) transparent adhesive (e.g., Scotch® type) tape. LePage's, a competing tape supplier, claimed that these bundled discounts were exclusionary, enabling 3M to maintain its market power in tape. Two similar cases also involved bundled discounts between manufacturers and "dealers," antibiotics to hospitals in the first[61] and blood virus screens to blood testing laboratories in the second.[62]

The key feature of all these cases is that unlike textbook models of tying or bundling, the buyers were not end users but other intermediate good providers in the production chain. Consequently, CMM techniques can be used. The relevant monopolized market is not the primary market in which the alleged monopolist operates but a complement used to make or sell that product. For example, in LePage's the market to examine is not tape manufacturing but the supply of retail outlets. If bundling is an exclusionary practice with anticompetitive effects, the retail market has to have been monopolized.

The critical and subtle question is the extent to which the arrangements between the bundler (e.g., 3M) and the complement suppliers (e.g., the tape retailers) constituted exclusive dealing. Analogizing bundling with exclusive dealing begins with the observation that exclusive dealing contracts can be breached by complement suppliers willing to pay the penalty. If such a contract is the standard for exclusion, the test is whether bundled discounts akin to 3M's rebate system impose a penalty on retailers who carry a competitor's products similar to the penalty for breaching an exclusive dealing contract.[63]

To see the implications of this CMM-derived standard for analyzing bundling, we examine the efficient damages penalty for breach of an exclusive dealing contract between incumbent manufacturer I and retailer R. These will be the lost profits to I if an entrant E gets to sell instead.[64] Absent any contract, R will sell E's product rather than I's to a customer if, all else equal,

$$P_E - W_E > P_I - W_I,$$

eral Trade Commission advising that review of the Court of Appeals decision would be premature. Brief for the United States as Amicus Curiae, 3M Company v. LePage's Inc., et al., http://www.usdoj.gov/atr/cases/f203900/203900.pdf, accessed Aug. 1, 2005.

[61] SmithKline Corp. v. Eli Lilly and Co., 427 F. Supp. 1089 (D.C.E.D. Penn. 1976), aff'd., 575 F.2d 1056 (3rd Circ. 1978), cert.denied 439 U.S. 838 (1978) (Lilly's policy of rebates over all versions of a certain type of antibiotic monopolistically impeded SmithKline's entry into the market, despite the price after rebate remaining above variable costs).

[62] Ortho Diagnostic Systems, Inc., v. Abbott Laboratories, Inc. 920 F. Supp. 455 (D.C.S.D. N.Y. 1996) (Abbott's discounts over sales of multiple blood virus screening tests were legal because Abbott's discounted prices were still above Ortho's costs).

[63] The up-front cost of the bundle is irrelevant, as is the price paid to retailers to sign exclusive dealing contracts. The issue is not profit sacrifice but competitive effect.

[64] The issuer of the contracts need not be a monopoly incumbent for them to be anticompetitive, but at some risk of perpetuating incorrect beliefs, I'll go with the usual cast of characters.

or

$$P_E - P_I > W_E - W_I,$$

where P and W are respectively retail price and wholesale price, and the subscripts refer to the entrant and the incumbent.

With an exclusive dealing contract, the cost of selling E's product rather than I's goes up by the breach penalty, which we would expect to be I's foregone profit, $W_I - C_I$, where C_I is the cost to I of producing that unsold unit. Adding that breach penalty into R's decision means that R sells E if

$$P_E - W_E - [W_I - C_I] > P_I - W_I,$$

or

$$P_E - W_E > P_I - C_I.$$

The effect of an exclusive dealing contract on R's incentive to sell E is to have R act as if the wholesale price charged to it by I just equals I's cost of producing that unit.

This suggests a two-step test for whether bundling is exclusionary:

- If the incumbent's rebate/bundling deal with a retailer implies that the retailer will treat the cost of selling a unit of the incumbent's product as no more than the incumbent's cost of producing that unit, the discount is tantamount to an exclusive dealing contract under basic standards for efficient breach. The relevant "cost" is the implicit cost calculated in determining what the expectation damages for breach of the exclusive dealing contract would be.
- The incumbent has entered into contracts with sufficiently many retailers to acquire pricing power in retailing services, the relevant complement market.

Using exclusive dealing contracts as the standard for identifying exclusive dealing suggests that one has exclusion if the retailer sees the incumbent's production cost as the incumbent's effective wholesale price when deciding whether sell a competitor's product. This might seem to indicate a link from the *Brooke Group*[65] below-cost predation test to bundling. However, cost is not relevant in the sense that it takes a price below that cost as predatory, but rather whether it makes bundling equivalent to exclusion. If the breach penalty is the lost profit to the incumbent from lost sales at the margin, the penalty will be the marginal cost of production up to the sales point. Unless the firm has to stretch capacity to make those sales, this cost would be short-run marginal cost, which may be quiet low.

The deeper question is whether exclusive dealing contracts are the appropriate standard for whether an arrangement is sufficiently exclusive to convey monopolistic control of the complement market. The standard may well be lower, in that a much lower penalty may suffice to convey such control. If so, the relevant

---

65 *Brooke Group*, *supra* note 30, 509 U.S. 209 (1993).

"cost" to the incumbent could be significantly above short-run marginal cost. However this question is resolved, it continues to remain relevant to check not just the first prong of this test but the second—to delineate the relevant complement market and to see if control over a monopoly share of that market was subject to these exclusionary contracts.

16.7. Game theoretic monopolization

16.7.1. Dynamic vs. static settings

Section 2 cases could go beyond complement market monopolization if they involve some kind of change to the game in the market resulting in reduced economic welfare. Holding preferences and technology constant, market outcomes depend on the set of allowed choices (e.g., prices, quantities, capacities, location, product characteristics), timing of moves, information available at any time, and the credibility of commitments. One should be concerned if a tactic can change the game, leading to a monopolized market.

Examples abound, although with different degrees of applicability. An early instance would be Spence's showing that adding committed capacity can reduce an incumbent's marginal cost, leading to a reduced post-entry price and thus deterring entry (Spence, 1977). Aghion and Bolton (1987) allow exclusive contracts to allow an incumbent and consumer to combine to extract rents for entrants with cost advantages, when the entrant's costs are unknown. Whinston (1990) sets up a model where a multi-market monopolist can deter entry into a potentially competitive market by committing to reduce sales in its monopoly market if it has to reduce sales in that competitive market.

Despite the proliferation of models of this type, most credible monopolization cases appear to involve the static and expected straightforward effects associated with cornering an otherwise competitive input market. One difficulty is verifying that the highly specific assumptions underlying these dynamic models in fact hold (Coate and Fischer, 2001).[66] A related problem is that in some of these models the change in the game is only assumed to follow from a change a practice, e.g., that vertical mergers in and of themselves allow price commitments that could be undertaken without it (Reiffen and Vita, 1995, commenting on Ordover et al., 1990). Finally, these models typically do not include the potential efficiencies from these practices and thus offer little guidance for the cost-benefit analyses that they require for successful implementation.

Looking again at the Microsoft litigation shows how static and dynamic stories may differ. We reviewed above how the Microsoft cases could be construed in complement market monopolization terms. However, Microsoft's practices could be and in many circles were regarded in a dynamic way. Preempting

---

[66] In many cases, these arguments become a kind of pseudo-evidence, in that if a practice can be harmful under some conditions, it may be harmful in the case at hand (Brennan, 2004a).

competition in web browsers today allegedly would boost Microsoft's position in gaining competitive advantage in subsequent competition between desktop-based and Internet server-based application platforms (Brennan, 2001; Carlton and Waldman, 2002).

It is essential to get the stories straight since, contrary to widespread belief, dynamic and static stories require different sets of evidence and imply different remedies. The following diagram illustrates the relevant differences.

Nature of theory	**Static**	**Dynamic**
Affected middleware	Generic	Specific (browsers)
Core market evidence	Power in relevant middleware distribution market	Entry into future application platform market
Remedy	Limit exclusive contracting over distribution	Divest crucial middleware (e.g., browsers)

The static story, reviewed above in discussing possible CMM applications, was essentially that Microsoft could exclude competitors in generic middleware through exclusionary contracts that tied up the market for distributing such programs, comprising primarily computer manufacturers and Internet service providers.

The dynamic story, on the other hand, rested on the question of how positions specifically in the browser market today would affect strategic positioning in application platforms tomorrow. It required a very specific story based on the special role of browsers in positioning for competition in future application platforms, as opposed to the degree of control Microsoft allegedly possessed over the ability to distribute middleware. Establishing the dynamic story would require the difficult job of establishing how one might enter future application markets and, anticipating such entry, nuanced game-theoretic analyses of how one might establish strategic advantage in, essentially, the market in potential competitive advantage to be the leading future application platform.

The most important difference is the remedy. The static theory identifies only middleware distribution as a monopolized input market. Accordingly, the appropriate remedy, and the one that ensued in the U.S., was not to change Microsoft's corporate structure in any meaningful way. Rather, it was only to halt or limit Microsoft's ability to control middleware distribution, to keep that market open. Had a dynamic case been successfully brought, the appropriate remedy would have been to preserve potential competition in future application platforms by having Microsoft divest browsers, leaving its operations and contracting practices in other middleware markets intact. The apparent difficulty of such a case, evidenced by its reduction to a concern over middleware distribution, indicates both the differences between dynamic and static cases and the temptation to try to reduce the former to the latter.

The broader lesson is that monopolization cases need not be dynamic. The CMM approach allows monopolization cases to resemble standard collusion and merger cases as not relying on a conjecture that practices that benefit consumers in the short run will make them worse off in the long run because of the effect of those practices on the subsequent strategic interaction of the parties. Collusion and merger are problematic because of direct price effects, and monopolization of complement markets can be understood exactly the same way. Dynamic considerations may be relevant and if so, as illustrated above, will require careful analyses that go beyond the straightforward identification of complement markets that have been monopolized. But the CMM approach shows that one need not introduce such considerations to bring a monopolization case, hence that one need not restrict monopolization cases to settings where dynamic games, inherently less robust and more speculative, are necessary.

16.7.2. Predatory pricing

Predatory pricing, the charging of inordinately low prices to drive out rivals and monopolize a market, had come to be criticized for resting on the theoretically implausible supposition that entrants would be discouraged by a low price but not encouraged to re-enter if a subsequent monopoly price were charged. For this reason, predation appeared to be an incredible threat, because accommodating entrants—e.g., through merger (McGee, 1958)—is usually more profitable than driving price below cost if high post-predation prices would just bring entry back (Easterbrook, 1984, pp. 26–27). Since the 1980s, however, predatory pricing was placed on dynamic game-theoretic foundations, relying on the entrant's inability to dismiss the possibility that the incumbent would rather keep a monopoly through predation than maximize profits (Kreps and Wilson, 1982; Milgrom and Roberts, 1982; Ordover and Saloner, 1989, pp. 545–562).

Although this theory has been invoked to restore the respectability of predation doctrine (Bolton et al., 2000), it has rarely if ever served as the foundation of an actual antitrust case.[67] Because predation cases remain largely static despite the game-theoretic analysis, some of the insights from CMM may be pertinent. The CMM critique of profit sacrifice in monopolization cases generally lends some insight into the debate about whether predatory prices themselves have to involve a profit sacrifice, e.g., be below some measure of marginal or average variable cost.

In a predation case we can identify six categories of welfare effects: predatory and post-predatory changes in welfare for the incumbent (predator) I, entrant/rivals (prey) E, and consumers C. The following table displays the notation, with subscripts indicating the relevant time period (1 for during predation, 2 for after).[68]

---

[67] Brennan (2001, pp. 1084–1085) discusses the foregone opportunity to apply this dynamic theory in *U.S. v. Microsoft*. One can contrast this dynamic theory with the traditional approach in *Brooke Group*, *supra* note 30.

[68] The "post-predation" effects may need to incorporate appropriate discount factors if the predatory period would entail a significant amount of time.

Agent	Time	
	Predatory period (1)	Post-predation (2)
Incumbent (I)	I_1	I_2
Entrant (E)	E_1	E_2
Consumers (C)	C_1	C_2

From an economic standpoint, predation is harmful if total welfare W falls, i.e.,

$$\Delta W = I_1 + I_2 + E_1 + E_2 + C_1 + C_2 < 0.$$

This condition can hold even without a profit sacrifice, i.e., with $I_1 > 0$. This suggests that it hardly makes sense to focus on profit sacrifice and the losses to a competitor. The emphasis in cases on the recoupment condition,[69] $I_1 + I_2 > 0$, seems to be follow from profit maximization. Recoupment in the sense that $I_2 > 0$ along with $I_1 + I_2 > 0$, seems to be at most indirect evidence (necessary but not sufficient) that $I_1 > 0$. But, like profit sacrifice generally, that condition speaks more to intent than effect. If we know that $I_1 < 0$, recoupment (actually, profit maximization directly) implies that $I_2 > 0$, but all else equal, that is an economic benefit, not a cost.

A finding that the incumbent's actions lead price to be below its marginal cost implies only that, along with $I_1 < 0$, predation-period welfare W_1 falls, i.e.,

$$\Delta W_1 = I_1 + E_1 + C_1 < 0.$$

However, that condition is not sufficient to show overall welfare losses. Moreover, unless one is concerned with rival firm welfare, it hardly seems the point of predation to make it illegal in and of itself for a firm to flood the market, benefiting consumers at the alleged predator's expense. Only the subsequent losses from higher prices would seem to matter.

The linkage between profit sacrifice $I_1 < 0$ (incumbent losses in the predatory period) and overall economic harm $\Delta W < 0$ seems to rest on the following steps:

Step 1: $I_1 < 0 \Rightarrow I_2 > 0$ (incumbent profit maximization)
Step 2: $I_2 > 0 \Rightarrow I_2 + E_2 + C_2 < 0$ (greater incumbent profit indicates social loss post predation)
Step 3: $I_2 + E_2 + C_2 < 0 \Rightarrow \Delta W < 0$ (future welfare loss outweighs any present gain)

Each step is problematic. The first is inconsistent with the possibility of "irrational" predation on which post-Chicago game-theoretic predation theory rests. The second step involves an implication which is neither necessary nor sufficient; as just noted, profits in and of themselves are good, not bad. The third is

69 *Brooke Group*, *supra* note 30, following Matsushita Elec. Indus.v. Zenith Radio Corp., 475 U.S. 574 (1986).

also neither necessary nor sufficient; it follows only if overall present welfare is negative as well, i.e., if $I_1 < 0$ implies $\Delta W_1 < 0$. But note that this is the exact opposite of the logic in Step 2, which rests on the belief that incumbent profits are negatively, not positively, correlated with overall welfare.

16.8. The fix: Delete "or maintain" from Section 2 practice

The characteristic case law phrase defining Section 2 jurisprudence is that it is intended to prohibit practices that would result in the "acquisition or maintenance" of monopoly power.[70] The second half of this phrase provides most if not all of the support for the fallacious syllogism in antitrust and its consequences. The doctrine of "monopoly maintenance" sets up entrants and small competitors as needing to be protected from encroachment by a dominant rival. This focus on rivals forces courts to adopt high if not impossible burdens, e.g., passing the absolute efficiency defense set up by the profit sacrifice screen.

Seeing whether a monopoly is being "maintained" also leads to the dubious prior dominance screen, when having a prior monopoly is irrelevant at best and perhaps should even be a defense against a monopolization charge. Monopoly maintenance leads one to look at the wrong market, the one the alleged monopolist is in, rather than one in which a market power that had not existed before is being created. This leads to both false positives and true negatives and placing intent ahead of effect in Section 2 law.

On the other hand, the "acquire" or "create" aspect of monopolization law is perfectly appropriate. The purpose of antitrust law in all of its aspects should be to prevent monopolies from arising where they would not otherwise occur. This is exactly the question asked under Section 1 or Section 7: Did price fixing, market allocation, or some other agreement prevent competition from otherwise taking place? Would a merger inhibit competition, either through the direct suppression of independent action by the merging firms or by increasing the likelihood of collusion among the remaining participants in the relevant product and geographic market?

The CMM approach restates this same question for monopolization. Where exclusion, foreclosure, or raising rivals' costs is alleged, the competitive harm in question requires the creation of market power over an input or complement market that did not exist before.[71] Such an analysis requires that we delineate relevant complement markets and ask whether sufficient control over that market has been acquired to raise that good or service's price to buyers. The concern is economically important whether or not the buyers are rivals of the alleged monopolist, and whether or not that alleged monopolist had a monopoly prior

[70] Grinnell, supra note 19 at 570–571.

[71] In the case of monopolization by regulated firms, vertical integration into unregulated markets may facilitate the exercise of input market power that was nominally controlled through price regulation (Brennan, 1987).

to acquiring control over the input or complement market. The extent to which new firms can enter to supply buyers, including entry by the buyers themselves into the complement market, is crucial, just as it is in standard horizontal merger analysis.

These together suggest that the path of legal reform that would better rationalize monopolization jurisprudence is to keep the good, "create," and delete the bad, "or maintain." This would strengthen monopolization's conceptual roots, and place it on the same sound foundation as the other threads of antitrust practice. The apparent paradox is that nominally reducing the scope of Section 2 by eliminating monopoly maintenance doctrines would broaden its reach by decoupling it from the criticism that it is about protecting competitors and not competition.

16.9. Summary

Section 2 monopolization law has resisted the economic consensus approach that has come to dominate the other two prongs of antitrust—collusion law and mergers—because of an undue focus on rivals. As the fallacious syllogism illustrates, this premise has been accepted by those who believe that monopolization cases should bear a high if not insurmountable burden. The fallacy is also shared by those who think that antitrust should be a vehicle for refereeing fair play among competitors.

This has led to two spurious screens that have dominated monopolization jurisprudence. The first, prior dominance, is essentially irrelevant, diverting attention away from competitive effects and toward the character of the alleged perpetrator. Not only is proving prior dominance contrary to proving that market power hinges on the alleged exclusionary practice, but prior dominance is more likely be a defense, in that the marginal harm for additional exclusion is likely to be small and the marginal benefit greater. The second spurious screen, profit sacrifice, also diverts attention from competitive harm to, ironically, the effect on the perpetrator. We show that it creates an absolute efficiency defense, and converts the issue from effect to intent. These errors are especially serious when regulated firms monopolize, particularly in network industries.

The complement market monopolization approach eliminates these difficulties. It is both necessary as a means for creating injury to downstream firms (whether or not rivals of the perpetrator), and should be *prima facie* sufficient for antitrust liability on its own, perhaps with prior dominance of a primary market as a defense rather than a condition of guilt. Moreover, by directing attention toward a monopolized input or complement market, it allows the tools of horizontal analysis—market delineation, concentration, entry barriers, competitive effects—to be employed in Section 2 cases. These appropriate screens replace the spurious profits sacrifice and prior dominance tests. Vertical relationships matter, but primarily only in the way that buyer preferences matter in standard horizontal merger cases. We examine but three of the many notable monopolization cases in recent years to illustrate how CMM can clarify the analysis.

CMM may inform bundling cases by comparing the lost benefits of a discount to breach payments for reneging on exclusive dealing contracts. Some cases, few in our opinion, require a more dynamic, strategic approach, but these are quite different from the static approaches often used in these settings, as the Microsoft cases illustrate. The CMM approach, in particular observing the peculiarities it suggests regarding the profit sacrifice screen, may inform the analysis of alleged predatory pricing.

A simple fix to Section 2 jurisprudence can refocus attention away from intentional harms done by dominant firms to protection-worthy rivals and toward the monopolization of previously competitive complement markets by anyone. This fix is to delete "or maintain" from the "create or maintain" standard set of Section 2 allegations. Emphasizing only the "create" aspect says that monopolization cases should turn on the same question asked in collusion or merger cases: Does the practice under scrutiny increase market power over what existed previously? Restricting monopolization doctrine in this way can save Section 2, restoring its appropriate standing in the antitrust family.

Acknowledgements

I thank Alden Abbott, Luke Froeb, Ken Heyer, Sanders Korenman, Mikhail Kouliatsev, David Krause, Donald Partridge, Dahlia Remler, Vincent Verouden, Michael Vita, and audiences at the U.S. Federal Trade Commission, Canada's Competition Bureau, the Baruch College School of Public Affairs, and the 2005 International Industrial Organization Conference for comments and suggestions. Special thanks go to Larry White and the referees and editors for this volume for detailed comments and trenchant criticisms. None of the above bears any responsibility for these observations; all errors remain the responsibility of the author. The author served as a staff consultant to the Bureau of Economics of the U.S. Federal Trade Commission during 2003–2005 and, for 2006, as the T.D. MacDonald Chair of Industrial Economics at the Canadian Competition Bureau; none the opinions here reflect those of the FTC or the Bureau or anyone on their staffs.

References

Aghion, P., Bolton, P. (1987), Contracts as a barrier to entry. *American Economic Review* 77, 389–401.

Antitrust Law Journal (1995), Symposium on post-Chicago economics. *Antitrust Law Journal* 63, 445–695.

Areeda, P., Turner, D. (1975), Predatory pricing and related practices under Section 2 of the Sherman Act. *Harvard Law Review* 88, 697–773.

Armentano, D. (1982), *Antitrust and Monopoly: Anatomy of a Policy Failure*. Wiley and Sons, New York.

Baker, J. (1991), Per se rules in the antitrust analysis of horizontal restraints. *Antitrust Bulletin* 36, 733–743.

Baker, J. (2003), The case for antitrust enforcement. *Journal of Economic Perspectives* 17, 27–50.

Baker, J., Rubinfeld, D. (1999), Empirical methods in antitrust litigation: Review and critique. *American Law and Economics Review* 1, 386–405.

Baumol, W., Ordover, J. (1985), Use of antitrust to subvert competition. *Journal of Law & Economics* 28, 247–265.

Bolton, P., Brodley, J., Riordan, M. (2000), Predatory pricing: Strategic theory and legal policy. *The Georgetown Law Journal* 88, 2239–2330.

Bork, R. (1978), *The Antitrust Paradox: A Policy At War With Itself*. Basic Books, New York.

Brennan, T. (1987), Why regulated firms should be kept out of unregulated markets: Understanding the divestiture in *U.S. v. AT&T*. *Antitrust Bulletin* 32, 741–793.

Brennan, T. (1988), Understanding raising rivals' costs. *Antitrust Bulletin* 33, 95–113.

Brennan, T. (1997), Industry parallel interconnection agreements. *Information Economics and Policy* 9, 133–149.

Brennan, T. (2000), Vertical excuses for horizontal practices: Should there be any *per se* rules? *Antitrust Bulletin* 45, 467–490.

Brennan, T. (2001), Do easy cases make bad law? Antitrust innovation or missed opportunities in *U.S. v. Microsoft*. *George Washington Law Review* 69, 1042–1102.

Brennan, T. (2003), Mismeasuring electricity market power. *Regulation* 25, 60–65. Spring.

Brennan, T. (2004a), The legacy of *U.S. v. Microsoft*. *Regulation* 26, 22–28. Winter.

Brennan, T. (2004b), Vertical market power' as oxymoron: Horizontal approaches to vertical antitrust. *George Mason Law Review* 12, 895–922.

Carlton, D., Waldman, M. (2002), The strategic use of tying to preserve and create market power in evolving industries. *RAND Journal of Economics* 33, 194–220.

Carlton, D., Perloff, J. (1990), *Modern Industrial Organization*. Scott Foresman and Co, Glenview, IL.

Clyde, P., Reitzes, J. (2004), Can mergers to monopoly, price fixing, and market division agreements raise welfare? *International Journal of the Economics of Business* 11, 69–90.

Coate, M., Fischer, J. (2001), Can post-Chicago economics survive Daubert? *Akron Law Review* 34, 795–852.

Competition Bureau, Canada (2001), Heinz Canada signs undertaking regarding jarred baby food and infant cereal. News Release, Aug. 1, 2000. http://www.competitionbureau.gc.ca/internet/index.cfm?itemID=570&lg=e.

Competition Bureau, Canada (2004), *Merger Enforcement Guidelines*. http://www.competitionbureau.gc.ca/PDFs/2004%20MEGs.Final.pdf.

Crandall, R., Winston, C. (2003), Does antitrust policy improve consumer welfare? Assessing the evidence. *Journal of Economic Perspectives* 17, 3–26.

Dewey, D. (1979), Information, entry and welfare: The case for collusion. *American Economic Review* 69, 588–593.

Department of Justice and Federal Trade Commission (1997), *Horizontal Merger Guidelines*. http://www.usdoj.gov/atr/public/guidelines/hmg.htm.

Easterbrook, F. (1984), The limits of antitrust. *Texas Law Review* 63, 1–40.

Eckbo, B.E., Weir, P. (1985), Antimerger policy under the Hart-Scott-Rodino Act: A reexamination of the market power hypothesis. *Journal of Law and Economics* 28, 119–149.

Edlin, A. (2002), Stopping above-cost predatory pricing. *Yale Law Journal* 111, 941–991.

Edlin, A., Rubinfeld, D. (2004), Exclusion or efficient pricing? The "big-deal" bundling of academic journals. *Antitrust Law Journal* 72, 119–157.

Elhauge, E. (2003), Why above-cost price cuts to drive out entrants are not predatory—and the implications for defining costs and market power. *Yale Law Journal* 112, 681–827.

Facey, B., Assaf, D. (2002), Monopolization and abuse of dominance in Canada, the United States, and the European Union: A survey. *Antitrust Law Journal* 70, 513–591.

Federal Energy Regulatory Commission (1996), Inquiry Concerning the Commission's Merger Policy under the Federal Power Act: Policy Statement, Order No. 592. http://www.ferc.gov/industries/electric/gen-info/mergers/rm96-6.pdf.

Fisher, F., McGowan, J. (1983), On the misuse of accounting rates of return to infer monopoly profits. *American Economic Review* 73, 82–97.

Froeb, L., Werden, G. (1996), Simulation as an alternative to structural policy in differentiated products industries. In: Coate, M., Kleit, A. (Eds.), *The Economics of the Antitrust Process*. Kluwer Academic, Norwell, MA, pp. 65–88.

Gelman, J., Salop, S. (1983), Judo economics: Capacity limitation and coupon competition. *Bell Journal of Economics* 14, 315–325.

Goldfine, D., Vorrasi, K. (2004), The fall of the *Kodak* aftermarket doctrine: Dying a slow death in the lower courts. *Antitrust Law Journal* 72, 209–232.

Greenlee, P., Reitman, D., Sibley, D. (2004), An antitrust analysis of bundled loyalty discounts. Economic Analysis Group Discussion Paper No. 04-13, http://ssrn.com/abstract=600799.

Harris, B., Simons, J. (1989), Focusing market definition: How much substitution is necessary? *Research in Law and Economics* 12, 207–226.

Katz, M. (1987), The welfare effects of third degree price discrimination in intermediate goods markets. *American Economic Review* 77, 154–167.

Katz, M., Shapiro, C. (2003), Critical loss: Let's tell the whole story. *Antitrust Magazine*, 49–56. Spring.

Krattenmaker, T., Salop, S. (1986), Anticompetitive exclusion: Raising rivals' costs to achieve power over price. *Yale Law Journal* 96, 209–293.

Kreps, D., Wilson, R. (1982), Reputation and imperfect information. *Journal of Economic Theory* 27, 253–279.

Lande, R. (1982), Wealth transfers as the original and primary concern of antitrust: The efficiency interpretation challenged. *Hastings Law Journal* 34, 65–151.

McGee, J. (1958), Predatory price cutting: The standard oil (N.J.) case. *Journal of Law and Economics* 1, 137–169.

Milgrom, P., Roberts, J. (1982), Predation, reputation and entry deterrence. *Journal of Economic Theory* 27, 280–312.

Nelson, P., White, L. (2003), Market definition and the identification of market power in monopolization cases: A critique and a proposal. Stern School of Business, New York University Working Paper 03-26. http://www.stern.nyu.edu/eco/wkpapers/workingpapers03/03-26White.pdf.

O'Brien, D., Wickelgren, A. (2003), A critical analysis of critical loss analysis. *Antitrust Law Journal* 71, 161–184.

Ordover, J., Panzar, J. (1982), On the nonlinear pricing of inputs. *International Economic Review* 23, 659–675.

Ordover, J., Saloner, G. (1989), Predation, monopolization, and antitrust. In: Schmalensee, R., Willig, R. (Eds.), *Handbook of Industrial Organization, Vol. 1*. North-Holland, New York, pp. 537–596.

Ordover, J., Saloner, G., Salop, S. (1990), Equilibrium vertical foreclosure. *American Economic Review* 80, 127–142.

Ordover, J., Willig, R. (1981), An economic definition of predation: Pricing and product innovation. *Yale Law Journal* 91, 8–53.

Posner, R. (1976), *Antitrust Law: An Economic Perspective*. University of Chicago Press, Chicago.

Posner, R. (2004), Keynote speech. Developments in the law and economics of exclusionary pricing practices: From classroom to courtroom. Antitrust Division, U.S. Department of Justice, Washington, DC (March 18).

Rasmusen, E., Ramseyer, M., Shepard, J. (1991), Naked exclusion. *American Economic Review* 81, 1137–1145.

Reiffen, D., Vita, M. (1995), Comment: Is there new thinking on vertical mergers? *Antitrust Law Journal* 63, 917–941.

Ross, T., Winter, R. (2004), The efficiency defense in merger law: Economic foundations and recent canadian developments. *Antitrust Law Journal* 72, 471–504.

Salop, S. (2005), Exclusionary conduct, consumer harm, and the flawed profit-sacrifice standard. *Antitrust Law Journal*, in press.

Salop, S., Scheffman, D. (1983), Raising rivals' costs. *American Economic Review Papers and Proceedings* 73, 267–271.

Scheffman, D., Coleman, M. (2003), Quantitative analyses of potential competitive effects from a merger. *George Mason Law Review* 12, 319–369.

Schwartz, M. (1989), Investments in oligopoly: Welfare effects and tests for predation. *Oxford Economic Papers* 41, 698–719.

Shenefield, J., Stelzer, I. (1998), *The Antitrust Laws: A Primer*. American Enterprise Institute, Washington.

Spence, A.M. (1977), Entry, capacity, investment and oligopolistic pricing. *Bell Journal of Economics* 8, 534–544.

Telser, L. (1960), Why should manufacturers want fair trade? *Journal of Law and Economics* 3, 86–105.

Werden, G. (2004), The effect of antitrust policy improve consumer welfare: What Crandall and Winston overlook. AEI Brookings Joint Center for Regulatory Studies Related Publication 04-09. http://aei-brookings.org/admin/authorpdfs/page.php?id=933.

Whinston, M. (1990), Tying, foreclosure, and exclusion. *American Economic Review* 80, 837–859.

CHAPTER 17

Private Antitrust Litigation: Procompetitive or Anticompetitive?

R. Preston McAfee[a], Hugo M. Mialon[b] and Sue H. Mialon[c]

[a]*Humanities and Social Sciences, California Institute of Technology, Pasadena, CA 91125*
E-mail address: preston@mcafee.cc
[b]*Department of Economics, Emory University, Atlanta, GA 30322-2240*
E-mail address: hmialon@emory.edu
[c]*Department of Economics, University of North Dakota, Grand Forks, ND 58202*
E-mail address: sue.mialon@und.edu

Abstract

The antitrust laws are intended to permit procompetitive actions by firms and deter anticompetitive actions. We consider firms' incentives to use the antitrust lawsuits for strategic purposes, in particular to prevent procompetitive efficiency-improvement by rival firms. Our main result is that, *ceteris paribus*, smaller firms in more fragmented industries are more likely to use the antitrust laws strategically than larger firms in concentrated industries.

17.1. Introduction

The antitrust laws were put in place to protect competition. Competition lowers prices and increases firms' incentives to innovate, to the benefit of consumers. However, the antitrust laws also have the potential to harm consumers if the laws are used to subvert competition. Whether the antitrust laws improve consumer welfare depends crucially on the incentives of those bringing antitrust lawsuits to court.

In the United States, the Antitrust Division of the Department of Justice and the Federal Trade Commission enforce the antitrust laws on behalf of the public. These agencies are charged with representing consumers. In addition, the antitrust laws are also enforced privately in the United States—firms directly harmed by anticompetitive acts have standing to sue under the antitrust laws. The Clayton Act, which offers the successful plaintiff treble damages, often makes such private litigation quite attractive.

Private firms will generally pursue antitrust actions when it is in the private firm's interest, an interest that could easily diverge from the social interest. Firms may have incentive to use the antitrust laws strategically, which may hinder rather than promote competition. The possibility of strategic abuse of the

CONTRIBUTIONS TO ECONOMIC ANALYSIS
VOLUME 282 ISSN: 0573-8555
DOI: 10.1016/S0573-8555(06)82017-1

antitrust laws has been raised by, among others, Baumol and Ordover (1985), Breit and Elzinga (1985), Shughart II (1990), Brodley (1995), and McAfee and Vakkur (2004). McAfee and Vakkur identify several ways in which firms can use the antitrust laws strategically. Let us illustrate several of them with important cases that have arisen in the U.S. courts.

Firms may use the antitrust laws to improve contractual conditions. The antitrust lawsuit filed by the Colorado Chiropractic Council (CCC) and 46 doctors of chiropractic against 9 Colorado hospitals is an example.[1] The suit came after a letter from CCC asking for staff privileges and mailed to 30 hospitals in the state. The 9 hospitals that did not respond or responded unfavorably were targeted by CCC. The suit alleged that these hospitals "have effectively restrained and suppressed the free flow of trade resulting in an uncompetitive marketplace." The lawsuit was dismissed from the U.S. States District Court. In his ruling, Judge Finesilver said, "the letter from plaintiffs' counsel ... requests a blanket grant of staff privileges ... closed with a threat to initiate litigation if the defendants fail to respond or respond negatively within 30 days. We find the contention of plaintiff's to be without merit and completely lacking substance as the basis for an antitrust action" (1986 U.S. Dist. LEXIS 17233, 650 F. Supp. 231 at 236).

Using the antitrust laws strategically to modify the terms of a contract can be damaging to the contractual parties and may discourage long term investments under a standard hold-up theory. The hold-up problem exists when parties refrain from working together because they are afraid that they may give the other party increased bargaining power once they cooperate. Contracts resolve the problem and improve efficiency as the parties are now willing to participate in jointly profitable actions. However, if the parties can use antitrust suits to alter the terms of the contract in their favor, then parties will anticipate such opportunistic behavior, which will make it harder for them to cooperate in the first place. Parties will end up experiencing more inefficiencies as they need to write more complex contracts to prevent hold-up and avoid renegotiation costs.

Firms may also take private antitrust actions simply to respond to existing private actions. Qualcomm owns around 40 per cent of the patents related to CDMA (Code-Division Multiple Access, a digital cellular technology that uses spread-spectrum techniques). While the others are held by Ericsson and Nokia, Qualcomm is credited with pioneering the commercial public use of the technology. In 2002, Qualcomm sued Maxim, a billion dollar a year supplier of analog integrated circuits and owner of Dallas Semiconductor, claiming that Maxim infringed five of its patents. As a part of its efforts to throw out the case, Maxim filed an antitrust suit against Qualcomm in 2004, accusing it of misusing its patents to exclude competition from the market for CDMA technology.[2]

These situations complicate the task of the courts by aggregating several actions. Moreover, they may have negative effects if they thwart antitrust actions

---

1 "D.C.s lose bid for hospital privileges," *The Chiropractic Journal*, November 1986.

2 Orlowski, Andrew, "Qualcomm hit with anti-trust suit," *The Register*, April 17, 2004.

that are pursued for good reason. Of course, they may also have positive effects if they thwart antitrust actions that are pursued strategically, but the counter-suits themselves may also be pursued strategically.

Private antitrust litigation may also be aimed at extorting profitable settlements from successful rivals. An example is AOL's antitrust lawsuit against Microsoft.[3] In 2002, just after the U.S. Department of Justice and Microsoft reached a settlement after Microsoft was found guilty of violating the antitrust laws in a government lawsuit begun in 1997, AOL filed the lawsuit against Microsoft through its subsidiary Netscape. AOL purchased Netscape in 1999 after the damage on Netscape had already been done by Microsoft, and waited for 3 years until Microsoft was found guilty of anticompetitive behavior before asking for relief. The settlement of this lawsuit paid AOL $750 million in damages. Although AOL sued on the grounds that the damages to Netscape reduced competition in the browser market, the settlement essentially put an end to competition in this market, by promising AOL a 7 year royalty-free license to use Microsoft's browser. AOL appeared uninterested in restoring Netscape, only in obtaining a profitable settlement from Microsoft.

Finally, private antitrust litigation may be aimed at impeding healthy competition from rival firms. For example, in September 1999, start-up Next Generation Realty sued the leading full-service real estate broker Iowa Realty Co. Inc. claiming that Iowa Realty used its size and influence to force the Next Generation Realty to pay $30 apiece for exclusive-right-to-sell listings.[4] Initially, Next Generation filed the suit to require Iowa Realty to share commissions, while Next Generation refused to share commissions on its listings sold. When Iowa Realty declined to reciprocate on that basis, Next Generation accused it of violating Iowa's anti-trust statute. The Iowa Supreme Court dismissed the action stating that the claims were without any merit or proof (686 N.W.2d 206; 2004 Iowa Sup. LEXIS 253).

Private firms usually have strong incentives to initiate antitrust lawsuits against rival firms that have violated the antitrust laws (procompetitive suits), but may also have incentives to initiate antitrust lawsuits against rival firms that have not violated the antitrust laws (anticompetitive suits), as in the various cases described above. Whether private antitrust enforcement is ultimately procompetitive or anticompetitive therefore depends on whether there are more procompetitive suits than anticompetitive suits, which in turn depends on whether a firm's losses from a rival firm's action are greater if the action is anticompetitive than if it is proticompetitive.

In the next section, we address this question in a Cournot model. We find that in industries with two or three firms, a firm with a share of the market greater than a half suffers a greater loss from an anticompetitive action than from a

---

[3] Glassman, James K., "AOL Antitrust Suit Against Microsoft," *Capitalism Magazine*, January 27, 2002.

[4] Evans, Blanche, "Iowa Anti-trust Suit Settled," *Realty Times*, September 6, 2004.

procompetitive action by a rival firm. In an industry with three firms, a firm with less than half the market suffers a greater loss from a procompetitive action than from an anticompetitive action by a rival firm. Moreover, we find that the value of stopping a rival's procompetitive action is more likely to be greater than the value of stopping an anticompetitive action the greater is the number of firms in the industry.

17.2. Theory

Consider a Cournot oligopoly. There are n firms, which we number $1, 2, \ldots, n$, and firm i chooses the quantity q_i. The price $p(Q)$ that arises depends on total industry output Q, where

$$Q = \sum_{i=1}^{n} q_i. \tag{17.1}$$

Firm i is assumed to have a constant marginal cost c_i and maximizes its profit π_i, which is given by

$$\pi_i = \big(p(Q) - c_i\big)q_i. \tag{17.2}$$

In what follows, we assume that the first-order conditions solve uniquely, and for interior solutions. Interior solutions satisfy

$$0 = \big(p(Q) - c_i\big) + q_i p'(Q). \tag{17.3}$$

Summing (17.3) over all the firms, we get

$$0 = np(Q) - \sum_{i=1}^{n} c_i + Qp'(Q). \tag{17.4}$$

Equation (17.4) shows that total industry quantity Q depends on the demand, the aggregate marginal cost, and the number of competitors. Totally differentiating Equation (17.4), we obtain:

$$0 = \mathrm{d}Q\big((n+1)p'(Q) + Qp''(Q)\big) - \mathrm{d}\left(\sum_{i=1}^{n} c_i\right). \tag{17.5}$$

For notational simplicity, it is useful to define

$$C = \sum_{i=1}^{n} c_i \tag{17.6}$$

and

$$\alpha = \frac{Qp''(Q)}{p'(Q)}. \tag{17.7}$$

Under the standard assumption of decreasing marginal revenue, $2p'(Q) + Qp''(Q) < 0$, and thus $\alpha > -2$. This implies that industry quantity is a decreasing function of the aggregate marginal cost, that is,

$$\frac{\mathrm{d}Q}{\mathrm{d}C} = \frac{1}{p'(Q)(n+1+\alpha)}. \tag{17.8}$$

The effect of a change in aggregate cost on price is

$$\frac{\mathrm{d}p(Q)}{\mathrm{d}C} = p'(Q)\frac{\mathrm{d}Q}{\mathrm{d}C} = \frac{1}{n+1+\alpha}. \tag{17.9}$$

The effect of a change in firm j's cost on firm i's quantity is (assuming $j \neq i$)

$$\frac{\mathrm{d}q_i}{\mathrm{d}c_j} = \frac{\partial q_i}{\partial Q}\frac{\mathrm{d}Q}{\mathrm{d}c_j} = -\frac{p'(Q) + q_i p''(Q)}{p'(Q)}\frac{\mathrm{d}Q}{\mathrm{d}c_j} = \frac{-(1+s_i\alpha)}{p'(Q)(n+1+\alpha)}, \tag{17.10}$$

where $s_i = \frac{q_i}{Q}$ is the market share of firm i. A change in firm i's cost affects its own quantity by

$$\begin{aligned}\frac{\mathrm{d}q_i}{\mathrm{d}c_i} &= \frac{\partial q_i}{\partial Q}\frac{\mathrm{d}Q}{\mathrm{d}c_i} + \frac{\partial q_i}{\partial c_i} = \frac{-(1+s_i\alpha)}{p'(Q)(n+1+\alpha)} + \frac{1}{p'(Q)} \\ &= \frac{n+(1-s_i)\alpha}{p'(Q)(n+1+\alpha)} < 0.\end{aligned} \tag{17.11}$$

Thus, a change in rival j's cost affects firm i's profits by

$$\begin{aligned}\frac{\mathrm{d}\pi_i}{\mathrm{d}c_j} &= q_i p'(Q)\frac{\mathrm{d}Q}{\mathrm{d}C} + \big(p(Q) - c_i\big)\frac{\mathrm{d}q_i}{\mathrm{d}c_j} = q_i p'(Q)\frac{\mathrm{d}Q}{\mathrm{d}C} - q_i p'(Q)\frac{\mathrm{d}q_i}{\mathrm{d}c_j} \\ &= q_i p'(Q)\left(\frac{\mathrm{d}Q}{\mathrm{d}C} - \frac{\mathrm{d}q_i}{\mathrm{d}c_j}\right) \\ &= q_i p'(Q)\left(\frac{1}{p'(Q)(n+1+\alpha)} - \frac{-(1+s_i\alpha)}{p'(Q)(n+1+\alpha)}\right) \\ &= \frac{q_i(2+s_i\alpha)}{n+1+\alpha} > 0.\end{aligned} \tag{17.12}$$

On the other hand, the effect of a change in firm i's cost on its own profits is

$$\begin{aligned}\frac{\mathrm{d}\pi_i}{\mathrm{d}c_i} &= q_i p'(Q)\frac{\mathrm{d}Q}{\mathrm{d}C} + \big(p(Q) - c_i\big)\frac{\mathrm{d}q_i}{\mathrm{d}c_i} - q_i \\ &= q_i p'(Q)\frac{\mathrm{d}Q}{\mathrm{d}C} - q_i p'(Q)\frac{\mathrm{d}q_i}{\mathrm{d}c_i} - q_i \\ &= q_i p'(Q)\left(\frac{\mathrm{d}Q}{\mathrm{d}C} - \frac{\mathrm{d}q_i}{\mathrm{d}c_i}\right) - q_i \\ &= q_i p'(Q)\left(\frac{1}{p'(Q)(n+1+\alpha)} - \frac{n+(1-s_i)\alpha}{p'(Q)(n+1+\alpha)}\right) - q_i \\ &= \frac{q_i}{n+1+\alpha}\Big(1 - \big(n+(1-s_i)\alpha\big) - (n+1+\alpha)\Big) \\ &= \frac{-q_i(2n+(2-s_i)\alpha)}{n+1+\alpha} < 0.\end{aligned} \tag{17.13}$$

Suppose firm 1 takes an action that is either procompetitive or anticompetitive. If the action is procompetitive, then it reduces firm 1's cost by an amount Δ. This reduces industry cost C by Δ. The competitive effect of this is to reduce market price by approximately $\frac{\Delta}{n+1+\alpha}$. If the action is anticompetitive, then it increases the cost of each of firm 1's rivals by an amount R. This increases the market price by approximately $\frac{(n-1)R}{n+1+\alpha}$.

For example, any investments that lead to innovations are acts that reduce the firm's costs. These acts are procompetitive since they may ultimately benefit consumers. Blocking access to crucial or related inputs, exclusive dealing arrangements with suppliers, or exclusive patent cross-licensing arrangements, are examples of strategies that are used to raise rivals' costs. These strategies are anticompetitive because they may harm consumers.[5]

If the two types of action have the same magnitude of effect on the price (but with the procompetitive effect having a positive sign and the anticompetitive effect having a negative sign), then $\Delta = (n-1)R$. The change in price corresponds to the change in consumer surplus, which approximates the change in social welfare for a small change in costs. The above condition simply says that the social gain from the action if it is procompetitive is approximately equal to the social loss from the action if it is anticompetitive.

Now consider the incentive for firm $i \neq 1$ to sue firm 1 for an alleged antitrust violation. This net gain of a suit is composed of three terms: the likelihood of prevailing in court, the size of the damages to the firm, and the cost of the action. Presumably, the plaintiff is less likely to prevail if the action of the firm is procompetitive than if the action is anticompetitive. However, we focus on the value of success to the plaintiff. From (17.12), the loss to firm i from a procompetitive action by firm 1 of magnitude Δ is, for small Δ,

$$-\frac{\partial \pi_i}{\partial c_1}\Delta = -\frac{q_i(2+s_i\alpha)}{n+1+\alpha}\Delta. \tag{17.14}$$

On the other hand, an anticompetitive action affects firm i's profits by increasing its own cost and also by increasing the costs of firm i's rivals. The change in firm i's profits from an across the board increase of magnitude R in rivals' costs c_j,

[5] There are numerous antitrust cases where the defendant has been accused or found guilty of raising rivals' costs. The Standard Oil case (221 U.S. 1, 1911) is one of the most famous. Standard Oil increased its share of U.S. refining capacity from 4% in 1870 to more than 90% in 1879. It achieved this market dominance through the railroad industry. Standard Oil and several other refineries arranged with the railroad companies, who were trying to enforce a cartel, to fix the market shares of each of the railroads in petroleum shipments, in order to reduce the incentives of cartel members to cheat, in exchange for lower shipping rates. This increased the shipping costs for other refineries that were not part of the arrangement, which reduced their profitability, allowing Standard Oil to buy many of them out. In the case of Aluminum Company of America (148 F.2d 416, 1945), Alcoa was charged with raising its rivals' costs by entered into exclusive dealing arrangements with electricity suppliers. And, more recently, expert witnesses for the government have accused Microsoft of raising rivals' costs in the Microsoft case.

for $j > 1$, $j \neq i$, and its own cost, for $j = i$, is

$$\begin{aligned}\sum_{j=2}^{n} \frac{\partial \pi_i}{\partial c_j} R &= (n-2)\frac{\partial \pi_i}{\partial c_j} R + \frac{\partial \pi_i}{\partial c_i} R \\ &= (n-2)\frac{q_i(2+s_i\alpha)}{n+1+\alpha} R + \frac{-q_i(2n+(2-s_i)\alpha)}{n+1+\alpha} R \\ &= \frac{q_i R}{n+1+\alpha}\big((n-2)(2+s_i\alpha) - \big(2n+(2-s_i)\alpha\big)\big) \\ &= \frac{-q_i R}{n+1+\alpha}\big(2(2+\alpha) - \alpha(n-1)s_i\big). \qquad (17.15)\end{aligned}$$

Equations (17.14) and (17.15) imply that, in general, firms with a larger market share have the most to gain from stopping an anticompetitive or a procompetitive action.

To keep the price effect the same from the two types of actions, we let $\Delta = (n-1)R$. Then (17.4) becomes

$$-\frac{\partial \pi_i}{\partial c_1}\Delta = -\frac{\partial \pi_i}{\partial c_j}(n-1)R = -\frac{q_i R(2+s_i\alpha)}{n+1+\alpha}(n-1). \qquad (17.16)$$

Firm i is more likely to sue firm 1 for taking an anticompetitive action than for taking a procompetitive action if its loss from an anticompetitive action is greater than its loss from a procompetitive action, which happens if and only if

$$\begin{aligned}R\sum_{j=2}^{n} \frac{\partial \pi_i}{\partial c_j} + \frac{\partial \pi_i}{\partial c_1}\Delta &= \frac{q_i R}{n+1+\alpha}\big((n-1)s_i\alpha - 4 - 2\alpha + (2+s_i\alpha)(n-1)\big) \\ &= \frac{2q_i R}{n+1+\alpha}\big(n-3+(n-1)s_i\alpha - \alpha\big) < 0. \qquad (17.17)\end{aligned}$$

For $n = 2$, if $s_i > \frac{1}{2}$, then $(-1 + s_i\alpha - \alpha) < 0$. This means that in a duopoly, the dominant firm's value of stopping an action by its smaller rival is greater if the action is anticompetitive than if it is procompetitive action. But if the non-dominant firm is sufficiently small relative to the dominant firm, then the non-dominant firm's value of stopping an action by the dominant firm is greater if the action is procompetitive than if it is anticompetitive.

For $n = 3$, $2s_i\alpha - \alpha < 0$ if and only if $s_i > \frac{1}{2}$. This means that in a triopoly, only a dominant firm suffers a greater loss from a rival's action if the action is anticompetitive than if it is procompetitive. A non-dominant firm always suffers a greater loss from a rival's action if the action is procompetitive than if it is anticompetitive. The implication is that, in highly concentrated industries, if a dominant firm sues a non-dominant firm then the lawsuit is probably procompetitive, but if a sufficiently small non-dominant firm sues a dominant firm, then the lawsuit is more likely to be anticompetitive.

Moreover, as n grows, it is more likely that $(n - 3 + (n-1)s_i\alpha - \alpha) > 0$. This means that a firm's loss from a procompetitive action by a rival firm is more likely to be greater than its loss from an anticompetitive action by the rival firm the more firms there are in the industry. The implication is that lawsuits are more likely to be anticompetitive in dispersed industries than in concentrated industries.

This striking result arises because firm i's loss from a procompetitive action increases as n grows while firm i's loss from an anticompetitive action decreases as n grows. Recall that firm i's loss from a procompetitive action is

$$-\frac{\partial \pi_i}{\partial c_1}\Delta = -\frac{\partial \pi_i}{\partial c_j}(n-1)R. \tag{17.18}$$

Firm i incurs the same amount of loss whether firm 1 lowers its cost by Δ or each of its rivals (including firm 1) lowers their cost by R. Therefore, as far as firm i is concerned, the effect of a procompetitive action is equivalent to a decrease in the costs of each of its rivals. This causes firm i to incur a loss as firm i is now less efficient relative to each of its rivals. And the greater is the number of rivals relative to which firm i is less efficient, the greater is firm i's loss. Hence, firm i's loss from a procompetitive action is greater the larger is the number of firms in the industry.

On the other hand, firm i's loss from an anticompetitive action (see Equation (17.15)) can be rewritten as

$$\begin{aligned}\sum_{j=2}^{n}\frac{\partial \pi_i}{\partial c_j}R &= (n-2)\frac{\partial \pi_i}{\partial c_j}R + \frac{\partial \pi_i}{\partial c_i}R \\ &= (n-1)\frac{\partial \pi_i}{\partial c_j}R + \frac{\partial \pi_i}{\partial c_i}R - \frac{\partial \pi_i}{\partial c_j}R \\ &= \frac{\partial \pi_i}{\partial c_j}(n-1)R - 2q_i R.\end{aligned} \tag{17.19}$$

This expression is clearly decreasing in n. An anticompetitive action by firm 1 imposes a loss on firm i, as firm i's costs are now increased relative to firm 1's costs (this effect corresponds to the term $\frac{\partial \pi_i}{\partial c_i}R$ in the above expression). But the anticompetitive action by firm 1 also increases the costs of each of firm i's rivals, which benefits firm i and therefore mitigates its loss from the anticompetitive action (this effect corresponds to the term $(n-2)\frac{\partial \pi_i}{\partial c_j}R$). Firm i's loss from firm 1's anticompetitive action is mitigated to a greater extent the greater is the number of other firms in the industry that also suffer the cost increase from firm 1's anticompetitive action. For this reason, firm i's loss from an anticompetitive action is decreasing in n.

Note that firm i's gain from the increase in the costs of each of its rivals other than firm 1 is equal to its gain from the increase in the costs of each of its rivals including firm 1 minus its loss from an equivalent decrease in firm 1's cost. The decrease in firm 1's cost and the increase in firm i's cost relative to firm 1 cause a double loss to firm i (corresponding to the term $-2q_i R$ in Equation (17.19)). On the other hand, the increase in the costs of each of firm i's rivals yields a benefit to firm i (corresponding to the term $(n-1)\frac{\partial \pi_i}{\partial c_j}R$). And firm i's benefit from the increase in the costs of each of its rivals from an anticompetitive action by firm 1, $(n-1)\frac{\partial \pi_i}{\partial c_j}R$, is exactly the same as firm i's loss from a procompetitive action by firm 1, which is increasing in n.

The loss from a procompetitive action is decreasing in n while the loss from an anticompetitive action is increasing in n. Thus, as n becomes larger, the loss from a procompetitive action is more likely to dominate. Hence, lawsuits are more likely to be anticompetitive in less concentrated industries than in more concentrated industries.

17.3. Conclusion

In this chapter, we developed a simple Cournot model to analyze the conditions under which private antitrust enforcement is procompetitive or anticompetitive. Our first result implies that in highly concentrated markets, antitrust lawsuits by non-dominant firms against dominant firms are more likely to be strategic abuses of the antitrust laws than lawsuits by dominant firms against non-dominant firms. The result suggests that the relative sizes of the plaintiff and the defendant will be correlated with the plaintiff's intentions in antitrust cases in highly concentrated markets. Our second result implies that lawsuits are more likely to be anticompetitive in more dispersed industries than in more concentrated industries. This result suggests that private antitrust enforcement should be more suspect in competitive industries than in concentrated industries.

We have pointed out the possibility of private antitrust lawsuits being abused, and derived conditions under which private lawsuits are more likely to be abused. These conditions may be useful to antitrust authorities in detecting private abuse of the antitrust laws.

Naturally, the next question is: what can be done to prevent private abuse of the antitrust laws? McAfee et al. (2005) construct a formal model that provides some answers. The obvious way to prevent private abuse of the antitrust laws is to reduce the scope of private enforcement, and expand the scope of public enforcement, of the antitrust laws. Private firms have greater incentives to abuse of the antitrust laws than the government. However, private enforcement also has advantages over public enforcement. For example, private firms tend to be better informed than the government about whether one of their rivals has taken an anti-competitive action.

In general, private firms have greater incentives to enforce the antitrust laws against rival firms, which provides a strong deterrent against anti-competitive actions, but also increases the possibility that the antitrust laws will be abused. Then the question is whether the antitrust system can be structured so that the abusive effect of private antitrust enforcement is minimized while its deterrent effect is maximized. This can be accomplished by multiplying and decoupling damage awards in antitrust cases, for example. Damage awards can be multiplied so that a loosing defendant is required to pay a multiple of the amount of damages that it caused the plaintiff by taking the anti-competitive action. Damages can be decoupled so that a winning plaintiff receives only a fraction of what the loosing defendant is required to pay. Multiplying damages reduces the incentives of firms to take anti-competitive actions, while decoupling damages reduces the incentives of firms to abuse of the antitrust laws.

Acknowledgements

We are especially grateful to Vivek Ghosal and an anonymous referee for helpful comments.

References

Baumol, W.J., Ordover, J.A. (1985), Use of antitrust to subvert competition. *Journal of Law and Economics* 28, 1.

Breit, W., Elzinga, K.G. (1985), Private antitrust enforcement: The new learning. *Journal of Law and Economics* 28, 405.

Brodley, J.F. (1995), Antitrust standing in private merger cases: Reconciling private incentives and public enforcement goals. *Michigan Law Review* 94, 1.

McAfee, R.P., Vakkur, N. (2004), The strategic abuse of antitrust laws. *Journal of Strategic Management Education* 1, 3.

McAfee, R.P., Mialon, H.M., Mialon, S.H. (2005), Private v. public antitrust enforcement: A strategic analysis. Emory Law and Economics Research Paper No. 05-20.

Shughart II, W.F. (1990), Private antitrust enforcement: Compensation, deterrence, or extortion? *Regulation* 13, 53.

CHAPTER 18

Antitrust in Open Economies[1]

Joseph Francois[a] and Henrik Horn[b]

[a] *Tinbergen Institute, Rotterdam, and CEPR, London*
[b] *Research Institute of Industrial Economics, Stockholm, and CEPR, London*

Abstract

We examine antitrust rules in a two county general equilibrium trade model, contrasting national and multilateral (cooperative) determination of competition policy, exploring the properties of the policy equilibrium. It is not imperfect competition, but variation in competitive stance between sectors that matters for trading partners. Beggar-thy-neighbor competition policies relate to countries' comparative advantages, and hurt the factor intensively used, or specific to, the imperfectly competitive sector. They also create a competitive advantage for export firms. FDI can be pro-competitive in this context, reducing the scope for beggar-thy-neighbor policies and reducing the gains from a multilateral competition agreement.

Keywords: antitrust policy, competition policy, merger policy, trade and imperfect competition, FDI

JEL classifications: L4, F12, F3

18.1. Introduction

The prospect of a multilateral agreement on antitrust, with far reaching consequences for national policy regimes, has sparked a nascent literature, including Graham and Richardson (1997), Head and Ries (1997), Horn and Levinsohn (2001), and Rysman (2001). While this literature addresses pertinent issues, it has a major weakness in that it builds on partial equilibrium frameworks. It thus implicitly assumes that the industry under study is the *only* industry with problems with competition, and furthermore, that this sector is sufficiently *small*

---

[1] This chapter benefits from comments at a CEPR workshop on international competition policy in Madrid and at a European Trade Study Group (ETSG) conference in Glasgow. It builds on a set of earlier papers, including Francois and Horn (1988).

CONTRIBUTIONS TO ECONOMIC ANALYSIS
VOLUME 282 ISSN: 0573-8555
DOI: 10.1016/S0573-8555(06)82018-3

relative to the rest of the economy to leave all factor prices unaffected by any competition policy intervention. This literature is consequently in effect concerned with the implications of *discretionary* policy interventions, rather than with the effects of competition rules that are meant to be applied to a range of industries and circumstances.[2]

The reliance on a partial equilibrium framework may be appropriate when the concern is with a regulatory problem in a particular sector. But when the focus is on the establishment of a general competition policy stance, such as when formulating merger guidelines, it is clearly much less adequate. In particular, the exercise of international competition policy will typically affect broad swathes of the economies of the countries involved and is thus likely to have strong cross-sectoral ramifications. The purpose of this chapter is to examine some aspects of an international competition policy agreement in a framework that takes account of such ramifications. This will allow us to relate strategic and distributional aspects of competition policy to basic trade theoretic concepts like comparative advantage and terms-of-trade manipulation.

A general equilibrium approach (whether or not it addresses open economy issues) generally offers a very different perspective on competition policy compared to one based on the partial equilibrium assumptions. The conflict is no longer between the "surpluses" of consumers and producers, or of different producers, but between the *real* incomes of different factor owners. Even under a consumer welfare standard, optimal policy may look very different when taking into account general equilibrium ramifications of competition policy. The general equilibrium approach also yields more interesting building blocks for examining political economy aspects of competition policy, by providing richer modeling of the determinants of income distribution. A second aim of this chapter is therefore to remind industrial organization analysts of the type of effects of competition policy that their traditional approach misses. While the focus here is on an international competition policy issue, several of the type of general equilibrium effects that the analysis highlights are likely to be at play also in a closed economy context. It seems to us that when addressing issues such as the appropriate general stance vis-a-vis collusion or merger, as opposed to the

---

2 Exceptions are Auquier and Caves (1979), and Francois and Horn (1998). The general equilibrium implications of monopoly were also recognized in the early antitrust literature. The rule of proportionality, proposed in the 1930s, targeted variations in markups across sectors. (See Kahn, 1935; Lerner, 1934, and Robinson, 1934.) In the modern antitrust literature, however, this is little more than a footnote. There is also, of course, a huge literature on the impact of market structures on trade policy in partial and general equilibrium. Traditionally, the general equilibrium branch of the theory of trade under imperfect competition emphasizes monopolistic competition, while firm-level interactions are modeled in partial equilibrium. (See Eaton and Grossman, 1986 and the papers collected in Grossman, 1992). While the older literature on trade and oligopoly is mostly focused on the partial equilibrium case (Markusen and Venables, 1988) a recent set of papers by Neary (2003) is focused on developing trade theory with oligopoly for the general equilibrium case. While the body of work is substantial, policy space in this literature covers trade policy, and not competition policy.

appropriate intervention in the case of an isolated case of collusion or a specific merger, the analysis should take such effects into account, or it may lead to erronous conclusions.

The chapter is organized as follows. Section 18.2 introduces a two-country, two-good model of trade with imperfect competition. Section 18.3 characterizes equilibrium competition policies, highlighting how the incentives for a beggar-thy-neighbor type antitrust regime are related to countries' comparative advantages. In order to determine the distributional impact of competition, in Section 18.3 we also adopt the two basic trade models for the determination of income distributional effects of trade—the Heckscher–Ohlin–Samuelson (H–O–S) model, and the Ricardo–Viner (R–V) model. In both frameworks, factors relatively specific to competitive sectors may win from imperfect competition, and hence may be a source of support in a political equilibrium with imperfect competition. Because the strategic competition policy drives a wedge between the international price of the product and relevant marginal costs, it also creates a competitive advantage (in terms of costs) for the imperfectly competitive industry. This in turn has important implications for the sustainability of strategic competition policy in a world with foreign direct investment (FDI), an issue addressed in Section 18.4.1, which shows that FDI can undermine the ability of an exporter to pursue a beggar-thy-neighbor competition policy. In this way, the workings and incentives for any international competition agreement are linked to the underlying FDI regime. Section 18.4.2 very briefly considers the impact of extra-territorial application of competition policy for the gains from an international agreement on competition policy. Section 18.5 summarizes the findings.

18.2. The model

Our focus is on structural, economy-wide aspects of competition policy, rather than on discretionary intervention in particular markets. In order to capture a government's ability to affect the general degree of competition in the domestic economy, we assume that it can directly or indirectly (without cost) influence markups over marginal cost. We embed this basic feature within a two-country, two-sector general equilibrium model, where costs are determined by a general equilibrium product transformation technology. The underlying production structure is general, and consistent with, for instance, a standard H–O–S or R–V general equilibrium framework. Our basic framework is summarized in the following list of assumptions (where subscripts denote partial derivatives and superscripts denote countries):

- There are 2 countries, indexed by $j = 1, 2$.
- There are 2 industries, X and Y, each producing a homogeneous product.
- Demands are identical and homothetic across countries.
- Factor markets are perfectly competitive.

- Both goods are produced under constant returns to scale.
- There is a standard concave transformation technology between X^j and Y^j:

$$Y^j = T^j(X^j), \quad \text{with } T^j_{X^j} < 0, \text{ and } T^j_{X^j X^j} < 0. \tag{18.1}$$

- Product X is sold at a price which might exceed marginal cost, in an internationally integrated market.[3]
- The governments control their respective domestic firms' markup levels in the X sector.
- Unless otherwise noted, product Y is sold in a perfectly competitive, internationally integrated market.

For the moment, we also assume governments seek to maximize national welfare, firms are purely national (they export without local presence), and there is no extra-territorial application of national competition policy.[4] These last assumptions are relaxed in a subsequent section. Their implications are that exporters are beyond the reach of the government in the importing country, and that for each country we have

$$p = (1 + m^j)c^j, \tag{18.2}$$

where c^j denotes the marginal cost faced by an oligopolist in country j as defined by the underlying product transformation technology, p is the price of the product X, and $(1 + m^j)$ is the domestic firms' markup over marginal costs. We can use any price as the numeraire, and find it convenient to normalize the unit cost of production of Y to unity. Because it is the difference in competition between sectors that matters (see Section 18.3), treating the Y sector as a competitive benchmark does not compromise the main thrust of our results.

We have outlined the model in a somewhat sparse manner, partly to preserve tractability. However, the structure is actually richer than it may first appear. Because we rely on a dual representation of the general equilibrium structure of the economy, we can interpret our general results with respect to a range of

---

[3] Identically, we could have assumed non-discriminatory ex-factory pricing. This is a requirement of the GATT antidumping code, which treats international price discrimination as actionable and hence punishable by import duties that force equality of ex factory prices. This implies uniform ex-factory pricing across markets, even with trading costs.

[4] The extent to which the welfare maximization assumption is descriptive of reality can obviously be questioned. On the one hand, competition laws have a strong flavor of consumer protection. However, domestic producer interests often make their voices heard, in particular when foreign firms have been involved in alleged abuses of dominant positions, or in concentrations. For instance, the tendency to allow and even support the creation of "national champions" in many countries reveals the readiness of governments to trade-off consumer welfare against producer interests. We view the assumption of welfare maximization as a convenient middle ground between the two extremes of straightforward consumer protection, and capture by producer interests. In any event, for the purpose of this chapter, other ways of weighing producer interests into country 1's objective function for competition policy would also suffice. Other possibilities are discussed briefly below in Section 18.3. The two last assumptions above will be relaxed in Section 18.4.

well-known trade models (Dixit and Norman, 1980). In addition, in the interest of relative generality, we have not explicitly modeled a particular strategic equilibrium between firms. Again, this allows us to drop down to more specific (competition) models when useful. For example, the simplest way of thinking about the model is to assume that in each country there is a single quantity-setting producer in the X sector. Unchecked these firms would be in a Cournot–Nash equilibrium. However, the respective government can force its producer to behave more or less competitively. Another representation consistent with this approach involves a fixed number of firms in each country that manage to collude perfectly with the aid or enforcement of the respective government. The governments can then enforce a target level of collusion within the industry concerned, such that markups are in the range between the perfect competition and the monopoly level of markup:

$$p = \left(1 - \frac{\lambda^j}{\varepsilon}\right)^{-1} c^j, \tag{18.3}$$

where ε^j is the perceived demand elasticity for the sector,[5] and $1 \geq \lambda^j \geq 0$ is an index of the effective degree of competition.

Let us now characterize the general equilibrium of this economy. Since factor markets are assumed to be perfectly competitive, the marginal cost in terms of product Y faced by an oligopolist in the X-sector must equal the amount of Y that is sacrificed for the marginal unit of product X:

$$c^j = -T_X^j(x^j). \tag{18.4}$$

Hence, by Equation (18.2) and Equation (18.4), we have

$$p = -(1 + m^j)T_X^j(x^j). \tag{18.5}$$

Let industry output of product X be x^j in country j. Market clearing for product X requires that world demand equals world supply, or formally that

$$S(p)\left[p(x^1 + x^2) + T^1(x^1) + T^2(x^2)\right] = p\left[x^1 + x^2\right], \tag{18.6}$$

where $S(p)$ is the budget share of product X in expenditures, and the bracketed term on the left-hand side is world income expressed in terms of product Y. Expressions (18.4), (18.5), and (18.6) constitute a system of equations sufficient to

---

[5] Equation (18.3) also follows if we assume that the government indirectly determines markup rates through concentration policy as proxied by the number of firms in the market, provided that there are no fixed costs involved. The Cournot–Nash equilibrium value of λ^j will then equal $\frac{\theta^j}{n^j}$, where θ^j is the quantity-based market share of the country j industry producing X, and n^j the number of firms. Since market share will itself be a function of the number of firms in equilibrium, λ^j can be set through an appropriate industrial concentration policy. This approach has been used in several of the recent partial equilibrium studies of international aspects of competition policy referred to in the Introduction.

determine the unknowns p, c^j, x^j as functions of the two markups m^j. Henceforth $P(m^1, m^2)$, $C^j(m^1, m^2)$, and $X^j(m^1, m^2)$ will refer to these equilibrium solutions for p, c, and x. It is straightforward to show that in equilibrium,

$$X^j_{m^j} < 0, \qquad X^i_{m^j} > 0, \qquad P_{m^j} > 0, \quad i \neq j. \tag{18.7}$$

We next turn to the definition of comparative advantage. To this end, let $D^j(m^1, m^2)$ be the domestic consumption of product X in country j. We will say that Country 1 has a comparative advantage in product X in the sense that it is a net exporter of X in the case where there is global perfect competition in this industry, i.e. $X^1(0,0) > D^1(0,0)$. Deviations from this equilibrium pattern can then be attributed to differences in competition, or identically to policy-induced competitive advantage. In order to simplify the discussion, we will assume that trade patterns are not reversed for any combination of markups:[6]

$$X^1(m^1, m^2) - D^1(m^1, m^2) > 0, \quad \forall (m^1, m^2). \tag{18.8}$$

We can define national welfare on the basis of identical homothetic preferences as follows:

$$W^j(m^1, m^2) \equiv \frac{1}{I(P)}\left[(P - C^j)X^j + C^j X^j + T^j(X^j)\right], \tag{18.9}$$

where $I(P)$ is the equilibrium value of the utility price index (an ideal consumer price index) for the representative consumer, defined over composite consumption good Q.[7] The first term in this expression represents profit, while the second and third terms represent factor incomes.

18.3. Antitrust in a trade-only equilibrium

Taking the social welfare measure in expression (18.9) as the government objective function, we can now characterize the properties of the policy equilibrium, with emphasis on aggregate and distributional effects of the choice of policies.

---

6 This will hold for the Nash equilibrium set of competition policies, see below. Outside the Nash equilibrium set of competition policies, we can construct cases where the direction of trade depends on markups/collusion. For example, with otherwise identical countries (and hence no traditional basis for trade in endowment or technology models of trade), differential markup policies will generate exports of X from the country with the lowest markup levels.

7 Given homothetic preferences, it follows directly from the properties of the social expenditure function $E(P, W)$ defined over welfare W and prices P. It allows us to deflate nominal income values directly. The terms $E_P = Q$ and $E_W = I(P)$ follow from the definition of the national expenditure function, and its properties. For a more detailed account of duality in trade theory, see the technical annex to Dixit and Norman (1980).

18.3.1. Aggregate effects

The typical industrial organization analysis would view significant markups in a particular industry as a clear indication that there is likely to be a socially wasteful misallocation of resources in the industry. Once the analysis is extended to a general equilibrium framework, the perspective changes fundamentally, however. In particular, once the interplay between monopolistic practices in different sectors is taken into account, it is the *difference* in competition between sectors that is critical. This finding is definitely not new—it can be traced back to Kahn (1935), Lerner (1934) and Robinson (1934)—but it seems to have gone unnoticed in the modern industrial organization literature. To demonstrate this feature, assume temporarily (and contrary to what has been assumed above) that there is an economy-wide markup rate $\tilde{m}^j$, a situation we will refer to as *Lerner proportionality*. In this economy, incomes for factor owners, as well as the aggregate profits, will depend on the markup. In particular, the higher is the markup, the larger is the share of GDP that accrues to profits. GDP itself will *not* be affected by the level of the markups, however: By our numeraire definition, the cost of producing Y remains unity, though the price of Y may change. We will then have income $(1+\tilde{m}^j)\cdot G(P^0, V^j)$ where G is the GDP function defined over the competitive equilibrium price vector P^0 and the endowment vector V^j. The indirect utility price index can then also be defined with respect to the competitive equilibrium price vector P^0 and our (symmetric) markups: $I(P)=(1+\tilde{m}^j)\cdot I(P^0)$. The real income is then

$$W^j(\cdot)=\frac{G(P^0, V)}{I(P^0)} \tag{18.10}$$

which as can be seen is independent of the markup level. Hence:[8]

PROPOSITION 18.1. *With Lerner proportionality, the impact of imperfect competition is to redistribute income from factor owners to recipients of profits. Aggregate welfare is unaffected.*

Note that Proposition 18.1 can be seen as providing some support for the use of a consumer surplus standard in competition policy. If problems of imperfect competition are pervasive in the economy, this may not be of primary concern from an aggregate welfare point of view, but could still be very harmful to consumers, by lowering their real incomes and hence having important distributional effects.

[8] It may help to imagine a process where the government imposes identical degrees of competition, as measured by markups, through a policy of industrial concentration. Individual oligopolists then try to raise prices by reducing output. In an economy-wide setting, this leads to falling factor prices. With falling marginal cost, oligopolists boost output, restoring full employment at lower factor prices. In this sense, an economy-wide equivalence in the degree of competition is like an economywide VAT or output tax.

For the rest of the chapter we focus on situations where there are asymmetries between sectors such that the markups differ. Consider the case where the Y sector is inherently competitive, but where markups can be encouraged (through mergers or collusion) in the X sector. The impact on real national income (deflated by the price of utility) of a marginal increase in the markup rate m in sector X is

$$W^j_{m^j} = \frac{m^j X^j_{m^j}}{I(P)} + \frac{X^j - D^j}{I(P)} P_{m^j}. \tag{18.11}$$

The first term in this expression is negative. It represents the loss of profits on existing sales as we reduce output further to boost the markup rate itself. The sign of the second term depends on whether the country is a net importer or exporter of product X, and is positive if and only if the country exports the product. It represents terms-of-trade gains made at the expense of the net importer. The net exporter will have an incentive to cartelize the sector since

$$W^j_{m^j}(0,0) = \frac{X^j(0,0) - D^j(0,0)}{I(P)} P_{m^j} > 0. \tag{18.12}$$

Hence, the net exporter of product X has an incentive to deviate from any perfectly competitive equilibrium.

PROPOSITION 18.2. *Absent an international antitrust agreement, national welfare maximization implies that the X importer will enforce marginal cost pricing among its X firms, and the X exporter will allow for positive markups by its X firms.*

By focusing on the Nash equilibrium competition policy and its relationship to comparative advantage, Proposition 18.2 means that we avoid potential indeterminacy about the effects of foreign competition on domestic competition policy in partial equilibrium.

Obviously, from a world point of view the Nash equilibrium is sub-optimal, as can be seen from

$$\frac{\mathrm{d}}{\mathrm{d}m^1}\left[W^1(m^1, m^2) + W^2(m^1, m^2)\right] = \frac{m^1}{I(P)} X^1_{m^1} + \frac{m^2}{I(P)} X^2_{m^1}$$

which is negative for m^2 sufficiently small. Consequently:

PROPOSITION 18.3. *An international agreement on antitrust policy could increase world welfare. However, to improve welfare for both countries, side payments are necessary.*

Proposition 18.3 suggests two separate reasons why attempts are underway to bring a competition policy agreement into the WTO, rather than let it stand by itself. First, our Country 1 prefers the non-cooperative equilibrium to the situation where marginal cost pricing is enforced globally. Hence, in order for both par-

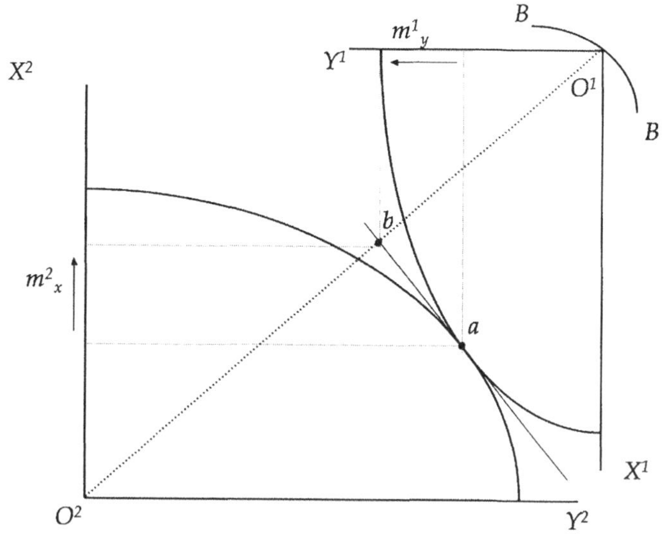

Fig. 18.1: Trade with perfect competition, and the Nash trade equilibrium with FDI and integrated markets.

ties to accept an agreement on competition policy it is necessary that Country 1 receives some form of side payment. The wide-ranging structure of the WTO agreements is likely to offer ample opportunities for such concessions. Note, however, that this is an argument for why the competition policy agreement may need the trade agreement to be politically viable, rather than vice versa. The second reason follows from the next proposition:

PROPOSITION 18.4. *An international antitrust agreement would increase trade.*

The strategic competition policy induces both countries to shift production toward their respective import sectors, and trade in both products is reduced (albeit not eliminated). The reduction in trade follows directly from price increases on the part of the Country 1 producers. At the same time, we know that exports will not be eliminated. Even if it were possible to choose $m^1 > 0$ such that trade ceased to exist, it would not be optimal, since at such a value of m^1,

$$W^1_{m^1} = \frac{m^1 C^1}{I(P)} X^1_{m^1} < 0. \qquad (18.13)$$

In terms of trade volumes, a trade and a competition policy agreement would thus be complementary. Therefore, considering the fact that the WTO is an organization with a pronounced "more trade is always better" attitude, the attempts to bring competition policy into the WTO are not surprising.

The equilibrium described by Propositions 18.2–18.4 can be summarized using Figures 18.1 and 18.2. In the figures, the Country 1 and Country 2 trans-

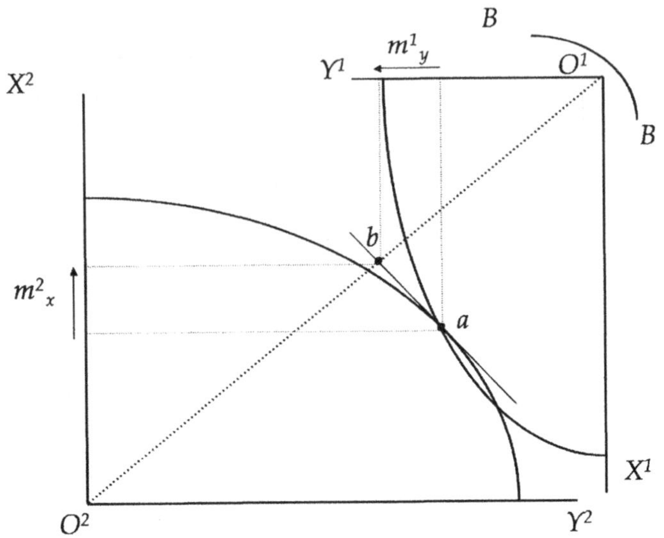

Fig. 18.2: The Nash trade-only equilibrium with integrated markets.

formation frontiers as defined in Equation (18.1) are mapped relative to origins O^1 and O^2. World production will be defined by point a while consumption is at point b. Perfect competition in both countries is represented by a tangency of the two production possibility frontiers. This is so because at point b we have equality between the marginal rates of transformation, prices, and marginal valuation in consumption. As prices and preferences are assumed identical across countries, consumption is along the diagonal from O^1 to O^2. International trade is then the re-allocation of quantities needed to let both countries consume at point b, given the global production point a. As such, the import quantities (the trade vector) are shown as m_x^2 and m_y^1.[9] The efficiency frontier BB is derived by tracing point O^1 as we move the Country 1 production frontier along the Country 2 production frontier, maintaining tangency.

In contrast to the competitive equilibrium in Figure 18.1, with the strategic competition policy equilibrium in Figure 18.2 production instead occurs at point a with non-marginal cost pricing by one country and marginal-cost (i.e. competitive) pricing by the other. Consumption takes place at a point b at goods prices given by a slope for the line ab that is higher, for good X, relative to the corresponding line in Figure 18.1. The positive markup in the home country is reflected in the non-tangency of price with the Country 1 frontier. Proposition 18.2 is reflected by the fact that point O^1 is below the global efficiency envelope without tangency.

---

[9] These variables are not to be confused with the markups.

18.3.2. Strategic competition policy and competitive advantage

We now turn to the policy interaction between the governments. To see the incentive for country j to intervene, consider the impact of an increase in the markup in its domestic sector on real factor incomes, as given by the last terms of expression (18.9). In general we have Equation (18.14).

$$\frac{\mathrm{d}}{\mathrm{d}m^j}\left[\frac{C^j X^j + T^j(X^j)}{I(P)}\right] = -\frac{C^j X^j + T^j(X^j)}{I(P)^2} I_P P_{m^j} + \frac{C^j_{m^j}}{I(P)} X^j_{m^j} < 0. \tag{18.14}$$

On the right-hand side, the first term in brackets represents the relative price effects (the price of X changes relative to that of Y), while the second term relates to the drop in factor income following from reduced factor demand (as firms try to constrain output). The second term flags a reduction in the cost of producing X and implies a drop in aggregate factor incomes. We can therefore also conclude the following:

PROPOSITION 18.5. *A strategic competition policy not only increases profits of domestic firms by permitting larger markups, but also tends to enhance the apparent competitive advantage of these firms by lowering their marginal costs.*

Note that Proposition 18.5 relates to a pure general equilibrium phenomenon. When an exporting country is large enough to affect international prices, a generally slack competition policy (or one that actively encourages exercise of market power) in this country will lead to lowered demand for factors of production, and this will in turn reduce their rewards.[10]

The strategic competition policy is similar in its effects to those of a strategic trade policy in a Cournot setting, in that it lowers the marginal costs for exporters and hence confers to them a cost advantage. However, in the case of the strategic trade policy, the lower costs are meant to capture market shares, whereas here with the strategic competition policy the exporting country loses market share. It is more like an optimal trade policy in the Bertrand case, which as shown by Eaton and Grossman (1986) often is a tax, even though here the gain comes only through the reduced competition between domestic firms. Hence, the competition policy here is not "strategic" in the sense of altering the competitive position of domestic firms vis-a-vis foreign competitors, but in the sense of affecting the competition between domestic firms.

---

[10] Though without formalization, Norman (1996) makes a similar observation.

18.3.3. The distributional effects of strategic competition policies

In standard industrial organization analysis, cartelization typically has positive externalities for outside firms in the industry. However, here the firms from the net importing country will not be able to profit from the cartelization, since their government continues to enforce marginal cost pricing. Therefore, since all income is factor income in this country, these factor owners as a group lose from the other country's competition policy. Hence, when we draw a line between (collective) factor owners and firm owners in the two countries, the *only* income group that gains in the aggregate from the cartelization is the owners of firms in the X industry in Country 1.

But while factor owners as a group in each of the countries lose from cartelization, it is still possible that certain factor owners gain. In order to determine possible winners and losers, and thus the likely sources of support for an international competition policy agreement, we must add further structure to the production technologies. We consider two standard trade models commonly employed to examine issues of income distribution.

First, assume that the underlying transformation technology in Equation (18.1) is the reduced form of a H–O–S economy. With positive markups in the X sector, output in this sector is constrained relative to the other sector (assuming full employment of both factors). It is this reduction in output, and hence in input demands, that forces factor incomes down relative to final goods prices, and makes profits possible. At the same time, the Y sector will not employ factors in the same proportion in which they are released by the X sector. Hence, from the well-known relationship between goods prices and factor incomes in the Heckscher–Ohlin model (aka the Stolper–Samuelson theorem), the fall in the relative value of C^j (i.e. marginal cost) will also involve a fall in income for the X-intensive factor greater than the reduction in C^j. Designating $\Omega^{X,1}$ as the equilibrium income of the factor used intensively in X production in Country 1:

$$P_{m^1} > 0 > C^1_{m^1} > \Omega^{X,1}_{m^1}. \tag{18.15}$$

The fact that price increases relative to marginal cost follows from the markup policy itself, and costs have to fall, as we have seen above. The third inequality follows from the basic Stolper–Samuelson theorem. In fact, the X-intensive factor will suffer the most, in real income terms, from cartelization of the X sector. The impact on the other factor will be ambiguous, since its income may fall relative to P (depending on markup levels), even as it rises relative to the other good Y:

$$P_{m^1} > 0 > C^1_{m^1} \quad \text{and} \quad P_{m^1} \gtrless \Omega^{Y,1}_{m^1} > 0. \tag{18.16}$$

The imposition of a markup in the X sector implies that the consumer price of X in terms of Y increases, whereas relative marginal costs fall. With competitive pricing in factor markets, and with constant returns to scale, we know from the Stolper–Samuelson theorem that there will be a reduction in the reward of the factor that is intensively used in this sector in terms of both products, and an increase in the reward of the other factor relative to both marginal costs. However, since the markup increases the price of X relative the marginal cost of X, it is not clear that the Y-intensive factor will actually gain in terms of the sector X price. This factor sees its income rise vis-a-vis the price of good Y, though it may rise or fall relative to good X. Consequently, the welfare effect is unclear with regard to this factor owner. This is directly analogous to the impact of a production tax in a H–O–S model.[11]

Consider next the alternative assumption that Equation (18.1) reflects a R–V transformation technology. Hence, we have a factor specific to each sector, and a factor that is fully mobile between sectors. Again, we know that markups are accomplished by constraining output in the X sector. This reduced demand for inputs will depress demand for the mobile factor and the X-specific factor, so that both lose unambiguously as we shift from competition to a positive markup. Again, there is a direct analogue to the impact of a production tax in the R–V model. In the Y sector, the Y-specific factor will experience rising productivity (as the mobile factor moves into the sector), and rising income in terms of the numeraire Y. However, because the price of X rises as well, the net effect is ambiguous.[12]

We can summarize the factor income effects as follows:

PROPOSITION 18.6. *The benefits from the strategic competition policy are focused on a specific income group—owners of firms in the imperfectly competitive sector in the country imposing a markup. The only factors that do not lose unambiguously from such a policy are those that are relatively specific (in a H–O–S or R–V sense) to the competitive sector.*

Hence, the support for an international agreement which prevents this type of behavior should stem from all factor owners except possibly for these latter groups, and the resistance would hinge on the ability of owners to form a coalition with the factor that is specific or intensively used in the competitive sector of the economy.[13]

---

[11] There are empirical issues raised by the factor market effects we have flagged here that go beyond this chapter, but that merit exploration. For example, we should expect relative factor prices to vary systematically with market structure. In addition, in rigid wage economies like those in continental Western Europe, we may expect variations along the employment margin (i.e. unemployment) rather than the wage margin, again as a function of variations in general degrees of competition.

[12] We could of course assume that the specific factor captures profits.

[13] A logical approach beyond the scope of this chapter is to introduce a formal political economy structure and embark on a detailed analytical treatment of political economy equilibrium competition policies in general equilibrium, starting with the basic winners and losers identified here. Combined with the political decision process (majority voting, coalition building, etc.) this will lead to the sustained policy set. Depending on the power of the beneficiaries of the strategic competition policy, in a politically determined equilibrium the net importer government may also support a domestic cartel, even though this is unambiguously bad for overall national welfare. Alternatively, with rent sharing between inside labor and firm owners, it might be possible to build a coalition of labor that includes the "losing" factor.

18.4. Antitrust with both trade and FDI

The results above may seem to provide a compelling economic rationale for an international antitrust agreement, such as the one currently under negotiation in the WTO. But there are several reasons not to jump to such a conclusion. First, as a practical matter, little is known about the empirical magnitude of the problem such an agreement is supposed to solve. But there are also more basic reasons for skepticism, as we will see. First, the analysis above assumes the absence of foreign direct investment (FDI). Once FDI is brought into the picture, the case for an international agreement becomes much weaker, as long as it is rendered "national treatment". Second, there are also unilateral actions that countries can take to mitigate the problem. In particular, as argued in the ensuing section, extra-territorial application of national antitrust laws can serve such a role.

18.4.1. Introducing foreign direct investment

While a standard assumption in trade theory (and even more so in industrial organization) is that firms serve foreign markets through exports without any local presence, in practice firms often serve foreign markets through local production. As we will argue, the possibility for firms to undertake FDI may have significant ramifications for the welfare-enhancing potential of a competition policy agreement. Indeed, in the policy debate and in parallel to the discussion concerning the desirability of an international agreement on competition policy, there is a similar (and politically much more charged) discussion about an international investment agreement. These issues are intertwined, circling partly around the question of whether these agreements are likely to increase or reduce trade, and whether agreements on competition policy and/or FDI should be brought into the WTO Agreement.

In order to examine the impact of FDI on the need for an international agreement on competition policy formally, we return to the model laid out in Section 18.2, but now relax our assumption regarding local presence, and assume that FDI means that firms can produce wherever they find it to be profitable. Firms in the imperfectly competition industry can thus divide their production between the two countries in any way they want. Firms come under the jurisdiction of each country in which they have some production. Importantly, the host country is assumed to give identical treatment to foreign producers in terms of, for instance, access to factors of production at the same prices as faced by domestic firms (there are thus no special taxes or input requirement imposed on foreign production), and that it enforces the same competition rules with regard to foreign producers for the production they undertake in the host country, as it applies to domestically owned firms. There are indeed already some WTO rules in the Trade-Related Investment Measures (TRIMS) Agreement that require such "national treatment", even though these rules are incomplete and relatively untested in WTO jurisprudence. The EU has a relatively recent set of rules following this principle, while the US, a much older customs union, has a long history of enforcing such rules internally under the Interstate Commerce clause of the US Constitution. In addition to TRIMS, in a WTO context we also have rules on imports and to some extent the WTO agreement on services (the GATS or General Agreement on Trade in Services) as further examples of non-discrimination provisions in international (and interstate) commercial rules.

It is instructive to conduct a thought experiment of introducing the opportunity for FDI in the trade-only type of equilibrium we examined before (summarized in Figure 18.2). In this equilibrium, firms located in Country 1 have a competitive advantage following from lax competition enforcement. Country 2 firms will hence find it profitable to shift production to Country 1, provided that they receive national treatment there. Assuming that the investing firms repatriate their earnings, this will shift profits to Country 2. At the same time, the optimal markup for Country 1 among its firms clearly falls because profit, including profit gained at the expense of domestic consumers, is now partially captured by foreigners. In terms of Equation (18.11), the terms-of-trade gain that followed from the partial monopolization is reduced. Country 2, on the other hand, will not find any reason to change its policy of marginal cost pricing. It takes advantage of the lower production costs in Country 1, induced by the partial monopolization of the industry, and it tends to gain both on account of the profit shifting, as well as the improved terms-of-trade.

How far will this reallocation process go if left unchecked? Country 2 firms will have incentive to shift production to Country 1 as long as there is any difference in production costs between the two economies, or until all production of X occurs in Country 1. This reallocation will continue either until all production of X occurs in Country 1, or until Country 1 ceases to allow/enforce prices above marginal costs. In the latter case, the production equilibrium would be exactly the same as in the case of a globally welfare maximizing competition policy agreement.

Formally, note that in the presence of foreign production, the welfare of Country 1 is

$$V^1(m^1, m^2) = \frac{1}{I(P)}\big[(P - C^1)X^1 + C^1(X^1 + Z) + T^1(X^1 + Z)\big], \tag{18.17}$$

where X^1 now refers to production of product X by Country 1 firms, and $Z(m^1, m^2)$ is production of X by Country 2 firms in Country 1. At what level of foreign production will Country 1 enforce marginal cost pricing in the Nash equilibrium? Differentiating with respect to m^1 and evaluating at $m^1 = m^2 = 0$:

$$V_1^1(0,0) = \frac{X^1 - D^1}{I(P)} P_{m^1} + \frac{Z}{I(P)} C_{m^1}. \tag{18.18}$$

The first term is positive as before. The second term is negative. Country 2 firms will hence shift production to Country 1 until their joint production is such as to make the right-hand side of this expression equal to zero. When this holds, there are no incentives for foreign producers to either increase or reduce their production in Country 1.

The pro-competitive effect of FDI identified here contrasts with that normally portrayed in the trade and the industrial organization literature. It is not the increased competition in a Cournot–Nash equilibrium due to an increase in the number of firms, nor is it the undercutting by external firms of the cartel price. Instead, FDI reduces the optimal degree of concentration for Country 1 for two reasons: first, it enables foreign firms to take a share of the surplus initially created through concentration for the domestic country; and second, the FDI increases marginal costs in the domestic industry, reducing competitive advantage. Hence, at the margin, we have less surplus created by a given markup. Basically, FDI acts to arbitrage away cost advantages created by the beggar-thy-neighbor competition policy.[14]

The findings can be summarized as follows:

PROPOSITION 18.7. *Inward FDI may induce Country* 1 *to enforce marginal cost pricing, as long as it provides national treatment to foreign production, thus removing the global efficiency gains from an international agreement on competition policy.*[15]

One reason why the policy discussion on the Multilateral Agreement on Investment proposed by the OECD has been so charged is that this agreement has been seen as providing national treatment protection (or even stronger protection) to investing firms, without imposing any constraints on their behavior. Hence, some have suggested that an international investment agreement must be complemented with an agreement on competition policy. The analysis above offers a rather different perspective. Proposition 18.7 suggests that (within our model) an agreement on national treatment may *weaken* the incentives for countries to pursue a beggar-thy-neighbor antitrust policy. Actually, the marginal cost pricing equilibrium achieved through FDI is exactly the same as the equilibrium that would arise if marginal cost pricing were enforced through an international agreement. To see this, note that the marginal cost pricing Nash equilibrium with FDI is characterized by the following expressions:

$$p = -T_x^j(x^j), \quad j = 1, 2, \tag{18.19}$$

$$S(p)\left[p(x^1 + x^2) + c^1 z + T^1(x^1 + z) + T^2(x^2)\right] = p(x^1 + z + x^2), \tag{18.20}$$

[14] We should note that if we were to introduce unions or rigid wages in our general equilibrium setup, factor costs may not adjust fully and the incentive for FDI may therefore be reduced.

[15] A tax on the earnings of foreign-owned plants could be used to limit this mechanism.

$$(x^1 - d^1)E_P P_{m^1} + zc^1_{m^1} = 0, \tag{18.21}$$

$$D^1 = S(p)\left[px^1 + c^1 z + T^1(x^1 + z)\right], \tag{18.22}$$

where $p = c^1$. Equation (18.19) defines marginal cost pricing, Equation (18.20) is our market clearing condition, Equation (18.21) follows from Equation (18.18) and relates the profit-shifting effect against terms-of-trade gains, while Equation (18.22) defines home demand. Equations (18.19) and (18.20) define a sub-system that yield equilibrium prices and output P and X^j. With identical demands, these are identical to those in the competitive equilibrium with trade only.

This finding can be illustrated graphically by again using Figure 18.1, assuming that we have started from the equilibrium in Figure 18.2. This new equilibrium imposes the conditions in Equations (18.19) through (18.22). Given Equations (18.19) and (18.20), FDI moves trade to the same level as under a competitive trade-only equilibrium (identical to the case originally illustrated in the figure). Hence, we have a tangency in the figure with both production possibility frontiers, and a trade vector identical to a competitive non-FDI trade vector. The only difference is that in the case of FDI, in Country 2 firm production is now split into the domestic production X^1 and the foreign production Z. However, since there is marginal cost pricing, there are no profits in this sector, and the ownership of firms in the sector is immaterial outside any transition process.

Country 1 loses from the FDI, since it suffers both a terms of trade loss and a loss of income through shifting of profits to Country 2 (assuming that firms repatriate their profits), and Country 2 correspondingly gains. The reason why there are unambiguous losses to Country 1 is that the investing firms do not bring with them either technology, or any productive resources. Consequently, Country 1 has an incentive to deny firms from Country 2 equal access to domestic resources, or to remove their incentives to invest by enforcing marginal cost pricing.[16]

PROPOSITION 18.8. *In the absence of side payments, Country* 1 *will oppose both an international agreement on antitrust, as well as an international agreement on investment that would enforce national treatment of FDI.*

18.4.2. Extra-territorial application of national competition policy

Clearly, one reason why the country with net exports of product X manages to pursue a strategic competition policy is the fact that the importing country

---

[16] Note that firm interaction/collusion in product markets may mean they are also able to erect entry barriers against FDI. See for example Campa et al. (1998).

has no jurisdiction over the exporting firms, by our assumption about extra-territoriality. Hence, an obvious solution from the point of view of the importing country would be to apply its competition policy extra-territorially. This is exactly the strategy followed in recent years by the European Commission vis-a-vis foreign mergers. Exporting firms in Country 1 would then come under two jurisdictions, and it would here seem reasonable to assume that the more stringent of the two applied. Therefore, Country 2 would enforce marginal cost pricing both at home and abroad, and the extra-territorial application of Country 2's competition policy would thus lead to a globally efficient outcome. This could also be accomplished by requiring marginal cost pricing. Ironically, anti-dumping laws encourage the behavior that extra-territorial competition policy would oppose. These laws effectively encourage price discrimination when it leads to higher prices in export markets. In this sense, they are anti-competitive.[17]

PROPOSITION 18.9. *A system of extra-territorial application of national competition policies would substitute for an international agreement on these policies.*

18.5. Summary

The purpose of this chapter has been to demonstrate the need to broaden the perspective in competition policy analysis. The currently prevailing approach in industrial organization theory, of implicitly restricting the analysis to the study of a discretionary intervention in a small distorted sector in an otherwise perfectly competitive economy that is closed to the rest of the world, is too limited for the analysis of many current policy issues. To highlight the difference an open economy, general equilibrium approach may make, we have pointed to certain basic aspects of antitrust in a very simple two-country, two-sector trade model in which countries can choose a general competitive stance. This has allowed us to highlight the role of relative opportunity cost, through the economy-wide interactions between goods and factor markets, for the design of national competition policies in a trade context.

The general equilibrium approach yields a significantly different perspective on antitrust than does the standard IO framework:

---

[17] See Head and Ries (1997) for a discussion of extraterritoriality. Note that while in the present model, the government of Country 2 faces the correct incentives from a global welfare viewpoint, this may conceal some drawbacks associated with extra-territoriality. In the present model, "maximal competition" is globally desirable. However, if we relax the assumptions of the present model, then a system of over-lapping jurisdictions may tend to lead toward too much competition, from a world welfare viewpoint. For example, in the presence of economies of scale, the issue may look different. In such a case it might be desirable to allow for some exploitation of market power, the private benefits of which may be unevenly distributed internationally, in order to enable exploitation of returns to scale.

1. It is the difference in the degree to which different sectors diverge from perfect competition that matters. The markup in a particular sector is hence not a valid predictor of misallocation of resources.
2. The rents created through imperfect competition will partly end up with factor owners through the interaction of factor and product markets. This "rent dissipation" does not require factor owners to be cartelized, as often maintained in the IO literature. As a consequence, indices of competition that rely on costs, such as Lerner indices, exaggerate the absolute price reduction that enforcement of perfect competition would entail. As competition is increased, not only will the price tend to fall, but marginal cost will also tend to increase.
3. The consumer–producer dichotomy may be misleading. What matters to consumers is their real income. Exactly how different consumers are affected depends on the underlying production structure. Certain consumers may lose from lack of competition both because they face higher prices, and because their incomes fall. Other consumers may benefit enough on the latter account to gain overall.

With regard to the more specific issue of the scope for an international agreement to curb beggar-thy-neighbor competition policies, we have observed:

4. Countries that are net exporters in the sectors that are more easily cartelized have incentives to pursue beggar-thy-neighbor competition policies.
5. There is a certain political logic to the fact that there are attempts to bring such a competition policy agreement into a structure like the WTO. This is, in part, because such an agreement would enhance trade. This is also because a competition policy agreement may require side payments, and a trade agreement, like the WTO or regional schemes, offers plenty of scope for members to trade off gains under one agreement with losses under another agreement. There is reason to believe that support for such an agreement could come from a wide spectrum of factor owners in both exporting and importing countries.

The discussion has also suggested that the gains from an international competition policy agreement may be limited due to certain other legal regimes:

6. If FDI is permitted and is provided national treatment, investment can be expected to respond to the competitive advantages created by national competition policies, and to undermine the scope for a competition policy agreement.
7. Extraterritorial application of competition laws may effectively prevent countries from pursuing beggar-thy-neighbor policies.

Finally, much of the development in trade policy analysis during the last 25 years has come from the importation of tools and insights from the industrial organization literature. We hope that this chapter contributes to convincing industrial organization economists that it is time to make the exchange of ideas more balanced.

Annex: Derivation of Equation (18.11)

This annex explains the derivation of Equation (18.11), which is the basis for subsequent welfare analytics within the chapter. The welfare expression (18.9)

$$W^j(m^1, m^2) = \frac{1}{I(P)}\left[(P - C^j)X^j + C^j X^j + T^j(X^j)\right]$$

can be simplified as follows:

$$W^j(m^1, m^2) = \frac{1}{I(P)}\left[(P)X^j + T^j(X^j)\right].$$

The derivatives with respect to the markup m^j are

$$W^j_{m^j}(m^1, m^2) = A + B,$$

where

$$A = \frac{[PX^j_{m^j} + T_{X^j}X^j_{m^j} + P_{m^j}X^j]}{I(P)}$$

and

$$B = -\frac{I_P P_{m^j}[PX^j + T^j]}{I(P)^2}.$$

Using Equation (18.4) we can rewrite A, as

$$A = \frac{[m^j X^j_{m^j} + P_{m^j}X^j]}{I(P)}.$$

And by Shepard's Lemma we can express demand D on its dual form

$$D = I_P W^j = I_P\left[PX^j + T^j\right]$$

implying that

$$B = -\frac{DP_{m^j}}{I(P)}.$$

Combining these expression, we have Equation (18.11):

$$W^j_{m^j} = \frac{m^j X^j}{I(P)} + \frac{X^j - D^j}{I(P)}P_{m^j}.$$

References

Auquier, A.A., Caves, R.E. (1979). Monopolistic export industries, trade taxes, and optimal competition policy. *The Economic Journal* 89, 559–581. September.

Campa, J., Donnenfeld, S., Weber, S. (1998). Market structure and foreign direct investment. *Review of International Economics* 6 (3), 361–380.

Dixit, A., Norman, V. (1980). *Theory of International Trade*. Cambridge University Press, Cambridge.

Eaton, J., Grossman, G.M. (1986), Optimal trade and industrial policy under oligopoly. *The Quarterly Journal of Economics* 101 (2), 383–406.

Francois, J., Horn, H. (1998), Competition policy in open economies. Tinbergen Institute Discussion Paper 98-092/2.

Graham, E.G., Richardson, D. (1997), Competition policies for the global economy. Institute for International Economics Policy Analyses in International Economics No. 51. November.

Grossman, G. (1992), *Imperfect Competition and International Trade*. MIT Press, Cambridge, MA.

Head, K., Ries, J. (1997), International mergers and welfare under decentralized competition policy. *Canadian Journal of Economics* 30 (4), 1104–1123.

Horn, H., Levinsohn, J. (2001), Merger policies and trade liberalization. *Economic Journal* 111, 244–273. April.

Kahn, R.F. (1935), Some notes on ideal output. *Economic Journal* 45, 1–35. March.

Lerner, A.P. (1934), The concept of monopoly and the measurement of monopoly power. *Review of Economic Studies* 1, 157–175. June.

Markusen, J., Venables, T. (1988), Trade policy with increasing returns and imperfect competition. *Journal of International Economics* 24, 299–316.

Neary, J.P. (2003), Globalization and market structure. *Journal of the European Economic Association* 1 (2–3), 245–271. June.

Norman, V. (1996), A small open economy perspective on international competition policy. Presented at the Oslo Competition Conference, Norwegian Competition Authority, June.

Robinson, J. (1934), *The Economics of Imperfect Competition*. Macmillan, London.

Rysman, M. (2001), Competition policy as strategic trade. Industry Studies Program Discussion Paper No. 46, Department of Economics, Boston University.

Subject Index

Printed and bound by CPI Group (UK) Ltd, Croydon, CR0 4YY
18/09/2026
14964964-0002